... but where do I sign?

Volume One
The Essentials

a guide to understanding the music industry and its contracts, copyrights, and licenses

by

Robert J. Nathan

&

Burgundy Morgan

Library of Congress Control Number: 2008909512

Published by
Music Law Press
Carson City, Nevada U.S.A.
http://www.musiclawpress.com

Cite as:

Nathan & Morgan, But Where Do I Sign?, (2008, Music Law Press) Vol. I

Music Law Press

http://www.musiclawpress.com

CONTENTS

Section I
THE BASICS

NA

SECTION II
MAKING DEALS

NA

Chapter 10 *(continued)*

CHAPTER 10 *(continued)*

NA

CHAPTER 10 *(continued)*

SECTION III
REMEDIES

RGAN

CHAPTER 12 *(continued)*

NA

INTRODUCTION

> ***"Think it over! If you don't understand it, and the laws under which it will be executed, then don't sign it! — no matter how much profit may appear to be in store. Too lazy and too eager can ruin you."***
>
> — *Robert A. Heinlein (1907 - 1988)*

The title of this book acknowledges a recurring and pervasive fact of life in the music industry. Artistic temperament being what it is, it's frequently difficult — if not impossible — to keep novice performers' and songwriters' signatures *off* of a contract long enough to thoroughly explain its terms, conditions and consequences. Artists — and particularly eager, fledgling performers and songwriters — can seldom contain their enthusiasm when presented with a "record deal" or other music industry contract. Never mind that they haven't read it... or understood all of its implications... or that it may subject them to a virtual indenture for little or no real compensation. *"But where do I sign?,"* is commonly the first question — sometimes the only question — which many of them interject when presented with a proposed contract... and the one question to which they seem most authentically interested in the answer.

When representing artists, this attitude can be a source of unending frustration. On the other hand, for record companies and other institutions within the industry, such bumptious exuberance makes it all too easy to take advantage of the inexperience of novice performers — and of their otherwise-qualified counsel — who are unfamiliar with music industry customs and practices.

Advocacy is a contest in which the weak go to the wall and devil take the hindmost, but we have put our adversarial roles to one side for this book. Here, we are only advocating for a level playing field — for the principle that when everyone thoroughly understands the terms of an agreement, and the laws and industry customs under which it will be enforced, only the scoundrels suffer.

In designing and teaching specialized classes in music business, copyright, contract law, negotiation strategies, and music industry legal issues for the Musicians Institute in Hollywood, California, we've learned that artists *want* to understand the business and legal aspects of the music industry... if they're presented in a familiar, music-related context This book is intended to do just that; to integrate specific contracts and legal issues into a discussion of how the music and entertainment industries are organized and operate.

Actually, it's probably easier for a musician to learn these areas of law than it is for a non-musician lawyer to learn the inherent quirks of the entertainment industry. This is a crucial point for lawyers interested in this field of practice to understand. There are aspects and nuances of the music industry which musicians can often grasp intuitively, but which remain elusive for those outside the entertainment industry. Without a comprehensive understanding of how the music business is organized and functions, even experienced attorneys will quickly be out of their depth in attempting to represent clients in this unique field. Therefore, although a primary purpose of this book is to educate artists about legal aspects of the music industry, it is equally directed to lawyers and other professionals who are unfamiliar (or insufficiently familiar) with how the music industry *really* works.

By way of example, everyone in the industry generally takes for granted that, in a record deal, 15% actually means, *at most*, 10¼% (or 7¼% for an "all-in" deal). A lawyer who doesn't have that nugget of information as part of his negotiating arsenal is at a disadvantage from the outset. (A detailed analysis of the contract would likely disclose the basis for that reduction — eventually — but that discovery may occur too late in the negotiations to best serve the client's interests.)* Seemingly innocuous terms such as "sold," "container," "recording cost," "delivery" and "satisfactory," can have far-reaching contractual consequences if their music-industry applications and usage are not thoroughly grasped.

We understand that for many (if not most) creative people, lengthy contracts and legal documents are a dreadful bore. That's unfortunate, because some of the most creative work in the entertainment industry appears in its contracts. (Although it's been said that the entertainment industry's *most* creative work occurs in its accounting departments... but that's an altogether different discussion.)

This is an amazing and exciting time in the music business, as the internet and developing technologies open entirely new markets and delivery methods for music of all kinds. Today, for a modest cost, an individual can enjoy a library of thousands of high-fidelity recordings kept in a small, pocket-size device. Music has never before been so accessible and inexpensive. Traditional record companies which have for decades been financially dependent on sales of physical albums are struggling to adapt and survive in this new environment, and music lawyers are working to create contract language and protocols which address rapidly evolving issues, seeking to develop terms and conditions fair to both sides in light of unprecedented changes in the industry. It's a trial-and-error process, since actual results can seldom be accurately predicted at the time of drafting an innovative agreement.

It is possible that traditional record companies may not survive in this new era, or that they may be unrecognizably transformed over the next few years. What is certain is that the *music* business — if not the *record* business — will survive and prosper. Music is a fundamental and indispensable part of the human experience. With new technologies making music more available and pervasive than at any time in history, the current challenge is to develop a new working model for the music business, appropriately

---

* No, we're not going to explain it here. The explanation requires several pages in the chapter on Recording Contracts, in VOLUME TWO. Suffice it to say that there are numerous reductions scattered throughout the contract itself, plus an overriding reduction which arises through adhesion of another, un-appended (and sometimes prospective and un-formed, but nonetheless referenced, integrated, and binding) third party agreement.

NA

rewarding artists for their creative efforts while seeking to preserve those entities which depend upon and market music as a viable, profit-making industry. Although an exact design for a transformed music industry remains inchoate, it is certain that its structural outlines will ultimately be drawn by the terms and conditions of contracts drafted over the next few years.

Our initial intention was to begin this book with an overview of the entire music industry as it is currently structured, stressing the contractual relationships which tie the various elements of the industry to each other. That discussion was moved to Chapter 5 when it became apparent that a grasp of certain legal fundamentals was a necessary precursor to understanding those relationships.

The next major revision to our original intention came about when we realized that the sheer mass of information which needed to be included could not be comprehensively set forth in a single volume.* In consequence, we opted to reorganize the material as a multi-volume set, of which this book is the first volume. We've organized the material into sections, with each section designed to lay a foundation of understanding for those which follow. Thus this VOLUME ONE ("The Essentials"), contains three sections which explain the essential concepts which underlie the remainder of the series:

Section I, "THE BASICS" covers legal fundamentals of contracts, intellectual property, and copyrights, concluding with our overview of the various roles and contractual relationships which comprise the music industry, tracing a song from its creation through the gamut of commercial exploitation.**

Section II, "MAKING DEALS" discusses basic contract organization, as well contract analysis and negotiation techniques. This section also includes "Clauses, Provisions and Boilerplate," containing common language likely to appear in music industry contracts, along with discussions of the intended purpose of each provision, alternative sample language, with analyses and explanations of the practical and legal effects of such provisions.

Section III, "REMEDIES" offers a brief overview and explanation of the American legal system, including both litigation and alternatives to litigation, examining potential options which are available when contracts go awry. These range from alternate dispute resolution methods such as mediation and arbitration, through the various causes of action available in court proceedings, including equitable relief (such as injunctions), contract actions, and tort theories of recovery, explaining the essential elements of each and the potential risks and rewards of pursuing such remedies.

Future volumes will include chapter-by-chapter discussions and analyses of particular types of music industry contracts, including:

---

* Recording Contracts alone required over 250 pages, and was moved to VOLUME TWO.

** Although the word "exploitation" may have a negative connotation in ordinary speech, it is a positive concept for the music industry, where it simply refers to the various means by which revenues can be legitimately generated by means of artists' creative efforts and personalities.

VOLUME TWO	Band Agreements & Recording Contracts;
VOLUME THREE	Songwriter Agreements, Publishing Contracts, Licenses & Assignments;
VOLUME FOUR	Miscellaneous Agreements, Contracts, Releases, & Licenses

If you read this first volume from cover to cover, you may note that some information is repeated in different places. Such redundancies are intentional, since many readers may choose to skip around, looking only at such portions as seem most relevant to their own interests, while others may use this book solely as a quick reference source. Be assured that when we've repeated information, it's because that information is critical and bears repeating.

Lawyers using this book will likely be tempted to skip the opening chapters. Before doing so, please recall that, on any given day, appellate opinions can alter — or legislatures repeal — almost anything we know. Besides, even though most contract fundamentals have remained constant for centuries, certain aspects of copyright law have been changing rapidly, and it never hurts to review the basics in any event. There might even be some new (or forgotten) bits of information to be gleaned from the introductory chapters.

For non-lawyers, the opening chapters of this volume may seem daunting, but working your way through them before trying to adapt or utilize the sample contract language from later chapters and volumes can mean the difference between a successful contract and a merely valid one. More importantly, ***anyone who can't fully comprehend the introductory chapters should not rely solely on themselves to draft, modify, review, or approve a contract without professional assistance.*** It's not our purpose to turn laymen into lawyers. While we hope that non-attorney readers will gain useful knowledge of music industry legal issues from the following pages, our principal intention is to create an awareness of the existence and nature of those legal issues, so that readers will recognize them before they become actual problems.

At the risk of sounding heretical, some laymen are perfectly capable of preparing simple contracts for themselves in their own areas of expertise without the assistance of counsel. That having been said, it is ***always*** better to have an attorney review contracts before signing them. Even lawyers commonly do this if a contract involves them personally, particularly where the subject matter is outside the scope of their regular practice. An important *caveat* should be mentioned here: While anyone is free to draft their own contracts, drafting a contract for someone else — that is, a contract to which the drafter is not a party — may constitute the unlicensed practice of law... a criminal offense in almost every jurisdiction. No matter how adept you may become at preparing your own agreements, do not start doing so for others, unless you're a licensed attorney.*

* And perhaps not even then. One licensed attorney of our acquaintance who gave up law for a successful career as a musician has learned from painful experience to <u>not</u> prepare his own contracts because of ethical considerations and the potential for conflict of interest claims by fellow band members.

NA

There is a hierarchy of laws in the United States, with the federal constitution at its apex, and with a complex structure of international treaties, state constitutions, state and federal laws, codes, regulations, statutes, public policies, and local ordinances arrayed below. Each of these portions of the overall body of law must conform to all of those which are superior to it in that hierarchy and, somewhere near the bottom of that hierarchy — but by no means the least of its components — are contracts. While contracts are only binding on the parties who enter into them (and their successors), contracts which conform to applicable laws and public policies have all of the force and effect of law themselves, and will be enforced as law by state, federal, and foreign courts. The adage that "the pen is mightier than the sword," is seldom more applicable than in the drafting and signing of contracts.

Winston Churchill defined "success" as "proceeding from failure to failure with no loss of enthusiasm." It is not our intention to dampen anyone's enthusiasm, but rather to provide information and insights sufficient to prevent or minimize avoidable failures on the way to eventual success. The entertainment industry is a strange and wonderful world, but the sad truth — especially for performers — is that only a very tiny percentage of those who devote themselves wholeheartedly to achieving a successful, lucrative career in this field actually manage to do so. In consequence, anyone who *can* be discouraged, probably should be. Lighting may strike, and overnight successes have been known to happen… but with somewhat less frequency than lottery millionaires. If you are one of those people who believes absolutely in themselves and their talent, and whom no amount of discouragement can possibly dissuade from seeking a career in the music business, then go for it! This book is definitely intended for you.

There is one last introductory observation we would like to make, which is relevant to those who pursue careers in any aspect of the music business, whether as performers, or as part of the vast legion of non-performers comprising the majority of the industry:

> *Musicians* are in the music business to make ***music***; everyone else is in the music business to make ***money*** … and *music* is secondary, at best.*

Keeping this fact in mind, and acknowledging honestly (at least to yourself) your own motives for being in the music business, will not only help you keep your head straight, but will also provide a valuable insight in dealing with other people in the industry. Into which category do they fall? Are they about the music, or the money? There is no good or bad, right or wrong here. Either motive is equally valid. But understanding this fundamental dichotomy of motivation is crucial to determining what will (and what will not) be perceived as an important contract consideration by others. If your own primary

---

* As a corollary, there is a distinction between *musicians* and those who simply want to be "rock stars." The latter group falls within the broad category of those in the business for the money, but their motivation is generally (in no particular order and in varying proportions) fame, sex, *and* money.

motivation is the music — but you don't particularly *want* to starve for your art — then you'll want to find someone — a music lawyer, business manager, personal manager, family member, or friend — whom *(a)* you trust, and *(b)* who will care more about the money than the music, on your behalf. (And you should still read this book for yourself, anyway, if only to be aware of what to look for — and what to avoid — in dealing with music lawyers, business managers, personal managers, family members, and friends.)

For many people, dealing with contracts is like watching a bad horror film — boredom combined with an expectation that something scary is about to happen. Hopefully, the information we've included in the following pages will alleviate both feelings. Once you understand contracts, and the laws under which they are interpreted and enforced, they can be both interesting and rewarding.

We hope you find this book informative, useful, and at least mildly entertaining. But, whether you do or not, we still get our royalties. After all, we're not among those who are in the music business just for the music.

Robert J. Nathan
Burgundy Morgan
August 14, 2008

SECTION I THE BASICS

... BUT WHERE DO I SIGN?

NA

CHAPTER 1

CONTRACT FUNDAMENTALS

"Given two experienced businessmen dealing at arm's length, both represented by competent counsel, it has become virtually impossible under recently evolving rules of evidence to draft a written contract that will produce predictable results in court. The written word, heretofore deemed immutable, is now at all times subject to alteration by self-serving recitals based upon fading memories of antecedent events. This, I submit, is a serious impediment to the certainty required in commercial transactions." Delta Dynamics, Inc. v. Arioto (1968) 69 Cal.2d 525, 532 (Mosk, J., dissenting.)

In the beginning was the words ... or the music ... or both. *Everything* in the music industry starts with the creation of a song or tune, without which there *is* no music industry.

Beyond their essential role in songwriting, words are also critical to the formation of express contracts which govern most relationships within the music industry (and elsewhere.) In fact, as discussed below, the term "express contract" is a short way of saying that the contract has been "expressed in words," rather than merely implied by the conduct of the parties. A basic understanding of what contracts are, and how they are formed, is the first step to being able to comprehend them; to enter into only such agreements as are intended, and to avoid the pitfalls of ill-considered agreements.

Unless you are a hermit, you enter into and perform contracts almost every day of your life. You may hire employees; agree to provide goods or services to someone; purchase goods or services from others; rent, lease or buy residential or business property; you may borrow money, open a bank account, or retain an attorney. Each of these involves the creation and performance of a contract. Anyone can create a potentially binding contract — ***sometimes without consciously realizing that an enforceable contract has been formed.***

A contract is no more than an agreement between two or more persons which creates an obligation to do — or to *not* do — a particular thing. The ability to freely enter into contracts is a ***fundamental right***. In fact, Article I Section 10 of the U.S. Constitution states, in relevant part: *"No State shall ... pass any Law ... impairing the Obligation of Contracts..."*

That constitutional prohibition is not absolute, and subsequent judicial interpretations have allowed exceptions where there is a pressing state interest in exercising protective powers to enforce laws and public policies. As Chief Justice Hughes observed, writing for the U.S. Supreme Court: *"[T]he question is no longer merely that of one party to a contract as against another, but of the use of reasonable means to safeguard the economic structure upon which the good of all depends. [...] [R]easonable exercise of the protective power of the States is read into all contracts ...*"[1]

Despite that doctrine, two or more people can form a binding agreement for *any lawful purpose* and, unless there is a specific statute or public policy which bars that purpose, **that contract has all the force and effect of law, and will be enforced as law by the courts.**

Principal Forms of Contract

Contracts fall into **three general categories**:

1. **Written contracts:** These are contracts where the terms are expressly set forth in some tangible medium. While that medium is almost always ink on paper, the legal definition of a "writing" is much broader, and a "written" contract may be memorialized by other means, such as video- or audio-recordings, under certain circumstances. (As discussed later, some types of contracts ***must*** be in writing, as a matter of law.) Manual signatures are *not* essential elements of a valid written contract.[2]

2. **Oral contracts:**[3] As the name states, these are agreements reached orally, without reducing the terms to a "writing." Note, however, that all five essential elements of a valid contract (discussed below) must still be present. As discussed *infra*, some types of contracts cannot be made orally, and the statute of limitations for oral contracts is generally a shorter period of time.

3. **Implied Contracts.** Sometimes binding contracts are created without their specific terms ever having been expressed in words, either written or spoken. Instead, the parties' respective conduct may *imply* the existence of a contract between them, with its enforceable terms inferred as a matter of logic through judicial analysis of that conduct. Situations where there is a reasonable assumption that a contractual relationship exists between parties, but without an express contract, are also referred to as *quasi* contracts, or as "tacit" agreements, since they are understood to exist without having been openly expressed or stated. Such contracts are instead inferred from the parties' actions, demeanor, silence, ratification, or acquiescence.

Stated somewhat differently, contracts are either "express"[4] or "implied." *Express contracts* can be either oral or in writing. *Implied contracts* are those which may be inferred from the

---

1 Home Building & Loan Assn. v. Blaisdell (1934) 290 U.S. 398

2 Signatures are, however, the most common presumptive evidence of agreement, consideration, and intent to perform, discussed *infra.*

3 Many people insist on erroneously referring to oral contracts as "verbal" contracts. Since "verbal" simply means "in words," **both written and oral contracts are verbal.** Only *implied* contracts are non-verbal.

4 *I.e.*, "verbal." Stated in specific words, either orally or in writing.

conduct of the parties. For legal reasons discussed below, some types of contracts are only valid if they are contained in "a writing" — which is not necessarily limited to ink on paper.

Essential Elements of a Valid Contract

Whether express or implied, a valid contract contains **five essential elements**:[5]

1. **Competent Parties** — There must be two or more parties who are not suffering from a condition which would impair their legal competence to formulate an intent to enter into a contract. Thus court intervention may be required to form a binding contract with a minor or person adjudged to be *legally* incompetent.

2. **Subject Matter** — The contract must relate to some real thing or purpose, which may be tangible or intangible, but which may nonetheless be described with reasonable particularity.

3. **Lawful Consideration** — Consideration is the value exchanged between the parties to the contract. The ancient formula is, "a hide, a hair, or a peppercorn," meaning only that there must be some tangible or intangible thing of at least minuscule **value** *to the receiving party* — a dollar, a million dollars, a glass marble, or some action or effort — that one party agrees to provide to the other. Consideration is the inducement to a contract; the price, right, interest, profit or benefit received; or some forbearance, detriment, loss, or responsibility given, suffered or undertaken, under the contract terms.

4. **Mutual Agreement (Meeting of Minds)** — There must be a "**meeting of minds,**" or (less poetically) an apparent, common understanding between the parties as to the subject matter of their agreement, the terms of that agreement, and a manifestation by each party of an intent to do or to refrain from doing some specific act or acts required by those terms.[6]

5. **Mutuality of Obligation** — This simply means that a contract must legally bind all parties to perform under the terms of the contract. A "contract" which requires one party to perform, but requires *nothing* of the other party, is not a contract. (But *mutuality* of obligation does not necessarily mean *equality* of obligation.)

---

5 Some authorities list only four elements by incorporating the fifth element, Mutuality of Obligation, into their Consideration element.

6 Signatures are a "manifestation" of agreement and intent to perform.

If any of those five essential elements are missing, the contract may be held to be legally defective, and void or voidable.[7]

Formation of Contract — Offer and Acceptance

A contract is **formed** when three things have occurred.

1. An **Offer**;
2. Unconditional[8] **Acceptance** of that offer; and
3. Some manifestation of **Consideration.**

These three steps comprise the elements of a legal doctrine called "**offer and acceptance.**" Simply stated, once there has been unqualified acceptance of an unequivocal offer, a binding contract *instantly* comes into existence once either party takes the *slightest* action (or inaction) in consideration of their agreement.

The "offer" must be a clear, unequivocal and direct approach to another party to enter into a contract. Mere advertisements such as a "For Sale" sign are not deemed offers, but rather "invitations to treat." In effect, they are "offers to make an offer," soliciting the commencement of negotiations with respect to some particular item. There are, however, exceptions. Where an advertisement is clear as to the salient terms necessary to a contract, lacking only the identity of a second party, it will likely be held to be a valid offer. Thus publishers' royalty schedules, setting forth the terms under which particular compositions may be licensed for specified types of use are firm offers, and use of those compositions constitutes acceptance of the published terms and conditions relating to such use.

With narrow exceptions, an offer may be revoked at any time before acceptance, and may expire by its own terms if a stated deadline for such acceptance passes. When there is no withdrawal or specified deadline, offers generally expire in a "reasonable" time, where "reasonable" usually depends on the nature of what is being offered. For an offer to sell fresh fish, a "reasonable time" might be limited to hours, while an offer to sell undeveloped land might be held to have remained open for months or years, unless the land has since been developed, or the offer withdrawn.

◆ ◆ ◆

7 A **void** contract will not be enforced under any circumstances. A **voidable** contract may be voided at the request of the disadvantaged party. (See "'Void' or 'Voidable'," *infra.*)

8 *Conditional* acceptance would constitute a **counteroffer**. There can be any number of counteroffers exchanged, back and forth, but no contract until an offer or counteroffer has been unconditionally accepted.

Now you know everything that there is to know about contracts… except of course for everything else that follows here and in later chapters… and in uncounted books, commentaries, and treatises on the subject.

◆ ◆ ◆

A *caveat* is appropriate at this point. The music industry has unique customs, standards, and practices in contracts which have developed over several decades, justified by historical realities of the industry, but which will likely seem unfair, or even unconscionable, to both novice and veteran attorneys who do not regularly practice in this field. On the other hand, it is not unheard of for a proposed music industry contract to include provisions which really *are* unconscionable. An *experienced music attorney* will know the difference.

◆ ◆ ◆

Form Contracts & Boilerplate

There are an abundance of written "form" contracts available from stationery stores and on the internet. These can generally be counted on to provide for all five essential elements necessary to formulation of a legally binding agreement. However, ***just because a contract is <u>valid</u> doesn't mean that it protects you adequately, or that it necessarily provides for everything that you believe you have agreed to.*** Be particularly wary of form contracts which allow you to "fill in the blanks" but not to edit the remainder of their terms and conditions.

"Boilerplate" refers to entire contracts or to contract provisions which are used repeatedly. Preprinted form agreements are a prime example of "boilerplate" contracts. **Being preprinted doesn't make it a "standard" contract or mean that it can't be modified.** Many of the "form contracts" which are readily available for the music industry are poorly written, one-sided, and generally range from the mildly repugnant to the thoroughly unconscionable. Such contracts are nonetheless regularly utilized by inexperienced parties, acting without benefit of legal counsel, in the naive belief that a "standard" contract equates to a *good* contract. Even experienced attorneys — if their practice has been outside the music industry — can be misled by seemingly-innocuous forms of agreement, and by words and phrases which have specific (and sometimes devastating) effect in their customary music-industry interpretation, usage and application.

Lawyers usually maintain their own libraries of "boilerplate" language which can be modified for inclusion in various contracts. It requires experience and skill, however, to determine if that language is appropriate (or desirable) in any particular agreement. Your attorney is best qualified to review or prepare a contract that will not only set forth the parties' intentions and obligations, but which will further address the broad range of potential circumstances which a layman is unlikely to consider or include. **The legal costs of untangling a poorly drawn contract through formal or informal dispute resolution will *always* exceed the cost of having had it properly written in the first place.** In other words, it's far less costly to *avoid* trouble than to *get* out of trouble.

Recitals

Recitals include the preliminary portion of a contract which identifies the parties, the date of their agreement, as well as other, foundational facts which may be materially or foundationally relevant to the contract, but which are not part of its specific terms and conditions. Formal contracts frequently commence with a section actually entitled "Recitals," in which the facts underlying the contract, and the parties' general intentions, are enumerated. Such recitals usually consist of concise statements of facts, each such statement traditionally commencing with the word, "Whereas."

Recitals are useful in understanding *why* a contract was formed, and may aid a court in subsequently determining how to interpret the intention, terms and conditions of the agreement, but are usually distinct from the clauses and provisions which comprise the main body and material terms of the contract. Recitals can be particularly useful by allowing the inclusion of extrinsic information and explanations which would otherwise be precluded by the Parol Evidence Rule, as discussed later.

Provisions and Clauses

Each of terms and conditions of a contract are generally embodied in separate paragraphs. Usually these paragraphs, and any subparagraphs, will be distinguished from each other by numbers or letters, and particular sections may also have specific titles or captions indicating the subject of that paragraph or section.

These paragraphs or sections of a contract are commonly referred to as the "provisions," or "clauses" of the contract. For practical purposes, there is no difference between the two designations, although purists may insist that **clauses** contain fundamental terms of the agreement while **provisions** relate to prospective conditions or occurrences. Negotiating and drafting contracts is a dynamic process which involves more than simply arriving at the fundamental terms of agreement. It also requires determining what provisions should be included or excluded from that agreement, and the specific language to be used to best serve the parties' requirements.

The following list of common types of contract provisions is far from all-inclusive. Many of the captions listed will be unnecessary in some contracts, while essential in others. Often, two or more of the listed provisions will be merged into a single section of a contract, or one caption may be split into separate sections. The goal is to arrive at a clear, ***unambiguous*** document which accurately reflects the parties' mutual understanding and agreement at the time of entering into the contract. Typical captions which appear in music industry contracts may include:

- Acceleration Provision
- Accounting Clause
- Adjustment Provision
- Advance Clause
- Advice of Counsel Clause
- Arbitration Provision
- Assignability Clause
- Availability Clause
- Attorney's Fees Provision
- Best Efforts Clause
- Buy-Sell Provision
- Choice of Law & Forum
- Compliance Clause
- Confidentiality Clause
- Conflict of Laws Provision
- Consideration
- Construction Provision
- Controlled Compositions Clause
- Credits Clause
- Cross-Collateralization
- Cure Provision
- Delivery Requirement Clause
- Entirety of Agreement Clause
- Exclusivity Clause
- Extension Provision
- Force Majeure Provision
- Grant of Rights
- Heirs and Assigns Provision
- Indemnity Provision
- Injunctive Relief Provision
- Insolvency Provision
- Integration Clause
- Leaving Member Provision
- Liquidated Damages Provision
- Mechanical License
- Mediation Provision
- Morals Clause
- Name and Likeness Clause
- Non-disclosure Provision
- Notice Provision
- Option Provisions
- Penalty Provision
- Personal Guaranty
- Renewal Provision
- Re-recording Restriction
- Reversion Provision
- Right to Audit Provision
- Royalty Clause
- Severability Provision
- Side Letter
- Supersedure & Novation Clause
- Sunset Provision
- Term
- Termination Provision
- Territory Clause
- Time of the Essence Provision
- Warranties & Representations
- Work For Hire Clause

These and other contract provisions are discussed at length in following chapters, but please remember that none of the contract language embodied in this book should be considered to be "set in stone." Each contract is *different*. Make certain that the language of your contract is clearly understood by all the parties, and that it unambiguously states what you have agreed upon. Contracts are said to "speak for themselves," and you will generally not be allowed to come back later and substitute your recollection of its terms for what it actually says.

Executed & Executory

In everyday speech, an "executed" contract usually refers to an agreement which has been signed by the parties, but the law (and lawyers) use the word "executed" to describe those contract provisions which have been fully completed, performed, or delivered. Thus, in legal terms, an "executed contract" actually refers to one under which nothing remains to be done. Conversely, "executory" contracts and provisions are those which have yet to be performed. Taking a record contract as an example, once the advance has been paid in full, then the advance clause is an "executed" provision of the contract, while the delivery and royalty clauses remain "executory" provisions.

The termination of a contract does not necessarily extinguish its executory provisions. Using the same example, the royalty provision — that is, the label's obligation to pay royalties on album sales — remains executory for so long as the album continues to be sold, unless there is a separate contract or other circumstance which terminates the obligation to pay further royalties. So-called "sunset provisions," which specifically address and limit the ongoing rights and obligations of the parties following termination of their underlying contract are a prime example of such executory agreements.

Contracts Which Must Be In Writing
(The Statute of Frauds, and Similar Laws)

Some types of contracts must be made or memorialized in writing to be valid. This has been true since the reign of Charles II of England when, in 1677, Parliament enacted the "Statute of Frauds and Perjuries," to put an end to a practice by which the existence and terms of *any* contract could be established by the oral testimony of witnesses alone. That law — more commonly referred to simply as the **statute of frauds** — has continued in most jurisdictions ever since that time, requiring that certain types of contracts must be memorialized in a writing signed by each party against whom enforcement of that contract is sought.

Traditionally, the Statute of Frauds requires that the following types of contracts be in writing:

- Contracts in consideration of marriage.
- Contracts which cannot be performed within one year.
- Contracts for the sale of an interest in land or otherwise affecting title to land.
- Contracts by the executor of an estate to pay a debt of the estate.
- Contracts for the sale of goods above a certain value (generally $500).
- Contracts promising payment or performance of another's debt or obligation.

The Uniform Commercial Code (UCC) contains a limited version of the Statute of Frauds, and most states have either adopted the UCC version, or enacted their own statute or code having much the same effect. Also, separate and apart from the Statute of Frauds, most states also have additional laws which impose a similar restriction in respect to certain other types of agreements, requiring that they, too, must be in writing. For example, most jurisdictions require that arbitration agreements, talent agency agreements, legal fee agreements, government contracts, home improvement contracts, and various other specific types of contracts, must be in writing to be enforceable. An attorney practicing within a particular state is best qualified to determine whether a specific type of contract must be in writing in that state, but many of these types of restrictions apply to contracts which also require one of the parties to hold some form of license as well, so that the licensee should be equally aware of the requirement.

These legal mandates requiring written agreements provide an affirmative defense to lawsuits brought to enforce an unwritten contract which falls within one of the specified categories. It must be emphasized that the Statute of Frauds is *only* an *affirmative defense.* The party alleging the existence and validity of a contract has no burden of proof on the issue unless and until a defendant timely alleges that the contract was invalid under the Statute of Frauds or equivalent statute. A defendant who admits the existence of the contract in pleadings or under oath, or who fails to timely raise the defense by answer or other responsive pleading, may have permanently waived (*i.e.*, forfeited) the defense which the Statute of Frauds (or equivalent statute) might otherwise provide.

Even in the absence of a signed, written agreement, a timely Statute of Frauds defense may still be limited or overcome under certain circumstances, based upon partial performance and the conduct of the parties. Courts are reluctant to allow parties to misuse the Statute of Frauds to avoid legitimate obligations, and may apply equitable principles such as severability, estoppel and waiver, or a claim of *quantum meruit* may be permitted, to strike a fair balance and avoid unjust enrichment.

If the parties have taken action in reliance on the agreement, those portions of the agreement which have been partially performed and are outside the scope of the Statute of Frauds may be severed and treated as separate contracts, with the remaining, unperformed portions (executory provisions) likewise treated as separate contracts. If those remaining executory provisions fall within the scope of the Statute of Frauds, then the defense would remain viable as to those remaining portions only, rendering them unenforceable. This equitable approach may not be applicable where the contract is wholly integrated, but it may be impossible to establish that an oral contract was wholly integrated, unless integration can be demonstrated by a party's admission, or by competent testimony, or where it may be judicially inferred from other established facts.

Contracts Speak for Themselves — The Parol Evidence Rule

A fundamental doctrine of contract law presumes that a written contract "speaks for itself," embodying the *entire and complete* agreement between the parties. Based on that presumption, the **parol evidence rule** generally forbids introduction of extrinsic evidence[9] which would modify the terms of a written contract. Although its name suggests that it is a procedural rule, the consensus of courts and legal analysts is that the rule constitutes substantive contract law. However, as with most rules of law, there are several established exceptions to the parol evidence rule.

First, the parol evidence rule only applies if the contract in question is an integrated writing, representing the final version of the parties' agreement. If the writing contains *all* of the final terms to which the parties ultimately agreed, then it would be a *complete integration.* If, on the other hand, it contains *some*, but not all, of the final terms to which the parties agreed, then it would be a *partial integration.* This distinction is essential to determining what evidence will be excluded under the parol evidence rule.[10]

Generally, any evidence which directly contradicts written terms will be excluded under the parol evidence rule, regardless of whether the contract is wholly or only partially integrated, but for a partial integration, evidence which merely adds to the contract's terms will not usually be excluded.

Notwithstanding these exclusions, extrinsic evidence can be admitted for the following purposes:

- To clarify the subject matter or intention of the contract;
- To resolve an ambiguity in the contract;
- To show that consideration has not actually been delivered;
- To identify the parties, or their successors or assigns;
- To imply or incorporate an unexpressed term of the contract;
- To show fraud, duress, mistake, or illegal purpose on the part of one or both parties;
- To show by clear and convincing evidence that an unambiguous term in the contract is actually a mistaken transcription of a prior valid agreement.

---

9 *I.e.*, evidence not contained within the language of the contract itself. *E.g.*, oral testimony or other evidence of communications between parties.

10 This is a principal rationale for the inclusion of an "integration," "merger," or "entire agreement" clause in most contracts, although such clauses may be held to present nothing more than a rebuttable presumption.

In order for evidence to fall within this rule, it must involve either: *(a)* a written or oral communication made prior to execution of the written contract; or *(b)* an oral communication made contemporaneously with execution of the written contract.

Evidence of a later communication will not be barred by this rule, but only to the extent that it is offered to show a later *modification* of the contract (although it might be inadmissible for some other reason, such as the Statute of Frauds.)

Similarly, evidence of a collateral agreement — a contract that would naturally and normally be included in a separate writing — will not be barred by the parol evidence rule. For example, if Abner contracts with Bill to record Bill's demo for $2,500, Bill can introduce extrinsic evidence to show that Abner also contracted to obtain and supply jewel cases and printed inserts for $225. The agreement to provide cases and printed inserts could logically be in a separate document from the agreement to record the demo.

The point here is that it is essential to have everything of material relevance to the contract appear within the four corners of the contract itself, since it may be difficult or impossible to introduce testimony which contradicts, explains, or expands upon the contract's written terms and conditions, or its apparent intent. This is where recitals can become crucial, since they provide an opportunity to present contemporaneous, otherwise-extrinsic explanations within the body of the contract itself. The parties' intentions, and the facts which they believed true and relied upon at the time of contract formation can be set forth in recitals. Such recitals are admissible as direct evidence, even where testimony about identical facts would be excluded by the parol evidence rule.

As a general rule of good practice, *everything* that is relevant and material to understanding the requirements, purpose, and intention of a contract should appear unambiguously "within the four corners" of the contract itself, since the parol evidence rule stands at the periphery to prevent intrusion of extrinsic facts into judicial determination of the contract's terms and conditions.

◆ ◆ ◆

A Cautionary Tale — *Third Story Music, Inc. v. Waits*

Parties have the right to make lawful agreements between themselves, and in the course of doing so are free to accept or reject the terms being offered. However, having once bargained for and accepted those terms, a party cannot look to the courts to amend contract language which, in one party's opinion, has proven unsatisfactory.

In *Third Story Music, Inc. v. Waits* (1995) 41 Cal.App.4th 798, Third Story Music ("TSM"), a music production company, had entered into agreements in 1972 and 1977 with Elektra/Asylum Records, a division of Warner Communications, Inc. (Warner), to produce master recordings which featured performances by one of TSM's singer/songwriters, Tom Waits. Under TSM's two agreements with Warner, Warner received the exclusive, worldwide rights to "'manufacture, sell, distribute and advertise records or other reproductions (visual or nonvisual) embodying such recordings'" and to "lease, license, convey or otherwise use or dispose of the recordings." (41 Cal.App.4th at 801)

However, the agreement also included a provision which allowed Warner to "'refrain from any or all of the foregoing'" ***at its sole discretion***. (Id.) In consideration for the rights which it conveyed to Warner, TSM received an initial payment plus a percentage of whatever revenues were thereafter generated by Warner through exploitation of the subject recordings.

In 1993, an affiliate of TSM sought to compile and market an album of previously-released recordings of Waits' compositions, including four which were the subject of the TSM/Warner agreements. Although Warner had no objection to the deal, its separate arrangement with Waits provided that he had a right to personally approve all such licensing requests.[11] Without stating his reasons, Waits refused to consent to the requested licenses, and Warner informed TSM that the licenses would not be granted. TSM then brought suit in California state court for, *inter alia*, contract damages based on breach of the implied covenant of good faith and fair dealing,[12] claiming that TSM was being unfairly deprived of its share of potential licensing income to which it was entitled under the 1972 and 1977 agreements. In effect, TSM's position was that Warner had a "good faith" duty to TSM to generate all possible income through exploitation of the subject master recordings, and that Warner's failure to do so breached an implicit (but not express) contractual obligation to at all times exercise its best efforts on TSM's behalf in exploitation of the subject recordings.

Both the trial court and the Court of Appeal found in favor of Warner and Waits, holding that it would be improper to recognize an implied covenant as overriding the

---

11 Tom Waits has a reputation for objecting to certain usages of his works. See, *e.g.*, Waits v. Frito-Lay, Inc. (1992, 9th Cir.) 978 F.2d 1093, cert. denied, (1993) 506 U.S. 1080

12 It is well settled that, in connection with every contract, there is an implied covenant which requires the parties to deal fairly and in good faith with each other. In practical terms, however, this merely requires that the parties cannot wholly disclaim their obligations, or deny the existence of the contract, or engage in conduct with respect to the other party which is patently deceitful or shocking to the conscience.

discretionary right for which Warner had bargained and which clearly appeared in the express terms of the agreements:

> "[C]ourts are not at liberty to imply a covenant directly at odds with a contract's express grant of discretionary power except in those relatively rare instances when reading the provision literally would, contrary to the parties' clear intention, result in an unenforceable, illusory agreement."[13]

So long as an agreement is supported by adequate consideration, the court will not recognize or enforce an implied term which is directly at odds with an express contractual grant of unrestrained discretion.

In *Third Story Music* there was no ambiguity to be resolved; the contract "spoke for itself," entirely and clearly. At the negotiating stage, TSM could have objected to Warner having unrestricted discretion to exploit or to refrain from exploiting the master recordings. TSM did not object — or perhaps even notice — that clear language within the contract's terms, but instead signed those agreements which contained that language, and was thereafter bound by that language.

◆ ◆ ◆

The moral which astute readers will have drawn from the foregoing is that ***no language of a contract is innocuous*****. Each contract should contain everything to which the parties have agreed, and *nothing* to which the parties have not specifically agreed.** Once the contract has been signed and consideration delivered, the words of the contract itself will be all that matters, and courts will not overrule or modify a contract's express terms except under extraordinary circumstances.

◆ ◆ ◆

Contracts with Minors

Generally, anyone entering into a contract with a minor does so at his or her own risk. The law normally permits minors to disaffirm most contracts[14] at any time, or within a reasonable period after reaching their majority, which usually occurs at the age of eighteen.[15]

---

13 41 Cal.App.4th at p. 808

14 Generally, a minor's contracts for "necessities" cannot be disaffirmed, but the burden of proof is on the other party to demonstrate that the subject matter of the contract was, in fact, a "necessity." The statutes of various states are not uniform in this regard, and vary as to the *types* of contracts which a minor may disaffirm. For example, in some states (*e.g.*, New York) a minor *seller* may be bound by a sales contract from the age of 14, while still entitled to disaffirm other types of agreement entered into before reaching 18.

15 The age of binding consent varies from state to state, and in some jurisdictions there are special statutes setting a lower age for certain types of contract, such as insurance agreements, student loans, or marriage contracts. For example, in Maryland, an insurance policy cannot be disaffirmed if the insured was 14 years old at the time of signing, although the age of majority in that state remains 18 years. Similarly, in Alaska, student loan agreements

This can be of crucial concern in the entertainment industry, where talent is often found (and exploited) well before legal age is reached. Record companies would be understandably reluctant to invest millions of dollars if their investment was free to walk out — or to accept a competitor's offer — at any time. Conversely, the law is disinclined to allow an immature person to make business decisions which could be binding for an indefinite period. Public policy favors protection of the child, and a minor's right to disaffirm his or her contracts "is conferred for his protection against his own improvidence and design of others."[16] For that reason, the law gives minors an opportunity, "after they have become capable of judging for themselves, to determine whether their acts or obligations are beneficial or prejudicial to them, and whether they will abide by them or not."[17]

California, New York and Tennessee have developed statutory schemes with respect to underage performers, in which a court pre-approves the minor's contract, setting certain conditions for protection of the minor's interests. Such court-approved contracts cannot be disaffirmed thereafter.

In 1938, California enacted the "Coogan Law"[18] — named after child-star Jackie Coogan who, upon reaching his majority, found that his mother and stepfather had *legally* squandered the millions he had made between the ages of five and fifteen. The Coogan Law required courts to establish a blocked trust fund for each minor performer, into which a portion of the minor's earnings must be deposited. The Coogan Law did not, however, bring all minors' contracts under court protection, nor change the laws which allows parents to claim and use their children's earnings as their own.[19] Coogan protection merely preserves a percentage (usually 15%) of the minor's earnings, requiring employers to deposit that portion of such earnings directly into a special blocked trust (a "Coogan Trust") from which no withdrawals may be made prior to the performer reaching legal age, unless by court approval.

Current California law [20] also allows parties to file a petition for court pre-approval of entertainment industry contracts involving minors. Once approved by the court, the minor's right to unilaterally disaffirm the contract is eliminated, and the minor performer is legally barred from backing out of that contract on the grounds that he or she was a minor when the contract was formed.[21]

---

are binding on a minor who is 16 or older. Other states have comparable laws creating exceptions with respect to a minor's right to disaffirm contracts.

16 Niemann v Deverich (1950) 98 Cal App 2d 787.

17 Hurley v Southern California Edison Co. (1950, 9th Cir.) 183 F2d 125.

18 Former California Civil Code § 36.1

19 Child star Shirley Temple supported a household of twelve family members, including her parents, throughout her film career. When that career came to a close, she found herself with only a few thousand dollars and a deed to the dollhouse in the yard of her parents' home.

20 California Family Code §§ 6712, 6750, 6751

21 See Morgan v Morgan (1963, 2nd Dist) 220 Cal App 2d 665

If the employer has any California offices or domicile, or if the minor is (or becomes) a resident of California, or if any portion of work under the contract is performed in California, the establishment of a Coogan Trust is mandatory. A minor's California work permit becomes void ten days from issuance unless a trustee's report is filed, verifying that a Coogan Trust exists and that the required contributions to that trust have been deposited. Those contracting with minor entertainers can find themselves subject to severe penalties for failure to comply with these requirements, even if they have paid all of their financial contract obligations to the minor (or to the minor's parents), in full.

New York law also authorizes judicial approval of minors' entertainment contracts. As with California, such approval applies to contracts by performing artists and professional athletes. However, under New York law, a judge may refuse to approve the contract until the parents (if entitled to the minor's earnings), or the minor, agree to set aside a portion of the earnings to be placed under the control of a trustee or guardian. New York courts generally have discretion to determine the amount of earnings to be set aside by considering *(a)* the parents' financial circumstances, *(b)* the needs of the minor's family and the parents' other children, if any, and *(c)* the minor's marital status.

Under New York law, most terms of the minor's employment contract may not exceed three years from the date of approval. California law does not specifically limit the term of a minor entertainer's employment contract, but California Labor Code § 2855 *does* limit the term of all personal services contracts — *except* those of recording artists — to seven years.

The Tennessee "Minor Performers Act,"[22] is perhaps the most comprehensive protection of the rights of underage entertainment professionals. While it echoes California in requiring that 15% of the minor performer's income be deposited into a blocked trust, it further provides: "If a contract is approved [by the court] pursuant to the provisions of this part, all earnings, royalties, or other compensation earned or received by the minor pursuant to such approved contract shall become the sole property of the minor who will be authorized to execute any contracts relating to administration or investments of such earnings."[23] Thus Tennessee has blocked the ability of parents or guardians to legally use a minor's income as their own.

Other states' legislatures are considering enacting similar laws with respect to underage performers and athletes, but New York and California currently remain the only states with both express statutes and a long history of case law interpreting and applying those statutes. That is not to say that the courts of other states would not implement an appropriate, protective trust scheme by judicial order, under common law and equitable principles, if petitioned to do so. However, such courts would generally be without any authority to negate a minor's legal right to disaffirm contracts, except in California, New York, Tennessee, and other states which have enacted specific laws containing such a provision.

22 Tennessee Code §§ 50-5-201, *et seq.*, enacted in 2003.

23 Id., § 50-5-209 subd. (b)

Unlawful Contracts and Unconscionable Contracts

Before proceeding further, it's important to understand that there are fundamental legal and equitable doctrines (and statutes embodying them) which will preclude or invalidate certain contracts, in whole or in part, as being unlawful or unconscionable. We should probably begin by clarifying what the *law* mean by the word "unlawful."

> **That is not lawful which is either: (a) contrary to an express provision of law; or, (b) contrary to the policy of express law, though not expressly prohibited; or, (c) otherwise contrary to good morals.**

When lawyers speak of a contract having an "unlawful" objective or element, this is the standard under which such a determination will likely have been made. There is something of a sliding scale between its three enumerated categories, with a court having to exercise increasing discretion and analytical caution at each step. Where there is an express law prohibiting some specific act or conduct — *i.e.*, it's *illegal* — then it's a "no-brainer" to decide that a contract which requires or attempts to accomplish that illegal act or conduct is unlawful, and likely void or subject to severance or avoidance. For example, a contract in which the stated consideration is a quantity of heroin is an illegal contract, and void on its face. This is not limited to contracts which call for violation of penal laws forbidding criminal conduct, but also includes violations of a vast array of civil statutes and other laws, including some which expressly ban certain matters from being included in otherwise-lawful contracts within the jurisdiction where such laws apply.[24]

A more thoughtful inquiry is required at the next level. What is the *intention* of a particular law? What is the public *policy* which it was intended to enunciate? If a contract takes advantage of an apparent "loophole" in the specific language of a statute by requiring or attempting to accomplish that which violates the *spirit* of a law, the court may find that the legislative intent or public policy underlying a law is being circumvented, and declare all or part of the contract "unlawful." To modify the prior example, suppose the contract were for a newly-developed "designer drug," not yet subject to penal statutes, as between a buyer and seller having no legitimate (*i.e.*, lawful) purpose for their transaction. Looking at the strong legislative policy criminalizing "recreational" narcotics, a court would have little doubt about the voiding such contract, although no crime was committed.[25]

---

24 *E.g.*, a state which prohibits gambling may declare a contract for payment of a gambling debt to be unenforceable in that state's courts (even though the debt was lawfully incurred in a state which permits gambling.)

25 Dealing in a drug which has not yet been made illegal is not a crime and the U.S. Constitution (Art. I, §§ 9-10) prohibits both federal and state legislatures from enacting *ex post facto* (after the fact) laws.

Finally, the "good morals" prong of the definition calls for the utmost in judicial discretion and caution, since it seeks to apply not a relatively clear policy, but rather a general sense of community standards as to what does or does not constitute "moral" conduct. Given our Constitutional guarantees, this is about as slippery as a slope can get, so the "good morals" prong is seldom utilized, or necessary. Rare indeed would be conduct which is sufficiently "contrary to good morals" to be deemed unlawful, yet not sufficiently repugnant to community standards to have already resulted in a law forbidding it. One would have to posit a truly *original* sin, not yet contemplated or forbidden by law or policy, to safely apply the "good morals" test for deeming such conduct unlawful.

Conscionability

Where the question of "good morals" *does* regularly come into play is in the area of "unconscionability." Perhaps it would be best to look first at what is meant by "conscionable."

> **conscionable** *(adj.)* In conformity with good conscience. Descriptive of that which is fair and just, or which demonstrates the attributes of conscience, fairness, probity, and good moral character.

In matters arising from contracts, a court may determine that the entire contract, or some portion thereof, is unreasonably unfair to one party, is oppressive, or otherwise unacceptably offensive to conscience — in other words, is *unconscionable.*

Procedural unconscionability occurs in the formation of the contract, or in the inducement to contract, consisting of unconscionable conduct by one party in the process of making the contract, rather than from any inherent unfairness or unreasonableness in the terms of the contract itself. Factors such as one party's ignorance or lack of comparative sophistication, or quantities of unexplained fine print, or provisions which allege informed consent or waiver in the absence of adequate information or opportunity to obtain independent counsel, or any other factor tending to have deprived one party of an opportunity to make an informed, meaningful choice to enter into the contract, may support a finding of procedural unconscionability.

Substantive unconscionability arises directly from the terms of the contract, where the court finds such terms to be unjust, overly harsh, or one-sided. Contracts which contain unreasonably disproportionate obligations and/or benefits, or which minimize one party's liability at the other party's expense (*e.g.*, a "liquidated damages" provision in a ridiculously small or unjustifiably large amount), may be held substantively unconscionable.

If a court, as a matter of law, finds a contract or any clause of a contract to have been procedurally or substantively unconscionable at the time it was made, the court may refuse to enforce the contract, or may enforce the remainder of the contract without the unconscionable clause, or it may so limit the application of any unconscionable clause as to avoid any unconscionable result.

In general, a contract which attempts to violate or circumvent the law or public policy, or to avoid a party's legal responsibility for actionable conduct, is an unlawful contract. A contract which takes unfair advantage of one party, either by its terms or in the manner of its formation, is an unconscionable contract.

Both are to be avoided.

"'Void' or 'Voidable'"

From time to time, particularly in litigation, a contract may be described as being "void or voidable." There is a subtle legal distinction between the two concepts, which deserves a brief explanation in light of the preceding discussion.

Contracts which have an unlawful purpose, or which violate an express, unequivocal policy of law, are "void." They are said to be a legal nullity which *never* had any lawful force or effect. Such contracts are said to be void *ab initio.*[26]

"Voidable" contracts, on the other hand, are those which contain some unlawful or unconscionable element which is detrimental to one party. The party who is adversely affected by those elements may have the option of asking the court to declare the contract void, on those grounds. In making that election, the affected party may also be sacrificing benefits which flow from the contract, and so may decide to instead seek severance of the offensive portions of the contract rather than avoidance of the entire contract, leaving the remainder of the contract in force. Because election to have a contract voided may be an irrevocable decision, all of the pros and cons should be weighed carefully before seeking that remedy.

◆ ◆ ◆

Anything that two or more people can agree on which isn't "unlawful" can become a binding contract ***with all of the force and effect of law*** and ***enforceable as law*** with respect to the contracting parties and their successors.

◆ ◆ ◆

26 From the beginning.

◆ ◆ ◆

You aren't entitled to what you want, or what's fair, or what you deserve... you're only entitled to what you have *negotiated and bargained for* ... and nothing else.

◆ ◆ ◆

NA

CHAPTER 2
INTELLECTUAL PROPERTY AND PERSONALITY RIGHTS IN THE MUSIC INDUSTRY

Every valid contract involves *something of value,* which is also a short definition of the word, "property."

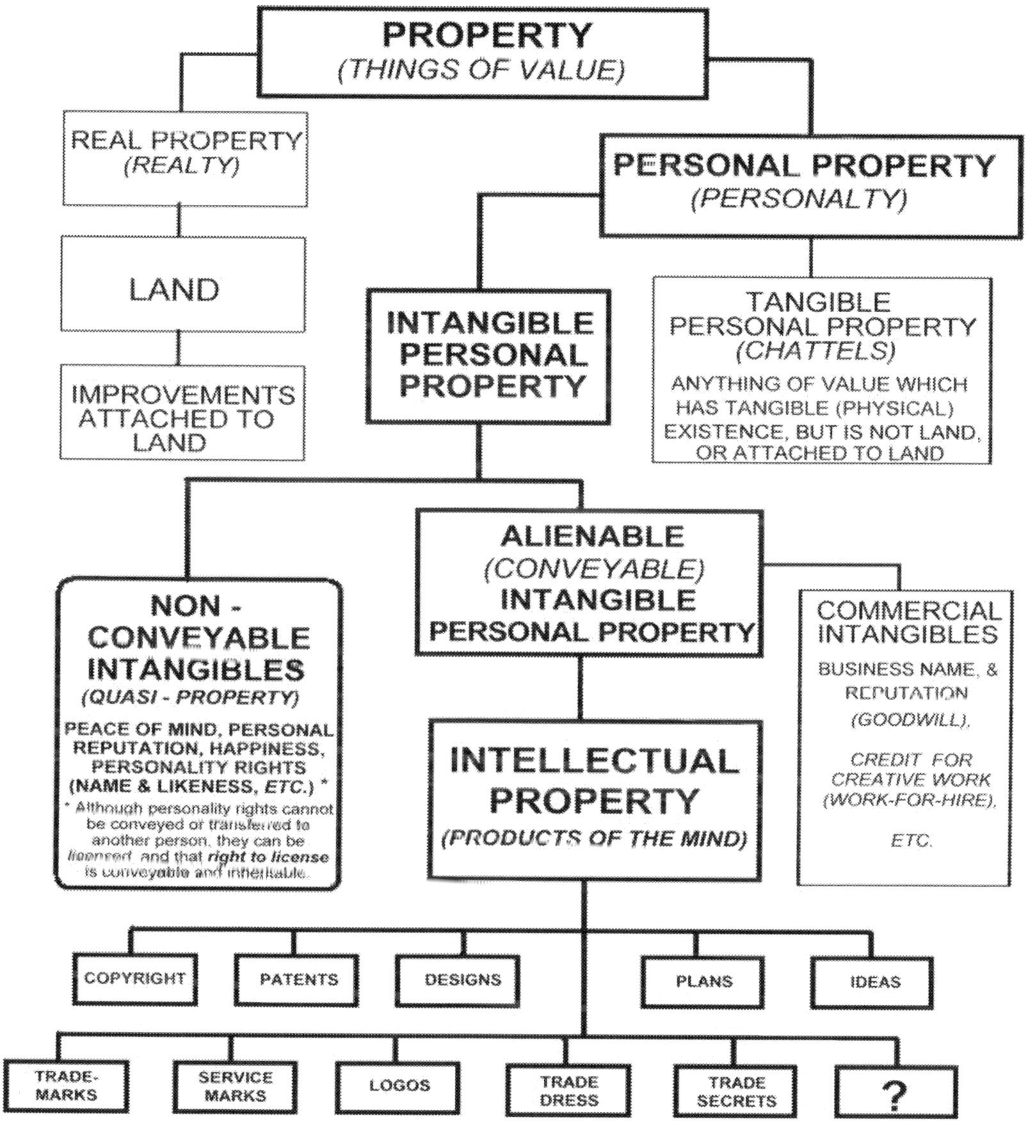

Categories of Property

As illustrated by the preceding chart, property is broadly divided into two primary categories:

(a) **Real Property** (or **realty**), which is limited to land and improvements attached to land,[27] and

(b) **Personal Property** (or **personalty**) which is everything and anything else of value, *regardless of whether or not it has a tangible, physical existence.*

While the primary attribute of property is that it has **value**, regardless of whether it is tangible or intangible, another distinguishing facet of most[28] property is that it is **alienable**; that is, it is capable of being transferred or conveyed from one owner to another. That which has value, but which is intangible and non-conveyable, is sometimes categorized as "*quasi* property."

Intellectual Property is a catch-all legal term which refers to certain types of information, ideas, and other intangibles — and to their expressed (tangible) forms — reflecting a legal precept which holds that creative products of the mind are as entitled to legal protection as are other forms of property.[29] Thus the term is broadly used to include copyrights, patents, trademarks, logos, plans, ideas, trade secrets, and other forms of creative or artistic expression, even though the specific laws governing each such form may be separate and distinct.

All such laws have the common purpose of granting and regulating exclusive rights over the products of intellectual or creative work, providing the owner of those exclusive rights a limited monopoly in respect to that property, usually for some set period of time[30] after which the monopoly terminates and the property is said to be in **public domain**. These laws vary from country to country, but the protections they afford have become more uniform and reciprocal through international treaties including the Universal Copyright Convention, the Geneva Phonograms Convention, the Berne Convention, the World Trade Organization ("WTO") Agreement, the World Intellectual Property Organization ("WIPO") Copyright

---

27 Discussions of the various aspects and distinctions of real property fill countless volumes of legal treatises, outside the purview of this book, and unrelated to the music industry.

28 Some forms of intangible personal property (or *quasi* property) — notably the bundle of personality rights commonly referred to as "name & likeness" — can be ***licensed*** to others, but *cannot* be transferred to someone else. A *beneficial interest* in those intangibles, and the *right to license* them, *can* be assigned, conveyed, or inherited. Also, some forms of *property* not relevant to this discussion, such as entailed real property, are *not* freely alienable .

29 The earliest known record of the term "intellectual property" appears in *Davoll, et al. vs. Brown*, an 1845 patent case (CCD Mass. 7 F. Cas. 197, 199) in which the court opined: *"[O]nly in this way can we protect **intellectual property**, the labors of the mind, productions and interests as much a man's own, and as much the fruit of his honest industry, as the wheat he cultivates, or the flocks he rears."*

30 For some types of intellectual property, such as trademarks, the right of exclusive use will generally continue indefinitely, provided that the owner continues to use and protect it.

Treaty, the WIPO Performances and Phonograms Treaty ("WPPT"), and the Agreement on Trade-Related Aspects of Intellectual Property Rights ("TRIPS").

In the music industry, typical forms of intellectual property include copyrights, trademarks, service marks, logos, and (from time to time) patents relating to new technologies and innovations. Each of these forms of intellectual property are protected by particular, but different, laws.

Quasi Property

The law recognizes that there are certain things of value which have many of the attributes of property, and which are almost, yet not quite, "property." Such almost-but-not-quite-property is referred to as *quasi*-property, which is entitled to many of the same legal protections as are afforded to traditional forms of property.

Personality Rights — the right to control exploitation of one's personal identity — are distinct from intellectual property but are nonetheless essential to the music industry. Commonly known as "Name and Likeness" rights, these are not property *per se*, but are treated as a form of intangible personal property (or *quasi*-property) and include the right to use (or to license others to use) aspects of one's individual personality, including name, likeness, voice, signature, and certain biographical information. When used commercially in this manner, these rights are more formally referred to as the **Right of Publicity** or **Publicity Rights**. These *quasi*-property rights are protected by common law in most states and, in some jurisdictions (*e.g.*, California), by specific statutes, as well.

The rationale behind personality and publicity rights flows somewhat incongruously, in part, from privacy rights, as well as from property laws. The logic is that, since a person is entitled to protect his or her personal life from uninvited intrusion or exposure, then he or she ought to be allowed to benefit from allowing such intrusion or exposure for a commercial purpose. This is particularly true in regard to those who have achieved some level of public recognition, and whose perceived involvement therefore adds value to a product or project.

The Clearance Tripod

Clearance refers to the process of determining that all necessary rights have been secured (cleared) prior to releasing a commercial recording, audiovisual project, or other created work which has the potential (whether by intention or inadvertence) of containing an infringement or misappropriation of another's rights, without consent. Clearance may consist of obtaining a license, release, or waiver of rights, or determination that necessary rights are available without license (*e.g.*, in public domain), or by copyright registration of a newly- created work.[31] Looking at each song on an album, these various property rights and their respective protections can be discerned:

- **The Song (Composition):** Consisting of the music and lyrics of a song, the composition is protected by a "Performing Arts" ("PA") copyright.[32] In order to release an album which includes a recording of that composition, the Record Label will need to have obtained a Mechanical License from the owner of such copyright, which allows the song (composition) to be recorded as a phonorecord.[33] On the album, the ownership of such copyrights — known as "publishing rights" — will be indicated by the "©" symbol, commonly referred to as a "circle-c."

- **The Recording:** The recorded sounds are themselves independently protected by a completely separate copyright which is usually owned and controlled by the Record Label. If the recordings are owned by someone other than the Record Label which is releasing the subject album, then the right to include such recordings must be obtained through a Master Use License from the owner of the Sound Recording ("SR") copyright <u>in addition</u> to a Mechanical License from the owner of the publishing rights to the composition. On an album, the ownership of sound recording copyrights will be indicated by the "℗" symbol, commonly referred to as a "circle-p" (for "phonorecord.")

- **Voices, Names, Photos & Biography:** As a "personality" right, performers' voices are their own personal property. Their inclusion in the recordings is by a contract, license, or release which allows such use, usually coupled with permission to use the performer's name, likeness and biographical information, as well. In the industry, this bundle of personality rights is generally referred to as **"name and likeness."**

All three of these distinct elements — *(1)* Mechanical License (for the composition); *(2)* Sound Recording copyright or Master Use License (for the recorded sounds); and *(3)* permission to use the performers' personality rights — are ***essential*** to lawful release of a commercial recording which contains vocals, or where the packaging includes performers' names or likenesses. Only in those rare instances where a recording is entirely instrumental *and* the performers are completely unidentified, would the two distinct copyrights be sufficient, either through ownership of those copyrights or by license from the copyright

---

31 The clearance process may also — with extreme caution — include a "fair use" determination, as discussed in a later chapter.

32 Although copyright exists as a matter of law from the moment the song is first fixed in tangible form, it is best protected by **registration**. A copyright for the music and for the lyrics may be registered separately or together, and generally will be owned by either the author or by a publisher ("copyright claimant").

33 For an audiovisual project, the composition rights are secured by a "Sync" license.

owners. This all seems fairly simple, but the distinction between the three forms of right lies at the heart of a great deal of confusion for most people who are not intimately familiar with the music industry. Even experienced judges and lawyers have been known to confuse the three rights, with the most common error being the mistaken belief that a legitimately obtained master recording automatically carries with it the other necessary rights. **It does not.** Both the *composition copyright* and the requisite *personality rights*, as well as the *sound recording rights*,[34] must be verified as part of the clearance process.

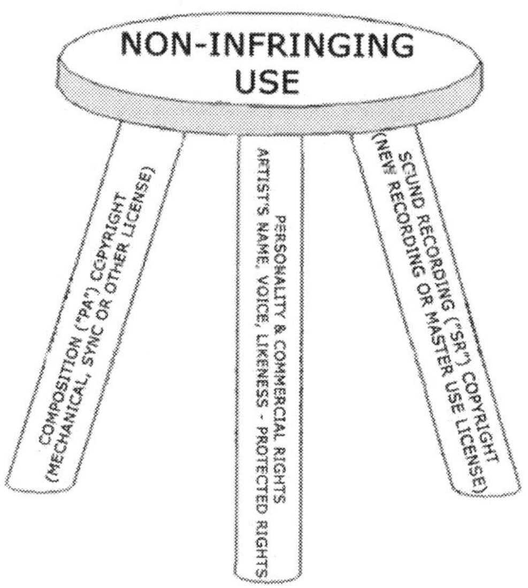

The distinction bears repetition: The *composition* is completely separate from a *recording* of that same composition, and their copyrights are likewise wholly separate and distinct. Permission to use the performers' *names, voices and likenesses* is also essential prior to any use of those personality rights. For a lawful commercial release, ***all three of these elements — composition, sound recording, and personality rights — must each be clearly established.***

Audiovisual Clearances

The clearance process for audiovisual projects may be even more daunting. The same three-element approach is still applied, with a "sync" license for the composition (instead of a "mechanical" license) being the only obvious difference. The complication arises in respect to various images which may be picked up by cameras, yet which may be subject to protection as a personality right, or as a proprietary trademark or service mark, or as a separate copyrighted work. Because of these possibilities, the "personality rights" leg of the clearance tripod must be viewed as embracing all possible protectable rights of third parties, and the entire audiovisual work must be carefully scrutinized for images which must be cleared (usually through obtaining a release), or else those images must be either eliminated or obscured. There are certain exceptions, such as for audiovisual coverage of news and

34 The late Bob Marley was renowned for paying off debts with copies of master recordings, but without conveying any *rights*. In consequence, there are hundreds of authentic copies of Marley master recordings which *cannot be legitimately licensed for use.* Without a valid master use license, traceable back to the original Sound Recording copyright — and a separate license from the owner of the *composition* copyright -- a "master recording" is nothing more than a tape recording which may be owned and enjoyed privately, with family and friends.

sporting events, but the general rule is that, absent specific releases, recognizable images of a person, or of protected marks or logos, or of copyrighted works, cannot be included in an audiovisual work without risking a lawsuit for infringement or misappropriation.

Constitutional Basis for Protection of Intellectual Property

Article I of the United States Constitution, which governs the Legislative Branch, provides, at Section 8, in relevant part:

> *The Congress shall have Power [...] to regulate Commerce with foreign Nations, and among the several States [...] to promote the Progress of Science and useful Arts, by securing for limited Times to Authors and Inventors the exclusive Right to their respective Writings and Discoveries; [...] and to make all Laws which shall be necessary and proper for carrying into Execution the foregoing Powers, and all other Powers vested by this Constitution in the Government of the United States, or in any Department or Officer thereof.*

Article II, governing the Executive Branch, at Section 2 provides (in relevant part) that

> *"[The President] shall have Power, by and with the Advice and Consent of the Senate, to make Treaties, provided two thirds of the Senators present concur..."*

Article III, governing the Judicial Branch, provides (in relevant part), at Section 1 that

> *"The judicial Power of the United States shall be vested in one supreme Court, and in such inferior Courts as the Congress may from time to time ordain and establish. [...]"*

and at Section 2 that

> *"The judicial Power shall extend to all Cases, in Law and Equity, arising under this Constitution, the Laws of the United States, and Treaties made, or which shall be made, under their Authority..."*

And finally, a "supremacy clause" is included in Article VI of the United States Constitution,[35] which provides (in relevant part):

---

35 The supremacy clause of the U.S. Constitution establishes a constitutional choice-of-law rule, makes federal law paramount, and vests Congress with the power to **preempt state law.** (see U.S. Const., art. VI, cl. 2; *Cipollone v. Liggett Group, Inc.* (1992) 505 U.S. 504, 516.) There are four basic types of federal preemption: *(1)* express; *(2)* conflict; *(3)* obstacle; and *(4)* field. (See *Bronco Wine Co. v. Jolly* (2004) 33 Cal.4th 943, 955.) *(continued)*

> *"This Constitution, and the Laws of the United States [...] and all Treaties made, or which shall be made, under the Authority of the United States, shall be the supreme Law of the Land; and the Judges in every State shall be bound thereby, any Thing in the Constitution or Laws of any State to the Contrary notwithstanding."*

Taken together, these constitutional provisions create the authority under which the statutory and regulatory framework protecting intellectual property has been created, implemented, adjudicated, and enforced. In erecting that framework, Congress instituted a fundamental difference between "authors" and "inventors," with wholly separate agencies regulating the protections afforded to each.

The Copyright Office, a division of the Library of Congress, registers the rights of authors[36] under authority of Title 17 of the United States Code and international copyright treaties to which the United States is signatory. Since copyright is of paramount importance to the music industry, the operations of the Copyright Office, and the statutes and regulations which govern copyright, are discussed at length in two following chapters.

The rights and interests of inventors, on the other hand, fall within the purview of the United States Patent and Trademark Office ("USPTO"), which is an agency of the Department of Commerce, governed by Title 35 and by portions of Title 15 and Title 44 of the United States Code.[37] Trademarks, service marks and logos are also of critical importance to the music industry, and are discussed later in this chapter.

Express preemption arises when Congress explicitly defines the extent to which its enactments pre-empt state law. "Preemption is fundamentally a question of congressional intent, and when Congress has made its intent known through explicit statutory language, the courts' task is any easy one." (*English v. General Electric Co.*, (1990) 496 U.S. 72, at pp. 78-79.) **Conflict** preemption occurs when simultaneous compliance with both state and federal directives is impossible. (*Hillsborough County v. Automated Medical Labs* (1985) 471 U.S. 707, 713.) **Obstacle** preemption arises when " 'under the circumstances of [a] particular case, [the challenged state law] stands as an obstacle to the accomplishment and execution of the full purposes and objectives of Congress.' " (*Crosby v. National Foreign Trade Council*, 530 U.S. 363 at p. 373, quoting *Hines v. Davidowitz* (1941) 312 U.S. 52, 67.) Finally, **field** preemption, *i.e.*, "Congress' intent to pre-empt all state law in a particular area," applies "where the scheme of federal regulation is sufficiently comprehensive to make reasonable the inference that Congress 'left no room' for supplementary state regulation." (*Hillsborough County v. Automated Medical Labs (supra)* 471 U.S. at p. 713, quoting *Rice v. Santa Fe Elevator Corp.* (1947) 331 U.S. 218, 230.)

36 In the context of copyrights, "author" refers to all creators of artistic works, including written, musical, dramatic, comedic, terpsichorean, and visual arts of any kind.

37 Title 35 USC §§ 1 - 376 embody the general statutory authority for administration of U.S. patent law as derived from the Patent Act of July 19, 1952 and subsequent congressional enactments and treaty obligations. 15 USC §§ 1051-1127 contain provisions of the Trademark Act of 1946 governing federal trademark registration, and 44 USC §§ 1337-1338 relates to administrative and business operations of the USPTO.

Patents

A patent is a limited monopoly granted to an inventor, preventing others from utilizing his or her invention during the term of the patent, except under license from the patent holder. Unlike copyright, there is no automatic protection for a patent. To the contrary, there is a rigorous application and registration process, and failure to timely apply for patent protection will result in a permanent forfeiture of any right to obtain a patent.

A patent cannot be granted for a mere idea or suggestion. A complete and technically detailed description of an actual device or other subject matter for which a patent is sought is required, and in some instances a working model or prototype may also be necessary. In order for an invention to be patentable under United States law, it must be both "new" and "useful" as defined in the patent law, which provides that an invention cannot be patented if: "(a) the invention was known or used by others in this country, or patented or described in a printed publication in this or a foreign country, before the invention thereof by the applicant for patent," or "(b) the invention was patented or described in a printed publication in this or a foreign country or in public use or on sale in this country more than one year prior to the application for patent in the United States . . ."

If the invention has been described by others in a printed publication anywhere in the world, or has been publicly disclosed, used, or on sale in the United States for more than a year before the application date, a U.S. patent cannot be obtained. It is immaterial when the invention was made, or whether the printed publication or public use was by the applicant or by someone else. If the inventor describes the invention in a printed publication or uses the invention publicly, or places it on sale, a ***U.S. patent application must be filed within one year***, or the right to a U.S. patent is forfeited. Internationally, the rule is even more stringent: failure to apply ***on or before the first date of public use or disclosure*** will destroy any right to patent protection in many foreign countries.

In consequence of these requirements an unavoidable but particularly tedious (and expensive) part of the patent application process is a comprehensive, worldwide search of available records to determine if, in fact, the proposed invention is eligible for patent.

There are three basic types of patents:

- **Utility patents**, which may be granted to anyone who invents or discovers any new and useful process, machine, article of manufacture, or composition of matter, or any new and useful improvement thereof;

- **Design patents**, which may be granted to anyone who invents a new, original, and ornamental design for an article of manufacture; and

- **Plant patents**, which may be granted to anyone who invents or discovers and asexually reproduces any distinct and new variety of vegetation.

The last of these types of patent has no application in the music industry (unless someone manages to cultivate a singing shrub), and design patents are principally concerned with visual or tactile ornamentation of products. Utility patents, however, have time-and-again significantly and fundamentally affected the music industry, and will continue to do so through innovations in media and technological devices which supplant their predecessors and introduce new methods and markets for the music business. Entire sectors of the music industry have come into existence, flourished for a time, and faded into obscurity or oblivion, all as a result of new patents.

Generally, the term of a new patent is twenty years. A United States grant of patent only operates within the jurisdiction of United States, and is essentially prohibitory in nature. That is, the U.S. patent holder is granted the right to *exclude others* from making, using, offering for sale or selling the patented invention in the United States, and from importing infringing products, goods or merchandise into the United States. The USPTO does not *enforce* these patent rights, it merely qualifies and registers those rights and, by grant of patent, empowers a patent holder to seek enforcement through other government agencies and judicial remedies.

Although the rights granted under a United States patent extend only to the United States and its territories and possessions, nearly every country has its own patent laws, and there are several international treaties that aid in applying for international patent protection. However, in the case of inventions made in the United States, U.S. law requires that a *license* be obtained from the USPTO *before* applying for a foreign patent if the foreign application is to be filed either *(a)* before an application is filed in the United States or *(b)* within six months from filing a U.S. patent application. An application for such license is regularly included as part of U.S. patent applications, and the applicant will usually be notified promptly as to whether or not a license for foreign application has been granted.[38]

In most foreign countries, any public disclosure or use of an invention before applying for patent will bar the right to a patent. It is therefore good practice to file a patent application prior to public disclosure of the invention, even though U.S. patent law allows a one year grace period, since prior disclosure may preclude subsequent international patent applications.

Most countries also require that a patented invention be manufactured in that country within a certain period, usually three years. This is generally referred to as the "working requirement," and if there is no manufacture within the required period some countries may void the patent. Additionally, most countries' laws provide for compulsory licensing of anyone wishing to manufacture under or utilize the patent in that country.

---

38 The license to apply for foreign patent protection is not required after six months from the U.S. application date, unless the invention has been ordered kept secret, which may occur in the case of sensitive technological innovations.

The Paris Convention for the Protection of Industrial Property — more commonly referred to as the Paris Convention — is an international intellectual property treaty which provides that each signatory country guarantees to the citizens of the other signatory countries the same rights in patent and trademark matters that it gives to its own citizens. It also provides for the **right of priority** in the case of patents, trademarks and industrial designs (design patents) so that after applying for patent in one signatory country one may, within a certain period of time,[39] apply for protection in other member countries. These later applications will be treated as if they had been filed on the same day as the first application.

It is this "right of priority" under the Paris Convention which allows public disclosure less than one year prior to filing of a U.S. patent application, before international applications are filed. Without this claim to priority, no international applications could be filed after initial public disclosure. For patent applications claiming priority under the Paris Convention, the relevant date for determining prior public disclosure is the filing date of the first application. Thus, disclosures permissible under U.S. patent law, are irrelevant to international applications under the Paris Convention, but only with respect to countries which are signatory to that international treaty. For countries not signatory to the Paris Convention, patent applications in such non-signatory countries should be filed before any public disclosure, if permissible under USPTO restrictions (discussed above) requiring a licence prior to any foreign application.

Another treaty, known as the Patent Cooperation Treaty ("PCT") provides that an application filed with the appropriate governmental agency in any PCT-signatory country may be taken as a concurrent application for patent in one or more (or all) signatory countries. Once the application is filed, only one initial patent search is required. When that search has been completed, the applicant may then elect to enter "Chapter II" of the process, in which a PCT-qualified governmental agency evaluates the application under PCT patentability standards. Eventually, the applicant will still be required to have the PCT application officially entered into the national patent office of each of the countries from which the applicant desires patent protection. This single application process is not only less time consuming than applying on a country-by-country basis, but is also considerably less expensive to initiate, allowing an eighteen month grace period during which the applicant can decide precisely where subsequent patent applications should be filed.

The patent application process is highly technical and a patent lawyer should be consulted before any public disclosure of an invention, particularly since the laws of various countries are inconsistent in their definitions of what constitutes "public disclosure," and premature disclosure may result in forfeiture of patent rights.

---

39 Twelve months in the case of utility patents, and six months in the case of industrial designs and trademarks.

Trademarks, Service Marks & Logos

A **trademark** is a word, phrase, symbol or design, or a combination of words, phrases, symbols or designs, that identifies and distinguishes a particular commercial entity or the source of commercial goods and products.

A **service mark** is the same as a trademark, except that it identifies and distinguishes the source of a *service* rather than a product. The terms "trademark" and "mark" are generally used in reference to both trademarks and service marks.

A **logo** is an emblematic design used as a trademark or service mark to identify goods or services. The silhouette of Gibralter adopted by the Prudential Insurance Company of America typifies this form of mark. One advantage of a unique, created logo as a trademark is that it may also qualify for additional protection under copyright, as a work of visual art.

Trademarks need not be limited to names, words or designs. Virtually anything which can be perceived by any means may be registered as a trademark if it identifies the source of a product or service. For example, the sound of a distinctive lion's roar has, since 1924, heralded MGM's motion pictures, and — since 1961 — three chimed notes have identified the National Broadcasting Company.[40] Even the *smell* of a product can serve as a trademark. In 1991, the registration for a line of sewing thread and embroidery yarn described its trademark as "high impact, fresh, floral fragrance reminiscent of plumeria blossoms." A common *color* can be a trademark, as well. Although the USPTO initially refused Owens-Corning's application to register the color *pink* for fibreglass insulation, that decision was reversed — and the trademark registered — when the company produced evidence that it had obtained a license from MGM for use of the animated Pink Panther character as a "celebrity" spokesperson, and had spent millions of dollars promoting the "pinkness" of its product. Architectural features can also be trademarks, as with McDonald's glaringly yellow "golden" arches.[41]

It's important to note that registration of trademarks is tied to a description of the particular types of goods or services to which the mark will be affixed. Descriptive categories, called "classes" for patent and trademark purposes, create a limitation on where and how the mark may be used. As an example of how trademarks are distinguished by "classes," the color pink and the Pink Panther character are also used by Cumberland Packing Corporation for its "Sweet 'n Low" brand of artificial sweeteners. Since food products and fibreglass insulation fall into different international classifications, there is no infringement as between Cumberland Packing and Owens-Corning. The rationale behind such permissible duplications of registered marks lies in the consumer protection aspects of

---

40 It may or may not be coincidental that NBC was a wholly-owned subsidiary of General Electric Corporation, and that the three chimed notes of NBC's audible trademark are G E C.

41 Note that the *phrase* "golden arches" is also a registered trademark of McDonald's.

trademark laws. Consumers are unlikely to assume or rely on a perceived common source, affiliation, sponsorship or endorsement as between the manufacturer of artificial sweeteners and the manufacturer of fibreglass insulation products.

Thus, a trademark registered only for one classification — say, for example, musical recordings (Class 9)[42] — *may* remain available for use by others in regard to other classes, such as for live performances (Class 41),[43] for a line of clothing (Class 25), for musical instruments (Class 15) or for printed material such as sheet music, books, photos, or posters (Class 16)... ***provided* that such use would not cause consumer confusion by implying sponsorship, affiliation, or endorsement with respect to the holder of the senior mark.**[44] Therefore, in addition to designating the appropriate class, applicants must also include a brief statement describing the proposed uses and particular goods or services to which the mark will be applied. A later expansion of a registrant's uses of their mark into areas or uses not disclosed in their application — even if within the same class of goods or services — may result in a complaint to the USPTO, an administrative review, and possible cancellation of the mark if such new uses infringe upon the rights of the holder of a senior mark, or are likely to generate consumer confusion in respect to that senior mark.

There are two factors to be balanced in determining which classifications should be applied for in seeking trademark registration: first, there is a nonrefundable application fee[45] to be paid for each class for which a particular trademark is sought to be registered, and second, failure to actually use the mark in commerce in respect to a class for which it is registered may result in loss of the mark for that class.

Just as copyright protects an original artistic or literary work, and a patent protects an invention, trademarks and service marks protect the identity of a commercial entity or product from competitors' infringement. There are significant differences, however, between these three forms of protection and how they are implemented. Copyright comes into existence automatically when a creative work is first fixed in tangible form, and registration of that copyright is optional. Patents, on the other hand, must be formally

---

42 "Scientific, nautical, surveying, electric, photographic, cinematographic, optical, weighing, measuring, signaling, checking (supervision), life-saving and teaching apparatus and instruments; **apparatus for recording, transmission or reproduction of sound or images;** magnetic data carriers, recording discs; automatic vending machines and mechanisms for coin operated apparatus; cash registers, calculating machines, data processing equipment and computers; fire extinguishing apparatus." (Class 9, International Schedule of Classes of Goods and Services)

43 "Education and entertainment." (But see, "Truth in Music," *infra.*)

44 That a mark has been registered in only one class does not automatically make that mark available to others for commercial use in other classes. For example, many band names are registered only under Class 9, for sound recordings. This does not leave Class 41 available for a competitor to register for live performances, since the ultimate intent of trademark protection is to prevent consumer confusion. If consumers associate the mark with a particular recording group, it would defeat the purpose of trademark protection to allow another, unaffiliated group to register the mark for public performances. It is nonetheless good practice to register a mark for each class in which it is being used, or will be used.

45 Currently $325 per class, per mark.

obtained through a governmental application process, or the right to patent is lost. Trademarks come into being through **legitimate commercial use**, and (as with copyright) registration is optional, but strongly recommended.

The trademark symbol ("TM") or service mark symbol ("SM") may be used at any time, without registration, to notify the public of a claim of proprietary interest in a mark. ***However***, the registered trademark symbol ("®"), commonly referred to as a "circle-R", ***may only be used after the mark has actually been registered*** (not merely applied for), and only in connection with the class or classes of goods or services listed in the trademark registration.

The advantages of obtaining federal registration of a trademark include:

- A legal presumption of ownership of the mark and of an exclusive right to use the mark;
- Constructive notice to the public of the claim of ownership of the mark;
- The ability to obtain an award of statutory damages and attorney's fees through federal court action for misappropriation of the mark;
- The ability to use U.S. registration as a basis for registration in foreign countries; and
- The ability to file the registration with U.S. Customs and Border Protection[46] to block importation of infringing foreign goods.

Once a trademark has been registered, it can be renewed indefinitely *if* it is still being used in commerce. The obvious goal of a trademark is to have the public favorably associate that mark with a specific product or service. Sometimes a trademark owner can succeed too well, and must act to prevent the public from adopting a trademark as the generic term for all similar products. The common, descriptive names aspirin, corn flakes, dry ice, escalator, kazoo, kerosene, lanolin, linoleum, nylon, raisin bran, shredded wheat, swiss cheese, trampoline, and yo-yo all began as proprietary marks which were lost by reason of their success. Over the years, other registered trademarks have also been on the verge of losing their protected status, and have retained it only through aggressive public advertising campaigns aimed at distinguishing their brand names from competing products. Among

---

46 Formerly the U.S. Customs Service. There is a fee payable when applying for this additional protection.

these have been Band-Aid, Frigidaire, Kleenex, Q-tips, Xerox, and Coke,[47] ... all registered trademarks which came close to being relegated to lower-case status.

A further distinction in trademarks should also be mentioned. "House" marks denote a company or other entity, while "product" or "service" marks denote particular goods, services, or slogans. Thus, "Chevrolet" is a house mark (owned by General Motors, which is also a house mark) while "Nova," "Impala," and "Blazer" are each product marks, owned by Chevrolet.

Trademarks are fundamentally protective, and their original function served to exclude importation of competing foreign goods. In the earliest common law cases, "foreign" was often interpreted as another state or county, but in today's global, free-trade economy, a more international approach is required. Some marks remain local, however, such as for businesses whose scope of activity is limited to a particular geographic region. Many such businesses — small restaurant chains, antique shops, grocery stores — do not bother with federal registration of their marks, but instead rely on state common law protection. ***A common law mark is as effective and exclusive within its geographic region as is a registered mark***, and where a conflict arises between the two types of mark it is the *senior* of the two (in terms of continuous commercial use in a particular geographic region) which will prevail *within that region.* Thus when a national restaurant chain with a federally registered name sought to expand into an area in which another, small restaurant chain with the same name had been in business for years, it was the national chain which was precluded from using its federally registered mark in any portion of the state in which the smaller (but older) common law mark was in use by its owner, *as well as other areas within the state into which the common law mark-holder might reasonably seek to expand its operations.*[48]

Although the Lanham Act is a federal law, it is not preemptive, and seniority of commercial use — balanced against the likelihood of consumer confusion — will be the ultimate test as to the right to exclusive use of a mark within any particular jurisdiction.

Internationally, beginning with the Paris Convention in 1883, which in turn led to the Madrid Agreement of 1891, there are a series of multinational agreements and treaties affecting trademarks. The intent of these treaties is to provide equal treatment of both

---

47 "Coke" is a special case which *began* as a popular name coined by consumers rather than as a trade name used by the manufacturer. *Coca-Cola* is arguably the world's most recognized and valuable brand name. First used in commerce in 1886, the name reflects two of the beverage's original ingredients: coca leaves and cola nuts. (Coca content was reduced to an infinitesimal trace amount in 1902, and eliminated entirely by 1929.) The name *Coca-Cola* was registered as a trademark in 1893, but "Coke" was merely a commonly-used term for the product, starting around 1909. That term became so popular that an enterprising competitor began marketing its beverage as "Koke." Coca-Cola successfully sued for trademark infringement, ***even though it had never used "Coke" in its advertisements or marketing.*** The Court nonetheless ruled that "*Coke*" was equated in consumers' minds with Coca-Cola, and hence was the exclusive property of Coca-Cola. "Koke" was therefore held to be "confusingly similar" and a trademark infringement. (See, *Coca-Cola Co. v. Koke Company of America, et al.* (1920) 254 U.S. 143) Even then, the word "*Coke*" did not appear in Coca-Cola's marketing until 1941, and was not registered until 1945.

48 See, *Spartan Food Systems v. HFS Corp.* (1987, 4th Cir.) 813 F.2d 1279

foreign and domestic trademark owners under the laws of all member countries, generally through conforming each member nation's laws to a common model, or by adopting a system wherein trademark rights are granted in many countries through a single "international" registration.

The United States is signatory to the Madrid Treaty and the resulting Madrid Protocol, but many nations are non-signatory to that agreement including Canada, Hong Kong, India, Israel, Mexico, New Zealand, the Philippines, South Africa, Taiwan, and most South American[49] countries.

As an alternative or adjunct to the Madrid Protocol, there is also a European Community regional trademark system ("CTM") which provides for a single application and examination process, and a unified court system for enforcement of trademark rights covering twenty-five countries. (Under the Madrid Protocol, there may be additional application fees and examinations required for each nation in which protection is sought.)

In the United States, the Trademark Law Treaty Implementation Act of 1998 ("TLTIA") (15 USC § 1051) substantially modified the prior Trademark Act of 1946 (the "Lanham Act") in dealing with international trademark considerations and treaty implementation. It's important to remember that the U.S. is also signatory to the Paris Convention, and enforces its standards regarding priorities. Essentially, this means that trademarks registered in any member nation, under the laws of that nation, will generally take precedence over a mark registered in another member nation. Sometimes, merely expanding on the use of an existing mark can create a conflict where none previously existed.

In 2005, the Irish band Westlife lost a five-year court battle to trademark the band's name for use in promotional merchandise when a judge ruled that "Westlife" is too similar to a German tobacco company's earlier-registered brand name, "West," which the company used on similar promotional merchandise. The court concluded that, "The relevant public might think that the origin of the goods and services marketed under the Westlife mark is the same as that of the goods and services marketed under the West mark, or at least that there is an economic link between the various companies or undertakings which market them. [...] In the light of all the foregoing, and in view of the fact that the goods and services in question are identical or similar, the court finds that there is a likelihood of confusion between the two trademarks."

The phrase "confusingly similar" is a crucial distinction and touchstone in commercial law. The very essence of trademark is that it brands particular goods and services as having come from a specific, known source, and the trademark laws are designed to prevent others from unfairly capitalizing on another's reputation through use of "confusingly similar" marks, packaging or advertising which might mislead or deceive consumers, either inadvertently or intentionally.

49 There is, however, a "Pan American Convention for Trade Mark and Commercial Protection."

More formally known as the Trademark Act of 1946, the Lanham Act (15 U.S.C.§§ 1051, *et seq.*) contains federal statutes governing trademark law in the United States.[50] That act and its subsequent amendments provide penalties for "Any person who, on or in connection with any goods or services [...] uses in commerce any word, term, name, symbol, or device, or any combination thereof [...] likely to cause confusion, or to cause mistake, or to deceive as to the affiliation, connection, or association of such person with another person, or as to the origin, sponsorship, or approval of his or her goods, services, or commercial activities by another person, or [...] in commercial advertising or promotion, misrepresents the nature, characteristics, qualities, or geographic origin of his or her or another person's goods, services, or commercial activities..." (15 USC § 1125) [51]

While ownership of trademarks carries with it enforceable legal rights, it also imposes certain responsibilities. To preserve exclusive rights in a mark, the owner has a duty to monitor and challenge third parties which apply for or use a confusingly-similar mark. Fortunately, there are computerized watch services which can monitor newly filed applications and trademarks, worldwide, providing their clients with early notification of potential infringements and the opportunity to take prompt action to protect their rights. Additionally, when new applications are filed with the USPTO, the review process may include giving notice to holders of marks potentially infringed upon by the proposed new mark.

Although trademark applications are far less complex than those for patents, lack of due diligence in the application process can result in the loss of a mark even years after it has been registered and used in trade. It's always a good idea to have a trademark attorney involved in the process, if at all possible. This is particularly true when — as is most often the case — the response from the USPTO is a written "action letter" or (in some instances) an outright rejection of the proposed mark. Unless the applicant chooses to abandon the registration attempt, the response to a USPTO action letter should probably be prepared by counsel, since there will be a number of legal issues to be addressed. The response to a rejection is an appeal process, which should almost certainly be handled by a qualified attorney versed in trademark law and the USPTO's rules and procedures.

Trade Dress

"The 'trade dress' of a product is essentially its total image and overall appearance."[52] While imitation may be the sincerest form of flattery, it can also be grounds for a claim of

---

50 The Act is not the sole source of U.S. trademark law, since international treaties, common law, and state statutes also control some aspects of trademark protection.

51 The phrase "confusingly similar" appears in that section [1125], as well as in 15 USC § 1129 (cyberpiracy) and 15 USC § 1114 (infringements).

52 *Two Pesos v. Taco Cabana* (1992) 505 U.S. 763, 764, n1.

trade dress infringement. Akin to trademark, trade dress is equally protected under the Lanham Act, even though it is not subject to registration, per se.[53] Trade dress refers to an inherent, non-functional distinctiveness or style of a product or service. Essentially, trade dress protection is extended to commercial image and overall appearance, and may include features such as size, shape, color or color combinations, texture, graphics, or even particular sales or presentation techniques. In a sense, trade dress is the commercial equivalent of personality — those elements which, taken together, evoke the unique identity of a commercial product or entity.

From the standpoint of the entertainment industry, trade dress can be a critical protection, since the overall style and manner in which a performance is presented or staged can be uniquely attributed to a particular performer or group, but not subject to trademark protection, *per se*. This federal protection can be particularly important in states which do not have statutory or common law protection for personality and publicity rights.

Essentially, a competitive usage which evokes the overall style, sense and image of another's product may be regarded as a trade dress infringement. The band Kiss is a good example of unique, non-functional trade dress. While their specific designs for make-up, costume and musical instruments may be subject to trademark, copyright, and even patent protection, the overall image, style and staging of their performances are not registrable, yet remain protected as trade dress. Thus an attempt by others to compete through use of different designs which nonetheless evoke an overall stylistic similarity to Kiss, could be an infringement of trade dress and subject to a claim under the Lanham Act.

In one sense, "trade dress" may be regarded as the institutional equivalent of publicity rights, discussed *infra*, although trade dress enjoys the protection of federal statutes under the Lanham Act, whereas personality and publicity rights currently exist only by virtue of state statutes and common law.

Publicity Rights — Name & Likeness

Personal image — and the components which make up that image — are arguably the most valuable assets for any performer or celebrity. Whether singing, acting, or endorsing some product or cause, an individual's *persona* — those elements which uniquely identify a specific performer such as name, voice, likeness and biography — have immense potential value as a saleable commodity. When those elements of *persona* are appropriated and used without permission, it not only deprives their owner of potential direct income (while unjustly enriching someone else), but it also causes indirect damage through dilution of the

53 Certain *components* of trade dress, such as trade name and logos may be registrable, or subject to copyright protection (*e.g.*, choreography, musical arrangements), or even patent protection (*e.g.*, design patents), but it is the overall *non-functional impression created by the totality of those components*, which forms the "trade dress" of a product or service.

commercial value of that *persona.* The law therefore recognizes that an individual should have the right to control commercial exploitation of his or her personal identity.

This concept is known to the legal profession as the right of publicity, but in the music and entertainment industries is more commonly referred to as "name and likeness" — although those are only two of the components of personality included within this bundle of rights. Most states now recognize at least a limited right to control commercial exploitation of a person's identity, but it is actually a relatively recent legal doctrine, derived from and expanding upon ancient rights to property and more recent concepts of the right of privacy. In fact, it was not until a 1953 case entitled *Haelen Laboratories, Inc., v. Topps Chewing Gum, Inc.*[54] that a court first expressly recognized the right of publicity — which the court's opinion simplistically defined as "the right of a man in the publicity value of his likeness…" — as being separate and distinguishable from the right to privacy. Following fifty years of judicial interpretation, a more comprehensive description of the right of publicity has evolved, as being the "inherent right of every human being to control the commercial use of his or her identity."[55]

While *Haelen Labs* and many other publicity rights cases are federal court opinions, common law and statutes regarding the right of publicity have evolved on the state level, but with the interpretation and enforcement of those laws often falling to the federal judicial system under jurisdiction based on diversity of citizenship or interstate commerce.[56] In some states and federal circuits,[57] the protection afforded by such laws is only minimal, and may be limited to a person's name and picture. In other states and circuits the protections afforded are broader and include those aspects of personality most commonly associated with celebrities and performers. (Not surprisingly, many of these cases have arisen in the Ninth Circuit, which includes California.) The American Bar Association, among others, has urged Congress to enact a federal statute defining and protecting personality rights, but no such *federal* statute yet exists — although a colorable argument could be made for bringing a federal action under the Lanham Act in instances of individuals whose *publicity* rights fall within the protections afforded to trade names or trade dress.[58]

---

54 (1953, 2nd Cir.) 202 F.2d 866, cert denied (1953) 346 U.S. 816

55 *E.g.,* Henley v. Dillard Department Stores (1999, N.D. Tex.) 46 F. Supp. 2d 587

56 Federal courts have jurisdiction to hear cases that either *(a)* raise a federal question (*i.e.,* where the relief sought is based on federal law, including laws which create federal jurisdiction in matters "affecting interstate commerce"), or *(b)* in cases where there is complete diversity of citizenship (*i.e.,* where no plaintiff resides in the same state as any defendant.)

57 The United States is divided into 94 federal judicial districts, which are organized into 12 regional circuits, each of which has a United States court of appeals. A court of appeals hears appeals from the district courts located within its circuit, as well as appeals from decisions of federal administrative agencies. In addition, the Court of Appeals for the Federal Circuit has nationwide jurisdiction to hear appeals in specialized cases, such as those involving patent laws and cases decided by the Court of International Trade and the Court of Federal Claims.

58 The available recovery for *unregistered* marks under the Lanham Act is limited to "actual damages" however, and the USPTO is extremely cautious when it comes to registering a living individual's name as a service mark.

In 1890 — sixty-three years before *Haelan Labs* — a Harvard Law Review article had proposed the idea of a protectable right of privacy, arguing that the law needed to shield private persons from the harm and embarrassment resulting from public disclosure of private facts, regardless of the truth of such facts.[59] That then-radical proposal soon gave rise to the now-familiar tort of "invasion of privacy," and the concomitant right of privacy which it recognizes. As a significant body of case law interpreting common law and statutory invasion of privacy actions began to focus on the harm resulting from unauthorized use of personal identity, the courts inadvertently laid one of the foundations upon which the right of publicity was later built.

But that body of privacy law offered no direct mechanism for claims based on unauthorized use of *celebrity* names or likenesses, since privacy rights are severely weakened for public figures. Courts generally held that, since performers, athletes, and other celebrities had voluntarily subjected themselves to public scrutiny through their choice of occupation, they had waived all but the smallest portion of their privacy rights, and could suffer no invasion of privacy except within a very narrow "zone of privacy" remaining to them. Essentially, the courts were unable to distinguish an invasion of privacy from a commercial misappropriation. In fact, at least one court implied that "greed" did not deserve judicial protection, and in a 1941 opinion the Fifth Circuit denied a famous sports figure's claim against a brewery which had, without permission, used his name and likeness in an advertisement for their beer, ruling that "the publicity he got was only that which he had been constantly seeking…"[60]

Haelan Labs changed everything. In that 1953 case, applying New York law to a claim involving an exclusive right to commercial use of baseball players' photographs, the federal court stated:

> "…in addition to and independent of that right of privacy (which in New York derives from statute), a man has a right in the publicity value of his photograph, i.e., the right to grant the exclusive privilege of publishing his picture, and that such a grant may validly be made 'in gross,' i.e., without an accompanying transfer of a business or of anything else. Whether it be labeled a 'property' right is immaterial; for here, as often elsewhere, the tag 'property' simply symbolizes the fact that courts enforce a claim which has pecuniary worth.
>
> "'This right might be called a 'right of publicity.' For it is common knowledge that many prominent persons (especially actors and ball-players), far from having their feelings bruised through public exposure of their likenesses, would feel sorely deprived if they no longer received

---

59 The Right of Privacy, 4 Harv. L. Rev. 193 (1890), Samuel Warren & Louis Brandeis.

60 O'Brien v. Pabst Sales Co., (1941, 5th Cir.) 124 F.2d 167, 170.

> money for authorizing advertisements, popularizing their countenances, displayed in newspapers, magazines, busses, trains and subways. This right of publicity would usually yield them no money unless it could be made the subject of an exclusive grant which barred any other advertiser from using their pictures." [202 F.2d at 868]

The court's pronouncement in *Haelan Labs* of a distinct right of publicity under property law was strongly supported and expanded upon by renowned intellectual property scholar Melville Nimmer, argued for an independent, common law right protecting economic rather than personal or emotional interests associated with the right of privacy, defining publicity rights as "the right of each person to control the profit from the publicity values which he has created or purchased."[61] Drawing on property law principles, Nimmer reasoned that significant commercial value exists in a celebrity's name or likeness as a result of the time, money and effort expended in establishing that value.

The California Supreme Court, in *Lugosi v. Universal Pictures* (1979) 25 Cal.3d 813, solidified the judicial foundation for a common law right of publicity grounded in property law. In *Lugosi,* the deceased actor's heirs sought to recover profits from Universal for its licensing of the Count Dracula character in subsequent films, arguing that Universal had misappropriated Lugosi's likeness to merchandise Count Dracula. The court held that Lugosi indeed had a proprietary interest in his likeness, but that such right was personal to the actor, and did not survive his death and entered the public domain after his demise. In response to this opinion, the California legislature enacted (former) Civil Code § 990 which made publicity rights inheritable — or *descendible,* in legal parlance — as a matter of law, from and after 1984.[62]

The common law right of publicity protects against the unauthorized commercial use of **name** and **likeness,** as well as other traits of identity which are less easily defined. Not only an individual's legal **name**, but **stage names** and **group names** are protected from unauthorized commercial use as being elements of the right of publicity.[63] **Likeness** refers not only to photographs and portraits, but to *any* recognizable visual rendering. In jurisdictions applying common law protections, this has been extended to unauthorized use of look-alikes and sound-alikes where circumstances might allow confusion as to whether a particular person (rather than an imitator of that person) authorized, is participating in, or is connected with such use in still photography, motion pictures, television, or live performance. If such possibility for confusion exists, the use may be an infringement.

In *White v. Samsung* (1992, 9th Cir.) 971 F.2d 1395, Samsung Electronics and its advertising agency, David Deutsch Associates, published a printed advertisement which

---

61 "The Right of Publicity," Nimmer, (1954) 19 Law & Contemporary Problems 203, 216.

62 Civil Code § 990 has since been substantially amended and renumbered as Civil Code § 3344.1.

63 Federal Lanham Act protection will also likely be available in many such cases.

depicted a robot dressed in a wig, gown and jewelry, selected to resemble the hair and dress of Vanna White, a well known television hostess, posed in a manner imitative of her television role. White never consented to, and was not paid or offered payment for the ad. She commenced a lawsuit alleging, among other claims, infringement of her publicity rights. Defendants attempted a novel, first amendment "fair use" approach,[64] arguing that the ad was a parody of plaintiff, and protected free speech rather than mere commercial speech.[65] Their argument was unpersuasive. The court held that unless the first amendment bars all right of publicity actions — and it does not — then it did not bar Vanna White's claims; she had the right to control commercial use of her likeness, whenever and however it might be recognizably presented.

While name and likeness can be defined with reasonable certainty, other elements of a personal identity under the common law right of publicity can be more elusive, as illustrated by some of the seminal cases in this area of law which are discussed below.

In the absence of a comprehensive federal statute, publicity rights cases can only rely on state laws and precedents. In consequence, identical actions filed in different states would likely receive inconsistent analysis and results. Although most states now protect the right of publicity to some degree, the nature and extent of that protection can vary widely from state to state.

In 1971, California enacted Civil Code § 3344, providing a detailed statutory scheme which forbids intentional unauthorized use of "another's name, voice, signature, photograph, or likeness, in any manner on or in products, merchandise, or goods, or for purposes of advertising or selling, or soliciting purchases of products, merchandise, goods or services, ..." The statute provides limited exceptions, such as for news and sports reporting, and imposes an award of actual damages (with a $750 per use minimum award), severe penalties (up to 100% of the profits received from the use), and an award of attorney's fees. It also provides that the statute is *cumulative*; that is, damages may also be awarded on other causes of action, including a common law right of publicity claim, permitting the court to go outside the enumerated list of protected personality traits contained in the statute. This is important, since the statute only protects against *intentional* use of specific, listed traits, so that mistake and inadvertence are defenses to a § 3344 action, but not to a concurrent common law action based on the same facts. Thus, the Ninth Circuit has held that the

---

64 "Fair use" doctrine is discussed at length in Chapter 3 ("A Primer on Copyright.")

65 "Commercial speech" refers to literal speech or, more usually, printed materials, "proposing a commercial transaction," (*Ohralik v. Ohio State Bar Ass'n, (1978) 436 U.S. 447*) or which are an "expression related solely to the economic interests of the speaker and its audience."' (*Central Hudson Gas & Electric Corp. v. Public Service Comm'n, (1980) 447 U.S. 557, 561*). Commercial speech is not afforded First Amendment protections unless it serves a public purpose (*Virginia State Bd. of Pharmacy v. Virginia Citizens Consumer Council (1976) 425 U.S. 748*) , or is "inextricably intertwined with otherwise fully protected speech." (*Riley v. National Fed'n of the Blind, (1988) 487 U.S. 781, 796.*)

California common law right of publicity includes "appropriations of identity" that extend beyond the statutory list of "name, voice, signature, photograph, or likeness."

> "The theory of the right is that a celebrity's identity can be valuable in the promotion of products, and the celebrity has an interest that may be protected from the unauthorized commercial exploitation of that identity.... If the celebrity's identity is commercially exploited, there has been an invasion of his right whether or not his "name or likeness" is used. [...] It is not important ***how*** the defendant has appropriated the plaintiff's identity, but ***whether*** the defendant has done so. [Prior cases] teach the impossibility of treating the right of publicity as guarding only against a laundry list of specific means of appropriating identity. A rule which says that the right of publicity can be infringed only through the use of nine different methods of appropriating identity merely challenges the clever advertising strategist to come up with the tenth."[66]

Undoubtedly owing to its jurisdiction over California, the federal Ninth Circuit has been at the forefront of publicity rights cases, and many (but by no means all) other federal circuits have frequently adopted Ninth Circuit opinions and analyses as precedent in these types of cases.

But not every jurisdiction recognizes a common law right of publicity. Even though the Second Circuit, applying New York law, was the source of the seminal *Haelen Labs* opinion, New York state courts have consistently denied the existence of common law protection for the right of publicity. The lack of agreement between state and federal courts applying the same state's laws in the same jurisdiction has resulted in unfortunate ambiguities in respect to publicity rights within that state. New York state courts have repeatedly held that the state's rather narrow publicity statutes, enacted in 1902, which encompass only "name, portrait, or picture of a living person," are the *sole* source for any right of publicity claim, and those statutes — Sections 50 and 51 of New York Civil Rights Law — are diluted by their inclusion of exemptions for a number of types of commercial use, which limit the scope of protection under the laws of that state. Additionally, New York law affords no protection in respect to the personality or publicity rights of a deceased person. Thus the publicity rights of New York residents pass into public domain upon their demise, whereas, since the 1984 enactment of California Civil Code § 990, the personality rights of California residents have been descendible and available for commercial exploitation by their heirs.

Although the Ninth Circuit and California have remained at the forefront of publicity rights jurisprudence, they have not been alone in defining these evolving rights. Following, in chronological order, are some of the more interesting (and illuminating) cases showing that evolution:

---

66 *White v. Samsung* (1992, 9th Cir.) 971 F.2d 1395, 1398

Motschenbacher v. R.J. Reynolds Tobacco Co.
(1974, 9th Cir.) 498 F.2d 821

Lothar Motschenbacher, a professional race car driver, sued R.J. Reynolds Tobacco Company and its advertising agency for injunctive relief and damages, alleging misappropriation of his name, likeness, and personality in a television commercial. The commercial "utilized a 'stock' color photograph depicting several racing cars on a racetrack. Plaintiff's car appears in the foreground, and although Plaintiff is the driver, his facial features are not visible." Defendants had altered the photograph by changing the numbers on all the racing cars depicted, transforming Motschenbacher's number "11" into "71," and photographically attaching a "'spoiler" to plaintiff's car with the word 'Winston' appearing on that spoiler. The Ninth Circuit held that the right of publicity affords legal protection to an individual's proprietary interest in his own ***identity*** and the fact that Motschenbacher's "likeness" was unrecognizable in the commercial; that the number of his racing car had been changed from "11" to "71"; and that a "spoiler" had been added to the car, did not preclude a finding that Motschenbacher was immediately identifiable, in view of his automobile's distinctive markings: white pin-striping, oval medallion, and red color.

Lugosi v. Universal Pictures
(1979) 25 Cal.3d 813

As discussed earlier, this decision preceded — and precipitated — the California legislature's subsequent 1984 enactment of (former) Civil Code § 990, which codified the descendability of publicity. In 1979, Bela Lugosi's heirs sued to enjoin and recover profits from Universal Pictures for licensing Lugosi's name and image on merchandise based on Lugosi's title role in the 1930 film, "Dracula." The California Supreme Court faced the question whether Lugosi's film contracts with Universal included a grant of merchandising rights in his portrayal of Count Dracula, and the descendability of any such rights. The court held that the right to control exploitation of one's name and likeness exists, but was personal to the artist and could be exercised, if at all, only during the artist's lifetime. The 1984 enactment of Civil Code § 990 (since renumbered and expanded as Civil Code § 3344.1) had the effect of overruling *Lugosi* as precedent in regard to descendability, making personality rights inheritable in California, from and since that time.

Clark v. Celeb Publishing, Inc.,
(1981, S.D. NY) 530 F. Supp. 979

In a New York action applying California law, the District Court awarded $25,000 in emotional distress damages based on unauthorized publication of Linda Clark's photographs in Celeb Magazine. Clark, a self-employed professional model and actress, had sued Celeb Publishing, Inc. for invasion of privacy and unauthorized use of her photographs which appeared "in a broad range of advertisements, as well as in Forum and Penthouse Magazine

..." Noting that Clark resided in California and suffered her alleged injuries in California, the federal district court for the Southern District of New York applied California law, rather than New York law, awarding $25,000 in damages for mental anguish resulting from the unauthorized publication of photographs in what was characterized as a low quality and very explicit pornographic magazine, plus $6,750 in lost compensation, and a $7,000 license fee for unauthorized use of the photographs.

Cher v. Forum International Ltd.,
(1982, 9th Cir.) 692 F.2d 634
cert. denied (1983) 462 U.S. 1120

Actress/celebrity "Cher" sued freelance writer Fred Robbins, on the basis of a published article billed as an "exclusive" interview. Cher had given Robbins an interview for a story to be published in "Us" magazine but, at Cher's request, Us declined to publish the article. Robbins eventually sold the interview to Forum International and Star. Based upon the headlines, cover page promotions, and related advertising, Cher brought suit alleging breach of contract, unfair competition, misappropriation of name and likeness, and misappropriation of her right of publicity. The Ninth Circuit held that Cher was not damaged by Star's allegedly exaggerated "exclusivity" claims and that the First Amendment protected the magazines from Cher's right of publicity claims so long as the article was not published with actual malice. However, the Ninth Circuit went on to hold that Forum misappropriated Cher's right of publicity by falsely indicating that she had revealed facts to Forum that she would not reveal to a rival magazine, and by falsely indicating that she endorsed the magazine. The Ninth Circuit affirmed an award of $100,000 in special damages, $69,000 in general damages, and $100,000 in punitive damages.

Groucho Marx Prod., Inc. v. Day and Night Company, Inc.
(1982, 2nd Cir.) 689 F.2d 317

Defendants produced a Broadway musical entitled "A Day in Hollywood/ A Night in the Ukraine," described by its authors as "a 'satiric comment' on Hollywood in the 1930's" it included a speculative depiction of how the Marx Brothers might have dramatized Chekhov's novel, *The Bear*. Although the Marx Brothers were not depicted by name, the script called for three principal performers to reproduce the appearance and comedy style made memorable by Groucho, Chico, and Harpo Marx. The Marx Brothers' assignees sued for interference with publicity rights. The federal Second Circuit held that "the descendability of the Marx Brothers' rights of publicity [was] governed by California law and that [prior to the 1984 enactment of California Civil Code § 990] ... such rights either [did] not survive death or at least [did] not entitle the plaintiffs to relief in this case."

Eastwood v. Superior Court
(1983) 149 Cal.App. 3d 409

In its April 13, 1982 edition, the Enquirer published a 600-word article about Clint Eastwood's alleged romantic involvement with two other celebrities, singer Tanya Tucker and actress Sondra Locke, featuring Eastwood's photograph on the magazine's cover page with the headline, "Clint Eastwood in Love Triangle with Tanya Tucker." Eastwood sued for false light invasion of privacy and for commercial appropriation of name, photograph and likeness under California common law and Civil Code § 3344. The California State Court of Appeal held that Eastwood had stated a viable claim, and broadly articulated the elements of California's common law right of publicity as follows:

> "A common law cause of action for appropriation of name or likeness may be pleaded by alleging (1) the defendant's use of the plaintiff's identity; (2) the appropriation of plaintiff's name or likeness to defendant's advantage, commercially or otherwise; (3) the lack of consent; and (4) resulting injury."

John W. Carson v. Here's Johnny Portable Toilets Inc.
(1983, 6th Cir.) 698 F.2d 831

Tonight Show host, Johnny Carson, brought suit against a Michigan company called Here's Johnny Portable Toilets Inc., for unfair trade practices under the Lanham Act, (15 USC § 1125(a)), and Michigan common law for unfair competition and invasion of the rights of privacy and publicity, for the company's use of the phrase "Here's Johnny," — a phrase closely associated with Carson. The Sixth Circuit noted that the test for relief under the Lanham Act and Michigan common law for unfair competition was the likelihood of confusion standard, which was not present in this case. The court also ruled that Carson's claim that his right of privacy had been invaded was not supported by the law or the facts. *However*, the court found that Carson's right of *publicity* had been violated, since a celebrity had a protected pecuniary interest in the commercial exploitation of his identity and that if the celebrity's identity was commercially exploited, there had been an invasion of his right whether or not his name or likeness was used. In essence, the Sixth Circuit ruled that Carson's famed tagline was a part of his *persona*, and that he could therefore withhold it from any use that he found offensive or for which he was not paid a licensing fee.

Midler v. Ford Motor Co.
(1988, 9th Cir.) 849 F.2d 460, cert. denied.

Singer Bette Midler sued Ford Motor Company and its advertising agency based on a television commercial which had used a "sound alike" vocalist to perform one of Midler's well known hit songs, "Do You Want to Dance." The Ninth Circuit held that Midler could not state a claim for violation of Section 3344 because her actual voice was not used in the commercial, but that she could nevertheless state a viable claim for violation of her common law right of publicity. Noting that Ford sought "an attribute of Midler's identity" and that "[i]ts value was what the market would have paid for Midler to have sung the commercial in person" [849 F.2d at 463], the court concluded:

> "We hold only that when a distinctive voice of a professional singer is widely known and is deliberately imitated in order to sell a product, the sellers have appropriated what is not theirs and have committed a tort in California. Midler has made a showing [that defendants] for their own profit in selling their product did appropriate part of her identity." [849 F.2d at 463-464].

Midler was awarded $400,000 in compensatory damages.

New Kids on the Block v. News America Publishing, Inc.
(1992, 9th Cir.) 971 F.2d 302

New Kids on the Block sued News America Publishing, Inc. (then publisher of "Star") and Gannett Satellite Information Network, Inc. (publisher of "USA Today"), alleging trademark infringement and misappropriation of rights of publicity based on defendants' pay-per-call, "900-number" public opinion polls asking which member of the group was the sexiest or most popular. The court held that the First Amendment protected the publishers against these claims because the polls were related to news-gathering and dissemination of information, and involved matters of "public interest." The Ninth Circuit affirmed, adding that the claims were not actionable because they fell within § 3344's exemption for use "in connection with any news, public affairs, or sports broadcast or account."[67]

Joplin Enterprises v. Allen
(1992, W.D. WA) 795 F. Supp. 349

Janis Joplin's heirs alleged that a two-act biographical play about the deceased Joplin was a misappropriation of Joplin's rights of privacy and publicity. The federal district court for the Western District of Washington concluded that Joplin's estate could not maintain a viable right of publicity claim under (former) California Civil Code § 990, because, by its

---

67 Plaintiffs' trademark (Lanham Act) claim was also defeated on the grounds that the use complained of fell within the "nominative fair use" exception, which holds that there is no consumer confusion — and hence, no infringement — "if three requirements are met: First, the product or service in question must be one not readily identifiable without use of the trademark; second, only so much of the mark or marks may be used as is reasonably necessary to identify the product or service; and third, the user must do nothing that would, in conjunction with the mark, suggest sponsorship or endorsement by the trademark holder." [971 F.2d at 308]

terms, that section applied only to "merchandise, advertisements, and endorsements" and exempted any "play," "book," or "musical composition" from liability.[68]

White v. Samsung

(1992, 9th Cir.) 971 F.2d 1395
cert. denied, (1993) 113 S. Ct. 2443

As more fully discussed earlier, Samsung's print advertisement depicting a futuristic robot game show hostess dressed in a wig, gown, and jewelry posed in a "Wheel of Fortune"-like game show set, violated White's common law right of publicity, which is not limited to appropriation of actual "name or likeness" but also includes *any* method of invoking an individual's "identity."

Ultimately, a jury awarded White $403,000 in compensatory damages.

Waits v. Frito-Lay, Inc.

(1992, 9th Cir.) 978 F.2d 1093
cert. denied, (1993) 506 U.S. 1080.

Singer and songwriter, Tom Waits, who generally refuses to write for or appear in commercials, sued Frito-Lay for a Doritos commercial which featured a voice strikingly similar to Waits' voice and singing style, performing a jingle based on Waits' song, "Step Right Up," which he had written as a cynical parody of advertising jingles. Waits obtained a $2.5 million verdict ($375,000 in compensatory damages, $2 million in punitive damages, and $125,000 in attorneys' fees). In affirming the award, the Ninth Circuit referred to clear evidence of Waits' outspoken public stance against doing commercial endorsements, his embarrassment when the commercial aired, and the injury to his good will and future publicity value.. Citing its own holding in Midler v. Ford Motor Co., (*supra*) 849 F.2d 460 at 463, the court reiterated that:

> "When a distinctive voice of a professional singer is widely known and is deliberately imitated in order to sell a product, the sellers have appropriated what is not theirs and have committed a tort in California."

68 The 1999 amendment of Civil Code § 990 (renumbering it Civil Code § 3344.1), retained these exceptions, stating: "a play, book, magazine, newspaper, musical composition, audiovisual work, radio or television program, single and original work of art, work of political or newsworthy value, or an advertisement or commercial announcement for any of these works, shall not be considered a product, article of merchandise, good, or service if it is fictional or nonfictional entertainment, or a dramatic, literary, or musical work."

Dora v. Frontline Video, Inc.

(1993) 15 Cal.App.4th 536

In 1987, Frontline produced a video documentary, "The Legends of Malibu," which chronicled the early days of surfing, showing footage of famous surfers, including Mickey Dora. Arguing that he was never interviewed nor photographed by Frontline and did not consent to use of his name, photograph, likeness, or voice, Dora sued for common law and statutory misappropriation of name and likeness. The California Court of Appeal held that Frontline was not required to obtain Dora's consent because the documentary contained matters of public interest and "public affairs," which are exempt from liability under California Civil Code § 3344.

Newton v. Thomason

(1994, 9th Cir.) 22 F.3d 1455

Country music performer and songwriter "Wood" Newton unsuccessfully sued television producers Harry Thomason and Linda Bloodworth-Thomason, as well as Burt Reynolds and Mozark Productions, Inc., alleging Lanham Act, common law, and statutory damages based on their use of his name for a character in the television series, "Evening Shade." The case was originally filed in the Northern District of Illinois, but transferred to the Central District of California. On appeal, the Ninth Circuit held that the use was coincidental and arguably consensual.[69] There was no evidence that Newton's name was used for a commercial purpose or that any particular commercial benefit was derived from the use. That use was therefore not an actionable violation of Newton's right of publicity.

Montana v. San Jose Mercury News, Inc.

(1995, Cal. 6th District) 34 Cal.App.4th 790

The California Court of Appeal affirmed summary judgment against football star Joe Montana's claim that a newspaper's poster reproducing its Super Bowl cover story violated his § 3344 and common law rights of publicity. Noting that § 3344 does not require consent for use of a "name, voice, signature, photograph, or likeness in connection with any news, public affairs, or sports broadcast or account, or any political campaign," the court held that the posters represented newsworthy events, and that a newspaper has a constitutional right to promote itself by reproducing its new stories.

---

69 Newton learned that Defendants' use of the name "Wood Newton" as a character name when his sister sent him a newspaper article about the series. He subsequently wrote, a letter to the show's producers which stated, in part: "I've been reading about your new show.... I want you to know I'm flattered that you are using my name, everyone who I've talked to about it thinks it's exciting and so do I."

Wendt v. Host International
(1995, 9th Cir.) 50 F.3d 18
(1997, 9th Cir.) 125 F.3d 806
cert denied (2000) 531 U.S. 811

In 1993, actors George Wendt and John Ratzenberger, who had portrayed the characters Norm Peterson and Cliff Clavin on the TV series "Cheers," sued Host International, which (under a license from Paramount Pictures) operated a chain of "Cheers"-themed airport bars, styled similarly to the bar featured in the TV show and which included a pair of animatronic likenesses resembling the two fictional characters. Paramount intervened in the case, contending that, since it owned all rights to the show and its characters, the actors who had played the roles had no rights with respect to the copyrighted characters which Paramount had licensed to Host. The actors' claims were dismissed by the trial court — twice — but the Ninth Circuit reversed and remanded the case for trial — twice — holding that "an actor or actress does not lose the right to control the commercial exploitation of his or her likeness by portraying a fictional character. [...] The ultimate issue for the jury to decide is whether the defendants are commercially exploiting the likeness of the figures to Wendt and Ratzenberger intending to engender profits to their enterprises."

(Following the Supreme Court's denial of certiorari review of the Ninth Circuit's remand, the two sides settled in 2001, leaving unanswered the question of whether an actor's right of publicity ultimately prevails over a studio's copyright claims.)

Kareem Abdul-Jabbar v. General Motors Corp.
(1996, 9th Cir.) 85 F.3d 407

During a televised NCAA basketball tournament, an Oldsmobile-sponsored trivia quiz referred to an NCAA record: Lew Alcindor's selection as Most Outstanding Player in three NCAA tournaments.[70] Abdul-Jabbar sued General Motors and its advertising agency for violations of, *inter alia*, his statutory and common law rights of privacy based on the use of his former name in Oldsmobile's trivia-quiz commercial. GMC's defense was that Abdul-Jabbar had abandoned all rights with respect to that former name when he legally changed it. The Ninth Circuit disagreed. Applying California law, the court held that both under common law and § 3344, "name or likeness" is not limited to present or current use. To the extent GMC's use of the Abdul-Jabbar's "birth name attracted television viewers' attention, GMC gained a commercial advantage." [85 F.3d at 415.]

70 Following his college career, Lew Alcindor, a Muslim, had legally changed his name to Kareem Abdul-Jabbar.

Astaire v. Best Film & Video Corp.
(1997, 9th Cir.) 136 F.3d 1208

Fred Astaire's widow, Robyn Astaire, sued Best Film & Video Corporation ("Best"), a New York corporation that manufactures, markets, and distributes pre-recorded videotapes, alleging that Best's use of her late husband's image in a series of dance instruction videotapes violated her statutory right to control the use of her deceased husband's name and likeness under (former) California Civil Code § 990. Each of Best's videotapes opened with about 90 seconds of footage of Fred Astaire from two of his motion pictures.

Although the federal trial court granted summary judgment to Astaire's widow, holding that Best's use of the Astaire film clips violated the "on or in products, merchandise, or goods" prong of § 990.(a), the Ninth Circuit later reversed that judgment, holding instead that Best's use of the Astaire clips was exempt from liability under § 990(n)(1). Although by its terms, that provision only exempted film and television programs, the court reasoned that pre-recorded videotapes were encompassed in the "film" exemption. The Court concluded that the exemption applied even if Best's use of the Fred Astaire film clips was an advertisement or commercial announcement.

> *(Robyn Astaire subsequently lobbied the California legislature to narrow the § 990 exemption to works which are "fictional or nonfictional entertainment, or a dramatic, literary, or musical work," in a revised descendability statute, renumbered as Civil Code § 3344.1 and entitled the "Astaire Celebrity Image Protection Act," which became law in 1999.)*

Kareem Abdul-Jabbar v. Karim Abdul-Jabbar
(1997, DC CD Cal.) Case No. CV-97-8162

In 1997, former basketball star Kareem Abdul-Jabbar sued Miami Dolphins running back Karim Abdul-Jabbar in the United States District Court, Central District of California, claiming that the latter's adopted Islamic name, and identical jersey number, infringed upon the former's commercial identity. The case ended with a stipulated settlement and order, pursuant to which the younger Abdul-Jabbar agreed to relinquish all commercial rights to use of the name.

Winter v. DC Comics, et al.
(2003) 30 Cal. 4th 881

Johnny and Edgar Winter, well-known musicians from Texas, sued DC Comics and others in the Los Angeles Superior Court, alleging, among other things, appropriation of their names and likenesses under California Civil Code § 3344. In the 1990's, DC Comics had published a series of comic books. Volume 3 of that series ended with a reference to two new characters, the "Autumn brothers," and the teaser, "NEXT: The Autumns of Our

Discontent." The cover of volume 4 depicts the Autumn brother characters, with pale faces and long white hair, with one of them wearing a stovepipe hat. Volumes 4 and 5 of the series featured "Johnny and Edgar Autumn," depicted as villainous half-worm, half-human creatures, who are shot and killed at the end of volume 5.

Plaintiffs alleged that the defendants selected the names Johnny and Edgar Autumn to signal readers that the Winter brothers were being portrayed; that the Autumn brothers were drawn with long white hair and albino features similar to plaintiffs'; that the Johnny Autumn character was depicted as wearing a tall black top hat similar to the one Johnny Winter often wore; and that the title of volume 4, "Autumns of Our Discontent," refers to the famous Shakespearian phrase.[71] They also alleged that the comics falsely portrayed them as "vile, depraved, stupid, cowardly, subhuman individuals who engage in wanton acts of violence, murder and bestiality for pleasure and who should be killed."

The trial court found for defendants on First Amendment grounds. The state appellate court reversed in favor of plaintiffs, and the California state Supreme Court reversed the appellate court, reinstating the original trial court's judgment upholding defendants' First Amendment rights, and stating:

> "The right of publicity cannot, consistent with the First Amendment, be a right to control the celebrity's image by censoring disagreeable portrayals. Once the celebrity thrusts himself or herself forward into the limelight, the First Amendment dictates that the right to comment on, parody, lampoon, and make other expressive uses of the celebrity image must be given broad scope. The necessary implication of this observation is that the right of publicity is essentially an economic right. What the right of publicity holder possesses is not a right of censorship, but a right to prevent others from misappropriating the economic value generated by the celebrity's fame through the merchandising of the 'name, voice, signature, photograph, or likeness' of the celebrity. Second, in determining whether the work is transformative, courts are not to be concerned with the quality of the artistic contribution vulgar forms of expression fully qualify for First Amendment protection. On the other hand, a literal depiction of a celebrity, even if accomplished with great skill, may still be subject to a right of publicity challenge. The inquiry is in a sense more quantitative than qualitative, asking whether the literal and imitative or the creative elements predominate in the work."
>
> "Application of the test to this case is not difficult. We have reviewed the comic books [and] can readily ascertain that they are not just conventional depictions of plaintiffs but contain significant expressive content other than plaintiffs' mere likenesses. Although the fictional characters Johnny and Edgar Autumn are less-than-subtle evocations of Johnny and Edgar Winter, the books do not depict plaintiffs literally. Instead, plaintiffs are merely part of the raw materials from which

71 The opening line of Shakespeare's Richard III. "Now is the winter of our discontent made glorious summer by this sun of York." (Punning on the words "sun" and "son.")

the comic books were synthesized. To the extent the drawings of the Autumn brothers resemble plaintiffs at all, they are distorted for purposes of lampoon, parody, or caricature. And the Autumn brothers are but cartoon characters--half-human and half-worm--in a larger story, which is itself quite expressive. The characters and their portrayals do not greatly threaten plaintiffs' right of publicity. Plaintiffs' fans who want to purchase pictures of them would find the drawings of the Autumn brothers unsatisfactory as a substitute for conventional depictions. [...] Comic books are no less protected [by the First Amendment] because they provide humorous rather than serious commentary."

John Doe, a/k/a Tony Twist v. TCI Cablevision, et al.

(2003, Mo.) 110 S.W.3d 363 (en banc),
cert denied (2004) 540 U.S. 1106,
appeal after remand (2006 Mo. App. E.D.)

In 2003, former hockey player Tony Twist, known as a notorious "enforcer" during his playing days, brought suit in the Missouri state court against the creator of the Spawn comic book series for creation, in the 1990's, of a character named "Antonio 'Tony Twist' Twistelli," portrayed in the Spawn comics as a violent Mafia boss. The original jury awarded Twist $24-million, but the trial judge overturned that verdict. On appeal, the Missouri Supreme Court, remanding the case for new trial, observed: "In this case, Twist seeks to recover the amount of the fair market value that respondents should have paid to use his name in connection with Spawn products and for damage done to the commercial value - in effect the endorsement value - of his name. Therefore, Twist's case, though brought as a misappropriation of name action, is more precisely labeled a right of publicity action [...] Despite the differences in the types of damages that may be recovered, the elements of the two torts are essentially the same. To establish the misappropriation tort, the plaintiff must prove that the defendant used the plaintiff's name without consent to obtain some advantage. [...] In a right of publicity action, the plaintiff must prove the same elements as in a misappropriation suit, with the minor exception that the plaintiff must prove that the defendant used the name to obtain a commercial advantage."

On remand and retrial, the new jury awarded Twist $15-million, upheld on further appeal (the U.S. Supreme Court having denied certiorari review.) As a result, Spawn creator Todd McFarlane was forced into bankruptcy.

> *(The U.S. Supreme Court's refusal to grant certiorari review left open the First Amendment question regarding comic books. There is no way to reconcile the Missouri Supreme Court's opinion in Doe, a/k/a Tony Twist v. TCI Cablevision with the California Supreme Court's opinion in Winter v. D.C. Comics,* supra.*)*

◆ ◆ ◆

Personality rights have attained *quasi*-property status and protection in most jurisdictions, and must be respected to the same extent as are intellectual property rights such as copyright and trademark. If nothing else, the foregoing cases — and the potential financial liability which can arise from unauthorized use of personality rights — should amply demonstrate that the outcome of court proceedings can *never* be taken for granted. These cases should also provide a suitable appreciation for the desirability of obtaining licenses or releases whenever possible from anyone whose name, voice, likeness, biographical information, or other identifiable element of persona is (or might be) associated with a commercial project.

◆ ◆ ◆

"Truth in Music" Statutes: State Law Protection of Artists' Names

At the time of this writing, twenty-six states have enacted so-called "Truth in Music" laws to protect recording artists from misappropriation of their *group* names for live performances by unauthorized imitators. The underlying premise of these laws is that ***art is not fungible***. Unlike hamburgers, which can be mass-produced and franchised, human beings (even musicians and singers) are unique and cannot be duplicated. Musical groups comprised of performers other than those who originally established the reputation and goodwill of the name under which that group appears may be viewed as defrauding the public when they fail to disclose that their group contains none of the original performers. Surprisingly, the legal history of this issue goes back to at least 1897.[72]

Imitation groups often misappropriate the names and reputations of the artists who established public recognition and goodwill for their band name, even when the names of the original, individual performers in those groups are relatively unknown. On any given night there may be public performances by a dozen different groups which have been promoted and have sold tickets by holding themselves out under the name of the same famous recording group. Usually these groups have *no legal right* to use the names under which they are promoted, booked, advertised, and appear. Frequently, they attempt to skirt current legal protections by booking themselves under expanded or modified names, but with advertising which downplays or omits entirely all but the famous name which they have misappropriated.[73] Occasionally, however, the promoters of these groups have —

72 Messer v The Fadettes (1897) 168 Mass 140, 46 NE 407, a trademark case in which the court held that a musical group's name rests on personal reputation of the original performers, and use of that name to designate a body of musicians different from those who earned a reputation under that name would be a fraud on the public.

73 In Williams v. SBE, etc., et al., U.S. District Court, Central District of California, Case No. 07-07006-GAF, Otis Williams — the last surviving original member of The Temptations — brought a Lanham Act suit against groups booked under the name "Legendary Lead Singers of the Temptations" which were being regularly advertised as "Legendary Lead Singers of **The Temptations**," including one such group which had been appearing nightly as a *(continued)*

legitimately or otherwise — obtained some colorable (if dubious) right to use of the recording group's name. But a bare, attenuated claim of right is insufficient under Truth in Music laws, which require that the group either include at least one performer who was a "recording member" of the original group and who holds a legal right to use of the group name, or that the group have a registered Federal trademark or equivalent rights,[74] or that it have express written consent from the original recording group *provided* that said original group is legally entitled to license others to use the name.

In Marshak v Green (1984, CA2 NY) 746 F2d 927, the court found that, under the Lanham Act, **a trade name has no significance independent of the goodwill which it symbolizes**. The name therefore cannot be sold or assigned apart from that goodwill, since use of the name in connection with a different group or product would result in a fraud on the public, with consumers reasonably assuming that a group performing under a recognized name would be the same group as had been previously identified by and which had recorded under that name. While it is true that, in many instances, only a few members of the public may be aware of the specific identities of the authentic members of a particular recording group, there is still a public reliance upon the integrity of the group as a whole; a shared continuity of identity, style, and quality which cannot be delegated through licensing or franchising.

Promoters who operate imitative groups with no legal right to the name they utilize may be sued in state or federal court under the Lanham Act for infringing on the trade name, mark, and trade dress of the original group *regardless* of whether or not there has been a trademark registration, *if* there is some plaintiff who can bring the suit and who has an unquestionable, superior right to the name. But those who *do* hold some attenuated connection to a famous group's name may be without a sufficiently provable right to prosecute a federal suit against imposters or, even when they do have such right, they may lack the *funds* necessary to such a suit.[75] Where the right to prosecute a Lanham Act suit may be questionable, or prosecuting such a suit may be financially impossible for the true holder of necessary rights, imposter groups may nonetheless be subject to Truth in Music laws on the theory that use by others of a well-known recording group's name confuses, deceives, and potentially defrauds consumers.

Certainly there are exceptions. Orchestral groups often create one or two smaller units of themselves, and no one expects the late Glenn Miller (1904-1944) to appear with the still-

---

"headline" act at the Sahara Hotel in Las Vegas under the "Temptations" name. Reaffirming its own order of preliminary injunction on a motion for reconsideration, the court stated: "[T]he Court is convinced that Defendants seek to mislead consumers…" (Order, 2/8/2008)

74 In *Marshak v. Treadwell*, (1999, DC NJ) 58 F. Supp.2d 551, affd. (2001, 3d Cir.) 240 F.3d 184, the promoter of an imitation "Drifters" group *had* obtained trademark registration. In a federal Lanham Act suit (which the registered trademark owner had originated), the court found that the application for that registration had contained fraudulent misrepresentations as to the applicant's alleged lawful commercial use of the name, and ordered the trademark registration cancelled.

75 A Lanham Act suit can easily cost $150,000 or more in attorneys' fees, plus costs, including the cost of obtaining a bond in order to secure an injunction to stop imposters from performing.

touring "Glenn Miller Orchestra." Similarly, there are so-called "concept" groups which, from their inception, were composed of interchangeable and replaceable members. But such groups do not confuse or deceive the public into believing that they will be seeing "the one and only" version of a famous recording group. The willful imposter groups, on the other hand, *count on* consumers being confused or deceived, and profit from consumers' mistaken belief that they are buying tickets to see "the originals."

Often these imitation groups may contain a "former member" of a famous group, but with that person having no legal right to use or license others to use the group's name. Sometimes the "former member" is no more than a session player who performed on one recording with the group, or who was a temporary replacement member of the group for a tour. Alternatively, the imitation group may purport to have been *licensed* to use the group's name by a "former member" (with no evidence that such "former member" had any right to issue a license), or by some heir or purported heir of such a "former member."[76]

The Pennsylvania-based Vocal Group Hall of Fame has been the prime mover in lobbying various state legislatures to adopt laws designed to stop promoters from deceiving the public with groups which have no connection (legal or otherwise) to the authentic groups. As throughout trademark law, the touchstone is the likelihood of consumer confusion, so Truth in Music statutes are essentially *consumer* protection laws, to prevent deception of ticket buyers. The model statute (which has been slightly altered by each state legislature) makes it mandatory for each live performance group appearing under the name of a recording group to either hold a legitimately registered federal trademark for the name, *or* to have an equivalent common-law trademark right, *or* to include at least one member who recorded as a member of that group ***and*** a who has a legal right to use the group's name. Unless the group can satisfy those requirements, their act must be clearly advertised and billed as a "tribute" or a "salute" to the original group, so that the public won't be deceived.

Of course, an ancillary effect of Truth in Music has been to protect the rights of original recording artists, many of whose livelihoods depend on touring and performing, often for decades after their last album was released.[77] The statute protects these artists from a form of commercial identity theft by empowering state authorities to promptly obtain injunctions to shut down imposter groups, and to impose financial penalties on those groups, their promoters, and (in most states[78]) venues which book them, for violation of Truth in Music laws.

---

76 At least one such imitation group claimed to be operating under authority of a license granted by the mother of a deceased former (non-original) member of a famous recording group. An investigation of that purported license disclosed that it was a *prima facie* forgery... the former member's mother had died nearly two years prior to the date upon which she had allegedly granted and signed that license.

77 Most such performers are from "oldies" groups which no longer record, but time marches on and, in the not-too-distant future, today's superstar recording artists may find themselves grateful for the protections which Truth in Music laws afford.

78 The notable exception is Nevada, where the Truth in Music statute contains an exception for venues, excusing them from liability unless they own, manage, or produce the imitation group.

NA

CHAPTER 3

A PRIMER ON COPYRIGHT

Because virtually every music industry contract relates in some way to copyrighted material, it is important to have at least a basic grasp of when and how copyrights are created, and what the term "copyright" covers.

What Is a Copyright?

Copyright is a government-sanctioned, limited monopoly providing certain almost-absolute rights to the creator of an original work of art to exclusively control that work for a period of time. While nearly every country in the world provides some form of copyright protection under its own laws, there are also international treaties which provide reciprocal protections for authors from other countries signatory to those treaties. In the United States, the national law is found in the Copyright Act (Title 17 of United States Code) which establishes protections afforded to the creators of "original works of authorship" which includes literary, dramatic, musical, visual, intellectual, and other forms of creative and artistic work.

Copyright protection applies to both published and unpublished creative work, in any medium, and (under the current Copyright Act) that protection begins the moment a work is first fixed in some tangible form — which can be anything ranging from a piece of scratch paper to a rough or final audio or visual recording. Basically, once a creative work is no longer simply "in your head" but has instead been memorialized in or on some physical object, copyright protection exists and it is illegal for anyone to violate any of the rights provided by the Copyright Act.

As a practical matter, however, the ability to enforce a copyright may be dependent upon proving both **creation** of the work and the **creation date** of that work. There are a number of methods for establishing ownership and creation date, but the most effective and practical is registration with the Copyright Office, which is a branch of the Library of Congress. Registration not only provides a presumptive record of the copyright's creation date and ownership, but is a mandatory requirement for obtaining statutory remedies through a federal lawsuit against an infringement of the copyright.

Who Can Claim Copyright?

Anyone who makes a contribution to the creation of a work which is subject to copyright protection is entitled to that protection. Even minors may claim a copyright, although state laws regulating minors' business dealings may impair a minor's ability to subsequently license or convey copyrights until they reach a specified age.

Mere ownership or possession of an original manuscript, painting, photographic negative, master recording, or any other creative work ***does not give the owner of that tangible object any copyright***. The law provides that transfer of ownership of any material object that embodies a protected work does not of itself convey any rights in the copyright.[79] Conversely, ownership of a copyright does not confer ownership in any tangible object. If you were to legitimately purchase the master recordings of a famous artist, you could not make any commercial use of them; you could only play them for your own entertainment because, as noted in the chapter on Intellectual Property, you do not have the three necessary rights.[80]

As stated above, copyright protection exists from the time a work is first created in a fixed form, and that copyright belongs to each and every person who made a discernable contribution to the creation of that work. *Contributors are regarded as equal co-authors of the entire work unless there is a contract providing otherwise.* In other words, if you are collaborating with others, or even simply creating a work in the presence of others — including musicians, producers, arrangers, or a sound engineer — they may also be legal "authors" of the work unless you obtain a release from each of them.[81]

Only the author or those deriving their rights from the author can rightfully claim copyright, unless the work is a "work made for hire," in which case it is the *employer* (not the employee) who is considered to be the author for all copyright purposes.

How Is a Copyright Established?

A copyright comes into existence *automatically* when a work is first created, and a work is "created" when it is first fixed in any tangible medium for the first time. If a work is prepared over a period of time, the part of the work that is fixed on a particular date constitutes the created work as of that date. Publication is no longer the key to obtaining statutory copyright as it was under the (former) Copyright Act of 1909. The Copyright

---

79 See 17 USC § 202.

80 Copyright in the composition (publishing right); copyright in the sound recording; and permission to use the artist's voice (name and likeness) if not granted and made assignable by contract in connection with the master recording.

81 An artist who does not obtain releases from everyone even marginally involved during the creative process may unwittingly end up having to share copyright ownership and co-writer credit with those individuals.

Office does not *grant* a copyright, it only *registers* claims of copyright ownership, as the public repository for such claims.

Even though copyright is established automatically under the current Copyright Act, and neither publication nor registration are required, there are definite advantages to registration, not the least of which is the ability to obtain an award of damages for copyright infringement in federal courts. The registration requirements and process for United States copyrights is discussed in the following chapter.

How Long Does Copyright Protection Last?

The term of copyright for a particular work depends on several factors, including whether it has been published, and, if so, the date of first publication. As a general rule, for works created after January 1, 1978, copyright protection lasts for the life of the author plus an additional 70 years.[82] For an anonymous work, a pseudonymous work,[83] or a work made for hire, the copyright endures for a term of 95 years from the year of its first publication or for a term of 120 years from the year of its creation, whichever expires first. For works first published prior to 1978, the term will vary depending on several factors.

Works that were created but not published or registered for copyright before January 1, 1978, have been automatically brought under the statute and are now given Federal copyright protection. The duration of copyright in these works will generally be computed in the same way as for works created on or after January 1, 1978. The law provides that in no case could the term of copyright for works in this category have expired before December 31, 2002, and for works published on or before December 31, 2002, the term of copyright cannot expire before December 31, 2027.

Under the law in effect before 1978, copyright was secured either on the date a work was published or on the date of registration if the work was registered in unpublished form. In either case, the copyright endured for a first term of 28 years from the date it was secured. During the last (28th) year of the first term, the copyright was eligible for renewal. The current copyright law has extended the renewal term for copyrights that remained in force as of January 1, 1978, making these works eligible for a total term of protection of 75 years.

The Copyright Act provides that **all terms of copyright run through the end of the calendar year in which they would otherwise expire.** This affects the duration of all copyrights and, for works eligible for renewal, the renewal filing period begins on December 31st of the 27th year of the copyright.

---

82 Where there are co-authors, 70 years after the death of the longest surviving co-author.

83 Unless the author's true name is disclosed in records on file in the Copyright Office.

What Types of Creative Work Are Protected By Copyright?

Copyright protects "original works of authorship" that are fixed in a tangible form of expression. The fixation need not be directly perceptible, so long as it may be communicated with the aid of a machine or device. The Copyright Office accepts creative work for registration in the following categories:

1. Literary works;
2. Musical works, including any accompanying words (lyrics);
3. Dramatic works, including any accompanying music;
4. Pantomimes and choreographic works;
5. Pictorial, graphic, and sculptural works;
6. Motion pictures and other audiovisual works;
7. Sound recordings; and
8. Architectural works.

These categories should be viewed quite broadly. For example, computer programs and most compilations of written works are registered as "literary works" using Form TX, while maps and architectural plans are registered as "pictorial, graphic, and sculptural works," using Form VA. Works which are intended to be **performed**, including "musical works, including lyrics," "dramatic works, including accompanying music," "pantomimes and choreographic works," and "motion pictures and other audiovisual works" are registered using Form PA. Recorded **sounds** — including recorded (audio only) performances of musical and vocal compositions, as well as dramatic and literary readings (*e.g.*, so-called "books-on-tape") — are registered using Form SR. Note, however, that audiovisual works such as films and music videos are registered using Form PA, even though their soundtracks may be identical to a sound recording registrable using Form SR.

United States copyright registration and protection are available for all **unpublished** works, regardless of the nationality or domicile of the author, but **previously published** works are only eligible for copyright protection in the United States if one or more of the following ten conditions apply:

1. If, on the date of first publication, one or more of the authors is a citizen of, or is domiciled or resides in the United States; *or*
2. If, on the date of first publication, one or more of the authors is a national, domiciliary, or sovereign authority of a foreign nation that is a party to a copyright treaty to which the United States is also a party; *or*
3. If, on the date of first publication, one or more of the authors is a stateless person wherever that person may be domiciled; *or*

4. If the work is first published in the United States or in a foreign nation that, on the date of first publication, is a party to the Universal Copyright Convention; *or*

5. If the work comes within the scope of a Presidential proclamation; *or*

6. If the work is first published on or after March 1, 1989, in a foreign nation that was a party to the Berne Convention on the date of first publication; *or*

7. If the work is not first published in a country party to the Berne Convention, it is published within 30 days of first publication in a country that is party to the Berne Convention; *or*

8. If the work , first published on or after March 1, 1989, is a pictorial, graphic, or sculptural work that is incorporated in a permanent structure located in the United States; *or*

9. If the work, first published on or after March 1, 1989, is a published audiovisual work, and all the authors are legal entities with headquarters in the United States; *or*

10. If the work is a foreign work that was in the public domain in the United States prior to 1996 and its copyright was restored under the Uruguay Rounds Agreements Act (URAA).

What Cannot Be Protected by Copyright?

Several categories of creative material are generally *not* eligible for protection under the Copyright Act. These include (among others):

1. Works that have not been fixed in a tangible form of expression. For example: choreographic works that have not been notated or recorded, or improvised speeches or performances that have not been scripted, transcribed or recorded.

2. Titles, names, short phrases, and slogans; familiar symbols or designs; mere variations of typographic ornamentation, lettering, or coloring; mere listings of ingredients or contents.[84]

---

84 Certain work within this category may, however, be protected as a trademark or service mark.

3. Ideas, procedures, methods, systems, processes, concepts, principles, discoveries, or devices[85] (as distinguished from a description, explanation, or illustration of them, which might be subject to copyright protection.)

4. Works consisting entirely of information that is common property and containing no original authorship. For example: standard calendars, height and weight charts, tape measures and rulers, and lists or tables taken from public documents or other common sources.

What Specific Rights are Protected by Copyright?

Section 106 of the Copyright Act generally gives the owner of copyright the ***exclusive*** right to do (and to authorize others to do) the following:

1. The right to **REPRODUCE** (*i.e.*, manufacture) the copyrighted work in copies or phonorecords;

   Under this right, no one can make or manufacture any copy of a protected work without the copyright owner's permission, usually given in the form of a license based on the payment of a royalty to be paid for each copy.

2. The right to prepare **DERIVATIVE WORKS** based upon the copyrighted work;

   Subject to certain exceptions discussed below, no one can make a "new" work which is based upon or derived from a previous work, without permission from the copyright owner of that earlier work. Note that this includes any substantial change in lyrics (including verbatim translation into another language), unless the changes constitute a *parody* under the fair use exception, as explained below.

3. The right to **DISTRIBUTE** copies of the copyrighted work to the public by sale or other transfer of ownership, or by rental, lease, or lending;

   Under this right, no one can sell, rent, or even give away any copy of a protected work without the copyright owner's permission,[86] which is usually given as part of a license to reproduce (manufacture) such

---

85 Patent protection may be available, however.

86 Permission is generally given on a "per copy" rather than "per transaction" basis. Thus, once a copy has been sold with the copyright owner's permission, that same copy can later be rented out, re-sold or given away without requiring further permission or royalty. This is referred to as the "**first sale doctrine.**" That copy cannot, however, be *re-copied*, nor publically *displayed*, nor can the contents be publicly *performed*, since those rights are not included in the original license, nor has a royalty been paid for such use.

copies, although the right to distribute is frequently limited to a particular geographical territory.

4. The right to **PUBLICLY PERFORM** the copyrighted work;

   A copyrighted work cannot be performed in public without the copyright owner's permission. This includes everything from poetry readings to concerts; from juke boxes to radio and television broadcasts; from karaoke to high school talent contests; from music-on-hold and ringtones to grand opera and motion picture theaters; from the choreography of a ballet to the unique movements of a mime.

   There are various types of licences with regard to this public performance right, each based on the nature of the copyrighted work and the type of public performance being licensed.

5. The right to **PUBLICLY DISPLAY** the copyrighted work.

   This right deals primarily with purely visual works of art such as photography, painting and sculpture, and has little direct application in the music industry. If, however, the original manuscript or copy of a composer's work were to be publicly exhibited, it would fall under this right.

In addition to these five *enumerated* rights, there is an implicit and pervasive right, generally referred to as "**First Use.**" With only very limited and narrow exceptions, authors (or other copyright owners) have an absolute right to *withhold* their works from initial publication, indefinitely.

Are there Exceptions to Copyright Protection?

Although the protections and prerogatives enumerated in Section 106 are "exclusive," there are nonetheless certain exceptions which limit those rights or which permit others to use a copyrighted work without the copyright owner's specific permission through statutory exceptions and exemptions.

Statutory Exemptions

In some cases, the limitations take the form of specified exemptions from liability for infringement. For example, libraries and archives are permitted to make limited copies for specific purposes (Section 108), the "first sale" doctrine permits the resale of a previously authorized copy (Section 109), non-profit educational facilities may perform or display copyrighted works in a classroom or equivalent setting (Section 110), and small business establishments of limited size and capacity may reproduce public broadcasts of copyrighted works, in real time, without infringement (Section 110). Various uses of copyrighted material by certain non-profit and governmental bodies are also exempt (Section 110) and additional limitations, exemptions and exceptions are enumerated in

17 USC § 110	(*"Exemption of Certain Performances and Displays"*);
17 USC § 111	(*"Secondary Transmissions"*);
17 USC § 112	(*"Ephemeral Recordings"*);
17 USC § 119	(*"Secondary Transmissions of Superstations and Network Stations for Private Home Viewing"*);
17 USC § 121	(*"Reproduction for Blind or Other People with Disabilities"*); and
17 USC § 122	(*"Secondary Transmissions by Satellite Carriers Within Local Markets"*).

Further limitations on the scope of exclusive rights in particular categories of copyrighted works also appear in

17 USC § 113	(*"Pictorial, Graphic, and Sculptural Works"*);
17 USC § 114	(*"Sound Recordings"*);
17 USC § 115	(*"Nondramatic Musical Works — Compulsory Licenses"*);
17 USC § 117.	(*"Computer Programs"*);
17 USC § 118	(*"Certain Works in Connection with Noncommercial Broadcasting"*); and
17 USC § 120	(*"Architectural Works."*)

Compulsory Licenses

Section 115 of the Copyright Act provides for a "**compulsory license**" for non-dramatic musical works which have previously been made available to the public in the form of a "phonorecord" to be newly recorded and released *only* in a new, different phonorecord.[87]

This narrow limitation is of vital importance to the music industry for two distinct reasons.

First, under the statutory scheme, anyone wishing to make a new recording of a

87 "Phonorecord" is a specific term of art in copyright law and refers to any physical object (*e.g.*, a vinyl record, compact disc, cassette tape, *etc.*) which is capable of preserving recorded only **sounds** (*e.g.*, music, voices, *etc.*) in a distributable form which permits those sounds to be reproduced and heard, usually through the use of some machine or device. An audiovisual work (*e.g.*, video, film, TV broadcast) is **not** a phonorecord.

The Digital Millennium Copyright Act ("DMCA"), discussed *infra*, also provides for compulsory licensing of sound recordings for the purposes of webcasting.

previously-recorded and publicly-released[88] composition may thereafter do so (but *only* as a phonorecord) without having to first obtain a mechanical license from the publisher. Instead, the statute sets forth the terms of the license, including the royalty rate to be paid.[89]

The second and more pervasive effect of this provision is that the royalty rate for compulsory licenses — which is periodically set by law and is called the **statutory rate** — is a benchmark used in contracts throughout the music industry as a multiplier for all publishing royalties. That is to say that a mechanical license will almost never state a fixed amount for royalties, but will instead state a percentage of the statutory rate. (*E.g.*, "Royalty rate shall be 80% of the statutory rate.") This usage has the effect of automatically increasing the amount of royalty paid under an existing license each time the statutory rate is raised, unless the license provides for the rate to be fixed as of a certain date (*i.e.*, "statutory rate in effect as of January 1, 2008").

At the present time, and since January 1, 2006, the **statutory rate** for phonorecords, for each composition, per copy manufactured or sold, is **9.1¢** *or* **1.75¢** for each minute (or fraction), whichever is greater. (The Copyright Royalty Board was required to set new statutory rates to be effective **January 1, 2008**, but (due to bureaucratic delays) that new rate has not yet been determined as of August, 2008. It is possible that a new rate may be made *retroactive* to January 1, 2008, and it is also possible that the CRB may decide to keep the 2007 statutory rates for an extended period.)

Because the statutory rate applies *only* to phonorecords, and only *after* the first commercial recording and public release of a phonorecord containing a particular composition, it does not control the royalty terms in a "first use" (or "incept") license. For a first use license, the copyright owner of the composition is free to demand whatever terms and royalty rate the market will bear. Even in this instance however, the royalty rate is likely to be *based* on the statutory rate. (*E.g.*, "125% of statutory rate.")

The most common use of compulsory licenses is for recording "cover" songs. So long as the full statutory rate is paid, the copyright owner cannot prevent anyone from making a new recording of a previously released song, provided that the new recording is released only in the form of a phonorecord[90] and has not been substantially changed[91] from the original.

Those who wish to record and sell albums of "cover" songs under a compulsory license may simply do so, but this requires filing complex monthly and annual reports with the

---

88 Publication by means other than phonorecord (*e.g.*, in a motion picture or music video) does ***not*** qualify the composition for a compulsory license. Likewise, the new recording must also be limited to a phonorecord; no other form of media is allowed.

89 Note that, under a compulsory license, a new recording cannot significantly alter the original composition, as this would constitute a derivative work, in violation of one of the enumerated rights of the copyright holder. The lyrics may be omitted entirely, however, and instrumental versions of a previously published phonorecord are permissible under compulsory licensing.

90 *I.e.*, a compulsory license is not available for audiovisual works.

91 Substantial modifications would violate the copyright owner's exclusive right to control derivative works.

Copyright Office, and monthly payment of royalties.[92] Failure to comply fully with any of these complex reporting and payment regulations may result in severe penalties, including a determination that the recording is an infringement, subject to civil action by the copyright owner.

Alternatively, for a fee, the Harry Fox Agency can provide licenses for most published recordings, and handle the reporting and royalty payments.

Beyond the fact that the requirements for statutory royalty payments and monthly reporting are incredibly complex and burdensome, a compulsory license will also generally cost more than a mechanical license negotiated directly with the publisher or publisher's agent. Under a negotiated mechanical license there is not only the opportunity to obtain a reduced royalty rate, but industry practice is to base that royalty on defined "actual sales," with royalty reports and payments made quarterly, semi-annually, or annually. Generally, the publisher will receive an advance payment for such concessions, but the advance is unlikely to be as much as the accounting costs for dealing with the statutory requirements for a compulsory license. The only exception would be where the publisher requires a *bonus*, or too large an advance, in which case the compulsory license alternative remains available.

There are also additional concessions which can be negotiated into mechanical licenses, such as a further-reduced royalty for discounted sales, a royalty waiver for promotional copies, a pre-arrangement for a sync license to make a video, or other specific agreements. Such concessions will not be available under a compulsory license. Most recording contracts contain a "negotiated" mechanical license as part of a "controlled compositions" clause under which artists who record their own material agree to accept a reduced royalty on that material. A controlled compositions clause may also compel artists to effectively subsidize a reduction in royalties payable for use of others' compositions by setting a "cap" on the total mechanical royalties which the label is required to pay for the entire album. Any royalties in excess of that "cap" amount are treated as an additional advance, recoupable from the Artist's royalties, or, in some cases, reimbursable upon demand.

The Fair Use Doctrine

One of the major exceptions and limitations of copyright protection is the doctrine of "**fair use**," which permits unauthorized copying and publication for certain purposes. It is essential to understand that "fair use" is *only an affirmative defense* and that, ultimately, the *only* definitive answer as to whether a particular use was, in fact, a fair use, must be provided within a court's judgment in a lawsuit for infringement.

---

92 The federal regulation which provides instructions for these required monthly reports and payments, and for CPA-certified annual reports, is 37 CFR § 201.19 ("Royalties and statements of account under compulsory license for making and distributing phonorecords of nondramatic musical works.") That regulation currently consists of 6,366 words — approximately 14 full pages of single-spaced text.

The fair use doctrine is codified in Section 107 of the Copyright Act, which states that *"the fair use of a copyrighted work, including such use by reproduction in copies or phonorecords or by any other means specified by that section, for purposes such as criticism, comment, news reporting, teaching (including multiple copies for classroom use), scholarship, or research, is not an infringement of copyright."* The doctrine is predicated on the premise that portions of a copyrighted work should be freely available for purposes of commentary and criticism of the work itself. It would be difficult to either comment upon or to criticize a work without the ability to reproduce portions of it. Without such freedom, copyright owners would be able to censor or block negative comments about their work.

Unfortunately, the only guidance provided by Section 107 as to what is — or is not — a "fair use," is a set of four somewhat nebulous factors:

> *"In determining whether the use made of a work in any particular case is a fair use the factors to be considered shall include -*
>
> *"(1) the purpose and character of the use, including whether such use is of a commercial nature or is for nonprofit educational purposes;*
>
> *"(2) the nature of the copyrighted work;*
>
> *"(3) the amount and substantiality of the portion used in relation to the copyrighted work as a whole; and*
>
> *"(4) the effect of the use upon the potential market for or value of the copyrighted work.*
>
> *"The fact that a work is unpublished shall not itself bar a finding of fair use if such finding is made upon consideration of all the above factors."*

When there is a dispute between a copyright owner and someone claiming "fair use" as a defense to an alleged infringement, the court must weigh the facts in light of the four statutory factors. This is always a highly subjective process which introduces a "fifth factor" — the judge's personal values and opinion of the character, demeanor and general conduct of the parties. These unlisted considerations may ultimately be determinative of the outcome.

There are no well-defined rules, only the four-factor guidelines and various (often inconsistent) court decisions. As with free speech, the fair use doctrine has a flexible definition that is constantly subject to new interpretations and applications. It is therefore best to be extremely cautious in borrowing from a copyrighted work in reliance on the fair use doctrine. Here are some points to consider:

- Because dissemination of facts or information benefits the public, it is safer to copy from factual works than from fictional works.
- Also, there will be a better claim of fair use if the material copied is from a published source rather than from an unpublished work. Fair use standards are

far more stringent for unpublished works, since authors have an almost absolute right to control the first use of their work.

- Another key factor is whether the contemplated use will deprive a copyright owner of actual or potential income from the copyrighted work. (Costing someone money is always a good way to touch off a lawsuit.)

Two common misconceptions about fair use have to do with **acknowledgments** and **disclaimers**.

Acknowledging the source of quoted material may be scholarly... it may be courteous ... it may even be a required condition of permissive use ... but it may also be taken as an admission of infringement. It is the copyright owner's initial burden to prove that the challenged use was actually taken from a particular copyrighted source. An acknowledgment *eliminates* that burden and, even though it may be a positive element in a court's fair use analysis, it is not equivalent to permission and will not prevent a finding of infringement. In fact, it may open the door to an additional claim for unauthorized commercial use of the copyright owner's personality rights.

Similarly, a disclaimer — that is, a statement that the use has not been authorized or approved by the copyright owner — may be a positive influence in a judicial fair use analysis, but will be of little ultimate effect if remaining factors weigh against a judicial finding of fair use.

In some cases, the amount of copyrighted material used is so small (*"de minimis,"* in legal parlance) that the court may allow the use without even conducting a formal fair use analysis,[93] but there is no *prima facie* test for determining a use to be *de minimus*, and even the briefest of uses may be held not to be a fair use.[94] Generally, the less taken, the more likely fair use will apply. However, even if the use is the tiniest possible fraction of a work, it will not be a fair use if it is a particularly memorable aspect of that work. For example, taking the single word "yesterday" accompanied by the three opening notes of the Beatles' song "Yesterday," would not be a fair use, unless it was a parody.

Since a **parody** intentionally ridicules someone or something by imitating or exaggerating it in a comedic or wry manner, it is necessary for a parody to borrow recognizable portions of the original work. Consequently, extensive use of the original is permissible in a parody, since identification of that parodied original is essential to the desired effect. The *de minimus* guideline is therefore wholly inapplicable to parody cases. The parodist is even allowed to borrow the "heart" of the original work since — as the U. S.

---

93 In Sandoval v. New Line Cinema Corp., (1998, 2nd Cir.) 147 F.3d 215, the use of ten copyrighted photographs which appeared briefly, without permission, in the background of the motion picture ,"Seven," was held to be a fair use.

94 In Ringgold v. Black Entertainment Television, Inc. (1997, 2nd Cir.) 126 F.3d 70, use of a copyrighted poster which appeared briefly, without permission, as one of several decorative, background set-dressing elements in the HBO cable television series, "ROC," was held *not* to be a fair use.

Supreme Court has acknowledged — "the heart is also what most readily conjures up the [original] for parody, and it is the heart at which parody takes aim." [95]

A parody may even be so memorable that it overshadows the original work to such extent that the original may never again be taken seriously. While a parody with such effect would undoubtedly be the proximate cause of financial damage to the copyright owner through the reduction in market value of the original work, such income loss is not the same *type* of loss as when a non-parody impermissibly borrows from that same work.

In regard to the "**educational**" fair use exemption of Section 107, a set of guidelines has been established by publishers and educators in an effort to provide "greater certainty and protection" for teachers and students. Although the guidelines are <u>not</u> part of the Copyright Act, they are recognized and published as an informational circular by the Copyright Office, and have been relied upon by judges as providing reasonable standards for fair use in education. It is important to note that, under those guidelines, "educational purposes" means, *and is limited to*, **non-commercial** instruction or curriculum-based teaching by educators to students at **nonprofit** educational institutions, planned **non-commercial** study or investigation directed toward making a contribution to a field of knowledge, or presentation of research findings at **non-commercial** peer conferences, workshops or seminars. Educators and students who comply with the guidelines can feel reasonably assured that they are not impermissibly exceeding a fair use of copyrighted materials.

The principal dilemma in going forward with a perceived fair use is that there is absolutely no predictable way to ensure that the use will actually qualify as a fair use. The best possible, good-faith, expert opinion that a use qualifies cannot prevent the copyright owner from commencing a lawsuit if he or she disagrees. Even if the court ultimately rules that the use *was* a fair use, the time, expense and aggravation of litigation will likely outweigh any benefit derived from having used the copyrighted work in the first place.

Because there are only nebulous guidelines and no hard-and-fast rules for judicial fair use analysis, the fair use exception may or may not apply in any given case. Extreme caution should therefore be employed in pre-analyzing a contemplated use before relying on the fair use exception.

Two typical situations are especially likely to result in litigation:

- When the use causes the copyright owner of the original work to lose income, or potential sources of income. This is most likely to occur when portions of a copyrighted work are included in a new *competing* work. For example, if someone were to borrow heavily from this chapter and include it in a book on music contracts or copyrights, we would probably sue them, since their book would compete with this one.

---

95 <u>Campbell v. Acuff-Rose Music</u> (1994) 510 U.S. 569.

- When the copyright owner is annoyed, insulted , or offended by the use, or considers it to be a "desecration" of his or her original work.

Note that these factors apply to *likelihood of litigation*, rather than the merits of a fair-use claim. The copyright owner's level of annoyance and loss of income will directly affect the odds that a lawsuit will be filed. However, just as some circumstances will increase the chances of a lawsuit, there are other situations in which those odds are lessened:

- When the use is *de minimus*, and for the purpose of news reporting, criticism, commentary, research, or scholarship;
- When there has been a comprehensive pre-use evaluation of the fair use factors in advance of the use and a resultant good faith belief that the use qualifies as a fair use. Ideally, this evaluation should be performed by a copyright attorney and the results memorialized in an opinion letter; and
- When, even after determining that the intended use falls within the fair use exception, there has been a diligent effort to locate the copyright owner, give notice of the intended use, and solicit permission prior to that use.

Remember, it is *always* better to obtain permission for the use whenever possible, because the results of a judicial fair use analysis are *never* predictable. Here are a few examples of how seemingly similar situations can yield diametrically opposed courtroom results...

Universal v. Sony Corp.
(1984) 464 U.S. 417

Commonly referred to as the "Betamax" case, the U.S. Supreme Court held that home videotaping of a television broadcast **was a fair use**. This is one *very* rare situation where **copying of an entire copyrighted work was held to be fair use.** The underlying rationale of the decision was that television viewers were merely "time-shifting" rather than building libraries of material which might impact the copyright owner's income. (But note that any attempt by a viewer to subsequently sell or otherwise profit from such videotape copy would be a separate violation of copyright law, having nothing to do with the fair use.) It is also worth noting that the original trial court's fair use analysis yielded a completely opposite result (*i.e.*, not fair use), which was reversed on appeal.

Salinger v. Random House
(1987, 2nd Cir.) 811 F.2d 90

An unauthorized biography of renowned author J. D. Salinger included paraphrased portions of unpublished letters written by Salinger. Those letters had been donated to university libraries and were readily available to the public, *but* Salinger had never authorized their reproduction. The court held that the paraphrasing was **not fair use**, and enjoined (prohibited) publication.

Wright v. Warner Books, Inc.
(1991, 2nd Cir.) 953 F.2d 731

A biography of African-American author Richard Wright included quotations from six of Wright's unpublished letters and ten unpublished journal entries. Although Wright had expressly denied the biographer, Margaret Walker, permission to use those materials, *the same court that had ruled "not a fair use" in Salinger four years earlier* held that the use of the Wright material **was a fair use.**

Roy Export Co. etc. v. CBS, Inc.
(1982, 2nd Cir.) 672 F.2d 1095

When a CBS television news program used 1¼ minutes from a 72-minute Charlie Chaplin film as part of a news report about Chaplin's death, the court found that the portions used were from the "heart" of the film and therefore held it was **not fair use**, affirming a $410,000 damage award against CBS for infringement.

Monster Communications v. Turner Broadcasting Systems
(1996, S.D. NY) 935 F. Supp. 490

Plaintiff owned the copyright to an 84 minute movie about the 1974 heavyweight title fight between Muhammed Ali and George Foreman. Defendants made a documentary film biography of Ali which used 41 seconds of film identical to plaintiff's copyrighted footage. The court held that this **was fair use** since Muhammed Ali was a public figure, his biography was informational and a matter of public interest, and the amount and substantiality of the footage used by defendant was small.

Los Angeles News Service v. KCAL-TV Channel 9
(1997, 9th Cir.) 108 F.3d 1119

A Channel 9 news broadcast had used 30 seconds from a four minute videotape of the 1992 beating of Reginald Denny. *Held*, **not fair use**. The use took the heart of the work, was commercial in nature, and directly affected the marketability of the video and hence deprived the copyright owner of prospective income.

Campbell v. Acuff-Rose Music
(1994) 510 U.S. 569

The musical group 2 Live Crew used the opening notes and words (but not the melody) from the first line of the Roy Orbison song, "Pretty Woman." The rest of the lyrics and music were new. 2 Live Crew had sought permission in advance of their use, but those requests were rejected, with the publisher expressly advising that the proposed use would be considered an infringement. The Supreme Court found that the use **was fair use.** Applying, in part, a **parody** standard to their analysis, the court found that the 2 Live Crew version had transformed the original work so that it was essentially a completely different piece of music, with only the opening line and musical tag being similar.

Hustler Magazine, Inc. v. Moral Majority, Inc.
(1985, C.D. Cal.) 606 F. Supp. 1526
(affirmed 796 F.2d 1148)

Hustler brought suit against Rev. Jerry Falwell for having made and disseminated "hundreds of thousands of copies of a single page from Hustler's November 1983 issue" as part of a fund raising campaign. The page in question, entitled, "Jerry Falwell talks about his first time," was itself a fair use parody of a Campari liquor advertisement, rife with *double entendres* and "scatological attempts at humor."[96] A purported disclaimer, reading, "Ad Parody — Not to Be Taken Seriously," was included at the bottom of the page. The court held that Falwell's copying of the copyrighted parody **was fair use,** since it did not impact sales of that issue of the magazine and was used for an "informational" purpose.

Dr. Seuss Enterprises, L.P.
v. Penguin Books USA, Inc.
(1997, 9th Cir.) 109 F.3d 1394

A tongue-in-cheek account of the O.J. Simpson murder trial was published in a work entitled "The Cat NOT in the Hat! A Parody by Dr. Juice," which was written entirely in the style of a Dr. Seuss book. The court determined that, despite its self-description, the book was a ***satire**, not a parody* — and therefore **not fair use** — because it did not ridicule *Dr. Seuss* but rather impermissibly used Dr. Seuss' characters and style to tell the story of the Simpson murder.

---

96 Falwell had brought suit against Hustler for defamation and intentional infliction of emotional distress on the basis of that same ad. In respect to those claims, the U. S. Supreme Court held that "public figures and public officials may not recover for the tort of intentional infliction of emotional distress by reason of publications such as the one here at issue without showing in addition that the publication contains a false statement of fact which was made with 'actual malice,' [... It is] our considered judgment that such a standard is necessary to give adequate 'breathing space' to the freedoms protected by the First Amendment." [*Hustler Magazine v. Falwell* (1988) 485 U.S. 46, 57]

Castle Rock Entertainment, Inc.
v. Carol Publishing Group
(1998, 2nd Cir.) 150 F.3d 132

Defendant had published a book of trivia questions about characters and events from 84 episodes of the television series, "Seinfeld," including direct quotations of dialogue from the show. There was a disclaimer stating that the book was not authorized by, nor affiliated with, the "Seinfeld" copyright owners. The court found that this was **not fair use**, since the book impacted the copyright owner's right to develop and exploit its own derivative works based on "Seinfeld" and its various characters, scripts, and other component elements.

◆ ◆ ◆

Confused yet? Synopses of such seemingly-inconsistent judicial rulings on fair use could fill an entire volume, but the foregoing examples should be sufficient to make the point that fair use is *only* an affirmative defense, and fair use analysis is *always* on a case-by-case basis — that even the most cautious pre-evaluation of fair use factors provides no assurance that a copyright owner won't bring suit — and that there are *never* any guaranties of the outcome in *any* lawsuit.

◆ ◆ ◆

Here's another important *caveat* to remember. ***Anyone* can sue *anyone* for *any reason* — or for no reason at all — at *any time!*** There are consequences for bringing a *completely* baseless lawsuit, and such suits can often be disposed of quickly, but judicial policy favors a trial on the merits if there is the slightest factual basis and legal theory to support the plaintiff's claim. Even the quickest and most favorable outcome won't negate the expense and aggravation which invariably accompany *any* litigation.

◆ ◆ ◆

With that in mind, the following page contains an evaluation chart which may be used *(at one's own peril!)* in deciding whether or not to proceed in reliance on the fair use exception:

"FAIR USE" EVALUATION GUIDE

Factor 1: "The **purpose and character of the use**, including whether such use is of a commercial nature or is for nonprofit educational purposes" *[17 USC § 107.(1)]*

PRO *(Fair Use)*	**CON** *(Not Fair Use)*
☐ Commentary	☐ Bad faith conduct
☐ Criticism	☐ Bad intent
☐ Limited access and dissemination	☐ Commercial activity
☐ News reporting	☐ Denial of credit to author
☐ Parody	☐ Entertainment
☐ Research	☐ For Profit
☐ Scholarship	
☐ *Nonprofit* Educational Institution	
☐ Teaching (including copies for classroom use.)	
☐ Transformation of original	
☐ Utilitarian (changes *use* of original.)	

Factor 2: "The **nature of the** [original] **copyrighted work.**" *[17 USC § 107.(2)]*

PRO *(Fair Use)*	**CON** *(Not Fair Use)*
☐ Educational intent	☐ Artistic work
☐ Factual or nonfiction content	☐ Imaginative work
☐ Published work	☐ Originality
	☐ Unpublished

Factor 3: "The **amount and substantiality of the portion used** in relation to the copyrighted work as a whole." *[17 USC § 107.(3)]*

PRO *(Fair Use)*	**CON** *(Not Fair Use)*
☐ *De minimus* quantity	☐ Large portion used.
☐ Portion appropriate for accepted educational purposes	☐ Entire work used
☐ Portion used not "heart" of work.	☐ Portion used is "heart" of work
☐ Portion used not particularly significant to entire work	☐ Portion used is significant to core of work

Factor 4: "The **effect of the use upon the potential market for or value of the copyrighted work.**" *[17 USC § 107.(4)]*

PRO *(Fair Use)*	**CON** *(Not Fair Use)*
☐ Copyrighted work is out of print or no longer available for sale.	☐ Affordable permission available for use of copyrighted work.
☐ Lack of means to contact copyright owner to request permission or license for use, despite diligent effort.	☐ Numerous copies made and available.
☐ No product similar to use is marketed by the copyright holder.	☐ Reasonably available licensing mechanism for use of the copyrighted work
☐ Only a few copies made of use. (No impact on market.)	☐ Repeated or long-term use
☐ Use does not affect any actual or potential market for copyrighted work or derivative work.	☐ Use competes for market (or potential market) for a derivative work.
☐ Original work identified and credited as source of use.	☐ Use made available in potential markets not yet exploited by copyright owner
	☐ Use competes for market (or potential market) for copyrighted work.

Finally, don't forget the unwritten "fifth factor." Which side of the question will most appeal to public opinion and to the sympathies of a judge or jury? In essence, who will come off as the "good guy" — and who the "bad guy" — if the matter goes to trial?

What are Copyright Licenses?

A license is a form of permission given by someone holding a right (the "licensor") to someone else (the "licensee"), allowing limited use of some portion of that right. As we've discussed, there are five enumerated rights in copyright, and previously-recorded music involves two separate and distinct copyrights — one for the composition and another for the recording of that composition. Whenever an intended use involves a *recording*, it will be necessary to have at least one licence from the publisher or a performing rights organization (for the composition), and another license from the owner of the recording itself (usually a record company.) This remains true even when only a "sample" of previously-recorded music is being used.

Whenever there is any performance or other use of music involving any one or more of the five enumerated rights, there will need to be at least one license obtained from the owner of that right, or from a designated agent of that copyright owner.

The most common example of a situation requiring multiple licenses is in the area of motion pictures, where a film's producers want to include a particular artist's recording of a song. In that situation there are two licenses required:

1. A **synchronization license** from the publisher, which allows the composition to be recorded as part of an audiovisual work; and
2. A **master use license** from the record company (or other owner of the sound recording copyright) to use a pre-existing recording of the composition.[97]

A unique example of a multiple license requirement which does not involve the sound-recording copyright is Karaoke, for which each of the following *composition* licenses are necessary:

1. A **mechanical license**, to record and manufacture a phonorecord containing an instrumental version of a composition. This may be obtained from the publisher or as a compulsory license; and
2. A **lyric printing license** from the publisher, allowing the song lyrics to be produced in printed form; and
3. A **synchronization license**, from the publisher, allowing the printed lyrics to be included as a synchronous, audiovisual presentation, accompanying the recording; and
4. A **performance license** permitting the composition to be publicly performed (even if badly) by customers. This license is usually obtained by the venue on an annual basis from performing rights organizations.

97 This license should also include warranties of the necessary personality rights of the performers appearing in that recording. When in doubt... verify and clear them separately.

What about Royalties?

The Copyright Office's primary function is the registration of copyrights and recordation of documents relating to copyrights. However, because the Copyright Office is also involved in compulsory licensing, its Licensing Division acts as administrator of those licenses, receiving royalty payments from compulsory licensees. After deducting its actual operating costs from such royalties as an administration fee, the remainder is invested in interest-bearing securities with the U.S. Treasury for eventual distribution of the remainder to copyright owners. This method of royalty collection and disbursement through the Copyright Office is the exception rather than the usual means by which copyright owners receive royalties for their works.

In order to understand how royalties are collected and distributed for various types of licenses, it's important to distinguish first between the "publisher's share" and the "writer's share" in a copyrighted work. For illustration, we'll look at a composition (PA) copyright, but the principles are the same for all forms of copyright.

Where the initial copyright claimant is the songwriter, he or she owns 100% of the rights to the copyright. Where the copyright claimant is a publisher — either at the time of the original registration or by subsequent assignment from the original claimant — then that publisher *collects* 100% of the royalties, but *retains* only half (the publisher's share), while forwarding the other half (the writer's share) to the songwriter. Of course, this presupposes that there are no recoupable advances outstanding. Generally, publishers acquire rights from a songwriter in consideration of a cash payment, or a cash advance against future royalties, or a combination of both. Sometimes the songwriter sells only a portion of the publishing in what are referred to as co-publishing deals, in which the songwriter retains 100% of the writer's share and (usually) half of the publisher's share as well. There are also "administration deals" in which the "publisher" merely acts as an agent and administrator for the songwriter, for a fee, which may be an annual fee, or a percentage of royalties collected, or a combination of both. Publishers and co-publishers also regularly deduct an "administration fee" (usually 10%-15%) from the writer's share, but such fees are negotiable.

Additionally, it is not unusual for a songwriter to *exclude* certain performance rights from the publishing assignment. In such instances, 100% of the royalties collected by the performing rights organization ("PRO") with which the songwriter is affiliated (*i.e.*, ASCAP, BMI, SESAC) are paid directly to the songwriter, minus the PRO's administration fee.

The larger interest a publisher has in the copyright, the more time, effort and money that publisher is likely to spend in seeking to license the composition. Thus "giving up" half of the copyright may make sense, especially for songwriters who do not have the industry contacts necessary for a successful, ongoing licensing business. On the other hand, an ineffectual, unmotivated publisher is merely a drain on the songwriter's income.[98]

---

98 These and other considerations are discussed in the chapters on publishing agreements, in VOLUME THREE.

Songwriters' royalties are usually paid on a quarterly basis by most publishers, although this, too, may be negotiable. In general, licensees pay royalties to publishers and to performing rights organizations, which in turn pay a portion of those royalties to the songwriter, on a contractual basis. It should be remembered, however, that where the songwriter is also the recording artist, these composition royalties are wholly separate and distinct from the "Artist's Royalties" payable under a record contract.

How Are Royalty Rates Established?

The general rule in copyright law is that the owner of a copyrighted work has the exclusive right to determine how that work is to be used. Anyone other than the owner wishing to use a copyrighted work must either: *(a)* obtain the owner's permission through a negotiated license; *(b)* be eligible for a statutory compulsory license, or *(c)* qualify for free use under a legal exception. Since there are various types of licenses to use copyrighted works in different manners and media, and different types of royalties payable in respect to those various licenses, the manner in which royalties are determined differs from type to type. Only in respect to compulsory licensing is there any fixed royalty rate determined by governmental authority.

For a "first use" (or "incept") license, the copyright owner dictates the royalty terms and conditions, which a prospective licensee is free to accept or reject. Thus the economic principle of supply and demand governs the process of negotiating the royalty rates for a first use.

Similarly, there is no fixed royalty rate for master use licenses to utilize an existing sound recording in a new audio or audiovisual work. The owner of the sound recording copyright can set any rate, which the prospective licensee can accept or reject.

The same negotiated, supply-and-demand royalty basis also prevails for sync licenses, "grand right" licenses, and other public performance uses of compositions. Frequently a blanket license will be published for some of these uses, establishing royalty rates for various types of use. Under the legal doctrine of "offer and acceptance," such publication constitutes an offer to license for a specified type of use at published royalty rates, and subsequent use of the work, without direct negotiation of other terms, constitutes an unconditional acceptance of that offer and an agreement to pay the published royalty rate and abide by the offered terms and conditions of use. Such published rates can often be found in published copies of works intended for performance, such as scripts for well-known plays and musicals.

For radio broadcasting, transcription licenses are negotiated on an industry-wide basis between various broadcasters, generally acting through broadcast associations, and the various performance rights associations, acting for the composers and copyright owners.

Similar contracts are also negotiated for royalties for jukeboxes,[99] music-on-hold, and even radio broadcasts when played in commercial settings. The performing rights organizations, or other designated agents, collect those royalties and distribute them to their member clients. When such agreements expire, but use continues and the parties cannot finalize new terms through negotiation, an agency of the Copyright Office may step in to help mediate an appropriate new rate.

Government involvement in setting and adjusting royalty rates began with the 1909 Copyright Act, which provided for only one type of compulsory license, allowing manufacture of phonorecords of previously recorded and publicly distributed compositions . The royalty rate for that compulsory mechanical license was set by statute at 2¢, which remained unchanged from 1909 to 1978.

Currently, it is the Copyright Royalty Board (CRB) which sets compulsory royalty rates, but between 1977 and 2007 there were other agencies of the Copyright Office charged with that function. In the 1976 Copyright Act, Congress recognized that the compulsory mechanical license was flawed because an inflexible, statutorily-set, royalty rate did not provide fair compensation. Also, the 1976 Act included additional types of compulsory licenses, and provided for creation of an administrative body to periodically adjust royalty rates for compulsory licenses, and to act as a distributor of royalties collected from users in situations where there were multiple claimants to the same funds, and where there were controversies as to how much each claimant was entitled to receive. From 1977 through 1993, these functions were fulfilled by the Copyright Royalty Tribunal, an independent regulatory agency, whose members were appointed by the President, with the advice and consent of the Senate.[100] Originally, the Tribunal consisted of five full-time commissioners, but in 1990, Congress reduced their number from five to three, and in 1992 established an *ad hoc* arbitration panel with jurisdiction over royalty rate adjustment and distribution proceedings. In 1993, the Copyright Royalty Tribunal was eliminated in favor of such *ad hoc* arbitration panels, designated as the Copyright Arbitration Royalty Panel system, or "CARP," which continued to operate until May 31, 2007.[101]

The Copyright Royalty and Distribution Reform Act of 2004 phased out the CARP system, replacing it with a panel of three Copyright Royalty Judges with authority to

---

99 The 1976 Copyright Act, provided a compulsory license for jukeboxes but, in 1988, Congress began eliminating such licenses to comply with the Berne Convention and, by 1990, there were sufficient private jukebox license agreements to remove jukebox licenses from the Copyright Act.

100 In Buckley v. Valeo (1976) 424 U.S. 1, the Supreme Court held that persons exercising executive branch functions "must be appointed in accordance with article II, sec. 2, clause 2 of the Constitution, the Appointments Clause." (424 U.S. at 126) which states that the President shall nominate, with the Senate's advice and consent, all "Officers of the United States." Having the president appoint the members of the Royalty Tribunal avoided a potential constitutional defect under Buckley.

101 For efficiency and continuity, the replaced CARP system was retained through May 31, 2007 to allow a sufficient transition and wind-down period during which the CRB was staffed, organized, and began assuming its duties.

determine royalty rates and terms for statutory licenses and make determinations on distribution of statutory license royalties collected by the Copyright Office. The Copyright Royalty Judges are full-time employees of the Library of Congress, appointed for six-year terms. This Copyright Royalty Board (CRB), is also charged with the responsibility for periodically adjusting statutory royalty rates, adjudicating disputes between copyright claimants, and establishing fair royalty rates where parties to common licensing agreements have been unable to negotiate such rates privately.

What is "Work for Hire"?

Section 101 of the Copyright Act defines a "work made for hire" as follows:

> A "work made for hire" is —
> (1) a work prepared by an employee within the scope of his or her employment; or
> (2) a work specially ordered or commissioned for use as a contribution to a collective work, as a part of a motion picture or other audiovisual work, as a translation, as a supplementary work, as a compilation, as an instructional text, as a test, as answer material for a test, or as an atlas, if the parties expressly agree in a written instrument signed by them that the work shall be considered a work made for hire. For the purpose of the foregoing sentence, a "supplementary work" is a work prepared for publication as a secondary adjunct to a work by another author for the purpose of introducing, concluding, illustrating, explaining, revising, commenting upon, or assisting in the use of the other work, such as forewords, afterwords, pictorial illustrations, maps, charts, tables, editorial notes, musical arrangements, answer material for tests, bibliographies, appendixes, and indexes, and an "instructional text" is a literary, pictorial, or graphic work prepared for publication and with the purpose of use in systematic instructional activities.

Simply put, there are only two circumstances in which a qualifying creative work is a "work made for hire" under the current Copyright Act: (1) When the creative work is part of an employee's regular duties *-or-* (2) when there is a ***written*** agreement stating that a work is being created or contributed to on a work-for-hire basis.

There is a legal presumption that a work is ***not*** a work made for hire, which presumption can be overcome only by proving that the work falls within one of the two statutory categories, and with the burden of that proof falling on the alleged employer.[102]

102 This is directly contradictory to the presumption of the Copyright Act of 1909, under which a work was presumed to have been made for hire if the writer received any consideration for that work before or during the process of its creation, with the burden on the creator to prove it was ***not*** a work made for hire.

By way of example, a advertising executive whose job is to create marketing campaigns may draw some sketches depicting an idea for an advertisement. His *employer* is the sole author of those creative works for copyright purposes (unless there is a written employment contract which provides otherwise) because such creative work is within the normal scope of his employment, and therefore a "work made for hire." On the other hand, if a clerical worker at that agency were to have drawn those same sketches, then it would not be a work for hire, because creative graphics are not within the normal course and scope of clerical work. In this latter instance, the agency would have to obtain a license or an assignment of rights from the clerical worker in order to be able to use the sketches — or to use *any new artwork or other material based on* (i.e., ***derived** from) those sketches or any original ideas embodied in those sketches* — for their advertisements.

Another example has to do with those hired as independent contractors to do specific jobs. Take, for instance, a photographer who is hired to take publicity photos. Even if he delivers all of the negatives and prints, the photographer retains the *copyright* unless there is a ***written contract*** stating that those photographs were work made for hire. Without a written work for hire agreement, the photos cannot be copied, or used commercially, without the *photographer's* consent, which is usually given in the form of a license, either for a one-time payment, or on a royalty basis.[103] Novice performers who attempt to use photographs of themselves for self-published CD's, or on T-shirts or other merchandise, are frequently shocked to receive a "cease and desist" letter from the photographer's lawyer, or worse, find themselves named as defendants in an infringement lawsuit.

There is one apparent "loophole" in the work-for-hire provisions of the Copyright Act, however, which is directly and uniquely applicable to the music industry. (And if the following explanation makes your head spin, you're not alone.)

The "work made for hire" provisions of the Copyright Act ***do not include sound recordings.*** Section 101 of Copyright Act (cited above) defining works made for hire, goes on to state:

> In determining whether any work is eligible to be considered a work made for hire under paragraph (2), neither the amendment contained in section 1011(d) of the Intellectual Property and Communications Omnibus Reform Act of 1999, as enacted by section 1000(a)(9) of Public Law 106-113, nor the deletion of the words added by that amendment— (A) shall be considered or otherwise given any legal significance, or (B) shall be interpreted to indicate congressional approval or disapproval of, or acquiescence in, any judicial determination, by the courts or the Copyright Office. Paragraph (2) shall be interpreted as if both section 2(a)(1) of the Work Made for Hire and Copyright Corrections Act of 2000 and section

---

103 Of course, if the photographs contain recognizable images of individuals, then the photographer cannot use them commercially either, without first obtaining a "name and likeness" release.

> 1011(d) of the Intellectual Property and Communications Omnibus Reform Act of 1999, as enacted by section 1000(a)(9) of Public Law 106-113, were never enacted, and without regard to any inaction or awareness by the Congress at any time of any judicial determinations. [*from* 17 USC § 101 (*"Definitions"*)]

What that boils down to is that, in 1999, Congress expressly **added** "sound recordings" to the list of what could be considered as a work for hire, but then, in 2000, they **retroactively *removed*** "sound recordings" from that list, but with the amended statute specifically stating that the 1999 insertion, of "sound recordings," and the 2000 retroactive removal of "sound recordings," did not, in effect, mean anything.[104] A court attempting to determine whether or not "sound recordings" are subject to the "work for hire" provisions of the Copyright Act, is forbidden from drawing any inferences from the abrogated 1999 amendment or from the 2000 retraction of that amendment. On the face of the statute, however, sound recordings remain ***excluded*** from (or at least not included within) the types of works which may be considered to be "works made for hire."

However, just to add to the confusion, Copyright Form SR ("Sound Recordings") nonetheless asks,

> *"Was this contribution to the work a 'work made for hire'?"*

and includes the following:

> *"NOTE Under the law, the "author" of a "work made for hire" is generally the employer, not the employee (see instructions)."*

Notwithstanding this language on the face of the Sound Recording (SR) copyright application form, there is no legal foundation for claiming authorship of a sound recording by reason of a work-made-for-hire agreement, alone. Instead, copyright interests must be obtained by transfer, conveyance or assignment from the creator or contributor to the copyright claimant.

The Copyright Act also provides that,

> In the case of a work made for hire, the employer or other person for whom the work was prepared is considered the author for purposes of this title, and, unless the parties have expressly agreed otherwise **in a written instrument signed by them**, owns all of the rights comprised in the copyright. [17 USC § 201.(b). Emphasis added.]

---

104 The Satellite Home Viewer Improvement Act of 1999 amended the definition of "a work made for hire" by inserting "as a sound recording" after "audiovisual work." Pub. L. No. 106-113, 113 Stat. 1501, app. I at 1501A-544. The Work Made for Hire and Copyright Corrections Act of 2000 amended the definition of "work made for hire" by deleting "as a sound recording" after "audiovisual work." Pub. L. No. 106-379, 114 Stat. 1444. The Act also added a second paragraph to part (2) of that definition. Id. These changes were made effective retroactively, as of November 29, 1999. [17 USC § 101, note 24]

Historically, even though there had been copyright protection for *compositions* since the 1909 Copyright Act, there was no copyright in sound recordings prior to 1976. The ownership of master recordings was construed solely under state and federal laws relating to property rights. Since labels had always owned — or at least absolutely controlled — master recordings under property law, they attempted to contract around the 1976 Copyright Act by adding "work for hire" language to their recording contracts. Recognizing that this might still be legally deficient, in light of the exclusion of sound recordings from 17 USC § 101, record companies also generally include an *assignment, transfer* or *conveyance* of all rights (exclusive of "mechanical" rights) from the Artist to the record company, in *addition* to"work for hire" language. This additional language also serves to conform recording contracts to the requirements of the Berne Convention which contains no express "work for hire" provisions, as well as those imposed by U.S. Copyright laws.

The point of all this is that creative work is presumptively ***not*** work for hire unless there's a written agreement to the contrary, and the addition of assignment, transfer, and/or conveyance language in a "work for hire" contract is a useful adjunct which serves to clarify any potential ambiguity in the statute, particularly with respect to sound recordings.

What Does "Co-Author" Mean?

Anyone who makes a creative contribution to a work is an author or co-author of that work, unless they have given a release or their contribution falls within one of the two categories of work-made-for-hire. Further, the legal presumption is that all such contributions are of *equal value*, so that contributors are equal co-owners of the copyright in the entire work, unless there is an agreement between them establishing different percentages of ownership.

In determining relative contribution, it is important to understand what constitutes a "work" for copyright purposes. Copyright in each separate contribution to collective work is distinct from copyright in the collective work as a whole, and the copyright vests initially with the author of the contribution. Thus, while an album may be a single work in one sense, the copyrights for the individual songs on it are independent of the album itself. Another aspect of co-authorship has to do with distinguishing collaboration from independent contribution. Suppose you write lyrics for a song and give them to someone else to compose music to accompany them. Even though the creation of the words and music occurred separately, this is a collaborative effort, and the lyrics and music will become inextricably linked to each other, with the lyricist and composer each owning half of the integrated song as co-authors.

Now, taking the same situation, suppose you were to write a *poem*, and subsequently ask someone to compose music to accompany it. In this instance the lyrics are an independent work, subject to separate copyright, and only the song derived from that work is collaborative. Conversely, a tune may be independently copyrighted before lyrics are ever added. In any event, it is always the best practice to get a written agreement between collaborators to establish the nature and extent of their working relationship in advance of any potential dispute over co-authorship percentages and entitlements.

Co-authors have certain legal rights and responsibilities in respect to each other. **Unless there is a written agreement between them forbidding it, each co-author can unilaterally negotiate and grant a non-exclusive license to use the co-authored work**, and is only responsible for paying his or her co-authors their proportional share of whatever money is received under that license. This can even be a "first use" license, creating the possibility for multiple, non-exclusive "first use" licenses negotiated by separate co-authors.

Is a "Copyright Notice" Required?

Before March 1, 1989, the inclusion of a formal copyright notice was mandatory on all published works, and any work first published before that date should continue to bear a notice or risk loss of copyright protection.

For works first published on or after March 1, 1989, inclusion of a copyright notice is optional, although strongly recommended because it informs the public that the work is protected by copyright, identifies the copyright owner, and shows the year of first publication. Furthermore, in the event that a work is infringed upon and that work does include a proper notice, the court will not allow a defendant to claim "innocent infringement"— that is, the infringer won't be allowed to say "I didn't know" as a defense. (Under United States copyright laws, "Innocent infringement" can subject an infringer to actual or statutory damages, but not to the punitive damages and other penalties which may be imposed for "willful infringement.") Also, copyright protection under the laws of foreign nations may, in some instances, be dependent upon the presence of the copyright notice. Including a specific copyright notice is therefore good practice, even though no longer mandatory under U.S. law in most cases.

Copyright notices are the responsibility of the publisher (copyright owner) and do not require advance permission or registration with the Copyright Office. Notice should be affixed to the work in such a manner and location as to "give reasonable notice of the claim of copyright." [105] The three elements comprising a copyright notice should appear together, usually on a single line:

105 The notice can be on the recording, or on its container (and preferably on both), so long as it provides reasonable notice of the claim.

1. For all works *other than* "Sound Recordings,"[106] the symbol © or the word "Copyright" or the abbreviation "Copr."; *followed by*
2. The year of first publication of the work; *followed by*
3. The name of the owner of copyright in the work, or an abbreviation by which the name can be recognized, or a generally known alternative designation of the owner.

For example:

© 2008, Robert Nathan & Burgundy Morgan

Sound recordings fixed in tangible form are "phonorecords," for which the "circle-p" symbol ("℗") is used for the copyright notice, followed by the year of first publication and identification of the copyright owner. A typical album will therefore contain both a "circle-c" notice (for the compositions) and a "circle-p" notice for the recordings (phonorecords) of those songs.

Do not use a "circle-p" notice on demos which you do not wish to have considered "published." Arguably, use of the "circle-p" symbol — denoting "phonorecord" — could open the door to compulsory licensing, thereby potentially foreclosing the opportunity to negotiate a "first use" license on better-than-statutory terms. To avoid an inadvertent publication, the author or other copyright owner should place a special "circle-c" copyright notice on any copies or recordings that might find their way into the hands of others, specifically stating that the work is not published. An appropriate notice for such a work would be:

Unpublished work, © [Year], [Copyright Owner].

On demonstration and promotional recordings, some or all of the following language should also be added to the notice.

For demonstration recordings ("Demos") the notice should read:

DEMO ONLY

<u>NOT FOR SALE, RELEASE, OR DISTRIBUTION.</u>

This recording is and remains the sole property of the copyright owner and is provided for demonstration purposes only. No portion hereof may be sold, leased, lent, broadcast, webcast, streamed, uploaded, downloaded, copied, distributed, disclosed, transmitted, transcribed, stored, or transferred by any means without written permission from the copyright owner.

---

106 Sound recordings are defined as works that result from the fixation of a series of musical, spoken, or other sounds, but ***not*** including sounds which are part of a motion picture, music video, or other audiovisual work.

For promotional recordings manufactured in connection with the release of a commercial recording, the notice should read something like this:

> **FOR PROMOTIONAL USE ONLY — NOT FOR SALE**
> **This recording is and remains the sole property of the copyright owner, and must be returned upon request. It is lent to the designated recipient for radio broadcast, internet streaming, critical review, and/or demonstration purposes ONLY. No royalties have been paid to the artist for this promotional phonorecord, and any sale, lease, loan, non-ephemeral upload or download, copying, distribution, transmission, transcription, storage, transfer or conveyance hereof, or possession hereof by any person not authorized by the copyright owner, is a violation of copyright and subject to prosecution under the laws of the United States and of foreign nations.**

Even the most comprehensive and explicit "demo" notice will *not* prevent a finding that the recording *has* been published as a phonorecord if the copyright owner has authorized the sale, lease, lending, or gift of even one such copy to a member of the general public.[107] Demonstration copies must remain exactly that, and should not be used for any other purpose. Remember, once publication has occurred in the form of a phonorecord, each and every composition included in that recording is available for re-recording by anyone, under a compulsory license.

What is "Publication"?

In simplest terms, *publication* is the action or process of making something available to the public. The Copyright Act defines "Publication" as

> *"...the distribution of copies or phonorecords of a work to the public*[108] *by sale or other transfer of ownership, or by rental, lease, or lending. The offering to distribute copies or phonorecords to a group of persons for purposes of further distribution, public performance, or public display, constitutes publication. A public performance or display of a work does not of itself constitute publication."* [17 USC § 101]

That statutory definition makes it clear that *any* sale of copies or phonorecords constitutes publication of all of the underlying work embodied in it, regardless of whether that work is

---

107 Allowing the broadcast or webcast of a demonstration recording is not publication. However, posting of an entire, downloadable recording to the internet may be taken as publication of a "phonorecord" (DPD) for the purposes of obtaining a compulsory license.

108 The phrase "to the public" has been interpreted as meaning distribution to persons without imposing explicit or implicit restrictions with respect to disclosure of the contents.

musical, dramatic, literary, or visual. However, if no material object changes hands — for example, performances or displays on television — it is not a publication no matter how many people are exposed to the work.[109] Conversely, when copies or phonorecords are offered for sale or lease to a group of wholesalers, broadcasters, or motion picture theaters, and if the purpose of that offer is further distribution, public performance, or public display of those copies or phonorecords, the *publication has occurred*, even if there is no subsequent sale, performance, display or further distribution.

Publication is a vital concept in copyright law for several reasons:

- A published work usually bears a notice of copyright to identify the year of publication and the name of the copyright owner and to inform the public that the work is protected by copyright.
- Works published before March 1, 1989, must bear the notice or risk loss of copyright protection.
- Works that are published in the United States are subject to mandatory deposit with the Library of Congress.
- Publication of a work can affect the limitations on the exclusive rights of the copyright owner.
- The year of publication may determine the duration of copyright protection for anonymous and pseudonymous works, and for works made for hire.

Can Copyrights be Sold or Transferred?

As with most forms of personal property, a copyright may be bequeathed, inherited, or transferred by court order. Also, as with other forms of personal property, conveyance will be subject to various state laws and regulations which govern ownership and transfers of property, the terms of lawful contracts and business conduct, and rules of inheritance.

Any or all of a copyright owner's exclusive rights, or any subdivision of those rights, may be transferred by a grant of rights, assignment, mortgage, exclusive license, transfer by will or intestate succession, or any other change in the ownership of any or all of the exclusive rights in a copyright, whether or not limited in time or place of effect. Unless by operation of law, a transfer of exclusive rights is not valid unless an instrument of conveyance, or a memorandum of the transfer, is in a writing signed by the owner of the rights conveyed, or by that owner's duly authorized agent.

---

109 ***However,*** uploading a full-length recording to a publicly-accessible website in an unrestricted, downloadable format constitutes publication of a "phonorecord," making the composition generally available for compulsory licensing.

The Copyright Office does not make or in any way participate in transfers of copyright ownership, but it will *record* a document of transfer after it has been executed by the parties. There are no special forms for such documents and notarization is unnecessary for such recordation, although use of the optional form entitled "Document Cover Sheet" is strongly recommended as an attachment to the transfer document.

Although recordation is not required for a binding transfer between contracting parties, it does provide certain legal advantages and may be required to validate the transfer or to allow the new owner to enforce copyright claims against third parties.

A *nonexclusive* license is not a transfer of ownership in a copyright and does not require recordation or a written agreement, although such an agreement is nonetheless strongly recommended.

Can a Grant of Rights Be Terminated?

Although a sale of property is usually "final," that is not always true of copyrights. In the context of copyright law, there is a right of *reversion*, under which an exclusive or non-exclusive grant of rights may be terminated after a fixed period of time and under certain circumstances. "Reversion" is an action or process by which ownership or control of property is returned to a former or original owner.[110]

Under the prior Copyright Act of 1909, the copyright in a work *automatically* reverted to the author, if living, or — if the author was not living — to other specified beneficiaries, provided that a renewal claim had been registered in the twenty-eighth year of the original term. That automatic reversion does not exist under current law.

Instead, Section 203 of the current Copyright Act permits authors (or specified successors of deceased authors) to terminate grants of copyright assignments and licenses that were made on or after January 1, 1978 when certain conditions have been met.

To be considered effective, a notice of termination must comply in form, content, and manner with specific statutory requirements (37 CFR § 201.10), may be served no earlier than twenty-five years after the execution of the grant or, if the grant covers the right of publication, no earlier than thirty years after the execution of the grant or twenty-five years after publication under the grant (whichever comes first). However, termination of a grant cannot be *effective* until thirty-five years after the execution of the grant or, if the grant covers the right of publication, no earlier than forty years after the execution of the grant or thirty-five years after publication under the grant (whichever comes first).

110 In the broader context of music contracts, reversion (sometimes called "turnaround") may also relate to a party's ability to recover or obtain ownership or possession of master recordings or other property, under certain circumstances.

For works already under statutory copyright protection before 1978, the present law provides a similar right of termination covering the newly added years that extended the former maximum term of the copyright from 56 to 75 years.

What is the "DMCA"?

The 1998 Digital Millennium Copyright Act ("DMCA") implements provisions of the two 1996 World Intellectual Property Organization treaties mentioned above: the Copyright Treaty ("WCT") and the Performances and Phonograms Treaty ("WPPT"). The DMCA also addresses a number of other copyright-related matters, attempting to harmonize long-standing copyright policies and doctrines with new issues raised by recent technological innovations and evolving media. The process initiated by the DMCA is ongoing, and many of those issues remain unresolved as the industry, the Copyright Office, the legislature, and the courts strive to interpret and implement copyright law in the face of technologies which provide instant, worldwide publication of countless copies of works, with and without copyright owners' consent.

The DMCA is not only technically complex from a legal standpoint, but — as noted above — it remains somewhat inchoate as new situations and issues arise which compel its further modification to implement additional regulations, legislative amendments, and judicial decisions construing its provisions and interpreting their application.

The most notable highlights of the DMCA — which appears as the newly-added Chapter 12 in Title 17 of the U.S. Code — are:

- Criminalizes circumvention of the anti-piracy measures which are built into most commercial software.
- Forbids and criminalizes the manufacture, sale, or distribution of devices used to illegally copy software. (But does permit development of code-cracking of copyright protection software and devices, provided the purpose is encryption research, or to assess product compatibility, or to test computer security systems.)
- Allows exemptions from anti-circumvention provisions for nonprofit libraries, archives, and educational institutions under certain circumstances.
- Establishes rules for webcasting, including compulsory licenses with a statutory royalty to owners of *sound recording* copyrights, and permits the making of "ephemeral" (temporary) copies of the work for that purpose.
- Generally limits internet service providers' liability for copyright infringement where their participation in the infringement is limited to simply transmitting information over the internet. (But service providers are required to promptly remove material from users' web sites whenever such material appears to constitute a copyright infringement.)

Although the DMCA specifically provides that it is not intended to "affect rights, remedies, limitations, or defenses to copyright infringement, including fair use, under [Title 17]" nor "enlarge or diminish vicarious or contributory liability for copyright infringement in connection with any technology, product, service, device, component, or part thereof.,"[111] there are two areas of copyright protection which have been particularly impacted by the DMCA, the extent of which impact remains largely indeterminate.

The **first sale doctrine**, codified in Section 109 of the Copyright Act (17 USC § 109), provides that a legally obtained copy of a protected work may be resold or otherwise conveyed by its owner, at any time, without any obligation to the copyright owner. However, this doctrine was developed when "copy" invariably meant *a single tangible object* which could change hands from one person to another and which had a *limited useful life-span.*

That is not the case with digital copies, where the original remains intact, and each sale is, in effect, a new copy. Moreover, since digital data does not degrade over time or with use, the life-span of such copies is effectively unlimited.

Another issue has to do with traditional **compulsory licenses** to make new recordings of compositions after their first publication in the form of a **phonorecord**. 17 USC § 115 provides a statutory license for the making and distribution of phonorecords of non-dramatic musical works, including the right to distribute a phonorecord by means of a "digital phonorecord delivery" ("DPD"). Thus a *digital download constitutes a "phonorecord" within the statutory definition.* By uploading an entire song to a website in an unrestricted, downloadable format, a songwriter has effectively "published" that song *as a phonorecord*, and has thereby made it available for compulsory licensing and waived the right to negotiate a first use license on better-than-statutory terms. The unresolved question, if any, is whether or not such publication was "incidental" under statutory language, and hence not truly "published." Unfortunately, current law does not clearly identify which DPDs can be classified as "incidental," nor provide guidelines for making this determination. Read literally, the Copyright Act provides that any composition uploaded to the internet in a publicly accessible and downloadable format is a DPD, making the compositions freely available for compulsory licensing under 17 USC § 115.

In order to clarify the many unresolved and evolving issues to which technological advances have given rise, the record industry continues to initiate litigation which not only seeks to protect the industry's interests but which also creates a means by which the courts can consider and rule upon these and other issues arising under the DMCA.[112]

---

111 17 USC § 1201.(c)

112 Under our judicial system, courts cannot issue rulings unless an action requiring adjudication is filed by a real party in interest. Only In ruling on that particular case can the court make findings which interpret — and sometimes overturn — laws. Thus each new case alleging violation under the DMCA affords the courts a chance to construe, distinguish, comment upon, and explain applicable portions of the law.

What is an "International" Copyright?

There is *no such thing* as an "international copyright," *per se.* Protection against unauthorized use in a foreign country generally depends on the laws of that country, but most countries' laws offer some protection to foreign works. There are, however, several international copyright treaties and conventions which have the force of law in countries which are signatories to them. These include...

- The Universal Copyright Convention ("UCC")
- The Berne Union for the Protection of Literary and Artistic Property (the "Berne Convention")
- The Agreement on Trade-Related Aspects of Intellectual Property Rights ("TRIPS")[113]
- The World Intellectual Property Organization ("WIPO") treaties, including,
  WIPO Copyright Treaty ("WCT"); and
  WIPO Performances and Phonograms Treaty ("WPPT")

In addition, there are a number of bilateral agreements with some countries which may afford protection even if that country is not signatory to more comprehensive treaties or conventions.

The United States was a founding member of the Universal Copyright Convention ("UCC") in 1955. Generally, a work by a national or domiciliary of a country that is a member of the UCC, or a work first published in a UCC country, may claim protection under the UCC if the work bears the notice of copyright in the form and position specified by the UCC. Such notice will satisfy and substitute for any other formalities a UCC member country would otherwise impose as a condition of copyright. A UCC notice should consist of the "©" symbol, accompanied by the name of the copyright owner and the year of first publication of the work.

For decades, the U.S. resisted joining the Berne Convention. However, on March 1, 1989, the United States gained protection for U.S. authors in all member nations of the Berne Union with which the United States formerly had either no copyright relations or had only a bilateral treaty arrangement. Members of the Berne Union agree to a certain minimum level of copyright protection and agree to treat nationals of other member countries like their own for purposes of copyright. A work first published in the United States or another Berne Union country (or first published in a non-Berne country, followed by publication within 30 days in a Berne Union country) is eligible for protection in all Berne member countries. There are no other requirements to obtain that protection.

An author who wishes copyright protection for his or her work in a particular country should first determine the extent of protection available to works of foreign authors in that

---

113 TRIPS was one of several agreements which comprised the 1994 Marrakesh Agreement under which the World Trade Organization (WTO) was created.

country. If possible, this should be done *before* the work is published anywhere, because protection may depend on the facts existing at the time of first publication, regardless of where that publication occurred.

If the country in which protection is sought is signatory to one of the international copyright conventions, the work generally may be protected by complying with the conditions of that convention. Even if the work cannot be brought under the aegis of an international convention, protection under the specific provisions of the country's national laws may still be possible. There are, however, some countries that offer little or no copyright protection to any foreign works. A regularly-updated list of signatories to the various treaties, conventions and bilateral agreements can be obtained from the Copyright Office, but it may be advisable to consult an expert familiar with foreign copyright laws to ascertain the amount of protection, if any, available for a specific work in a particular country.

What are "Droits Moral?"

Pronounced "DWA'•more•AL," this phrase literally translates as "moral rights," but the French word "moral" doesn't mean quite the same thing as does its English counterpart. In a French context, "moral" has connotations of "personal," "spiritual," "intangible," "eternal," "inalienable," "non-economic" and "indefinable." Although many statutes, courts, and commentators use the translated English phrase, "moral rights," it is perhaps better practice to think and speak of *droits moral* when referring to this aspect of artists' rights, in order to retain all of those Gallic nuances which are inherent to the concept.

There is a fundamental, philosophical distinction as to the nature of copyright between English common law (upon which U.S. laws are primarily based) and French and European legal systems. In English law, copyright arose as a governmental grant extended to publishers to protect their economic interests, while simultaneously imposing governmental restrictions and censorship.[114] France, on the other hand, regarded the right to control artistic creations to be a "natural" right vested in the artist, separate from the economic rights related to publication of the work itself. These two distinct views of the foundational basis for copyright impeded development of international cooperation and treaties, as various countries sought compromises which preserved their own legal traditions, yet afforded their citizens the benefits of international protection for creative works. The United States was particularly recalcitrant in these efforts, and only joined the Berne Convention after years of negotiation and compromise. The 1988 amendments to the Copyright Act represented, in large part, concessions by the United States which brought U.S. copyright laws into conformity with the dictates of the Berne Convention, including adoption of some of the European *droits moral* ideals.

114 These censorship and control aspects never arose in the United States, as a direct result of the First Amendment to the U.S. Constitution.

Historically, the *droits moral* doctrine holds that a work of art is forever linked to its creator in an intangible, yet fundamental and unassailable manner, giving the artist certain rights which transcend and survive both copyright and ownership interests. Some countries[115] have long recognized these rights as being personal to artists, wholly apart from the economic publishing interest represented by copyrights. The extent to which those rights are enforceable varies from country to country, but a limited form of *droits moral* protection is included in the Berne Convention, and is therefore binding on all signatory countries, including the United States.

Specifically, the Berne Convention provides:

> "Independently of the author's economic rights, and even after the transfer of said rights, the author shall have the right to claim authorship of the work, and to object to any distortion, mutilation, or other modification of, or other derogatory action in relation to, the said work, which shall be prejudicial to his honor or reputation."[116]

The list of all those particular rights which comprise *droits moral* is lengthy, and varies from country to country, but the two most significant aspects of *droits moral* are the rights of **attribution** and of **integrity**.

The **attribution** right is essentially the right to be publicly known as the author of a work. Collaterally, this includes a bundle of additional rights related to the author's name and reputation. The **integrity** right refers to the work itself, and consists of an author's (or his or her successors' or heirs') rights to prevent others from making deforming modifications to the work.

There are at least five distinct, traditional rights falling within these two broad categories of *droits moral*,[117] and those rights remain enforceable in France (where they first evolved) and to lesser extent in many other countries — particularly those jurisdictions which have a French legal heritage.

While the traditional *droits moral* are "inalienable" and continue to be regarded as such in those European countries where they developed, the Berne Convention does not expressly include that perpetual aspect of the rights, and does not specifically preclude waiver, transfer, or assignment of *droits moral*. In consequence, an informed waiver of rights which expressly includes *droits moral* will generally be held enforceable in the U.S. and other countries not

---

115 Most notably France and Germany.

116 Article 6*bis*, Berne Union for the Protection of Literary and Artistic Property (the "Berne Convention")

117 The traditional Droits Moral include the following: *Droit au respect du nom* (the right to have one's name respected); *Droit à la paternité* (right to be publicly acknowledged as the father (creator) of a work); *Droit au respect du l'oeuvre* (right to have the work itself respected and protected from deforming changes, desecration, or destruction); *Droit de divulgation* (right to publish a work, or to withhold it from the public); and *Droit de retrait* or *Droit de repentir* (right to retract or withdraw a work from distribution or display, particularly where it no longer represents the artist's views.)

bound by specific laws against such waivers.

In the United States, there has nonetheless been a steady trend toward recognizing certain aspects of *droits moral*, particularly in regard to works of visual art such as painting, sculpture, and photography. Both Congress and a number of state legislatures have enacted statutes which limit the rights of the legal owners of such works from doing anything with their property which would destroy or diminish its artistic integrity. Some of the more stringent of these laws impose a legal duty upon the owners of works of fine art, essentially making them trustees or conservators obliged to protect and preserve those artistic works for posterity.

For the music industry, the **attribution** right has come to refer primarily to claims of a creative contribution made by someone other than the named author of a work. For example, suppose a band is working on recording a new composition, and a friend of the recording engineer just happens to be at one session. The band members are arguing about a particular lyric, and the engineer's friend — without invitation — suggests a word or phrase. The band later releases a song which contains that word or phrase and, *voila!*... the "friend" (whom no one has seen or talked to since) suddenly reappears and claims co-authorship rights.

If he or she can prove that even a small contribution actually occurred, then a claim for an *equal* co-author's share in the song could likely succeed, since the law will generally presume all creative contributions to be of equivalent value unless a contract between the co-authors provides otherwise. This potential for a *droits moral* claim by an inadvertent or casual contributor is one reason why it has become essential to obtain releases (including *droits moral* waivers) from anyone and everyone who has been even remotely involved in the creative process.

What Does "Clearance" Mean?

In the music industry, and throughout the entertainment business, clearance is the process of verifying that a project does not infringe upon or misappropriate anyone's rights. This refers not only to copyrights, but to all of the intellectual property and personality rights referred to in the preceding chapter, since unauthorized use of any copyright, trademark, trade dress, name, voice, likeness or any other protected property or *quasi*-property right can create an exposure to liability for infringement or misappropriation.

From the standpoint of entertainment contracts, clearances are critical. It is essential to confirm that all necessary rights have been secured (or that a well grounded legal exemption is applicable) before releasing a commercial product. Contractual "Warranties and Representations" clauses are generally not sufficient by themselves, since they only provide for indemnification and cannot excuse liability to third parties. (An indemnity is only as valuable as the indemnitor's ability to pay, which may be insufficient to offset the costs arising from an infringement or misappropriation claim.) For that reason, most labels and production companies insist on conducting their own due diligence, either in-house or through outside firms or attorneys specializing in clearances. This is especially true with regard to artists whose works include "sampling." Contrary to popular belief, *no* amount of sampling is permissible without a license from both the publisher of the composition and the owner of the master recording which is sampled. For rap, hip-hop, and urban artists — where sampling concerns are most applicable — labels will often insist on the artist retaining (at artist's expense, as part of the "recording cost" advances) the services of an independent, bonded clearance service to certify that all necessary licenses have been obtained and verified.

Clearance can often be a tortuous process. At a minimum, it requires that all personnel involved in the composition and recording process — the songwriters, musicians, vocalists, recording studio, engineer, producer, and arranger — sign agreements which either specify their continuing rights and interests in the work or assign those rights and interests, or releases which waive their rights (including *droits moral*), and grant the necessary permissions in respect to personality rights.

Obtaining all of the necessary clearance documents can be difficult enough in the controlled situation of recording a new album. When the project is audiovisual, or where it is otherwise dependent on licenses to use previously written or recorded materials (such as with sampling), the level of diligence required goes up significantly.

Suppose, for example, you obtain a master use license from someone. In addition to a copy of the master recording itself, you'll need to verify that all of the necessary clearances for that master have been completed, and that the person licensing the master to you has all of the necessary rights to do so.[118] The reputation and financial capability of your source can be crucial, since you may need to seek indemnification from them in the event that an unknown party suddenly sues for infringement, alleging that your license is invalid, inadequate, defective, or fraudulent. (And to reiterate an earlier caveat, you're still the one liable for the infringement, even if it was unwitting.[119] All you can do is go after your source, based on their warranties and representations, to defend and indemnify you against the infringement claim. If your license source is insolvent, or can't be located, you're out of luck.)

◆ ◆ ◆

A thorough understanding of copyright, and of related intellectual property rights, and of those personality rights which amount to *quasi*-property, is indispensable in almost every aspect of the music industry, since those rights permeate every commercial recording, and are integral to all products, marketing, and promotional efforts, throughout the field of entertainment.

---

118 A *valid license* is paramount. Once a valid license has been obtained, a commercially- purchased CD may be used as a "master recording" — provided it is not copy-protected — since its digital quality will be identical to that of a traditional "master" copy.

119 An unintentional infringer is not subject to additional *punitive* damages, but is still liable for the general damages resulting from that infringement. If the infringement is intentional, however, substantial punitive damages can be added, as well as attorney's fees, and potential criminal liabilities.

CHAPTER 4

COPYRIGHT REGISTRATION AND DEPOSIT

The Copyright Office is essentially a registry and repository of public records. Except in certain limited situations, registration in the Copyright Office is not a condition of copyright,[120] although it may be required as a legal prerequisite to certain remedies afforded by the Copyright Act.

In general, copyright registration is simply a legal formality intended to create an official public record of the basic facts of a particular copyright. Since current law permits registration of unpublished works, formerly common "self-help" methods of establishing creation and creation date have become superfluous, although they may still be used to provide additional evidence of the original, independent creation of a registrable work.[121]

Registration is a reasonably simple process which may be done at any time within the life of the copyright, although earlier registration is preferable, and is necessary to obtain some of the benefits listed below. Unlike the former law, it is no longer necessary to re-register a work when it becomes published, although **there is a mandatory requirement for *deposit* of copies of works which have been *published* in the United States**.

Even though registration is not required for creation of a valid copyright, there are definite advantages to registration and current law provides several inducements to encourage copyright owners to register their work.

- Registration establishes a public record of the copyright claim, creating a legal presumption which must be overcome by any rival claimant seeking to challenge a registered copyright;
- Before a Title 17 infringement suit may be filed in court, U.S. registration is required for works of U.S. origin and for foreign works which originate in a country which is not signatory to the Berne Convention;

---

120 Copyright registration may be required in order to preserve a copyright on a work first published before March 1, 1989, that would otherwise be invalidated because the copyright notice was omitted from the published copies or phonorecords, or the name or year was omitted, or certain errors were made in the year date.. (See 17 USC §§ 405 & 406)

121 The Copyright Act of 1909 generally did not allow for registration of unpublished works. Authors consequently resorted to various *ad hoc* methods to prove their rights including, among others, depositing copies with unofficial registries such as the Writer's Guild, notarized affidavits of authorship, and/or sending themselves copies of their work by certified mail in envelopes which could remained sealed until needed as evidence. These and other self-help methods of seeking to establish ownership are sometimes referred to as a "poor man's copyright."

- If made before or within five years of publication, registration constitutes *prima facie* evidence in court of the validity of the copyright and of the facts stated in the certificate;
- If registration is made within three months after publication of the work — or prior to an infringement of the work — statutory damages and an award of attorney's fees will be available to the copyright owner in court actions. Otherwise, only injunctive relief and recovery of actual damages and the infringer's profits are awardable to the copyright owner; and
- Registration allows the owner of the copyright to record the registration with U.S. Customs and Border Protection Service to block importation of infringing copies.

Who Can File a Copyright Registration?

Under the Copyright Act, only four categories of persons are legally entitled to submit an application for copyright registration. They are...

(1) **The author**. This can be either a person who actually created the work, or — if the work was made for hire — the employer or other person for whom the work was prepared.

(2) **The copyright claimant.** The copyright claimant is *either* the author of the work (see above) *or* a person or organization that has obtained ownership of all the rights under the copyright by contract or by operation of law.

(3) **The owner of exclusive right(s)**. Under copyright law, any exclusive rights in a copyright, and any subdivision of those rights, can be transferred and owned separately, even though the transfer may be limited in time or place of effect, and subject to a statutory right of subsequent reversion. With respect to any of the exclusive rights contained in a copyright, the term "copyright owner" refers to the owner of that particular right. An owner of an exclusive right may apply for registration of their particular claim of interest in the work.

(4) **A duly authorized agent of the author, copyright claimant, or owner of exclusive right(s).** Any person authorized to act on behalf of the author, other copyright claimant, or owner of exclusive rights may apply for registration.

Copyright application forms include a formal certification, and a person who does not fall within one of the four listed categories cannot sign the application without committing a punishable federal offense.

What Is Required for Registration?

Generally, copyright registration requires three elements:

(1) The correct application form, properly completed;

(2) A nonrefundable filing fee for each application;[122] and

(3) A nonreturnable deposit[123] of the work being registered.

The three elements should be sent in a single envelope or package addressed to:

Register of Copyrights
Copyright Office
Library of Congress
101 Independence Avenue, S.E
Washington, D.C. 20559-6000

If the application package for an unpublished work is incomplete through insufficiency of, or failure to include, any of the three elements, it will not be processed and ordinarily will be returned. In the case of published works, the deposit copy or copies will usually be retained by the Library of Congress, even if the remainder of the application is returned as incomplete or incorrect. In this circumstance there has been no *registration* of that published work, and a new, complete application package, including a new deposit of the work, will need to be submitted to secure registration.

Which Copyright Form Should Be Used?

The Copyright Office publishes a wide variety of applications and related forms, including (among others) the following:

---

122 As of July 1, 2006, the basic fee was raised to $45 per application, although a different fee structure applies to certain specialized copyright applications (*e.g.*, those requiring Form SE/GROUP or Form G/DN.) The current fee can be ascertained from the Copyright Office's website (http://www.copyright.gov) or by telephoning (202) 707-5959.

123 There are special deposit requirements for some types of work such as three-dimensional objects and computer programs, among others. In general, however, the guidelines for the deposit are as follow:

If the work is **unpublished**, the required deposit will be **one complete copy or phonorecord** of the work.

If the work was **first published in the United States**, the deposit will be **two complete copies or phonorecords** of the "best edition" of the work (if published after January 1, 1978) or of the work "as first published" (if published before January 1, 1978).

If the work was **first published *outside* the United States**, then the deposit will consist **one complete copy or phonorecord** of the work "as first published."

Form PA	*(Performing Arts)* This form is used for registration of both published and unpublished works which are performed or which are intended to be performed, including musical compositions, plays and other dramatic works, pantomimes, choreographic works, motion pictures, videos (including music videos), and other audiovisual works.
Form SR	*(Sound Recordings)* This form is used for registration of both published and unpublished sound recordings, which are defined as a fixation in tangible form of a series of musical, spoken, or other sounds, but ***not*** including sounds embodied within a motion picture, video, or other audiovisual work.
Form TX	*(Text)* This form is used for registration of both published and unpublished non-dramatic literary works such as short stories, fiction and non-fiction books, poems, computer programs, and all other forms of written text which are not intended to be performed.
Form VA	*(Visual Arts)* This form is used for registration of both published and unpublished works of visual art including photographs, paintings, graphics, sculptures, and architectural works.
__/CON	*(Continuation)* This form is used as an attachment to other copyright application forms to provide additional information when the primary form has insufficient space. In using this form, the leading blank line should be filled in with the designation of the form being augmented. *(E.g.,* PA **/CON.***)*
Form CA	*(Correction/Amplification)* This form is used to supplement, correct or amplify information contained in a prior application for an earlier *registered* copyright.
Short Forms	In addition to their standard-length versions, Forms PA, TX, and VA are each available in "short form" versions, as well. These simplified application forms may **only** be used by an **individual, living author** who is also the **sole author** *and* the **sole owner** of the copyright in the work. The work must be **completely new** (*i.e.*, contain no previously published or registered material, or any public domain material) and **not a work made for hire**. If there is more than one author, or if an entity appears as the copyright claimant, then a standard (long) form must be used.
Document Cover Sheet	This form is used when submitting transfers of copyright ownership or other copyright-related contracts and documents (other than applications or renewals) for recordation in the Copyright Office.
Form RE	*(Renewal)* This form is used to claim a renewal of copyright in works copyrighted under the former copyright law which was in effect through December 31, 1977.
Addendum to Form RE	This is a special, mandatory form which must accompany Form RE when applying for renewal of any work published between January 1, 1964, and December 31, 1977, which was not registered during its first 28-year term.

Form SE	*(Serial)* This form is used for registration of serialized works issued or intended to be issued in successive parts bearing numerical or chronological designations and intended to be continued indefinitely (*i.e.*, periodicals, newspapers, magazines, newsletters, annuals, journals, *etc.*)
Form G/DN	This is a specialized form to register a complete month's worth of issues of a daily newspaper under certain regulatory conditions.

These and other copyright forms are available from the Copyright Office by mail, or by download from http://www.copyright.gov.

Can Musical Compositions and Sound Recordings Be Registered Together Using a Single Application?

As emphasized earlier (and throughout this book), there is a critical difference between a **musical composition** copyright and a **sound recording** copyright. Although those copyrights are and remain wholly separate and distinct, an application for copyright registration where there is ***exactly identical ownership*** of both the composition copyright and the sound recording copyright is the *only* instance in which that distinction is of little importance.

A **musical composition** consists of music, including any accompanying words, and is normally registered as a work of performing arts. The authors of a musical composition are generally the composer and the lyricist. The deposit for a musical composition may be in the form of notated written copy (*i.e.*, sheet music) or in the form of a phonorecord (*e.g.*, cassette tape, CD, DAT, *etc.*).

A **sound recording** results from the fixation of a series of musical, spoken, or other sounds. The author of a sound recording is the performer or performers whose performance is fixed in that recording, or the record producer or engineer who processes the sounds and fixes them in the final recording, or both.

Copyright in a sound recording is therefore never the same as — nor a substitute for — copyright in the underlying musical composition. ***However***, even though they are separate works and separate copyrights, a musical composition and a sound recording ***may*** be registered together on a single application **if, *and only if*, ownership of the copyrights in both the *musical composition* and in the *sound recording* is <u>exactly</u> the same.** In that one circumstance, a single Sound Recording application (Form SR) may be filed. **This is the only situation which results in both a "circle-c" and a "circle-p" copyright registration issuing from a single application.**

In almost all instances, it is better practice to register the composition separately under Form PA, even though the *deposit* for that registration may be in the form of a sound recording. Remember, the sound recording ("circle-p") copyright is intended to protect an infringement of a particular recording, not the composition. Since the initial deposit in respect to the composition is more than likely *not* going to be a final, mastered recording, registering the copyright to that particular sound recording may be premature or unnecessary.

Regardless of the application form used, it is critical when submitting a recording as the deposit for registration of a composition that the lyrics and musical elements be clear and comprehensible. If there is any doubt that the lyrics can be heard and understood from the recording, Form PA should be used and typed lyrics included as part of the deposit. (If the lyrics were originally created separately as poetry, they may be independently registered as such using Form TX, in which event the Form PA application should reflect that the composition which includes those lyrics is a derivative work. Similarly, if the tune was composed and completed independently in advance of the addition of lyrics, the tune could be registered separately using form PA, and subsequent registration of the song (with lyrics) should state that it is a derivative work based on that previously-registered tune.)

How Many Songs Can Be Registered Using a Single Application?

Under federal regulations,[124] **two *or more*** unpublished songs, song lyrics, or other musical works may be registered as a **collection**, under a single, common title, using only one application and paying only a single fee, *provided* that certain conditions are met.

One of those conditions is that **the copyright owner(s) must be the same for all the songs.** Additionally, there must always be at least ***one* author who is common to *all* the songs in the collection**, even if there has been a transfer of ownership.

If those conditions are satisfied, then there is no upper limit on the number of compositions which can be included in registering a collection. However, where there are multiple authors with only one common to every song in the collection, experience has shown that the better practice is to combine songs into separate collections so that the authorship is completely identical for that collection. For example...

Hypothetical: Assume that Abner, Bill, and Cathy have composed the following songs:

"One."	Lyrics by Abner; Music by Bill
"Two."	Lyrics by Abner; Music by Cathy
"Three."	Lyrics by Abner; Music by Bill & Cathy
"Four."	Lyrics by Abner; Music by Bill & Cathy
"Five."	Lyrics by Abner; Music by Bill
"Six."	Lyrics by Abner & Bill; Music by Bill & Cathy
"Seven"	Lyrics by Bill; Music by Cathy
"Eight"	Lyrics and Music by Abner
"Nine."	Lyrics by Abner; Music by Bill & Cathy

---

124 37 CFR § 202.3 subd. (b)(3)(i)

In this hypothetical example, there *cannot* be a single copyright application for a collection of all nine songs because there is not a single author who is common to *all nine* of them. *Technically*, a single registration application could be filed for the eight songs in which Abner appears as an author, and a separate application could be filed for the single song ("Seven") to which he did not contribute.

(1) Collection"ONE"
("One," "Two," "Three," "Four," "Five," "Six," "Eight," & "Nine.")
Lyrics by Abner & Bill; Music by Abner, Bill & Cathy

(2) "Seven"
Lyrics by Bill; Music by Cathy

The problem with this approach begins when it comes time to issue licenses, or to divvy up royalties. Even if there is a carefully crafted contract between the three co-authors, disputes are almost inevitable. For example, a third party, in reliance on the copyright registration, might obtain a non-exclusive license from Cathy or Bill for use of the song "Eight," even though neither Bill nor Cathy contributed to that song.[125] Nonetheless,"Eight" appears within the collective copyright, with Bill and Cathy listed as co-authors, so a third party's reliance on their right to grant a non-exclusive license would be justified, and the license would likely be valid. In this hypothetical, the better practice would therefore be to file six separate applications, as follow:

(1) Collection"ONE"
("One" & "Five")
Lyrics by Abner; Music by Bill

(2) "Two"
Lyrics by Abner; Music by Cathy

(3) Collection "THREE"
("Three," "Four," and "Nine")
Lyrics by Abner; Music by Bill & Cathy

(4) "Six."
Lyrics by Abner & Bill; Music by Bill & Cathy

(5) "Seven"
Lyrics by Bill; Music by Cathy

(6) "Eight"
Lyrics and Music by Abner

The only disadvantage to this approach is an increase in the copyright registration fees [126] On the other hand, it has the distinct advantage of avoiding any confusion as to each author's

125 Co-claimants of a copyright generally have the right to grant non-exclusive licenses to third parties without the knowledge or consent of other co-authors, providing that they share equally with those co-authors whatever consideration they obtain for that license.

126 Currently, $270 instead of $90 (or $210 instead of $70, for electronic, on-line filing.)

contribution by making each registration an accurate reflection of the individual co-author's rights. This will be of inestimable importance in the event of a future controversy over royalty distributions or the right to grant licenses.

The same federal regulation which permits single registrations of collected musical works also permits collections of literary and other types of registrable work on the same single-application, single-fee basis, provided that the one-claimant, one-author-in-common requirement is met.[127]

How Should Form PA Be Completed for a New Work or Collection?

Form PA is for registration of published or unpublished works which are intended to be performed. That includes: *(a)* musical works (music and lyrics); *(b)* dramatic works (including any accompanying music); *(c)* pantomimes and choreographic works; and *(d)* motion pictures and other audiovisual works (including any accompanying music). Here, we are primarily discussing registration of "non-dramatic musical works."

The title of the new work or "collection" should be entered in under "Title of This Work" (**Space 1**) of the Form PA application, and it should also appear on the deposit copy or recording. For a collection, individual song titles may also be listed on the application using Form PA/CON. Remember, the *name* given to the collection ***doesn't matter*** and can be completely arbitrary. **Neither the collective title nor individual song titles are protected by copyright.**

When unpublished works are registered as a collection, only the collection title will appear in the catalogs and indices of the Copyright Office, even if individual titles have been listed on a PA/CON form. Individual titles will appear in Copyright Office records only if each song is originally registered separately, or if Form CA applications for supplementary registration are submitted to specify individual titles in a *previously-registered* collection. Applications for

---

127 37 CFR § 202.3 subd. (b)(3)(i), which states:

For the purpose of registration on a single application and upon payment of a single registration fee, the following shall be considered a single work:

(A) In the case of published works: all copyrightable elements that are otherwise recognizable as self-contained works, that are included in a single unit of publication, and in which the copyright claimant is the same; and

(B) In the case of unpublished works: all copyrightable elements that are otherwise recognizable as self-contained works, and are combined in a single unpublished "collection." For these purposes, a combination of such elements shall be considered a "collection" if:

(1) The elements are assembled in an orderly form;

(2) The combined elements bear a single title identifying the collection as a whole;

(3) The copyright claimant in all of the elements, and in the collection as a whole, is the same; and

(4) All of the elements are by the same author, or, if they are by different authors, at least one of the authors has contributed copyrightable authorship to each element.

Registration of an unpublished "collection" extends to each copyrightable element in the collection and to the authorship, if any, involved in selecting and assembling the collection.

supplementary registration may not be submitted until *after* a certificate of registration has been issued for the collection.

In **Space 2** of the Form PA application, each individual author who contributed to any of the works included in the collection should be identified. If the authors are members of a performing group, this may be indicated after each name, but naming *only* a performing group as author does not properly identify the authors and may be grounds for rejection of the application. Remember, if the work was a work for hire, *"the* ***employer*** *or other person for whom the work was prepared is considered the author."* If there are more than three individual authors who contributed to the work or collection, use Form PA/CON to identify the additional authors.

In **Space 3**, under "Year in Which Creation of this Work Was Completed", write in the *latest* (most recent) year in which any copyrightable element of the collection or work was completed.[128]

In **Space 4**, under "Copyright Claimant," give the name and address of the owner(s) of the copyright, even if this is the previously-named author or authors. If the listed copyright claimant is not identical to the author, then how the claimant acquired the copyright from the author in the space entitled "Transfers." This explanation need be no more than a few words. *E.g.*, "inherited from deceased author," or "by written contract."

Space 5 relates to previously registered works. As a general rule, only one basic copyright registration can be made for the same *version* of a particular work. If the new work is a only a modification or revision of a previously-registered work, a second registration is generally not possible unless: *(a)* the prior registration was for an unpublished form of the work and the new, second registration is for a first published edition; or *(b)* someone other than the author is identified as copyright claimant in the earlier registration, and the author is now seeking registration in his or her own name. If the work has been substantially changed from an earlier-registered version and the new registration is to cover additions or revisions, check the last box in Space 5, give the prior registration number and date,[129] and complete both parts of Space 6.

Space 6 of the PA application is for works which incorporate all or portions of one or more earlier works that have already been *(a)* published, or *(b)* registered for copyright, or *(c)* which have fallen into the public domain. These include **changed versions** of earlier- registered works, **compilations**, or **derivative works.**

Compilation refers to a work formed by collecting and assembling preexisting materials in such a way that the resulting work, taken as a whole, constitutes an original work of authorship.

---

128 See 37 CFR § 202.3 subd. (b)(3)(ii)

129 If there has been more than one earlier registration of the work, give the number and date of the *latest* prior registration.

Derivative work refers to a work which has been based on one or more preexisting works, *regardless of whether those works are registered or subject to copyright protection.* Musical arrangements, dramatizations, translations, abridgments, condensations, motion picture versions, or "any other form in which a work may be recast, transformed, or adapted," are all derivative of earlier works, including earlier works which are in public domain. Derivative works also include works "consisting of editorial revisions, annotations, or other modifications" if such changes, as a whole, represent an original work of authorship.

Remember, except under certain *narrow* exceptions,[130] **works which include or are derived from copyrighted material require the consent of the original copyright owner.** This includes any work which incorporates ***sampling*** from previously recorded material.

The remainder of Form PA (**Spaces 7, 8 & 9**) are generally self-explanatory. For those who frequently file applications for copyright registration, a **Deposit Account** can be established to facilitate processing. For those who have not previously established a Deposit Account, leave Space 7a blank and include payment of the required fee with the application. The processing of the application will generally not commence until the fee has been credited, so payment by check may delay the application by as much as ten days, although the registration will still be retroactive to the date the application was first received.

However, the application will not be considered "received," nor will it be accepted or processed, unless it bears a signature **date** and an original, handwritten ink **signature** of the author, other copyright claimant, owner of exclusive rights, or of a duly authorized agent of one of them, certifying the application.

What Are the Deposit Requirements for Copyright Applications?

The general rule for deposits is one copy of unpublished works, and two copies of published works, but special deposit requirements exist for many types of registrable work. In some instances, only one copy is required for published works, in other instances only identifying material is required, and in still other instances, the deposit requirement may be unique. The following are prominent examples of exceptions to the general deposit requirements:

- If the work is a **motion picture** (including **videos**), the deposit requirement is one complete copy of the unpublished or published motion picture and a separate written description of its contents, such as a continuity, press book, or synopsis. (Form PA)

130 See "*Are There Exceptions to Copyright Protection?*," in the preceding chapter. Additionally, derivative works based on materials in public domain do not require consent.

- If the work is a **literary, dramatic or musical work published *only* on phonorecord**, the deposit requirement is one complete copy of the phonorecord. (Form PA / Form SR)

- If the work is an **unpublished or published computer program**, the deposit requirement is one visually perceptible copy in source code of the first and last 25 pages of the program. (Form TX)

- For a **computer program *of fewer than 50 pages***, the deposit is a copy of the entire program. (Form TX)

- If the work is in a **CD-ROM format**, the deposit requirement is one complete copy of the CD-ROM, the operating software, and any manual(s) accompanying it. If the identical work is also available in print or hard copy form, one complete copy of that printed version and one complete copy of the CD-ROM version are required. (Form TX)

- In the case of **3-dimensional works**, identifying material such as photographs or drawings are ordinarily required. (Form VA)

Other examples of works with special deposit requirements include (without limitation) works of the visual arts such as greeting cards, toys, fabric, and oversized works; video games and other machine-readable audiovisual works; automated databases; and contributions to collective works. When in doubt, the applicant should contact the Copyright Office in advance to determine the appropriate deposit to accompany a particular application.

Even though registration is not required to establish copyright, the Copyright Act requires a **mandatory deposit for works published in the United States**. In general, the owner of the copyright or the owner of the exclusive right of publication in the work has a **legal obligation** to deposit in the Copyright Office, within 3 months of publication in the United States, two copies (or, for sound recordings, two phonorecords) for the use of the Library of Congress (of which the Copyright Office is a division). **Failure to make the deposit can result in fines and other penalties**, even though it does not affect copyright protection.

A single deposit will satisfy *both* the deposit requirements for the Library of Congress *and* the Copyright Office registration requirements *if* the required deposit copies or phonorecords accompany the original application for registration and filing fee.

When Does the Registration Become Effective?

Copyright registration is effective **as of the date the Copyright Office receives the application and all of the required elements in acceptable form**, regardless of how long it subsequently takes to process the application. It is advisable to send applications using "delivery confirmation" or by registered or certified mail with return receipt requested, since the Copyright Office does not send any formal acknowledgment that an application has been received. The Copyright Office will, however, send a letter or will telephone if further information is needed to complete their processing of the application. At the conclusion of their review process — which can, and usually does, take several months — the Copyright Office will send either a Certificate of Registration to indicate the work has been registered, or a letter explaining why registration has been refused.

Can Corrections Be Made After a Certificate of Registration Has Been Issued?

Information in a copyright registration can be corrected or amplified by filing a **Form CA** supplementary registration form. The information provided in such a supplementary registration augments ***but does not supersede*** information contained in the earlier registration. Note that a supplementary registration is ***not*** a substitute for an original registration, for a renewal registration, or for recording a transfer of ownership.

Original registration must be on the appropriate form for the type of registrable work being submitted — **PA**, **SR**, **TX**, or **VA**, *etc.*, — as discussed above. For works which are subject renewal, use **Form RE**, and for recordation of a change of ownership, use a **Document Cover Sheet**, with the applicable transfer instrument attached.

Online Copyright Registration

As of July 1, 2007, in conjunction with the release of new, revised copyright registration forms, the Copyright Office was scheduled to begin a trial program of online registration for a reduced fee of $35 per application. Unfortunately (if predictably) technical complications delayed the scheduled implementation of this program, while "beta testing" by selected registrants was being used to verify the system and eliminate problems. In theory, the appropriate copyright registration form can now be completed and filed online, the fee paid by credit card or through a deposit account, and the deposit of materials made either by uploading or by separate mailing. Current availability of the online registration system can only be determined by going to the official United States Copyright Office website (http://www.copyright.gov.)

For simple applications, online registration offers an ideal method for quickly completing the process, but — at least until all of the "glitches" have been isolated and dealt with — more complex or critical copyright registrations should probably be made through the traditional, mail-in process.

CHAPTER 5

MUSIC INDUSTRY ROLES AND RELATIONSHIPS

(AN OVERVIEW)

Originally, this was to have been the first chapter of this book, but it became obvious during the writing process that a rudimentary grasp of contract basics, copyright fundamentals, intellectual property concepts, and personality rights were all necessary as a foundation for the following discussions of the primary, secondary, and ancillary occupations, professions, and businesses which make up the music industry.

Primary roles belong to songwriters and performers — the essential creators of music. Secondary roles are those of the record companies, publishers, and distributors — those who are essential to converting music into a business. And finally, the ancillary roles facilitate the interface between music and the business of selling music to the public — those who record, polish, sweeten, package, present, and otherwise convert music into a saleable product — as well as those who market, promote and sell that product and those whose function is to maintain a smooth working relationship between the public, the artists, and the more pragmatic aspects of the industry. These ancillary roles include everyone else in or affiliated with the music business, from lawyers, agents and managers, to producers, arrangers, recording engineers, promoters, venue operators, graphic artists, printers, merchandisers, photographers and videographers. While not essential to music, *per se*, they have made themselves indispensable to the *business* of music. Together, these primary, secondary and ancillary roles comprise the entire scope of the industry, taking a song from its original creation through all of the steps likely to be involved in bringing it to a final commercial form as a source of direct and indirect income, and with all of the various industry roles linked to each other, directly or indirectly, through a network of contractual relationships.

Independent Lyricists and Composers (Songwriters)

In popular music, songs are often created by a single individual who writes both the lyrics and the music. Just as often, however, the song may result from a collaborative effort of two or more individuals. The first contract to be considered in the music business is therefore a **co-authorship agreement** between collaborators, determining their respective rights in the final song or composition. This may be no more than a recital of their respective rights on the copyright registration form, but if they collaborate on a regular basis — particularly in the case of members of a performing group — then a more formal agreement between them is strongly recommended. Such contracts fall into two basic categories: co-authorship and separate works.

In co-authorship, the lyricist and composer share an indivisible interest to all rights in the entire work, unless they agree that the lyrics and the music are separate and distinct and copyright them separately. Sometimes a lyricist may send completed lyrics to a composer for the addition of music. Likewise a composer may send completed music to a lyricist for the addition of lyrics. Unless they have established a copyright to their own independent work before sending it on to a collaborator — or unless they have an express agreement between themselves severing their respective interests in the final work — that final work is one of co-authorship, with the rights to the lyrics and to the composition wholly integrated and not easily separated thereafter; the lyricist would own half the music rights, and the musical composer would own half the lyric rights. Determining who owns how much of which rights is a critical contractual issue for all songwriters. Also, in order to avoid having someone's casual participation turn into a claim of co-authorship, a **release** should be obtained from anyone who was in any way involved in the process but who is not intended to be a co-author.

Next, there are **publishing agreements**, in which the rights are assigned to a publisher in consideration of an advance against a percentage (usually 50%) of future royalties. There are also **co-publishing agreements**, in which only a portion of the rights are assigned to a publishing house which administers the copyright and collects the royalties and license fees on the songwriter's behalf, retaining a percentage of those royalties and fees for their services. Generally co-publishing agreements provide for little or no advance, but a larger future percentage of royalties.

Songwriters often form their own "publishing" companies, usually through registering the company name with a performing rights organization.[131] Songwriters who are affiliated with more than one performing rights organization will have a *different* publishing company name for each of them, and will have to determine which of their company names (and therefore which performing rights organization) will be attached to each new composition. Additionally, the Harry Fox Agency acts as a general licensing agent and clearinghouse for its affiliates, which include most music publishers in the United States. Artist-owned publishing companies are seldom actively involved in marketing the songs which they control, but instead enter into publishing, co-publishing, or administration agreements with commercial publishers for that purpose.

Next comes the means for turning all this creative work into money, which is done through issuance of **licenses** to perform or record the work, or through sale or license to a record label which may thereafter select an artist to record it. Songwriters and composers who do not intend to perform their own work (and who do not want to directly market their work themselves) may employ a manager, agent, or representative to shop their songs to an artist, group or label. Obtaining these services will require a **management contract**, **agency agreement**, or **shopping agreement** empowering someone else to negotiate on their behalf. If a lawyer is employed to shop the songwriter's work, then there is likely to be a conflict of

---

131 Performing rights organizations (*e.g.*, ASCAP, BMI, SESAC, *etc.*) are organizations which grant licenses and collect fees and royalties for public performance and broadcast use of their members' copyrighted works.

interest which may prevent that attorney from acting as legal counsel, as well. For legal services there should always be a separate, written **retainer agreement**, and no other type of agreement should exist between an attorney and client unless it has been reviewed and approved by another, independent attorney acting for the client.

A special *caveat* is appropriate here regarding **shopping agreements** and **demo deals**. There are a number of legitimate facilitators in the industry who, for a fee or percentage, will agree to seek placement of material for publication. Unfortunately, there are also a number of individuals who will offer to provide such facilitation on terms that are tantamount to an indenture or confiscation. Not surprisingly, the less scrupulous the facilitator, the less credibility he or she is likely to have in the industry, and the less able to obtain a favorable deal. Shopping agreements should therefore be approached cautiously, and should *always* be reviewed by an independent attorney before being signed.

If the songwriters are also the intended *performers* of the song, then licences are seldom formalized beforehand, although it is good practice to do so, particularly where not <u>all</u> of the performers participated in the songwriting process, or if they participated to differing degrees or at different times. If the copyright has not been previously established, minor adaptations and changes which regularly occur during rehearsal or recording may result in an unintended co-authorship, entitling casual contributors to an equal share of the publishing rights and royalties. This is especially true when the publishing rights have not been previously formalized, and there are no prior agreements or releases.

There are numerous types of licenses granted in respect to musical compositions, with the four most common being:

- A license to record a song or non-dramatic musical composition in a phonorecord, called a **mechanical license**;
- A license to publicly broadcast a recording of that song on the radio, called a **transcription license**;
- A license to use the song or composition as part of an audiovisual presentation, such as in a motion picture, a video, or in a TV commercial, known as a **synchronous** (or "**sync**" or "**synch**") **license**; and
- A license to publicly perform a nondramatic musical work, called a **performance license** or **small right**.[132]

The songwriter/publisher is entitled to receive fees and/or royalties for any use of a copyrighted work, in any medium, except under narrow legal exceptions previously discussed. The purpose of a license is to establish a contractual basis for the terms and conditions of that use, and the amounts and frequency of payments.

132 For a "*dramatic* musical work," such as an opera, ballet, or musical comedy, the performance license is referred to as a "grand right."

For the independent composer or lyricist, the contracts and related documents with which to be generally familiar are:

- **Co-authorship Agreements**
- **Publishing & Co-publishing Agreements**
- **Administration Agreements**
- **Single Song Agreements**
- **Releases**
- **Copyright Registration Forms**
- **Performing Rights Society Agreements**
- **Management Contracts**
- **Agency Agreements**
- **Shopping Agreements**
- **Retainer Agreements**
- **Mechanical Licenses**
- **Sync Licenses**

◆ ◆ ◆

Work-for-Hire Lyricists and Composers (Songwriters)

As discussed more fully in the chapters on Intellectual Property and on Copyright, the right to control when and how a song or composition is first used, and to be entitled to financial benefit from any use of that work, belongs to whoever created that work and first put it into tangible form, unless it is a "work made for hire," in which case it is the ***employer*** who is generally considered to be the "author" (creator) of the work for copyright purposes. It is astonishing how many famous popular composers have limited songwriting skills. Perhaps their actual contribution may be no more than a snatch of melody, a few lyrics, or a song title. What they do have is the reputation and financial ability to hire others to anonymously create the balance of the work.

Work for hire agreements take two basic forms. The first is an **employment agreement,** which need not necessarily be in writing. If the scope of an employee's job includes composition of music or lyrics, then it is the *employer* (rather than the employee-songwriter) who is the legal author and who owns and controls all copyrights in that work. This is true even when songwriting is only *incidental* to employment, such as when an advertising executive composes a jingle for a client's account. Unless there is a written employment agreement which provides otherwise, creative work which is done within the "normal and customary scope of employment" is the property of the employer. This is not true where creative work is outside such normal scope, however. If, for instance, it was the janitor at the advertising agency who composed the jingle for a client's product, it would not be a work made for hire since, presumably, the janitor's job description did not embrace artistic creativity.

Sometimes an employee will be asked to sign a **release** of their creative work. Such releases are often no more than a formality, but should be viewed with caution if there is doubt as to whether or not a creative contribution was, in fact, a work made for hire.

The second instance of works made for hire is where there is a specific, *written* **work-for-hire agreement** in which the songwriter agrees to provide creative work on specified terms, which may or may not include future royalty participation. It is the other party to the contract, however, who is the employer and who owns the copyright under such arrangement.

In work for hire situations, it is the copyright owner (employer) who will deal with the copyright registration, publishing, and licensing . The work-for-hire songwriter's contractual concerns will therefore generally be limited to:

- **Employment Agreements**
- **Work for Hire Agreements**
- **Releases**
- **Grants of Rights**
- **Reservation of Rights**

◆ ◆ ◆

Performers — Musicians & Vocalists

Music is a performing art, so instrumental and vocal performers are obviously (if sometimes lamentably) indispensable. Without them, there is no *music* — only words and notes on a page.

For most people, vocal performances are limited to singing in the shower, and musicianship never goes beyond tabletop-drumming and air-guitar. For aspiring and active professionals however, there is an intricate maze of contractual relationships. Performing artists frequently avoid considering or formalizing those relationships until they are compelled by circumstances to do so. Invariably, the terms of such "eleventh hour" agreements are less than ideal. It is far better practice to formalize these contractual relationships early, and not hastily.

Traditionally, performers often begin their careers in bands consisting of a few friends who get together and start playing, possibly trying to get gigs at parties, schools, or in small local venues. There are numerous legal issues which they should take into consideration from the outset, but of which they seldom become aware until a problem arises. **Inter-band agreements** should be formalized as early as possible in the relationship to reduce liability and to prevent (or at least minimize) friction and disputes later on. The initial agreement can be as simple as a one-or two-page, handwritten memo. It can always be expanded and modified later, with the original band members' mutual consent, but it's best to get the key points down on paper from the very beginning.

Some singers and musicians do not regularly perform as members of a particular group. In some instances, a performer is hired by others to provide a vocal or musical contribution for a performance, tour or recording under an **employment contract**. For live performances, such contracts are often oral, at-will employment agreements, but for recordings — or where the employee's name and likeness are used for advertising or promotion, a written agreement, with appropriate releases and conveyances, is essential. For union members — generally the American Federation of Television and Radio Artists (AFTRA) for vocalists, and the American Federation of Musicians (AFM) for instrumentalists — the minimum terms for such employment are governed by a **collective bargaining agreement**. For non-union performers, there is no standard agreement, but familiarity with union contracts and scales will provide reasonable guidelines for what to ask or look for in a contract.

Sometimes it is the solo performer who is a "star," hiring musicians and/or vocalists to provide back-up for his or her performance, tour, or recording under **employment contracts**. In those instances, the band members have only such rights and interests as their contracts provide, and they are generally employees-at-will who can be replaced at any time. It is not unusual for such "groups" to have one set of musicians in the recording studio, and a different set of musicians who tour, with only the star performer remaining the same.

Another situation in which artists are employed to perform are concept groups, such as so-called "boy bands" in which the band is created, owned and controlled by a non-performing, third-party entrepreneur who hires individual members to perform, and who may terminate or replace them at will. Performers may also be employed by a particular event, or by an orchestral organization, or by a venue, for terms ranging from a single performance to an open-ended career. Unless there is a contract which provides otherwise, an artist who is employed by another to perform is regarded as an **employee at will** whose employment may be terminated at any time, for any good reason, or for no reason at all. (But not for an *improper* or *unlawful* reason, such as discrimination or retaliation for privileged conduct.)

A *caveat* previously given for songwriters regarding **shopping agreements** and **demo deals** needs to be repeated here for performers There are individuals who may offer to seek a "record deal" for performers under an agreement that contains unconscionable terms which amount to co-ownership and control of the performers' entire future career and income. There are even a number of readily-available, preprinted form agreements which include such confiscatory terms, and which should be avoided. *However,* there actually are some qualified individuals in the industry who can and will provide such shopping and demo services on far more reasonable terms, and these latter, more scrupulous professionals are likely to have both the credibility and the industry contacts necessary to actually obtain a deal. Such agreements should therefore be approached with extreme caution. Investigate the credentials and reputation of anyone who proposes such an agreement and *always* have it reviewed by an independent attorney before signing.

Whether or not in a band, performers may at some point retain the services of a personal manager to guide their careers. Generally, the manager receives a percentage of the performers' revenues under the terms of a **management agreement**. Managers often include a **power of attorney** as part of their agreement, but these should be approached with caution since they permit the manager to sign contracts which are legally binding on the performers.

Agents[133] are not the same as managers. Agents are generally responsible for securing employment for performers. They are usually required to be licensed by the state in which they conduct business, and are subject to legal regulations. Agents' compensation is commonly a percentage of the performers' income, which may be limited to the specific bookings arranged by that agent, or which may include other income earned by the performer during the term of the **agency agreement**, and sometimes for an additional term thereafter, depending upon the language of the agreement. Licensing laws which govern talent agents frequently require that the form of contract being used be pre-approved by the governmental body charged with regulating such agencies.

In entering into various contracts, performers may also want to obtain the services of an attorney who can negotiate terms on their behalf and who can advise them on contractual and other legal matters. Generally, attorneys work for an hourly fee but, in some instances, may agree to accept a percentage of a performer's income as full or partial payment for legal services. The contract by which an attorney is employed is generally referred to as a **retainer agreement** or **legal services agreement**.

Performers' incomes are generally derived from four revenue sources:[134]

- performances,
- recordings,
- merchandising, and
- endorsements.

The arrangement for an artist or group to perform is referred to as a "booking." The terms of a **booking contract** or **tour agreement** can range from large cash advances and participation in ticket sales and concession revenues at one end of the spectrum, to **pay to play** agreements at the other. Bookings can involve a single performance, a particular tour, or an open-ended employment.

---

133 In broader legal context, an "agent" is anyone who acts for and with the authority (or apparent authority) of another person (called a "principal.") Here, we are speaking more narrowly about talent agents and booking agents.

134 Publishing income is not listed here because it derives from songwriting rather than performing. Where the performer is also the composer of the music performed, this additional source of royalty income can be substantial, but will also likely be subject to significant reduction through a "controlled compositions clause" in the artist's recording contract.

Recording income can range from session work through a multiple album **recording contract**, which provides for the label to pay royalties from both sales and from licensing of recordings made pursuant to that agreement. There are also supplemental sources of income from recording, such as reuse fees which are paid when a previously recorded work is utilized in another medium such as in a television broadcast or motion picture soundtrack. (If the performer retains an *ownership* interest in master recordings, there may also be additional income from various types of licensing.)

Merchandising income is obtained from the sale of items which relate to the performer or group, such as T-shirts, posters or other items bearing the performers' name, photograph, logo or other proprietary imprints. Unsigned performers also derive merchandising income from the sale of self-produced recordings.[135] For performers operating on a larger scale, the manufacture and distribution of such items will be the subject of a **merchandising contract**, where the performer will receive a fee and/or royalty based on the number of items manufactured or sold. The more successful the performer or group, the broader the range of merchandising available.

Performers may also receive compensation for endorsing others' products or services. Sometimes the compensation may be no more than free or discounted items of the endorsed merchandise (*e.g.*, musical instruments, electronic gear, clothing, *etc.*) or it may be payment of a cash fee or other form of consideration, which will be set forth in an **endorsement agreement**. Such agreements may also involve public appearances at various events. The availability and value of an endorsement deal will be based on the level of public recognition which the performer has achieved.

In preparing publicity, performers will generally have photographs taken of themselves. If such photographs are going to be used for commercial purposes — particularly for merchandise or on album covers or inserts, then it is essential to have a **photography contract** in which the photographer assigns all copyrights, or otherwise licenses commercial use of the photographs. In addition to the copyright, it is also necessary to obtain a **release** from anyone whose image appears in the photos, since likenesses are protected personal property which cannot be commercially exploited without permission.

The same concerns arise in respect to videos as well as photographs. The **video contract** should specify the copyright ownership of the final video, and each person appearing in the video must sign a **release**, which may be a separate document or a provision within a more comprehensive agreement.

As a performer's income becomes more substantial, it may be advisable to hire a business manager to oversee finances and accounting matters. Unlike personal managers, business managers are generally paid a monthly or quarterly fee, although they may also receive an additional sum based on a percentage of the money which they handle for their client.

---

135 Generally, CDs and other media which embody the recorded music are referred to as ***product***, while posters, T-shirts, and other ancillary items are ***merchandise***.

Business managers are generally employed under a **retainer agreement** or **business management contract**.

The contracts and related documents with which performers should be generally familiar are:

- **Band Agreement**
- **Co-authorship Agreement**
- **Employment Contract**
- **Work for Hire Agreement**
- **Shopping Agreements / Demo Deals**
- **Management Contract**
- **Power of Attorney**
- **Agency Agreement**
- **Booking Contract**
- **Pay to Play Agreement**
- **Releases**
- **Recording Contract**
- **Retainer Agreement**
- **AFM Master Agreement**
- **AFTRA Recording Code**
- **Merchandise Contract**
- **Endorsement Agreement**
- **Video Contract**
- **Photography Contract**
- **Tour Agreement**
- **Liability Insurance**

◆ ◆ ◆

Publishers, Co-Publishers & Publishers' Agents

Although little considered outside the music industry, publishing is the holy grail of the music business. Publishing rights and the royalties they provide continue to generate income long after the original recordings and recording artists have been forgotten.

In the simplest terms, publishers are in the business of acquiring rights to songs and musical compositions, which they then license others to perform or record, for which they collect fees and royalties. Sometimes the publisher acquires these rights through purchase from the songwriter through a **single song agreement** or a **publishing agreement**, or the publisher may be partnered with the songwriter (or other copyright owner) under a a **co-publishing**

agreement, or may simply act as the copyright owner's agent through an **administration agreement**.

The agreement between the publisher and original copyright owner of the work may limit the rights which the publisher is permitted to license, or it may impose other restrictions. Essentially, the publisher negotiates and grants licenses, collects money from those licenses, maintains the bookkeeping records and periodically provides an accounting and payment to the author or other copyright owner in accordance with their contract terms. The amount of effort which the publisher expends will generally be proportionate to the type of agreement utilized and the resulting percentage of licensing income to which the publisher is entitled under that agreement.

The **Harry Fox Agency** acts as a clearinghouse for publishers, issuing **mechanical licenses** and **performance licenses** on their behalf. Similarly, performing rights organizations such as ASCAP, BMI, and SESAC issue **transcription licenses** and **performance licenses** on behalf of their respective members.

Another particularly lucrative source of publishing income is **synchronization licenses** — more often referred to as **sync** (or **synch**, and pronounced "sink") licenses — which authorize use of a composition (but not any particular *recording* of that composition) in an audiovisual medium such as motion pictures, video and television.

An additional, rapidly-developing source of publishing revenue is licensing **ringtones** for use in cellular phones, PDA's, and similar electronic devices. Essentially, any recognizable use of any portion of a copyrighted composition is a source of publishing income, either through compulsory or negotiated licensing, or through imposition of statutory penalties for infringement.

The songs and compositions owned or controlled by a publisher are referred to as that publisher's catalogue. Agencies, on the other hand, do not own catalogues, but rather act as central clearinghouses and middlemen between publishers and potential licensees, for a fee.

In operating a music publishing business or agency, the contracts and documents with which to be generally familiar will include:

- **Songwriter Agreement**
- **Grant of Rights**
- **Foreign Publishing Agreement**
- **Publishing Agreement**
- **Co-Publishing Agreement**
- **Administration Agreement**
- **Single Song Agreement**
- **Mechanical License**
- **Sync License**
- **Festival License**
- **Master Use License**

- **Transcription License**
- **Clearances**
- **Copyright registration forms**
- **Assignments**

◆ ◆ ◆

Performing Rights Organizations (PRO's)

Almost everyone is familiar with the acronyms ASCAP and BMI, but those outside the entertainment industry would be hard-pressed to recall why, or what words they abbreviate. Where they've seen them, of course, is on album covers and in the music credits for films and television shows, usually in parentheses following the name of the publisher of a particular composition. Another acronym, SESAC, is less widely known, but is perhaps the most prestigious of the three U.S.[136] performing rights organizations, which are collectively referred to by yet another acronym; PRO's.

Each musical composition carries with it a distinct "bundle of rights" which allow copyright holders to receive licensing fees and royalties for various uses of that composition. Among those rights are the so-called "performance" rights, which entitle the copyright owner to royalties whenever the composition is publicly performed, whether by live or recorded performance. The PRO's are principally involved in collecting such performance royalties for radio and television broadcasts, webcasts, jukeboxes, karaoke, and other performance of copyrighted compositions in clubs, theaters, and other venues. Although all performing rights organizations provide essentially identical services, they each operate somewhat differently.

ASCAP ("American Society of Composers, Authors, and Publishers") was the first Performing Rights Organization, formed in 1914. Any songwriter can become an ASCAP member, but publishers must either be actively engaged in exploitation of published works, or hold publishing rights to works which are regularly performed. ASCAP tracks performances of songs by surveying AM, FM, public, and college radio; local, network, cable, and public television; airlines; Muzak™ and similar background music services; licensed web sites; live performances in symphony and concert halls, colleges and universities; and a wide range of other venues. In some areas they conduct a census survey, while in others they use statistical analysis based on a sample survey.

SESAC ("Society of European Stage Authors and Composers") is a privately-owned company originally established in 1930 to serve European artists who were not adequately represented in the United States. SESAC is the smallest of the three PRO's but, unlike its two

136 SOCAN ("Society of Composers, Authors and Music Publishers of Canada") is yet another American performing rights organization, headquartered in Toronto, and with offices throughout Canada.

larger counterparts, not every songwriter is invited to join; SESAC carefully selects songwriters and publishers with which it wishes to be affiliated. There is no cost for songwriters to join SESAC, but publishers must pay a fee for affiliation. SESAC utilizes high-tech BDS and MusiCode systems to track radio and TV performances. BDS maintains a digitally encoded database of titles, using electronic listening devices to monitor virtually all radio and TV broadcast frequencies, matching what it hears with the digital "fingerprints" of songs in its database. MusiCode utilizes digital audio watermarking to track songs on radio, TV, and the Internet.

BMI (Broadcast Music, Inc.) is a non-profit corporation formed in 1940. There is no cost to songwriters for affiliation with BMI, and any songwriter may join. BMI's survey procedure consists of tracking radio and TV performances by monitoring "a scientifically chosen representative cross-section of stations each quarter. The stations being monitored supply BMI with complete information as to all music performed." BMI also tracks some live music, background music services, and music performed on licensed websites.

One of the five enumerated rights under the Copyright Act is the "performing right," which entitles the owners of musical compositions to license those works for public performance. Businesses which typically license music include broadcast radio and TV stations, cable radio and TV stations, enterprises such as nightclubs, bars, hotels, and other establishments which feature live or recorded music (including Karaoke), as well as those which merely provide background music in an effort to enhance their business.[137]

There are countless establishments throughout the United States where music is publicly performed. It would be impossible for individual copyright owners to monitor all of these establishments personally, let alone determine the extent to which each establishment might owe them royalties or attempt to collect such royalties from each of them. Instead, each of the PRO's acquires rights from writers and publishers and, in turn, grants to commercial users of music various types of licenses to use the entire repertoire of that PRO. Most commercial licensees, such as broadcasters and performance venues, are required to periodically file "cue sheets," reporting which compositions have been performed, how frequently, and the dates and times for each composition. The PROs do not entirely rely on the accuracy of these cue sheets, however, and each has different methods for "spot checking" the accuracy of their licensees' reports.

Each of the three organizations has its own royalty payment formula for determining the monetary royalty value of each performance and, after collecting the calculated fees from its licensees, and deducting its own administration fee, each PRO sends periodic payments to

---

137 Except for small businesses and other entities entitled to limited exemptions under 17 USC §§ 110, *et seq.*, it is unlawful for any business to play music within its facility without a performance license. **This includes radio broadcasts, MP3s, and CDs.** Violation can be punishable by up to five years in prison and $250,000 in fines, or more. Offenders can also be held civilly liable for actual damages, lost profits, or statutory damages of up to $150,000 per composition. This is why business facilities which provide "background" music do so through a music service which is licensed by, and pays royalties to, the various PROs.

members entitled to performance royalties, based on reported and tracked performances of the member's compositions. Although each PRO has a different delay period from performance to actual royalty payment, each pays their affiliated writers and publishers on a quarterly basis.

PRO's only license non-dramatic performing rights, referred to as the "small right." A license to stage and perform an entire musical show (*e.g.*, "Cabaret," or "Phantom of the Opera") — known as the "grand right" - must be obtained directly from the publishers or other copyright owner, or their agents.

The various types of licenses issued by each of the PRO's may have different names, and modified licenses may be available for non-profit users, but the basic agreements and licenses utilized by the PRO's are essentially the following:

- **Songwriter Affiliation Agreement**
- **Publisher Affiliation Agreement**
- **Live Performance Licenses (Non-Dramatic Musical Works)**
- **Recorded Performance Licenses**
- **Electrical Transcription Licenses**
- **Website Licenses (Streaming)**

◆ ◆ ◆

Record Companies (Major, Distributed & Independent Labels)

Record companies — or Labels, as they are known in the industry — are divided into categories based on the distribution channels through which their products reach the public.

- **Majors** — or **major labels** — are those which maintain their own distribution system, selling directly to retail outlets. Currently, the majors — sometimes called the "Big Four" are EMI-Capitol, Sony-BMG, Universal, and Warner Music. Mergers and acquisitions, as well as market forces, have changed the identities of the major labels over the years, and are likely to continue to do so in the future.
- **Distributed labels** are those which have an ongoing contractual relationship with a major label or distributor, so that all of the distributed label's releases reach retail outlets through regularly established distribution channels. Many of the larger distributed labels are actually subsidiaries of major labels.
- **Independent labels** — or **indies** — arrange for distribution through another label or through an independent distributor on an *ad hoc*, case-by-case basis, which may be for a single release or for a limited number of releases. Recent industry data indicate that independent labels account for 80% of new releases in major

markets, but receive only 30% of the revenues generated in those same markets. This disparity results from the major labels' ability to largely control many distribution channels, and to support costly marketing, promotion, and advertising efforts. The upsurge in online music sales has been a boon to indies, since it places them on almost-equal footing with larger labels in this newly developing market.

Contractual arrangements between a major label or distributor, and a distributed or independent label can take several forms: *(a)* **pressing and distribution contracts** (P&D deals) ; *(b)* **distribution only contracts**; *(c)* **fulfillment contracts**; *(d)* **production agreements**; *(e)* **joint venture agreements**; *(f)* **participation agreements** (equity deals); *(g)* **licensing agreements**; or *(h)* **buyouts**. There are a number of factors which will influence the type of contract utilized, and its specific terms. In particular, the financial strength and sales record of the smaller label, the marketability of its artists, and the degree to which it (and its personnel) are qualified and available to actively participate in the promotion, marketing and distribution of the product, will influence the nature and terms of distribution arrangements.

Whether major, distributed, or independent, each label is usually organized and operated as a separate company, even though it may be a subsidiary of another label, or owned by a diversified corporation or conglomerate.

The organizational structure of each label may vary, but it will generally be divided into departments which include:

- **A&R (Artists & Repertoire)** is responsible for locating new talent for the label and for acting as the ongoing liaison between the label and its signed talent. "Talent" may include both recording artists and songwriters, and an A&R representative will often be instrumental in the selection of material to be recorded. The A&R representative is also likely to be involved in the selection of a producer, arranger, recording studio and all other elements necessary to completion of an album.

- **Business Affairs** is generally staffed by lawyers and accountants, and (if there is no separate **Legal Affairs** department) its attorneys are responsible for negotiating and preparing the label's various contracts, and particularly its recording and songwriting contracts with artists, as well as acting for the label in various legal and transactional matters. Preparation of copyright applications, licenses for sound recordings, negotiation for first use or other mechanical licenses, clearances of all necessary rights, and most other business negotiations for the label will fall within Business Affairs' purview, although larger labels will have separate departments for **Royalty Accounting** and for **Licensing**. Accountants in Business Affairs oversee the label's bookkeeping, payroll, general finances, royalty reporting, and prepare projections and forecasts to help guide in the label's decision-making processes.

  At larger labels, Business Affairs and Legal Affairs may be completely separate departments, but they will generally work closely with each other, since disputes and litigation are often the best means for identifying new issues to be considered in determining trends and preparing new contracts and licenses.

- **Publicity & Promotion** are often a single department in smaller labels, but separated in larger organizations. Publicity deals with spreading the word about a label's artists, arranging for media coverage, on-air interviews, and for articles in print media.

  While Publicity focuses on the *artist*, Promotion's function is to get airplay for the artist's *music* — since that's what the label is in the business of selling. This not only involves radio airplay, but may also include on-air performances for television programs, music videos, and tour support. It usually falls to Promotion to coordinate the efforts of all other departments, to assure that their respective activities are not counterproductive and that the artist and music are receiving maximum exposure.

- **Artist Development** usually doesn't rate a separate department at smaller labels, where its functions are split between A&R and Publicity, and larger labels have also largely dispensed with this department in recent years, or have renamed it "Product Development." Artist Development is (was) involved with grooming the label's artists to deal with the public and media, and in planning artists' long term careers, working closely with each artist's own management team as well as with the label's Publicity and Promotion departments. The extent to which a label supports development of long-term careers may be a reasonable gauge of its level of commitment to its artists.

- **Marketing** develops overall, unified plans for how each album will be presented to the public, coordinating the advertising campaign and the efforts of the promotion, publicity and sales departments to determine the best release date, as well as pre-release buildup publicity and post-release promotion, advertising, and sales efforts.

- **Liaison** refers to coordination between the label and the distributor, particularly in regard to timing of a release and a determination of quantities to be manufactured and shipped to the distributor, and coordinating advertising and promotional efforts. For majors, where distribution is an in-house, function, this department may be minimized or eliminated. At small labels, liaison functions may divided among Business Affairs, Marketing, Promotion, and Sales.

- **Sales** works with retail outlets (*e.g.*, record stores) to get the label's products (albums) onto retailers' shelves and into other retail outlets, generally coordinating with Promotion and Publicity departments to seek prominent placement and retailers' support for the label's products.

- **New Media** deals with new and developing technologies. This may include coordination of video productions, internet sites, and other potential methods for promoting or marketing the label's artists and products. As new technologies become more commonplace and established, they will generally be shifted away from this department. For example, online music stores now generally fall within the purview of the Sales Department, and music videos are often handled by Promotion or by a specialized department.

- **Art** prepares visual elements for a label's albums, promotional materials, publicity, marketing and advertising. These may include graphic art, photography, and the entire gamut of visual arts. For smaller labels, much (if not all) of an Art Department's functions are outsourced to independent contractors on a work for hire basis.

Regardless of the organization or size of a particular label, the primary function of any label is to convert music into saleable product, and hence into money. To accomplish this they enter into contracts with performing artists, advancing funds which are recoupable from revenues generated by sales of the artists' albums. Through recoupment, the artist ultimately pays for almost everything, assuming that the album's sales and licensing revenues are sufficient to offset the label's total expenditures. This break-even point — referred to as reaching recoupment — is the first major hurdle for any release, and *most releases never achieve it!* The most recent studies indicate than only one released album in twenty reaches recoupment. For most artists then, whatever portion of the advance they actually receive is likely to represent their entire income from the album.

When you consider that not every "signed" artist's or group's album gets released — in which case there are no revenues to offset the label's advance — the ratio between advances and recouped albums is even worse. These unfavorable odds are the primary justification behind many of the apparently-skewed terms which appear in recording contracts. The revenues from one successful album out of each twenty-plus advances, must ultimately offset all of the label's unrecouped advances and expenditures for all of those albums, as well as providing the profits required to keep the label (and the industry) alive and flourishing.

Most recording contracts are "all inclusive" — usually referred to as "all in"— contracts. This means that the artist's advance includes the entire recording budget for the album, including all advances and fees for the producer, arranger, session musicians and others who will contribute to recording the album. In addition to these withheld sums, it may also be a "split advance" with only a portion payable immediately, and with the remainder disbursed to cover the recording budget. One or more subsequent "advance" payments may actually go to the artist — usually triggered by completion of certain phases of the recording process, or by release of the album — *if* there is any money left over after payment of all of the recording costs and related expenses.

In addition to split advances, recording companies also hedge their bets by a number of other contract provisions which reduce their risk, including such devices as container fees, free goods, return allowances, discount sales and cutout provisions, and controlled composition clauses. These and other details of recording contracts are discussed in the chapter devoted to them, but the point here is that record companies operate as do venture capitalists — high-risk investment in expectation that a few of those investments will generate profits sufficient to offset less successful endeavors.

The contracts and documents with which record companies will be readily familiar include:

- **Recording Agreements**
- **Songwriter Agreements**
- **Producer Agreements**
- **Distribution Agreements**
- **Mechanical Licenses**
- **Master Use Licenses**
- **Work for Hire Agreements**
- **Employment Agreements**
- **Copyright Registrations**
- **Waivers and Releases**
- **Universal Product Code (UPC) Applications**
- **Pressing Agreements**
- **One Sheets**

◆ ◆ ◆

Distributors

The primary job of a Distributor is to get record companies' products (albums) into retail outlets. Distributors are the initial wholesale purchasers of quantities of albums from various labels, under **distribution agreements** which afford the distributor a variety of special terms and conditions. Generally those terms will include delayed payment for product received (anywhere from two to four months, or more, after invoice), a supply of **free goods** to be used as sales incentives for retailers, and additional **promotional copies** for complementary use to support sales efforts and for distribution to the media.[138] There is also likely to be a provision for cooperative ("co-op") advertising, with the distributor charging back to the label a portion of the distributor's media advertising expense. The extent of these and other concessions are usually negotiable as between the record label and distributor. Even when the label and the distributor are commonly-owned and are, in effect, one and the same company, there will be distribution contracts spelling out the terms and conditions of the "distribution deal" between them. This not only helps preserve the appearance of an arm's-length relationship but (as will be discussed later) certain terms of the distribution contract have a direct effect on the label's recording contracts, and on Artist's royalties under those contracts.

Most distributors publish a catalogue which lists the record labels for which they distribute, and the specific titles available through them. Distributors also work closely with a record

---

138 Free goods and promotional copies, and their impact on royalties, are discussed in the chapters on Recording Contracts and Songwriter Agreements.

label's liaison, and with its promotion and marketing departments, to develop co-op advertisements and promotional campaigns for the label's products.

There are several different kinds of distributors, ranging from major distributors with worldwide operations (and most of which are themselves major record companies, or are owned by or affiliated with a major record company),[139] to small independents covering only a limited geographic area or specializing in one genre of music. With the advent of the internet, many record companies have bypassed traditional distributors and have begun to deal directly with online retailers such as Napster and Apple Computer's iTunes. The ultimate role of distributors in the electronic download market therefore remains undetermined.

In general, distributors require that the record companies that they deal with have a proven track record of operation and successful releases. As a general rule, most distributors are reluctant to deal with a record company that has been in business for fewer than three years, at a minimum. This was often an insuperable obstacle for small, start-up labels in the past, but the ability to distribute via the internet has altered that situation, allowing new labels to start generating revenue and reputation in advance of securing more traditional distribution. Conversely, the growth of the internet as a competing retail outlet for record sales has had a direct effect on traditional distributors, as their regular customer base of record stores and retail outlets has dwindled due to internet competition. Some distributors have responded to the changing marked by an increased willingness to enter into so-called **pressing and distribution agreements** ("P&D deals") under which the distributor undertakes the manufacturing costs for an album, paying a negotiated fee to the record company for each copy sold.

While there is no hard-and-fast rule, the terms of any distribution agreement will reflect the label's operational history and financial condition. The more established and successful the record company, the more favorable will be the rates and terms of their distribution agreement.

The documents and agreements with which distributors will be most familiar will be:

- **Distribution Agreements**
- **Pressing and Distribution (P&D) Agreements**
- **Purchase Orders**
- **One Sheets**
- **Catalogues**

◆ ◆ ◆

139 The list changes from time to time, but at present the "major distributors" are Sony Music Entertainment / Bertelsmann Music Group (SONY/BMG), EMI Music Distribution (EMI/Capitol), Warner-Elektra-Atlantic Corporation (WEA), and Universal Music Group (UMG), each of which owns or controls multiple subsidary distributors.

Music Producers

Selecting a producer is often the single choice which most influences the final appearance, sound, and overall tone of an album. In a very real sense, a producer is the principal "author" of a sound recording, except for the fact that the producer is almost-invariably subject to contract provisions which transfer that authorship interest to a record company.

Record producers — or music producers, as they are often called — have broad responsibilities in the creative process. They not only control the recording sessions, guiding the musicians in much the same way a conductor guides an orchestra — while concurrently supervising the recording engineer (or engineering the session themselves) — but they also participate in the selection of material to be recorded, the studio in which it will be recorded, and oversee the mixing and mastering of the album after the recording phase has been concluded. This may even involve going back into the studio to add additional tracks, with or without the original performers. It is the producer who determines when a recording is completed, and who must sometimes convince performers that the recording (or their part of it) *is* completed. An ability to work and communicate with performers, and to have them accept the producer's dictates, is one of the most vital skills in music production.

In the industry's early days of monaural recording, the producer and recording engineer were often one and the same, and were generally employees of a record company which maintained its own, in-house recording facilities. With the development of new technologies and independent recording studios, producers were elevated to a new and more influential role in the industry.

Independent producers now frequently select and arrange songs — sometimes writing or collaborating on the material — oversee recording sessions, occasionally engineer those sessions, and direct the mixing and mastering sessions as well, adding additional elements and tracks as necessary to fulfill the producer's intention of how the final recording should sound.

Sometimes this is done "on spec," with the producer owning the resulting sound recordings, which may then be licensed to a record company for manufacture and distribution. In other instances, the producer works under a contract, either with the artist or the label, or both. Typically, a producer retained on such a contractual basis receives an advance against a royalty ranging from 2% to 5% of the suggested retail price ("SRLP") of the album. High profile producers may also receive a "bonus" or fee for their services, in addition to royalties.

Many producers have created pseudonymous "groups" composed of session musicians under employment-at-will contracts. While the "boy bands" of the 1980's and 1990's are the most familiar example of such endeavors, the practice has existed continuously since the industry's earliest days. The Markettes (1950's-1960's), the Monkees (1960's-1970's) and the notorious Milli Vanilli debacle (1988-1990) are each examples of such producer-created groups. (Although the Monkees performers successfully divorced themselves from their TV-producer creators and struck out on their own with moderate success.) Some producers have effectively become recording artists in their own right, utilizing new computer and sampling technology to assemble compositions without involving individual performers at all. Conversely, a number of successful recording artists have developed adjunct careers for themselves as producers of other performers' recordings.

Because of their influential role in the selection of material, control of recorded performance, and determination of the final form in which a recording is presented to the public, producers can strongly affect and set trends in popular music and in performers' careers.

The contracts with which producers will be most readily familiar include:

- 𝄞 **Producer Agreements**
- 𝄞 **Employment Agreements**
- 𝄞 **Work for Hire Agreements**
- 𝄞 **Recording Contracts**
- 𝄞 **Songwriter Agreements**
- 𝄞 **Copyright Registrations**
- 𝄞 **Recording Services Agreements**
- 𝄞 **Releases**

◆ ◆ ◆

Transcribers & Arrangers

Surprisingly few of today's popular musicians and songwriters can read or write standard musical notation. Transcription is the process of creating such notation for a piece of music, transferring musical sounds into a printed form. Those who perform this process are known as transcribers, and while many trained transcribers continue to practice this basic aspect of their craft, computer software now exists which can convert source material, such as a MIDI file, into musical notation quickly and accurately.

Transcription has also come to include arranging a composition originally intended for one instrument or group of instruments so that it may be performed on other instruments or vocally.[140] Such minimal arrangements rely on the phenomenon that any particular note can sound both the same and yet entirely different when performed on different instruments, since it remains identical in pitch, while altered in timbre. Many popular compositions include transcriptions of classical music phrases rendered almost unrecognizable through changes in instrumentation and tempo. Computer programs are less successful at this aspect of transcription, since it involves artistic choices and creative musical arrangement.

---

140 Transcriptions of orchestral and other works for piano or keyboard are known as "reductions," with dozens of separate instrumental parts reduced to what one (or sometimes two) performers can manage to play.

Arrangement refers to either rewriting a piece of existing music through addition of newly-written material, or to expanding a lead sheet or compositional concept into a performable work. Arrangers often add parts for orchestral or band instruments involving new material, thereby making significant changes to the original composition. Sometimes this process even occurs after an initial performance has been recorded, since modern recording techniques allow for the introduction of new material onto additional tracks.

As a general rule, arrangement refers to the addition of new musical material or elements, and merely altering existing material is transcription. Notwithstanding their indubitably-creative contributions to the final work, arrangers are not co-authors of that final work, since those contributions occur after the work was first "fixed" by others for copyright and royalty purposes.

Transcribers and arrangers should be familiar with:

- **Work for Hire Agreements**
- **Releases & Assignments of Right**
- **Employment Agreements**

◆ ◆ ◆

Recording Technology, Studios, & Engineers

In 1877, Thomas Edison recited "Mary had a little lamb…" into an oversized horn with an attached, diaphragm-mounted needle which mechanically scratched an analogue of his voice's vibrations onto a rotating, wax-covered cylinder. Edison thought he was creating a dictation machine for business use,[141] and could little have realized that he was also laying the foundation for today's multi-billion-dollar recording industry.

By 1900, Edison's cylinders had begun to give way to the now more familiar flat, circular disks, originally made of hard rubber and later of a composite material called shellac.[142] The era of these primitive, monaural, direct acoustic recordings lasted for nearly forty years — quite a feat by today's standards of rapid technological change.[143]

---

141 Edison's invention was successful for that purpose, as well. Although cylinders were soon replaced by celluloid (and later plastic) belts, Edison's original technology remained virtually unchanged for a century in products such as Dictaphone™.

142 Vinyl was introduced by RCA Victor in the 1930's but was not immediately successful for a variety of reasons, not least of which was the Great Depression (1929-1939), since vinyl recordings required purchase of a new turntable capable of a slower, 33⅓-rpm playing speed.

143 Mention should be made of the separate and contemporaneous invention of the player piano, which was at least as commercially successful as the acoustic recordings of that era. Piano rolls have been in constant production since the 1880's, although MIDI technology has largely taken over the field of preserving performance data. Even today, piano rolls (and their MIDI successors) continue to generate publishing and artist *(continued)*

During those four decades of acoustic recordings, studios were simply soundproof rooms which only minimized *outside* noise. Master recordings were made on the spot, by a direct-to-disc cutting process, with performers gathered around a large funnel-shaped horn connected directly or electrically to a cutting lathe.[144]

By the late 1920's, technological innovations such as the microphone, amplifier, potentiometer, mixing board, and speakers had brought an end to mechanical recordings, and new studios were designed to accommodate both emerging technology and the genres of music being commercially recorded. Early studios were principally intended for live recording of symphonic works, so they tended to be large spaces with an acoustically "live" ambience. In fact, many of these early studios were converted churches, since their original designs had been intended to create both open space and superb acoustics. Microphones and groups of performers were strategically located on the studio floor in an effort to best capture the tonal and harmonic qualities of a live performance in a monaural recording. Engineers who worked in these studios developed complex effects based on the unique acoustic properties of their studios.

The singular characteristics of each major studio lent an identifiable acoustic character to the recordings made there. Also, since most of those studios were owned and controlled by major record labels — which had their own research and development departments — each studio often had one-of-a-kind equipment and control consoles with which only the label's in-house engineers were familiar.

As tastes in popular music changed, so did recording techniques and the design of recording studios. Anechoic — or acoustically "dead" — studios became preferred for smaller groups, with performers isolated from each other, monitoring themselves and their accompaniment through headsets. Also, the development of multi-track recording had made it possible to record instruments and singers separately, on different tracks and often at entirely different times.

Even the most anechoic of studios have unique sonic qualities however, best known to the engineers who regularly record in them. Recording artists also have their own preferences, and many have been known to refuse to record except in a particular studio. Smaller, independent studios, often owned by skilled engineers who built their own boards and equipment, developed techniques and technologies which they jealously guarded as trade secrets of that studio. Many now-common devices such as equalizers and compressors were first developed in this manner.[145]

---

royalties. In a very real sense, piano rolls were the first digital recordings.

144 The nature of this process, cutting a continuous groove into a metal surface which could be used as a mechanical master mold for pressing records, led to the term "mechanical license," denoting permission given by a composer or publisher which allowed the creation of such mechanical copy of a composition.

145 Because they are frequently at the cutting edge of new technologies in the industry, many key patents have been developed by recording studios and engineers, who are consequently likely to be somewhat familiar with that aspect of intellectual property protections.

Multi-track recording also brought a new level of creative participation to the engineer and music producer. A "finished" recording could be re-mixed and sweetened; new arrangements could be introduced, vocal and instrumental tracks could be added, subtracted, or replaced; tonal qualities, pitch and timbre could be altered, and the entire effect of the recording could be changed dramatically or subtly under the hands of a skilled engineer. Only after the engineer had completed such post-recording work would the multi-track recording be converted to a master recording for delivery to the label.

Before the introduction of electronic digital recording, twenty-four track analogue machines were the industry standard, and a number of such 24-track machines could be slaved together to provide more tracks as needed, limited only by the number of potentiometers ("pots") on the engineer's console. In digital recording, however, the number of tracks is only limited by the capacity of the mixing board or computer interface, and even that limitation can be avoided by blending completed tracks into one or two tracks, thereby freeing up console channels for new material. Unlike analogue recordings, digital data does not degrade with each generation, so engineers are able to make unlimited successive copies with no loss of fidelity.

These factors, and other developments in electronics, and advances in computer and digital recording technologies particularly, brought a radical change to the industry. The compactness of such devices, and their relatively modest expense and ease of operation, allowed quality recordings to be made in almost any location, often by the musicians themselves. Suddenly, *everyone* was an "engineer," and small "project studios" began to appear in garages, basements, and similar locations throughout the country. While most of the recordings made in these small studios might initially have been intended only as demonstration recordings ("demos"), many became self-released albums sold directly by the musicians at venues, by mail, or through small, independent distributors, and (more recently) over the internet.

Although digital systems now predominate commercial recording methods, some studios and artists still prefer to record in analogue, believing that digital recordings sound "harsh" in comparison. (Digital recording takes thousands of tiny samples of a sound wave each second,[146] whereas analogue captures the entire, continuous sound wave.) Since this is an issue of artistry rather than science, there can be no resolution to the debate. It is worth noting, however, that regardless of the in-studio recording method, current manufacturing technology requires that a master recording be delivered in digital format to allow for production of CDs.[147]

The creative contribution of a skilled recording engineer to the final product should not be underestimated, and goes far beyond merely controlling the recording process. Placement of microphones and baffles, location of the performers in the studio, selection of particular microphones, instruments and equipment, and even the introduction of resonant or sound-

---

146 1,411,200 bits per second at a 44.1 kHz sample rate with a 16-bit word size.

147 CD manufacture generally requires a pre-mastered recording on 3/4" broadcast-quality tape cassette (Sony U-matic™ PCM-1630), commonly referred to as a "1630."

dampening physical objects onto the studio floor, or suspended above it, can all make a distinct change to the recorded sounds. The engineer's participation during the actual recording process, and later in the editing, sweetening and mixing process, are often a key factor in the ultimate sound of the finished recording. Thus a recording engineer might reasonably be considered to be a co-creator of recorded sounds for copyright purposes[148] but — since recording studios and engineers are generally retained under agreements containing waivers, releases and assignments of rights, and usually work-for-hire provisions, as well[149] — they do not usually receive royalties from their creative contributions, although their names are often included in an album's credits.[150]

The contracts and documents with which recording studios and engineers will be most familiar include:

- **Recording Services Agreements**
- **Releases**
- **Work for Hire Agreements**
- **Employment Agreements**
- **Equipment Rental Agreements**
- **Equipment Leases**
- **Patent Applications**

◆ ◆ ◆

Personal Managers & Agents

Although grouped together for this discussion, there are fundamental legal and pragmatic distinctions between a personal manager and an agent.

Personal managers are precisely that — they guide and manage the career choices of an artist, and are often empowered to enter into binding contracts on behalf of the artist under a **power of attorney**. Their services are provided on the basis of a **management contract** between themselves and the artist, specifying their responsibilities and the manner and extent of their compensation, which will usually include (but not necessarily be limited to) a percentage of anywhere from 10% to 25% of the artist's income. Because most states regulate

---

148 As we've mentioned before — and will reiterate many times throughout this book — sound recordings are subject to their own distinct copyright, completely separate and apart from the copyright in a *composition* embodied in such recordings.

149 As noted earlier, sound recordings are excluded from the list of works which may be "works made for hire," but work-for-hire language is nonetheless included in most sound recording contracts.

150 This is not merely a courtesy, but usually a contractual obligation insisted upon by the recording studio. (Although if an individual engineer's name is to be added to the credits, a separate release should be obtained, in addition to the contract with his or her employer.)

and license booking agencies, managers are generally precluded from providing booking services directly, and their contracts may be invalidated — in whole or in part — when they provide such services in violation of a state's licensing requirements.[151]

An agent's role is generally limited to seeking and obtaining employment and other income sources for an artist. The principal distinction between agents and managers is that agents are generally required to be licensed, with specific laws governing and regulating their services, the manner in which they perform those services, and the maximum compensation which they may receive for those services. Most states require that an agent's *pro forma* agreement with represented artists be pre-approved by whatever governmental body regulates talent agencies within that state.

Also, governmental regulation of agents also frequently provides for an exclusive method of dispute resolution, usually through a semi-formal proceeding before an administrative law tribunal within the relevant government agency. Contract disputes between artists and managers, on the other hand, are more likely to result in protracted and expensive litigation, unless they contain provisions for alternative dispute resolution such as a binding arbitration clause. More than one successful artist has spent a significant part of his or her career (and income) in courtroom battles with a former manager, years after terminating their working relationship.

As a practical matter, it is often difficult for an aspiring new artist to obtain the services of a well-established professional agent, while managers are generally more accessible. Caution should be exercised however, since many "managers" lack the industry experience and qualifications which are necessary to effectively furthering an artist's career. If "artist management" is a sideline rather than the full time career of a prospective manager, artists would be well advised to verify the manager's references, background and qualifications before entering into a contractual arrangement.

Another category of agents consists of so-called "middle agents." These agencies work with venues, talent buyers, and promoters, usually on a "package" basis, and obtain artists' services from the artists' primary agent or manager, usually at a significant discount by guarantying a minimum number of appearances over a set period of time. In effect, middle agents buy artists' performances wholesale, and then resell them retail to a number of different venues, generally within a particular geographic area. Their role is often one of dual agency, representing both the venues and other talent buyers on one hand, and the performers on the other. In states where their activities are not subject to licensing requirements which impose maximum fees for agency services, middle agents can generate significant profits by reselling performances for considerably more than the agent pays for those services. For example, suppose a

151 *See* Marathon v. Blasi (2008) 42 Cal. 4th 974, in which the California Supreme Court applied the doctrine of severability to prohibit an unlicensed manager from claiming any portion of an artist's income from employment which the manager booked in violation of California's Talent Agencies Act (California Labor Code, §§ 1700, *et seq.*), but allowing the manager to claim remuneration for other services provided under the contract which did not violate the Act.

particular artist normally gets $10,000 per night for one-night shows. The middle agent negotiates a deal for twenty shows at only $5,000 per night ($100,000), then resells those shows to twenty different venues at $9,000 per night ($180,000). The venues save $1,000 over the "regular" price, the artists get a guaranteed $100,000 (less their primary agent's and/or manager's percentage) and the middle agent makes a profit of $80,000.

In the recent opinion mentioned above,[152] the California Supreme Court made the following observations as to the distinction between managers and agents:

> Agents are effectively subject to regulation by the various guilds [*i.e.*, unions][... which] may require agents to agree to a code of conduct and restrictions on terms included in agent-talent contracts. ... Most significantly, those restrictions typically include a cap on the commission charged (generally 10 percent), a cap on contract duration, and a bar on producing one's client's work and obtaining a producer's fee. These restrictions create incentives to establish a high volume [*i.e.*, high revenue, much-in-demand] clientele, offer more limited services, and focus on those lower risk artists with established track records who can more readily be marketed to talent buyers.
>
> Personal managers, in contrast, are not franchised by the guilds. They typically accept a higher risk clientele and offer a much broader range of services, focusing on advising and counseling each artist with an eye to making the artist as marketable and attractive to talent buyers as possible, as well as managing the artist's personal and professional life in a way that allows the artist to focus on creative productivity. "Personal managers primarily advise, counsel, direct, and coordinate the development of the artist's career. They advise in both business and personal matters, frequently lend money to young artists, and serve as spokespersons for the artists."[153] Given this greater degree of involvement and risk, managers typically have a smaller client base and charge higher commissions than agents (as they may, in the absence of guild price caps); managers may also produce their clients' work and thus receive compensation in that fashion.

While there is a fundamental difference between personal managers and agents, both are principally concerned with enhancing an artist's career and generating new sources of income for that artist, since that is the source from which their own income is derived. They are therefore motivated to be familiar with all of the various types of agreement through which artists obtain revenue. The agreements and other documents with which they will be particularly familiar include:

- **Agency Agreements**

---

152 *Marathon Entertainment, Inc., v. Blasi* (2008) 42 Cal.4th 974

153 *Park v. Deftones* (1999) 71 Cal.App.4th 1465, 1469-1470

- Management Agreements
- Powers of Attorney
- Fidelity Bonds
- Band Agreements
- Employment Contracts
- Work for Hire Agreements
- Booking Contracts
- Pay to Play Agreements
- Releases
- Recording Contracts
- Retainer Agreements
- AFM Master Agreement
- AFTRA Recording Code
- Merchandise Contracts
- Endorsement Agreements
- Video Contracts
- Photography Contracts
- Tour Agreements

◆ ◆ ◆

Business Managers

The scope of a business manager's role is significantly different from that of a personal manager. A business manager advises the artist in regard to business decisions and is generally responsible for disbursing payments of the artist's financial obligations and overseeing the artist's income and investments. This will often include regular reviews of royalty statements and other sources of an artist's income. It may also include controlling bank accounts and funds for the artist, paying bills on his or her behalf, and generally managing the artist's financial interests. Because of the level of control which this relationship often creates over an artist's money, it may be advisable to obtain a **fidelity bond** to guarantee that those funds will only be disbursed for the artist's benefit or in accordance with the artist's instructions.

Business managers are frequently trained and licensed accountants, or may have equivalent experience in the field of music business. The relationship between the artist and business manager will be governed by a **management contract**, but the compensation will most likely be a fixed monthly amount plus some percentage of funds received and/or disbursed on the artist's behalf.

Because they oversee artists' business interests, Business Managers should be readily familiar with the entire scope of the documents and contracts to which artists are signatory, as well as tax regulations and other purely financial considerations, but particularly including:

- **Agency Agreements**
- **Management Agreements**
- **Power of Attorney**
- **Fidelity Bonds**
- **Employment Contracts**
- **Booking Contracts**
- **Recording Contracts**
- **Retainer Agreements**
- **Publishing Agreements**
- **Tour Agreements**
- **Federal & State Tax Regulations**
- **Royalty Reports**

◆ ◆ ◆

Publicists

Publicists generate and manage publicity. Their job is neither more nor less than intentional manipulation of the public's perception of some celebrity, performer, group, or company, or of a project such as an album, film, or publication. Publicists may be employed by a large public relations firm, or be "in-house" employees of a record company or other organization, or work alone, or be part of a small, "boutique" firm. Regardless of the manner in which they operate, their goal remains the same: ***to get the media to accept and report as "news" whatever information is disseminated by the publicist***, either directly through press releases, or surreptitiously through manipulated "leaks" and "plants." Although publicity is primarily an informational activity, its ultimate goal is to increase a client's revenue by enhancing[154] the public image and reputation of a person, product, or project, and thereby generating public interest and demand.

A publicist's most basic tool is the **press release**, but for such releases to be reported by the media they must be of interest to the public — or at least to a segment of the public targeted by a particular media outlet. Press releases are frequently tailored to appeal to a particular sector at which they are being aimed, and often contain more creative writing than accurate reporting. In consequence, journalists generally view press releases with skepticism. The personal reputation and relationships of a particular publicist can make a significant difference in whether or not a press release is "picked up" and utilized in the media.

---

154 "Enhance" is a relative term in the music business. Reportedly, Donny Osmond's manager once suggested that it would enhance Osmond's marketability as a rock vocalist if he could arrange to be arrested for drug possession. (Osmond rejected the suggestion.)

Publicists know that getting media coverage is dependent on presenting the right material at the right time, and are constantly looking for a "hook" — some issue or story that has *already* caught public interest and to which a client's press release can be made to appear relevant. Press releases related to topics of current public interest are referred to as "news pegs," and they tend to be particularly successful. Publicized celebrity statements regarding AIDS, global warming, world hunger, and any number of other issues can generally be traced to a publicist, regardless of the sincerity and authenticity of the celebrity client's commitment.

Besides press releases, publicists employ a number of other techniques to generate publicity, including press conferences with the client (both in person and by telephone), media tours, junkets, video news releases ("VNR's"), wire-service stories, and internet postings. These may not be enough, however, to accomplish their publicity goals, so publicists may also adopt a more proactive approach by creating their own "news." This can take the form of contests, invented awards,[155] sponsorships, charity events, or by having their client publicly espouse a controversial position on some high-profile, newsworthy subject.

As compared to commercial advertising, publicity is both lower in cost, and higher in credibility, since it is perceived by the public as journalism rather than advertising. The primary disadvantage of publicity is the lack of control over if, when and how disseminated information will be reported. The adage that "any press is good press," has a number of notable exceptions, and many publicity campaigns have been necessitated as a means of damage control to repair the effects of bad press. That adage nonetheless remains generally true in the long term, if the client has the ability and staying-power to persevere regardless of what is being reported. Some celebrity careers have been based on nothing *but* publicity, and often bad publicity at that. Paris Hilton's public antics are perhaps the most notable current example. Not only has she become personally famous through notoriety, but discernable trends and spikes in Hilton Hotels' revenues reportedly correlate to the amount of publicity which she and her more outrageous public debacles have received.

In the music industry, a label's staff publicist has the job of getting the media to report about both the label and its artists. Part of this involves generating — sometimes inventing — a favorable public image for the artist... something that will enhance public interest and album sales. Since staff publicists must necessarily put the label's interests ahead of the artists', and may be responsible for publicizing several artists at one time, many artists have their own publicist as a member of their management team. The goal of both the artist's and the label's publicist should be the same: to garner as much positive media exposure for the artist as possible. To accomplish this, publicists should be masters of networking, with personal contacts throughout the industry and media. Not surprisingly, publicists spend a lot of time on the telephone, at social functions, and at media events where they can promote the artist personally while seeking out potential new leads and contacts for future publicity.

---

155 More than one publicist has formed his or her own impressively-titled foundation which has the sole function of presenting prestigious-sounding awards to the publicist's clientele — and often to the publicist, as well.

Publicists also monitor the media in a number of ways, including "clipping" services which search worldwide publications, both online and in print, providing them with regular updates on what's being reported about their clientele. This allows publicists to gauge the impact of their efforts, and to alter or redirect those efforts when the apparent result is less than ideal. Such data collection is also, in one sense, the publicist's "report card" — a means by which to demonstrate to the client the extent to which the publicist has produced measurable results.

Independent publicists and public relations firms are usually retained under a **publicity agreement** or **publicist agreement**, generally for a term of two or three years. (It takes time for a publicity campaign to generate discernable results, so short-term agreements tend to be counterproductive.) For their services, publicists generally receive a monthly (sometimes weekly) fee, plus reimbursement of their expenses and (sometimes) a markup on those expenses. Determining the legitimacy of a publicists's expense claims is one of the most common points of contention between an artist and publicist, and establishing mutually-agreed guidelines for those expenses should therefore be an important consideration in the contract.

Another key consideration is creative control over information released to the media. While the publicist cannot guarantee that the contents of a press release will be reported accurately, completely, or at all, press releases containing information which the artist did not want disseminated can quickly lead to a breakdown in the working relationship. Since publicists tend to be on the periphery of an artist's management team, they are seldom interested in the specific terms and conditions of the artist's contracts, but will want to know the high points for press release purposes. They will eagerly inform the press that their artist has signed a "six album deal at 15%," with little interest in the fact that the contract is for one album with five options, and the net percentage is reduced to less than 7% by other contract provisions.

The documents and contracts with which publicists should be thoroughly familiar are:

- **Publicity (Publicist) Agreements**
- **Research Agreements**
- **Press Releases**

◆ ◆ ◆

Music Lawyers

The legal profession has a limited number of certified specialties, **and music law *is <u>not</u> one of them*.** Any licensed attorney can hold himself or herself out as being an "entertainment lawyer" or "music lawyer" without ever having demonstrated any particular expertise in those complex areas of legal practice.[156] The music industry has customs and practices which are in many instances contrary to those of "normal" businesses, so even the most experienced of lawyers can easily go astray without a comprehensive working knowledge of how the music business is organized and functions. What may be highly-favorable terms in the music industry will frequently seem unfair, unreasonable, or unconscionable to a lawyer unfamiliar with the music business.

On the other hand, there are a number of attorneys who *do* have the necessary expertise, usually obtained through years of working in the music industry, either representing artists, or inside the Business Affairs or Legal Affairs departments of a record label, or through having themselves been professional performers at some time in their lives. These lawyers are an established part of the industry in their own right, and their clients can benefit from their industry contacts as well as from their valuable legal advice and advocacy. In consequence of their stature in the industry however, the very best of these attorneys can be as hard to contact as are major record company executives.

Although locating a qualified music attorney may seem an insuperable obstacle, particularly for unestablished artists at the beginning of their careers, entering into contracts without qualified legal representation is potentially disastrous. Personal references, networking, internet searches, music business schools, and specialized legal referral services, are all viable methods for finding a possible candidate. Remember that — as with any other member of a management team — there are trade-offs between different levels of qualification; a high-powered, "super-star" music lawyer will be more expensive and yet unlikely to expend a lot of personal time or attention for a new client, whereas a less-established attorney will probably cost less, be more available, and be able to devote more time and effort. What's most important is that there be confidence in the attorney's competence in this field, and comfort with the financial arrangements agreed upon.

In representing artists, music attorneys generally charge for their services in one of three ways: an hourly fee that can range from $75 - $750 per hour (or more); a percentage arrangement, where the attorney will receive anywhere from 3% to 30% of whatever contract

---

156 In the legal profession, the word "specialist" (or its equivalent) is reserved for those attorneys who have been recognized and certified by an accredited independent authority as having satisfactorily demonstrated particular expertise and experience within a defined area of legal practice. **Currently, there are no legal specialization programs in either entertainment law or music law recognized by any state**, although counsel to the American Bar Association's Standing Committee on Specialization has suggested that "they certainly would be areas ripe for board certification."

he or she negotiates;[157] and a flat-fee arrangement, where the attorney receives a pre-agreed sum for each contract negotiated, which could be anywhere from $500 to $50,000, or more, depending on the attorney and the nature of the contract under consideration. Regardless of the type of fee arrangement, it is essential — indeed, it is legally required in most jurisdictions— that the terms be memorialized in a **written** legal services agreement.

Because this book deals with music contracts, our focus here is on an area of legal practice referred to as "transactional law," dealing primarily with the negotiation and formation of contracts. Other areas of music law include "intellectual property" (copyrights, trademarks, *etc.*) and litigation (adversarial proceedings), which are discussed in Part III ("Remedies"). A music lawyer may be qualified in these additional areas, or may refer you to other lawyers experienced in those fields, or may be part of a "full service" law firm which has partners or associates who are skilled in those areas of practice. If it is a matter of litigation, however, the trial attorney should be completely familiar with the music industry and its legal aspects, since they are likely to be essential to effectively presenting the case to a judge or jury. A trial lawyer's lack of familiarity with subtle legal distinctions of the music industry, or inability to effectively educate the court on those issues, has led to more than one erroneous judgment at trial.

A qualified music lawyer should be thoroughly familiar with every type of contract and document discussed throughout this book, but the specific contracts to which attorneys are themselves parties will include:

- **Retainer Agreements - Hourly fee arrangement**
- **Retainer Agreements - Flat fee arrangement**
- **Retainer Agreements - Participation arrangement** [158]
- **Retainer Agreements - Contingent fee arrangement**
- **Retainer Agreements - Hourly fee, plus percentage**
- **Shopping Agreements** [159]

◆ ◆ ◆

---

157 A recently-published opinion has called into question whether an attorney violates talent agency licensing requirements under this "participation" type of contract if it amounts to securing employment for the client. (See Ferrer v. Preston (2006, 2nd Dist.) 145 Cal. App. 4th 440.) *Cf.*, *Marathon v. Blasi* (2008) 42 Cal.4th 974

158 There is some question as to whether such agreements violate talent agency licensing laws if the services involve securing employment for an artist. Attorneys will sometimes enter into a "Shopping Agreement" on a participatory basis, but such agreements do not (and should not) cover legal services. Before signing a shopping agreement with anyone, it should be reviewed by an *independent* attorney.

159 Here's another of those reiterated *caveats*. For ethical reasons, an attorney should not enter into a shopping agreement with anyone who is also a client, and should never offer legal advice as to the merits of a shopping agreement (or *any* contract) to which that attorney is a party. *Always* get the opinion of a qualified, *independent* attorney before entering into a shopping agreement with anyone.

Promoters

Promoters are perhaps the most entrepreneurial figures in the music industry. Their job is simple; *to bring entertainment to an audience* — but "simple" and "easy" are far from the same, and the number of tasks which must be accomplished to fulfill that simple job are legion, and seldom easy.

Radio promoters are single-mindedly devoted to getting clients' recordings public exposure through airplay and, more recently, webcasting. Such promoters constantly walk a legal tightrope between permissible promotion efforts and impermissible inducements commonly known as "payola." (The easiest way to get a DJ to air a particular recording is to give him money or something else of value. However, because broadcasting is a "public trust" licensed by the federal government, such *quid pro quo* arrangements are illegal.) Radio promoters have repeatedly been the focus of investigations by the Justice Department, and central figures in a number of music industry scandals as a result. Record companies generally maintain an in-house promotions department, but many labels have sought to distance themselves from potential scandal (and possible indictments) by utilizing independent radio promoters as outside contractors who are (ostensibly) employed by recording artists rather than the record company. Even though the record company pays the promoter, they do so as an "accommodation" to the artist, and treat some or all of the money paid to the promoter as a recoupable advance to the artist.

Show promoters may work with a single performer or with a small number of performers or groups, arranging for them to perform in particular venues and taking a share of the proceeds, or — on a larger scale — promoters may plan and organize an entire tour, which can be regional, national or worldwide, or promote a major event which brings together performers from around the world while providing (or obtaining) financing and guarantees for both the performers and the venues.

The artists with whom these show promoters work may be signed — in which case an artist's label may be entitled to pre-approve any bookings — or they may be seeking to be signed, in which case the promoter may want a participation interest in any deal they make as a result of appearances arranged by the promoter. There are likely to be merchandising tie-ins, which will also be dependent upon the existence of prior contracts. There may also be other concessions involved, as well as venue owners, fire marshals, other state, county or city officials, all of whom will have requirements which the promoter must address and satisfy. Additionally, there will be advertising — which can range from flyers to national radio and television spots — and all of which may need to be approved by a range of interested parties, in advance. If a tour is involved, there are also the logistics of transporting the artists, crew, instruments, equipment and other physical elements of the production from one location to the next, and arranging accommodations in each location. There may also be "advance" men who arrive several days prior to each show to handle local promotion and advertising arrangements, accommodations, local hiring for support positions, and a range of necessary activities which may vary widely from one location to the next.

Because of the scope of promoters' activities, they should be familiar with a broad range of contracts, industry standards, and governmental regulations including, but not limited to:

- **Booking agreements**
- **Deal Memos**
- **Engagement Letters**
- **Bonds & Guarantees**
- **Concession agreements**
- **Promotional consideration agreements**
- **Endorsement agreements**
- **Employment agreements**
- **Equipment rental agreements**
- **Performance licenses**
- **Subleases and "fourwall" agreements**
- **Collective bargaining agreements**
- **Licenses and permits**
- **Liability insurance**
- **Fire and safety regulations**
- **Finance agreements**

◆ ◆ ◆

Performance & Tour Support

In the music business, the term "tour support" refers to the technical and logistical components and personnel necessary to present a performance or series of performances, including not only the technicians, engineers, electricians and stagehands required for each show, but also securing venues, transportation of performers and key personnel from one location to another, accommodations for performers and staff in each location, hiring of local personnel, security, local and national advertising, publicity, and a wide range of ancillary requirements. Most of those relationships and arrangements will be by contract, and in the case of union members, those contracts will fall within the scope of a collective bargaining agreement.

When live performances are involved, there are certain legal issues which should be borne in mind, particularly by small, unsigned groups. "Roadies" and other support personnel — whether paid or unpaid for their services — may be legally presumed to be employees falling within the scope of a doctrine called *Respondeat Superior*. In simple terms, this doctrine says that an employer is legally responsible for the acts and omissions of an employee in the course of employment. Since most start-up groups have not formalized themselves as a limited liability company or corporation, they are legally presumed to be a general partnership, with each member 100% personally liable for the obligations of the group. Putting the two doctrines together, individual group members can be held personally responsible for whatever their support personnel (or other group members) may do or cause to happen in the course of setting up, performing, packing out, or traveling to or from a show. *E.g.*, when a band's tour bus driver carelessly discharged a holding tank of toilet waste off of a bridge and onto a boatload of unsuspecting tourists below, the band was held liable, even though no band member was present at the time. (And yes, this really happened.)

In the context of music *contracts*, "tour support" also refers to the funds necessary to pay for some or all of the above… including liability insurance. But getting a record label to agree to provide such funds may be one of the trickier issues in negotiating a recording deal.

No one in the industry will dispute that the more a group or artist tours, the more their recordings sell. This is even truer for new artists still in the process of building a widespread fan base. Since labels are in the business of selling albums, they are always pleased to have their artists touring as much as possible, and may even make it a requirement in their recording contracts. They are less pleased, however, at the prospect of paying for such tours, and will generally contribute only grudgingly unless contractually obliged to do so. Tour plans should therefore be discussed, in detail, as part of recording contract negotiations, with the label's tour support commitments specified from the outset.

Some examples of tour support items to seek in recording contract negotiations might include:

- Promotional support (photography, graphic arts, posters, flyers, promotional CD's, website, sponsorship solicitation, merchandising subsidy, *etc.*)
- Publicity support (press releases, media interviews, publicist attachment or budget, *etc.*)
- Advertising support (ad copy and slicks, booking of ads or co-op ads, advertising agency attachment or budget, *etc.*)
- Logistical support (lighting and show design, advance man, road manager, roadies, light and sound technicians, equipment rental, transportation (*e.g.*, vehicle rent or lease and driver), *per diem*, accommodation subsidy, *etc.*)

It would be difficult (if not impossible) to obtain all of the suggested items, but the artist can always *ask*, and it actually *is* in the label's best interests to support artists' touring efforts, since tours increase album sales. The trade-offs in negotiating for tour support will be the artist's commitment to participate in the label's marketing efforts as an adjunct to the tour, as well as additional contract concessions.[160] These commitments and concessions from the artist would likely include:

- Giving media interviews in advance and while on tour;
- Radio and television appearances;

160 These issues are covered at length in the section on Recording Contracts, in VOLUME TWO.

- In-store promotional appearances;
- Label approval of overall visual and technical show design;
- Label selection or approval of tour cities and venues;
- Label selection or approval of opening act or supplemental act;
- Label approval of song selections or set list;
- Label approval of advertising and promotional materials; and
- Label recoupment of some or all of tour support funds as additional advances under recording contract.

The most important point here is that *tour support should never be an afterthought.* The artist should have some reasonably comprehensive touring plan in mind at the time of initial negotiations for a recording contract. Ideally, the tour can then become a joint effort of the label and artist, with each benefitting from the other's contributions. In return for the artist's additional efforts to support the label's marketing goals while on tour, the label lends its personnel and advances funds to make that tour successful. Properly structured, it can be a win-win arrangement.

Unless the tour or performance is being arranged through an independent promoter, tours are usually organized and run by a tour manager, who is likely to be working closely with a booking agent. Whoever is managing and planning the tour or performance should be familiar with the following:

- **Booking Agreements**
- **Pay to Play Agreements**
- **Engagement Letters**
- **Side Letters**
- **Bonds & Guarantees**
- **Concession Agreements**
- **Promotional Consideration Agreements**
- **Endorsement Agreements**
- **Employment Agreements**
- **Equipment Rental Agreements**
- **Performance Licenses**
- **Subleases and "Fourwall" Agreements**
- **Collective Bargaining Agreements**
- **Licenses and Permits**
- **Liability Insurance**
- **Fire and Safety Regulations**
- **Finance Agreements**

◆ ◆ ◆

Clubs & Other Venues

The location in which public performances occur is referred to as a "venue," which can be virtually anywhere, indoors or out. As a practical matter, professional venues are most often clubs, theaters, auditoriums, stadiums, and concert facilities. The owners or operators of such facilities may enter into a **booking contract** directly with the performers or their agent, or they may deal with a promoter or "middle agent" who arranges to provide performers to the venue on a contractual basis. Where the promoter takes over the operation of substantially all of the venue for certain dates, the contract may be in the form of a **four wall agreement**. Sometimes performers or their management guarantee certain minimum revenue, often prepaying all or a portion of that guaranteed sum. Such contracts are often referred to as **pay to play** agreements, whether made with the promoter or directly with the venue.

In most instances, the venue operator will employ a staff which includes a house manager, maintenance personnel, stagehands, and lighting and sound engineers, although these technical personnel may be provided by the performers or promoter. If the venue serves food and/or beverages, there may also be kitchen staff, bartenders and serving staff. For larger venues, these "food services" may be provided by outside contractors under a **concession agreement**. The venue (or promoter) may also provide space for the sale of promotional merchandise or products, which is also generally the subject of a concession agreement, which may be a separate contract or part of a more comprehensive **lease** or **booking contract**.

When photography or audio or visual recording are to take place in the venue, the venue may need to give or obtain **releases**, depending on who retains the rights to the photographs or recordings. It may also be advisable to obtain releases from patrons, both as to liability and as to the possible commercial use of photographs or recordings taken within the venue. This can often be accomplished by posted notices and/or by the use of contract language printed on admission tickets for the purpose of establishing the patrons' informed consent.

Notably, it is the venue operator who is generally accountable for payment of royalties to performing rights organizations (*i.e.*, BMI, ASCAP, SESAC) in respect to songs and compositions performed within the venue, whether by live performance or by recordings (including karaoke and jukeboxes). Performers can generally grant all rights necessary for live performance of their own original material, but not for compositions owned by publishers or by other artists, and certainly not for recorded music played in the venue as background music or during performance intervals.

The contracts and documents with which a venue operator should be generally familiar are:

- **Leases and Rental Agreements**
- **Booking Agreements**
- **Pay to Play Agreements**
- **Employment Agreements**
- **Concession Agreements**
- **Equipment Rental Agreements**

- **Performance Licenses**
- **Subleases and "Fourwall" Agreements**
- **Collective Bargaining Agreements**
- **Licenses and Permits**
- **Liability Insurance**
- **Fire, Health, and Safety Regulations**
- **Bonds and Guarantees**

◆ ◆ ◆

Visual Artists & Photographers

In addition to music itself, the business of music requires other creative components as well. Even at the "garage band" level, musicians are certain to have photographs taken of themselves, and the creation of a commercial album usually involves both photography and graphic art as an integral part of its packaging and overall presentation.[161] Additionally, there are likely to be posters, one-sheets, catalogues, signs, billboards, T-shirts, and a wide range of marketing and promotional materials and merchandise which are dependent upon visual arts. Such usages create potential legal entanglements arising under both copyright and trademark laws, and under statutes and common law regarding personality and publicity rights. Consideration of those issues is critical each time a visual image is used for advertising or promotion, or incorporated in a product or merchandise.

Photographers and visual artists create and preserve images that depict something or someone, or which tell a story or record an event. To accomplish this, these artists must have both creativity and technical expertise. Currently, most photographers use digital rather than traditional film cameras (although some use both types), plus an array of other equipment ranging from lenses, filters, and tripods to flash attachments, reflectors and specially constructed lighting equipment. Graphic artists employ a variety of methods and an assortment of materials, including oil paints, watercolors, acrylics, pastels, pencils, pen and ink, and computers. Their work may be realistic, stylized, or abstract, and may depict objects, people, nature, events, or some completely internal, personalized vision.

Most photographers are self-employed, while most graphic artists work for a firm. The distinction between freelance artists and those employed by others is important in determining copyright ownership of the visual images they create. The person who first puts creative work into tangible form is the author and owner of that work for copyright purposes *unless* it is a "work made for hire," in which case it is the *employer* who is the "author" and owns the copyright.

---

161 The cost and expense of developing these visual elements, together with the cost for actual physical manufacture of a saleable commercial album, are the rationale behind the "container" or "packaging" reduction of artist's royalties which appears in most recording contracts.

Art directors develop design concepts and review material that is to appear in printed or digital media, directing the efforts of photographers and visual artists, and deciding which photographs or artwork to use. They oversee the design, layout and production of visual elements, determining how best to present it for maximum effect.

Photographers, artists and art directors may be regular employees of a record company, or they may be independent contractors hired on a project-by-project basis. While those who are full-time employees may need to be conversant only with their own craft and the terms of their employment agreement, freelance artists should be familiar with:

- **Copyright Registration**
- **Name & Likeness laws**
- **Proposals**
- **Photography Contracts**
- **Graphic Arts Contracts**
- **Employment Agreements**
- **Work for Hire Agreements**
- **Releases**
- **Permissions**
- **Licenses**

◆ ◆ ◆

Broadcasters, Cablecasters & Webcasters

Broadcasting refers to transmission of audio content to the public by means of AM or FM radio signals, or of audiovisual content by means of VHF or UHF television signals. In contrast, webcasting refers to transmission (streaming) of audio or audiovisual content over the internet, and cablecasting refers to transmission of encrypted audio, visual or audiovisual content by wire but *excluding* transmissions over the internet or computer networks. In addition, there is also satellite broadcasting, which transmits encrypted audio and audiovisual content from geosynchronous orbit. The laws, rules and regulations which govern these types of transmission are all somewhat distinct from each other, particularly in respect to copyright materials and royalties payable for such transmission.

Some broadcasters — such as National Public Radio (NPR) and the Public Broadcasting System (PBS) — operate on a not-for profit basis, supported by subsidies and donations, and are afforded special dispensations in royalty rates. Cable and satellite systems, and some internet sites, operate on a subscription basis, receiving payments from their subscribers. For traditional broadcast and other commercial operations, income is dependent on advertising revenues. Regardless of their income sources, broadcasters, cablecasters and webcasters must use that income to pay salaries, operating expenses, and royalties.

In traditional AM and FM radio broadcasting, stations pay royalties to the publishers (copyright owners) of musical *compositions* which they broadcast, but not for the *sound recording* of that composition which they actually transmit.[162] The royalty rate which they pay is determined by contracts signed with the various performing rights organizations (ASCAP, BMI, SESAC), which establish a royalty scale based on station format, broadcast area, day of the week and time of broadcast, and other factors. Royalties are paid through the performing rights organizations, which (after deduction of their fee) disburse royalty payments and statements to their members. Stations are required to keep a journal of all music which they play, and to file periodic reports with the performing rights organizations. While the performing rights organizations (PRO's) generally rely on the broadcasters' reporting, they also periodically monitor broadcasts to verify the accuracy of broadcasters' airplay reports. The advent of computer-driven monitoring equipment and software, and the inclusion of detectible, non-audible "watermarks" in many recordings, has vastly expanded the extent and effectiveness of such monitoring in recent years.

In webcasting, royalties are not only paid for the composition, but also for the sound recording being streamed. SoundExchange is a nonprofit performance rights organization designated by the U.S. Copyright Office to collect statutory sound recording copyright royalties and to and distribute those royalties to the copyright owners and recording artists.

For television and other audiovisual media there is an additional complication. Each composition requires a sync license from the publisher, and each sound recording requires a separate master use license. There are music catalogues and blanket licenses available for many compositions and recordings, specifying royalty rates for their use in an audiovisual medium and with that rate usually determined by medium, type of program, broadcast day and time, and other factors. Where there is no rate being offered by a catalogue rate sheet or blanket license, then the two required licenses — sync and master use — must be negotiated with the publisher and record company. (If the composition is to be *performed* during the audiovisual program, rather than reproduced from a prior recording, then only the sync license is required.)

Both broadcasters and webcasters need to be aware of their liabilities for music royalties. Some broadcasters erroneously assume that royalties paid to BMI, ASCAP and/or SESAC cover their entire royalty obligation, even when they concurrently stream (simulcast) their content over the internet. Those licenses cover only *simultaneous* streaming of their broadcast material, and *only* with respect to the composition. If a broadcaster is operating a "side channel" of music content which is not being broadcast over-the-air, a separate internet-only license must also be obtained from one of those performing rights organizations, and a separate royalty for the recording must be paid through SoundExchange.

While ASCAP, BMI, and SESAC continue in their role of licensing and receiving royalty

---

162 In December 2007, a bill entitled the "Performance Rights Act"(H.R. 4789) was introduced in Congress. If passed by the House and Senate (and signed by the President) it would require radio stations to pay performance royalties to record companies and recording artists for radio airplay.

payments for public performance of compositions, for webcasting those licenses are usually on the basis of a minimum fee plus royalties based on either website usage or on website revenue, rather than on broadcast calculation methods. Regardless of the royalty formula adopted, those composition royalties are only one part of a webcaster's royalty obligation.

The Digital Millennium Copyright Act (DMCA) requires royalties to be paid to the *performers* for all digital uses of music except those limited to over-the-air broadcast, so webcasters must also pay an additional, statutory royalty to SoundExchange for the sound recording itself. Half of the fees collected by SoundExchange go to the performers, and half to the copyright owner of the sound recording, which usually means the record company. A "compulsory license" allows webcasters to use recordings without express permission, provided that the statutory royalty is paid, and there is compliance with certain additional restrictions.

Anyone streaming copyrighted material over the internet needs to be aware of the rules governing such transmissions. Broadcasters are accustomed to paying royalties for the use of music to the traditional performance rights organizations — ASCAP, BMI, and SESAC — and any internet simulcasts of their content are covered by those agreements, but *only* in respect to the underlying composition, not the sound recording.

Although principally intended as a means to make unlawful copying difficult, the DMCA and regulations adopted to implement it also make traditional broadcast practices difficult to adapt for internet application. Broadcast stations which fail to adequately modify their procedures to accommodate these changes risk both fines and possible loss of license.

To qualify for a compulsory license, webcasters must either meet specific requirements or else obtain permission directly from the copyright owner. Failure to obtain either a directly-negotiated license, or to qualify for a compulsory license, may result in an action for damages and penalties for copyright infringement.

To qualify for the compulsory license, a webcaster must:

- File a "Notice of Use of Sound Recordings Under Statutory License" with the Copyright Office ***before*** commencing service, together with a filing fee. (A single filing can be paid for multiple streams on the same website.)
- Comply with performance restrictions which prevent copying of streamed material. This requires that there be no "interactive" service allowing the listener to directly select content, that the relevant copyright information (title, source album title, and artist, at a minimum) be simultaneously transmitted with each selection, that there be no posting of advance scheduling of playlists, and that selections by the same artist or from the same album are not played too frequently.[163]

---

163 This last restriction is referred to as the "sound recording performance complement," and has two components: *(a)* Webcasts cannot contain more than three selections from any one album or CD on a particular channel within any three-hour period, and no more than two such selections can be played consecutively; and *(b)* Webcasts cannot contain more than four different selections by the same featured artist or *(...continued)*

- Implement and comply with all mandated "anti-piracy" measures.
- Transmit only lawful recordings — no bootlegs.
- Accurately calculate, report and pay royalties.

In registering with the Copyright Office, an applicant for compulsory webcast licensing will need to determine if a Section 114 or a Section 112 license is required. Section 114 relates to the right to perform a musical work, while Section 112 relates to the right to make temporary "ephemeral" copies. Since an ephemeral copy is indispensable to any digital transmission process, webcasters need *both* licenses. Although ephemeral copies have no discernable independent value, a small portion of the royalty is nonetheless allocated for the making of that copy.

The Federal Communications Commission (FCC) regulates interstate and international communications by radio, television, wire, satellite, and cable. It does not, however, directly regulate the internet, although it indirectly affects it through its jurisdiction over transmission media and its programs related to suppression of child pornography.

The Communications Act of 1934 established the FCC as an independent US government agency responsible directly to Congress, with jurisdiction covering all 50 states, the District of Columbia, and all U.S. territories and possessions. The Act was intended to regulate interstate and foreign commerce in communications via wire and radio to help make available a rapid, efficient, nationwide, and worldwide wire and radio communications service, and the FCC's jurisdiction has been subsequently expanded to include television (as being within the scope of "radio"), and it has assumed oversight of the satellite and cable telecommunications media, as well.

Within the FCC, the Mass Media Bureau licenses and regulates amplitude and frequency modulation (AM & FM) radio, broadcast television (VHF & UHF), and direct (unencrypted) satellite broadcasting. The FCC does not license radio or television *networks*, but rather the owners of particular stations (affiliates) within those networks, as well as unaffiliated stations. The FCC also does not regulate internet content, or transmission by means of closed-circuit radio or television, and it has no authority over news-gathering organizations, music-licensing organizations, record companies and distributors, video and film production companies and distributors, or the print media.

In theory, it is the broadcasters alone who are solely responsible for selecting all program content, since the Communications Act and the U.S. Constitution *prohibit* the FCC (or any government agency) from censoring content. In practice, however, the FCC wields tremendous power through its control of broadcast license issuance and renewal. Without FCC approval, no broadcast station can be built, modified, purchased, sold or operated. The FCC's authority to levy fines against broadcast stations, and virtually absolute autonomy in regard to withholding, revoking or denying renewal of broadcast licenses, allows the FCC to

---

from any set or compilation on a particular channel within any three-hour period, and no more than three such selections can be played consecutively.

effectively censor any content which does not comply with its regulations or conform to its unilateral standards of "decency." (Since cable television is available by subscription only, cable operators are subject to a different set of FCC regulations and standards than are broadcast television stations.)

In addition to applicable licensing requirements, broadcasters, webcasters, cablecasters and satellite broadcasters will necessarily enter into an number of contracts with others. For music content, they will have agreements with the various performing rights organizations, usually through collective agreements negotiated by trade associations of which they are members. For webcasters, this will also include an agreement with SoundExchange. If their content involves broadcasting of prerecorded audiovisual programs (*i.e.*, films, television shows, music videos, *etc.*) they will obtain those through contracts with producers or distributors. If they are part of a network, there will be a network affiliation agreement, as well. To the extent that broadcasters employ on-air talent, they may also be signatory to a collective bargaining agreement with AFTRA. And finally, if they are commercial operations, there will be contracts with their advertisers.

From the standpoint of music, the contracts and related documents with which radio broadcasters, webcasters and cablecasters will be most familiar will include:

- **Cue Sheets**
- **Transcription Licenses**
- **AFTRA Agreements**
- **ASCAP, BMI, and SESAC Agreements**
- **SoundExchange Agreements**
- **FCC Regulations**

◆ ◆ ◆

Video & Film Producers

Whether for a music video, a motion picture, a television broadcast, a TV commercial or any other audiovisual presentation, synchronized sound — and the licencing of compositions for such synchronization — forms the basis of a significant income source in the music industry.

MTV, its progeny, and its imitators, have created a dedicated market for music videos. This form of synchronous presentation of music and visual images has become a distinct segment of the modern music industry in its own right, to satisfy that market. Of course, integration of music with images in a recorded audiovisual medium had been around since the 1920's,[164] and an important part of the film industry since that time. Television continued the

164 Contrary to popular belief, the 1927 film "The Jazz Singer," was *not* the first of these. *(...continued)*

practice of synchronous music use as an integral part of a visual medium. Music videos are distinct because they are a generated by the music industry itself, both as promotion and as a distinct product of that industry, and are comprised solely of the audiovisual presentation of a particular song.

Producers of audiovisual products undertake to bring together all of the various arts, professions, trades, crafts and other elements necessary to convert a concept into a final, commercial presentation. Once a project has been "green lighted" (*i.e.*, approved to commence, which generally means a commitment of funds based on a preliminary budget) the process is divided into three phases:

- **Pre-production**, which includes securing the services of any principal talent (screenwriter, stars, director, cinematographer or videographer, composer, choreographer, set designer, costume designer, *etc.*) not previously attached to the project by a commitment letter; casting the remainder of the required talent; finalizing the script; preparing storyboards; finalizing the budget; arranging for studio facilities and locations; preparing shooting schedules; arranging for equipment, costumes, set pieces, transportation and support for production; *etc.*
- **Production**, which involves not only the actual shooting of the film or video footage, but providing all of the personnel and equipment (cameras, lighting, sound, costumes, makeup, dressing rooms, special effects, screening facilities, *etc.*) necessary to do so, transportation to and from locations, caterers to feed the cast and crew, and a plethora of unforeseen adjustments to the script, schedule and budget.
- **Post-production**, during which all of the raw materials obtained in pre-production and production are assembled into a final form through editing and the inclusion of re-recorded sounds and dialogue, music, effects, titling, and additional elements, including stock footage and any "second unit" footage shot independently of the main production.

Film and television producers must obviously deal with a vast number of contracts, regardless of the particular medium in which they work. Not least of their contractual concerns is making certain that releases for personality rights have been obtained not only from each performer who appears in the final film or video, but also from each and every person whose name, voice or likeness is in any way contained within the body or credits of the film. Inclusion

---

D. W. Griffith's 1921 short feature, "Dream Street," included a singing sequence and background audio effects, but no recorded dialogue. Similarly, in 1926, Warner Brothers' first Vitaphone feature, "Don Juan" had a synchronized instrumental score and sound effects throughout, but no recorded speech. "The Jazz Singer" is regarded as the first "talkie" because it contained not only a synchronized instrumental score and sound effects, but also numerous synchronized singing sequences, as well as the first-ever synchronized, recorded dialogue in a commercial film, although that dialogue was limited to only a few, short sequences. Certainly "The Jazz Singer" marked the point at which the entertainment industry first took serious notice of the enormous economic potential of synchronized sound.

of identifiable images which appear even incidentally within a film or video can lead to claims of infringement or misappropriation unless releases have been obtained or the use falls within narrow (and often ambiguous) legal exceptions. This even applies to identifiers of *corporate* "persons." Obtaining necessary releases, and particularly music clearances, can be among the most painstaking (and frustrating) aspects of the audiovisual production.

Commercial use of *any* portion[165] of a copyrighted work requires permission from the copyright owner, except under very narrow exceptions. The first exception is when the work has entered the public domain, and is no longer subject to copyright protection. This can occur either because the copyright has expired (*i.e.*, the work is really old) or because the copyright owner has voluntarily put the work into the public domain. The second exception is "fair use" — a complex legal doctrine which, under very special and limited circumstances *may* allow use of copyrighted work without permission.[166] Unfortunately, fair use is only a defense to an infringement claim, so one never really knows for sure if a use was a "fair use" or not, until a final judgment provides the answer. There are also limited statutory exceptions, discussed earlier, which will have little application in film and video production.

In respect to obtaining music clearances, music videos are often easiest, since the owners of the master recording and publishing rights are probably involved in the production from the outset. If, however, the publishing rights are not controlled by the artist, and no sync license or option was obtained at the time a mechanical license was negotiated, then getting that sync license becomes the most important pre-production goal, since the entire project is valueless without it. Music videos are unique in this regard, since for other types of audiovisual projects, the addition of music, and clearances for that music, most often occur in post-production.

Because most record companies are signatory to union contracts, and there is consequently a compliance clause in their recording contracts, commercial music videos (other than self-produced videos by unsigned bands) will be "union shoots." This refers not only to the musicians being AFM members, and the vocalists being AFTRA members, but may also require that all performers also be members of the Screen Actors' Guild (SAG). Union compliance does not stop there, since *everyone* involved — crew, technicians, *etc.*, — will also need to either be union members or fall within limited exceptions.

For film and video productions other than music videos, the inclusion of music takes two forms: *(1)* music specially composed and recorded for the project; and *(2)* music acquired by license from outside sources. Unlike music videos, finished audio components will be among the very last things added to the project in post production. There are very practical reasons for this. Although the film's composer may have been working on the themes and score since

165 There's a pervasive myth that a "few notes" may be used without permission. ***Wrong!*** While it might be difficult for a copyright owner to *prove* that one, two, three, or a few more notes were actually taken from a copyrighted work — either from a composition or sampled from a recording — it is nonetheless an infringement unless it falls within a recognized legal exception.

166 For a more comprehensive discussion of the fair use doctrine, including a fair use evaluation checklist, see Chapter 3 ("A Primer on Copyright.")

early in the production, and rough tracks may have been used for playback during production — particularly when choreography is involved — the soundtrack cannot be finalized until the film has been completed and edited, since the music and other audio effects must be synchronized to each scene of the edited film.

Music composed for the film or video will be subject to written work for hire agreements, both with respect to the composer and to the musicians who perform for the soundtrack recording. Appropriate "name and likeness" releases will be incorporated into those agreements.

For the film to include songs and recordings from other sources, however, a sync license will be necessary for each composition, and a master use license (with appropriate releases) will be required for each pre-existing recording.

Sync rights are generally (although not always) controlled by a music publisher, while master recording rights are usually (but not always) controlled by the record label, which will also generally (but not invariably) also have the contractual ability to license the necessary personality rights associated with that recording.[167] To use the recording lawfully, all three rights — sound recording, composition, and personality — must be cleared.

Sometimes the process can be facilitated by seeking clearance through the Harry Fox Agency (HFA) Theatrics Department. Even if HFA is not able to grant a license directly, they can generally identify the individuals or entities authorized to do so, usually both for the publishing and for master recordings.[168] Publisher identification and contact information is also available through ASCAP, BMI, SESAC, and SOCAN. Searches can also be conducted through the U.S. Copyright Office for registered composition and sound recording copyright owners, but — since failure to register does not dilute the copyright itself — the absence of a Copyright Office record does not mean the work is free for the taking.

A number of factors come into play in negotiating music licenses. How much of the composition or recording will be used? Where and how will it be used in the film? Will the tune or lyrics be altered? What is the nature of the project? What rights are being sought? How will the film be distributed or exhibited? Each of these factors can radically alter the price of a license.

Because there are no standard fees for sync licenses, publishers and their licensing agents are free to set whatever amount they choose. It's often a process of back-and-forth negotiation which continues until there's either an agreed price and terms, or the producer (or director, or

---

167 Even unquestioned legal ownership of a master recording does not necessarily permit commercial use or licensing of that recording. Documentary evidence of commercial exploitation and licensing rights, particularly including the personality rights of vocalists whose performances are embodied in the recording, and of performers' individual and group names which will be credited in respect to that recording, must also be verified as part of the clearance process.

168 A composition may have been re-recorded under compulsory licenses, so HFA is a good starting point for locating sources, since they can often identify several such licensees.

music director, or whoever has the final say at the production company) decides that the film doesn't *really* have to have that particular song in the soundtrack, at which point the process starts all over again with a different song and (most likely) a different publisher.

Bear in mind that this process needs to be repeated for each composition that will be included in the audiovisual product — regardless of whether that project it is a feature film, a documentary, an animation, a television commercial, a public service announcement, or any other audiovisual form — and that sync licenses are only the first step.

Having obtained sync licenses from the publishers, it will be time to go after master recordings. Again, there is no standard rate, but this time it's most likely a record company[169] which will be quoting fees for a master use license. If the recording artist or group is well known, the price for licensing even a few seconds from a recording can be exorbitant. Further, the price will vary based on the intended use. An "all use" license covers theatrical exhibition , video, television broadcast, cable, and any possible use of the film. This is the most expensive type of master use license. At the other end of the spectrum, "festival" and "student film" licenses are the least expensive, and can contain options locking in a rate for expanded uses, if and when the project attains wider distribution. Usually, for a film, the license should cover theatrical exhibition, cable/satellite transmission, television broadcast, DVD/video release, and soundtrack rights. In addition to the original fee, the license will generally call for further payments to be made as each of these rights are exploited, and may require royalty or residual payments on a per use or per unit basis thereafter.

In obtaining the master use license, it's vital to verify that the person granting the license has all of the necessary rights to do so, including the performers' personality rights. Additionally, the license needs to state who is responsible for payment of "reuse fees" to the performers.[170]

Sometimes, no amount of negotiating skill is sufficient to bring the price of a master use license down sufficiently to meet budget constraints. This is a principal reason why soundtracks often contain familiar songs re-recorded by unfamiliar artists,[171] which is permissible under the authority granted by the publisher's sync license for the composition.

Failure to fully clear all necessary rights is probably the biggest single sources of non-

169 In some instances, the record company may have sold or leased the masters to a licensing company, or masters may be owned by the recording artist, producer, etc.

170 Under the terms of music industry collective bargaining agreements, union vocalists (AFTRA) and musicians (AFM) are entitled to receive additional monies when their previously recorded performances are "re-used" in an audiovisual medium. The re-use fee for each song is generally equivalent to the minimum scale which the performer would receive for a single recording session under the collective bargaining agreement applicable to new recordings made for film or television productions.

171 Caution must be exercised to avoid "sound alike" performances which too-closely imitate the original recording or recording artist. See *Midler v. Ford Motor Co.* (1988, 9th Cir.) 849 F.2d 460, and *Waits v. Frito-Lay, Inc.*, (1992, 9th Cir.) 978 F.2d 1093, which are discussed in Chapter 2 ("Intellectual Property and Personality Rights.").

contract disputes and litigation regarding audiovisual works, and even a hint of potential problems with clearances can stop a project dead in its tracks. No distributor or broadcaster will accept or release a project until they are completely satisfied with the clearances. There are attorneys and companies which specialize in providing clearances, and while the cost for such services may seem prohibitive, it is often the best assurance that can be provided to a potential distributor, since clearance services generally provide warranties, agreeing to indemnify the producers and others in the event of infringement or misappropriation claims.

A final issue in respect to music licenses for audiovisual projects has to do with compliance with the licensing terms, since failure to fully comply can lead to an entirely different range of contract-based disputes. The license will specify that the producer must deliver certain items to the licensor, such as payment, music cue sheets, one or more copies of the film, copies of any soundtrack album (if the license allows for a soundtrack album), video and DVD releases (if allowed by the license), an initial release and distribution schedule, and periodic updates on current and upcoming exploitation of the film, as well as other articles. These "deliverables" should be reviewed carefully before signing the license, since they may impose future obligations that are infeasible. Once the license has been signed, its obligations should be adhered to conscientiously to avoid contract disputes and litigation which can arise long after the project has been concluded.

One need only look at the lengthy list of credits which appear at the end of a film or television program to get an idea of the many varied contracts with which an audiovisual producer must deal. Each person and entity appearing in those credits have contractual relationships with the production, and have given written permission for (and probably insisted upon) the inclusion of their names in those credits. All of these various types of contracts could easily fill a book of their own, but our principal focus here is on music-related contracts and documents with which film and video producers will be familiar, including:

- **Sync Licenses**
- **Master Use Licenses**
- **Releases**
- **Work for Hire Agreements**
- **Attachment Letters**
- **Collective Bargaining Agreements**
- **Clearances**
- **Copyright Registrations**
- **Cue Sheets**

◆ ◆ ◆

Merchandisers

In the music industry, the words **product** and **merchandise** have distinctly different meanings. *Product* refers to those items which actually embody recorded performances, such as CD's and music videos,[172] along with their packaging, whereas *merchandise* refers to ancillary items such as posters, T-shirts, action figures, lunch boxes, bottle openers, cigarette lighters, and virtually anything else (other than "product") which capitalizes on being identified with a particular performer, group, entity, project, logo, trademark, or product, through use of name and likeness, or other identifiable traits.[173]

Promotional merchandise — sometimes known as "freebies" or "giveaways" — are distributed *gratis* or at minimal cost as a means of generating public awareness and support for product. The right to utilize performers' personality rights for such merchandise is usually included in their recording contracts, providing the label with a license to manufacture and distribute such promotional materials with no additional fee or royalty being paid to the artists whose names or likenesses may appear in that merchandise.

Commercial merchandising, on the other hand, is a for-profit business which manufactures and sells such merchandise under license, and pays fees and royalties for the right to do so. The first critical step for merchandisers must be determining who has a legal right to grant the necessary license and receive payment for such use.

Tie-ins are a form of promotional merchandising in which an artist's or project's name and likeness are used in connection with a commercial product which is otherwise unrelated to that artist or project. Tie-ins are distinct from endorsements (where an artist's name is used to advertise a product ostensibly used by the artist) and from commercial or promotional merchandising in which the merchandise is exclusively centered around a particular artist or project.

Placement or *product placement* is similar to tie-ins, but the product or promotional material will visibly appear in the context of an otherwise unrelated entertainment program, such as a motion picture or television show, such as when a poster is displayed as set decoration. Where the product appears *audibly*, a sync license and master use license are required, but these can be negotiated on favorable terms if a prominent promotional credit for the performer and album is provided in consideration for reduced licencing fees.

Almost all music industry contracts signed by performers will grant the other party a license to use the performer's name and likeness to some extent. Performers must be wary of the distinction between an "exclusive" and a "non-exclusive" grant of such right of use, and be

172 Inside some record companies, *Artists* are sometimes referred to as "product."

173 An exception to this distinction between "product" and "merchandise" occurs in relation to live performances. Artists frequently sell copies of their CD's as well as other merchandise at what is colloquially referred to as a "merch" table, usually set up in the lobby or adjacent to the venue. Permission to conduct such an operation usually needs to be negotiated as part of the artists' booking contract with the venue.

especially concerned about the phrase "license others to use..." in such contracts. If the artist has contractually granted someone an "exclusive right" to use the artist's name and likeness, then that artist may no longer be legally entitled to grant anyone else a license to use his or her personality rights during the term of the original contract.[174] Even a non-exclusive license can create a conflict if it permits the non-exclusive licensee to "license others to use" the artist's personality rights, since the original licensee becomes the artist's direct competitor in licensing those same rights to others.

A curious paradox arises when a contract grants an exclusive right to use personality rights, but does *not* grant a right to license others to use those rights. The original, exclusive licensee cannot grant licenses to others, but neither can the artist... at least not without breaching the exclusivity provision of the original contract. A number of solutions to this conundrum are discussed elsewhere, but the simplest is to make the license non-exclusive, or to limit the scope and territory of each exclusive license, restricting it to only particular types of use and to specified geographic areas.

Generally, a **merchandising license** requires the merchandiser to pay an advance against royalties, and will specify the types of merchandise allowed under the license, the period of time (term) during which the license will remain in effect, and the geographical territory in which the merchandise may be sold. Additionally, many artists will insist on a right of approval of a prototype for each item manufactured, to prevent their names or images being associated with an item with which they do not wish to be associated, and to assure themselves of the quality of merchandise bearing their names or images. There may also be concerns about where and how merchandise will be manufactured. Learning, after the fact, that one's name has been linked to goods being made in third-world countries by underpaid children working in sweatshop conditions, or items which contain dangerous materials, can create a public relations nightmare more costly than the royalties received from the merchandising license. Other considerations may include a sell-off provision (limitation on continuing to sell previously-manufactured merchandise after expiration of the license term), renewal options, free or discounted merchandise to the artist or label, and tour support commitments.

The primary concern will remain the question of who has the right to grant a merchandising license, and there will invariable be a warranties and representations clause, coupled with and indemnification provision. It is not unusual for an artist or group to learn, after the fact, that they have lost their right to grant a valid merchandising license because of terms contained in a recording contract, management agreement, or shopping agreement.

The contracts and related documents with which merchandisers will be most familiar include:

---

174 This was the situation in Haelen Laboratories v. Topps Chewing Gum (1953, 2nd Cir.) 202 F.2d 866, cert denied (1953) 346 U.S. 816, a New York case which provided the first legal recognition of personality rights as a commercial commodity. (See Chapter 3, *"Intellectual Property and Personality Rights in the Music Industry."*)

- **Merchandising Licenses**
- **Manufacturing Contracts**
- **Concession Agreements**
- **Fulfillment Agreements**
- **Purchase Orders**
- **Form VA Copyright Registration**
- **Trademark Registration**
- **Customs Regulations**

◆ ◆ ◆

Wholesalers & Retailers

Ultimately, the largest part of the billions of dollars generated each year by the music industry comes from consumers' retail purchases. In this era of digital downloads, traditional retail outlets have felt the impact of online competitors. Some seemingly- unassailable retail record store chains have been forced into bankruptcy by declining sales, while others have downsized their operations through store closures and diversification, and still others have refocused their marketing strategies to include website sales to supplement faltering in-store revenues. (Approximately 588.2 million albums were sold in 2006 — a 4.9% decline from 2005 — while digital sales increased by 65% during the same period.).

At the wholesale level, there are only two potential sources from which albums can be initially purchased: the distributor, and (in some instances) the record label itself. Some of those sales will be to intermediate (secondary) wholesalers, which purchase in large quantity and, in turn, resell lesser quantities to small retailers. Albums which are originally sold by the distributor will generally be those which are considered to be within "normal" or "regular" retail distribution channels. Sales by the record company are more likely to be discounted sales to alternative wholesalers, earning little for the artist unless the recording contract prohibits such sales or specifics royalty payments are to be received from such sales.

Traditionally, retail sales of albums has been conducted through various outlets, with the immediate source of wholesale products to those outlets was equally varied.

- **Record Stores** (major chains) purchase directly from the distributor, usually at the lowest regular dealer price. They seldom receive discounts in that price, *per se,* but rather are provided with "free goods," — a contractual device which is the equivalent of a cash discount to the retailer, but which shifts the burden of that discount onto the Artist (unless the Artist's recording contract prevents it.) Such chains also regularly obtain promotional support from the label, including display materials, giveaways, and in-store appearances by Artists.

- **Record Stores** (small chains and single store operations), often referred to as "Mom & Pop"operations, do not have the buying power of major chains, and generally purchase their product from secondary distribution sources, such as one-stops, rather than directly from the label or distributor. In consequence, they are likely to pay a higher wholesale price, and their retail prices usually reflect that fact.

- **Department Stores / Retail Chains** which have music departments often do not purchase recordings at all. Instead, they deal with a "rack jobber" who outfits and supplies the department, and pays the store a monthly minimum fee for the concession, plus a percentage of record sales, which is deducted from record sale monies collected by the store. (Such an arrangement, known as a "leased department" is not uncommon for department stores. Fine jewelry departments are another example of merchandise which is usually provided on this basis.)

- **Record Clubs** generally manufacture their own version of albums, operating under a license obtained directly from the record label, and ship directly to their customers at below-retail prices. Most recording contracts provide for a reduced artist royalty (or no royalty) for such licensing arrangements, so artists may receive little if any income from such sales, unless their contract provides otherwise, or shifts such sales to the "licensing" provision.

- **Online Retailers** such as Amazon and others operate as do major chain record stores, but without the same overhead, delivering product to their customers by mail or parcel delivery service. Many such retailers are actually divisions of traditional record store operations which maintain online "stores" to augment their in-store sales.

- **Downloads** are an ever-increasing segment of retail music sales. Between 2005 and 2006, digital download sales increased 65 percent, with 582-million individual tracks and nearly 33-million complete albums sold by electronic delivery retailers. As a result, even though traditional album sales (CD's and vinyl) fell 4.9 percent for 2006, there was an overall increase in music sales (including all albums, singles, music videos and digital downloads.) of 19 percent for that same year.[175] Because digital downloading allows consumers to purchase single songs, rather than complete albums, record labels have been faced with falling profits and are developing experimental strategies to increase their income from these new, digital retail outlets. (One tactic employed by record companies to increase profits from electronic transactions is by treating downloads as "sales" (rather than licensing) in calculating Artist's Royalties due under recording contracts.)

All sales, whether retail or wholesale, involve contracts. At the retail level, these will generally be implied, or expressed only by a published offer (a price tag), acceptance (picking it up and taking it to the cash register), and exchange of consideration (giving the clerk the

---

175 Based on Neilsen SoundScan™ figures for 2006 sales by reporting retailers.

money and taking the album home.) At the wholesale level, the contractual relationship will be more defined, either by the distributor's published terms (*i.e.*, a one-sheet or published catalogue and policies), or by a written purchase order or purchase agreement. A key contractual component as between distributors and retailers, whether by specific contract or published policy, will be the "return privilege" which sets the terms under which the retailer can receive credit for unsold product.

In the case of record clubs and for downloads, there will be a licensing agreement, permitting them to both manufacture and sell their own edition of the album.

Here are the documents with which wholesalers and retailers will be most familiar:

- **One Sheets**
- **Catalogues**
- **Order Forms**
- **Purchase Orders**
- **Purchase Contracts**
- **License to Manufacture**
- **License to Distribute Electronically**

◆ ◆ ◆

The foregoing is by no means an exhaustive list of all of the occupations, professions, and trades which make up the music industry, but it does provide a general overview of the primary and secondary industry roles, as well as many of the more visible ancillary aspects of the music business.

SECTION II

MAKING DEALS

Caveat

Here's another of those redundancies that we promised in the Introduction.

None of the following contract language or sample contracts should be taken as being set in stone. Every contract is — and should be — tailored to fit the particular needs of the contracting parties, but any modifications must reflect legal considerations, as well. If your changes eliminate one or more of the five essential elements of a valid contract, or if you include provisions which are contrary to law or public policy, or create ambiguous or contradictory terms, then all or part of the contract may become invalid. Also, if your modifications result in ambiguities within the contract, it may require a court to adjudicate the legal meaning and intent of your agreement. An attorney is best qualified to formulate and implement necessary contract modifications while avoiding these potential pitfalls.

The cost of untangling a poorly drafted contract will invariably exceed the cost of having it properly prepared by a qualified attorney in the first place.

We understand that the expense of hiring an attorney can be daunting for new companies and fledgling performers, but that expense can be minimized by taking your own "best shot" at a draft agreement, first, and then having an attorney review, edit, and improve it. The more complete and comprehensive the deal points or draft agreement you present to an attorney, the less time it will take to convert into a final form. This is not only less expensive for you, but easier for the attorney as well. It takes time to interview a client and draw out their contractual intentions. It's far easier when those intentions have been clarified in advance and in writing.

NA

CHAPTER 6
NEGOTIATING CONTRACTS: DEAL POINTS AND DEAL MEMOS

Deal points are the salient terms of an agreement; its most important and crucial elements. A "deal memo," on the other hand, is a short form of legally binding contract which is usually intended to be superseded by a longer form of agreement at a later date.

Contact negotiations are often no more than a comparison of each party's proposed deal points couples with a series of compromises aimed at achieving a mutually-acceptable list of deal points and common agreement as to terms for each point. Before commencing negotiations, it's vital to have an understanding of the particular deal points which should be included in the specific type of contract being negotiated, and an agenda of the terms you're looking for in respect to each of those points. The best place to start is by creating a checklist of deal points for the prospective contract.

That checklist need not be formal or elaborate, but it should be *complete.* A good starting point for compiling that checklist is to review earlier, similar types of agreements, looking not so much at their specific terms, but rather at the *types* of terms which are included. If the paragraphs or sections have captions, those will be a good indicator of the items to be included in a checklist for that type of contract. The language of each paragraph should also be analyzed to determine what it covers, since captions are not necessarily indicative of the entire scope of the sections to which they relate. For example, a paragraph or section simply entitled "Disputes" might include a number of distinct checklist items such as an arbitration provision, an attorney's fees provision, a cure provision, an injunctive relief provision, a waiver of bond, a liquidated damages provision, and a choice of law and forum provision, all under a single, nondescript heading.

Becoming completely familiar with all of the salient deal points which should be addressed in any particular type of agreement should <u>precede</u> the negotiation process... not be a part of it.

For example, suppose the contemplated agreement is a recording contract. A deal points checklist (in no particular order) might look something like the following:

Record Contract Deal Points Checklist

- ☐ Parties
- ☐ Exclusivity
- ☐ Term
- ☐ Territory
- ☐ Album Guarantees / Options
- ☐ Royalty Rate ("at source" for foreign)
- ☐ Royalty Base (digital download (DPD) provisions; shift to "licensing")
- ☐ Advance provisions
- ☐ Recording Budget / All-Inclusive
- ☐ Distribution / Retail Channels
- ☐ Creative Control
- ☐ Packaging / Container fees
- ☐ Recoupment (list, define, and limit recoupable costs)
- ☐ Cross-Collateralization / Sources & limits
- ☐ Free Goods, cutouts, etc. (Royalty Waivers & Discounts)
- ☐ Warranties and Representations
- ☐ Indemnification
- ☐ Grant of Rights
- ☐ Trademark Rights
- ☐ Controlled Compositions / Caps
- ☐ Accounting Provision
- ☐ Right to Audit
- ☐ Union compliance
- ☐ Assignability
- ☐ Name & Likeness / Approval provision
- ☐ Licensing Rights (splits, and inclusion of certain types of "sale" *i.e.*, DPDs)
- ☐ Merchandising Rights
- ☐ Website design & hosting
- ☐ Choice of Law/Conflict of Law:
- ☐ Dispute Resolution / Cure Provision
- ☐ Injunctive Relief / Bond Waiver
- ☐ Force Majeure
- ☐ Liquidated Damages
- ☐ Attorneys' Fees
- ☐ Delivery Requirements
- ☐ Notice Provision
- ☐ Re-recording restrictions
- ☐ Key Man Provision
- ☐ Leaving Member Provision
- ☐ Release guarantee / Reversions
- ☐ Ownership of Masters
- ☐ Recording Budget
- ☐ Tour support
- ☐ Promotional Budget / Guarantees
- ☐ Reservation of Rights (Rights not specifically granted, reserved.)
- ☐ Heirs & Assigns

Most, if not all, of these deal points should be discussed (or at least mentioned) in recording contract negotiations, and agreed-upon language in respect to each should then be embodied in the contract. In the interim — between preliminary negotiations and signing a formal record contract — a short form of contract, or **deal memo**, may be signed as a temporary — but legally binding — agreement between the parties.[176]

176 For music industry contracts, there is frequently a variation in this protocol, with a "deal memo" which precedes *any* substantive negotiations. As discussed below, such deal memos can be dangerous, since they may create an exclusive, long term relationship, devoid of equitable consideration.

Negotiations, if successful, will result in what is referred to (in the music business) as a "short form" contract. This misnomer is usually applied to a formal agreement which can be anywhere from twenty to fifty pages long.[177]

Negotiating Deals

Negotiating contracts is a specialized skill — almost an art — at which a label's Business Affairs or Legal Affairs attorneys will be highly adept. An artist who attempts to negotiate a record contract without his or her own equally-experienced *music* attorney is at a severe disadvantage. (And this book is no substitute for years of negotiating experience and professional expertise.) As a general rule, if the other side has an attorney at the table, then you want one, too… and it shouldn't be your second cousin who just graduated from law school (although you might invite him to sit in and listen; he might learn something and, who knows, with a few years of "hanging out," he might be able to represent you in music deals.)

Regardless of whether it's a record contract being negotiated, or some other type of agreement, be prepared with your list of deal points, first. If you're working with an attorney, go over all of your deal points with him or her in advance of substantive negotiations with other parties. Have a good idea of what you're looking to get for yourself… and what you're willing to give up. Determine your *realistic* "walkaway point," beyond which you cannot go, and be prepared to say, "Thank you…," and leave, if further negotiations won't get you close to those minimum requirements. The most powerful party at a negotiating table is generally the one most willing to walk away from the potential deal. It's not unusual for negotiations to come to a halt, resume another day, be stalled yet again and again… and still result in a successful contract after several aborted negotiating sessions.

Now, here's the hard part. When you get to the negotiations, just listen and let the other side talk as much as possible. As a general rule, the side that proposes a number first…loses. If you think about it, you'll see why this must be so. Say we're talking about a record deal, and you walk in and say "I want a 15% royalty." Well, from that moment on, 15% becomes the most you will be able to get. On the other hand, if the label starts out offering a 10% royalty, then you know that they are prepared to pay at least that much, and that number can only go *up*.

Of course there are other factors which can make those percentages *effectively* greater or smaller without actually changing the numbers themselves. This is where an experienced music lawyer earns his or her fee; by eliminating or minimizing the additional contract provisions which can have the effect of turning a 15% agreed royalty into an actual yield of only 7% (or less) through deductions, charges, exceptions, and qualifications hidden away in

177 A "long form" agreement (often 70 or more pages in length) may eventually be completed, but it is not unusual for such superseding agreements to be delayed for years, when all but ongoing executory provisions (*i.e.*, royalty payments and accounting) have become moot.

apparently-unrelated provisions of most recording contracts.[178]

Make notes during the negotiations. Keep referring to your checklist to see what's been covered or agreed to, and what remains to be discussed. Even if the negotiation appears to have broken down, make a summary of all of the points agreed upon, the details of any disagreements, and the points which remain to be covered. This will be particularly useful if and when negotiations resume, as well as providing the basis for a deal memo or final contract if an agreement is reached.[179]

The deal memo itself doesn't need to be elaborate or formal, but it should be ***complete*** with respect to ***all*** of the important material terms which will ultimately appear in the contract. Alternatively, it should contain an "escape clause" to terminate it if a formal contract is not completed within a reasonable time.

◆◆◆

Caveat: A&R representatives will often offer artists a "deal memo" which does not contain all of the necessary terms of a recording contract, but which nonetheless binds the artist exclusively to the label for an indefinite period of time while the contract terms are being "worked out" — which generally means until the artist surrenders completely to the label's terms, since the artist can't sign with anyone else after signing the deal memo. **Artists should not sign such memos**, no matter what the A&R rep says or promises, unless it contains an escape clause which releases the artist from any obligation to the label if a formal contract is not competed and signed within a set period (*e.g.* 45 - 120 days.) Otherwise, the artist has virtually no bargaining power in respect to critical terms of the recording contract, yet may be indentured to the label for the next seven years.

Such A&R "deal memos" are often no more than one or two paragraphs:

> For and in consideration of an Advance of $10,000.00, receipt of which is hereby acknowledged, the undersigned Benjamin Tover ("Artist") agrees to become, and does hereby become, an exclusive recording artist of and for QQQQ Records ("Company") or its assignee, for the purpose of recording phonorecords pursuant to the terms and conditions hereof and as may be set forth in such standard "six album" record contract as Artist and Company shall hereafter agree upon. This memorandum of agreement constitutes the entire, integrated agreement between the parties, and shall remain in full force and effect until superseded by a more formal contract.

---

178 Learning how to calculate — or, at least, *estimate* — the net "penny rate" is an essential skill in music industry contract and license negotiations, as this is the only meaningful gauge of the monetary compensation being offered.

179 Such notes can also provide compelling evidence, or valuable aids to testimony, if a dispute later arises in respect to the contract.

No artist should *ever* sign any such "deal memo," regardless of how large or tempting the attached "advance" may be, unless it includes, at a minimum, an escape clause along the following lines:

> Notwithstanding the foregoing, this agreement shall terminate and shall be of no further force nor effect, and Artist shall be entitled to retain all Advances received hereunder as earned compensation, in the event that Company shall fail to enter into good faith negotiations with respect to a superseding agreement within thirty (30) days hereof, or the parties shall fail to agree upon final terms for such superseding agreement within ninety (90) days from the date hereof.

◆◆◆

An *acceptable* deal memo is nonetheless possible, *if* it addresses all of the necessary, salient terms of a final agreement. For the hypothetical record contract negotiations discussed earlier, using your checklist and notes from the negotiations (and assuming that everything went smoothly in those negotiations), a *comprehensive* deal memo might look something like the one which appears on the following pages.

Record Contract Deal Memo *(Sample)*

1. Between QQQQ Records, Inc. ("Company") and Benjamin Tover and Victoria Timm, p/k/a "Nos Morituri," (jointly and severally "Artist").

2. Exclusive recording contract, limited to the U.S. and Canada ("Territory") Contract to be for 1 album, with Company to have option for up to 5 additional albums thereafter (released approximately 1 year apart), upon terms and conditions herein. Automatic termination 1 year from later of USNRC release of, or 18 months from Artist's tender of masters required for, any album hereunder, unless option is exercised and advance paid prior to such date.

3.. Artist shall receive a 15% royalty ("Artist's Royalty") based on SRLP for each physical album actually sold., to be paid to Artist semi-annually after recoupment. Artist's royalty for sales of DPDs will be on the same basis as hereinafter provided for "licensing" of recordings produced hereunder.

4.. Company shall pay Artist an"Advance" of $250,000 (USD) for first album, to be delivered to Artist as follows: (a) $25,000 on Artist's signing; (b) $75,000 on signing Producer; and (c) residue (if any) of remaining $150,000 ("Recording Budget") to be paid to Artist within 30 days of delivery of no fewer then 14 finished tracks, after deduction therefrom of all recording costs and expenses including, without limitation, producer's advance and fees, and all recording studio costs. Recoupable advance for option albums to be 10% of total gross retail sales for best-selling prior album, or $250,000, whichever is greater, to be allocated and with split delivery, as above

5. For physical albums actually sold, the Royalty Base shall be the SRLP (set by Company, but not less than $14.95 USD), minus no more than 25% for all allowances and reserves, including container fee.

6. Master recordings produced and delivered hereunder shall be property of Company. Artist shall receive an Artist's Royalty equal to 50% of all revenues accruing to Company from any and all exploitation and licensing of said master recordings (excluding physical albums released hereunder), and specifically including (without limitation) sales of digital downloads, whether as singles or as albums, and royalties for webcasting. No packaging or other deductions apply.

7. Company shall be entitled to withhold all Artist's Royalties from any and all albums produced hereunder, and from any licensing revenues from master recordings, until such time as Company shall have fully recouped all Artist's Advances and recoupable costs incurred in the recording, manufacture, release and distribution of any and all albums recorded hereunder. Costs and expenses shall not be recoupable unless specifically so agreed. Nothing herein shall require Artist to reimburse or repay Company for any monies received by Artist.

8. If Company distributes as "free goods," saleable copies of albums released hereunder, the total number of such "free goods" shall at no time exceed 10% of the number of the same album "actually sold," and Artist shall receive for such "free goods" an Artist's Royalty equivalent to 50%of the Artist's Royalty which would have been payable had such albums been "actually sold." For discounted goods, including cutouts, record clubs, and other sub-prime means of distribution of albums released hereunder, Artist shall receive Artist's Royalty equivalent to 25% of the Artist's Royalty payable had such albums been sold at a regular, wholesale price.

9. Artist to make all customary warranties and representations as to exclusive ownership and control of rights in and on album(s). Artist to provide all necessary licenses and releases. Artist to indemnify and hold Company harmless from third party claims contradictory to warranties and representations.

10. Company shall pay no more than 75% of statutory rate for no more than 10 tracks per album for mechanical licenses. Artist shall be solely responsible for all publishing royalties in excess of that aggregate sum. Mechanical Royalties paid by Company which are in excess of such limitations shall be deemed advances to Artist, and recoupable as such. Nothing herein shall permit Company to withhold mechanical royalties payable to Artist (at the agreed 75% of statutory rate) for compositions controlled by Artist. Nothing herein constitutes a grant of rights in or to any musical composition, or any portion thereof, to Company.

Page 1 of 3

11. Producer shall be as Company and Artist shall mutually agree. Producer's advance, fees and royalties shall be deducted from Artist's Advance and Artist's Royalties, when and as they become due. Producer, Artist and Company shall each be signatory to Producer's work-for-hire contract. Producer shall have creative control over album(s), including selection of material from Artist's controlled compositions, except that Artist may unilaterally select 3 selections, which Producer may designate as "bonus tracks." Selections other than from Artist's controlled compositions shall only be with Artist's express consent. Producer's agreement to include work-for-hire provision in favor of Artist with respect to contributions to compositions and arrangements, and in favor of company as to sound recordings. Company shall have right to approve or disapprove selected compositions.

12. Company to provide Artist with Royalty Statements and post-recoupment Royalty Payments on semi-annual basis following USNRC release. Accounting to be per GAAP. 15%, one-year holdback for return allowance. Holdback to earn interest at then-current prime lending rate from relevant Royalty Statement date. Artist to have right to GAAS audit, once per year, at Artist's expense. Under-reporting of royalties by 10% or more during any reporting period shifts audit cost to Company, as non-recoupable expense. Under-reporting of royalties by 10% or more during any two consecutive reporting periods, or appearing in two or more successive audits, constitutes a material breach of contact by Company. Unreported royalties to be paid to Artist immediately, plus 10% annual interest.

13. Full union compliance in respect to collective bargaining agreements to which Company is or may become signatory is required for albums and all ancillary performances. Artist to join AFM &/or AFTRA (if not already a member) prior to commencing recording sessions hereunder. All state and federal laws to be complied with.

14. Contract obligations are not assignable by either party without written consent of other party.

15. Artist grants Company right to use, and to license others to use, Artist's name, voice, likeness and biographical information in connection with packaging, marketing, publicity and promotion for albums released hereunder. No likeness or biographical information shall be used or released by Company without Artist's express written consent, which will not be unreasonably withheld. All rights not expressly granted by written contract are specifically reserved to Artist.

16. In the event Company fails or refuses to release any album hereunder for a period of 12 months or more from the date of Artist's Company-scheduled delivery of master recordings, Artist may give Company a 120-day written termination notice. If, at the end of that 120 day period, Company has still not released that album, then ownership and possession of those masters shall revert to Artist, and Company shall deliver the same.

17. Company to have right to use name & approved likenesses for promotional merchandise only. All other merchandising rights are reserved by Artist.

18. Choice of law, California. Choice of non-arbitration forum, L.A. Superior Court. Prevailing party entitled to award of costs and attorney's fees.

19. Parties agree to binding arbitration under AAA at Los Angeles, CA. Company to pay all fees.

20. No breach material until after 30 days written notice and opportunity to cure. No breach if delay or non-performance results from force majeure.

21. In action for injunctive relief, and only on clear and convincing evidence showing imminent harm for which monetary damages would be insufficient, injunction may issue without bond.

22. Delivery of Master Recordings for first album, no fewer than 10 tracks, in technically satisfactory format and condition, to be within 18 weeks from date subscribed hereto.

23. All notices to be in writing delivered by Certified Mail or equivalent private courier to the address of the other party hereto subscribed. Notice effective on receipt.

///

///

Page 2 of 3

24. Artist not to re-record any selection released hereunder for release within Territory for a period of *(a)* 5 years from the first release of that selection hereunder; or *(b)* 2 years from termination of this agreement, whichever is later.

25. If Artist's A&R rep, Jane Doe, leaves the employ of Company at any time during the term hereof, Artist shall have right to terminate this agreement, provided all unearned advances, plus 10%, shall be repaid to Company as a condition of termination. Unreleased master recordings shall revert to Artist on termination, and Company's sole obligation thereafter shall be accounting for and payment of royalties which are due or thereafter. become due hereunder.

26. If any individual comprising "Artist" ceases to perform as a member of Artist, Company shall have the right, at its sole discretion, to: *(a)* terminate agreement in entirety or as to any individual; *(b)* require the leaving individual to fulfill all obligations hereunder, as a solo performer or otherwise; or *(c)* require the remaining individual(s) to fulfill all obligations hereunder, as solo performer(s) or otherwise; or *(d)* require all individuals to fulfill all obligations hereunder, as a solo performers or otherwise.

27. Company shall provide Artist with tour support consisting of a reasonable number of promotional copies of any album released hereunder, and financial support to Artist of not less than $50,000 as a recoupable additional advance hereunder, during each year in which Artist tours within the Term hereof and by assisting in publicity and advertising of Artist's tour(s) through Company's normal personnel and outside agencies. One half of costs and expenses thereby actually incurred by Company (other than for promotional copies and Company personnel) shall be recoupable hereunder. Artist shall cooperate with Company's marketing and publicity departments and make Artist reasonably available for promotional appearances and interviews during tour and in scheduled tour cities.

28. Company to expend, as non-recoupable expense, exclusive of in-house services, not less than $75,000 as promotional and advertising budget for each album released hereunder.

29. Parties agree to cooperate with each other in the formation of a more comprehensive agreement which shall supercede this agreement. Until such supersedure, this writing forms the entire agreement between the parties, and is binding on them and their respective trustees, successors, representatives, heirs, and assigns.

AGREED ____________, 20___, at Los Angeles, California, by and between:

Company: ____________________ Artist: ____________________

____________________ ____________________

Address: ____________________ Address: ____________________

____________________ ____________________

Tax I.D. ____________________ Tax I.D. ____________________

and Artist: ____________________

____

Address: ____________________

____

Tax I.D. ____________________

Page 3 of 3

The foregoing sample approaches the next stage in the contract process; the so-called "short form" contract. As noted earlier, such "short forms" often take the form of a lengthy business letter from the label to the artist, can often be *twenty or more pages*, and are often the only formal contract which ever gets signed. Eventually, however, the label is likely to send a "long form" agreement to supersede the "short form." Long forms can run to seventy or more pages, and should be read carefully, as they supersede the short form, and have been known to contain terms and conditions contradictory to those of the short form.[180]

Blame Your Lawyer... Even If You Don't Have One

If you don't have a lawyer representing you in the negotiations and drafting, be firm in refusing to sign *anything* until you have had a chance to have it reviewed by your own attorney. No reputable company will object. Be particularly wary if the proposed agreement states that you've been given ample opportunity to consult with an attorney before signing... especially if you *haven't*.

Feel free to make your attorney the bad guy at this point. Tell them, "My attorney said he'd [hit me / break my legs / poison my dog] if I signed anything without him seeing it first." Say this even if you don't *have* an attorney yet, then run out and get one. Having a proposed contract in hand will open most attorneys' doors for you. But, as we've said before, you're better off having a qualified attorney with you throughout the negotiation and drafting process.

The foregoing three-page sample deal memo is about as elaborate and lengthy as such memos ever get. One or two page memos are more common, and four page (or longer) memos are unusual. It may take months (or more) for even a "short form" contract to be completed... and the "long form" frequently never gets finished at all. Unless and until there is a superseding agreement, the deal memo — sometimes called an "interim contract" — will be all there is to memorialize the parties' agreement and to protect their respective rights.

Occasionally, negotiations may result in a semi binding quasi-agreement, called an **agreement in principle**. Usually, this means that the parties have been able to reach an accord on most of the key points of a deal, but that certain other critical items remain unresolved. Essentially, an agreement in principle only commits the parties to continue or resume their negotiations, and to forbear entering into a conflicting agreement with others without first notifying the other party. Sometimes, a "first refusal," may be included, permitting a party to match someone else's bonafide competing offer rather than abandon the potential deal.

---

180 Without naming names, a major label recently sent a long form for a major artist's multiple-album deal, nearly a year after the final album under that deal had been released. The proposed long form contained entirely new provisions, including a changed royalty structure for future payments on previously released albums. It took six hours to analyze the proposed long form and compare it with the short form agreement, after which it was sent back to the label, ***unsigned*** and with the word ***"N O !"*** scrawled across the signature page. The short form therefore remains the only operative agreement between that artist and label.

Basic Negotiation Strategies

Here are some key points to remember in negotiating any contract:

- **Know the relevant deal points for the type of contract you'll be negotiating.** Do some research, talk to colleagues and friends, talk to your *lawyer*, and make a comprehensive list of "bullet points" that covers every issue you can think of that should be addressed in the agreement.

- **Know what you want.** Once you know what the deal points are, decide on what specific terms you want in respect to each of those points. Find out (if you can) what terms others have been able to obtain in recent, similar agreements. This will essentially be your "wish list" of ideal terms, not a set of intractable demands. (And leave *lots* of blank space in between the items on your list, for notes. Having only one or two points per page is ideal.) **Only put your "wish list" numbers — and *never* your "bottom line" numbers — in a written form which the other side might somehow get a chance to see during the negotiations!**[181]

- **Know your walkaway point.** Before negotiations, decide on realistic, minimum or maximum requirements for critical deal points. Be prepared to terminate negotiations — or to postpone that issue and address others — if the other side can't or won't meet your requirements. If you're being represented by counsel in the negotiations, go over these carefully, in advance, to be certain that he or she understands where your "wiggle room" ends.

- **Let the other side commit to a number first.** Raise individual issues from your list of deal points, but try to get the other side to state their *numbers* before you state yours. In this context, "numbers" can be an amount of money, a percentage rate, a period of time, a specific date, or a quantity. Remember, once a number has been stated by the other side, it can likely change only in your favor, if at all.

- **Calculate the penny rate.** In the music industry especially, many critical numbers being negotiated will be expressed as percentages. Be prepared to calculate what those percentages represent in dollars-and-cents terms, and to discuss those calculations as part of the negotiations. Ultimately, the *net* penny rate — after all other contract deductions have been factored in — is the only meaningful representation of the monetary consideration being offered, and the only means of estimating the sales figures which will be necessary to achieve recoupment.

---

181 Never assume that the other side won't take the opportunity to peek at anything you've left behind if you're out of the room. Make certain that your notes disclose nothing that would give the other side an advantage in negotiations. This can be turned to your advantage in some situations if, for example, you "inadvertently" allow the other side to see a "walkaway" number which is *really* your ideal optimum.

- **Be prepared to give something up.** Keep one or more demands on the table that you don't really care that much about. If and when necessary, you can — oh, so reluctantly — give up one or more of those demands in exchange for the other side's concession on an issue you really *do* care about. You can even be magnanimous and use them as "giveaways" to obtain the other side's goodwill, *provided* they believe that the issue you're conceding was important to you.

- **Recognize the other side's legitimate needs.** Remember that the other side probably has a list just like this one. The negotiations will only work if each side can get something *valuable to their side* out of a contract. Determine what they really need to get out of the deal, and be willing to give it to them, if you can do so without critically damaging your own needs.

- **Take notes, and keep your notes.** Whenever there is agreement on a particular point on your list, make a clear note of that fact in the blank space you've left for that purpose on your "wish list." Do the same if there is an irreducible disagreement on a point, noting each side's position. Some of these latter disagreements may be resolved, or the parties' positions may alter somewhat, at which point make a new note, below the old one. Draw a single line through the old note, but don't obliterate it. It can also be helpful to write the date and time for each such note, as well as who said what (if there are a number of people involved in the negotiations.) Retaining your notes can be of inestimable value to you, later, for a number of reasons.

- **Be prepared to *really* walk away.** If you've been honest with yourself in creating realistic "walkaway" numbers, then stick to them. You're far better off taking a pass than you would be by agreeing to a deal you can't live with. An *authentic* willingness to walk away can often be the turning point in obtaining concessions from the other side (although there may be a few intervening days of anxiety before negotiations resume), but don't walk out simply as a pose or a tactic. If the other side can't or won't meet your absolute requirements, and you can't or won't meet theirs, then the deal probably shouldn't be made. (And remember, "requirements" does not mean your hopes, dreams, wants, or desires. It refers to your "walkaway" points.)

- **Let your lawyer be the "bad guy."** It's part of what lawyers get paid for. If your attorney is with you in the negotiations, let him or her be the unreasonable one. If the deal works out, you'll be working with these people in the future, so why have them think that it's you (rather than your attorney) who's an obtuse, intransigent, demanding jerk. If for some reason you're negotiating without counsel present, you can still make him or her the scapegoat. "My lawyer told me that I have to …" And, of course, your absent (and perhaps not-yet-hired) attorney has threatened you with grievous bodily harm if you even consider signing something he hasn't seen yet.

- **Let the other side do the drafting.** First, why should you be the one paying counsel for a first draft? (You'll be paying enough for your lawyer to review and revise the other side's drafts.) Second, there's a legal doctrine which construes ambiguities against the drafter, so there's a slight advantage if the contract has to be judicially interpreted later. Once you've received the other side's draft, compare it to your negotiation notes. If your notes indicate that something was agreed to, and you can't find it in the draft, call the other side (or have your attorney call), remind them (from your notes) exactly what was agreed, and ask where it is in the draft. If it's not there, or isn't clear, ask them to insert or clarify it in a redraft. Repeat this process until the final draft contains everything you agreed to, and nothing that you didn't. (And you still want to keep your notes from the negotiations, even after the final contract has been approved and signed.)[182]

No matter what type of contract you're negotiating, following these steps will prove invaluable in developing contract terms and conditions that meet your needs. Contract negotiations can be risky if you're unprepared, or if you're eager to make a deal on any terms. On the other hand, if you've done your homework and are willing to abandon a prospective deal that doesn't meet your objective minimum requirements, contract negotiations can be a lot of fun... a bit like playing poker, but with potential millions on the table. (If large sums make you anxious, just pretend it's play money and concentrate on the game for its own sake.) And above all, ***listen to your lawyer.*** You may not always *take* his or her advice, but you're paying for it anyway, so at least consider it before deciding to rely on your own better judgment.

182 If you're wondering why, it's because disputes sometimes arise in even the best of contractual relationships. Having concise, contemporaneous notes can sometimes make all the difference in resolving a dispute informally, or they can lend credibility to your testimony if the dispute escalates into arbitration or litigation. Also, if and when a "long form" contract is eventually proffered, it's useful to have a record of what was agreed to (and what was rejected) in negotiations, to be certain that the proposed superceding contract actually conforms to the agreements reached.

CHAPTER 7

WHAT IF …?

CONVERTING DEAL POINTS INTO CONTRACTS

Once the parties have reached a "meeting of minds" on the salient points of their agreement, the conversion of those terms into a formal contract can begin. But a well crafted contract needs to not only memorialize those key points of agreement; it should also recognize the likelihood that not everything will go exactly as expected, and make provisions for those eventualities. Unforeseen events, altered circumstances, unrealized expectations, or thwarted intentions can drastically alter the relationship between contracting parties, and their contract should take that possibility into account.

To minimize the detrimental effect of unwanted changes in circumstances, the contract should include provisions for as many of them as can be reasonably foreseen by asking and answering hypothetical, "What If?" questions. For example,

- What if the delivery is delayed?
- What if one party isn't satisfied with what's been delivered?
- What if a third party sues one of the contracting parties?
- What if a contract payment isn't made on time?
- What if artistic differences arise?
- What if it becomes impossible for one of the parties to perform?
- What if one of the parties *refuses* to perform?
- What if lightning strikes?

Tailoring such speculative questions to the particular contract under consideration, and determining answers which are acceptable to the negotiating parties, will likely lead to other, related questions which should also be addressed in the contract. Remember, there are no "right" answers to any of them; merely answers which are acceptable to the parties… provided that those answers conform to law and public policy. Not every conceivable contingency can be anticipated, but dealing with the most obvious of them when drafting the contract can avoid potential future disputes.

Another source for these types of drafting considerations is looking at recent disputes and relevant court decisions relating to similar contracts. Could the controversies in those cases have been avoided by including, excluding, or modifying something in an underlying agreement? The law is constantly evolving, and what was "good" contract language when drafted could, through legislation or a subsequent court opinion (in someone else's lawsuit), suddenly become questionable, unenforceable, unconscionable, or voidable. One of the things that lawyers do (or should do) is keep themselves regularly apprised of such changes in the law, especially in their own areas of practice. For the music industry — particularly in light of the still-evolving body of intellectual property law relating to the internet and the DMCA — significant changes and judicial pronouncements can be expected to continue for a number of years, as courts and legislatures around the world fine-tune the law as it relates to these areas.

Many possible answers to these "What if...?" questions appear in Chapter 10 ("Sample Clauses and Provisions"), but there is no way to determine if all of the necessary questions have been asked and answered. Only the contracting parties, familiar with their own peculiar intentions, needs, and circumstances, can do that. Most importantly, they should do it as early in the contract formation process as possible, since consideration of these types of questions is intended to address possible issues and potential disagreements *before* they can materialize. Sometimes this process can actually kill a deal before it begins, but it's likely that such agreements were effectively doomed from the outset if a reasonable consideration of foreseeable circumstances causes either party to withdraw.

The best example of this situation arises in the area of pre-marital agreements. Two people, presumably in love with each other, committed to spending their lives together, try to formulate an agreement which will treat each of them fairly in respect to their individual rights and obligations during their marriage and, more critically, in the (presumably unlikely, but statistically likely) event that the marriage fails. If an ostensibly-loving couple can't agree on fair answers to those "What if?" questions, they probably shouldn't be married to each other in the first place. On the other hand, it is most likely that only at the outset will affection and commitment override selfish interests sufficiently to allow formation of an equitable arrangement addressing those questions. (Agree on what's fair *before* the deal is done. You probably won't get another chance.)[183]

During negotiations and drafting, when each party wants something from the other, is the best time — perhaps the only time — when the parties can and will approach these questions with a maximum of equanimity. Although re-negotiation of an existing contract is not unusual in the entertainment business, it is generally a costly and painful process, often involving accusations and recriminations which are, at best, unpleasant.[184]

---

183 A brief digression here on the subject of premarital agreements. Anyone in the music business contemplating marriage should have one, and it should particularly address intellectual property and publishing issues. Royalties received during marriage are normally community property (in community property states), but what about new works created during the term of a marriage? Which spouse will own those copyrights, and the royalties derived from them, if the marriage is dissolved? Far better to make that determination in a prenuptial agreement, rather than leaving it to a divorce court's discretion.

184 With a bit of creative negotiating and drafting skill, a contract provision can be included to set certain financial performance standards which, when achieved, trigger an automatic increase in royalties and/or provide for renegotiation of the agreement.

It's Far Easier to Avoid Trouble Than to Get Out of Trouble

In posing the relevant "What if…?" questions, there may be a tendency for the other party to respond, "*That* would never happen!" or to treat the inquiry as a personal affront: "Are you suggesting that we would…" Point out that you have no doubts about the other side's honesty/integrity/good intentions… but that the contract is intended to anticipate all reasonable possibilities, many of which are outside the control of either party, and the contract could conceivably pass to a successor about whom you know nothing, or performance might become dependent on the conduct of others over whom the parties have no control. Also, the proposed contract provisions are aimed only at what *might* happen, not at what you *expect* to happen… if you expected such occurrences you wouldn't be entering into a contract with them in the first place. Finally, these are merely *provisions*… without any force or effect unless and until a contemplated and unlikely event actually occurs.[185]

Once you've identified all of the additional issues which should be addressed by such provisions, and agreed on a protocol for how each will be handled, the contract drafting process can truly begin.

Creating a Contract Outline

If you've completed a deal memo, it can usually be expanded into a formal first-draft contract. If not, start with your negotiation notes, determining each salient deal point and the agreement reached as to that point. Begin with an outline, grouping the deal points into a logical and consistent arrangement which will make sense to someone reading it for the first time. Here is a typical outline:

- Title of Contract
- Date of Agreement
- Names and capacities of parties
- Recitals (general scope, intention, and background facts.)
- Term
- Specific obligations & consideration of first party (multiple sections)
- Specific obligations & consideration of second party (multiple sections)
- Grants of rights
- Exclusions and limitations
- "Housekeeping" (Accounting, reporting, notice requirements, etc.)
- Provisions and remedies

185 If they continue to balk at inclusion of certain provisions, recall Shakespeare's observation: "The lady doth protest too much, methinks." (Hamlet, Act III, Sc. II)

- "Boilerplate" (Choice of law/forum, dispute resolution, attorney's fees, integration, novation/supersedure, heirs and assigns, advice of counsel, *etc.*)
- Definitions of special words and phrases (if not integrated or included earlier.)
- Signature lines (including name, capacity, date, and location.)
- Counsels' countersignature lines (as to form, or as to form and content.)

Keep reviewing your original checklist while preparing your outline, to be certain that you haven't omitted anything. It's a good practice to add the contract paragraph numbers as a marginal notation to your original checklist, so that you know *where* in the contract each deal point has been covered.

Contract Organization

This is another of those areas of practice in which there's no "right" way to do it, and a number of equally effective styles may be used. The key, however, is consistency, since use of multiple styles within a single contract may create an *impression* of ambiguity, even where the actual language of the contract is unambiguous. The touchstone for all contract organization and drafting is to consider a hypothetical stranger, years in the future, being able to peruse the contract, readily determine the parties's intentions, and locate all of the salient terms and conditions of the agreement with relative ease.

A well organized contract goes a long way toward satisfying that test.

Following are examples of four common styles of contract organization:

Style 1. (Letter Format)

Identity of First Party **(Letterhead)**	[Party 1] [Address] [City, State Zip Code] [Phone Number] / [Fax Number]
Date of Agreement	[Date]
Identity of Second Party	[Party Two] [Address] [City, State Zip Code]
Recitals:	Dear [Party Two]: This letter, when signed by you, will constitute the entire agreement between us with respect to [scope of agreement], as follows:
Text of Agreement:	1. [First clause or provision] a. [or (a.)] [Optional subparts of first clause or provision] b. [or (b.)] [Optional subparts of first clause or provision] 2. [Second clause or provision] a. [or (a.)] [Optional subparts of second clause or provision] 3. [Third clause or provision] *Etc...*
Closing:	Very truly yours, [Authorized Signatory / Party 1]
Acceptance:	AGREED AND ACCEPTED: Date: ___________ ____________________________ [Party 2]

Style 2. (Simple, short agreements)

Title of document.	"_______ Agreement"
Names of parties.	"By and between [Party 1] and [Party 2], who [or which] agree as follows:"
Recitals: [optional]	"WHEREAS, [underlying fact, circumstance, or intention]; and "WHEREAS, [underlying fact, circumstance, or intention]; and *Etc...* WHEREFORE the parties agree as follows:
Text of Agreement:	1. [First clause or provision] a. [or (a.)] [Optional subparts of first clause or provision] b. [or (b.)] [Optional subparts of first clause or provision] 2. [Second clause or provision] a. [or (a.)] [Optional subparts of second clause or provision] 3. [Third clause or provision] *Etc...*
Closing:	Executed at [City or County], [State], on [Date]
Signatures:	(Include capacity in which parties are signing.)

Style 3. (Longer agreements)

Title of document.	"_______ Agreement"
Names of parties.	"By and between [Party 1] (hereinafter "Party 1")and [Party 2] (hereinafter "Party 2"), as follows:"
Recitals: [optional]	"WHEREAS, [underlying fact, circumstance, or intention]; and "WHEREAS, [underlying fact, circumstance, or intention]; and *Etc...* WHEREFORE the parties agree as follows:
Text of Agreement:	A. [or I.] [TITLE OF FIRST SECTION] 1. [First clause or provision of first section.] a. [or (a.)] [Optional subparts of first clause or provision of first section] i. [Optional] ii. [Optional] 2. [Second clause or provision of first section.] *Etc....* B. [or II.] [TITLE OF SECOND SECTION] 1. [First clause or provision of second section.] a. [or (a.)] [Optional subparts of first clause or provision of second section] 2. [Second clause or provision of second section.] *Etc...*
Closing:	Executed this [day] day of [month], [year], at [City or County], [State] by and between,
Signatures:	(Include capacity in which parties are signing.) (If countersigned by counsel, indicate whether their approval is "as to form" or "as to form and content.")

Style 4. (Long or more technical agreements)

Title of document.	"________ Agreement"
Names of parties.	"By and between [Party 1] (hereinafter "Party 1")and [Party 2] (hereinafter "Party 2"), as follows:"
Recitals: [optional]	"WHEREAS, [underlying fact, circumstance, or intention]; and "WHEREAS, [underlying fact, circumstance, or intention]; and *Etc...* NOW, THEREFORE, the parties hereby agree as follows:
Text of Agreement:	1. [TITLE OF FIRST SECTION] 1.1 [First clause or provision of first section.] 1.1.1 [Optional subparts of first clause or provision of first section] 1.1.1.1 [Optional] 1.1.1.2 [Optional] 1.2 [Second clause or provision of first section.] 1.2.1 [Optional subparts of first clause or provision of first section] 1.2.1.1 [Optional] 1.2.1.2 [Optional] *Etc....* 2. [TITLE OF SECOND SECTION] 2.1 [First clause or provision of second section.] 2.1.1 [Optional subparts of first clause or provision of second section] 2.2 [Second clause or provision of second section.] *Etc....*
Closing:	Executed this [day] day of [month], [year], at [City or County], [State] by and between,
Signatures:	(Include capacity in which parties are signing.) (If countersigned by counsel, indicate whether their approval is "as to form" or "as to form and content.")

There are countless variations of the foregoing styles of contract organization, but the intention and effect should always be *clarity*. Some contracts can run into hundreds of pages, so the organizational method used should allow for quick identification and location of particular clauses or provisions, without having to search through the entire document each time. Particularly long contracts may even have a table of contents and/or an index to aid in locating particular provisions within them. Inclusion of **boldface** captions to designate sections and subsections is also helpful for this purpose, but when captions, tables of contents, or indices are used, a construction clause should state that these are for convenience only and are not material terms of the agreement.

Basic Drafting Considerations

In preparing or reviewing a draft contract, consider the following:

- Contract language should be clear and specific.
- Sentences should be short and non-complex, to avoid confusion and potential ambiguities.
- Be certain that the names and capacities of the parties are accurate.
- Use recitals to state the basic intention and common understandings of the parties in forming the contract.
- Define all special terms clearly, and use those defined terms consistently (using ALL CAPITALS, *or* Leading Capitals, *or* other distinctive method) throughout the agreement. Whichever method you choose to identify defined terms, use only <u>one</u> such method, and do not alter it.
- Use a logical numbering or outline format to distinguish and identify paragraphs and sections. Keep related clauses and provisions together or in consecutive paragraphs or sections. Captions are optional, but will aid in clarity. (However, if you use captions, include a construction disclaimer which makes clear that the captions themselves are not material terms of the contract.) **Boldface** captions can be particularly helpful to quickly locate particular provisions. For longer contracts, consider including a table of contents.
- If a paragraph is deleted from an earlier draft, and you don't want to renumber all of the subsequent paragraphs (usually because some sections may contain internal references to certain paragraph numbers, all of which would need to be located and changed) then leave the deleted paragraph <u>number</u> in place, followed by the words, "INTENTIONALLY OMITTED."

- Avoid blank space. Use slash marks ("///") at the left margin to indicate that blank lines are intentionally blank, or draw a diagonal line or "X" through the blank portion of the page.
- Anticipate potential disputes by including choice of law and forum and attorney's fees provisions. If there is to be a mediation or arbitration provision, consider including a space in the margin for each party to initial at that section, to indicate express acceptance of that provision.
- Establish what constitutes "notice" by one party to another, and include mailing addresses, telephone numbers, fax numbers, email addresses or such other delivery information as may be necessary to perfect notice by the prescribed method. State when and how notice will be deemed "delivered."
- All parties should sign the contract. If they are signing in some particular capacity, that should be expressly indicated at their signature line. If they are signing in more than one capacity (*e.g.*, as an individual, and as an officer of a corporation), then there should be multiple signature lines for them - one for each capacity in which they are signing.
- If the parties will be signing in different geographic locations using counterparts (*i.e.*, with each party signing a different copy of the same document) make certain to include language indicating that executed counterparts are deemed integrated as a single document, and that facsimile signatures (*i.e.*, faxed signature pages) or other electronically transmitted signatures, are deemed to be original signatures.
- Pages should be numbered, and the total number of pages indicated on each page (*e.g.*, "Page 3 of 7" rather than simply "3.") For critical contracts, consider having each signing party initial each page, as well.
- Each page of each *version* of a contract draft should be numbered or marked and dated (*E.g.*, "First Draft," "Fourth Draft, 1/17/07" "Rev. 5," "5/23/07 Draft," *etc.*) to avoid possible confusion or commingling of pages from one draft with those from another.
- Keep copies of interim drafts, particularly those with notes written on them. Correspondence relating to contract changes should also be kept.
- Go back over your original checklist and negotiation notes one last time, to be certain that everything is included as agreed, and that nothing has been omitted. Add the contract paragraph or section numbers to your notes or checklist, to verify and cross-reference the inclusion of each agreed point in the final contract.
- Proofread carefully. (If possible, wait a day or more between completing a draft and proofreading it.)

◆ ◆ ◆

Congratulations! You now have a finished contract document, ready to be signed. All that's left to do after that is to faithfully perform all of your obligations under its terms... while hoping that the other side will do the same.

CHAPTER 8

DRAFTING CONTRACTS;

THINGS TO INCLUDE, AND THINGS TO AVOID

Clauses are the fundamental terms and conditions of a contract from its inception. *Provisions* are most commonly designed to provide answers to the "What if…?" questions, and can often be identified by their inclusion of the conditional predicate phrase, "In the event…" or the words "if" or "should." "Clauses" are the absolute conditions of agreement, while "provisions" are conditional terms of that agreement which only come into effect if occasioned by some specified occurrence.

As a practical matter, this distinction between the two words — "clause" and "provision" — has no meaning in modern practice. The words "clause" and "provision" are regularly used interchangeably, since separation of the two concepts is often impossible in the real world, where they often merge with each other in the drafting process. For example, a "right to audit" would be an absolute, bargained for condition of agreement; a clause. However, the results of that audit may trigger specified remedies or adjustments, which are provisional. It is possible to separate the two elements into distinct paragraphs or sections, but practicality and a desire for clarity in contracts suggest that the better practice would be to merge both the clause and the provision into a single section (usually the same section which sets forth the "accounting" clause) of the contract. Since the overarching goals of contract drafting include simplicity and clarity, related concepts should be kept together wherever possible. This not only makes the agreement easier to read and understand, but also minimizes potential ambiguities. Nonetheless, an appreciation of the technical distinction between absolute and provisional contract terms can prove helpful in contract negotiations and in the drafting process.

Also, certain phrases simply seem to flow more comfortably off the tongue, so it is common to speak of an "attorney's fees *clause*," even though it is a purely provisional part of the contract, and to refer to an "advance *provision*," despite the fact that advances are an absolute condition of the contract — a clause. It makes no difference if something is *called* a clause rather than a provision, or *vice versa*, provided that the parties understand that some parts of the contract are absolute terms, while others are provisional conditions which become effective only in the event of some occurrence or non-occurrence.

Regardless of what you call them, some contract language is meant to be effective throughout the term, or even to survive the term. Other contract language is only intended to address speculative contingencies which *might* occur. To put it another way, *provisions* don't matter until they matter… and then they *matter!*

In the following chapters, several specific categories of contract clauses and provisions are discussed and analyzed, with alternative versions given for most of them. Once again, there is no "right" version of any of them. Take the version that comes closest to approximating your needs, and modify it until it says precisely what the parties actually intend to agree to. (And, if you're not a lawyer yourself, have an attorney do these modifications, or — at the very least — have an experienced music attorney review it afterwards, to be certain that your changes haven't introduced a violation of law or public policy.)

A Few Simple Rules

In editing or creating contract language, here are a few guidelines to keep in mind:

- Eschew obfuscation.[186]
- Avoid "lawyer" words (unless you're a lawyer, and mostly even then.)
- Say what you mean to say — don't just come close.
- Define your special terms carefully, and then use them consistently.
- Verify that everything negotiated and agreed to has been included.
- Do not include anything *which has not been negotiated and agreed upon.*
- Check your spelling.
- Check your punctuation.[187]
- Use a consistent, logical system for numbering sections and subsections, with related matters in the same or successive sections.
- Proofread your work — or, better yet, have someone else proofread it first, and then proofread it yourself.

The Dangers of Colloquialisms

One question we hear frequently is, "Why do lawyers use so many 'old' words in contracts? Why not just use everyday words that everyone understands?"

Contrary to popular opinion, archaic words aren't used to cause confusion, but rather to *avoid* confusion. *The meaning of these words and phrases are unlikely to change over time!*

---

186 Avoid obscure words and phrases.

187 In the 1916 British case of Sir Roger Casement, the defense hinged on the presence or absence of a comma in the Treason Act. An original parchment draft of that Act (written in 1351) was located and examined. It had no comma. Casement was convicted and hanged.

There's an inherent danger in using common, colloquial expressions from a modern, living language in contracts. Commonly used words and expressions can change their meaning, seemingly overnight, and may even assume a temporary meaning which is antithetical to prior or subsequent "dictionary" meanings. By way of example, there was a decade-long period when the word "bad" was commonly used to mean "good" in colloquial speech. Imagine a contract which required the Artist to deliver "ten bad master recordings." Pity the poor judge who, twenty years later, must decipher the parties' intention.

This does not mean that contract language should be limited to Latin or to the Elizabethan English of Shakespeare, but only that colloquial uses should be avoided unless specially defined within the contract itself.[188] When in doubt, use a dictionary to determine the accepted definition before using a word. If necessary, the contract can even include a reference to the particular dictionary used for that purpose in its construction clause, although only hyper-technical agreements commonly resort to such inclusion. The law presumes that, unless the contract specifies otherwise, words will be interpreted according to their commonly-understood meanings, and it is not unusual for judges to consult a standard dictionary and to base a legal decision upon the definition which it provides.

"Magic" Words

> *Whilst counselors at law, with a predilection for verbosity and verbiage, may, as scriveners, inculcate their tomes with a plethora of polysyllabic circumlocutions of dubious provenance, meaningless to the theretofore uninitiated absent a concordance, irrespective of erudition or wit, such stylistic obfuscation ought be abated, forthwith and ab initio.*

The foregoing sentence actually makes sense… if you're a lawyer or scholar. Here's what it says in English:

> Lawyers have a tendency to talk too much and use too many words when they write. They may include lots of long words which obscure their actual meanings. This makes it hard for non-lawyers to understand without a specialized legal dictionary, even if they're intelligent and well-educated. Lawyers should stop it, right now, and they should never have started doing it in the first place.

There, now. Isn't that better?

188 As we've noted elsewhere, contracting parties can invent whatever meaning they want for words, provided that agreed-upon, unambiguous definitions are included in the contract. If the contract says "The word BLACK, as used herein, shall mean and refer to that color which is commonly, usually, and generally referred to as 'white.'" … then BLACK ***is*** white, so far as that contract is concerned.

◆ ◆ ◆

We began our Introduction with a quotation which states, in part:

> "If you don't understand it, and the laws under which it will be executed, then don't sign it!"

As a corollary to that rule,

> "If you don't understand it..., don't ***write*** it!"

◆ ◆ ◆

Many specialized legal words can be avoided in writing contracts. Non-lawyers (and some lawyers) include such words in an apparent attempt to have their drafts appear professional and "lawyerly." The problem is that certain words and phrases have a distinct legal meaning and effect. Using them carelessly in a contract, without a thorough grasp of their legal implications, can have catastrophic results. On the other hand, some of those words can hardly be avoided, since they *can* reduce complex legal concepts into a single word or phrase. For example, which of the following is easier to read and understand?

(A) Studio shall have a *pro tanto* lien against Masters recorded hereunder.

-or-

(B) Studio shall have a specialized quasi-ownership interest in master recordings recorded under the terms and conditions of this agreement, which interest shall be based upon Studio's expenditures and efforts in creating those recordings, and which interest will give Studio the right, but not the obligation, to retain possession of the master recordings, and a right to offer them for sale to others, but without warranty of any ancillary right, and Studio's interest and rights in respect to those masters shall remain in force and effect, for the benefit of Studio, only until Studio receives payment in full for its work on the masters, and payment of less than the full amount due shall only reduce Studio's claim in proportion to the amount paid as compared to the original amount owing.

Both of the foregoing sentences have identical meanings. Of course, to use the shorter form, you need to understand what "*pro tanto*" and "lien" mean. Additionally, there are also common, ordinary words which have particular legal meanings when used in contracts. It's perfectly acceptable to use these legally-fraught words *provided* the parties understand their specialized meanings and legal ramifications. If you're uncertain, try to avoid them.

Here's a list of a few of those words and phrases to be particularly aware of:

ab initio
abandon
accommodate / accommodation
acknowledge
agent / agency
agree
attest
aver
bar
bind / binding
certify / certification
cloud / clouded / unclouded
common
conditional / unconditional
condition
    condition precedent /
    condition concurrent /
    condition subsequent
consent / mutual consent
covenant
customary
customary usage
customary practice
deliver
discretion / discretionary
essence
estopped / estoppel
exclusive / non-exclusive / excluding
forbear / forbearance
forthwith
grant
guaranty / guarantee / guarantor
harmless
inclusive / including
joint / several / joint and several
license
lien
limitation / without limitation /
    not limited to
liquidate / liquidated / unliquidated
material / not material (or nonmaterial)
normal
novate / novation / supercede
prejudice / without prejudice
quiet
quit / quitclaim
reasonable / reasonably
recourse / non-recourse / without recourse
release
rely / reliance / reliable
remit / remise
represent / representation
reserve / reservation / without reservation
revert / reversion
revocable / irrevocable
satisfy / satisfaction / satisfactory
sole
subscribe / subscribed / subscription
waive / waiver
warrant / warranty

The foregoing list is far from complete. There are hundreds of such words and phrases which have a legal meaning which may differ substantially from what those same words may mean in everyday speech. Specialized legal dictionaries can provide accurate definitions, and there's nothing *wrong* with including such words in a contract, *if* they are being used correctly and *if* the parties understand precisely what those words mean in their legal context. If a word is unfamiliar, or if a familiar word seems to be used strangely, then either change it to something that makes sense to the parties, or verify the parties' common understanding of its legal meaning and effect before signing the contract.

Common Words Fraught With Meaning

The more common and familiar a word is, the easier it will be to overlook its legal implications. The principal culprits in this category are:

a, any	(non specific, as distinguished from "the," "that," or "said.")
and	(elements both before and after the word are mandatory)
or	(elements before and after the word are mutually exclusive of each other)
and/or	(at least one of the elements is mandatory, but not exclusive, with the remainder being optional)
may, can	(conduct is optional)
shall, will, must	(conduct is mandatory)
the, that, said	(specific, as distinguished from "a" or "any.")

Useful Archaisms

Another category is that of words unlikely to be encountered other than in lawyers' speech or writings. Words which lawyers employ regularly, but which faded from common usage centuries ago, include: *henceforth, hereinafter, heretofore, hereinabove, forthwith, infra, supra, whereas, wherefore* (and *wherefor)*. Such archaisms actually have simple meanings, and they can be useful in navigating legal documents. Here's what lawyers mean when they use these types of words:

aforesaid	Mentioned earlier.
forthwith	Immediately. At once.
henceforth	From this moment forward in time. From now on.
herein	Within this document; within these proceedings.
hereinabove	At some earlier point in this particular document.
hereinafter	From this point forward within this particular document or proceeding.
hereinbelow	At some later point in this particular document.
heretofore	Before now; up until now; prior to this point in time.
infra	As some point later in this document. Below.
instant	This specific document, matter, pleading, or proceeding which is currently under consideration.
notwithstanding	Despite something else which may appear to be to the contrary.
supra	At some point earlier in this document. Above.

thence From that place; from there -or- from that circumstance or source.

thenceforth From a specified moment forward in time. From then on.

therefor For that purpose.

therefore For that reason.

thereon Upon this, that, or it.

theretofore Prior to a certain date, time or occurrence.

thereupon Concerning some particular matter -or- immediately following or concurrently with some occurrence.

whence From where or from which. From what place. From what origin or source.

whereas Because.

wherefor For which purpose.

wherefore For which reason.

whereupon At which time -or- at the time of which occurrence.

within In this transaction; in this proceeding.

◆ ◆ ◆

The point of all this is that there are words to use, and words to avoid… and the latter category should include any word which you don't fully comprehend in its legal application. The "magic" here is not supernatural, but misuse of certain words can have a potential for catastrophe beyond anything a sorcerer's apprentice might inadvertently invoke.

The touchstones of contract writing are *clarity* and *completeness*. Can a hypothetical stranger, having no information beyond what appears within the four corners of the contract, immediately grasp both the intention of the parties and all of the facts necessary to a complete understanding of their agreement? If the answer to that question is "No," then the draft language should be augmented or clarified until it can pass that test.

The following chapters contain detailed discussions and alternative language for many clauses and provisions which may appear in contracts. Most of them will contain a some of the "magic" words discussed above. Be certain you fully understand all of their legal implications before attempting to use or adapt any of them.

CHAPTER 9

COVERING THE ESSENTIAL ELEMENTS

In the chapter on contract basics, we discussed the five elements which are essential to a valid contract. For reference, those essential elements are:

1. Two or more **Competent Parties**;
2. Describable **Subject Matter**;
3. Legal **Consideration**;
4. Mutual Agreement or a "**meeting of minds**"; and
5. Mutuality of **Obligation**

There are a number of common contract clauses in which those indispensable requirements may appear, but each and every one of them needs to be included *somewhere* in the contract, either expressly or by unambiguous, clear implication.

1. Two or More Competent Parties

At the very beginning of the contract, the names of the contracting parties should be stated with sufficient specificity to prevent any dispute as to the actual identity of any party. Their respective *capacities* and *domicile* should also be recited. For example,

> "… QQQQ Records, a Delaware corporation…"
>
> "…John Jones, an individual resident of Nevada…"
>
> "…William Preston and Theodore Logan, individually and as a California general partnership p/k/a[189] 'Wyld Stallyns'…"
>
> "…Happi Toones LLC, a New Jersey limited liability company, f/s/o[190] Janet Smith…"

It is not unusual to have a contract section actually captioned "Parties," which fully identifies the contracting parties. The parties' names and capacities should also appear at the signature page. In the remainder of the contract, however, the common practice is to assign

---

189 "Professionally known as."

190 "Furnishing services of." The acronym "p/s/o" ("providing services of") is also sometimes used. These acronyms are generally only seen in "loan out" agreements.

a defined term which will be used throughout the contract to refer to the parties in a more convenient and comprehensible manner. Expanding upon the above examples, such definitions would appear as follow:

> "... QQQQ Records, a Delaware corporation (hereinafter 'Company')..."

> "...John Jones, an individual resident of Nevada (hereinafter 'Artist')..."

> "...William Preston (hereinafter 'Preston') and Theodore Logan (hereinafter 'Logan'), individually and as a California general partnership p/k/a 'Wyld Stallyns' (hereinafter collectively and severally referred to as 'Artist')... "

> "...Happi Toones LLC, a New Jersey limited liability company f/s/o Janet Smith (hereinafter 'Artist')..."[191]

Although the defined terms "Company" and "Artist" are commonly used throughout entertainment industry contracts — and throughout this book — such terms are defined by each individual contract. Once again using the above examples, here are some alternatives:

> "... QQQQ Records, a Delaware corporation (hereinafter 'QQQQ')..."

> "...John Jones, an individual resident of Nevada (hereinafter 'Jones')..."

> "...William Preston (hereinafter 'BILL') and Theodore Logan (hereinafter 'TED'), individually and as a California general partnership, p/k/a 'Wyld Stallyns' (hereinafter collectively and severally referred to as the 'BAND')..."

> "...Happi Toones LLC, a New Jersey limited liability company (hereinafter 'Loan-Out') f/s/o Janet Smith (hereinafter 'Artist')..."

There is no prohibition against using such alternative definitions in a contract. The only caveat is that, once defined, the defined term should be used consistently throughout the agreement thereafter. What is essential is that the parties bound by the contract be unambiguously identified within the contract. This often goes beyond merely identifying the persons signing the original contract, since others may also become bound by the contract's terms. Clauses and provisions which can affect the identity of parties bound by the contract may include, but are not limited to, the following:

- Assignability Provision
- Buyout or Buy-Sell Provision
- Heirs and Assigns Clause
- Leaving Member Provision
- Side Letter / Inducement Letter

---

191 Note, however, that "Artist" here refers to the loan out company, not to the individual "artist," who is not personally a party to the contract and not bound by its terms. (But see, "side letter," *infra.*)

- Termination Provision

2. Describable Subject Matter

The subject matter of a contract must relate to some thing or purpose which can be described with reasonable specificity. Such description is often fragmented throughout the contract, but a single, concise overview may appear in the Recitals, or in a specific contract section entitled "Subject of Agreement," or "Scope of Agreement" (or simply "Scope"), or some other caption.

The purpose of such a specialized section can be more than simply reciting the subject matter of the agreement; it will also likely be intended to implicitly or expressly *exclude* anything not recited. This is most often accomplished by limitation language such as:

> "The scope hereof shall include only the following…"; or
>
> "The purpose of this agreement is, and shall be limited to…"

Conversely, the scope may be made open-ended with similar language:

> "The scope hereof shall include (without limitation) the following…"; or
>
> "The purpose of this agreement includes, but is not necessarily limited to, …"

Sometimes, and particularly where the contract may be construed as having a broad, open-ended scope, there may be *specific* (or *express*) exclusions, generally made part of the subject matter provisions or in a separate section labeled "Exclusions," such as:

> "Nothing herein shall be construed as requiring Company to…"
>
> "The following are expressly excluded from the scope of this agreement, to wit;…"

Subject matter provisions will be closely linked to those provisions which recite consideration, and both essential elements are often satisfied by the same contract language. That is to say that, in describing what each party is required to do or not do, the contract describes both the subject matter and the consideration of the contract, at the same time. Caution should be used to avoid creating an overly broad or vague scope, as it may result in a void or voidable agreement if the intention of the contracting parties cannot be readily ascertained.

Contract sections devoted to subject matter may include the following captions:

- Recitals
- Scope

- Subject Matter
- Object of Agreement
- Consideration
- Obligations

3. Legal Consideration

We began an earlier chapter on Intellectual Property with the statement that, "Every contract involves something of value, which is a short definition of the word, 'property.'" That statement is true, but somewhat misleading. Contracts definitely require "something of value" but not *every* "thing of value" is necessarily "property," since *services* also have value… they simply are not "things." In circumstance where parties to a contract are only exchanging services with each other, it would be possible to have a valid contract devoid of any tangible or intangible property. For example,

> ***Hypothetical:*** *Abner and Bill agree that Abner will pilot Bill's plane on a trip, in consideration of Bill performing at Abner's daughter's party.*

In the foregoing hypothetical, no money or other property changes hands, but the consideration is valuable and the contract is valid.

Consideration is the value which each party to a contract agrees to deliver to the other party, and so can be readily confused with the "subject matter" or "obligation" of the agreement. Often they are, in fact, one and the same. In the example just given, the *subject matter* of Abner's and Bill's agreement it twofold: it is a contract for *(a)* piloting a plane; and *(b)* providing entertainment at a party. The *consideration* for piloting the plane is the providing of entertainment, while the *consideration* for providing entertainment is piloting the plane. Likewise, Abner's *obligation* is to pilot Bill's plane, and Bill's *obligation* is to perform at Abner's daughter's party.[192]

If, on the other hand, the agreement were that Abner would pilot Bill's plane for $1,000.00, then the subject matter would *only* be piloting the plane, while the consideration would be both *(a)* piloting the plane; and *(b)* $1,000.00. Thus there is a subtle but important distinction between consideration, obligation, and subject matter.

---

192 "Value" is often subjective. While it can be money, goods, services, or *anything* which is lawful and which has intrinsic value, it can also be something which *only has value to the receiving party*. One person's worthless dustrag may be another person's priceless heirloom baby blanket. Where such extrinsic considerations are a part of the transaction, it is good practice to refer to relevant extrinsic factors in recitals, to justify apparent disparities.

Even more than with subject matter, the consideration for a contract is likely to be fragmented throughout the agreement, even where there is a clearly labeled section entitled "Consideration," since each obligation of either party to the other is part of the consideration. Some aspects of consideration may be crucial (*i.e.*, "material") to the agreement, while other aspects are secondary or incidental. Primary considerations are likely to appear in contract sections which might be entitled:

- Consideration
- Compensation
- Obligations
- Royalties
- Advances
- Payments

Secondary and incidental considerations, however, are likely to be scattered throughout various sections within an agreement.

4. Mutual Agreement ("Meeting of Minds")

There must be common understanding between the parties as to the subject matter of their agreement, the terms of that agreement, and a manifestation by each party of an intent to do or to refrain from doing some specific act or acts required by those terms. This is not something readily reduced to a specific set of words, but rather requires that the overall language of the contract be clear and unambiguous, so that an impartial arbiter, upon reading the agreement, cannot believe that a reasonable person would fail to understand its broad purpose and intention.

Recitals can be particularly useful in demonstrating that the essential meeting of minds element has been satisfied, since they can include a series of simple declarative statements as to the common understandings and intentions of the parties in forming the agreement.

What should be included specifically in the contract is not a separate section, but rather specific language which indicates that the parties have, in fact, agreed to the contract terms and conditions. This recitation, containing some form of the "magic word," *agree*, will almost invariably appear at the beginning and end of the contract, but may also appear earlier. Here are a few examples:

At the very beginning	"Agreement by and between _____ and _______..."
Following the recitals	"Wherefore the parties hereby agree as follows:"

In a particular clause	"The parties, and each of them, further agree that..."
Above the signature lines	"Executed and agreed by and between ....."

There's no upper limit on the number of times you can insert the word "agree" or its variants in a contract. The whole point of "meeting of minds" is to demonstrate that the parties have reached agreement on the contract as a whole, and on each of the specific clauses and provisions contained in that contract.

5. Mutuality of Obligation

Since a contract must bind all parties to perform *something* under its terms, this element is not so much a particular contract provision as it is a verification process. Is each party required by the contract to do some particular thing, or to refrain from doing some particular thing? A "contract" which requires one party to perform, but requires *nothing* of the other party, is not a contract.[193] Make certain that your contract requires each party to deliver some form of consideration to the other. Remember, too, that there is no requirement that each party's consideration be of equal value, merely that the parties agree that whatever consideration is to be received is "good and sufficient" recompense for the consideration given. It is up to the parties to agree on this point and to determine if what they are to receive is fair compensation. Except in situations where the law establishes a minimum compensation, courts will generally not overturn a contract solely for inequality of consideration. (There are exceptions, however, mostly in cases where there has been a mutual mistake or fraudulent misrepresentation as to the *value* of one party's consideration.)

◆ ◆ ◆

Having all of these elements included within the agreement will establish a *valid* contract, but will not necessarily assure you of the contract you want or intended. *That* requires careful negotiation, drafting, and detailed analysis of the various clauses and provisions of the final agreement.

193 It may, however, be a *promise*, which may be enforceable under certain circumstances. The distinction between enforceable and unenforceable promises is outside the scope of the present discussion, but generally depends upon the presence or absence of conduct undertaken in justifiable reliance on the promise being performed, and the intention of the person making the promise *at the time the promise is made.* (A promise made without a contemporaneous intention to perform it, but rather intended solely to induce someone to rely on it, and to do or refrain from doing something on the basis of that reliance, may be an actionable fraud. (See "Understanding Remedies") However, actually *proving* a promisor's contemporaneous lack of intent to perform is usually extremely difficult.)

CHAPTER 10

SAMPLE CLAUSES AND PROVISIONS

It's time to repeat one of our caveats. None of the sample contract language we've used in this book should be regarded as set in stone. Each contract is a unique creation which embodies — or should embody — the intentions and agreements of the parties. The circumstances which underlie the following samples are unlikely to match those of your contemplated agreement and so should not be used *verbatim* without careful comparison to your own situation and intentions. Also, piecemeal adoption of clauses from various contracts can create ambiguities through inconsistent treatment of a single issue.

With that in mind, this chapter provides a number of "boilerplate" sample provisions and clauses which may (or may not) be applicable or useful in drafting a contemplated agreement. They are arranged alphabetically, rather than in the order in which they would likely appear within a contract, to aid in locating them within this chapter. While each of them might appear in almost any contract, it is highly unlikely that *all* of them (or even a majority) would ever appear in any single contract.

◆ ◆ ◆

"Good writers borrow from one another's work.
Great writers steal outright."
— Aaron Sorkin[194] ("The West Wing")

◆ ◆ ◆

The provisions and clauses included in this chapter have been taken from a number of different contracts, and may not be suitable for any other agreement. They are provided solely as examples of various types of contract language. At most, they may serve as rough templates from which appropriate contract terms might be formulated. There's no "right" way to prepare a contract, but there are countless *wrong* ways. **Any use of the following samples, or interpolation and integration based upon these samples, is best left to a qualified attorney.**

---

194 But under the doctrine that it espouses, we'll take credit for it.

Acceleration Provision

Acceleration provisions are a special, permissible[195] form of penalty, or in some instances a bonus. In the event of a default, or other specified occurrence, an acceleration provision requires that certain obligations be performed sooner than originally provided by the contract. Loan agreements are the most likely place to find such provisions, where they are used to make an entire unpaid balance due and payable immediately in the event of an uncured default in payments. Implementation of a acceleration provision is generally at the sole option of the party to whom the obligation is due. A typical acceleration provision might read as follows:

Acceleration (Loan):

> **In the event that Borrower shall default upon any payment due hereunder, and shall thereafter fail to cure that default by delivery to Lender of all past due sums and earned fees within ten (10) days from the date of Notice of that default, then the entire unpaid Balance due hereunder, principal and interest, shall become all due and payable, immediately upon expiration of the aforesaid ten (10) day period.**

An acceleration provision is appropriate where there is an overall obligation which is to be reduced by scheduled part performance, decreasing the remaining obligation. In the event that the obligated party fails to make a timely, scheduled delivery of the reduction (*e.g.*, a payment or shipment), or there is a fundamental change which affects the contractual relationship, then the entire remainder of the obligation can be declared immediately due under an acceleration provision.

Acceleration (Termination, Forfeiture and Lien)

> **In the event that Company shall cease operations, dissolve, or be adjudicated insolvent, whether voluntarily or involuntarily, or be merged into or otherwise acquired by another entity without Artist's express consent, all obligations of Company to Artist hereunder shall immediately become due, and all grants of right hereunder shall be deemed immediately cancelled and all rights thereunder forfeited. All unpaid obligations of Company to Artist**

195 Contract provisions which are only punitive, without a reasonable justification for the nature or amount of the penalty imposed, are generally disfavored, and will usually be severed or otherwise disallowed.

> **hereunder are hereby acknowledged and stipulated to be a secured, priority claim against Company, or any successor of Company, and to constitute an enforceable and recordable lien against any and all assets of Company or any successor-in-interest, as security for performance of any unfulfilled obligations of Company to Artist hereunder.**

Such provisions may also be a useful adjunct to a right to audit provision, particularly where there are funds being withheld for returns or other hold-backs, since an acceleration provision may be structured to deem withheld funds to immediately payable as a penalty in the event of under-reporting or under-payments discovered by the audit.

For the "bonus" aspects of acceleration, see "Adjustment Provision," *infra.*

◆ ◆ ◆

Accounting Clause

An accounting clause establishes when and how one party will account to the other for monies or other benefits earned under a contract, as well as when and how payments will be made in accordance with that accounting. In many music industry contracts, the accounting clause may be subsumed in a royalty clause, rather than being identified as a separate section.

Accounting clauses are appropriate in any contract where funds or other things of value are received by one party, and portions thereof are to be disbursed to other parties, or held for the benefit of other parties, as apportioned by the contract's terms. Generally, the party which calculates and makes disbursements is required to provide accountings to the party or parties entitled to receive those disbursements.

As a matter of music industry usage and custom with respect to royalty payments, Artist's Royalties are usually paid semi-annually, most often by October 1st (for the period from January through June of the current year) and by April 1st (for the period from July through December of the prior year.) Mechanical and other publishing royalties are more often paid quarterly, with payments (and accountings) due sixty to ninety days following the end of each calendar quarter.

As with most contract terms, an accounting clause can be drafted to favor one party over the other in a number of ways. For consistency with standardized language found in many music contracts we have referred to the party responsible for providing the accounting as the "Company" and to the party entitled to receive the accounting as the "Artist." Please note that a "Right to Audit" clause is not included here, but is instead discussed separately, later in this chapter. It is nonetheless a better practice to integrate the right to audit into the same contract section as the accounting clause.

The highest level of duty which one party can owe to another is a *fiduciary duty*, and logic would suggest that when one party receives all of the income from common efforts, and is contractually obliged to account for that income and pay a portion to the other party, that a fiduciary relationship and duty would exist. Unfortunately, in the case of royalty accounting, the courts do not agree. Record companies and publishers are pleased to be considered merely "agents" in this regard, and thus excused from a heightened legal duty, since any failure on their part to accurately account for and pay royalties promptly and in full carries with it no additional liability beyond paying whatever underpayment may be discovered through an audit. Conversely, if they were held to have a fiduciary duty, identical underpayment could result in a further award of punitive or exemplary damages, which are often three to ten times the amount of underlying "contract" damages. Unless and until the legislature enacts a statute which expressly establishes a fiduciary duty upon those who collect, account for, and distribute royalty payments, the *only* way to impose this higher level of duty is by incorporating it by stipulation in the underlying contract. For the reasons stated, however, record companies and publishers will resist the inclusion of such language. From the artist's standpoint, it is worth fighting for, but it may prove to be a "deal killer" for the other side. (Bear in mind that a vehement refusal to accept the role of fiduciary in respect to royalty accountings is tantamount to an admission that those accountings will be inaccurate and unreliable.)

***Generic Accounting Clause** (Non Royalty):*

Company shall maintain current, accurate, and complete financial books and records of accounts of all transactions relating hereto, which books and records shall at all times be maintained in accordance with Generally Accepted Accounting Principles, and the originals (or true, accurate and current copies) of which shall at all times be available for inspection at the principal offices of the Company.

Royalty Accounting (Short Version) — Company Favorable:

Accounting statements as to royalties payable here-under shall be sent by Company to Artist within ninety (90) days after the expiration of each calendar quarter for the preceding quarterly period, ending the last fiscal day of February, May, August or November. Notwithstanding the foregoing, Company may, if Company elects, change the aforesaid time and dates, provided, however, in the event of such change, statements shall be rendered to Artist no less frequently than semi-annually. Concurrently with the rendition of each statement, Company shall pay Artist all royalties shown to be due by such statement, after deducting all Recording Costs paid by Company, all payments made to Artist, and all Advances made to Artists prior to the rendition of the statement, and all reserves against returns. No statements need be rendered by Company for any such quarterly period for which there are no sales, nor after the expiration of the Term for which there are no sales of Records derived from Masters hereunder. Company shall be entitled to maintain a single account with respect to all Recordings subject to this agreement or any other agreement. Artist shall be deemed to have consented to all accountings rendered by Company hereunder and said accountings shall be binding upon Artist and not subject to any objection by Artist for any reason unless specific objection, in writing, stating the basis thereof, is given to Company within six (6) months after the date Company renders the applicable statement and any action (i.e., lawsuit), if any, must be instituted by Artist withing one (1)

year after the date Company renders the applicable statement. Company shall be deemed conclusively to have rendered to Artist each statement on the date prescribed in this paragraph unless Artist notifies Company otherwise with respect to any particular statement within thirty (30) days after the date that Company has failed to render that statement.

Royalty Accounting (Short Version) — Artist Favorable:

Company shall furnish Artist with reasonably detailed, complete and accurate royalty statements, prepared in accordance with Generally Accepted Accounting Principles, indicating the number of Records sold and the date, source and amounts of all income received and all expenses paid, within thirty (30) days following the end of each calendar quarter, ending each March 31, June 30, September 30 and December 31, together with payment in full of all revenues due to Artist.

Royalty Accounting (Comprehensive) — Company Favorable:

(1) Company will compute Artist's royalties as of each June 30 and December 31 for the prior six (6) months, in respect of each such six (6) month period in which there are sales or returns of Records or other exploitations of Masters on which royalties are payable to Artist. On or before the next September 30 with respect to the period ending June 30, and on or before March 31 with respect to the period ending December 31, Company will send Artist a statement covering those royalties and will remit to Artist the net amount of such royalties, if any, after deducting any and all unrecouped Advances and chargeable costs under this agreement and such amount, if any, that Company may be required to withhold pursuant to the applicable state tax laws, the U.S. Tax Regulations, or any other applicable statute, regulation, treaty, or law. In computing the number of Records sold, only Records for which Company has been paid or credited will be deemed sold, and Company will have the right to deduct returns, rebates and credits of any nature and to withhold reasonable reserves therefor from payments otherwise due Artist. No royalty statements will be required for periods during which no additional royalties accrue. If Company makes any over-payment to Artist (e.g., by reason of an accounting error or by paying royalties on Records returned later), Artist will reimburse Company to the extent Company does not deduct such sums from monies due

Artist hereunder. Company may at any time elect to utilize a different method of computing royalties provided such method does not decrease the net monies received by or credited to Artist hereunder. The parties expressly acknowledge that royalty accounting is a complex procedure in which inadvertent errors may from time to time occur, wherefore the parties expressly agree that failure to timely or accurately account for royalties hereunder shall not be a material breach of this agreement.

(2) Royalties for Records sold for distribution outside the United States ("foreign sales") will be computed in the same national currency and at the same rate of exchange as Company is accounted to by its licensees with respect to the sale concerned and will be subject to costs of conversion and any taxes applicable to royalties remitted by or received from foreign sources. Royalties on Records sold outside the United States are not due and payable by Company until payment or credit therefor has been received by Company in the United States in United States dollars. For purposes of accounting to Artist, Company will treat any foreign sale as a sale made during the same six (6) month period in which Company receives its licensee's accounting and payment for that sale. For purposes of accounting to Artist, Company will use reasonable efforts to have its wholly owned licensees account to it on a semi-annual basis. If Company does not receive payment or credit in the United States in United States Dollars and is required to accept payment in foreign currency or in a foreign country, Company will deposit to Artist's credit (at Artist's request and expense) in such currency in a depository selected by Artist in the country in which Company accepts payment Artist's share of royalties due and payable with respect to such sales. Such deposit will fulfill Company's obligations in connection therewith. If any law, government ruling or other restriction affects the amount that any Company licensee can remit to Company, Company may deduct from Artist's royalties an amount proportionate to the reduction in such licensee's remittances.

(3) Company will compute Mechanical royalties as of each March 31, June 30, September 30, and December 31 for the prior three (3) months, in respect of each such three (3) month period in which there are sales or returns of Records or other exploitations of Masters on which Mechanical royalties are payable. On or before the next May 31 with respect to the period ending March 31, on or before August 31 with respect to the period ending June 30, on or before November 30, with respect to the period ending September 30, and on or before March 1 with respect to the period ending December 31, Company will

send Artist a statement detailing those royalties and will remit to the respective publisher of each composition for which such Mechanical royalties are due the net amount of such royalties, if any. To the extent that the aggregated Mechanical royalties for any period exceed the maximum amount which Company is obliged to pay in respect to such Mechanical Royalties hereunder, Company shall be entitled to require Artist to reimburse Company for any and all such overages, or Company may deem such overages to be additional Advances to Artist hereunder. Company's treatment of mechanical royalty overages as additional Advances shall not constitute a waiver or limitation in respect Company's right to subsequently reverse any such Advances and to instead demand reimbursement by Artist of any and all mechanical royalty overages hereunder. No royalty statements will be required to be delivered to Artist for periods during which no additional Mechanical royalties accrue. Company may at any time elect to utilize a different method of computing Mechanical royalties provided such method does not decrease the net monies payable to the respective publishers of subject compositions hereunder. To the extent that Company has obtained mechanical licenses from third parties in regard to compositions embodied in any Recording hereunder, then the terms and conditions of that third party mechanical license shall supercede the terms of this subsection, but only in respect to such composition or compositions as are the subject of that third party mechanical license.

(4) All royalty statements rendered by Company will be conclusively binding upon Artist and not subject to any objection by Artist for any reason unless specific objection in writing, stating the basis thereof, is given to Company and an audit for that statement (as herein elsewhere provided) is completed, within two (2) years after the date such statement is rendered. Failure to make such written objection or to conduct the audit within such time period will be deemed to be Artist's express approval of such statement, Artist's full and complete waiver of any and all contractual and statutory rights to audit or for an accounting, and Artist's further express waiver of any right to sue Company for additional royalties in connection with the applicable accounting period. Each statement will be deemed rendered when due unless Artist notifies Company that the applicable statement was not received by Artist and such notice is given in writing within sixty (60) days after the applicable due date specified in subparagraph (1) above, in which event the statement will be deemed rendered on the date actually sent by Company. Artist will not have the right to sue Company in connection with any royalty accounting, or to sue

Company for monies claimed as due on account of the exploitation of Masters hereunder during the period which a royalty accounting covers, whether from the sale of Records or otherwise, unless Artist commences the suit within two (2) years after the date such statement is rendered.

Royalty Accounting (Comprehensive) — Artist Favorable:

(1) Company will compute Artist's royalties in accordance with generally accepted accounting principles (GAAP) as of each June 30 and December 31 for the prior six (6) months, in respect of each such six (6) month period in which there are sales or returns of Records or other exploitations of Masters on which royalties or a share of licensing revenues are payable to Artist. On or before each September 30th with respect to the period ending each June 30th, and on or before each March 31st with respect to the period ending each December 31st, Company will deliver to Artist a statement covering those royalties and revenues, and will remit to Artist the net amount of such royalties and revenues, if any, due to Artist after deducting any and all unrecouped Advances and such amount, if any, that Company may be required to withhold pursuant to the applicable state tax laws, the U.S. Tax Regulations, or any other applicable statute, regulation, treaty, or law. Royalties payable for any semi-annual accounting period will not be charged with Advances paid after the end of that accounting period. In computing the number of Records sold, Company will have the right to deduct actual returns, rebates and credits and to withhold reasonable reserves therefor from payments otherwise due Artist. Company will liquidate any such reserves within two (2) full accounting periods after the period in which such reserves were initially established. In establishing reserves, Company will take into consideration Soundscan reports (or similar retail sales reports) and reports from Company's distributor regarding to what extent the Album concerned is "selling through" at retail outlets. Returns will be treated as units sold or Free Goods in the same proportion as appears in Company's customer account in respect to the customer(s) from which such returns originated. If Company makes any overpayment to Artist (e.g., by reason of an accounting error or by paying royalties on Records returned later), such overpayments will be deemed additional Advance, recoupable from Artist's royalties subsequently due Artist hereunder. Company may at any time elect to utilize a different

method of computing royalties provided such method conforms to GAAP and does not decrease the net monies received by or credited to Artist hereunder. Company's duty to timely and accurately report and pay royalties to Artist hereunder is an essential and material condition of this Agreement.

(2) Royalties for Records sold for distribution outside the United States ("foreign sales") will be computed in the same national currency and at the same rate of exchange as Company is accounted to by its licensees with respect to the sale concerned, as remitted by or received from foreign sources. Royalties on Records sold outside the United States are not due and payable by Company until payment or credit therefor has been received by Company in the United States in United States dollars. For purposes of accounting to Artist, Company will treat any foreign sale as a sale made during the same six (6) month period in which Company receives its licensee's accounting for that sale. Company's wholly owned licensees shall account to Company on a semi-annual basis. If Company does not receive payment or credit in the United States in United States Dollars and is required to accept payment in foreign currency or in a foreign country, Company will deposit to Artist's credit in such foreign currency in a depository selected by Artist in the country in which Company accepts payment Artist's share of royalties due and payable with respect to such sales.

(3) Company will compute Mechanical royalties in accordance with generally accepted accounting principles (GAAP) as of each March 31, June 30, September 30, and December 31 for the prior three (3) months, in respect of each such three (3) month period in which there are sales or returns of Records or other exploitations of Masters on which Mechanical royalties are payable. On or before the next May 31 with respect to the period ending March 31, on or before August 31 with respect to the period ending June 30, on or before November 30, with respect to the period ending September 30, and on or before March 1 with respect to the period ending December 31, Company will send Artist a statement identifying each publisher and detailing all mechanical royalties accrued during the preceding accounting period, and to date, in respect to each Recording hereunder, and will remit to the respective publisher of each composition for which such Mechanical royalties are due the net amount of such royalties. To the extent that the aggregated Mechanical royalties for any period exceed the maximum amount which Company is obliged to pay in respect to such Mechanical Royalties hereunder, such overages shall be deemed additional Advances to Artist, and reflected as such within the next

following semi-annual report of Artist's royalties hereunder. Company may at any time elect to utilize a different method of computing Mechanical royalties provided such method accord with GAAP and does not decrease the net mechanical royalties payable to the respective publishers of subject compositions hereunder. To the extent that Company has obtained mechanical licenses from third parties in regard to compositions embodied in any Recording hereunder, then the terms and conditions of that third party mechanical license shall supercede the terms of this subsection (3), but only in respect to such composition or compositions as are the subject of that third party mechanical license, and without relieving Company of the obligation to report all information in regard thereto in the quarterly Mechanical Royalty Report provided to Artist.

Fiduciary Duty Addendum to Accounting Clause:

The parties, and each of them, hereby expressly agree that, in undertaking to collect revenues for, and to account for and pay royalties to Artist hereunder, Company, and its agents, employees, and representatives responsible for such royalty accounting and distribution, shall at all times owe to Artist the highest possible fiduciary duty in respect to the timeliness and accuracy of said accountings and distribution of royalty payments hereunder.

◆ ◆ ◆

Adjustment Provision

Sometimes a contract will contemplate future changes in an underlying situation or circumstance and will provide for such changes to automatically alter certain contract terms, if and when those changes occur. A common use of such an adjustment provision in music contracts provides for an increase in an Artist's Royalty rate based on album sales, but there are other situations were a pre-agreed adjustment to a party's obligation or entitlement is a good means for staving off potential disputes when altered circumstances make the original contract terms too one-sided at some point in the future.

Here are samples of a few adjustment and royalty acceleration provisions:

Royalty Acceleration *— Favorable to Company:*

> **Notwithstanding anything to the contrary contained hereinabove, with respect to top-line USNRC Net Sales of any Standard Album in excess of 500,000 units, Artist's basic royalty rate applicable only to such excess units shall be prospectively increased by one percent (1%), on an album-by-album basis. Notwithstanding the foregoing, with respect to top-line USNRC Net Sales of any Standard Album in excess of 1,000,000 units, Artist's basic royalty rate applicable to such excess units only shall be increased prospectively by one percent (1%), on an album-by-album basis.**

Royalty Acceleration *— Favorable to Artist:*

> **Notwithstanding anything to the contrary contained hereinabove, with respect to retail sales of any Standard Album in excess of 500,000 units, Artist's basic royalty rate applicable to such excess units, and the rate stated hereinabove for each subsequent album thereafter, shall be increased by one percent (1%). Notwithstanding the foregoing, with respect to retail sales of any Standard Album in excess of 1,000,000 units, Artist's basic royalty rate applicable to such excess units, and the rate stated hereinabove for each subsequent album thereafter, shall be further increased by an additional one percent (1%). For the purposes hereof, "retail sales" shall be as reported by RIAA, SoundScan, or an equivalent, recognized reporting service.**

Of course royalty acceleration provisions are not the only type of adjustment provisions which appear in contracts. The term "adjustable rate mortgage," refers to a contract in which the adjustment clause is a paramount element of the agreement, altering the basic amount of consideration in accordance with periodic fluctuations in lending rates.

The most common form of adjustment provision will generally be linked to a quantity, and modify consideration — up or down — based upon increases or decreases in that quantity. Modification of consideration is not the only purpose for such clauses, however. Sometimes an adjustment clause will instead relate to time requirements of a contract, extending or shortening time for certain contract obligations (*e.g.*, delivery) on the basis of stated, possible events or contingencies.

◆ ◆ ◆

Advance Clause

For most contracts based on royalties, a primary inducement will be the amount of advance being paid, and the scheduling of its payment. An advance clause addresses both of these issues.

In many entertainment industry agreements (*e.g.*, record contracts), "Advance" will be a specially-defined term applied to *any* money which is subject to recoupment. That is, every dollar which is either paid *to* the artist, or for the *ostensible benefit* of the artist, or for any expense or cost for which the artist is ultimately responsible under the contract terms, becomes an "advance" which is recouped by withholding money which would otherwise be payable to the artist. In recording contracts, virtually every dollar that a label pays out other than for overhead expenses, direct manufacturing costs, and earned royalties, will be considered an "advance" to the Artist, unless a specific exception has been included elsewhere in the contract.

For typical, multiple album recording contracts, the advance can be quite complex, since there will other provisions which modify the stated advance based on sales performance adjustments (see "Royalty Acceleration," above) as well as the so-called "min-max" formula, which may override the sums stated in the Advance clause of the contract.

For other types of contracts, such as licenses and publishing agreements, the Advance Clause will be much more straightforward. The key feature of any advance is that it is recoupable from future income to be derived from the contract. This is in contrast to a *bonus*, which is in *addition* to future income under the contract.

***Advances** (Simple - Favorable to Company):*

> **Upon signing of the instant agreement, Company shall deliver to Artist an Advance in the sum of $_____, which shall constitute a prepayment of Artist's future earnings hereunder, and which Company shall be entitled to recoup through withholding of all monies otherwise payable to Artist hereunder until such time as the entire amount of the Advance shall have been thereby recouped.**

***Advances** (Simple - Favorable to Artist):*

Upon signing of the instant agreement, Company shall deliver to Artist an Advance in the sum of $_____, which shall constitute a prepayment of Artist's future earnings hereunder, and which Company shall be entitled to recoup through withholding of, and the source of which recoupment shall be limited to, Artist's Royalties payable hereunder with respect to the Album to which the said Advance directly relates, until such time as the entire amount of the Advance shall have been thereby recouped. All mechanical royalties, Artist's share of licensing fees, and other sources of income payable to Artist hereunder, including any Artist's Royalties for prior or subsequent Albums, are exempt from such withholding for purposes of recoupment.

***Advances** (Multiple Album Recording Contract) - Company Favorable:*

(1) All monies paid to Artist, or paid to anyone on Artist's behalf, or otherwise paid to or on behalf of any Person representing Artist, or otherwise paid in respect to any Album or other Recordings recorded by Artist hereunder, excluding only Artist's royalties and mechanical royalties payable to Artist pursuant to this Agreement, shall constitute fully recoupable Advances hereunder.

(2) Artist agrees that the Advances hereunder include prepayment in full of union scale of all recording session work performed by Artist hereunder, in accordance with, and as provided by, the applicable union codes, and Artist agrees to provide, or to otherwise cooperate in the preparation of, any documentation required by the applicable union to memorialize and acknowledge Artist's actual receipt of said union scale payment.

(3) Company may recoup Advances from any royalties or other monies otherwise payable to Artist pursuant to this Agreement.

(4) The amount of the Recording Fund for the First Album Delivered pursuant to Artist's Recording Commitment for the Initial Contract Period shall be ____ Dollars, ($___) payable as follows:

(a) Upon, or promptly following the signing of this agreement, the sum of________Dollars ($___) shall be paid to ______________; and

(b) Upon, or promptly following the signing of this agreement, the sum of __________Dollars ($___) shall be paid to ____________; and

(c) Within ____ days following the signing of this agreement, the sum of ________________Dollars ($___) shall be paid to

______________.

The balance of the Recording Fund shall be disbursed when and as set forth hereinbelow.

(5) In the event that Company shall exercise its option(s) to extend this Agreement for the recording of Standard Albums subsequent to the First Album hereunder, then for each subsequent Standard Album, the Recording Fund for each such subsequent Album shall be determined by calculation (the "Formula Amount," as defined hereinbelow) which shall reflect the amount, if any, by which the sum designated as Recording Fund exceeds Recording Costs, as follows:

(a) For the Standard Album required to be delivered during the first Option Period, if any, the Recording Fund shall be the Formula Amount, but no less than _________ Dollars ($____) and no more than ___________ Dollars ($____).

(b) For each Album required to be delivered during the second Option Period, the Recording Fund shall be the Formula Amount, but no less than _________ Dollars ($_____) and no more than ___________ Dollars ($____).

(c) For each Album required to be delivered during the third Option Period, the Recording Fund shall be the Formula Amount, but no less than _________ Dollars ($_____) and no more than ___________ Dollars ($____).

(d) For each Album required to be delivered during the fourth Option Period, the Recording Fund shall be the Formula Amount, but no less than _________ Dollars ($____) and no more than ___________ Dollars ($____).

(e) For each Album required to be delivered during the fifth Option Period, the Recording Fund shall be the Formula

Amount, but no less than ________ Dollars ($____) and no more than ________ Dollars ($____).

The "Formula Amount" for a particular Album recorded and Delivered hereunder in fulfillment of Artist's Recording Commitment shall mean an amount equal to sixty six and two-thirds percent (66.66%) of whichever of the following amounts is lesser:

(A) the amount of the royalties credited to Artist's account on Net Sales Through Normal Retail Channels in the United States ("USNRC Net Sales"), of the immediately preceding Album Delivered hereunder in fulfillment of Artist's Recording Commitment after deduction of reserves for returns and credits; or

(B) the average of the amounts of such royalties so earned by Artist hereunder on the two (2) immediately preceding Albums delivered hereunder in fulfillment of Artist's Recording Commitment.

In either case, the amount of royalties with respect to any preceding Album shall be computed as of the end of the month immediately preceding the month in which such the Album concerned is to be Delivered and will be determined by Company's or Distributor's most recent "trial balance" as of such date (taking into account Company's reasonable, good-faith estimate of "pipeline" royalties.)

(6) With respect to each Album (other than the First Album), Company shall pay to Artist ___ percent (__%) of the applicable minimum Recording Fund promptly following receipt of written notice indicating that recording sessions for the applicable Album have been commenced in accordance with the terms and conditions hereof.

The remaining balance of any Advance payable to Artist, if any, (after deducting all Recording Costs), shall be paid to Artist upon Company's acceptance of Delivery of the subject Master Recordings, in accordance with all of the terms and conditions hereof, reduced by the amount, if any, of any anticipated costs for mastering, re-mastering or re-mixing any Master Recordings for inclusion within an Album, and the estimated amount for any Recording Costs incurred but not yet billed to Company; any such amounts which are deducted

but not thereafter incurred shall be remitted to Artist prior to release of the subject Album.

(7) Notwithstanding anything to the contrary contained herein, fifty percent (50%) of all sums paid or incurred by Company in connection with the independent promotion and marketing of records hereunder.

***Advances** (Multiple Album Recording Contract) - Artist Favorable:*

(1) Monies actually paid by Company to Artist or on Artist's behalf in respect to and Albums recorded by Artist hereunder, other than Artist's royalties and publishing royalties payable pursuant to this Agreement, shall constitute Advances.

(2) Artist agrees cooperate in the preparation of any documentation required by any applicable union to memorialize and acknowledge Artist's receipt of union scale payments and Pension & Welfare contributions, provided that such payments and contributions have, in fact, been timely received and made.

(3) Company may recoup Advances only from Artist's Royalties accruing to Artist's benefit pursuant to this Agreement. Mechanical royalties and Artist's share of any licensing revenues or performance royalties are expressly excluded from being applied toward Recoupment.

(4) The amount of the Recording Fund for the First Album Delivered pursuant to Artist's Recording Commitment for the Initial Contract Period shall be ____ Dollars, ($____) payable as follows:

(a) Upon, or promptly following the signing of this agreement, the sum of __________Dollars ($__) shall be paid to Artist, as a non-recoupable "signing bonus"; and

(b) Upon, or promptly following the signing of this agreement, the sum of __________Dollars ($__) shall be paid to Artist as a partial Advance toward the First Album; and

(c) Within ___ days following the signing of this agreement, the sum of __________Dollars ($__) shall be paid to _________.

The balance of the Recording Fund shall be disbursed when and as set forth hereinbelow.

(5) In the event that Company shall exercise its option(s) to extend this Agreement for the recording of Standard Albums subsequent to the First Album hereunder, then for each subsequent Standard Album, the Recording Fund for each such subsequent Album shall be determined by calculation (the "Formula Amount," as defined hereinbelow) which shall reflect the amount, if any, by which the sum designated as Recording Fund exceeds Recording Costs, as follows:

(a) For the Standard Album required to be delivered during the first Option Period, if any, the Recording Fund shall be the Formula Amount, but no less than _______ Dollars ($____) and no more than _______ Dollars ($____).

(b) For each Album required to be delivered during the second Option Period, the Recording Fund shall be the Formula Amount, but no less than ________ Dollars ($____) and no more than __________ Dollars ($____).

(c) For each Album required to be delivered during the third Option Period, the Recording Fund shall be the Formula Amount, but no less than ________ Dollars ($____) and no more than __________ Dollars ($____).

(d) For each Album required to be delivered during the fourth Option Period, the Recording Fund shall be the Formula Amount, but no less than ________ Dollars ($____) and no more than __________ Dollars ($____).

(e) For each Album required to be delivered during the fifth Option Period, the Recording Fund shall be the Formula Amount, but no less than ________ Dollars ($____) and no more than __________ Dollars ($____).

The "Formula Amount" for a particular Album recorded and Delivered hereunder in fulfillment of Artist's Recording Commitment shall mean an amount equal to seventy-five percent (75%) of whichever of the following amounts is greater:

(A) the amount of the royalties credited to Artist's account on Net Sales Through Normal Retail Channels in the United States ("USNRC Net Sales"), of the immediately preceding

Album Delivered hereunder in fulfillment of Artist's Recording Commitment after deduction of reserves for returns and credits; or

(B) the average of the amounts of such royalties so earned by Artist hereunder on the two (2) immediately preceding Albums delivered hereunder in fulfillment of Artist's Recording Commitment.

In either case, the amount of royalties with respect to any preceding Album shall be computed as of the end of the month immediately preceding the month in which such the Album concerned is to be Delivered and will be determined by Company's or Distributor's most recent "trial balance" as of such date (taking into account Company's reasonable, good-faith estimate of "pipeline" royalties.)

(6) With respect to each Album (other than the First Album), Company shall pay to Artist ___ percent (__%) of the applicable minimum Recording Fund (the "Cash Advance"), as follows:

(a) A sum equal to 15% of the Cash Advance concurrently with Company's notification of its intention to exercise its option to have Artist record another Album hereunder; and

(b) A sum equal to 10% of the Cash Advance within ten (10) days following Artist's delivery to Company of the Recording Budget for the subject Album;

(c) A sum equal to 75% of the Cash Advance upon Company's receipt of written notice indicating that recording sessions for the applicable Album have been commenced.

Eighty percent (80%) of the remaining balance of the Recording Fund, after deduction of all Recording Costs and paid advances, shall be paid to Artist upon Company's acceptance of Delivery of the subject Master Recordings, the retained twenty percent (20%) thereof being withheld for the purpose of paying any Recording Costs incurred but not yet billed to Company.

The entire remaining balance (if any) of the Recording Fund shall be remitted to Artist prior to release of the subject Album.

(7) **Notwithstanding anything to the contrary contained herein, fifty percent (50%) of all sums paid or incurred by Company in connection with the independent promotion and marketing of records hereunder, up to a maximum of __________ Dollars ($____) per any Single (or Album track), but in no event more than an aggregate total of _______ Dollars ($____) per Album, shall constitute additional Advances.**

◆ ◆ ◆

Advice of Counsel Clause

It is always preferable to have an attorney involved in the negotiation and formalization of contracts, but that often is not the case. Being represented by counsel creates a stronger presumption that the represented party fully understands a contract's terms and conditions, and the absence of counsel may, in some circumstances, provide grounds for the (rarely successful) defense that a party did not understand the agreement and that there was no "meeting of minds" necessary to a valid contract. To avoid even that slight possibility, many contracts make clear that the parties have had an *opportunity* to consult with an attorney before entering into the agreement, and have either done so, or are intentionally waiving their right to do so, and are voluntarily accepting any consequences which may result.

Advice of Counsel:

> **Artist warrants and represents that he or she is fully aware of his or her right to be represented by legal counsel in respect to and throughout the negotiation of this agreement, and that he or she has been afforded ample opportunity to engage an independent attorney of his or her own choosing for that purpose prior to executing this agreement, and that he or she is entering into this agreement as a matter of his or her own free will and informed consent.**

To make certain that a party cannot make a credible claim that they were unaware of this provision, many contracts will include it in ALL CAPITAL LETTERS so that it stands out prominently and would be difficult to miss.

Advice of Counsel (Alternative):

> **ARTIST SPECIFICALLY ACKNOWLEDGES HAVING BEEN NOTIFIED AS TO THE ADVISABILITY AND RIGHT TO BE REPRESENTED BY AN INDEPENDENT ATTORNEY IN REGARD HERETO, AND HAVING BEEN AFFORDED AMPLE TIME AND OPPORTUNITY TO SEEK AND OBTAIN THE ADVICE OF SUCH INDEPENDENT COUNSEL CONCERNING INTERPRETATION AND THE LEGAL EFFECT OF THIS AGREEMENT. ARTIST HEREBY WARRANTS AND REPRESENTS THAT ARTIST HAS EITHER OBTAINED SUCH PRIOR ADVICE OF COUNSEL, OR HAS INTENTIONALLY REFRAINED FROM DOING SO, AND IS KNOWINGLY, INFORMEDLY, AND VOLUNTARILY WAIVING THE RIGHT**

TO ADVICE OF COUNSEL IN REGARD HERETO, AND FURTHER WAIVING ANY AND EVERY CLAIM, WHETHER NOW KNOWN OR UNKNOWN, WHICH IS OR MIGHT BE BASED UPON THE ABSENCE OF SUCH COUNSEL IN RESPECT HERETO.

Caveat: Do not include these or an equivalent clause *unless* the parties actually *have* had an opportunity to confer with legal counsel. *Do not sign a contract in which such a clause appears if you have not, in fact, been given sufficient time to consult with an independent attorney.*

◆ ◆ ◆

Approval Clause

In virtually every music contract, there will be some reference to "name and likeness," and when artists are involved such provisions can be broad and far-reaching, often allowing the other party to "use and license others to use Artist's name and/or likeness" in various ways in relation to products, merchandise, advertising, publicity, and promotion. From the artist's standpoint, it is advisable to protect his, her, or their public image through a contract clause which requires the artist's express approval before any such use or licensing. From a label's, publicist's, or other contracting company's standpoint, it is preferable to have *carte blanc* to use the artist's name and likeness whenever and however they may choose. Depending on how it is drafted, an approval clause can afford the artist with varying degrees of control over such usage.

***Name & Likeness Approval** — Minimal control:*

> **Company shall use, or license others to use, only such likeness or likenesses of Artist as Artist shall have previously approved for use.**

***Name & Likeness Approval** — Moderate control:*

> **No image containing any likeness of Artist, or biographical information regarding Artist, shall be used, released, licensed or otherwise disseminated or exploited for any purpose, without Artist's express, prior, written consent, which will not be unreasonably withheld.**

Name & Likeness Approval — *Maximum control:*

> **No use shall be made of Artist's name, likeness or biographical information, nor of any aspect or component of Artist's personality or Artist's rights related thereto, for any purpose hereunder or in relation hereto, without Artist's express, written consent and approval of each such use. Artist's right of approval hereunder specifically includes final approval of all such inclusions of any component of Artist's personality rights in such final form and medium as is proposed to be published, distributed, or disseminated. Artist's approval of any particular likeness or other component of Artist's personality rights for any particular use or**

in any particular format or medium shall not constitute approval of the same or equivalent likeness or component for any other use, or in any other format or medium. Company may not authorize others to use any aspect of Artist's personality rights, except in connection with the manufacture, advertising, promotion, marketing and sale of Recordings hereunder. All rights not herein expressly granted are reserved to Artist.

Of course approval clauses are not limited to name and likeness. In recording contracts alone, labels will generally want an approval right as to choice of recording studio, producer, recording personnel, and song selection. If it's an independent label, the artist will also want approval rights as to Distributor and as to the Distribution Agreement, particularly where no Distribution Agreement is yet in place with respect to the Artist's recordings at the time of signing the recording contract, or if the Distributor or Distribution Agreement may be changed, later.[196] Outside the recording industry, there are an infinite number of circumstances where one party to a contract will want to approve a prospective choice made by another party. Such circumstances would include...

- A choice of supplier. The eventual recipient may want the right to approve the sources of material being used as part of a final product.
- Assignment of rights or obligations. As discussed in the section on Assignability (below), one party to the contract is likely to want a right to approve any substitution of the other party. Perhaps the most familiar example of such circumstance is in the area of leases, where the landlord retains the right to approve or disapprove any prospective sub-tenant or co-tenant.

The key negotiating point with respect to approval rights will be establishing the manner and timing of notice and approval, and the basis for approval or denial of approval. The party who must obtain the other's approval will want to insist on a limited time and a presumption of approval thereafter, and insertion of the phrase "... which shall not be unreasonably withheld," to avoid delays and capricious denials. The party which must give approval will want little if any limitation, and absolute discretion to deny without having to supply a rationale for that denial.

---

196 Most recording contracts contain provisions which integrate the Distributor's policies, and the terms and conditions of the Distribution Agreement, making them binding on the Artist, even when such Distribution Agreement is merely prospective and its terms are unknown at the time of negotiating the recording contract.

Sub-Tenancy Approval - Landlord Favorable

Tenant shall not assign all or any portion of this Lease, nor enter into any agreement with any third party in regard to the Premises including, without limitation, any agreement for co-tenancy or sub-tenancy of all or any portion of the Premises, without first obtaining Landlord's written approval. Tenant shall provide Landlord with all such information as Landlord may request or require with regard to any prospective assignee, co-tenant or sub-tenant, and the determination as to approval or disapproval thereof shall be solely within Landlord's discretion. Under no circumstances may Landlord's silence or delay be deemed approval.

Sub-Tenancy Approval - Tenant Favorable

Tenant shall not sub-let the Premises without first obtaining Landlord's approval, which shall not be unreasonably withheld. Landlord's failure to disapprove a proposed sub-tenancy in a writing which states with particularity the reasons for such disapproval, or Landlord's failure to deliver such writing to Tenant within five (5) days following notice to Landlord of a proposed sub-tenancy of the Premises, shall be deemed to constitute Landlord's express approval of such sub-tenancy.

◆ ◆ ◆

Arbitration Provision

Arbitration is an alternative method for dispute resolution in which the case is tried before one or more arbitrators in an informal forum, rather than in a courtroom before a judge or jury. Arbitration can be either binding or non-binding. Binding arbitration has much the same effect as a court judgment, and a binding arbitration award can be entered with the court as a judgment, and enforced as such. In non-binding arbitration, the parties have an opportunity — usually a period of time after the award is announced — to disregard the arbitrator's determination and instead pursue the matter in court.

Procedurally, arbitration is the submission of a dispute to an impartial third person or persons. The arbitrator or arbitrators are either selected directly by the parties, or are chosen in accordance with the rules of a particular arbitration organization specified in the parties' contract. If there is no such specification in the contract, each party usually chooses one arbitrator, and the two arbitrators select a third. When parties submit to arbitration, they are agreeing to be bound by and comply with the arbitrators' decision, which will be given following an informal proceeding at which each side presents evidence and witnesses.

Arbitration usually comes about in one of four situations:

(1) When the law requires that a particular type of dispute be submitted to arbitration, such as in most labor (employee/ employer) disputes;[197]

(2) When a court orders it, usually in an attempt to seek resolution of a lawsuit without the expense of a formal trial;

(3) When the parties to an existing dispute agree to submit the matter to arbitration; and

(4) When a contract between the parties provides for arbitration of disputes between them.

For our purposes here, only this last category — arbitration provisions within a contract — need be discussed further.

There are a number of organizations which provide arbitrators, and which maintain their own arbitration rules and which, in many locales, have facilities in which arbitrations may be conducted. Notable among these are the American Arbitration Association (AAA) and JAMS,[198] although there are numerous other non-profit and for-profit alternative dispute resolution (ADR) organizations which provide similar services. Each generally promulgates

---

197 Although this type of arbitration is generally non-binding, it may be a mandatory prerequisite to commencing a lawsuit on the claim. "Failure to exhaust administrative remedies" is an affirmative defense which can defeat a lawsuit which is filed without first complying with a mandated administrative arbitration procedure.

198 Originally an acronym for "Judicial Arbitration and Mediation Service," the the company is now simply JAMS.

its own procedural rules which govern the arbitration process, unless the contract's arbitration provision includes a modification of the organization's standard rules.[199] Each organization also maintains lists of available arbitrators, who may be attorneys, retired judges, or other qualified, impartial individuals who are paid for their services. The costs for arbitration can range from nothing for some non-profit services, to $20,000 or more per day. Costs will depend on the service used, the rates charged by each arbitrator, whether the matter is heard by a single arbitrator or by a panel of arbitrators, and the number of hours or days which the arbitration continues.

While using an established arbitration service is recommended, it is not mandatory. It is perfectly acceptable to devise an integrated, standalone arbitration scheme within the contract itself, independent of any arbitration organization. In any event, the arbitration rules and procedures for the selected method of arbitration should be reviewed and understood prior to incorporating them by reference into your contract.

It is also strongly recommended that the contract specify *where* a prospective arbitration is to take place, since omission of this detail may render the arbitration provision uncertain.

Additionally, arbitration rules generally preclude the discovery process which normally allows litigants a means by which to obtain evidence through depositions, interrogatories, requests for admissions, inspections, and demands for production of documents and other tangible things. Where one party has custody or control of the majority of relevant evidence, the absence of discovery procedures can be a significant disadvantage to the other party, which may be unable to obtain or produce evidence necessary to presenting their side of the case. Because arbitration is based in contract, it is possible to modify the arbitration clause to incorporate discovery procedures. Be aware, however, that such modification may negate a substantial part of the potential savings of arbitration as compared to litigation, since discovery can be costly.

Finally, there are certain types of equitable relief which lie outside the jurisdiction of arbitration, and which may therefore be pursued in court even where there is a binding arbitration clause. Such equitable actions would commonly include injunctive relief, and petitions to compel arbitration against a party who refuses to participate in a contractually-agreed or statutorily mandated arbitration process.

Statutes of Limitations and Tolling Agreements

Each jurisdiction has statutes which establish time limits within which particular claims must be filed. Failure to timely commence litigation within the time prescribed by the

---

199 Arbitration rules seldom provide for any form of pre-arbitration discovery, which creates an advantage for the side having possession of necessary evidence or control over witnesses. It is therefore good practice to include a discovery provision within the contractual arbitration language, to level the playing field by allowing for depositions, interrogatories, and other discovery procedures.

applicable statute of limitations erects an almost impenetrable bar to asserting such claim, unless the parties have expressly agreed to waive the statute of limitations. Where there is no such waiver, it may be necessary for a party to file a lawsuit even though obligated to proceed with mediation or non-binding arbitration, in order to preserve the right to pursue the claim should such alternative dispute resolution fail.

Tolling agreements waive a party's right to assert a defense based on a statute of limitations. The purpose of such agreements is to allow additional time before it becomes necessary to commence formal litigation. During whatever period is specified, any applicable statutes of limitations are said to have been "tolled," and the time during which a lawsuit may be filed is extended by the tolled period. It is generally good practice to include a tolling agreement when providing for alternative dispute resolution, so that a delay in the mediation or arbitration will not result in an inadvertent forfeiture of rights.

The American Arbitration Association ("AAA") suggests the following arbitration provision:

> **Any controversy or claim arising out of or relating to this contract, or the breach thereof, shall be settled by arbitration administered by the American Arbitration Association in accordance with its Commercial [or other applicable] Arbitration Rules [including the Optional Rules for Emergency Measures of Protection], and judgment on the award rendered by the arbitrator(s) may be entered in any court having jurisdiction thereof.**

(An alternative AAA arbitration clause, requiring mediation as a prerequisite to arbitration, is as follows:)

> **If a dispute arises out of or relates to this contract, or the breach thereof, and if the dispute cannot be settled through negotiation, the parties agree first to try in good faith to settle the dispute by mediation administered by the American Arbitration Association under its Commercial Mediation Procedures before resorting to arbitration, litigation, or some other dispute resolution procedure. If they do not reach such solution within a period of 60 days, then, upon notice by either party to the other, all disputes, claims, questions, or differences shall be finally settled by arbitration administered by the American Arbitration Association**

in accordance with the provisions of its Commercial Arbitration Rules.

JAMS suggests the following arbitration provision:

Any dispute, claim or controversy arising out of or relating to this Agreement or the breach, termination, enforcement, interpretation or validity thereof, including the determination of the scope or applicability of this agreement to arbitrate, shall be determined by arbitration in (insert the desired place of arbitration), before (one) (three) arbitrator(s). At the option of the first to commence an arbitration, the arbitration shall be administered either by JAMS pursuant to its (Comprehensive Arbitration Rules and Procedures) (Streamlined Arbitration Rules and Procedures), or by (name an alternate provider) pursuant to its (identify the rules that will govern). Judgment on the Award may be entered in any court having jurisdiction. This clause shall not preclude parties from seeking provisional remedies in aid of arbitration from a court of appropriate jurisdiction.

(Optional) ***Allocation of Fees and Costs*****: The arbitrator may, in the Award, allocate all or part of the costs of the arbitration, including the fees of the arbitrator and the reasonable attorneys' fees of the prevailing party.**

(JAMS Optional "Step Clause" requiring mediation, and which is intended to be added following their arbitration clause, above, is as follows:)

The parties agree that any and all disputes, claims or controversies arising out of or relating to this Agreement shall be submitted to JAMS, or its successor, for mediation, and if the matter is not resolved through mediation, then it shall be submitted to JAMS, or its successor, for final and binding arbitration pursuant to the arbitration clause set forth above. Either party may commence mediation by providing to JAMS and the other party a written request for mediation, setting forth the subject of the dispute and the relief requested. The parties will cooperate with JAMS and with one another in selecting a mediator from JAMS panel of neutrals, and in scheduling the mediation proceedings. The parties covenant that they will participate in the

mediation in good faith, and that they will share equally in its costs. All offers, promises, conduct and statements, whether oral or written, made in the course of the mediation by any of the parties, their agents, employees, experts and attorneys, and by the mediator or any JAMS employees, are confidential, privileged and inadmissible for any purpose, including impeachment, in any arbitration or other proceeding involving the parties, provided that evidence that is otherwise admissible or discoverable shall not be rendered inadmissible or non-discoverable as a result of its use in the mediation. Either party may initiate arbitration with respect to the matters submitted to mediation by filing a written demand for arbitration at any time following the initial mediation session or 45 days after the date of filing the written request for mediation, whichever occurs first. The mediation may continue after the commencement of arbitration if the parties so desire. Unless otherwise agreed by the parties, the mediator shall be disqualified from serving as arbitrator in the case. The provisions of this Clause may be enforced by any Court of competent jurisdiction, and the party seeking enforcement shall be entitled to an award of all costs, fees and expenses, including attorneys' fees, to be paid by the party against whom enforcement is ordered.

Location of Arbitration (to be inserted into or appended to arbitration provisions.)

Arbitration proceedings hereunder shall be conducted within the County of {County}, State of {State}, unless the parties shall otherwise agree, in writing, to an alternative location.

As noted earlier, the parties are not required to designate an established arbitration service in order to provide for arbitration of disputes, but may instead develop their own, unique arbitration scheme. Here's an example:

In the event that a dispute arises out of or in relation to this contract, or in respect to any breach of the terms and conditions hereof, and if said dispute cannot be resolved through informal negotiation between the parties, the parties hereby agree that either may give written notice to the other, demanding binding arbitration, pursuant to the following procedures. Within thirty (30) days following the date of notice demanding arbitration, the parties shall either (a) agree upon a single arbitrator to hear the dispute, or (b) each party shall independently designate a single

arbitrator, and those designated arbitrators shall, within ten (10) days following their acceptance of that designation, agree upon and designate a third arbitrator, with the three arbitrators comprising an arbitration panel which shall hear and determine the dispute. Arbitration shall be conducted in {County} County, {State} in accordance with the statutes and rules of the State of {State}, as applied to judicial arbitration in said state. The determination of the arbitrator, or of a majority of the arbitrators if there is more than one arbitrator, shall be final and binding upon the parties, and any arbitration award hereunder may be entered as a judgment of and by the highest court of the forum having jurisdiction in respect hereto.

To allow for discovery during arbitration, the following may be added:

Notwithstanding anything stated hereinabove or any arbitration Rule to the contrary, the parties hereby expressly agree that, in respect to any arbitration proceeding commenced in regard hereto, each party shall be entitled to conduct discovery to the fullest extent permitted by the Discovery and/or Civil Procedure Rules and/or statutes of the State of ____, including the right to petition a court of competent jurisdiction for issuance of such process and/or commissions as may be necessary to conducting such discovery in accordance therewith, and the arbitrator(s) is/are hereby authorized and empowered to interpret and apply those discovery rules and statutes in regard hereto, and to make such findings and directives as may be authorized and appropriate thereunder. In the event that either party shall fail to participate in good faith in the discovery process, or shall fail or refuse to comply with the directives of the arbitrator(s) in regard thereto, the discovery-related issue may be submitted to any court of competent jurisdiction for an order compelling compliance with said directives, and for such further orders, including imposition of allowable sanctions, including monetary sanctions, issue sanctions, and/or terminating sanctions, as the court may deem just.

Tolling Agreement — Addendum to Arbitration or Mediation Provision

In the event that either party shall demand arbitration [or mediation] pursuant to the foregoing, then such demand shall toll all statutes of limitations in respect to any and all claims arising hereunder. Nothing herein shall be deemed to reinstate any claim for which an applicable statute of limitations shall have expired prior to the date of demand for [mediation or] arbitration hereunder. For the purposes of determining the applicability of any statute of limitations in respect hereto, the date of any written demand for [mediation or] arbitration hereunder shall be deemed to be the filing date in respect to any claim hereunder, provided that litigation is commenced not later than ninety (90) days following the earlier of: conclusion of [mediation or] arbitration proceedings hereunder, or a party's failure or refusal to participate in scheduled [mediation or] arbitration proceedings hereunder. [A demand for arbitration within sixty (60) days following unsuccessful mediation shall extend the tolling period hereinabove provided.]

◆ ◆ ◆

Assignability Clause

Assignment is the act of conveying to another person certain rights or obligations. The person who gives the assignment is referred to as an "assignor," while the person who accepts the assignment (and the rights, privileges and/or obligations which go with it) is referred to as the "assignee."

Contract-based rights, benefits and obligations are, in general, freely assignable *except*: (1) obligations of a personal nature; or (2) when there is some public policy against the assignment.

Thus an artist cannot appoint someone else to provide entertainment services which the artist agreed to provide personally, but *may* assign his or her beneficial interest (*i.e.*, income) from that same contract. On the other hand, since distributing records is not a "personal" service, a label may assign its entire interest in a contract (*i.e.*, sell an artist's contract to another label), unless the contract expressly prohibits such assignment. Sports contracts are perhaps the best examples of both concepts. Players regularly assign a portion of their income to managers or agents, but they can't have someone other than themselves show up to play. Conversely, players are regularly "traded" between teams, which simply means that their contracts have been sold (*i.e.*, assigned) to another company, and the athlete has no say in the matter unless his or her contract expressly contains an assignability provision gives the athlete a right to approve or disapprove a proposed assignment.

It's fairly simple to determine whether or not a contract obligation is "personal." Is one of the parties obligated to provide a unique service, and were the personal qualifications of that party a consideration for which the other party bargained in negotiating the contract? If so, then that aspect of the contract is likely "personal," and not assignable.

The "public policy" aspects of assignability questions can be more elusive, and have been the source of a number of inconsistent judicial rulings. In general, public policy tends to favor a contracting party's right to choose the person or entity with whom or which he or she will be in a contractual relationship, and to disfavor assignments to which the other party objects, unless the contract plainly contemplates the possibility of assignment. This is far from being a rule, however, and when the goods or services being provided are fungible, or the differences between them are commercially negligible, the contract will be freely assignable unless it expressly provides otherwise.

One area where there is a common law doctrine of non-assignability has to do with licensing of intellectual property — an area which directly affects the music industry.

The Copyright Act defines "transfer of copyright ownership" as including "... an assignment, mortgage, exclusive license, or any other conveyance, alienation, or hypothecation of a copyright or of any of the exclusive rights comprised in a copyright, whether or not it is limited in time or place of effect, **but not including a nonexclusive license.**" (17 USC § 101. Emphasis added.)

Where a copyright license limits assignability, such provisions will be enforced. Where the license is silent, courts have held that a *nonexclusive* copyright license "is personal to the transferee ... and the licensee cannot assign it to a third party without the consent of the copyright owner."[200] Courts are split, however, over the assignability of *exclusive* licenses, where the contract makes no provision for assignment. Some courts have held that an exclusive licensee is entitled to all the rights and protections afforded to a copyright owner, and may freely transfer those rights by assignment,[201] but at least one Ninth Circuit opinion interprets the Copyright Act as mandating an opposite conclusion, holding that "exclusive [copyright] licenses are only assignable with the consent of the licensor."[202]

Because most non-personal contract rights *are* assignable, so called "assignment" or "assignability" clauses are often more aptly described as "Non-Assignability" clauses, since their intention is usually to limit or preclude the assignment of contract rights which would otherwise be freely assignable. However, where — as in the case of copyright licenses — the legal question of assignability may be unresolved, or where law and public policy disfavor assignment, the parties should memorialize their specific intentions regarding possible assignment, within the contract itself.

In summary, it is generally the best practice for the contract to specify both permissions and restrictions regarding assignability. Other than rare instances where the law expressly precludes assignment under any circumstances,[203] the express language of the contract itself will likely govern the question of future assignability of all rights arising out of that contract.

Non-Assignable:

> **Neither party may assign any right or obligation arising hereunder without first obtaining the express written consent of the other party [, which shall not be unreasonably withheld].**

---

200 See, *e.g.*, Harris v. Emus Records Corp., (1984, 9th Cir.) 734 F.2d 1329, 1333-34 (applying 1909 Copyright Act); In re Patient Educ. Media, Inc., (1997, S.D.N.Y. Bankr.) 210 B.R. 237, 240; see also Michaels v. Internet Entm't Group, Inc., (1998, C.D. Cal.) 5 F.Supp.2d 823, 834.

201 See I.A.E., Inc. v. Shaver, (1996, 7th Cir.) 74 F.3d 768, 775; In re Patient Educ. Media, *(supra)* 210 B.R. at 240.

202 Gardner v. Nike, Inc., (2002, 9th Cir.) 279 F.3d 774, holding that "[17 USC] § 201(d)(2) only conferred [to an exclusive licensee] the 'protections and remedies' [of a copyright owner] ... but not the rights."

203 The right to sue for tort claims (*e.g.*, assault, etc.) is generally not assignable.

Freely Assignable by any party:

All rights and obligations of each and all parties hereto and arising hereunder are expressly acknowledged and agreed to be non-personal in nature, and freely assignable by either party.

Freely Assignable by one party only:

Company shall have the right to freely assign all or any portion of Company's rights and obligations hereunder.

Obligations Non-Assignable by Artist:

Artist may not assign any portion of Artist's obligations hereunder, and any purported assignment thereof shall be null and void.

Assignable Only by Consent:

This license is not assignable without the express permission of Licensor[, which shall not be unreasonably withheld].

Limited and Conditional Assignability:

This license is not assignable by Company without the express permission of Licensor, which shall be granted in respect to an established, financially responsible, and solvent assignee, *provided* that Company is not then in default in respect to any obligation of Company hereunder. It is expressly agreed and stipulated that no portion hereof may be assigned to any person or entity, and that this Agreement is subject to automatic termination and reversion of all rights granted herein, upon any act of insolvency or bankruptcy by Company, as is herein elsewhere provided. [204]

◆ ◆ ◆

204 See discussion at Insolvency Provision, *infra.*

Availability Clause

One of those contract clauses which is peculiar to the entertainment industry has to do with a performer making himself or herself available to perform certain future obligations. A label may anticipate having the Artist appear at promotional events, or for radio or television interviews, or any number of other promotional opportunities. Since there will be no scheduled dates for any such prospective events at the time of contract formation, there will instead be a generic provision requiring that the Artist be "available" — usually on a "reasonable notice" basis — to participate in such events.

An alternative form of "availability clause" also frequently appears in so-called "attachment letters" or "letters of intent" which are conditional agreements to participate in a future project, if and when some predicate event (usually funding) has occurred. This form of the clause is most often seen in respect to motion pictures, where a director, producer or star agrees to participate in a proposed film, stating when and for how long they will be available for such participation. Under the doctrine of "offer and acceptance" such letters become binding deal memos upon satisfaction of the stated conditions, and some manifestation of consideration.

Recording Artist Availability (Neutral):

> **Subject to conflicting obligations, Artist shall be available to Label at all reasonable times, and upon reasonable notice, for the purpose of supporting Label's advertising, marketing and promotional efforts, including, without limitation, press interviews, photo shoots, and promotional appearances, which may include live, taped, filmed, or broadcast performances, as the Label may, from time to time, request.**

Recording Artist Availability (Label Favorable):

> **Throughout the Term, Artist shall be available to Label for the purpose of providing press interviews, photo shoots, promotional appearances, and similar events which may include, but are not limited to, live, taped, filmed, or broadcast performances, or for such other personal appearances as the Label may, from time to time, require.**

Recording Artist Availability (Artist Favorable):

Upon reasonable advance notice and request, in writing, and subject to Artist's availability, Artist will endeavor to support Label's promotional, advertising and marketing efforts in regard to any Album released hereunder by participating in press interviews, photo shoots, and promotional appearances, which may include, but are not limited to, live, taped, filmed, or broadcast performances for which Label receives no remuneration or other valuable consideration. Label shall be required, in connection therewith, to provide Artist and such additional personnel as Artist may reasonably require to support Artist in regard to such appearance, with first class travel and accommodations, and *perdiem* subsistence, for each such appearance, and Label shall further pay, or shall promptly reimburse to Artist, all reasonable costs and expenses (including salaries and subsistence for Artist's support personnel) incurred or accrued in respect to such appearances. Except as herein provided, Label shall not be required to pay Artist a fee (other than subsistence) for such promotional appearances, except as may be required under any applicable Union agreement. Nothing herein shall relieve any third party of an obligation to pay Artist for services rendered hereunder in accordance with the terms and conditions of any applicable collective bargaining or other agreement, or by operation of law. No monies paid, disbursed or allocated by Label pursuant to this subsection, or in regard to any promotional appearance hereunder, shall constitute an Advance to Artist, nor shall any portion thereof be recoupable hereunder.

Availability (Commitment Letter — Film Director):

> **In respect to that certain proposed motion picture tentatively entitled "___ " (the "Picture"), I will hold myself available for __ weeks of pre-production, __ weeks of principal photography, and a total or no more than __ weeks of post-production (with no more than __ elapsed days between any phases of such post-production), provided that all of the foregoing occurs within a aggregate period of not more than ____ months. I shall thereafter be further available for no more than __ non-consecutive days for promotional events which are approximately contemporaneous with commercial release dates for the Picture, subject to reasonable notice in advance of each such promotional event. The foregoing availability is conditional upon pre-production commencing not later than ______ 20__ or, in the event of postponement, following not less three (3) months written notice to me, in advance of the revised commencement date, and further subject to my withdrawal or modification of all or any part of the foregoing availability commitments due to any conflicting commitment(s) which may arise in the interim, as to which potentially-conflicting commitments I will give you prompt notice within a reasonable time following my agreement to such commitments. The foregoing commitments with respect to the Picture, and each of them, shall be deemed automatically withdrawn and void in the event that my involvement in pre-production of the Picture does not commence prior to _______, 20__.**

◆ ◆ ◆

Attorney's Fees Provision

Under the so-called "American Rule," the prevailing party to a lawsuit is only awarded attorney's fees under two circumstances: *(1)* if the lawsuit is pursuant to a statute which expressly authorizes an award of attorney's fees; or *(2)* if a contract between the parties *specifically provides for attorney's fees.*

Very few contract actions fall within a statutory provision which permits an award of attorney's fees, so the presence or absence of an attorney's fees provision can make all the difference in deciding whether or not to pursue a remedy through adversary proceedings such as arbitration or litigation.

For example, suppose that you're owed $10,000.00 under a contract, and the other party refuses to pay you. You go to an attorney who is willing to handle your case, but you will have to pay a $5,000.00 retainer and, by the end of the case, it has cost you a total of $25,000.00 in legal fees. You prevail at trial, and are awarded $10,000.00. But, if the contract did not have an "attorney's fees" provision, that $10,000.00 judgment is *all* you get, and you're still out-of-pocket the $25,000.00 in legal fees. Even if the other party actually pays the judgment — and collecting on judgments can be a problematic and expensive proposition all by itself — you will still have a *net* loss of $15,000.00 for nothing more than the satisfaction of having "won" your case.

Most often, attorney's fees clauses provide for an award of "reasonable" attorney's fees and costs to the "prevailing party." However, under the doctrine of reciprocity, even a one-sided attorney's fees provision will generally have that effect. If you are the prevailing party (*i.e.*, the winner), then you may have your legal fees and costs reimbursed by the other side. However, if the other side wins, you may be required to reimburse *their* legal fees. Carefully consider all the issues relating to your agreement before determining whether inclusion of an attorney's fees clause is appropriate.

Some examples of attorney's fees provisions would include:

Attorney's Fees Provision — Simple:

> **In the event of a dispute between the parties, the prevailing party shall be entitled to attorney's fees.**

Attorney's Fees Provision — General:

In the event of any action, suit, or proceeding arising from or based upon this Agreement brought by either party hereto against the other, the prevailing party shall be entitled to recover from the other its attorney's fees in connection therewith, in addition to the costs of such action, suit, or proceeding.

Attorney's Fees Provision — Party Specific:[205]

_______________ shall be entitled, at its sole election, to recover any and all attorney's fees and other costs incurred in the enforcement of the terms of this Agreement or for the breach thereof, whether or not litigated, arbitrated, reduced to final judgment or settled, arising out of or occasioned by any breach or alleged breach hereof, or any claims inconsistent with any agreement, covenant, representation, warranty or grant made or assumed hereunder, or otherwise arising with respect to the rights granted herein and the exercise thereof, arising form any portion of this agreement, including but not limited to any fees and costs in connection with any claim by a third party.

---

205 Even though it is not unusual for an attorney's fees provision to identify only one party as being entitled to attorney's fees in the event of a dispute, the equitable doctrine of reciprocity makes the provision equally applicable to both parties whenever either party has pled for an award of attorneys' fees. The potential usefulness of a one-sided provision lies in the pleading stage of a lawsuit. If the party designated by the provision is the party which initiates the lawsuit, that party may elect ***not*** to include a prayer for attorney's fees. If it is the other party which first includes a prayer for attorney's fees based on the contract provision, that portion of their pleading might be subject to a motion to strike on the basis that the option to plead for contract based attorney's fees was not theirs to make. The outcome of such argument is debatable, however, and wholly dependent upon the jurisdiction in which the action occurs, as well as on the court's perception of applicable facts and law. For example, the argument would undoubtedly fail in California, where a statute (Civil Code § 1717) makes all contractual attorney's fees provisions fully reciprocal, as a matter of law.

An interesting paradox arises in respect to pleading for attorney's fees. If plaintiff pleads for attorneys' fees alleging that a contract so provides, and the court finds that there is no such contract or provision, a prevailing defendant may nonetheless be awarded attorneys' fees under the (nonexistent) contract provision, on the ground that plaintiff pled it affirmatively and fairness requires that a prevailing defendant be entitled to the benefit which plaintiff unsuccessfully sought by that pleading.

Attorney's Fees Provision — Comprehensive:

In the event that any party hereto shall reasonably retain counsel for the purpose of enforcing any term or condition of this Agreement, or in order to prevent or remedy any actual or reasonably anticipated breach of any term or condition of this Agreement, then that party, or the prevailing party in any adversarial proceeding (including, without limitation, arbitration), shall be entitled to recover any and all costs and expenses of any and every kind or nature thereby reasonably incurred or accrued, including (without limitation) all related attorney's fees and costs. In addition to an award of attorney's fees and costs arising in the course of litigation or arbitration of the dispute, all such costs and expenses incurred or accrued by the prevailing party prior to commencement of that litigation or arbitration may be awarded as a judgment for special or consequential damages.

Addendum to Attorney's Fees Provision
(to encourage mediation):

Notwithstanding the foregoing, neither party may initiate any adversarial action through litigation or arbitration as against the other party [, other than for the purpose of obtaining injunctive relief,] without having first attempted informal resolution of any dispute hereunder through mediation, as provided in paragraph ___ of this Agreement. Failure to initiate, or failure to participate in good faith in, the mediation process, prior to commencement of an adversarial proceeding [(other than for injunctive relief)] shall constitute an irrevocable waiver by the party failing to mediate of the benefits of the foregoing attorney's fees provision, without prejudice to the other party's right to claim such benefit. [An affidavit or declaration by the designated mediator, attesting as to a party's failure to participate in good faith in the mediation process, shall be presumptive evidence of such failure to participate in good faith.]

◆ ◆ ◆

Best Efforts Clause

Contracts generally require one or more of the parties to perform certain acts in the future. In the entertainment industry, this often requires one party to make an artistic contribution. On the other side, a production company or label must package, distribute, promote and market a product which embodies that artistic effort. The potential problem for the parties is how to assure themselves that the other party will perform its obligations fully, rather than half-heartedly, and to embody that assurance in contract language which is clear, meaningful, and legally enforceable.

To address this concern, many contracts include a provision by which a party, or all parties, warrant and represent that they will employ their "best efforts," in fulfilling their obligations under the contract. Theoretically, anything less than such an effort would constitute a breach of contract, but for certain types of obligations proof of a party's less-than-best effort may be difficult... particularly where the obligation is artistic in nature and may only be judged subjectively. (Consider that all but one of Van Gogh's paintings were unsaleable during his lifetime. Had he produced the others under a work for hire agreement, could his employer have claimed breach of a "best efforts" clause?)

In effect, a "best efforts" clause is the antithesis of, and negates, a provision which grants discretion, since it not only eliminates any choice as to whether an effort will be made, but mandates that it must be a "best" effort rather than a merely perfunctory or superficial effort.

Artist's Best Efforts (Label Favorable):

In performing Artist's obligations hereunder, Artist shall at all times exercise Artist's best efforts to provide compositions, recordings and performances which employ Artist's capabilities to the fullest extent possible, and which are technically and commercially satisfactory.

Label's Best Efforts (Artist Favorable):

In performing its obligations hereunder, and particularly with respect to the distribution, marketing and promotion of Artist's Recordings released hereunder, Company shall at all times exercise its diligent and best efforts toward assuring the commercial and critical success of such recordings.

Generic Best Efforts Clause:

> **The parties, and each of them, agree, warrant and represent that they shall each, and at all times throughout the term hereof, exercise their best efforts in fulfilling their respective obligations hereunder.**

◆ ◆ ◆

Buy-Sell Provision

Buy-sell provisions generally appear in agreements for the formation of partnerships, joint ventures, or other business entities which are owned by more than a single individual. Their purpose is to allow a partner, shareholder or investor to withdraw on a fair and equitable basis, and to prevent a departing stakeholder from conveying their interest to an outside party without consent. Such provisions are essential to inter-band agreements, where the various performing members may have an equity stake in the group and its assets. When a band member leaves or is ejected, or becomes disabled or dies, there needs to be a contractual mechanism in place for disposition of the departed member's interest.

Because these provisions must reflect not only the nature of the business relationship and capacity of the business entity, but also the personal relationship and intentions of the original stakeholders, it would be difficult to offer a standardized or generic provision. This is particularly true with inter-band partnership agreements, where the personalities and respective creative contributions of the group members will play a substantial role in formulating an equitable buy-out protocol.

For partnerships and limited liability companies, the buy-sell provisions will usually be included within the partnership or operating agreement, while for corporations it will more usually be a wholly separate document.[206]

For multi-owner businesses in general, the agreement usually takes one of three forms:

<u>*Cross-Purchase:*</u> In this simplest type of buy-sell agreement, the withdrawing owner agrees to sell his or her interest to the remaining owners. This is the simplest form of buy-sell agreement and is best suited to businesses which have only a few owners.

<u>*Entity-Purchase:*</u> For entities with more than a few owners, this form of the buy-sell agreement provides for the withdrawing owner to sell his interest to the entity itself, which retires that portion of ownership interest. (*E.g.*, if an entity was owned by fifty equal partners, and the entity itself "buys out" one of the partners, each remaining partner's interest would automatically increase from 2% (1/50th) to 2.041% (1/49th) of that entity.)

<u>*Hybrid (Two-Step):*</u> In this combined form, the withdrawing owner must first offer his interest to the business entity. If the entity declines or is unable to make the purchase, then the interest must next be offered to the other owners on a *pro rata* basis.

There are endless variations and possible modifications to these three basic types of buy-sell agreements and (as discussed below) the issues which must be addressed for performing groups can be quite complex.

---

206 Some states ***require*** that there be a buy-sell agreement between the shareholders, stakeholders, or partners of closely-held entities.

The following hybrid buy-sell provision is structured for a corporation, and consequently refers to "shares" rather than to "membership interest" (LLC) or "equity interest" (partnership), but the principles would be the same for any entity, subject only to changes in nomenclature:

Buy-Sell Agreement — Corporate Shares

> **No shareholder or successor shareholder may offer all or any portion of his or her shares in the corporation for sale or transfer to any person or entity, nor sell, transfer or convey, nor purport to sell transfer or convey, nor enter into any agreement with respect to the sale or transfer of, all or any portion of such shares to any person or entity, except as hereinafter provided:**
>
> **(a) In the event that shareholder (or a successor, heir or trustee of shareholder) desires to sell all or any portion of held shares, a written offer to sell those shares must first be sent to the Secretary of the corporation, at its principal offices. The corporation shall have and option period pf sixty (60) days following actual receipt of such offer during which the corporation shall have the exclusive right to purchase the said shares, or any portion thereof.**
>
> **(b) In the event that the corporation fails to respond to the aforesaid offer to sell within the said sixty (60) day period, or agrees to purchase only a portion of the shares being offered for sale, then the shareholder must next offer those shares (or such portion thereof as the corporation has declined to purchase) exclusively to the remaining shareholders, on identical terms who shall have an additional sixty (60) day option period, following expiration of the aforesaid sixty (60) day corporate option period, during which to accept or decline said offer. In the event that some or all of the remaining shareholders agree to purchase the offered shares, those shares shall be apportioned between such shareholders in proportion to their respective, current ownership interest in shares of the corporation.**
>
> **(c) Following expiration of the aforesaid one-hundred-twenty (120) day combined option period, the shareholder or successor shareholder may offer any remaining shares which the corporation or other shareholders have not agreed to purchase for sale to outside parties, upon identical terms as offered to the corporation and remaining shareholders, and**

subject to any restrictions or conditions imposed by law or public policy in respect to such offer or sale. In the event that such sale has not been concluded, upon the said terms and no others, and the transfer of shares and terms of sale registered with the corporation within ninety (90) days following expiration of the aforesaid one-hundred-twenty (120) day combined option period, then all such offers to sell shall be automatically withdrawn, and any subsequent or renewed offer to sell all or any portion of the subject shares must be resubmitted to the corporation, and to the remaining shareholders, in the manner set forth hereinabove.

(d) **In the event that a shareholder shall die or become disabled, the corporation may, by a majority vote of the remaining shareholders, compel a shareholder, or such shareholder's trustees, successors, heirs, or estate administrators, to sell the said shareholder's shares to the corporation, or to the remaining shareholders, in the manner set forth hereinabove. The purchase price for such shares shall be set by the following formula: The percentage of ownership of the corporation represented by the subject shares, multiplied by the net worth of the corporation as of the fiscal year last ended as of the date of the shareholder's death or disability, plus an additional five percent (5%) of the said sum. The subject shareholder, or such shareholder's trustees, successors, heirs, or estate administrators estate may, at their own expense, cause the said purchase price to be verified by audit of the corporation's books and records, provided that such audit is commenced and concluded within sixty (60) days following the date upon which the purchase price is first calculated and tendered by the corporation.**

In regard to the "death or disability" aspect of these provisions, it is not unusual for a business to purchase an insurance policy to provide some or all of the necessary purchase money with which the company can buy out a deceased or disabled owner's interest. In some agreements, the purchase of a deceased owner's interest is mandatory, and the company *must* purchase that interest. Where such a provision exists, an appropriate insurance policy becomes essential.[207]

207 In any event, it is good practice to include (usually elsewhere in the agreement) a provision which requires individual owners to submit to medical examinations if required for insurance purposes.

For inter-band agreements, there are a number of special issues which must be factored into the buy-sell agreement.[208] The possible variations, based on the makeup and dynamics of the group itself, are so numerous as to preclude generally applicable sample provisions, since this aspect of the agreement will need to reflect the attitudes, perceptions, and intentions of various group members.

To begin with, there are three distinctly different situations in which the provision might need to be implemented:

1. A group member dies or becomes disabled; or
2. A group member decides to leave the group; or
3. The other members of the group decide to eject a member.

Each of these three circumstances calls for a different form of buy-sell provision, although the last two may be consolidated.

Death or Disability

In this situation, the purpose of the provision will be to recompense a leaving member (or his or her heirs) for that partner's equity interest in the group assets. Where the group has had some success, and there is current or expected royalty and licensing income, it needs to be determined whether the former member or heirs will continue to receive such income, or if there will be a one-time buy-out payment for all future royalties and licensing revenues. If the latter, a formula for calculating a fair present value of future royalties will need to be included. Having life and disability insurance policies on each of the members is probably the best method for dealing with this type of buyout, but the expense of policy premiums may be outside the financial ability of smaller groups.

> **In the event that a member shall die or become permanently disabled, then the partnership shall purchase, and that member or his/her heir(s) shall sell, all of the said member's present and future interest in the partnership and partnership income for a sum equal to ___% of the then-current net worth of the partnership, plus ___% thereof. The said purchase and sale shall expressly [include/exclude] royalty income and licensing fees customarily and previously paid by third parties directly to the said member for [publishing royalties,] [Artist's royalties,] [licensing fees,] and/or [reuse fees].**

---

208 See VOLUME TWO, "Band Agreements."

Disaffection — Withdrawal or Ejection

It's a rare group which achieves success with all of its original members intact. Personality clashes, creative differences, dissatisfaction with a current situation, finances, or schedule conflicts can all lead to a member's departure. In partnership law, the general rule is that the departure of any member automatically dissolves the entire partnership, unless there is a partnership agreement which provides otherwise. As a practical matter, this results in the remaining partners automatically constituting a "new" partnership, which must then negotiate to acquire the assets of the "dissolved" partnership. It is clearly advantageous to avoid this particular operation of law by having a written agreement which addresses the issue of leaving members *without* a dissolution of the partnership. Here, we have treated both withdrawing members and ejected members equally, although it can be argued that a member who voluntarily withdraws should be penalized by less favorable severance terms than are afforded an ejected member.

In the event that a member shall, with or without notice, withdraw from the partnership, then the partnership shall nonetheless continue, and that leaving member shall thereby forfeit all rights and interests in and to all partnership business, assets, and income, current and prospective, except as herein provided, and upon the following terms and conditions:

(a) In the absence of express notice of a member's intention to withdraw from the partnership, and for the purposes of this section, a member's repeated, protracted, or unexcused failure to attend and diligently participate in rehearsals, performances, recording sessions, writing sessions, or promotional events, shall be deemed such member's withdrawal from the partnership. Notwithstanding the foregoing, a member may be designated as "withdrawn" for the purposes hereof if, by unanimous consent of the remaining partners, the partnership decides to disassociate itself from and eject that member for good cause, or for irreconcilable differences, or for dissatisfaction with the nature or quality of that member's contribution to the partnership.

(b) In the event of a member's withdrawal or ejection from the partnership, then that former member shall be entitled to thereafter receive, in the form of a promissory note and upon those terms and conditions hereinafter provided, the following;

(I) Such unpaid, earned income as may have accrued to that former member's benefit prior to the date of withdrawal, which shall be paid to the former member when and as hereinafter provided; and

(ii) A sum equal to ___% of the then-current net worth of the partnership, reflecting all partnership assets at the value appearing upon the partnership's books and records as of the fiscal year last ended prior to the member's withdrawal, minus all outstanding and accrued partnership liabilities.

(c) The withdrawn or ejected member shall, and does hereby, relinquish, release, assign, convey and transfer to and for the benefit of the partnership, each, every, any and all rights or claims of right which the withdrawing partner has or may have in or to any and all property of any kind or nature in which the partnership, or any of the other partners, currently holds any interest. This expressly includes all intellectual property rights, including copyrights, trademarks, trade names, logos, trade secrets, customer lists, fan lists, musical arrangements, transcriptions, recordings, and every form of proprietary information and property in which the partnership holds an interest, and hereby acknowledges and agrees that the consideration therefor, as herein provided, is good, full, and sufficient.

(d) In full and complete consideration of and for the foregoing, the partnership shall tender to the withdrawn or ejected member a Promissory Note in a principal sum calculated pursuant to subsections (b)(I) and (b)(2) hereinabove, bearing simple interest at the rate of ___ percent (__%) per year, payable in quarterly installments over a term of ___ years, with the first payment thereunder due ___ months following the date of the member's withdrawal.

(e) Nothing herein shall be deemed to excuse a withdrawing member from any obligation to any third party.

Note the importance of giving the leaving member reasonable and fair consideration — even if on the basis of a long term payoff plan — rather than attempting an unremunerated forfeiture of all partnership rights and interests. An "overreach" in this respect can easily lead to protracted litigation.

◆ ◆ ◆

Choice of Law & Forum

A Choice of Law and Forum clause determines which state's or nation's laws will govern any disputes arising under the agreement, and designates (by stipulation) precisely *where* any adversarial action relating to the contract will occur.

Labels and other entertainment companies often use this clause to select a state with laws perceived as being more favorable to their legal position. Legal doctrine requires that there be some logical nexus between the parties — or the subject matter of the agreement — and the selected forum. Companies generally satisfy this requirement by maintaining offices within what they perceive to be the most favorable jurisdiction, even if those offices are not their primary headquarters.

Most entertainment agreements select either California or New York law and forum.[209] California's laws and courts are commonly regarded as more favorable to artists and entertainers, while New York's are regarded as more favorable to record companies and other large businesses. Not surprisingly, most major label's contracts specify New York law and forum, even when all of the underlying transactions and personnel are in California. However, the Choice of Law and Forum can designate *any* state or nation with which the contract (or either party) has *any* jurisdictional connection.

Some companies don't want to litigate *anywhere* in the United States, even though they may maintain offices and do much of their business here. In addition to designating another specific country in the Choice of Law and Forum clause, such companies may even insist that the contract be *signed* somewhere other than the United States, (*e.g.*, a "free" trip to Acapulco, to sign the contracts) to ensure that there is no possible legal grounds to argue for U.S. jurisdiction. If a contract designates a foreign nation in its choice of law and forum clause, be certain to obtain competent legal advice from an attorney familiar with the laws and litigation procedures of the designated nation before agreeing.

The seemingly innocuous "Choice of Law and Forum" provision should not be disregarded as mere "boilerplate." It can not only change the manner in which a contract must be interpreted, but can make any litigation of disputes prohibitively expensive by forcing repeated travel to a location thousands of miles away in order to enforce that agreement.

---

209 For the music industry, Tennessee is the next most common alternative, after California and New York.

Choice of Law and Forum — General:

This Agreement has been entered into in the State of New York and its validity, construction, interpretation and legal effect shall be governed by the laws of the State of New York applicable to contracts entered into and performed entirely within the State of New York.

Choice of Law and Forum — Specific:

This agreement has been entered into in the State of California. California law, applicable to contracts entered into and to be performed entirely within California, shall govern all disputes arising out of or related to this agreement and all interpretation, performance or enforcement of this agreement. State and federal courts located within the County of Los Angeles, California will have exclusive jurisdiction over any controversies regarding this agreement, all disputes arising out of or related to this agreement or the interpretation, performance or enforcement of this agreement. The parties hereto consent to the personal and subject matter jurisdiction of said courts. Without limiting the means and manners of service otherwise available, any process in any action, suit or proceeding arising out of or relating to this agreement may, among other methods, be served upon Licensor by delivering it or mailing it to Licensor in accordance with the Notice provision set forth herein. Any such delivery or mail service shall be deemed to have the same force and effect as personal service.

Choice of Law and Forum — Comprehensive:

This Agreement is entered into, and shall be construed, in accordance with the laws of the State of California applicable to contracts entered into and to be performed entirely within California. Further, as an bargained for consideration hereof, the parties agree that the judiciary of the State of California, in and for the County of Los Angeles, West District, is and shall be the sole and exclusive forum, through trial or final resolution, of each, any, every, and all disputes arising hereunder or related hereto, except in a case involving federal issue preemption of the matter in controversy, in which case the United States District Court, Central District of California, Western Division, shall be the sole and exclusive forum, through trial or final resolution, of each, any, and all federally preempted disputes arising hereunder or related hereto. The parties hereby submit themselves to the in personam jurisdiction of the above-stipulated courts, and as a bargained for condition hereof expressly waive any and all rights which either has or may have, in law or in equity, now or in future, as to any and all other forums or jurisdictions, regardless of whether any grounds for such alternative forum or jurisdiction is now known or unknown, extant or prospective.

(Note: The last part of the foregoing version is intended to prevent removal to a federal bankruptcy court located in a party's state of residence in the event that such party files for Title 11 protection.)

◆ ◆ ◆

Confidentiality (Non-Disclosure) Clause

Frequently seen in employment agreements, confidentiality clauses impose a heightened duty to keep secret certain information which is likely to be exposed within or as a result of the contract. Often, however, confidentiality may be the essence of a contract, which is then more commonly referred to as a Non-Disclosure Agreement. Such agreements are common in the entertainment industry in connection with discussions of proprietary information in advance of a prospective project. The intention of such agreements is to prevent premature public disclosure of creative ideas or plans, and to thereby minimize the resulting potential for an identical or derivative competing project being rushed into public release.

Financial arrangements are also frequently made the subject of confidentiality clauses in entertainment contracts. For example, booking contracts regularly contain non-disclosure requirements to prevent others from learning the terms under which an Artist may have agreed to work. Artists (and their agents) prefer to negotiate for bookings without the potential talent buyer knowing what terms the artist may have recently accepted for another, comparable booking. Likewise, venues may not want artists (or their agents) to learn how much the venue was willing to pay for a comparable act.

Confidentiality agreements are also used when one party has a "secret" which it wants someone else to evaluate, often with the intent that such evaluation will lead to financing or assistance in further development. Obviously, few people are willing to invest in something without knowing what it is, but the holder of the "secret" can't afford to reveal it unconditionally, since its "secrecy" is often its principal value. In this circumstance, the non-disclosure agreement amounts to "I'll tell you, but once I do, you can't tell anyone else, or do anything with it except in conjunction with me." If the disclosed information is subsequently used, or revealed to another who uses it, the disclosing party has an action for breach of contract, and can seek injunctive relief and monetary damages.

One hyper-technical use of confidentiality agreements lies in the area of patent rights. As discussed in a previous chapter, public use or disclosure of a patentable idea may result in forfeiture of the right to obtain a patent. Disclosure under a properly drafted confidentiality agreement is not "public" however, and can avoid an unintended forfeiture of patent rights.[210]

Whether included as a clause within a broader contract, or as stand-alone agreements in their own right, confidentiality agreements should define what information can and cannot be disclosed. This is usually done by way of specially defining certain information as confidential or proprietary, with such definition being subject to the parties' negotiation. The types of information that can be deemed "confidential" are virtually unlimited, and any information

---

210 This type of Confidentiality Agreement is best left to an attorney who specializes in patent law, since applicable laws and court decisions of various nations may need to be taken into consideration in creating an agreement which satisfies all necessary legal requirements.

that flows between contracting parties may be designated as confidential. Most confidentiality agreements therefore *exclude* certain types of information from their definition of confidential information. Common exceptions are information that the recipient already had prior to the disclosure, information that is in the public domain, or which enters the public domain through no fault of the recipient, information that becomes available from a third party with a right to disclose the information, and information independently created, developed or discovered by the recipient.

The agreement can also limit a party's use of the disclosed information. For example, it may specify that the information is to be used only for evaluation of the disclosing party's idea or proposal, but that such information, or anything derived from or based on the disclosed information, cannot be used by the recipient for any other purpose. Breach of this restriction on use would give the disclosing party grounds for an action for injunctive relief and monetary damages.

Another important aspect of confidentiality agreements is the standards and protocols under which the parties handle confidential information. Generally, each party will be required to treat the other party's confidential information in the same manner in which it treats its own. Unfortunately, not everyone has regular procedures for handling confidential information. It is therefore prudent for the agreement to contain some minimum standards for how confidential information will be protected whenever a recipient party's security practices are questionable.

A common defect in poorly drafted confidentiality agreements relates to two essential time periods which must be established. The first is the period during which subject disclosures have been or will be made, including the commencement and termination of such period, and the second is the period of time during which the disclosed information must be kept confidential. Generally, the best practice is to link the first period to the Term of the underlying agreement, and to set the second period as a term of years following termination of the Agreement.

As a further drafting consideration, confidentiality agreements should contain a clear statement to the effect that no license to the disclosed information is being granted to the recipient, either expressly or by implication, that all tangible embodiments of the disclosed information remain the property of the disclosing party and must be returned upon request, and in no event later than the end of the Term, and that no copies thereof shall be retained by the other party.

Simple, Mutual Confidentiality:

[Note: This simple version is only appropriate when the parties do not contemplate the exchange of much confidential information.]

Throughout the Term, and for __ (__) years after the termination of this Agreement, each party shall hold in confidence and shall not use for said party's benefit outside the scope of this Agreement, any confidential information obtained from the other party herein or during the Term hereof. [All financial arrangements as between the parties hereto are expressly understood and agreed to be "confidential information" for the purposes hereof.]

Mutual Confidentiality with Exclusions:

The parties may, herein and, from time to time, in connection herewith, disclose confidential information to each other ("Confidential Information"). To the fullest extent authorized by law, each party will use reasonable efforts to prevent the disclosure of any of such Confidential Information to third parties for a period of not less than ____ (__) years following termination of this Agreement, provided that the recipient party's non-disclosure obligation shall not apply to information which is: (a) not disclosed in writing, either herein or subsequent hereto; or (b) already in the recipient party's possession at the time of disclosure thereof; or (c) already, or later becomes, part of the public domain through no fault of the recipient party; or (d) received from a third party having no obligations of confidentiality to the disclosing party; or (e) independently developed or discovered by the recipient party; or (f) required by law or regulation to be disclosed. [This Agreement, and all terms and conditions hereof, are hereby expressly designated as Confidential Information hereunder.]

In the event that any portion of the aforesaid Confidential Information is required to be disclosed by law or regulation (*e.g.*, by subpoena), the party required to make such disclosure shall, if and only to such extent as may be allowable by law, promptly notify the other party thereof, in order to allow such other party an opportunity to assert whatever privileges, exclusions or exemptions may be available under applicable law or regulation.

Unilateral Confidentiality (Employment Agreement):

Throughout the term hereof, and for so long as possible thereafter, and for at least seven (7) years following termination hereof, Employee shall not, without the prior written consent of the Company, use, divulge, disclose or make accessible to any other person, firm, partnership, corporation or other entity any Confidential Information obtained by Employee during the Term hereof, or obtained at any time in connection with his employment by the Company, pertaining to the business of the Company or any of its affiliates, except when required to do so by a court of competent jurisdiction, by any governmental agency having supervisory authority over the business of the Company, or by any administrative body or legislative body (including a committee thereof) with jurisdiction to order the Employee to divulge, disclose or make accessible such information. For purposes of this Agreement, "Confidential Information" shall mean non-public information concerning the financial data, strategic business plans, product development, proprietary product data, customer lists, technology (whether or not patented or copyrighted), marketing plans and other non-public, proprietary and confidential information of the Company and its affiliates and customers that, in any case, is not otherwise available to the public.

Employee and the Company agree that any breach of this confidentiality agreement or the covenants contained therein would irreparably injure the Company. Accordingly, Employee and Company mutually agree that, in the event of breach thereof, and in addition to such other remedies as may be available in law or in equity, Company may obtain an injunction from any court having jurisdiction over the matter, restraining any violation thereof, and/or further enjoining any person or enterprise from operating in whole or in part upon the basis of information obtained through violation of the foregoing confidentiality agreement and covenants. To the extent permissible by applicable law, such injunction shall issue without bond, or upon a bond in the least amount which shall be within the court's authority to impose as a condition for injunction.

Standards of Confidentiality:

The word "confidential" and phrases "maintain confidentiality," and "keep confidential," and any similar terms shall be taken to require that the party having a duty to keep information confidential will maintain custody of all tangible manifestations of such information within a locked facility, and will maintain all electronically stored manifestations of such information in password protected files, to which facility and files no one not bound by the within confidentiality covenants will have access, and said terms shall further require that no one bound by the within confidentiality covenants and restrictions will disclose any portion of such information to, nor discuss the same with, any person not authorized hereunder.

◆ ◆ ◆

Conflict of Laws Provision

The phrase "conflict of laws" acknowledges that the laws of different countries, or even of different jurisdictions within the same country, may be inconsistent with each other, or even in direct opposition to each other, on identical issues or subject matter requiring adjudication. Although the very nature of this circumstance precludes any binding rules, a few general guidelines have been more-or-less universally accepted:

A. Every nation possesses an exclusive sovereignty and jurisdiction within its own territory. The laws of every state, therefore, affect and bind directly all property, whether real or personal, within its territory; and all persons situate within it, whether citizens or aliens, natives or foreigners; and also all contracts made, and acts done within it.[211]

B. A state may therefore regulate the manner and circumstances under which property situated within it, whether real or personal, shall be held, transmitted or transferred by sale, barter or bequest, or recovered or enforced; the condition, capacity, and state of all persons within it as to the validity of contracts and other acts done there; the resulting rights and duties growing out of these contracts and acts; and the remedies and modes of administering justice in all cases.

C. A state or nation cannot by its laws directly affect or bind property outside of its own territory, or persons not resident therein,[212] whether they are natural born or naturalized citizens or subjects, or others. This results from the principle that each sovereignty is perfectly independent.

D. Whatever force and obligation the laws of one country have in another depends entirely upon the laws and regulations of the latter. If a jurisdiction's statutes or common law forbid recognition of a foreign law, that foreign law is of no force whatever within such jurisdiction.

E. When a question arises as to which of conflicting laws is to have effect, the decision must necessarily depend on a variety of circumstances which cannot be reduced to any certain rule. No nation will willingly suffer the laws of another to interfere with its own, or to injure the person or property of its citizens.

---

211 Notwithstanding such sovereignty, ambassadors, credentialed diplomats, heads of foreign states and other public ministers while in the territory of the state to which they are delegates, are exempt from local jurisdiction. Likewise those composing a foreign army or fleet present in the territory of another state with whom the foreign nation whose armed forces they are is in amity, are generally exempt from local civil and criminal jurisdiction.

212 To this general rule there appears the exception that a nation has a right to bind its own citizens or subjects, regardless of where they may currently reside, but such exception is not without some qualifications.

F. In a conflict of laws, it must often be a matter of doubt as to which should prevail; and, whenever a doubt does exist, the court which decides the issue will prefer the law of its own country to that of a foreign nation.

When a controversy is placed before a court, one of the first questions to be resolved will be a determination as to the particular body of law which will govern the issues of the case. This is far from being a trivial matter, as what is proper and legal under the laws of one state or nation, may be forbidden by the laws of another.

Courts faced with choice of law issues generally have only two options: The court can apply the law of the forum (*lex fori*), and will usually do so when the question of what law to apply is procedural, or the court can apply the law of the site of the transaction or occurrence that gave rise to the litigation (*lex loci*), which will usually be the controlling law selected as to substantive issues of the case. This process of determining what law to apply to a particular issue is sometimes referred to as "classification" or "characterization" of a case, and the determination must be made in accordance with the law of the forum. For example, a federal court in a case based on diversity of citizenship will determine substantive conflict of law issues as if it were the highest court of the state in which that federal court is situated, or of the state the laws of which are applicable to the action *(lex loci)*, while applying Federal Rules of Civil Procedure and federal statutes *(lex fori)* to all procedural issues.[213]

In contract cases, much of the complexity of a conflict of laws dispute may be resolved by the simple expedient of including an express provision within the contract itself. Such a provision will generally be accepted as binding by the courts of all states and nations *provided* that there is some logical and factual basis for the selection. If, for example, a resident of New York were to enter into a contract with a resident of South Carolina, for the purchase and sale of real property located entirely in Arizona, and they were to sign that contract in New Jersey and Maryland, respectively, with payment of the purchase price being made through an escrow located in Virginia, any one of those various states' laws could reasonably be designated within the contract's choice of law or conflict of law provision. If, however, such provision were to state that the contract was to be construed under the laws of the African nation of Chad, there would be no nexus to that body of law, and the provision would be unlikely to be accepted by a court.[214] Conversely, if one of the parties were a citizen of Chad, the nexus would exist, the provision would likely be deemed valid, and an American court would determine the substantive issues of the case in accordance with the laws of Chad, even if those laws were contrary to (but not expressly forbidden by) state or federal law in respect to the same issue.

---

213 The Federal Rules of Civil Procedure ("F.R.Civ.P."), together with Title 28 of the United States Code, embody the rules and procedural statutes which govern all federal courts.

214 Although, if a suit were to be filed in Chad, and the conflict of law question raised there, the courts of that nation might decide to retain the case and adjudicate the issue. (See "F," on the preceding page.)

Conflict of Laws Provision:

In the event of any controversy arising hereunder or in respect hereto, the terms and conditions of this agreement shall be construed exclusively pursuant to and in accordance with the applicable laws of the [state/nation] of ____________, and any questions of procedure or of substantive law in respect to such controversy shall be resolved by and in favor of the laws, rules and jurisprudence of the said [nation/state] to the fullest extent permissible under the laws of the forum.

◆ ◆ ◆

Consideration Clause

Even though the words "contract" and "agreement" are often used interchangeably, there is a distinct difference between the two That difference is the presence or absence of *consideration.*

As we've discussed earlier (and repeatedly), "lawful consideration" is one of the five essential elements of a valid contract. Without it, there is at most only an agreement, not a contract.

In its most basic sense, consideration is the inducement, compensation, price, or motive which causes a party to enter into an agreement or contract. In effect, it answers the question "What do I get out of it?"

Consideration can be *anything* which is of value to the party receiving it, given by one party in exchange for receiving something from another party. Consideration may even be a *negative* which has beneficial effect, such as avoidance of an inconvenience.[215] Consideration of some sort is so absolutely necessary to formation of a valid contract that an agreement under which one party receives no compensation is void as a matter of law,[216] and its performance cannot be compelled. But "compensation" has broad meaning, and its value may be wholly personal to the recipient, even though devoid of any discernable intrinsic value.

Valid consideration must also be "new." That is, it cannot be something to which the recipient is already legally entitled. Contracts which provide *no* new consideration to a party will generally be insupportable, and void or voidable, as a matter of law.

It is easy to mistake the consideration of a contract for its subject matter or for the parties obligations, for the simple reason that they are often (but not always) one and the same. Where a contract is for personal services, then those services are the subject matter of the contract, as well as one party's obligation, and the other party's consideration. Because of this potential for multiple characterizations of a single contract element, not all consideration will necessarily appear in a single section of the contract, but will more likely be distributed, in bits and pieces, throughout that contract. Nonetheless it is good practice to include the primary consideration which the parties are to give and receive in a separate section, which may be captioned "Consideration," but may also be entitled "Obligations of the Parties," "Compensation," "Payments," or any of a number of possible captions.[217]

---

215 Caution must be exercised in such agreements, however, to avoid *unlawful* consideration. An agreement to refrain from an illegal or unprivileged act, thereby benefitting the person who would otherwise be the victim of that act, is not lawful consideration, but may instead be the crime of extortion.

216 Based on the doctrine that "Mutuality of Obligation" is an essential element of contracts.

217 In a "construction clause" it will generally be established that the captions and section titles *(...continued)*

Nondescript consideration (Traditional):

> **For one dollar received in hand, and other good and valuable consideration, the receipt of which is hereby acknowledged...**

Nondescript consideration (Modern):

> **For good and valuable consideration, the receipt and sufficiency of which is hereby expressly acknowledged...**

Both of the foregoing "nondescript" consideration clauses are generally used at the beginning of conveyance instruments, such as grant deeds, quitclaims, assignments or releases of rights, or bills of sale, where the parties do not want to make a public record of the actual consideration received by the conveying party from the other party. The consideration which is received by the *purchaser* however — *i.e.*, the property or other thing of value being conveyed — will nonetheless be identified with specificity, later in that document, since the contract is required as evidence to prove that a conveyance of the described property or right has, in fact, occurred.

Consideration Clause (Master Use License):

(a) For and in consideration of the foregoing non-exclusive license, Licensor shall be compensated a flat fee in the amount of $_____, as follows:

(1) $_____ to be paid upon execution of the instant Agreement;

(2) $_____ to be paid upon commencement of principal photography; and

(3) $_____ to be paid prior to public release or distribution of the Film.

(b) Further, and in addition to the aforementioned flat fee, Licensor shall receive ____% of net profits earned by Company (or its successors) from the Film, to be paid to Licensor in the manner hereinafter provided. [218]

---

which appear in the contract are for organizational and convenience purposes only, and are not themselves material terms of the contract.

218 Accounting and Right to Audit provisions must appear elsewhere in the license, giving *(...continued)*

(c) Licensor shall further receive a fee equivalent to ____% of gross sums received by Company, or its successors, licensees or assignees, for any exhibition or exploitation of the Film in any manner other than U.S. theatrical exhibition (e.g., for foreign markets, TV, Cable, Satellite, in-flight, video, DVD, etc.)

Consideration (Commission) Clause (Artist's Manager):

Commission. **As consideration and compensation for the services to be rendered to Artist by Manager hereunder, Artist agrees to pay Manager a Commission in an amount equal to Fifteen percent (15%) of Artist's Gross Earnings (as defined below) commencing as of the date of this Agreement and continuing thereafter through the remainder of the Term and thereafter as specifically provided for herein.**

Consideration (Services) Clause (Artist's Manager):

Manager's Services. **In consideration of and for the Commission herein provided, Manager agrees to render such advice, guidance, counsel, direction and other services as Artist may reasonably require to further Artist's career as may be determined in consultation with Artist, including, but not limited to, the following services:**

(a) To the extent permitted by law, to represent Artist and act as Artist's negotiator;

(b) To supervise on Artist's behalf and to consult with employers and prospective employers so as to assure the proper use of and continued demand for Artist's services; To be available at reasonable times and places to advise, counsel and confer with Artist in connection with all matters concerning Artist's professional career, business interests, employment and publicity;

(c) To advise and counsel Artist with respect to all matters pertaining to media, and in connection therewith to approve (subject to prior approval by Artist in each instance) and permit, for the purpose of trade, advertising and publicity, the use, dissemination, reproduction or publication of Artist's name, approved

---

Licensor a mechanism by which to verify sums owed under this and the following subparagraph.

photographs, approved likenesses, voice, sound effects, approved caricatures, literary, artistic and approved musical materials; and

(d) To assist, advise and counsel Artist regarding whether to engage, discharge and/or direct such theatrical agents, booking agencies, business managers, attorneys and employment agencies consultants who may be retained for the purpose of securing contracts, engagements or employment for Artist.

Consideration (Recording Studio Agreement):

1. Client agrees to the following rates:

1.1 Hourly and daily rate:

1.1.1 $50.00 per hour, for five or fewer hours, or

1.1.2 $ 280.00 each day, for 6 hours per day, plus

1.1.3 $75.00 for each hour or fraction over 6 hours per day, up to 10 hours, maximum.

1.2 Mastering: $ 35.00 per track or $ 500.00 complete CD up to 20 tracks;

1.3 Transfer of Digital Wave or Audio Files: $35.00 per 650 megabytes;

1.4 Cost of Recordable Media:

1.4.1 DAT: $ 17.00

1.4.2 Blank DVD-R: $ 15.00

1.4.3 Blank CDRs: $ 1.00

Consideration (Website Design & Hosting Agreement):

1. CONSIDERATION

1.1 Website Design and Development

Company agrees to provide certain design and other creative services to Client as an independent contractor on a work-made-for-hire basis, and Client agrees to pay for those services in the amount of $______, upon the terms and conditions contained in this Agreement. Based upon initial consultation with Client, it has ben tentatively concluded that the desired number of individual web pages to be designed and developed hereunder will be no more than ______ pages. Additional pages may be added at the rate of $________ per additional page.

1.2 Post Website Development

If Client wishes to make any minor changes in text after the completion of the website, this is acceptable under the terms of this Agreement at the rate of $___ per hour. If Client wishes to make substantial changes in text, or any change in graphics or layout whatsoever once pages are completed, Company reserves the right to charge Client $___ per hour. In order to install the design in question, Company must be granted read/write access to Client's storage directories; and those directories must be accessible via FTP.

1.3 Search Engine Registration

Company strongly recommends that Client employ the use of Internet Marketing techniques to fully maximize exposure of Client's website on the Internet. Multiple search engine registration, occurring on a monthly basis, can be provided at a rate of $_______ per month. A search engine registration log will be emailed to Client each month via email upon completion of that month's search engine registration. Company has sole discretion to determine which directories are the most widely used Internet directories and search engines.

1.4 Website Hosting

Unless otherwise agreed upon, Client empowers Company to choose which Internet Service Provider (ISP) the website will reside upon, and Company may, from time to time, at Company's discretion, change to an alternate ISP. Furthermore, Client acknowledges that Company will act in behalf of the Client for the administration and technical contact for the website. Depending upon the Client's needs, the monthly website hosting rate will be $_____ , which shall include

__POP mail accounts, __ IMAP mail accounts, _____ Megabytes of dedicated storage space, remote email administration, and FrontPage Extensions, as standard service features. Additional features including, but not necessarily limited to, detailed website statistics, SSL, and SQL database setup will require additional fees, which shall be charged to Client at the rate of $______ per hour, unless made the subject of a separate price quotation. Website hosting is billed in monthly cycles and a thirty-day notice must be given upon cancellation. Company reserves the right to determine refunds of prepaid website hosting fees.

Officer Compensation (Employment Agreement):

(a) *Salary.* As full compensation for the services to be rendered by the Employee hereunder as Company's Vice President of Business Affairs, and as consideration therefor, Company shall pay Employee, and the Employee shall accept, a salary at the rate of Two Hundred and Fifty Thousand Dollars ($250,000.00) per annum. Such salary shall be payable in increments not less frequently than once per month. In the event that the Employee's employment shall be terminated by death or Permanent Disability, the Employee, or his legal representatives, as the case may be, shall receive: (I) all salary earned by the Employee through the last day of his employment; (ii) a lump sum severance payment equal to two (2) years of his base salary; and (iii) immediate vesting of all outstanding shares of the Employee's Company stock options, notwithstanding anything to the contrary in the agreement(s) granting such options.

(b) *Benefits.* Participation in group life, medical, pension, profit sharing and other employee benefit plans (collectively hereinafter referred to as "Fringe Benefit Plans"), and other provisions of the Employee's employment not herein specifically provided for shall be consistent with, and in no event less than, benefits provided to senior executives of the Company or its parent corporation.

(c) *Bonus.* In the event that Employee shall remain employed by the Company for the entire Term hereof, Company shall pay to Employee a bonus equal to two (2) years of his base salary at the rate then in effect.

(d) *Stock Options.* Company has granted Employee an option to purchase up to 1,000,000 shares of the Company's common stock. The per share exercise price of the option is Five Dollars and Forty-Five Cents ($5.45) per share. The term of such option is 10 years from the date hereof,

subject to earlier expiration in the event of the termination of Employee's employment. Such option is immediately exercisable, but the purchased shares shall be subject to repurchase by the Company at the exercise price paid per share in the event that Employee's employment terminates prior to vesting in the shares. This stock option grant is subject to the Company's standard form of Stock Option Agreement (together with Notice of Grant), a copy of which is attached hereto as an exhibit, and which notice must be executed as a condition of the grant. Employee shall have the right to exercise his option while he remains employed by the Company by delivering a full recourse promissory note secured by a pledge of the shares purchased thereunder. If required under the laws of the Company's state of incorporation, Employee shall pay cash for the par value of the exercised option shares. Interest on the promissory note shall accrue at a rate no less than the minimum applicable federal rate under the Internal Revenue Code to avoid imputed income. The principal balance and interest shall be due in full on the earlier of (a) the fourth anniversary of the date the promissory note is executed or (b) six (6) months after the termination of Employee's employment, whichever first occurs. The note shall be subject to such other terms and conditions as may be agreed to by the Company and Employee. The principal balance of the note shall not exceed the aggregate option price payable for the purchased shares. Company will take all reasonable steps at its sole cost and expense to register on Form S-8 Employee's stock if acquired via exercise after an initial public offering so that Employee may sell any vested shares of stock if he so chooses following the expiration of any applicable lock-up period. Nothing herein will be interpreted as requiring the Company to breach any regulations regarding the registration of securities under the Securities Act of 1933.

Obviously there is no hard and fast rule for *how* to memorialize consideration in a contract, just the *invariable* rule that lawful consideration from and to each party must be included somewhere. Perhaps the simplest approach is to ask the "What's in it for me?" question on behalf of each party, and make a list of the results. Those lists will comprise the parties' respective consideration, and it remains to the drafter to decide whether those responses should be scattered throughout various sections of the contract, consolidated into a single section, or split between both methods. As a practical matter, the last approach generally ends up being used, since at least some elements of consideration will be inextricably linked to other contract clauses and provisions.

◆ ◆ ◆

Construction Clause

Construction clauses should not be confused with choice of law or conflict of laws clauses. While those clauses are intended to establish the substantive and procedural laws under which a contract is to be interpreted (or *construed,* in legal jargon), a construction clause is essentially "housekeeping," intended to provide a reader of the contract with instructions as to the intended meaning (or, in some instances, non-meaning) of certain words and phrases which appear within the contract. The English language contains certain vagaries, many of which relate to its pronouns, word forms, and tenses. Construction clauses seek to eliminate potential ambiguities which may result through the use of an inappropriate or confusing pronoun or word formation.

Construction Clause:

> **The use of captions, paragraph titles, or section titles herein is for organizational and convenience purposes only, and none of the said captions or titles shall be construed as being in any manner material portions of this Agreement. For the purposes of interpreting the within Agreement, and unless the context dictates otherwise: (a) singular pronouns and word forms shall be taken to include their plural forms; (b) plural pronouns and word forms shall be taken to include their singular forms; (c) masculine pronouns or word forms shall include their feminine and neuter forms; (d) feminine pronouns or word forms shall be taken to include their masculine and neuter forms; (e) neutral pronouns or word forms shall be taken to include their masculine and feminine forms; (f) nominative pronouns and word forms may include their equivalent objective forms; and (g) objective pronouns and word forms may include their equivalent nominative forms. Terms of art appearing herein shall have the meanings established through and by reason of common industry custom, usage and practice. Except for (A) terms of art and (B) terms otherwise specially defined herein, the words and phrases used herein shall be taken as having their commonly-understood meanings.**

◆ ◆ ◆

Controlled Compositions Clause

At the risk of turning this into a polemic, controlled composition clauses have wrought an overwhelming change in the music industry over the past few decades, and have effectively ended the era of the non-performing songwriters who were once the dominant source for new compositions.

There are a number of critical clauses and provisions in recording contracts which relate to Controlled Compositions, in addition to the Mechanical License granting a right to manufacture and sell phonorecords embodying the Artist's compositions. Such clauses and provisions not only directly affect (and reduce) the Artist's *publishing royalties* from recordings made under the contract, but can also directly impact *Artist's* Royalties, or even require the Artist to *reimburse* the label for excess mechanical royalties. The effect of a controlled composition clause is that the Artist will end up subsidizing publishing royalties, one way or another; either by a reduced royalty for "controlled" compositions, or by an obligation to absorb (or reimburse) all or a portion of royalties for non-controlled composition.

Labels will want to define "controlled compositions" as broadly as possible, to include not only songs actually written by the Artist, but those written by a producer or by anyone remotely affiliated with the Artist, or published by a company in which the Artist or an affiliate of Artist has any interest.

Controlled Compositions (Definition) - Company Favorable:

> **"Controlled Composition" - a Composition which is written or composed, in whole or in part, by Artist or by any affiliate of Artist, or which is published, owned, or controlled, in whole or in part, directly or indirectly, by Artist or by any Person or entity in which Artist or any affiliate of Artist has any direct or indirect interest.**

Controlled Compositions (Definition) - Artist Favorable:

> **"Controlled Composition" - a Composition for which Artist, or any entity in which Artist holds a majority interest, is, in whole or in part, the "Author" or "Copyright Claimant" in respect to such Composition, as provided under Title 17 of the United States Code or Title 37 of the Code of Federal Regulations.**

The Copyright Act of 1909 set a fixed statutory rate of 2¢ per composition, which stayed unchanged for nearly seven decades. In the Copyright Act of 1976, Congress enacted a more flexible scheme, taking the rate out of the *statute* and instead making it a matter of *regulation*, with periodic escalations which could be adjusted by the Copyright Office, without requiring a further Act of Congress. The current (2007) rate is 9.1¢ flat rate, or 1.75¢ per minute (or fraction), whichever is *greater*. (In practice, this means that recordings of five minutes or less are 9.1¢, while longer recordings pay the 1.75¢ "per minute or fraction" rate.) Of course, *all* recordings of Controlled Compositions are considered to be under five minutes in length for royalty purposes, regardless of their actual playing time.

Essentially, the label is required to pay **mechanical royalty** for each "mechanical reproduction" (*i.e.*, for each "phonorecord," including downloads) of the recording. The mechanical royalty rate will be fixed in perpetuity by the terms of the mechanical license,[219] usually as a *percentage* of the applicable, statutory rate (*e.g.*, "75% of Statutory Rate") **as of a certain date.** Because these statutory rates are periodically adjusted upward, labels will often try to fix the rate as being the rate which is in effect on the date of the recording contract, although public policy considerations may prevent avoidance of future royalty rate escalations in that manner. The three most common dates for fixing the mechanical royalty rate for Controlled Compositions are: *(a)* the *recording* date; *(b)* the *Delivery* date; and *(c)* the *Release* date. The label will favor the earliest date, while the Artist will favor the latest date, but (unless the Copyright Office has announced an impending increase) there is little likelihood that the date selected will have much practical effect. The point is that for Controlled Compositions the **penny rate** for mechanical royalties will not escalate with future Copyright Office increases in the statutory rate.

Mechanical royalties should be paid from "Record One" and not used to cross-collateralize recoupment. Artists (and their counsel) should object adamantly to any contract provision which provides otherwise. (Such cross-collateralization provisions can also become a particular problem for artists who have independent publishing deals, since the publisher will likely insist that at least the publisher's share of mechanical royalties be paid from Record One, regardless.) Fortunately, the label will not be able to expropriate the artist's share of *performance* royalties collected by performance rights organizations (ASCAP, BMI, SESAC) for radio airplay and other performance uses of the composition.

If the label gets its way, any composition with which the Artist has even the remotest, attenuated connection will be considered to be a "Controlled Composition," while artists will want to define that term as narrowly as possible. In essence, a "controlled" composition is one for which the artist — *or the record producer* — holds some or all of the publishing rights, generally as an author or co-author, or as an owner or part-owner of the copyright claimant. Under the recording contract, the Artist will be required to give the Label a perpetual mechanical license, at a reduced mechanical royalty rate. Usual industry practice for controlled

219 The mechanical license will be either a section which appears within the recording contract (for controlled compositions), or a separate agreement negotiated with the publisher.

compositions is generally seventy-five percent (75%) of the current statutory rate, but that is by no means a universal standard, but few labels will seek a rate lower than 60%, or agree to a rate of more than 90% of the statutory rate, for controlled compositions.

Categorizing excess mechanical royalties as an Advance constitutes only one part of a mechanical royalty "cap" which labels generally insist upon in their recording contracts. In effect, regardless of who controls the publishing, the Artist is agreeing that all mechanical royalties over the amount which would be paid for *controlled* compositions will ultimately be paid for by the Artist, through Recoupment. That's not the only element of the "cap," however. The label is also likely to put a limit on the number of *songs* for which it will pay *any* mechanical royalties for any particular album. That aspect of the cap, generally set at only ten (10) songs per album — regardless of how many songs the Artist is required to Deliver — places the burden entirely on the Artist for the balance of mechanical royalties. That is, the label will pay no more than a calculated, maximum penny rate (at the reduced, controlled compositions rate) for mechanical royalties, per record, and anything over that amount becomes an additional, recoupable Advance, or a reimbursable expense.

For example, if the cap is 75% of the statutory rate for no more than 10 songs, and the album contains fourteen songs, only eight of which are controlled compositions, and the remainder of which are at full rate, then (using the current statutory rate of 9.1¢), the total mechanical royalties for the album would be $1.092 per unit [*i.e.*, (8 x 0.091 x 0.75) + (6 x 0.091)] However, under the cap, the label will only pay $0.6825 per unit [*i.e.*, 10 x 0.091 x 0.75], with the remaining 41¢ ($0.4095) treated as an Advance to the Artist. If the penny rate for Artist's Royalties is $1.17 per album, then in this example the mechanical cap would have the effect of reducing that Artist's Royalty to 76¢ per unit sold, in perpetuity.

In fact, the impact may be even greater, since mechanical licenses for non-controlled compositions are unlikely to be limited to the same definition of "sold" as is imposed on the Artist, or subject to the same reserves or configuration discounts. That is, the label may have to pay mechanical royalties for albums for which the Artist receives *no* royalty, but for which the Artist is still charged back for the mechanical royalties in excess of the mechanical royalty cap. In many contracts, such additional mechanical royalty payments by the label are deemed *reimbursable* (rather than merely recoupable), with the label making an actual cash demand on the Artist for repayment of mechanical royalties which exceed the cap.

If the artist were to record an album which contained eighteen tracks and *no* controlled compositions, and the songwriters insisted on full statutory rate, then even assuming that none of the recordings exceeded five minutes, the total mechanical royalty payable for each album sold would be $1.638 per copy. But under the cap, the label will only pay $0.6825 of that amount, and can ask the artist to reimburse the label $0.9555 per record sold. Even if and when Recoupment is reached, this situation would reduce the net Artist's Royalty from $1.17 to less than 21½¢ per record sold. But wait... there's more. Many controlled composition clauses include a provision which further adjusts the mechanical royalty rate by the same percentage as the Artist's Royalty is adjusted for other than "top line, U.S. normal retail channel sales." In practical terms, this will average out to a further 30% reduction, which means the label will only pay 47¾¢ per sale, reducing the Artist's Royalty to… *nothing.* In fact, pending Recoupment, the label can demand that the Artist pay the label $1.16 as reimbursement for mechanical royalty "overages" for each record sold.

It's also a "carrot and stick" situation. Because mechanical royalties are usually a flow-through payable from Record One, an Artist who records only controlled compositions stands to actually *receive* that 47¾¢ per record sold. Pending Recoupment, this will likely be the only income which the Artist receives from the label for a long while.

To return to the point at which we began, the era of the great non-performing songwriters appears to have ended, and controlled compositions clauses have been the proximate cause of that demise. Recording artists simply cannot *afford* to record songs which they didn't (ostensibly) write themselves… even if their songwriting talents are less than stellar.

Having *defined* "Controlled Compositions" elsewhere in the recording contract, the actual Controlled Compositions Clause will generally appear as part of the "Mechanical License" section of that recording contract:

Mechanical Royalty Rate (Controlled Compositions) — Company Favorable:

Mechanical royalties shall be payable for each Controlled Composition on Net Sales of Records and at the following rates:

(a) "United States Mechanical Rate": seventy-five percent (75%) of the minimum statutory royalty rate (without regard to playing time) provided for in the United States Copyright Act in effect as of whichever of the following dates is earlier: (I) the date of completion of Delivery of the Master Recordings constituting the Album project (or other recording project) concerned; or (ii) the date of expiration of the time within which the Recording concerned is required to be Delivered under the terms of this Agreement.

(b) "Canadian Mechanical Rate": seventy-five percent (75%) of the prevailing rate agreed upon by the Canadian recording industry and the Canadian music publishing industry or its mechanical collection representative in effect as of the applicable date specified in subparagraph (a) above; provided, however, in no event shall the Canadian Mechanical Rate be greater than the applicable United States Mechanical Rate.

(c) Notwithstanding anything to the contrary contained herein, solely in the event USNRC Net Sales of any Standard Album exceed five hundred thousand (500,000) units on an album by album basis, the

phrase "eighty-seven and one-half percent (87.5%) "shall be substituted for the phrase "seventy-five percent (75%)" in subparagraphs (a) and (b) above. Notwithstanding the foregoing, solely in the event USNRC Net Sales of any Standard Album exceed one million (1,000,000) units on an album by album basis, the phrase "one hundred percent (100%)" shall be substituted for the phrase "eighty seven and one-half percent (87.5%)" in subparagraphs (a) and (b) above.

(d) The maximum aggregate mechanical royalty for all Compositions on any Album, including Controlled Compositions, shall be limited to ten (10) times the amount which would be payable on the Album if it contained only Controlled Compositions. The maximum aggregate mechanical royalty shall be limited to two (2) times that amount on any Single, five (5) for EPs and three (3) for Long-Play Singles or any other Record which is not an Album, EP or Single. If the aggregate mechanical royalty rate applicable to all of the Compositions embodied on any Record hereunder shall exceed the applicable maximum aggregate royalty rate set forth above for that Record, then the aggregate mechanical royalty rate for the Controlled Compositions, if any, contained thereon shall be reduced by an amount equal to such excess. If the aggregate mechanical royalty rate applicable to all of the Compositions embodied on that Record shall, even as reduced in accordance with the immediately preceding sentence, still exceed the applicable maximum aggregate mechanical royalty rate for that Record, then Artist shall, upon Company's demand, pay Company an amount equal to the additional mechanical royalties payable as a result of that excess and Company may, in addition to all of Company's other rights or remedies', deduct that amount from any monies payable by Company hereunder or under any other agreement between Artist and Company.

(e) Mechanical royalties on Net Sales of Records which are not top-line, top-tier records sold through U.S. Normal Retail Channels shall be calculated in accordance with provisions of this Agreement appertaining thereto.

[Note: Although the foregoing subparagraph (e) may seem innocuous, it automatically further reduces virtually *all* mechanical royalties by 10%, 20%, 50%, or more (and eliminates them altogether in some instances), by making them subject to the same reductions as are applied to Artist's Royalties, which are generally only paid in full on "top line" "normal retail channels" "U.S. Sales" of vinyl records.

Any other type of sale will be subject to a reduction or elimination of the royalty.]

Mechanical Royalty Rate (Controlled Compositions) — Artist Favorable:[220]

Mechanical royalties shall be payable for each Controlled Composition at the following rates:

(a) "United States Mechanical Rate": eighty percent (80%) of the minimum statutory royalty rate provided for in the United States Copyright Act and Code of Federal Regulations in effect as of [...]

[...] the date upon which the Recording containing said Composition was Delivered in respect to the subject Album.

[-or-]

[...] the date upon which the subject Album embodying a recording of that Controlled Composition was first released in the United States.

(b) "Canadian Mechanical Rate": eighty percent (80%) of the prevailing rate agreed upon by the Canadian recording industry and the Canadian music publishing industry or its mechanical collection representative in effect as of the applicable date specified in subparagraph (a) above;

(c) Notwithstanding anything to the contrary contained herein, solely in the event that U.S. Reported Retail Sales of any Standard Album exceed five hundred thousand (500,000) units, the phrase "ninety percent (90%) "shall be substituted for the phrase "eighty percent (80%)" in subparagraphs (a) and (b) above. Notwithstanding the foregoing, solely in the event that U.S. Reported Retail Sales of any Standard Album exceed one million (1,000,000) units on an album by album basis, the phrase "one hundred percent (100%)" shall be substituted for the phrase "ninety percent (90%)" in subparagraphs (a) and (b) above.

(d) [OMIT -or-] The maximum aggregate mechanical royalty for all Compositions on any Album, including Controlled Compositions,

---

220 Actually, *no* controlled compositions provision is favorable to the Artist, but this version is less onerous and confiscatory than most.

shall be limited to twelve (12) times the amount which would be payable on that Album if it contained only Controlled Compositions. The maximum aggregate mechanical royalty shall be limited to two (2) times that amount on any Single, five (5) for EPs and three (3) for Long-Play Singles. If the aggregate mechanical royalty rate applicable to all of the Compositions embodied on any Record hereunder shall exceed the applicable maximum aggregate royalty rate set forth above for that Record, then the aggregate mechanical royalty rate for the Controlled Compositions, if any, contained thereon shall be reduced by an amount equal to such excess. If the aggregate mechanical royalty rate applicable to all of the Compositions embodied on that Record shall, even as reduced in accordance with the immediately preceding sentence, still exceed the applicable maximum aggregate mechanical royalty rate for that Record, then the sum of additional mechanical royalties payable as a result of that excess shall be deemed an Additional Advance to Artist hereunder.

◆ ◆ ◆

Counterpart, Facsimile & E-Signatures Clause

A counterparts clause is another of those "housekeeping" provisions intended to clarify certain procedural aspects of the contract. It is not unusual, particularly in today's global economy, for parties to a contract to reside half a world apart. Getting together physically to sign the contract may be impractical, and transmitting an original multi-party agreement from one necessary party to the next for signature may be time consuming and awkward. The solution is to provide that the contract may be signed electronically, by facsimile, and/or in counterparts.

On the other hand, it may be advisable to expressly *limit* the extent to which electronic signatures will be considered binding manifestations of intent in respect to a particular contract. In *Stevens v Publicis S.A.* (2008) 50 AD3d 253, a New York state appellate court held that a series of emails was sufficient to create or modify a contract, because the emails (which included the sender's typed name) counted as "signed writings" under the statute of frauds, and contained details of contract terms, as well as a clear expression of each party's unqualified acceptance of those terms.

Counterparts, Facsimiles and Electronic Signatures Clause:

> **This Agreement may be signed by the parties in counterparts, and counterparts of the signature page(s) hereof, when [manually] signed by all parties, shall constitute a single, integrated, signed original signature page hereof. A [manually] signed counterpart transmitted electronically or by facsimile shall be deemed a duly signed original for all purposes. [This agreement may not be enacted, ratified, amended, or modified except by a writing manually signed by all parties. For the purposes hereof, and notwithstanding any statutory or other definition to the contrary, "writing" shall be taken to expressly *exclude* e-mails and any similar or equivalent form of electronic communication, and "signed" shall mean and be limited to a party's manual signature which [shall be deemed to include electronically transmitted facsimiles of such manual signatures, but which] shall expressly *exclude* typewritten, printed, and electronic signatures.]**

◆ ◆ ◆

Credits Clause

This is one of those contract clauses which is unique to the entertainment industry. The "billing" which entertainment industry professionals receive on an album, in film or TV credits, and elsewhere, is a significant part of their bargained for consideration. And it's not just a matter of having their name appear. The placement, type size and font, and the relationship to the placement, type size and font used for others' names and for the title, all become critical negotiating points.

To illustrate the seriousness of the issue to performers, a story is told of how Katherine Hepburn tried to convince her long time co-star (and lover) Spencer Tracy, to allow her name to be billed above his for an upcoming film. He refused. "But, Spence," she complained, "What about 'women and children first'?" "It's a movie, Kate," he replied, "Not a damned lifeboat! And the operative rule is 'every man for himself.'"

This may seem silly, but the manner of credit placement has a direct impact on public perception, which equates to future earning power.

The issue of credit and billing has led to some interesting compromises, conventions, and guidelines. Here are a few.

Bigger is better.

Before is better than after

Last is better than between.

Higher is better than lower.

Left is better than right.

High-right & Low-left are approximately equal

Alone is better than shared.

Staggered is better than aligned,

Sustained is better than brief.

High contrast is better than low contrast.

Unique is better than uniform.

Under these conventions, a single name appearing centered, large, and alone on the screen for a sustained period of time, in sharp contrast and before anything else, would seem to be an ideal credit for a film or television program, but only one such "best" placement exists, and determining who (if anyone) will get it, as well as all the other factors — size, placement, duration, *etc.* — can often take days, or even weeks, of back-and-forth negotiations and compromises.

For a printed medium, such as album covers, the process is somewhat less frustrating, but can be nonetheless intense. Various contributors to the album are likely to have contracts which specify minimum standards for the manner in which they will receive credit. Care must be exercised to avoid irreducible conflicts which may arise where the guaranties contained in one participant's contract is contradictory to, or excludes, a guaranty which appears in another participant's contract. For example…

Suppose we have two sidemen performing as musicians on the album… let's call them Abner and Bill. Abner's sideman contract states,

> *Musician may not receive front cover album credit or credit on advertisements placed in connection with such records, or any other credit except on album labels or liner notes of records embodying the Musician's performances as a side-man, which shall appear in a size and placement which is no less prominent than is accorded to side-man musicians and backing vocalists other than the Musician whose performances are also embodied in that album.*

Bill, on the other hand, is a signed recording artist who is appearing under a side-man exception in his recording contract, and his label has insisted on the following contract language:

> *Musician shall receive front cover album credit, in the lower right or left corner thereof, in size not less than one-quarter that of the name of the Principal Artist as it appears thereon, and Musician's name shall be preceded by the words "Featuring performance by," and followed by the words "Courtesy of [Record Company]," which additional phrases shall be in a typeface size no smaller than one-half that of Musician's name as it appears thereon. Musician's name, followed by the phrase "(appearing courtesy of [Record Company])" shall also appear on the reverse of all album covers, and in any liner notes of records embodying Musician's performances as a side-man, in a size which is not less than one-and-one-half times the size accorded to any side-man musician or side-vocalist other than Musician whose performances are also embodied in that album.*

So Bill's name must appear on the cover, in a type size which is at least one quarter the size of the name of the Artist whose album it is, and at least one and a half times the size of Abner's name. ***But*** Abner's contract says that no other side man's name can be larger or more prominently placed than his. This is the kind of contractual snafu that keeps labels' lawyers awake at night.[221]

221 This actually happened. After weeks of wrangling, during which the other label wouldn't budge from their position, their signed artist's tracks were removed from the masters and replaced by recording another musician.

***Credit Clause** (from Sideman Exception — Recording Contract):*

Artist will not accept any sideman engagement unless the Person for whom the recordings are being made first agrees and warrants in a writing, directed to the Company, and for Company's express benefit, that:

(1) The member of Artist's name will appear with a courtesy credit to Company on the Album liners used for such Records, in the same position as the credits accorded to other sidemen or side-vocalists, and in type identical thereto in size, prominence, color, and all other respects; and

(2) Except as expressly provided hereinabove, neither Artist nor Artist's name (or any similar name), nor any picture, portrait or likeness of Artist, or of any member of Artist, will be used in connection with such Recordings, including, without limitation, on the front covers of Album containers, on sleeves or labels used for Singles, or in videos, advertising, publicity or any other form of promotion or exploitation, without Company's express written consent, which Company may withhold in its unrestricted discretion.

Before any member of Artist accepts any sideman or side-vocalist engagement, Artist will notify Company of the name of the Person for whom the recordings are to be made, and identify the record company which will have the right to distribute the resulting Records.

Of course performers are not the only ones looking for credit on the album. The producer, the recording studio, the engineer, the songwriters, their publishers, and anyone with whom the Artist has an endorsement deal (musical instrument manufacturers, clothing lines, etc.) will all be looking to have their names appear somewhere on the album cover or in the liner notes. Moreover, their respective contracts usually *require* that they receive album credits, and leaving them off can result in a breach of contract claim.

Songwriter/Publisher Credit *(Mechanical License):*

In each and every instance where the title of any song licensed for mechanical reproduction hereunder appears in print on or in relation to any Recording thereof, the title of such song shall be immediately followed by the following: "([Songwriter's Name] / [Publisher's Name] - [PRO])." Where the song title appears in boldface, the said songwriter/publisher credit shall be in the same type size, not bolded. Where the song title is not bolded, the songwriter/publisher credit may be italicized and in a font size no more than two points smaller than the font size of the song title. In each instance, the songwriter/publisher credit shall appear prominently, either immediately to the right of, or centered directly below and adjacent to, each song title. Any proposed alternative presentation of songwriter or publishing credit must be approved in advance by Licensor, in writing, which approval will not be unreasonably withheld.

Recording Studio Credit:

The cover and any liner notes of any album or other phonorecord manufactured utilizing any recordings recorded by Client hereunder, including both published and unpublished recordings (*i.e.*, "Demos" as well as commercial recordings) shall include the following statement, printed in a manner which shall make it legible and appropriately prominent: "Recorded at QQQQ STUDIOS, Hollywood, California / Recording Engineer, ______," with the name of the engineer inserted therein. Label warrants and represents that Client and Client's assignees are hereby granted all necessary permissions for use of the said names in the manner provided herein.

◆ ◆ ◆

Creative Control Clause

Many artists, and particular novice performers signing their first record contract, are unduly concerned with what they perceive as "creative control" of "their" album. If the label didn't have respect for the artist's creative talent, and confidence that the artist's efforts would yield a profitable album, they wouldn't be offering a recording contract at all. That having been said, the label is about to lay out a substantial amount of money in advance, and reasonably expects some control over where, when and how that money is going to be spent, including to assuring itself that the personnel and facilities which the artist intends to utilize meet the label's standards, and that the songs to be recorded are in line with what the label believes can best be promoted and sold. That having been said, label's also realize that the final product is ultimately dependent on the artists' authentic and enthusiastic creative efforts, which can't be obtained through coercion. Out of an abundance of caution, some artists may insist on a specific contract provision guaranteeing that the artist will have the last word in making creative decisions. Such provisions are seldom truly necessary, however, and the artist may end up conceding far more critical deal points in order to achieve this purely nominal concession. Having a good rapport with the label, and particularly with the artist's A&R rep — will ultimately prove far more effective than any contract clause in assuring that the artist's creative vision is determinative in guiding an album through to its completion.

To the extent that there is a "creative control" clause in recording contracts, it will generally appear in a section entitled "Recording and Delivery Procedures" (or some equivalent caption) which sets forth the label's expectations as to not only *what* will be recorded, but also when, where, and by whom (besides Artist) it will be recorded. The purpose is *not* to take creative control away from the artist. Instead, is intended to motivate the artist to meet and confer with the label to discuss and plan the logistics of recording an album. If the label feels that some of the artist's choices are questionable, it is likely to ask the artist to consider alternatives, but will more than likely go along with most of the artist's reasonable suggestions. The label may, however, elect to withhold the recording budget until an accord can be reached.

Ultimately, the label *always* has creative control over an album, because they don't have to *release* it. Generally, however, the label will *want* to release the album. They'll *want* to accept Delivery of the Masters. After all, that's how they recoup the money they've already advanced. If the label is reluctant to accept Delivery or to release the album, it's time for the Artist to take a second look at the album itself, or to ask an independent expert to listen to it and render an objective opinion.

"Creative Control" — Recording Contract - Company Favorable
(from "Recording & Delivery Procedures")

Artist shall prepare and submit to Company, for Company's approval, a written designation of each of the following:

(a) The producer or producers whom Artist proposes to employ in respect to each of the Master Recordings, including prior credits and relevant *curriculum vitae* for each proposed producer;

(b) The names and a synopsis of qualifications for each other individual whom Artist proposes to employ in respect to services to be rendered in connection with the recording of those Master Recordings, or in respect to the providing of materials which shall be embodied in those Master Recordings; and

(c) An identification of the recording studio or studios at which Artist proposes those Master Recordings shall be recorded, and the anticipated dates of recording of those Masters (the "Recording Elements").

(d) A written list, for Company's approval, of the Compositions which Artist proposes to record hereunder, including any "demos" or "scratch tracks," embodying those Compositions.

"Creative Control" — Recording Contract - Artist Favorable
(from "Recording & Delivery Procedures")

In connection with recording sessions hereunder, Artist shall select and engage all artists (including musicians and side vocalists), producers, engineers, and other personnel and the places of recording. Any place of recording shall be a first-class recording studio subject to the following conditions, (a) its use would not be inconsistent with any of Label's union agreements, (b) its use would not cause labor difficulties for other reasons, (c) the studio takes appropriate measures to secure any material recorded on its premises, and (d) its use will not require expenditures inconsistent with the authorized budget.

Artist and Label shall mutually approve the Compositions to be recorded hereunder.

At least fourteen (14) days prior to commencement of recording of the Album concerned, Artist agrees to submit the names of the producers of the Masters to be recorded hereunder and the authorized budget to Label for approval, such approval not to be unreasonably withheld or delayed. If Label disapproves of the foregoing, for stated

reasons amounting to good cause, Artist shall promptly submit alternative proposals, but in all instances allowing Label no less than fourteen (14) days to review each such alternate proposal prior to the proposed first date of recording.

One type of contract where it may be of importance to fight for "creative control" is in so-called "Demo Deals" or "Shopping Agreements."[222] Typically, these contracts bind the artist to an exclusive relationship with a company or individual whose sole obligation may be to pay for (or provide facilities for) the recording of demos by the artist, which the company then "shops" to various labels in the hope of getting a recording contract for that artist.

"Creative Control" *— Shopping Agreement -* ***Company Favorable:***

The selection of material, individual producers and similar creative matters with respect to the recording of Demos and Masters (but not budgets or other business matters which shall be solely within Company's discretion and control) shall be mutually determined by Artist and Company provided that, in the event of a disagreement, Company's decision shall be final and controlling.

"Creative Control" *— Shopping Agreement -* ***Artist Favorable:***

Artist and Company shall mutually select all material to be recorded by Artist hereunder, but Artist's decisions as to choice of material to be recorded shall be determinative and controlling.

◆ ◆ ◆

222 Since many of these types of contracts closely hug the line of confiscatory unconscionability anyway, every aspect of them must be scrutinized carefully.

Cross-Collateralization Provision

Although the concept of cross-collateralization is common in many different areas of finance, the manner in which it is applied in the music business is distinctive. In most other businesses, cross-collateralization merely means that a creditor will have recourse against several different assets (the collateral) in the event of a default. While such arrangement may prevent the obligated party from further encumbering or conveying the collateral without satisfying the underlying obligation, it does not interfere with that party's income, so long as the underlying obligation is not allowed to go into default. For example, suppose a landlord owns five apartment buildings and borrows $1,000,000.00, using all five buildings as collateral. Suppose further that the loan is for five years, and must be repaid at the rate of $25,000 per month. If the rental income from the five buildings is $100,000 per month, the landlord pays the debt service ($25,000) and keeps the difference. If the landlord decides to sell one of the buildings, arrangements will need to be made with the lender to either pay off or reduce the outstanding obligation from the sale proceeds, since that portion of the collateral will no longer be available as security for any unpaid balance of the obligation.

That's not how it works in the music business.

First off, the collateralized obligation is the unrecouped portion of all Advances to — or for the (ostensible) benefit of — the recording artist. Under most recording contracts, all expenditures other than actual manufacturing costs and label overhead are treated as recoupable advances. Moreover, the amount of that obligation is subject to upwards adjustment, at the label's discretion. Labels can generally expend money for post-release record promotion, and treat half of that new expenditure as an additional recoupable advance to the artist.

The real difference, however, has to do with the manner in which that obligation is reduced. Under most recording agreements, the label withholds 100% of the Artist's royalty income until all Advances have been fully recouped. Thus an artist whose first three albums are selling well and generating royalties may find that the income from those prior albums has been entirely cut off and diverted toward recoupment of the label's advances for a fourth album.

Since there's little chance of avoiding cross-collateralization altogether, there are a few ways to minimize its financial impact on the Artist:

First, ***publishing income should never be treated as collateral or applied toward recoupment.*** It is essential to firmly establish that the artist has two distinctly different roles: one as a recording artist, and the other as a songwriter/publisher of musical compositions. Even though both of those roles are recognized in the recording contract, it is vital that the income which each role generates not be allowed to become commingled with the other. As a practical matter, the money which an artist receives from a publishing interest in the recorded compositions — *i.e.*, mechanical royalties and licensing fees — is likely to be the *only* post-release money that the artist receives from the label for a very long time, and possibly ever. Without that income, the artist may be reduced to touring and merchandise sales — or a "day job" — just to survive until recoupment has been reached. Of course, once recoupment has been reached, the label is likely to exercise its next option, pay the required advance for that option, and stop all royalties once again. Cross-collateralization should therefore *only* apply to the "Artist's Royalties" due for the artist's work *as a recording artist*, and not to publishing royalties or fees. (There should also be no cross-collateralization between a publishing agreement and a recording contract, even if they are with the same company, but some labels attempt this as well by referencing "other contracts" with the label or its affiliates.)

Second, the artist should negotiate for a "bracket" on cross-collateralization, limiting it to the immediately preceding one (or two) albums, so that income from Album One continues, even though Album Three (or Album Four) is not yet recouped. With such a bracket, cross-collateralization will apply to no more than two or three albums at a time, while royalties from any earlier albums would continue to flow through to the artist.

Third, the artist should take cross-collateralization into account when negotiating the amount of Advance for each subsequent album. The sum remaining from that Advance will need to replace the Artist's Royalty income until such time as the new album has recouped. (This can take some complex calculations, since that Advance will become part of what then needs to be recouped. The larger the Advance, the longer until recoupment. This is where knowing the net "penny rate" becomes critical.)

Finally, specify the extent (if any) to which cross-collateralization will continue in respect to a "leaving member" whose option is picked up the label. Will the remaining members be on the hook for recoupment of that former member's new albums? Will income from the former member's new albums be attributable to recoupment under the original contract?[223]

The underpinning for cross-collateralization will likely appear in multiple locations throughout a recording contract. There will probably be a definition of the term itself in a "Definitions" section; the cross-collateralization formula will appear in the "Royalty Accounting" or "Advances" section, and will be dependent on the calculation of royalties and recoupable advances (and various factors which affect them) which appear throughout the contract.

223 These issues should be addressed in the "Leaving Member" section of the contract.

"Cross-Collateralization" (Definition) - Company Favorable

"Cross-Collateralization" - accounting practice by which all income accruing to Artist from any and all sources under this Agreement, and under any and all other agreements now or hereafter existing as between Company and Artist (or as between Company and any Person included within "Artist" hereunder), may be withheld by Company until such time as all Advances and other Recoupable expenses incurred or accrued by Company hereunder shall have been fully Recouped.

"Cross-Collateralization" (Definition) - Artist Favorable

"Cross-Collateralization" - accounting practice by which certain, specified Artist's Royalties hereunder may be withheld by Label only until such time as certain specified Advances or Recoupable expenses, as hereinafter expressly provided, shall have been fully Recouped.

Cross-Collateralization Clause - Company Favorable

Company shall be entitled to recoup Advances from any royalties or other monies otherwise payable to Artist pursuant to this Agreement or pursuant to any other agreement between Artist (or any individual member thereof) and Company or any affiliate of Company.

Cross-Collateralization Clause - Artist Favorable

Company may recoup Advances only from Artist's Royalties accruing to Artist's benefit pursuant to this Agreement, and only from such Artist's Royalties as are attributable to the Album to which such Advances directly relate, and from Artist's Royalties attributable to the one (1) Album released hereunder (if any) which immediately preceded the Album to which such Advances relate. (*E.g.*, Artist's Royalties from the First and Second Album may be withheld until the Second Album is Recouped; Artist's Royalties from the Second Album and Third Album — but not from the First Album — may be withheld until the Third Album is Recouped; *etc.*) Except as herein expressly provided, no other royalties or income may be withheld for the purposes of Recoupment hereunder. Mechanical royalties, licensing revenues, performance royalties, and all income from Artist's appearances or live performances, are expressly excluded from being applied toward Recoupment.

◆ ◆ ◆

Cure Provision

Cure provisions establish a notice requirement and grace period to permit a contracting party to remedy a perceived failure to perform a contract obligation before the other party can take any action against them on the basis of that failure to perform. While cure provisions provide some "wiggle room" to fix problems, they should be closely scrutinized for both reasonableness and fairness. If the notice period or subsequent cure period are too long, any damages resulting from the default may become irremediable. Conversely, if those periods are insufficient to permit a cure to be effectively implemented, the provision becomes mere formality, without practical benefit. Most cure provisions require some form of "Notice" to the other party regarding the specifics of any breach of contract. However, if a breach is *intentional*, then such "intentional breach" should not require the same notice requirements. Once a breaching party knows, or should have known, of a breach, they are required to cure that breach.

Cure Provision — Simple:

> **No failure to perform any obligation hereunder shall constitute a breach hereof unless the party which has failed to timely perform is first given written notice of such failure and is allowed an additional thirty (30) days following such notice in which to perform that obligation.**

Cure Provision — Basic:

> **No breach or failure by either party to perform any terms of this Agreement, which would otherwise constitute a material breach of this Agreement, shall be deemed or declared to be a material breach of this Agreement unless, within sixty (60) days after acquiring actual knowledge of such breach or failure to perform, or of a fact sufficient to put the non-breaching party on notice of any such breach or failure to perform, the non-breaching party serves the other with written notice of such breach or failure to perform, and the breaching party does not cure, or commence a good faith effort to cure, the same, within a further period of thirty (30) days after receipt of such written notice. Except as may be otherwise required by law, the date of mailing of such notice shall be deemed the date upon which such notice was given, and it shall be deemed received three days thereafter. Notice by facsimile transmission (fax) or by electronic**

mail (e-mail) shall be deemed to have been received when transmitted. Failure to give notice hereunder is not material, and shall in no event be deemed a waiver or limitation in respect to any breach or non-performance of any contractual obligation hereunder.

Cure Provision — Comprehensive:

Neither party may assert that the other party has committed a material breach of any term or condition of this Agreement, or is in default in respect to this Agreement, unless and until written notice shall have first been given by the non-breaching party to the breaching party, setting forth in reasonable detail the nature and extent of the perceived breach or default, and allowing a period of thirty (30) days from the date of such notice for such breach or default to be cured to the satisfaction of the non-breaching party. Except as may be otherwise required by law, the date of mailing of such notice shall be deemed the date upon which such notice was given, and it shall be deemed received three days thereafter. Notice by facsimile transmission (fax) or by electronic mail (e-mail) shall be deemed received when transmitted. In consequence of this cure provision, neither party may initiate any legal proceeding for breach of contract against the other without first giving that other party the written notice and thirty (30) day opportunity to cure any breach or default, as hereinabove provided. Failure to give notice hereunder is not material, and shall in no event be deemed a waiver or limitation in respect to any breach or non-performance of any contractual obligation hereunder. The foregoing restriction on commencement of legal proceedings applies only to actions for actual breach, and is without effect as to actions for anticipatory breach, injunctive relief, declaratory relief, or in tort.

◆ ◆ ◆

Delivery Requirement Clause

"Delivery" is one of those common, plain-English words fraught with legal meaning. In its everyday sense, the word is more closely akin to what (in legal parlance) is referred to as "tender" — the act of attempting to deliver something to another — while *delivery* only occurs if the recipient *accepts* the tender.

The word is particularly critical in recording contracts, and should therefore be specially defined in those contracts. In the absence of a special definition, the rules of legal construction will apply a definition based upon the normal usage and custom of the industry. For the record business, that usage and custom provides that *acceptance* (and hence "delivery") does not occur until the label has decided that the tendered recordings are "satisfactory." Under that definition, it's impossible to be certain that "delivery" of master recordings has occurred until the album is actually manufactured and released.

Because certain recording contract rights and obligations are linked to the "Delivery Date," establishing what does (and what does not) constitute "Delivery," and formulating a means for determining the precise date upon which "Delivery" occurs, can become a critical issue in respect to option periods and release commitment dates.

Even when an artist honestly believes that all of the necessary recordings for an Album have been finished and delivered, any one of a number of factors may prevent "Delivery," from having actually occurred. The most common of these are:

- Incomplete or questionable clearances.
- Someone at the Label considers one or more of the recordings "unsatisfactory," for some specific or non-specific, disclosed or undisclosed reason.

The "satisfactory" requirement can be insuperable, particularly where *that* word is not further defined, or where its definition sets a subjective, rather than objective standard. Of course, regardless of the standard applied, if the Label doesn't want to release the Album, they won't... and the technicality of whether or not "Delivery" occurred will make little difference unless the matter actually ends up in court.

"Delivery" *(Generic, favorable to delivering party)*

> **"Delivery" shall be conclusively presumed to have occurred upon the date and at the time of tender [, unless the recipient shall, within ___ [days/hours] thereof, return the same, intact, unaltered, unused and undamaged, together with notice in writing that delivery has not been accepted and stating with specificity the reason or reasons for non-acceptance].**

"Delivery" *(Generic, favorable to receiving party)*

"Delivery" hereunder shall not occur unless and until recipient shall have had ample opportunity to inspect and approve any tender hereunder, and thereafter acknowledge, in writing, that said tender is satisfactory and has been accepted as having been delivered. Language appearing on or in connection with any "delivery receipt" or similar instrument prepared by anyone other than recipient, and signed contemporaneously or in connection with receipt of the tender shall not satisfy the requirements of this provision.

"Delivery" *(Master Recordings)* ***Company favorable:***

"Delivery" shall be the actual receipt and acceptance by Company and by Distributor of no fewer than [number] fully mixed and edited Master Recordings of original compositions never previously released by any artist or Company, recorded by Artist hereunder entirely within the term of this Agreement, each of which Master Recordings shall have a playing time of no less than [minimum time], and no more than [maximum time] and none of which shall be a re-recording of any composition previously recorded and commercially released by Artist in any territory, market or medium, at any time, and each of which shall be deemed satisfactory to Company and Distributor, in their sole discretion, and ready for Company's and Distributor's manufacture of Phonograph Records, and shall include therewith all necessary licenses, consents, approvals, union compliance, and payments to any and all third parties. Artist's tender of the foregoing shall not be deemed "Delivery" hereunder unless and until the Company shall either (a) acknowledge, in writing, that Delivery hereunder has occurred as of a certain date (the "Delivery Date") or, (b) the Company shall release a phonorecord containing no fewer than [number] of the aforesaid Master Recordings, in which event the Delivery Date shall be deemed to be the Initial Release Date of such phonorecord in the United States through normal retail channels. The release of a Single or EP shall not be deemed an acknowledgment of Delivery of any Master Recording not contained within such Single or EP.

Alternatively, some record contracts split the definition of Delivery into three separate definitions: Delivery, Acceptance, and Delivery Date, as follow:

"Delivery" *(Master Recordings)* ***Company favorable*** *(alternative):*

> **"Delivery" — Company's receipt of two (2), two track stereo tapes, fully edited, mixed, leadered and equalized, or a digital equivalent in a format which the Company has approved in writing, together with a track by track list ("Personnel List") of all featured vocal performers, background vocal performers, and instrumental performers on each Master Recording identifying their performances, and all necessary licenses, approvals, consents and permissions, including copies of all Union-required session reports.**
>
> **"Acceptance" — Each Master Recording shall be subject to Company's approval as satisfactory for the manufacture and sale of records. Upon Company's request, Artist shall record additional Compositions and/or re-record any Composition recorded hereunder, as necessary, until a Master Recording which in Company's sole judgment is satisfactory for the manufacture and sale of records shall have been obtained.**
>
> **"Delivery Date" — for each Album recorded hereunder, shall be the date upon which the Company unreservedly "Accepts" the final Master Recording required to complete Delivery of such Album.**

"Delivery" *(Master Recordings)* ***Artist favorable:***

"Delivery" shall be Artist's tender to Company or Distributor of no fewer than [number] fully mixed and edited Master Recordings of original compositions recorded by Artist, of sufficient aggregate playing time to comprise a normal and customary "Album," and each of which shall be technically satisfactory for manufacture of phonorecords, together with all necessary licenses, consents and approvals in respect to said Master Recordings. The "Delivery Date," thereof shall be the date upon which such tender occurred. The Company shall have a period of thirty (30) days following the date of tender to advise Artist, in writing, if the Company deems Delivery not to have been completed thereby, specifying with particularity each element of the Delivery which Company deems absent, insufficient, defective, or technically unsatisfactory. Artist shall have an additional forty-five (45) days following receipt of such notice, during which to cure the specified deficiencies, or to meet and confer with Company in respect to the actual necessity, if any, of so doing. The "Delivery Date" shall nonetheless remain the original date of Artist's tender, except to the extent that such date may be hereinafter used to fix a date certain for release or distribution of recordings hereunder. For that limited purpose, any such provision mandating release or distribution shall be extended by no more than one hundred twenty (120) days, to accommodate any agreed-upon, necessary correction or augmentation of Artist's original tender hereunder.

◆ ◆ ◆

Escape Provision

It is unlikely that a contract will actually contain a section or provision entitled "escape," but such provisions are not uncommon, either as an adjunct to another contract section, providing for release in the event that a stated obligation of that section is not timely or fully performed, or as a section bearing a less ominous-sounding name, such as "Early Termination," or "Automatic Termination," or they may be part of a cure provision.

Whatever it's called, or even if it is unnamed, such a provision is intended to allow a party to terminate the contract whenever certain stated events occur or fail to occur. For example, in an earlier chapter we discussed the dangers of one type of record company "deal memo," and stressed the importance to Artist of insisting on an escape provision in such deal memos:

Escape Provision - Record Label Deal Memo - Artist Favorable:

> **In the event that Company does not initiate formal contract negotiations with Artist within ten (10) days following the date subscribed by Artist hereto, or if, within sixty (60) days following that date, Artist and Company shall have failed to agree upon and enter into a formal record contract which supercedes the instant memorandum, then this memorandum agreement shall automatically terminate and be of no further force nor effect, and any "Advance" and/or other consideration tendered to Artist in connection herewith shall be retained by Artist as fully earned and due compensation for the time during which Artist was bound to Company hereunder.**

(See also, "Termination Provision")

◆ ◆ ◆

Exclusivity Clause

In contracts, the word "exclusive" means precisely that. Certain otherwise-available alternative agreements with others are excluded, and one or both of the parties will limited to dealing with the other party *only,* in respect to those portions of the agreement which are made "exclusive." Thus, under an "exclusive" recording contract, the artist cannot enter into a competing agreement with any other recording company. Note that this does not preclude entering into a non-competing agreement, however, such as one which is for a different territory, or which is for services which are outside the scope of the exclusive contract. It is not unheard of for an artist to be signed "exclusively" to one label for the United States and Canada, while signed "exclusively" to a different label in Europe or the U.K.[224]

It should be noted that public policy disfavors exclusivity when it amounts to unfair competition, or a restraint of trade, or would violate antitrust laws, and such provisions may be void, voidable, or severable, as a matter of law. For example, a number of cable operators and satellite providers had for years included exclusivity provisions in their contracts with residential building owners, mandating that no competing service could be installed in their facilities. This restricted tenants' right to chose a competitor's services, creating a virtual monopoly within that facility. The FCC stepped in, making such "exclusivity" provisions unenforceable.

For personal services, however — particularly long-term personal service agreements in the entertainment industry — exclusivity is the norm rather than the exception, and there is no law or public policy against such agreements.[225]

Care should be exercised *whenever* the word "exclusive" (or any variant of that word) shows up in a contract, particularly in respect to licenses or grants of right. For example, if an artist grants an *exclusive* right to use, and to license others to use, the artist's personality rights, then the artist cannot enter into any other agreement with respect to those rights. This effectively forecloses any opportunity for the artist to obtain endorsement or merchandising deals, since *only* the company (and not the artist) can thereafter license others to use artist's name and likeness.

Generally, exclusivity must be expressly stated, and non-exclusivity is to be presumed. It is nonetheless good practice to specifically state that a particular grant or license is "non-

---

224 Caution must be exercised in respect to the "re-recording restrictions" in such contracts, however, to avoid a breach resulting from recording the same song for both labels.

225 California does have "minimum compensation" statutes with respect to such contracts, which preclude the employing party from obtaining injunctive relief against a performer who breaches the exclusivity provisions of a personal service contract, unless the employing party has paid the performer certain minimum amounts of consideration during the contract term. See California Civil Code, § 3423, subd. (5) and California Code of Civil Procedure § 526, subd. (5). *Cf.,* MCA Records, Inc. v. Newton-John (1979) 90 Cal. App. 3d 18.

exclusive" whenever that it the intention, particularly where the contract contains exclusivity in respect to other aspects of the agreement.

Exclusivity Clause — Company Favorable:

> **Company hereby engages Artist's exclusive personal services as an entertainer and recording artist in connection with the entertainment industry, including recording services, performances, and all talent-related services in the field of entertainment, and Artist hereby accepts such engagement and agrees to exclusively render such services for Company in and throughout the Territory during the Term, including the initial period of this agreement and all extensions and renewals thereof.**

Exclusivity Clause — Artist Favorable:

> **Company hereby engages Artist's exclusive personal services as a recording artist in connection with the production of Recordings and/or Records and Artist hereby accepts such engagement and agrees to exclusively render such services for Company in the Territory during the Term hereof.**

Exclusivity of Name and Likeness — Company Favorable:

> **Company shall have the worldwide exclusive right to use, and to license others to use, Artist's name, likeness, other identification, and biographical material relating to Artist, for and all purposes of or related to trade and advertising. This right shall be perpetual in respect to any and all uses which are in any way related to any Recordings recorded hereunder including, without limitation, any and all packaging, marketing, sales, advertising, publicity, promotion and merchandise which is in any manner related to such Recordings.**

Non-Exclusive Name and Likeness — Artist Favorable:

Label shall have the perpetual, non-exclusive right, throughout the Territory, to use Artist's name, likeness, other identification, and biographical material relating to Artist, for promoting, marketing, distributing, advertising, packaging, and/or sale of Recordings recorded hereunder by Artist. All rights in respect to Artist's personality not expressly granted or licensed by the foregoing are expressly reserved to Artist.

◆ ◆ ◆

Force Majeure Provision

A maxim of jurisprudence states that, "The law never requires impossibilities." Contracting parties are generally required to perform only such contract obligations as they have not been "excused or prevented" from performing. (And "excused," in its legal context, does not refer to bringing a note from home.)

Translated literally, "force majeure" means "major force," but the legal concept of force majeure refers to unpredictable, significant occurrences which are (1) outside the control of a contracting party, (2) could not by a party's due care have been avoided, and (3) which impede or wholly preclude a party's ability to perform a contract obligation. Typically, force majeure arises by reason of natural disasters or other "Acts of God,"[226] war, or an unforeseeable failure by third parties — e.g., subcontractors, transport companies — to perform obligations which are indispensable to performance of the contracting party's obligations.

For example, a band may be excused from failure to perform at a concert, if their tour bus is hit by lightning and explodes on the way to the gig. If, on the other hand, they fail to show up because their manager gave the driver the wrong date, or bad directions, and it's now become impossible for them to fulfill the obligation, their failure to perform would *not* be excusable under force majeure. Even though performance was "impossible," that impossibility flowed from their manager's avoidable negligence.

Thus force majeure provisions recognize legal precepts regarding impossibility of performance, while to some extent defining and limiting the types of occurrences which will excuse a party from liability if some unforseen event beyond that party's control makes performance impossible. Note, however, that the availability of such excuse will require that the failure to perform could not have been avoided by exercising of due care.

As a drafting consideration, force majeure provisions should apply equally to all parties, and not seek an inequitable application benefitting only one party. It is also good practice to include specific examples of occurrences which will typically excuse performance ("*e.g.*, wars, natural disasters, Acts of God, *etc.*") Such examples will clarify the parties' intent that the provision not apply to failures to perform for reasons which were within the parties' reasonable control.

226 ***Practice note:*** For religious reasons, some parties will be unable to subscribe to a writing which includes the word "God" spelled in full. The convention, if the word cannot be avoided, is to redact the "o," so that the phrase above would appear as "Acts of G_d."

Force Majeure Provision:

Neither party shall be or become liable for damages hereunder, nor subject to injunction or other court order, nor shall there be any right for either party to terminate this Agreement, by reason of any delay or default in performance hereunder which delay or default is proximately caused by, or unavoidably results from, occurrences or conditions beyond the control of the party whose delay or default thereby results. The types of occurrences and conditions contemplated by the foregoing include, but are not necessarily limited to: default or delay by third parties in respect to essential materials or services necessary to the party's performance hereunder; natural disasters (e.g., hurricanes, earthquakes, floods, etc.); other Acts of G_d; governmental restrictions (including, but not limited to, judicial orders, incarceration, detention, denial or cancellation of any visa, work permit, import license, export license, or other required license or permission); wars; insurrections; acts of terrorism; and/or any other event or occurrence beyond the reasonable control of the party whose performance is affected thereby.

Force Majeure Provision *(with Notice and Extension Clauses):*

Neither Party shall be liable for any failure or delay in performance under this Agreement (other than for delay in the payment of royalties or other monies which are or may become due and payable hereunder) to the extent that any such failures or delays are proximately caused by, or unavoidably result from, events beyond that Party's reasonable control, (including, without limitation, natural disasters, , Acts of God, and default, defect, or delay of suppliers, subcontractors, or carriers) which have occurred without the Party's fault or negligence, provided that, as a condition to a claim of non-liability hereunder, the Party experiencing an impediment to performance for reasons within the scope of this provision shall give the other Party prompt written notice, following the occurrence of the cause relied upon, stating the precise nature and details of the occurrence and its impact upon performance hereunder. Dates by which performance obligations are scheduled to be met will be extended hereunder for a period of time equivalent to such time as is lost due to any delay so caused, including such time as may be required to restore the affected Party to status quo ante.

◆ ◆ ◆

Grant of Rights Clause

In every contract which conveys any interest in intellectual property (or equivalent rights), or exclusive personal services, a contract section entitled "Grant of Rights" will usually be included. Even in contracts where such a section appears, however, grants of right may be scattered throughout the agreement. For example, in recording contracts and publishing agreements, a grant of rights to use name and likeness will probably appear elsewhere in those contracts, although each will nonetheless have a specific Grant of Rights section for personal services or copyrights which are primary subjects of the contract.[227]

The purpose of a "grant of rights" clause is to enumerate the specific rights being granted by the owner of those rights to the other party, *and to impose limitations and exclusions in respect to the scope of rights being granted.* It is critical to make certain that limitations with respect to the particular Rights,[228] Term, Territory, included media and configurations, as well as any other special considerations, are established unambiguously. It is also good practice (for the grantor) to conclude the section with an unequivocal statement to the effect that all rights not expressly granted are reserved to the grantor.

Another current consideration are the so-called "e-rights" for various types of electronic exploitation. While a blanket reservation of rights will likely preserve these rights (unless the grant contains an "all media whether known or unknown" statement), it will be better practice to include within the grant of rights the specific e-right which are *intended* to be granted.

Songwriting agreements, recording contracts, publishing agreements, distribution agreements, graphic arts contracts, and photographer's contracts (among others) are all likely to contain grants of rights.

The scope of a grant of rights clause can vary widely, so its wording must be scrutinized carefully in negotiations and draft reviews. For example, the grant could be *all inclusive* and *exclusive*, or narrowly drawn as *non-exclusive* and *limited.* The crucial point will be to establish that the grantee may only exploit those rights which have been specifically granted — and no other rights.

To avoid controversies over electronic rights ("e-rights"), then the specific inclusion of (and limitations upon) such rights should be made part of the grant of rights clause. This, together with a "reservation of rights" statement will likely be critical to determining the

227 In recording contracts, a "Mechanical License" or "Controlled Compositions" section will likely contain the grant of rights with respect to composition copyrights, while the "Grant of Rights" section will address exclusive personal services, sound recording copyrights, and (sometimes) "name and likeness" — although this last is more usually included in a separate section, by itself.

228 For copyright grants, look to the five enumerated statutory rights in copyright — reproduction, derivative rights, distribution, public performance, and public display — and be specific as to what aspect(s) of which right(s) are to be included in (or excluded from) the grant.

respective rights of the grantor and grantee as to control and exploitation of all or part of the subject work through present electronic means and potential new technologies.

The type of contract being negotiated or drafted will necessarily dictate the rights being granted, and hence make a significant difference in the grant of rights section of that contract. In recording contracts, in particular, there will be a sweeping number of "rights" which label will want the Artist to convey, waive, assign or license. The names given to these various rights may vary from contract to contract, but their substance will include: (1) exclusivity as to Artist's personal services; (2) license to use Artist's personality / publicity rights ("name and likeness"); (3) licenses for controlled compositions (mechanical licenses and, in some instances, agency authorization for other licensing); and (4) the most critical of these rights for the label (under whatever name is used) a "work for hire" provision with respect to master recordings to be recorded under the agreement, coupled with conveyance, transfer and sale language duplicating that grant.[229] While inclusion of each of these *categories* of grants will be non-negotiable in every recording contract, their *scope* will be negotiable to some extent, depending on the reputation, prior success, and resultant bargaining power of the Artist.

Grant of Rights *(Basic) - Record Contract - Company Favorable:*

> **Company and any Person authorized by Company shall have the exclusive and unlimited rights to own, control and exploit Artist's services as a recording artist during the Term and to all the results and proceeds of Artist's services as a recording artist during the Term, including, but not limited to, the following exclusive, unlimited and perpetual rights throughout the Territory:**
>
> **(a) to manufacture, advertise, sell, lease, license, distribute or to otherwise use, exploit or dispose of, in any or all fields of use by any method now or hereafter known, Records embodying Masters;**
>
> **(b) to release Records derived from Masters under any name, trademark or label which Company or its subsidiaries, affiliates licensees may from time to time elect;**
>
> **(c) to perform such Masters publicly and to permit public performances thereof by means of radio broadcast, television, or any other method now or hereafter known; and**

229 As noted elsewhere, sound recordings are technically *excluded* from the types of work which may be designated as "works made for hire" under the U.S. Copyright Act. Although labels still generally include "work for hire" statement regarding sound recordings in their recording contract, they include transfer, sale and conveyance language, as well. Such language is necessary to comply with Berne Convention requirements, in any event.

(d) to reproduce, adapt, transmit, communicate or otherwise use Masters, all upon such terms and conditions as Company may elect, or at its discretion, to refrain therefrom.

Grant of Rights *(Basic) - Record Contract - Artist Favorable:*

Company shall have the non-exclusive right to exploit Artist's services as a recording artist in connection with the Project during the Term, including, but not limited to, the following rights throughout the Territory:

(a) to manufacture, advertise, sell, lease, license, distribute or to otherwise use or exploit Records embodying Masters recorded hereunder;

(b) to release Records derived from Masters recorded hereunder under Company's name;

(c) to perform such Masters publicly and to permit public performances thereof by means of radio broadcast, television, or any other method now or hereafter known; and

(d) to reproduce, adapt, transmit, communicate or otherwise use Masters, provided such uses directly relate to the Project.

All other rights are reserved by Artist.

Grant of Rights *(Comprehensive) - Record Contract - Company Favorable:*

(1) Company and any Person authorized by Company shall have the exclusive and unlimited rights to own, control and exploit Artist's services as a recording artist during the Term and to all the results and proceeds of Artist's services as a recording artist during the Term.

(2) Each Master Recording made under this agreement will be considered a "work made for hire" for Company within the meaning of U.S. Copyright Law, to the fullest extent permissible thereunder. Artist hereby assigns, transfers, conveys, sells and releases to and for the benefit of Company each, every, any and all rights which Artist has or may have in or to the said Master Recordings, and each of them, to the fullest extent permissible by law, except such interest therein as may be expressly provided to Artist by the terms of this Agreement.

(3) As between Artist and Company, each, every, any, and all Master Recordings, from the inception of the recording thereof, and all Records and other reproductions made therefrom, together with the performances embodied therein and all copyrights therein and thereto throughout the Territory, and all renewals and extensions thereof, shall be entirely Company's property, and Artist hereby expressly agrees, warrants and represents that such Master Recordings shall be and shall forever remain free of any and every claim whatsoever by Artist or by any other person, firm, or corporation.

(4) Company shall have the exclusive right to register all copyrights, including all renewals and extensions thereof, in and to all Recordings hereunder, in Company's name as the exclusive owner and author thereof.

(5) In the event that Company shall be deemed not to be the author of any recording hereunder, or should any recording hereunder be deemed not to be a "work made for hire" under the Copyright Law of the United States, then this agreement shall constitute an irrevocable transfer and conveyance from Artist to Company of any and all rights of ownership of copyright, including (without limitation) any and all rights to renewals and extensions thereof, from Artist to Company, in respect to each, every, any and all recordings hereunder. Artist shall, upon Company's request, cause to be executed and delivered to Company any and all such transfers of ownership of copyright, renewals, and extensions in respect to those recordings, and any other documents which Company may deem necessary or appropriate, to vest in Company the rights granted to Company under the terms of this Agreement, and Artist hereby irrevocably appoints Company as Artist's attorney-in-fact for the purpose of effecting those transfers of ownership and other documents in Artist's name.

(6) Without limiting the generality of the foregoing, Company and any person, firm, or corporation designated by Company shall have the exclusive, perpetual and worldwide right to manufacture, sell, distribute and advertise Records embodying those Master Recordings under any trademarks, trade names, or labels, and to lease, license, convey or otherwise use or dispose of those Master Recordings by any method now or hereafter known in any field of use and to perform publicly Records and other reproductions embodying those Master Recordings, all upon such terms as Company may approve, or Company may refrain from doing any or all of the foregoing.

Grant of Rights (*Comprehensive*) - *Record Contract - Artist Favorable:*

(1) Master Recordings Delivered hereunder, together with the performances embodied therein, shall be the property of Company, except as may be herein elsewhere provided.

(2) Nothing contained in the within Agreement shall convey to Company any right whatsoever in respect to the ownership of, or any right to publish, or to administer, or to in any manner participate in, any copyright or other right in or to, or in respect to, any musical composition, except as embodied in sound recordings made hereunder, and subject to the mechanical licensing terms provided herein in respect thereto.

(3) Company shall have the right to register Sound Recording copyrights in Master Recordings Delivered hereunder, in Company's name as Copyright Claimant and owner of such , provided that Artist appears as the author thereof, and no right or interest in or to any composition embodied in such Sound Recording is purported to be included within such Sound Recording copyright.

(4) Without limiting the generality of the foregoing, Company and its designees shall have the exclusive and perpetual right, but not the obligation, throughout the Territory, to manufacture, sell, distribute and advertise Records embodying those Master Recordings, and to lease, license, or otherwise use those Master Recordings by any method now or hereafter known in any field of use, and to perform publicly Records and other reproductions embodying those Master Recordings. Each, every, any and all rights not expressly granted to Company herein are reserved by and to Artist exclusively.

Grant of Rights (*Basic*) - *Worldwide Publishing - Company Favorable:*

Author hereby grants exclusively and irrevocably to the Publisher all rights in and to the work of musical composition tentatively entitled _________ (the "Work") during the full term of copyright (and all renewals and extensions thereof) throughout the world, including (without limitation) the sole and exclusive right to reproduce, publish, distribute, sell copies in any medium (other than as a sound recording embodying a performance of the work), and the further exclusive right to license any or all of such rights granted herein, specifically including (but not limited to) the right to grant mechanical, synchronous, or other licenses for the recording of performances of the Work in any and every medium, and through any technological method, regardless of whether such medium and/or technology is now know or unknown.

***Grant of Rights** (Basic) - Worldwide Publishing - Author Favorable:*

Author hereby grants to Publisher the following enumerated rights, and only those rights, in and to the work of musical composition tentatively entitled __________ (the "Work") during the full term of copyright (and all renewals and extensions thereof) throughout the world; the sole and exclusive right to print or otherwise reproduce, publish, distribute and sell the Work in printed form, and to grant to others mechanical licenses to record the Work as a phonorecord, and to grant to others licenses to record the work for synchronous embodiment in an audiovisual work, and such subsidiary rights as are specified in paragraph __, with the exclusive right to license any or all of such rights. The rights herein granted are revocable, pursuant and subject to terms and conditions set forth in paragraph __ hereof.

(See, also, "Reservation of Rights.")

◆ ◆ ◆

Heirs and Assigns Provision

This is an especially critical "housekeeping" provision which should appear in every contract. In essence, it memorializes a legal doctrine which says that whoever takes the benefit, also assumes the burden. Even when a contract precludes assignments, there are other mechanisms by which the identity of a contracting party may change. For example,

- A company or individual may go bankrupt, and the court may appoint a trustee to take charge of all assets (including contract benefits) and liabilities (including contract obligations);
- Creditors may force a company into receivership, and the court may appoint a receiver to take over the company's operations;
- One company may merge with another, so that the original company disappears into a new entity;
- An individual may die, with or without a will, at which point an estate administrator or trustee will be appointed;
- An individual may lose capacity (*i.e.,* become mentally incompetent or unstable) at which point a conservator may be appointed.

And, of course, if the contract does not preclude assignment, the original party may sell or assign its interests in the contract to someone else.

The purpose of the "Heirs and Assigns" provision is to make clear that the terms and conditions of the agreement are equally binding upon any successor individual or entity stepping into the role of a party to the contract. In addition, it clarifies the fact that all affiliates of a contracting party are bound by the contract's terms and conditions, as well.

Heirs and Assigns (Basic):

> **This Agreement is binding upon the Parties, and upon their respective employees, representatives, agents, successors, heirs, and assigns.**

Heirs and Assigns (Comprehensive):

> **This Agreement is binding upon the Parties hereto and upon their respective employees, principals, officers, directors, managers, representatives, agents, affiliates, subsidiaries, successors, conservators, administrators, trustees, legatees, nominees, devisees, heirs and assigns.**

◆ ◆ ◆

Indemnity Provision

Parties to a contract cannot, by the language of their agreement, dispense with or shift a liability which either may have with respect to a non-party. To put it another way, the contract cannot directly affect any of the rights or remedies of anyone who is not a party to the contract. For example,

> *Abner owes Bill $1,000.00. Abner and Charlie enter into a contract, the terms of which state that Charlie will be 100% responsible for paying Abner's obligation to Bill. That agreement does not stop Bill from suing Abner for the debt. Abner is still liable to Bill, and must pay the obligation. However, under the contract with Charlie, Abner can make a claim against Charlie for indemnity, compelling Charlie to either pay Bill directly, or else to reimburse Abner for the costs and expense of not only paying the debt to Bill, but also the costs of the lawsuit.[230] But, unfortunately, Charlie has filed for bankruptcy protection, and has no assets. Abner is out of luck. He must pay Bill, and is unlikely to ever see a dime of reimbursement from Charlie.*

An indemnification is only as good as the indemnitor's ability to pay.

In recording contracts, the indemnification provision will almost-invariably be a part of the Warranties and Representations section. Its purpose is to make the Artist ultimately liable in the event that a third party sues the label based upon fact which are inconsistent with the Artist's representations to the label in respect to rights being conveyed to the label by the contract. As with our friend Abner, however, the label will have to pay the third party if the claim is proven, and will have only the Artist to look to for indemnification of that expense. Fortunately for the label, however, it will have the ability to withhold virtually all of the Artist's income until the indemnification is paid off.

---

230 Depending on the language of the contract between Abner and Charlie, this may also include the cost of Abner's attorney's fees.

Indemnity Provision (Recording Contract) - Company Favorable:

Artist will at all times indemnify and hold harmless Company from and against any and all claims, losses, damages, liabilities, costs and expenses, including, without limitation, all legal expenses and attorneys' fees of any party or third party, arising out of or regarding any alleged breach or actual breach by Artist, or of any individual comprising Artist hereunder, or any person actually or ostensibly acting for or on behalf of Artist, of any warranty, representation or agreement made by Artist herein, which has resulted in a final judgment or has been settled with Artist's written consent (it being understood that Artist's consent is hereby given, in advance, to any settlement which does not exceed Twenty-Five Thousand ($25,000) Dollars). Notwithstanding the foregoing, if Artist withholds consent to any settlement which Company is willing to make, the foregoing indemnity shall apply and Company may settle such claim in its sole discretion unless Artist promptly assumes all costs of defending against such claim, demand or action including, without limitation, court costs, reasonable attorneys' fees, and direct expenses theretofore incurred by Company in connection with said claim, demand or action; provided that in the event Artist assumes said costs, Company shall nonetheless have the right to settle such claim, demand or action in its sole discretion without Artist's consent, provided that, in such event, the foregoing indemnification shall not apply with respect thereto. Artist will reimburse Company on demand for any payment made at any time after the date hereof in respect of any liability or claim in respect of which Company are entitled to be indemnified. Upon the making or filing of any such claim, action or demand, Company shall be entitled to withhold from any amounts payable under this agreement such amounts as are reasonably related to the potential liability in issue. Notwithstanding the foregoing, Company shall liquidate such withheld amounts if within twelve (12) months no lawsuit has been commenced and active settlement discussions are not then taking place. Notwithstanding the foregoing, Company shall release to Artist all such withheld payments upon Artist's posting of a bond in an amount equivalent to the sum being withheld by Company in respect of such third party claim with a good and sufficient surety approved by Company, provided that such surety agrees unconditionally, in writing, to pay all costs, fees, damages, etc. incurred by Company by reason of such third party claim. Artist shall be promptly notified of any such third party claim, action or

demand and shall have the right, at Artist's own expense, to participate in the defense thereof with counsel of Artist's own choosing; provided, however, that Company's decision in connection with the defense of any such claim, action or demand shall be final.

Indemnity Provision (Recording Contract) - Artist Favorable:[231]

Artist will indemnify and hold harmless Company from and against proven claims, losses, damages, liabilities, costs and expenses, including a third-party's reasonable attorneys' fees, arising out of any proven breach by Artist of any warranty, representation or agreement made by Artist herein, and which has resulted in a final judgment or has been settled with Artist's written consent. Notwithstanding the foregoing, if Artist withholds consent to any settlement which Company is willing to make, the foregoing indemnity shall apply and Company may settle such claim in its sole discretion unless Artist promptly assumes all further costs of defending against such claim, demand or action including, without limitation, court costs, reasonable attorneys' fees, and direct expenses in connection with said claim, demand or action; provided that in the event Artist assumes said costs, Company shall nonetheless have the right to settle such claim, demand or action in its sole discretion without Artist's consent, provided that, in such event, the foregoing indemnification shall become inoperative, ineffective, and inapplicable with respect thereto. As a material condition of this indemnity provision, Company shall promptly notify Artist of any such third party claim, action or demand. Artist shall have the right, at Artist's own expense, to participate in the defense thereof, and all settlement discussions and correspondence in respect thereto, either personally or through independent counsel of Artist's own choosing.

---

231 Counter-intuitively, the most favorable deal for the Artist would not be omission of an indemnification provision, since the law will enforce an *equitable* indemnification in the absence of a contractual one when a party has been damaged through detrimental reliance on insupportable warranties. This provision establishes a less onerous obligation for Artist than a court might impose as an equitable remedy.

Indemnity Provision (Generic, Comprehensive) — Company Favorable:

Artist agrees to indemnify Company, Company's successors, assigns, and licensees, and their respective directors, officers, agents and employees, and to hold Company, its successors, assigns and licenses and their respective directors, officers, agents and employees harmless against any damages, cost, expenses, fees (including costs and reasonable attorneys' fees) incurred or accrued by Company its successors, assigns and licenses and their respective directors, officers, agents and employees in any claim, suit or proceeding instituted by or against Company its successors, assigns and licenses and their respective directors, officers, agents and employees by a third party in which any assertion is made which is inconsistent with any warranty, representation or covenant made by Artist and which is reduced to final non-appealable judgment or settled with Artist's prior written consent, which shall not be unreasonably withheld. Company shall notify Artist of any claim, demand, or action covered by this indemnity, and Artist shall have the right, at Artist's sole expense to participate in the defense of any such claim, demand, or action through counsel of Artist's choice. The defense and settlement of the claim, however, shall be controlled and determined in Company's sole discretion.

◆ ◆ ◆

Injunctive Relief Provision

Injunctive relief is an equitable remedy by which a court issues an order — an injunction — which compels a party to cease some current conduct, or to not undertake a planned action, or which requires the party to perform some legally required action or duty.[232] Where the injunction is framed in the negative — requiring that certain activities cease, or that those activities not commence[233] — the injunction is termed *prohibitory*. Where the order commands the performance of a duty or obligation, it is referred to as a *mandatory* injunction.

Also, injunctions can be temporary, preliminary, or permanent. Temporary injunctions (more often referred to as restraining orders) are generally issued on an emergency basis, for a short period of time, and are usually only made effective until a full hearing can be held upon the underlying issue. Preliminary injunctions — which usually issue as a result of a hearing on a temporary restraining order — generally last for the duration of the underlying lawsuit, precluding the enjoined conduct until the entire case and all of its legal and factual issues have been resolved. Finally, upon final judgment and disposition of that case, that injunction, or some portions of it, may be made permanent if the facts and legal issues warrant a permanent order.

The party seeking the injunction or restraining order must demonstrate a number of elements to the satisfaction of the court: (1) that imminent and irreparable harm, for which monetary damages are insufficient remedy, will result if the injunction does not issue; (2) that there is no readily available remedy at law which could prevent that harm; (3) that the "balance of harm" favors the party seeking injunction; and (4) that the party seeking injunction will likely prevail on the merits of the underlying case. A bond for the purpose of indemnifying the enjoined party is usually a requirement for issuance of a restraining order or preliminary injunction.

By way of example...

> *Hypothetical:* Abner is a recording artist under an exclusive recording contract with Baker Records. Baker learns that Abner has recorded an album for Competitor Records, which is about to publicly release that album. Baker rushes to court with a complaint against Abner and Competitor, together with

---

232 A petition for writ of mandate *(mandamus)* is an injunctive procedure which seeks an order from one court directed to a *lower* court, tribunal, or administrative agency, commanding that the lower institution perform some particular duty which the higher court has held is required of them, as a matter of law, Characterized as an "extraordinary writ" procedure, writs of mandate can be either *peremptory* (absolutely commanding that the lower body perform as ordered), or *alternative* (commanding that the duty either be performed, or that a real party in interest appear before the issuing court and show cause why the commanded duty or action should not be performed.) The procedure involved in *alternative* writs therefore mirrors that of restraining orders and injunctions.

233 Injunctions against actions which have not yet occurred are difficult to obtain, due to Constitutional considerations with respect to "prior restraint."

an application for an emergency restraining order to which copies of relevant evidence (e.g., Abner's contract, Competitor's press releases, declarations of witnesses, etc.) are attached, as proof that Competitor is about to release an album by Abner in violation of the exclusivity of Baker's contract with him. The court issues the temporary order, commanding that Competitor and its affiliates not release the album, and ordering Abner and Competitor to appear in court on a certain date to show cause why that restraining order should not be made a preliminary injunction. (As a condition for obtaining that temporary order, Baker will likely have to post a bond with the court, for the defendants' benefit if they should ultimately prevail on the issue.)

At the hearing on the order to show cause, both sides argue their respective positions, with Competitor arguing (among other things) the amount of financial harm it will suffer if the album is not released, requesting that, if a preliminary injunction issues, there should be a much larger bond than was posted for the temporary order.

The court issues the injunction on an increased bond, Baker posts that additional amount with the court, and the case proceeds normally through discovery and eventual trial...assuming the parties don't settle first. Absent a successful motion to dissolve the injunction earlier, it will stay in effect throughout the entire litigation process.

Now, here's why all of that is relevant to drafting contracts...

In many types of contracts, and particularly exclusive personal service agreements like recording contracts, it is possible to limit or expand the right to injunctive relief, and to stipulate to certain facts and conditions required for injunctive relief, within the contract itself. Such contract language can *preclude* injunctive relief,[234] or *allow* it only for one party, or in respect to limited circumstances only.

More importantly, the parties may stipulate as to the essential "irreparable harm" element of proof, to "imminent" harm, or to other facts, thereby taking those fact out of the scope of what must be proven to the court. Stipulated "facts" will generally be accepted as true by the court, without further need for proof. The parties may even (within limits) waive the bond requirement, or stipulate to a nominal sum for such bond.[235]

---

234 Usually included as part of a "Liquidated Damages" or "Cure" provision.

235 Such stipulation would be ineffectual in regard to the example given above, since the enjoined entity (Competitor) is not party to the underlying contract, and hence not bound by any waiver or stipulation which it contains.

Injunctive Relief (Generic - Employment Contract):

> **The parties acknowledge, agree and stipulate that any breach of this Exclusive Employment Agreement by Employee would cause Employer irreparable harm, and that it would be difficult, if not impossible, to determine the monetary damages that Employer would suffer as a result thereof. Therefore, upon a preliminary finding by a court of competent jurisdiction that there is a likelihood that Employee has breached this Agreement, Employer shall be entitled to temporary and permanent injunctive relief. Employer's right to injunctive relief is in addition to and does not limit any other right, remedy or relief that is available to Employer at law or in equity, including but not limited to damages.**

In recording contracts, references to injunctive relief may appear in regard to different issues in separate parts of the same contract. For example, where Artist has an approval right with respect to name and likeness, and label breaches its duty to obtain Artist's approval before releasing materials containing the un-approved images, the contract is likely to contain a preclusion of injunctive relief:

No Injunctive Relief *(Record Contract — Name & Likeness):*

> **No inadvertent failure to comply with this subparagraph** *[requiring Artist's approval before use of images]* **will constitute a material breach of this agreement, and Artist shall not be entitled to injunctive relief to restrain the continuing use of any material used in contravention of this paragraph provided, however, that Label shall exercise its reasonable and best efforts to cure any such breach on all manufacturing runs involving materials used subsequent to Label's receipt of Artist's timely disapproval or notice of breach.**

Another passing reference to injunctive relief will generally appear in connection with a recording contract's "Minimum Compensation" clause, which is included solely for purposes of compliance with California statutes which bar injunctive relief for breach of exclusive personal services agreements if the employee does not receive a statutorily mandated minimum compensation for each year of the contract.

Injunctive Relief Available *(Record Contract - Minimum Compensation Requirement under California law):*

> **Artist acknowledges that this** *[Minimum Compensation]* **paragraph is included to avoid compromise of Label's rights (including Label's entitlement to injunctive relief) by reason of finding of applicability of California Law, but does not constitute a concession by Label that California Law is actually applicable.**

Injunctive Relief — Recording Contract - Company Favorable:

> **This Agreement constitutes a contract whereby Artist is obliged to provide Artist's unique entertainment services as a recording artist to Company on an exclusive basis, throughout the Term and Territory, and refrain from violating certain covenants contained herein (*e.g.*, re-recording restrictions) for a stated term following termination hereof. Artist hereby acknowledges, agrees and stipulates that any breach of this Agreement by Artist would result in imminent and irreparable harm to Company, and that it would be difficult, if not impossible, to determine a monetary sum as adequate damages for the loss, damage and harm which Company would suffer as a result of Artist's breach. Therefore, a court of competent jurisdiction may, upon finding that Artist likely breached the terms hereof, or that Artist has unequivocally stated an anticipatory breach hereof and is imminently likely to breach, may grant, and Company shall be entitled to have, in respect to such breach, injunctive relief on an ex parte, emergency, temporary basis, and a preliminary or permanent injunction thereafter. The parties expressly agree and stipulate, as a bargained for condition hereof, that the bond required for any injunction hereunder shall be a sum of not more than $25,000.00. Company's foregoing right to injunctive relief is in addition to, and does not limit or waive, any other right, remedy, or relief that is or may become available to Company, either in law or in equity, including, but not limited to, such damages as may be allowable by law.**

Injunctive Relief — Recording Contract - Artist Favorable:

In respect to the within Agreement, and any alleged breach, Company shall be entitled to injunctive relief only upon regularly noticed motion and only upon clear and convincing evidence of imminent and irreparable harm for which no amount of pecuniary compensation or damages would be sufficient.

[*Note:* The foregoing, limiting injunctive relief to "regularly noticed motion," prevents the Company from seeking or obtaining a temporary restraining order on an expedited, *ex parte* application, and sets the highest possible standard of proof which must be met before any injunction will issue.]

◆ ◆ ◆

Insolvency Provision

Many contracts contain provisions which make the bankruptcy or insolvency of one party a triggering event which allows the other party to terminate the contract. When such provisions appear in music industry contracts and licenses, they generally include a reversion of rights, which can become problematic.

Sometimes referred to as "Ipso Facto"[236] provisions, these contract clauses commonly provide for *automatic* termination of the contract, without notice or any necessity for the other party to perform any action to implement that termination. **For reasons explained below, most such provisions, either with or without a notice requirement, are *unenforceable*, as a matter of law.**

Insolvency Provision (Generic):

> **This Agreement shall terminate, without notice, (a) upon the institution by or against either party of insolvency, receivership or bankruptcy proceedings or any other proceedings for the settlement of either party's debts, (b) upon either party making an assignment for the benefit of creditors, or (c) upon either party's dissolution or cessation of business operations.**

Variations of this provision will be found in licenses, leases, and other types of contracts, but most especially in those in which the solvency of a party is critical to performance of ongoing obligations to the other party, and where insolvency would put the other party at risk of future loss or harm. While many such provisions state that termination is automatic (as above), others may include a notice requirement following the occurrence of a triggering event. Common triggers may include:

- Filing of petition in bankruptcy, either voluntarily (by the party), or involuntarily (filed by creditors, forcing the party into bankruptcy);
- Making a general assignment for the benefit of creditors;[237]
- Becoming "insolvent."[238]

---

236 "By the fact alone." (Latin) The mere existence of a fact is all the proof necessary for all consequences which flow from that fact.

237 This is a voluntary procedure recognized by the laws of most states as an alternative to bankruptcy, generally requiring liquidation of the indebted party's assets.

238 This term is often included as a vague "catchall," without being further defined.

- Admitting *in writing* to being insolvent; or
- Violating a "financial condition" covenant[239] within or supplemental to the contract.

While these automatic termination provisions may be common, two key provisions of the Bankruptcy Code render them largely ineffective. First, 11 U.S.C. § 541(c) provides that a debtor's interest in property becomes "property of the estate." A contract provision "that is conditioned on the insolvency or financial condition of the debtor, on the commencement of a case under this title, or on the appointment of or taking possession by a trustee in a case under this title or a custodian before such commencement, and that effects or gives an option to effect a forfeiture, modification, or termination of the debtor's interest in property," cannot be used to deprive a debtor or property of contractual benefits. This means that a clause which purports to terminate a contract because of the "insolvency" or "financial condition" of the debtor, or due to the filing of a bankruptcy case, will be unenforceable once a bankruptcy case has been filed.

Yet another Bankruptcy Code provision, 11 U.S.C. § 365(e)(1), governs insolvency clauses in *executory* contracts, such as entertainment contracts which provide for future royalty payments or licensing fees. "[A]n executory contract or unexpired lease of the debtor may not be terminated or modified, and any right or obligation under such contract or lease may not be terminated or modified, at any time after the commencement of the [bankruptcy] case solely because of a provision in such contract or lease that is conditioned on — (A) the insolvency or financial condition of the debtor at any time before the closing of the case; (B) the commencement of a case under this title; or (C) the appointment of or taking possession by a trustee in a case under this title or a custodian before such commencement." This section of the Bankruptcy Code generally makes Insolvency provisions in *executory* contracts and leases unenforceable.

However, there is an important exception to these rules, having less to do with the bankruptcy itself than the rules governing *assignability* of certain types of contracts, and particularly intellectual property licenses.[240]

11 U.S.C. § 365(e)(2), read in conjunction with § 365(c)(1), provides that an insolvency clause *can* be enforceable whenever the debtor or trustee ***is not permitted by applicable law to assume or assign the contract.*** Thus if "applicable law" provides that a copyright license or other executory contract cannot be assumed by the estate or trustee without the other party's consent, and consent to assignment does not appear within the contract itself, then the contract cannot be assigned to, or assumed by, the bankruptcy estate or its trustee, which are legally separate entities from the contracting debtor. In such circumstance, the insolvency provision may be used to force termination of the contract and reversion, generally by applying to the

---

239 Some contracts include an express provision which requires a party to maintain a certain minimum "net worth" and/or cash flow position throughout the Term.

240 These issues a more comprehensively discussed in the section on Assignability Provisions.

bankruptcy court for an order to that effect. It is therefore critical to draft the Assignability Clause with the potential for insolvency in mind.[241]

The narrowness of these exceptions begs the question, "Why bother putting insolvency provisions into contracts in the first place?" Well, the easy answer is... inertia. Prior to 1979, under the old Bankruptcy *Act* of 1898, such provisions *were* enforceable, and lawyers got into the habit of including them. Since contract drafting is often a matter of modifying and augmenting earlier, similar agreements, outdated but apparently innocuous boilerplate language is often retained from year to year, without alteration. Since these provisions are inoffensive (even if ineffectual), and the possibility always exists that Congress may further amend the current Bankruptcy Code, restoring the effect of such provisions, there is no reason to delete them.

Perhaps more importantly, the rules which render these provisions ineffective apply *only* if a bankruptcy is commenced. If the insolvency provision states that the contract will terminate on the occurrence of listed triggering events, and no bankruptcy petition is filed prior to the occurrence of such event,[242] it's possible that the insolvency provision could be effectively utilized to terminate the contract.

---

241 If the contract states that it is freely assignable, this exception to transfer in bankruptcy will be unavailable. Also, in most federal circuits, "applicable law" makes a distinction between *exclusive* and *non-exclusive* intellectual property licenses, with exclusive licenses being freely assignable (except in the Ninth Circuit, as of this writing), *unless* the contract states that it is non-assignable, or only assignable by consent, in which case that contract language will be dispositive of the issue.

242 Or within a short period thereafter. If a bankruptcy filing seems imminent, good practice would dictate sending a formal termination and reversion notice immediately following the triggering event, *before* a bankruptcy petition may be filed. While a bankruptcy court would have jurisdiction to examine the issue and negate the termination, such notice would shift the burden to the debtor to show that the *termination* should be deemed ineffective, rather than leaving Artist with the burden of proving that assumption of the contract is precluded by applicable law.

Insolvency Provision - Recording Contract - Artist Favorable:

It is expressly understood that the continued financial stability and solvency of the Company are a critical and material consideration and covenant of this Agreement, particularly with respect to the executory provisions hereof including, but not limited to, royalties and licensing fees with respect to intellectual property and personality rights falling within the scope hereof. This Agreement shall therefore terminate, without the necessity of notice, and, except as hereinafter provided in respect to existing inventory, all grants of copyright, personality rights, licensing, and other rights personal to Artist contained herein shall revert immediately to Artist, (a) upon the institution by or against Company of insolvency, receivership, or bankruptcy proceedings or any other proceedings for the settlement of Company's debts, (b) upon Company making or purporting to make a general assignment for the benefit of Company's creditors, or (c) upon Company's dissolution or cessation of regular business operations. Notwithstanding anything appearing elsewhere herein to the contrary, the aforesaid rights, and each of them, are not assignable, except to the limited extent that a particular right may have been expressly and unconditionally designated as assignable elsewhere herein. Notwithstanding the foregoing, nothing in this section shall be deemed to preclude Company, or its trustee, receiver, or other successor, following termination and reversion under this section, from selling or otherwise disposing of merchandise actually existing in Company's inventory at the time of such termination *provided* that it is expressly agreed that all remaining, unpaid financial obligations of Company to Artist hereunder, and most especially royalties accruing to Artist by reason of such aforesaid inventory, constitute a secured, priority debt of Company to Artist, secured by such inventory and by Company's accounts receivable. With respect to the aforesaid royalties accruing by reason of existing inventory, and notwithstanding any contrary provision for accounting and royalty payments contained elsewhere herein, all such royalties, including both mechanical royalties and Artist's Royalties attributable thereto, shall be payable to Artist, in full and without reduction or regard to Recoupment, immediately upon, and as a condition of, the sale of any such inventory, or any portion thereof.

◆ ◆ ◆

Insurance Requirement Clause

Insurance is nothing more nor less than regulated, institutionalized, legal bookmaking. Lloyds of London's venerable underwriters began as dockside coffee house habitués, taking bets on whether or not particular ships would return safely from their voyages. Insurance has since grown into a highly sophisticated and respected industry, which nonetheless still consists of taking bets, although the determination of odds is now based on extremely complex statistical analysis and calculations.

In effect, an insurance company's bet goes something like this: "We'll bet that certain things won't happen within a certain period of time. You pay us a small amount now (or every month or year), and if one of those things *does* happen, we'll pay you a certain amount in compensation." Insurance companies will even take bets which they're *certain* to eventually "lose," because they have calculated that the investment income which they will have generated from premiums will almost certainly exceed whatever amount they must eventually pay. Life insurance companies aren't betting that you won't die... they're simply betting that you wont die before they've turned your premium payments into far more money than the eventual payoff amount. If you drop dead sooner, that's the risk they take, and a possibility which was taken into account when they calculated the premium.[243]

Sometimes, insurance companies simply don't like the odds for a particular individual, and will refuse to issue a policy. Some people are just too "high risk" for the insurance company to be willing to take the chance. In the case of large-sum disability and life insurance policies, most insurance companies will require a medical examination of the proposed insured, as a precondition to issuing a policy.

Now, back to the music business...

Insurance requirements are likely to appear in almost any type of contract, whenever the acquisition of some form of insurance is either a mandatory condition or a prospective option within the agreement. The wording of the insurance requirements provision will necessarily reflect the type of insurance coverage required or contemplated, which party is responsible for obtaining that policy, the beneficiary of the policy, and the obligations of the other parties in respect to obtaining and maintaining that policy.

In entertainment contracts, it is usual to include a clause which requires artists to agree that they will submit to medical examinations for insurance purposes. If the company is concerned about the artist's health or lifestyle, it will have the option to apply for a policy of insurance before it must decide whether to pay an advance or exercise an option. If the artist refuses to be examined, it's a breach of the contract. If the artist fails the medical exam, the company can

243 Insurance companies also *hedge* their bets by reinsuring them with other insurance companies, so that if the original insurer's total policy payout exceed a predetermined amount, the reinsurer will compensate the insurance company.

decide whether or not to risk its own money on the artist's ability to complete the project. And, of course, if insurance policy is issued, then the *company* will recover from the insurance company if the artist dies or becomes unable to work. Labels seldom insure all of their recording artists, but for artists who represent major "product" (and income) labels will frequently obtain insurance policies which will compensate the label if that artist's career is cut short.

For motion pictures, such insurance policies are the rule rather than the exception. Lending institutions which provide film financing impose a requirement for life and disability insurance policies on the film's star performers (and often its director, as well) as a mandatory condition of financing. In consequence, many 'deal memos" for film actors will contain an insurance requirement, coupled with an "escape clause" if the performer is uninsurable.

Such insurance provisions and policies are by no means unique to the entertainment industry. Most often referred to as "key man" insurance, many businesses regularly insure the lives and continuing ability to work of employees, officers, and principals whose contributions to business operations are considered so vital that their death or disability would have a direct, measurable financial impact on the company. Such policies are also obtained for the purpose of providing the business with cash to pay contractual obligations to a disabled employee or heirs, especially where there is a contract provision calling for the buy-out of a contractual benefit or equity interest upon death or disability. For example, such insurance and buy-out provisions are strongly recommended for inter-band partnership agreements or corporate bylaws.[244]

Liability, fire, theft, and loss insurance may also be required for various types of music industry contracts. For example, a record label may require that its artists only record in studios which have adequate insurance coverage, and that the studio provide proof of such insurance — often with a rider showing the label as additional loss payee in the event of claim — before the label will approve the use of that studio by its artists.

Workers compensation insurance will be *mandatory in almost every instance, as a matter of law*, regardless of whether or not it is mentioned in the contract.

Artists' booking agreements for live performances should include a requirement that the tour promoter or venue in which they will be appearing will have adequate insurance coverage, and major artists' contracts usually do provide for such insurance coverage.[245]

---

244 Even though it might seem an unaffordable luxury for start-up bands, the fact is that a modest policy ***with guaranteed non-cancellation and the right to increase policy limits later*** can be obtained for relatively small initial premiums. The relevant portions of the agreement or bylaws should provide for annual reevaluation and increase of the policy limits to reflect a sum *greater* than current net value of a stakeholder's buy-out, and as much more as seems appropriate. A bit of foresight and negotiating skill early in a band's career can provide guaranteed insurance coverage for artists who might be uninsurable at a later date.

245 Major artists' booking agreements may also require the venue to provide chilled Dom Perignon in their dressing rooms, or any of dozens of other perqs that go with star billing. Fledgling performers generally feel lucky if the venue gives them a discount on draft beer.

Insurance Requirement — Generic, Mandatory:

Company is to be protected to the maximum extent feasible against loss or losses which would significantly affect Company's personnel, property, finances, or the ability of Company to continue it normal operations without interruption or to fulfill its obligations to third parties. {Contractor} shall therefor, prior to commencing work hereunder, provide satisfactory proof(s) of insurance from established carriers, acceptable to Company, for the following types and amounts of insurance coverage [, including written acknowledgment that Company has been designated as an additional Loss Payee in respect thereto]:

[Workers' Compensation, with coverage limits of not less than $____

General Liability, with coverage limits of not less than $____

Premises Fire/Theft/Comprehensive, with coverage limits of not less than $____

Automobile/Vehicle Liability, with coverage limits of not less than $____

Business Interruption, with coverage limits of not less than $____

Professional Liability, with coverage limits of not less than $____

***Etc.*]**

The above-specified insurance coverage shall remain in effect, and acceptable evidence thereof shall remain current and on file with Company, throughout the Term of the within contract, in order for {Contractor} to be entitled to receive any payment whatsoever hereunder. Nothing contained in this section shall be deemed to impose or create any limitation with respect to indemnification obligations which may arise pursuant to other sections of this Agreement.

Insurance Requirement *(Alternative, with Attached Schedule of Coverage)* — ***Generic, Mandatory:***

A. Insurance Requirement: {Contractor} will maintain insurance to cover its operations throughout this Contract and any Contract extensions.

1. The insurance must meet the requirements set forth in Schedule __, attached hereto and incorporated by this reference.

2. Any insurance or self-insurance maintained by Company will apply only in excess of, and shall not contribute to, insurance maintained by {Contractor}.

3. {Contractor} will give Company 30-days written notice prior to modifying the insurance obtained under this section. Company may object to the modification within 15 days of receiving the notice. Failure to maintain insurance acceptable to Company shall be deemed a material breach, and may, at Company's option, be grounds for early termination hereof, without waiver or limitation in respect to such other relief as may be available to Company at law or in equity.

4. This section does not limit {Contractor}'s indemnification obligation as set forth in Paragraph __, or elsewhere herein.

B. Involuntary Policy Modifications: If {Contractor}'s insurer modifies its insurance in any manner that affects the specifications in Schedule __, {Contractor} must notify Company within 48 hours of {Contractor} receiving notice of such modification. Company may demand that {Contractor} obtain additional coverage sufficient to comply with the said specifications, or may terminate this Contract in the manner herein elsewhere provided.

Insurance Option — Recording Contract — Company Favorable

Company shall at all times during the Term have the right, but not the obligation, to obtain for Company's exclusive benefit one or more policies of life insurance, disability insurance, and/or other forms of insurance with respect to Artist (or any one or more individuals who comprise Artist, or are affiliated with Artist in respect to Artist's obligations hereunder.) As a material condition of this Agreement, Artist, and each individual member comprising Artist hereunder, shall promptly submit to such medical examination as may be reasonably required by any insurance company in respect to the obtaining or maintaining of any such policy of insurance. For the purposes hereof, "medical examination," shall include, but not be limited to, providing a complete and accurate medical history, submitting to physical examination, submitting to psychological examination, submitting to x-ray or other scanning technologies, blood tests, testing of other fluids or secretions, and cooperating fully in any established, diagnostic medical procedure.

Insurance Option — Recording Contract — Artist Favorable

Company shall at all times during the Term have the right, but not the obligation, to obtain one or more policies of life insurance, disability insurance, and/or other forms of insurance with respect to Artist (or any one or more individuals who comprise Artist) and Artist agrees to cooperate in regard to a non-invasive physical examination, if reasonably necessary as a condition for the obtaining of such insurance.

◆ ◆ ◆

Integration Clause

Often referred to as an "Entire Agreement" or "Entirety of Agreement" clause, an Integration clause is an essential bit of housekeeping language which defines what documents comprise the contract, and, by exclusion, what documents or oral agreements *are not* part of the contract.

Integration clauses are also used where there is an extrinsic agreement contemplated or already in place, and the new agreement takes the terms and conditions of that separate agreement into itself, as though the terms and conditions of the other agreement had been expressly re-stated in the new agreement. For example, a recording contract may include by reference (*i.e.*, "integrate") the terms and conditions of a separate Distribution Agreement or Collective Bargaining Agreement, making the recording contract subject to terms and conditions which appear in those agreements, even though those terms and conditions do not appear in the recording contract itself.

Integration Clause (Generic, no outside agreements)

This Agreement, and no other writing except as hereinafter enumerated, constitutes the entire contract and agreement between the Parties. The Parties, and each of them, hereby revoke any and all prior or contemporaneous oral or written agreements between them that are inconsistent with this Agreement. The Agreement between the Parties contains no terms or conditions not in writing, and the Agreement may only be amended or otherwise modified by a further writing, executed by the Parties, and by no other means. This Agreement consists exclusively of, and is limited to, the instant Agreement as wholly integrated with the following writings which are incorporated herein by reference:

A. [Schedule -*or*- Exhibit] [A -*or*- 1] {Title of Schedule or Exhibit}

B. [Schedule -*or*- Exhibit] [B -*or*- 2] {Title of Schedule or Exhibit}

C. [*Etc.*]

Entirety of Agreement Clause - Employment Agreement (with warranties of diligence):

Employee and Company each warrant that they have satisfied themselves as to the substance and terms of this Agreement, through independent investigation and diligence, and mutually agree that this Agreement embodies the entirety of the agreement between them, and that neither has relied upon any representation, term, condition, promise or covenant not expressly set forth herein.[246]

Integration Clause — Investor Subscription Agreement (with integration of separate writing.)

Investor understands and agrees that this Subscription Agreement ("Agreement") is wholly integrated with, and part of, the Private Placement Memorandum ("Memorandum"), and that all terms, conditions, executory provisions, caveats and recitals of the Memorandum are included as part of this Agreement, by reference, as though the entirety of the Memorandum were here set forth and reiterated, in full.

Integration Clause — Recording Contract (integration of Distribution Agreement as superceding terms of contract.)

Artist hereby acknowledges that Label has entered into a Distribution Agreement with {Distributor} dated____ (the "Distribution Agreement"). Artist hereby agrees that the terms and provisions of {Distributor}'s standard form recording agreement (annexed hereto as Exhibit "A" and referred to herein as the "Form Contract") will be and is incorporated herein, as a wholly integrated part of this Agreement. In the event of a conflict between the terms of this Agreement and those of the Form Contract, the terms of the Form Contract shall control.

---

246 **Extreme caution should be exercised with respect to this example.** If, hypothetically, the employee had made false representations as to qualifications for that employment, this language will ***excuse*** that conduct, *unless the false representations appear as warranties or recitals within the contract itself.*

Integration Clause — Recording Contract (integration of Distribution Agreement, superceding only as to administrative issues.)

Artist hereby agrees that the terms and provisions of any current or prospective Distribution Agreement (also referred to herein as the "Form Contract") will, upon implementation thereof, be or become incorporated herein, as a wholly integrated part of this Agreement. In the event of a serious, material conflict between the terms of this Agreement and the Form Contract, then this Agreement shall control, but in minor and administrative matters the terms of the Form Contract shall control.

◆ ◆ ◆

Key Man Provision

This is one of those odd contract provisions which is found in entertainment contracts with some frequency, but only seldom seen elsewhere.[247] The purpose of the provision is to assure an artist that some particular person with whom they share a special relationship will continue to be available to work with that artist, and provides the artist an option to terminate the agreement if that person becomes unavailable.

As discussed in an earlier chapter, there is usually a strong bond between artists and the A&R representative who signed them to their label and who has been their liaison with the label ever since. Not surprisingly, the "key man" designated by these provisions will therefore most often be a particular A&R rep.

The biggest concern for labels is that an A&R rep will accept a better offer from another label, or will decide to strike out on his or her own as an independent label, taking a number of the label's artists along with the A&R rep to that new label. For artists, the biggest issue will be obtaining a reversion or buy-back right as part of the key man provision, since terminating under this provision will not normally affect the re-recording restrictions which would prevent the Artist from recording any material — even unfinished or unreleased recordings — recorded under the contract.[248]

Key Man Provision (Simple) — Recording Contract.

> **Company acknowledges, accepts and agrees that in the event that {Individual employee of Company} is no longer employed by Company, Artist may elect, in Artist's sole discretion, to (a) continue this Agreement with Company or (b) terminate this Agreement with Company.**

---

247 Equivalent provisions are sometimes seen in advertising agency client agreements, where the client reserves the right to terminate if a particular employee is no longer with the agency.

248 In negotiating the re-recording restriction, the Artist should seek to have it apply only to recordings *recorded and released* under the recording contract, rather than simply to those *recorded* under that contract.

Key Man Provision (Comprehensive) — Recording Contract.

It is hereby expressly agreed that, in the event that {Individual employee of Company} shall, for any reason, cease to be employed by Company, that Artist may elect, in Artist's sole discretion, to (a) continue this Agreement with Company or (b) terminate this Agreement with Company withing ninety (90) days following Artist's receiving notice that such employment has terminated. Upon termination of this Agreement pursuant hereto, Artist shall have the further option to acquire, and Company shall upon exercise of such option convey to Artist, all interest which Company has or may have in and to any unreleased Recordings recorded by Artist hereunder, to the same extent, in the same manner, and upon the same terms and conditions as herein elsewhere provided in respect to Recordings which Company has failed to timely release hereunder.[249]

◆ ◆ ◆

249 This last refers to provisions which should be included in the "Release Commitment" section of the recording contract, providing for either a "buy-back" option, an "override royalty" license, or an outright reversion of unreleased master recordings. The above key man provision should be modified to reflect the appropriate remedy incorporated into the Release Commitment with respect to unreleased recordings.

Leaving Member Provision

Whenever the "Artist" is comprised of two or more individuals, prudence — and the vagaries of human nature, not to mention artistic temperament — require that contracts take into account the possibility that one or more of those individuals may decide to leave the group, or the other members may decide to eject a member from the group, during the term of a contract under which they are jointly and severally obligated to perform.

When a recording group breaks up, their label will generally have several options:

1. Terminate all agreements with the group and any members of the group;
2. Terminate all agreements with the leaving member(s), and continue the existing contract relationship with the remaining members and any substitute member(s).
3. Terminate all agreements with the remaining members, and continue the existing contract relationship with the leaving member(s).
4. Continue the existing contract relationship with the remaining member(s) and any substitute member(s), ***and*** continue a separate but identical contractual relationship with the leaving member(s).

When an entire group disbands, their label can retain any one or more of the former members under contract. Some "Leaving Member" provisions grant the *label* the option of determining whether the remaining members or the leaving members will be entitled to use the group's name, although contrary provisions contained within an inter-band partnership agreement may negate that option, or render its enforcement problematic. It is more usual for the name to be retained by the remaining members, but the question of what to do when the group splits into equal factions is best addressed in an inter-band agreement, rather than being left to the label's discretion or predilection.

One of the critical issues in any Leaving Member provision will be how to handle cross-collateralization for recoupment of pre-dissolution advances. Many labels which elect to retain their relationship only with a leaving member will attempt to have future royalties accruing to the retained leaving member's recordings apply toward recoupment of prior, pre-dissolution advances. It is unlikely that a retained leaving member will be able to "start fresh" and avoid any liability for recoupment of pre-dissolution advances, but the equitable compromise is usually to transfer only a percentage of those unrecouped advances, *pro rata*, based on the number of individuals who comprised Artist prior to dissolution of the group. (*Viz.*, 33⅓% for a three-member group; 25% for a four-member group; 20% for a five-member group; *etc.*)[250]

---

250 It is generally *substitute* members who get the "short end" of the deal when the label retains the remaining members rather than (or in addition to) the leaving member, since he or she will receive an advance for new albums recorded with the group, but no royalties from such albums until the group's *prior* advances (of which the substitute member received no portion) have been recouped,

Leaving Member Provision — Recording Contract:

(1) Artist's obligations under this agreement are joint and several, and all references to "Artist" herein include all members of the group collectively and individually, including members of the group as presently comprised ("Present Members") and such other individual(s) who at any time during the term hereof shall become members of the group ("Substitute Members"). The substitution of, addition to, or subtraction from the membership of the, group shall be done only with the prior written approval of Company. Any Substitute Member will be automatically deemed a party to this Agreement, and shall promptly execute an instrument expressly binding said Substitute Member to all terms and conditions of this Agreement.

(2) If any individual ceases to perform as a member of the group ("Leaving Member"), Artist shall promptly give Company written notice of such occurrence ("Leaving Member Notice"). If the group disbands or dissolves, each member of the group shall be deemed a Leaving Member. If Company so requests, within ninety (90) days after Company's receipt of the Leaving Member Notice, Artist shall promptly deliver to Company a "demo recording" made at Company's expense pursuant to an approved budget, embodying the performances of such leaving member and/or the remaining members of the group.

(3) Each of the Present Members and Substitute members agree that, without limiting any of Company's other rights and/or remedies, if there is a Leaving Member during the Term hereof:

(a) Company shall have the right to terminate the Term of this agreement with respect to the remaining members of Artist by notice given to Artist at any time before the expiration of ninety (90) days after Company's receipt of the Leaving Member Notice (or, if later, the date of the delivery to Company of Leaving Member's demo recording). If Company elects to do so all members of Artist shall be deemed Leaving Members and subparagraph (3)(b) (below) shall then apply.

(b) Each individual member of Artist hereby grants to Company an irrevocable option to engage the exclusive services of any Leaving Member as a recording artist. Said option, with respect to such individual, may be exercised by Company by giving Artist notice at any time before the expiration of ninety (90) days following Company's receipt of the Leaving Member Notice (or, if later, the date of the delivery to Company of the Leaving Member's demo recording.) If Company exercises said option, Company and such Leaving Member shall be deemed to have entered into a new agreement upon all the terms and conditions of this agreement except that: (I) the provisions for pre-approved recording budgets

contained herein shall not be applicable, but rather Company shall pay all recording costs for Masters to be recorded by such individual up to the amount of the budget approved by Company therefor; (ii) any unrecouped Advances in Artist's account at the time such member leaves may be recouped out of royalties earned by such Leaving Member under this paragraph; (iii) a portion of any future royalty earnings from Master Recordings embodying such Leaving Member's performances recorded prior to his departure from the group shall be applied to recoup any future Advances to such Leaving Member, such portion to be determined by applying a fraction having a numerator of one (1) and a denominator equal to the number of members of Artist at the time immediately prior to the Leaving Member Notice; and (iv) recordings by such individual shall not be applied in reduction of Artist's Recording Commitment set forth in this agreement.

(4) A Leaving Member shall not, without Company's consent, use the professional name of the group for any purpose beyond inclusion in such Leaving Member's biographical information, it being understood and agreed that such professional name shall remain the property of the remaining members, subject to Company's rights to use such name as granted pursuant to this Agreement.

◆ ◆ ◆

Liquidated Damages Provision

Liquidated damages provisions are antithetical to provisions which stipulate to injunctive relief, although they each begin with an identical stipulated fact as their foundation, from which they then proceed in diametrically opposed directions.[251]

An essential factual element for both liquidated damages and injunctive relief is that damages are difficult or impossible to reduce to a precise monetary sum. At this point, the two provisions radically diverge; injunctive relief provisions go on to state that *no* amount of monetary damages would ever provide a sufficient remedy, while liquidated damages provisions instead use the assumption that damages are incalculable as a basis for establishing, by agreement of the parties, an *arbitrary but reasonable* sum that is neither capricious nor punitive, to be the exact, stipulated amount of damages in the event of a breach.

That stipulated amount must be neither ridiculously low, nor punitively high, but — unlike Goldilocks — the law does no require that liquidated damages be "just right." Instead, the parties may pre-agree on a fixed sum which will constitute the amount which a breaching party must pay the other party, *regardless of the amount of "actual" damage resulting from the breach*, so long as that sum falls somewhere within the broad range between "too little" and "too much."

The first issue for analysis of a liquidated damages provision will be, is it punitive? Too small an mount is punitive to the non-breach party, and amounts to unjust enrichment of the breaching party. Too large an amount has the opposite effect.

The provision will not be held punitive, however — and hence invalid — simply because it is intended to motivate performance of contract obligations, *provided* that the amount stipulated represents a reasonable attempt to anticipate losses to be suffered. But if the *sole* purpose is to coerce performance, rather than to provide compensation for damages resulting from breach, the provision will be deemed a unenforceable penalty.

Liquidated damages provisions are likely to be found unreasonable (and unenforceable) whenever they bear *no reasonable relationship to the range of actual damages which parties could have anticipated as resulting from a breach.* The amount set as liquidated damages must therefore represent a reasonable effort to estimate fair compensation for loss that might be sustained, rather than some number picked capriciously from thin air. Consequently, courts generally look to the circumstances existing *at the time the contract was negotiated and formed*, including the following:

---

251 Although injunction provisions and liquidated damages provisions are essentially antithetical, they are *not* mutually exclusive. A contract may specify injunction with respect to one party or type of breach, while stipulating to liquidated damages for another party or breach. However, a court may apply an equitable balancing test to determine whether the remedies are so disproportionate as between the parties as to create an unconscionable disparity, which the court cannot allow.

1. A cognizable relationship between the stipulated amount and the range of potential harm that could be reasonably anticipated *at the time of contract formation*;
2. Equality or disparity of bargaining power as between the parties *at the time of contract formation*;
3. Participation by counsel for either or both parties in formation of the contract;
4. Parties' belief *at the time of contract formation* that proof of actual damages would be difficult or impossible;
5. The actual difficulty of quantifying damages;
6. The actual difficulty of proving causation, and
7. Whether the liquidated damages provision is included in a preprinted form contract, rather than a specially prepared agreement.

There is no bright line rule to determine the validity of a liquidated damages provision, but California Civil Code § 1671.(b) comes about as close as possible to enunciating the guideline for judicial analysis in most[252] contract cases:

> "A provision in a contract liquidating the damages for the breach of the contract is ***valid*** unless the party seeking to invalidate the provision establishes that the provision was ***unreasonable*** under the circumstances existing ***at the time the contract was made***." [Cal. Civ. § 1671,(b). Emphasis added.]

Since "reasonableness" is undoubtedly the slipperiest of legal standards, care should be exercised in the drafting process to address those issues into which a court may eventually enquire. Using recitals within the liquidated damages provision itself to summarize the parties' *reasons* for stipulating to liquidated damages, and their *rationale* for the amount agreed upon, will minimize the chance that a court will later invalidate the provision.

252 The statute provides that, for certain residential leases, liquidated damages are rebuttably presumed to be void, placing an affirmative burden on the party seeking to enforce the provision, rather than the reverse. Also, it "does not apply in any case where another statute expressly applicable to the contract prescribes the rules or standard for determining the validity of [liquidated damages]" [Cal Civ. § 1671 subd. (a)]

Liquidated Damages (Generic, Comprehensive)

The parties have agreed that, by reason of the nature of this Agreement, it would be extremely difficult, costly, inconvenient, impractical or impossible, in the event of a breach hereof by {Party B}, to calculate the actual damages which {Party A} would suffer thereby. The parties have further agreed, taking into account all reasonable possibilities, that foreseeable estimated damages which {Party A} might suffer as a proximate result of material breach hereof by {Party B} would in no event be likely to exceed $____, nor to be less than $____. In order to expedite the resolution of any dispute arising from a breach hereof, and to avoid the inconvenience, expense, delay, and difficulty of attempting to quantify actual damages in such event, and as a specially bargained for condition hereof intended to provide appropriate compensation for damages resulting from non-performance or inadequate performance of obligations hereunder, the parties hereby irrevocably stipulate and agree that, in the event of any material breach by {Party B} hereunder, the damages awardable to {Party A} on account of such breach shall be deemed to be the sum of [$______, precisely.] *[-or-]* [$____ for each [month/week/day], or portion thereof that the breach continues [, up to the remainder of the Term, including any renewals thereof].] [The foregoing is expressly limited to contract damages, and nothing therein shall be deemed to reduce, limit or waive any claim of consequential or special damages, nor an award of costs and expenses of suit herein, nor awardable attorney's fees, nor damages arising under any cause of action sounding in tort, negligence, equity, or statute, regardless of any reference therein to the within contract.]

◆ ◆ ◆

Mechanical License

This is one contract provision — or entirely separate agreement — which is absolutely unique to the music industry, since its sole purpose is to authorize the use of copyrighted works for the making of phonorecords. *Mechanical Licenses serve no other purpose.* As discussed (at length) in Chapter 4 ("A Primer on Copyright"), Mechanical Licenses (other than Compulsory Licenses) are issued by the publisher or other copyright owner of a *composition.*

Mechanical License (Letter format; Basic)

With respect to the within-identified Copyrighted Work(s), you shall have such rights, and no other, which are granted to, and all obligations which are imposed upon, users of a copyrighted work under the compulsory license provisions of the Copyright Act within or upon instruments serving to reproduce mechanically a copyrighted work (*i.e.*, in phonograph records, audio-cassettes, compact discs, and all forms of phonorecord media now known or unknown, but specifically excluding any and all media which embodies synchronous visual images) by another person, except that with respect to phonorecords thereof made and distributed by you, you shall pay royalties and account to us, as Publisher, quarterly, within forty five (45) days after the end of each calender quarter, on the basis of records made, distributed and not actually returned, and for all such records made and distributed, the royalty shall be ________ percent (__ %) of the statutory rate in effect at the time the record is made and distributed.

Mechanical License — Recording Contract —
***Company Favorable** (Controlled Compositions):*

(1) Artist hereby grants to Company and to Company's designees an irrevocable, non-exclusive license, under copyright law, to reproduce each Controlled Composition hereunder on Records, and to distribute those Records in the United States and Canada.

(2) Notwithstanding the non-exclusivity of the foregoing license, Artist agrees and warrants that no mechanical license for any Controlled Composition recorded hereunder shall be granted by Artist nor by any agent or affiliate of Artist to any third party prior to expiration of a period of either (I) one hundred twenty (120) days following initial U.S. release by Company or its designee of a Recording embodying that composition, or (ii) one (1) year from the date upon which a Master recorded hereunder which embodied that Controlled Composition was first tendered to Company by Artist, whichever shall first occur.

Mechanical License — Recording Contract —
***Artist Favorable** (Controlled Compositions):*

Artist hereby grants to Company a non-exclusive license, to run concurrently with the life of the relevant copyright, including any renewals thereof, under and as limited by applicable copyright law, to reproduce as a phonorecord, as such term is defined by copyright law, each Controlled Composition recorded hereunder, and to distribute those Records within the Territory, in consideration of and conditional upon Company's timely payments to Artist or Artist's designee or successor of all mechanical royalties on account thereof, as hereinafter set forth.

Mechanical License (Comprehensive):

Mechanical License

Date:

Territory:

Licensee:

Licensor:

Composition:

Writer(s)

Timing (approximate):

Mechanical Royalty Rate:

Artist

Distributor/Label:

Record/ Catalogue No.:

Anticipated Date of Release:

1. Licensor warrants and represents that
   (a) Licensor holds, as owner or publisher, a valid United States copyright in the above musical composition (the "Composition"), *and*
   (b) The Composition is original and does not violate or infringe upon the rights of any person. firm or other entity, *and*
   (c) Licensor has full right, power and authority to grant this license, *and*
   (d) Licensor will be responsible for payment of all sums due to the writer(s) of the Composition by reason of Licensee's exercise of the rights granted hereunder.
2. Licensor grants to Licensee the nonexclusive right, privilege and license, irrevocable during the term of the copyright and all renewals and extensions thereof, to reproduce the Composition (either words or music or both) in phonorecords, to be manufactured and sold for distribution in the Territory (as identified above), including the right to reproduce the lyrics of the Composition on the packaging of such phonorecords.
3. Licensee shall pay to Licensor mechanical copyright royalties at the rate stated hereinabove for each phonorecord containing the Composition which is manufactured and sold by Licensee for distribution in the Territory and not actually returned. Phonorecords which are distributed as promotional units or as so-called "free goods" shall not be deemed sold. In no event shall the total number of such "free good" exceed ten percent (10%), nor the number of "returns" exceed fifteen percent (15%), of the number of phonorecords for which royalties are due and payable hereunder.
4. This license is intended to cover and is limited to a single commercial recording of the Composition by the above artist on the above phonorecord (and re-releases thereof).

Page 1 of 2

5. Licensee shall render to Licensor quarterly statements of royalties payable hereunder, within forty-five (45) days after the end of each calendar quarter, together with payment of all royalties shown to be due. Licensee shall have the right to withhold a reasonable portion of royalties otherwise due as a reserve against returns. A reserve equivalent to no more than the royalties due upon 10% of phonorecords (exclusive of "free goods") shipped during any accounting period shall be deemed reasonable. Each royalty statement rendered by Licensee shall be binding upon Licensor and not subject to objection by Licensor for any reason unless such objection in made in writing, within two (2) years from the date rendered.

6. Licensor shall have the right, upon written notice and during regular business hours, to inspect and/or independently audit Licensee's books, records and accounts. All costs and expense of such inspection or audit shall be borne exclusively by Licensor, unless the results of such inspection or audit discloses a discrepancy in favor of Licensor which exceeds five percent (5%) of sums previously reported by Licensee, whereupon Licensee shall become solely liable for all costs and expenses of said inspection or audit, without prejudice to such further remedies as may exist in law or equity.

7. Licensor does hereby indemnify, save and hold Licensee harmless from any and all loss or damage arising out of or connected with any claim by a third party which is inconsistent with Licensor's warranties and representations contained herein. In any action, including audit, mediation, arbitration or litigation, to enforce the terms and conditions hereof, or to prevent or remedy a breach hereof, the prevailing party in any such action shall be entitled to recover all costs and expenses thereby incurred including, without limitation, attorney's fees.

8. As an expressly bargained for condition of this agreement, the United States District Court, Central District of California, and no other court or forum, shall have exclusive, original jurisdiction over any and all disputes arising hereunder, and the parties do hereby expressly submit themselves to the jurisdiction of that Court, for all relevant purposes.

9. This agreement shall inure to the benefit of and be binding upon the parties hereto and their respective heirs, legal representatives, successors and assigns. The execution of this agreement shall constitute and is accepted by Licensor as full compliance with all obligations of Licensee to Licensor, statutory and otherwise, arising from or connected with Licensee's use of the Composition as provided herein.

Licensor

By: ______________________________

Address: ______________________________ Fed. Emp. ID. No.: ____________________

____

____

Licensee

By: ______________________________ Fed. Emp. ID. No.: ____________________

Page 2 of 2

◆ ◆ ◆

Mediation Provision

Mediation provisions in contracts are intended to forestall and potentially avoid more costly arbitration or litigation of the parties' contractual disagreements.[253] Where there is no written agreement to mediate, parties may nonetheless attempt mediation either before or after filing a lawsuit or arbitration. In some cases, courts in which an action has been filed may order the parties to attempt a settlement through mediation.

Although mediation has many of the attributes of an adversarial proceeding, no one actually "wins" a mediation. Instead, the process is designed to motivate the parties to compromise. Successful mediation has been characterized as achieving a settlement agreement which leaves each side with an equal sense of having lost.

Mediation usually occurs in two formats, and sometimes shifts from one to the other. In "roundtable" mediation, the parties and their counsel are generally in a single room, with the mediator acting to guide their interactions toward a settlement. In "shuttle" mediation, the respective parties and their counsel will be in separate rooms, with the mediator going back and forth between them, with offers, counteroffers, and arguments aimed obtaining concessions from each party, in an attempt to achieve a settlement.

The *sine qua non* of effective mediation is the presence of all parties necessary to sign a binding settlement agreement, either in person or by a power of attorney authorizing someone present at the mediation to execute such binding agreement on that party's behalf. This enables successful mediation to conclude with a final, enforceable agreement. If nothing is signed to implement a binding agreement at the time, it may be impossible to get that same settlement agreement signed later. Parties will invariably think of "one more thing" by the next day, which effectively negates the entire effort.

There are pros and cons for including a mediation provision in any contract. Contractual mediation can be a relatively inexpensive and speedy method for resolving disputes, but a failed mediation merely delays commencement of arbitration or litigation, and may result in premature disclosures of evidence or legal theories, which may be a tactical disadvantage later.[254]

Often, when a dispute is "hot and heavy," it may be difficult to get the parties to agree to sit down and mediate. Angry parties often want their "day in court" as soon as possible, and believe that mediation will be a completely pointless waste of time and money. Nor is that

---

253 Chapter 11, "Understanding Remedies," includes a discussion of mediation and other forms of alternative dispute resolution.

254 This can generally be avoided by utilizing the "shuttle" protocol for the mediation, and submitting evidence only to the *mediator* in confidence, and putting legal arguments into the form of a "Confidential Mediation Brief" which only the mediator will see. The mediator can then informedly argue as to the relative strength or weakness of a party's position on an issue, without disclosing the specifics which support the mediator's conclusions.

assessment always inaccurate.

However, if the contract requires mediation, a party's failure to mediate before commencing litigation — other than litigation limited to injunctive relief, or to *compelling* mediation or arbitration — may be grounds for an effective affirmative defense based on the failure to comply with a contractual obligation to mediate.

Where the parties do decide to include a mediation provision in their contract, the most effective method for coercing them to go forward with that mediation in the event of a dispute is by linking the mediation requirement to the contract's "attorney's fees" provision. Essentially, such provisions state that a party's failure or refusal to participate in mediation as a condition precedent to commencing arbitration or litigation will constitute an *irrevocable waiver and forfeiture* of that party's right to seek or obtain an award of attorney's fees under the contract, regardless of the outcome of that arbitration or suit.

There are a number of organizations which provide mediation services. Notable among these are the American Arbitration Association (AAA) and JAMS, although there are numerous other non-profit and for-profit alternative dispute resolution (ADR) services, as well as attorneys, retired judges, or other qualified, impartial individuals who regularly act as mediators, and are paid for their mediation skills. The costs for arbitration can range from nothing for some non-profit services, to thousands of dollars. Costs will depend on the mediator or mediation service selected.

The American Arbitration Association ("AAA") suggests the following mediation provision:

> **If a dispute arises out of or relates to this contract, or the breach thereof, and if the dispute cannot be settled through negotiation, the parties agree first to try in good faith to settle the dispute by mediation administered by the American Arbitration Association under its Commercial Mediation Procedures before resorting to arbitration, litigation, or some other dispute resolution procedure. If they do not reach such solution within a period of 60 days, then, upon notice by either party to the other, all disputes, claims, questions, or differences shall be finally settled by arbitration administered by the American Arbitration Association in accordance with the provisions of its Commercial Arbitration Rules.**

JAMS suggests the following mediation provision:

> **The parties agree that any and all disputes, claims or controversies arising out of or relating to this Agreement shall be submitted to JAMS, or its successor, for mediation, and if the matter is not resolved through mediation, then it shall be submitted to JAMS, or its successor, for final and binding arbitration pursuant to the arbitration clause set forth above. Either party may commence mediation by providing to JAMS and the other party a written request for mediation, setting forth the subject of the dispute and the relief requested. The parties will cooperate with JAMS and with one another in selecting a mediator from JAMS panel of neutrals, and in scheduling the mediation proceedings. The parties covenant that they will participate in the mediation in good faith, and that they will share equally in its costs. All offers, promises, conduct and statements, whether oral or written, made in the course of the mediation by any of the parties, their agents, employees, experts and attorneys, and by the mediator or any JAMS employees, are confidential, privileged and inadmissible for any purpose, including impeachment, in any arbitration or other proceeding involving the parties, provided that evidence that is otherwise admissible or discoverable shall not be rendered inadmissible or non-discoverable as a result of its use in the mediation. Either party may initiate arbitration with respect to the matters submitted to mediation by filing a written demand for arbitration at any time following the initial mediation session or 45 days after the date of filing the written request for mediation, whichever occurs first. The mediation may continue after the commencement of arbitration if the parties so desire. Unless otherwise agreed by the parties, the mediator shall be disqualified from serving as arbitrator in the case. The provisions of this Clause may be enforced by any Court of competent jurisdiction, and the party seeking enforcement shall be entitled to an award of all costs, fees and expenses, including attorneys' fees, to be paid by the party against whom enforcement is ordered.**

The parties are not required to designate an established arbitration service such as the AAA or JAMS in their contract in order to provide for mediation of disputes, but may instead develop their own, unique mediation provision. Here's an example:

> **In the event that a dispute arises out of or in relation to this contract, or in respect to any breach or anticipated breach of the terms and conditions hereof, and if said dispute cannot be resolved through informal negotiation between the parties, the parties hereby agree that either may give written notice to the other, demanding formal mediation of the dispute, pursuant to the following procedure. Within ten (10) days following the date of said notice demanding mediation, the parties shall either (a) agree upon a mediator; or (b) each party shall independently designate a single, impartial person, and those designated persons shall, within ten (10) days following their designation, agree upon and designate a mediator or mediation service located within the [City/County] of __________, which mediator shall not be one of the persons designated to make such selection, nor affiliated with such person. In the event that no such designation is made within the time period prescribed, then the mediation shall be conducted by [JAMS -or- the American Arbitration Association -or- any qualified mediator or mediation service selected by the party which first gave written notice demanding mediation hereunder], within the aforesaid [City/County]. Upon notice of the amount required to be paid in advance for costs and/or fees in order commence mediation, the parties shall each promptly tender their proportional share of such total amount to the designated mediator. All mediation hereunder shall be conducted in accordance with the statutes and rules of the State of ________.**

To add a coercive element as motivation for the parties to mediate their disputes, the following may be appended to any of the foregoing, or to any alternative mediation provision:

> **Notwithstanding any other term or condition of this agreement to the contrary, a party which, prior to commencing any arbitration proceeding, or commencing any judicial action (other than an action for injunctive relief, or an action to compel mediation or arbitration), fails or refuses to participate in a reasonable and good faith effort to mediate any dispute hereunder in the manner hereinabove provided, shall by such failure or refusal automatically and irrevocably waive and forfeit any and all claims which said party has or may have to recover, by award or otherwise, in whole or in part, any attorney's fees or expenses of any suit or arbitration related hereto, notwithstanding the outcome of such suit or arbitration. Notwithstanding any confidentiality requirements imposed by any mediation provision or agreement, the declaration or testimony of a mediator designated to conduct mediation in respect hereto shall be admissible evidence, and shall be given considerable presumptive weight, in regard to a party's failure or refusal to participate in good faith in said mediation.**

◆ ◆ ◆

Morals Clause

Although the concept may seem quaint or outdated to performers, morals clauses (sometimes referred to as "morality" clauses) remain viable throughout music industry contracts, and are invariably included in *endorsement* contracts, where the endorser is understandably reliant upon the public's perception of the performer, and on the continuing value of that performer's name and public image in connection with the endorser's products or services.

Morals clauses are a special type of termination clause, setting forth an enumerated list of specific grounds for termination of the contract whenever the performer's public image (and hence the performer's value to the other party) has been tarnished. Because performers are under constant scrutiny from the media, with their private lives matters of morbid interest to "inquiring minds," certain types of conduct may be perceived as an embarrassment for those in contractual relationships with them, particularly where the conduct involves the commission of a crime, or acts of "moral turpitude."

In addition to allowing unilateral termination upon conviction for a crime, morals clauses may prohibit a broad range of conduct deemed to be unacceptable, including the use of illegal drugs, acts of public disrepute (which is a euphemism for sexual misbehavior in public), and virtually *any* conduct which could be perceived as repugnant to good morals, or which is likely to result in public approbation.

Interestingly, some socially conscious performers — if they have sufficient bargaining power to achieve it — require a morals clause which allows the *performer* to terminate the contract if their label or endorser engage in conduct which the performer considers objectionable, such a becoming involved with tobacco advertisements or production, creating environmental hazards, utilizing goods or services produced by child labor, or any of a number of other acts which the performer considers reprehensible or morally repugnant.

Because a morals clause gives one party a right to terminate the entire contract without penalty, negotiation and drafting of these clauses requires a certain amount of both finesse and diplomacy, so that the party benefitting from the clause feels adequately protected, while the party whose conduct is constrained by the clause does not feel that their personal liberties are being violated or lost.

Another problem arises if and when it comes time to actually *invoke* a morals clause. Our legal system presumes innocence unless and until there has been an adjudication to the contrary.[255] Invoking the clause based on anything short of conviction for a crime can lead to a protracted and costly court battle.[256]

---

255 In many jurisdictions (*e.g.*, California) there are statutes which expressly forbid an employer from terminating or taking other adverse action against an employee based on an arrest that has not yet resulted in conviction.

256 In 1996, Aaron Spelling fired actress Hunter Tylo from "Melrose Place" after learning she had become pregnant. Instead of the morals clause, however, Spelling elected to terminate her contract under a clause which referred to "any material change" in her physical appearance, asserting that her pregnancy was *(... continued)*

In December, 2007, MTV announced that Brittany Spears' sixteen year old sister, Jamie Lynn Spears — star of Nickelodeon's squeaky-clean series "Zoey 101" — was twelve weeks pregnant. Fortunately for Nickelodeon, the fourth (and presumably final) season of the show had already completed shooting before the pregnancy was announced, relieving them of having to make any immediate decision as to whether they should invoke the morals clause of her contract,[257] change fundamental aspects of the show's plot to account for the pregnancy, try to "shoot around" and ignore it in future episodes, or simply allow the series, or her character, to fade away.

To repeat an earlier caveat: just because you *can* do something, doesn't mean that you *should*. Invoking a morals clause to terminate a contract epitomizes a circumstance where a "wait and see" attitude is likely the most prudent course. As a practical matter, labels are unlikely to terminate any artist whose records are continuing to sell, no matter what they've done — while willing to use any excuse to terminate an artist whose records are failing to sell.

Morals Clause (Simple):

> **Artist shall not commit any act indicative of dishonesty or moral turpitude, or that otherwise could materially injure Artist's or Label's public reputation.**

certain to cause such a "material change." In the resulting wrongful termination and discrimination suit, the jury disagreed with Spelling's rationale, awarding Tylo $,5,000,000 in damages.

257 While getting pregnant isn't a crime, there is nonetheless a potential criminal issue which complicates this matter, depending on where the baby was *conceived*. The putative father was Spears' 19-year-old ex-boyfriend. Spears had lived in California for the prior two years and, under California penal statutes, any person who engages in an act of unlawful sexual intercourse with someone under the age of 18, and who is not more than three years older or younger than the age of the other person, is guilty of a *misdemeanor*. *But* if conception occurred in the ex-boyfriend's home state of Louisiana, he could face *felony* charges for "carnal knowledge of a juvenile" under Louisiana's laws which mandate that a person must be at least 17 to legally consent to sex and that the accused partner must not be more than two years older.

Morals Clause (Basic):

Artist shall not commit any act, or do any thing, or engage in any conduct, which might tend to bring Artist into public disrepute, contempt, scandal, or ridicule, or which might tend to reflect unfavorably on Company, or upon any affiliate of Company, or upon any product, service or business practice of Company or of Company's affiliates, or which might tend to injure or impede successful promotion or marketing of any Album released by Company hereunder.

Morals Clause (Comprehensive):

Artist shall at all times during and throughout the Term, conduct himself (or herself) with due regard to public conventions and morals. Artist shall not, either while rendering services to Company hereunder, or in public, or in private life, commit any offense involving moral turpitude under Federal, state or local laws or ordinances. Artist shall not do or commit any act or thing which might tend to degrade him (or her) in society or bring him (or her) into public hatred, public disrepute, contempt, scorn, or ridicule, or which would tend to shock, insult or offend community or public morals or decency, or prejudice the Company or the entertainment industry in general. Conduct in violation of these provisions shall include, without limitation and by way of example only: (a) public intoxication, whether caused by lawful or unlawful substances; (b) public or private use of illegal drugs or substances; (c) public acts of indecency including, but not limited to public exposure of any part of Artist's body which law, community standards, or ordinary decency dictate should remain covered in public; (d) any public conduct which is lewd, lascivious, or which amounts to "obscenity," under such legal definition(s) as may be current at the time and place of such conduct; (e) any conduct which endangers or would tend to endanger any person under the age lawful consent; or (f) any conduct which contributes or would tend to contribute to the delinquency of any person under the age of lawful consent.

◆ ◆ ◆

Name and Likeness Clause

The right to exploit an individual's persona is an essential component of virtually every entertainment industry contract. Because one element of those personality rights (*i.e.,*voice) is likely to be embodied in a recording itself, while other elements (*e.g.*, name, photos, and biographical information) are likely to appear in packaging and promotional materials, those rights are *essential* to recording contracts, and comprise a substantial part of both the subject matter and consideration within those contracts.

Because of statutory and common law limitations on use of personality rights, both in respect to the right of publicity and the right of privacy, labels must clearly and unequivocally secure these rights by contract. Clauses most commonly captioned merely "Name & Likeness" will therefore be a non-negotiable part of every record contract, and will necessarily include a license for perpetual use of an Artist's personality rights not only in albums and their packaging, but also for a wide range of related uses, such as for advertising, promotional materials, press releases and other forms of marketing and publicity related to the Artist's recordings.

Three *aspects* of this clause *will* be negotiable, however: *(1)* exclusivity; *(2)* Artist's right to approve materials used; and *(3)* merchandising and other uses not directly related to albums.

Exclusivity

Labels need to have an ongoing right to use of Artist's name and likeness, even after the Artist's record contract terminates, so they can continue to promote and sell recordings made during the contract term. A license to use Artist's name and likeness it therefore both reasonable and necessary. Labels will generally ask for an *exclusive* right to Artist's personality rights — at least for the term of the contract — but such exclusivity can be a problem for artists subject to a conflicting license for ongoing use under a prior contract, or where an artist has a career apart from music, such as acting or other occupation where personality rights are inherently necessary.

An exclusive grant to the record company can even affect public appearances, since only the label is technically empowered to authorize use of the Artist's name and likeness for marquees, posters, advertisements and promotional materials. Remember, if the label has the "exclusive" right to the artist's personality rights, ***even the Artist is prohibited from authorizing anyone else to use any portion of those rights.***

Since the artist's *recording services* are likely already exclusive to the label, there's really no reason for the label to insist on an exclusive personality rights license, too, unless the label is anticipating re-licensing those rights for merchandising, as discussed below.

Approval Rights

Because artists have a vested interest in preserving their public image — and often spend considerable effort to create and maintain a particular public image and reputation — Artists should insist on an approval right in respect to photographs and biographical information which may be used by their label. For example, many artists use a pseudonym for their professional lives, and prefer not to have their legal names generally known. Among other things, this allows them to use their legal names freely in their private lives, to own property, enter into contracts, or have their phone number listed, without being harassed as a result. Unless they have preserved an approval right however, there is nothing to prevent the label from disclosing their true names to the public, as "biographical information." Likewise, the label may choose to use photos which the Artist considers inconsistent with the public image that he or she is trying to maintain, or which are embarrassing or otherwise objectionable to the Artist.

In consequence, artists will want total control over the label's ability to use their personality rights, while the label will want unrestricted freedom to use every aspect of those rights in any way it sees fit. The compromise will usually be that Artist will be granted limited approval rights, with a specified period of time in which to approve or reject material in advance of its proposed use, with Artist's failure to formally reject that proposed material within the allotted time constituting approval. As a practical matter, this allows the label to move forward with its planned use if the Artist is unreachable or unresponsive. The specified time period for Artist's consent is generally short however; usually no more than five days. Also, labels will generally try to limit the approval right to uses within the United States. Artists will want the approval right to cover material in every country, especially in regard tp advertising layouts and worldwide campaigns.

As an added restriction regarding photo approval, most labels will want to include a "single session" provision, under which the label is only responsible for the cost of the first photographs submitted to the artist for approval. If the artist rejects all of the submitted photos, then the costs for any additional photography must be borne by the Artist.

Merchandising

The "name & likeness" clause may not actually contain the word "merchandising" at all, but may nonetheless convey all relevant merchandising rights to the label by the seemingly-innocuous inclusion of five other words: *"and license others to use,"* or an equivalent phrase. Where the label's "name & likeness" license is exclusive, and such "and license others" phrase is included, the Artist may find that he or she has given the label all merchandising rights, for no additional consideration.

Records are expensive to manufacture, release and promote; tours can be costly, with little profit margin as compared to the time, effort and overhead which they require; but merchandising, on the other hand, is *almost pure profit.* [258]

Many artists — and particularly those who don't write their own songs— may never make any significant money from sale of their records, but will instead generate revenue through licensing the manufacture and sale of posters, T-shirts, caps, key-chains, coffee mugs, and a wide array of other "merchandise." Some artists may even cut out the "middleman," and offer merchandise for sale directly, through a website, or at an on-site "merch table" while on tour or at local shows.

Labels generally feel that, since they've invested substantial money to develop the artist's image — which is what makes merchandising possible — they should enjoy the profits to be derived from that investment. The artist, on the other hand, will generally feel that, since he or she is already committed to reimbursing the label for 100% of its investment through recoupment, and merchandising is primarily based on the artist's personal image — the label shouldn't participate in merchandising profits.

On balance, the artist's argument is the stronger. The label profits far more than does the artist from record sales, and successful merchandising is generally related to successful record sales. Nonetheless, labels will often try for at least *part* of the merchandising income, or may require that all merchandising or merchandise manufacture be done through a company which the label either owns, or with which it has an ongoing arrangement.

Ultimately, the value of merchandising rights will fluctuate with the success (or otherwise) of the artist's career. Fighting to keep the merchandising rights in the hope of negotiating a deal with the "highest bidder," at a later time, may or may not eventually yield significant income for the artist. Conversely, where the label participates in merchandising income, it provides an additional incentive for them to promote the artist over the long term, and participation in merchandising can be a useful bargaining lever in obtaining "tour support" commitments from the label, as part of the record contract.

---

258 For those interested in accounting, the gross profit *margin* for merchandise will generally be between 80% and 98+% of the selling price.

Name & Likeness Release (Generic)
Company Favorable:

For valuable consideration, the actual receipt and sufficiency of which are hereby acknowledged, the undersigned hereby grants to Company an express and irrevocable release and permission for unlimited use of the undersigned's name (including any stage, professional or group name), voice, likeness, and biographical information, to use the same, or any portion thereof, at Company's sole discretion, within, in connection with, or in any manner related to, that certain *[insert type of project, e.g., Album; film; etc.]* tentatively entitled *[insert working title]*.

Name & Likeness Release (Generic)
Favorable to Releasor:

The undersigned hereby grants to Company a non-exclusive license and permission for limited use of the undersigned's name, voice, likeness, and biographical information, subject to and conditional upon the undersigned's right to first approve or disapprove, at the undersigned's discretion, any proposed use of the same, and of any portion thereof, and further limited to use thereof only within, or reasonably related to the packaging, advertising or promotion of, that certain *[insert type of project, e.g., Album; film; etc.]* tentatively entitled *[insert working title]*.

Name & Likeness Clause — Recording Contract —
Company Favorable:

(1)(a) Company, and any person, firm or entity designated by Company, and each of them, shall have the worldwide right to use. and to license others to use, Artist's name, likeness, other identification, and biographical material relating to Artist, and the name, likeness and biographical material of any producer, musician, vocalist or other person rendering services in connection with Master Recordings recorded by the Artist hereunder, for purposes of trade and advertising. This right shall be perpetual in respect to any and all uses which are in any way related to any Recordings recorded hereunder including, without limitation, any and all packaging, marketing, sales, advertising, publicity, and promotion which is in any manner related to such Recordings.

(1)(b) Company shall have the further right to refer to Artist, throughout the Term, as Company's exclusive recording artist. Artist shall, in all Artist's activities in the entertainment field, cause the Artist to be billed

and advertised, during the Term, as Company's exclusive recording artist.

(1)(c) The rights hereinabove granted to Company with respect to Artist's name, likeness, other identification, and biographical material shall be exclusive to Company during the Term hereof, and nonexclusive thereafter. Artist shall not, during the Term hereof, authorize or permit any person, firm, or entity other than Company to use the Artist's legal or professional name or the Artist's likeness in connection for any commercial purpose, without Company's express written consent.

(2)(a) Company will make available to Artist, for Artist's approval, which Artist may not unreasonably withhold, any pictures or other likeness or identification of the Artist, and any biographical material about the Artist, which Company proposes to use for packaging, advertising or publicity in the United States during he Term of this agreement. Company will not use any such material of which Artist disapproves, in writing, within five (5) business days from the time such materials are made available to Artist, provided that Artist shall furnish substitute material, satisfactory to Company in its sole and reasonable discretion, in time for use within Company's production and release schedules.

(2)(b) In no event shall Company be required to incur expenses for photography beyond those expenses customarily incurred for one (1) photographic shooting session for each Album hereunder. Artist shall submit biographical material of Artist to Company, and may also submit photographs, artwork and other materials. Artist's submission thereof shall constitute Artist's approval of Company's subsequent use thereof. Artist shall not be entitled to injunctive relief to restrain the continuing use of any material used in contravention of this section provided, however, that Company shall exercise reasonable efforts to remove from future manufacturing runs those materials of which Artist reasonably disapproves.

(3)(a) It is hereby expressly agreed that, as between Artist and Company, Company shall exclusively own and control all materials comprising the artwork (including, without limitation, art, photographs, graphic designs, etc.) and other items created or used in connection with the exploitation of Records hereunder, including, without limitation, all materials provided by Artist, and all copyrights and the right to secure copyright throughout the world and in perpetuity.

(3)(b) Notwithstanding the foregoing, Artist may retain the copyright and the right to secure copyright in any visual artwork or related materials supplied by Artist for which Artist paid not less than one hundred percent (100%) of the cost, and which were approved by Company after having

received reasonable prior notice of Artist's desire to retain the copyright in such materials, provided however that Company shall have a perpetual license to use such artwork, without royalty, for and in connection with the reissue of any Record recorded by Artist hereunder.

Name & Likeness Clause — Recording Contract — Artist Favorable:

(1)(a) Company shall have a perpetual, non-exclusive license, throughout the Territory, to use Artist's name, likeness, other identification, and biographical material relating to Artist, for purposes of trade and advertising related to any Recordings recorded by the Artist hereunder.

(1)(b) Company shall have the further right to refer to Artist, throughout the Term, as Company's exclusive recording artist.

(1)(c) The rights hereinabove granted to Company with respect to Artist's name, likeness, other identification, and biographical material, shall be limited to use by Company to advertising or sale of Records recorded by Artist hereunder. Artist shall not, during the Term hereof, authorize or permit any person, firm, or entity other than Company to use the Artist's professional name or the Artist's likeness in connection with the advertising or sale of Records, excluding records previously made or released pursuant to any earlier contract, or as may be otherwise provided herein.

(2)(a) Company will make available to Artist, for Artist's approval, any and all photographs, pictures or other likenesses or identification of the Artist, and any biographical material about the Artist, and any graphic artwork which Company proposes to use for packaging, advertising or publicity in any way related to Artist or to any Recordings hereunder. Company will not use any such material unless and until Artist shall approve the same, in writing. Artist's failure to expressly disapprove such proposed material within five (5) business days from Artist's actual receipt thereof shall be deemed approval. Artist shall have ten (10) business days following Artist's disapproval of proposed materials, in which to submit alternative proposed materials to Company.

(2)(b) In no event shall Company be required to incur expenses for photography beyond such expenses as are customarily incurred for one (1) photographic shooting session for each Album hereunder. This subparagraph will not apply to materials previously approved or submitted to Company by Artist. Artist shall have the right, but not the obligation, to submit photographs, likenesses, and biographical material of Artist, and

Artist's submission thereof shall constitute approval.

(3)(a) It is hereby expressly agreed that, except as provided in the following subsection, then as between Artist and Company, Company shall exclusively control all materials comprising the artwork (including, without limitation, art, photographs, graphic designs, etc.) and other items created or used in connection with the exploitation of Records hereunder, including, without limitation, all copyrights and the right to secure copyright throughout the world and in perpetuity. Nothing herein shall grant to Company any right to use any such materials, or any portion thereof, except with respect to materials used during the Term, and for purposes reasonably related to Recordings recorded by Artist hereunder, only. Notwithstanding the foregoing, Company shall, and does hereby, grant to Artist a perpetual, free license to use any and all such materials.

(3)(b) Notwithstanding the foregoing, Artist shall retain the copyright and the right to secure copyright in any visual artwork or related materials supplied by Artist. Company shall have a perpetual license to use such artwork, without royalty, in connection with any Record recorded by Artist hereunder.

◆ ◆ ◆

Non-Competition Provision

Non-competition provisions — more properly termed agreements (or covenants) not to compete — are hyper-technical contracts wherein a party, while employed by a business, and/or upon leaving that business, agrees not to enter into competition with that business. **Such contracts and contract provisions are generally disfavored by law and policy, and defects in their formation will often be sufficient to deem them invalid, unenforceable, or severable.** Most states allow agreements not to compete only in very limited circumstances, while other states may allow greater latitude in respect to such agreements. In consequence, a non-competition provision should *only* be implemented as directed by licensed attorneys familiar with the laws of the jurisdiction in which the contract will be operative.

As a general rule, such agreements *will* be enforced against the seller of a business, or a departing partner in a business, provided that they are drawn narrowly to avoid *competition*, rather than to punitively prevent someone from practicing their occupation or profession in a non-competing manner or locale. With respect to employees, generally, most states will not enforce these agreements unless it can be shown that the employee has obtained **trade secrets** of the employer or former employer, and is utilizing or likely to use those trade secrets in competition with the employer. A few states will enforce a covenant not to compete, even in the absence of a showing of trade secrets, as against former executives, management level employees, or professional staff, but such states (*e.g.*, Colorado) are the rare exception rather than the rule.

Requiring an agreement not to compete as a condition of employment can be costly mistake. If a proposed agreement is legally unenforceable within a particular jurisdiction, an employee likely has a *right* to refuse to sign it, and termination upon the basis of such refusal may be a wrongful discharge under public policy exceptions to the employment-at-will doctrine. Court decisions in various states are conflicting on this issue, with some courts allowing employers to discharge employees for refusal to sign an unreasonable or unenforceable agreement not to compete, but with a majority of state courts recognizing the public policy exception and allowing damages. One California jury awarded $1.2 million in damages for wrongful discharge to an employee who was fired for refusing to sign a covenant not to compete.[259]

259 "We hold an employer cannot lawfully make the signing of an employment agreement, which contains an unenforceable covenant not to compete, a condition of continued employment, even if such agreement contains choice of law or severability provisions which would enable the employer to enforce the other provisions of the employment agreement. We further hold that an employer's termination of an employee who refuses to sign such an agreement constitutes a wrongful termination in violation of public policy." D'Sa v. Playhut, Inc. (2000) 85 Cal.App.4th 927, 929

No one should attempt to utilize an agreement not to compete under any circumstances except upon the advice of an experienced attorney practicing within the state under the laws of which the contract will take effect.

In the music industry, agreements not to compete are not uncommon, but are difficult to enforce. For example, leaving member provisions of an inter-band partnership agreement may include a covenant not to compete, and acknowledge that certain proprietary information of the band — fan mailing lists, lists of venue contacts, musical arrangements, or certain styles or techniques developed by the band — are "trade secrets." Nonetheless, even with the unquestioned existence of "trade secrets," it would be difficult or impossible to keep a musician or singer from pursuing artistic endeavors under the rubric of a contractual covenant not to compete, particularly where such endeavors constitute a primary means of livelihood. The nature of the music industry does not lend itself to the type of geographic restrictions which are normally necessary to a valid covenant not to compete. An enforceable covenant would therefore likely require substantial additional consideration in the form of a severance package amounting to subsidy in order to justify a requirement that a leaving member not engage in any "competing" activities.

!!! WARNING !!!

THE "EMPLOYEE'S COVENANT NOT TO COMPETE" WHICH FOLLOWS IS GENERALLY UNENFORCEABLE IN MANY JURISDICTIONS AND ITS USE OR ATTEMPTED USE WILL LIKELY RESULT IN SUBSTANTIAL LIABILITY. It contains several provisions which are contrary to public policy, and is provided here **only to illustrate the concept of non-competition agreements, and is not to be taken as a sample form intended for use by any person.**

Employee's Covenant Not to Compete

1. For good and valuable consideration, the receipt and sufficiency of which is acknowledged, the undersigned, ____________, ("Employee"), shall not engage in a business which is in any manner similar to, or which operates in competition with, ______________, ("Company") during the term of his or her employment.

2. Further, Employee shall not engage in a business which is in any manner similar to, or which operates in competition with, Company's business for a period of ____ (_) years from the date of termination of Employee's employment by Company within a geographical area consisting of a ____ (_) mile radius of any office of Company.

3. For the purpose of this agreement, Employee shall be regarded as engaging in "a business which is in any manner similar to, or which operates in competition with, Company's business " if, directly or as an independent contractor or employee of any business, Employee is engaged in the business of ______ or such other business or businesses as Company is engaged in either individually or as part of some other business entity or affiliate during the term of Employee's employment by Company.

4. Employee shall not request any customers of any business then being conducted or contemplated by Company or its affiliates to curtail or cancel their business with Company or its affiliates.

5. Employee shall not disclose to any person, firm, or corporation any trade, technical or technological secrets, any details of organization or business affairs, any names of past or present customers of Company or its affiliates or any other information relating to the business or businesses or their affiliates.

6. Employee shall not solicit, canvass, or accept any business or transaction for any other person, firm, corporation, or business similar to any business of Company or its affiliates.

7. Employee shall not induce, or attempt to influence, any employee of Company or its affiliates to terminate employment with Company or its affiliates or to enter into any employment or other business relationship with any other person, firm, or corporation.

8. Employee acknowledges and agrees that the above restriction is reasonable as to duration and geography, that it is fully enforceable, and waives any objection thereto and covenants to institute no suit or proceeding or otherwise advance any position or contention to the contrary.

9. Employee recognizes and stipulates that immediate and irreparable damage will result to Company if Employee breaches any of the terms and conditions of this agreement and, accordingly, Employee hereby consents to the entry of temporary, preliminary, and permanent injunctive relief by any court of competent jurisdiction against him or her to restrain any such breach in addition to any other remedies or claims for money damages that Company may seek; and Employee agrees to render an equitable accounting of all earnings, profits and other benefits arising from such violations; and to pay all costs and counsel fees incurred by Company in enforcing this agreement, which rights shall be cumulative.

10. Employee represents and warrants to Company that his or her experience and capabilities are such that he or she can readily obtain employment in business without breaching the terms and conditions of this agreement and that his or her obligations under the provisions of this agreement, or the enforcement of the covenants herein contained by injunction or otherwise, would have material, adverse effect upon him or her, nor in any manner impede his or her ability to earn a livelihood.

11. The existence of any claim or cause of action of Employee against Company, whether predicated on this agreement or otherwise, shall not constitute a defense to the enforcement by Company of this covenant by injunction or otherwise.

12. In the event that Employee is in material breach of any of the provisions of this agreement as set forth above, the period of proscription from doing the act or acts that constitute a breach of this agreement shall be extended for a period of ______ (__) years from the date that Employee ceased, whether voluntarily or by court order, to engage in or do said actions.

13. Employee recognizes and agrees that Company does not have a remedy at law adequate to protect Company's rights and interests as set forth in this agreement, and Employee therefore agrees that Company shall have the right to an injunction enjoining Employee from violating the provisions of this agreement. Nothing herein contained shall be construed as prohibiting Company from pursuing any other remedies available to Company for such breach or threatened breach.

14. If any action at law or equity is necessary to enforce or interpret the terms of this agreement, Employee agrees to pay Company reasonable attorney fees, costs, and necessary disbursements, in addition to any other relief and/or damages to which Company may be entitled.

15. In the event that a court of competent jurisdiction determines that this covenant not to compete is unenforceable in whole or in part for any reason, including, without limitation, the duration, scope, and remedies set forth above, then same shall not be void, but rather shall be enforced to the extent that same is deemed to be enforceable by said court, as if originally executed in that form by the parties hereto.

16. Service of all notice under this agreement shall be sufficient if made by certified or registered mail to the specific party involved herein at his or her respective address hereinafter set forth or as such party may provide from time to time in writing:

Company: ___________________________ (Address)

Employee: ___________________________ (Address)

17. This agreement constitutes the entire agreement between the parties hereto and supersedes all prior negotiations, understandings and agreements, whether oral or written, of any nature whatsoever with respect to the term of employment that is the subject matter hereof, and there are no representations, warranties, understandings or agreements other than those expressly set forth herein between Company and Employee.

18. This agreement may not be modified, amended or terminated unless in a writing signed by the parties hereto.

19. The validity, interpretation, construction and enforcement of this agreement shall be governed by the laws of the State of _________________.

20. The invalidity or unenforceability of any particular provision of this agreement shall not affect any other provision(s) hereof, and the agreement shall be construed in all respects as though such invalid or unenforceable provision had been omitted.

IN WITNESS WHEREOF, the parties hereto acknowledge, understand, and agree to this agreement. The parties understand and intend to be bound by all of the clauses contained in this document and further certify that they have received signed copies of this agreement on this date.

There will be circumstances in which an agreement not to compete ***will*** be appropriate and enforceable, ***but only an attorney should attempt to make that determination in respect to any particular circumstance and jurisdiction.***

Without diluting that *caveat*, circumstances where an agreement not to compete would likely be appropriate and enforceable include the sale of an ongoing business, or ownership interest in such a business, particularly where the value of goodwill (and clientele) which accompanies such sale would be diluted or lost if the seller were to commence a competing business thereafter. Examples of circumstances which would likely justify the use of non-competition clauses in the music industry and related businesses might include:

- Sale of a nightclub or other venue;
- Sale of a record store;
- Sale of a publicity agency;
- Sale of a talent agency;
- Sale of a photography studio;
- Sale of a graphic arts studio.

Note that these all relate to the sale of ongoing businesses, and the agreement not to compete would bind the former owners (sellers) but likely would not affect the *employees* of the purchased business, apart from the possibility of a "trade-secrets" issue.

Subject to review by an attorney to verify conformity with the laws of a particular jurisdiction, the following would typify a non-competition clause appearing within an agreement to purchase an existing business.

Covenant Not To Compete — Business Purchase Agreement:

As a specially bargained-for and material condition of this Agreement, Seller shall not directly or indirectly engage in any business which is similar to, or which operates in competition with, the within Business in any location within a geographical area consisting of a __ (_) mile radius of the Business, or any office or other facility thereof, including the current primary location of the Business, and any and all secondary or subsidiary locations of the Business, whether currently operating or which may subsequently be operated by Business, for a period of ____ (__) years from the date upon which transfer of the Business to Purchaser hereunder is concluded, as established by the Closing Date of escrow. Notwithstanding the foregoing, in the event that Seller shall enter into a competing or similar business outside said geographic area, and Business shall thereafter open or operate a secondary or subsidiary operation of Business within said area, it shall not be deemed a breach by Seller of the within covenant. For the purposes hereof, the phrase "directly or indirectly engage in any business" shall be taken to include, but not necessarily be limited to, owning in whole or in part, personally or through the agency of another (except as hereinafter qualified), managing, being employed in any capacity by, serving as a consultant to, serving as an officer or director of, acting as advisor to, being spokesperson for, or publicly endorsing in any manner, any business which, either directly or through an affiliate or subsidiary, operates in competition with, or which is similar to, the within Business. During the aforesaid period, Seller shall at all times refrain from any public utterance which is in any degree disparaging of Business or of Purchaser. Nothing herein shall be deemed to prevent Seller from owning not more than ____ percent (__%) of the outstanding shares of a publicly listed and traded company which is similar to or which directly or indirectly operates in competition with Business. Seller acknowledges, agrees and stipulates that the foregoing are reasonable and valid restrictions against unfair competition, intended to preserve to Purchaser so far as possible the undiluted goodwill of the Business purchased hereunder, and that the consideration received by Seller hereunder is good and sufficient compensation therefor. Seller further warrants and represents that Seller has a ready ability to earn income through means not falling within the scope of the foregoing restrictions, and that the foregoing restrictions will in no way adversely affect Seller nor Seller's livelihood.

◆ ◆ ◆

Notice Provision

Notice provisions address three questions: How? When? and Where? While this may seem to be a "housekeeping" provision, it is actually quite critical, especially for contracts which have long-term executory aspects, such as royalty accounting and payments.

First, a Notice Provision is intended to specify the *manner* of effective notice. Is leaving a phone message good notice under the contract, or must notice be sent in writing by certified mail with a return receipt requested? Modern contracts frequently provide for facsimile transmission (fax) or email, but they may also include regular first-class mail, or even require personal service into the hands of a designated recipient. However, as with many elements of contracts, courts will generally not allow frivolous, overly burdensome, or impractical specifications. If the contract states that notice must be given in skywriting, or by carrier pigeon, or hand-embroidered on a silk handkerchief delivered personally by one party to the other, such requirements will not be enforced.[260] Courts will generally deem *any* method sufficient if it resulted in actual notice to the party entitled to such notice, and the *manner* of giving notice will be of little consequence. Nonetheless, the contract should specify a practical, preferred method.

The second aspect of the provision is more crucial, since it specifies *when* notice becomes effective, which is particularly important in regard to options, cure provisions, and other time-sensitive contract terms. The *length* of a required notice period (*e.g.*, "30 day notice") will likely not appear within this provision, but rather in those portions of the contract which refer to giving notice as to a particular occurrence or matter.

The third element specifies *where* notice must be sent. This may be a physical address, a mailing address, a fax number, an email address, or any combination of these. In some instances, the particular person to whom notice should be directed may also be named, either individually or by their title.

Although contracts will generally contain a section captioned "Notice," that section will often include only one or two of the above elements expressly, with the remaining one or two elements operative by reference. For example, the provision will invariably state the method by which notice is to be given, but include the place where it is to be delivered as "at the address of the parties subscribed hereto," or "at the address(es) first appearing above," or similar reference. However the address is designated — either within the Notice section or by reference — the notice section should conclude its address designation with, "or such other address as may from time to time be designated in writing," or similar phrase. This allows the parties to change their address for notice, later, by *giving notice* (in the manner provided) of

260 Many older contracts contain notice requirements specifying once-common delivery methods — *e.g.*, cablegram. telegraph, Telex, *etc.* — which have been supplanted by newer technologies. Some current record contracts still contain these vestigial reminders of a bygone era which should be deleted from new agreements.

a new address for purposes of notice. **If you have a beneficial future interest in a contract — such as possible royalty payments — it is your responsibility to provide the other party with a current address for notice.**[261]

The amount of time required with respect to giving notice will more likely appear elsewhere in the contract, and probably in several locations in the contract. One aspect of the contract may require a five day notice period, whereas another section may specify a thirty day notice for a different purpose. Wherever a contract refers to "notice," it implicitly, and sometimes expressly, references the Notice section. The *effective date* of the notice — that is, the date upon which notice will be conclusively presumed to have been given — will likely appear within the Notice section, particularly where notice is to be given by regular mail. For example, that notice would be *"effective as of the third day following the date upon which said notice shall have been deposited into the United States mail."*

Notice (Basic notice by mail):

> **All notices required under this agreement shall be given in writing, transmitted by first-class mail to the designated address for notice stated herein, or to such other address for notice as a party may provide from time to time by written notice. Notice shall be deemed effective as of the date upon which the same is deposited into the United States Mail, and the notified party shall be presumed to have actually received such notice not later than five (5) calendar days following such deposit.**

261 Time and again, artists have threatened lawsuits against a former label for non-payment of royalties, only to discover that such non-payment resulted from the Artist's failure to provide formal notice of a new address. Labels will keep mailing accountings and checks to the address required by the contract, even when such mail is returned as undeliverable year after year. The label will have done everything which the contract requires, and the artist has no claim beyond the amount of any *uncashed* royalty checks delivered to an old address. (If someone other than Artist received and cashed some of Artist's royalty checks, it's not the label's fault.) Even if past royalty checks have not been cashed, there may be a one or two year maximum "look back" accounting provision, barring recovery of other, earlier payments not received by Artist, and excusing the label from *ever* having to pay them.

Notice (Typical) - Recording Contract:

Except as otherwise specifically provided herein, all notices hereunder shall be in writing and shall be given by courier or other personal delivery, or by registered or certified mail, at the respective addresses hereinabove set forth, or such other address or addresses as may be designated in writing by either party. Such notices shall be deemed given when mailed or tendered to a commercial courier service, except that notice of change of address shall be effective only from the time of its actual receipt. Notice may be given by telefacsimile (fax) to such telefacsimile number as a party may, from time to time, designate in writing, and such notice shall be effective upon electronic verification of successful transmission thereof.

[Notwithstanding the foregoing, and in addition thereto, a true and correct copy of each notice given by Artist to Company pursuant to the foregoing must thereafter be sent by certified mail addressed to: "Vice President, Business Affairs, *{Company Name} {Address}*"]

[Notwithstanding the foregoing, and in addition thereto, all Royalty Statements and payments from Company to Artist hereunder shall in each instance be delivered only by certified mail, return receipt requested, or by bonded courier, to such address as Artist may from time to time specially designate for such delivery.]

◆ ◆ ◆

Option Provision

In general, an Option is an agreement, or a provision within an agreement, which allows one party to enforce some future right, without any obligation to enforce that right. In terms of basic contract doctrines (*i.e.*, "offer and acceptance") an option may be regarded as an exclusive offer which cannot be withdrawn for a specified period of time, during which period the other party is free to accept or decline that offer, with acceptance forming a new, binding contract (or new element of an existing contract) as between the parties.

In general, option agreements usually relate to a contemplated purchase, setting a firm price and terms. For example, it is possible to rent a property "with option to purchase," so that the landlord is obligated to sell the property to the tenant upon terms specified in the lease agreement. Options can also be stand-alone agreements, where one party tenders consideration to another to "lock in" a certain price and terms for a period of time. Options are therefore a speculative investment in many instances, with the speculator paying a small amount to preserve a future right to purchase, then waiting to see if market forces make executing the option a favorable or unfavorable deal. For example ...

> *Hypothetical:* Abner owns a piece of property, which has a current market value of $1,000,000. Bill and Abner enter into an option agreement under which Bill gives Abner $25,000.00 for an exclusive option to purchase Abner's property for $1,250,000 at any time during the next five years. Abner now cannot sell the property to anyone but Bill (or Bill's successor or assignee) for the next five years. Three years into that option period, the market price of Abner's property has tripled, and it's now worth $3,000,000. At that point Bill can wait another two years to see if the value continues to increase -or- he can exercise the option and purchase the property by paying Abner $1,250,000 -or- if Bill doesn't have $1.25-million, he can sell the option to someone else. A prospective purchaser would likely prefer to pay Bill $1,000,000 for the right to purchase the property from Abner for $1.25-million, rather than wait another two years to purchase at its then-current market value... gambling that Bill's option will have been allowed to expire without being exercised before that.
>
> Of course, if the value of Abner's property remains constant or goes *down*, Bill might be out his initial $25,000... unless he is able to recover some or all of it by selling the option to some other speculator.

There is an entire sector of the investment business devoted to the buying and selling of *options* to purchase shares of stock at a particular price, profiting on the differences between values *then, now,* and *later.*

In the music business, however, the term "option" most often relates to a label's option to extend the term of a recording artist's contract. Most record contracts are for one album "firm," with a series of time-dependent options for additional subsequent albums. For established artists, the first *two* albums may be firm commitments, and options may likewise be for more than one album. Whether or not such options will be exercised, however, always lies solely within the discretion of the label — the *Artist* has no option. The truth is that most new artists will not get past their first album, and, if they are fortunate enough to get a chance at a second album, that second release is even more likely to be their last. The real problem for artists is that the label may have a year or more (depending on the contract language) in which to decide whether or not to exercise its option. For as long that period may be, the artist can do nothing but tour, rehearse, work on new material, promote the last album, and worry incessantly about whether or not his or her recording contract will be allowed to lapse. Until the option period expires, or the option is picked up, the Artist remains in an anxious state of contractual limbo.

Thus, when an artist speaks of a "six album deal," it is almost certainly a *one* album deal, with five options. After each album is released the label will have an extended period during which to decide whether or not another album by that artist would be a good investment.[262]

Option Provision — Recording Contract — Company Favorable:

> **Company will have five (5) separate Options, each of which shall be designated as a "Contract Period Option" to extend the Term for additional Contract Periods, as hereinabove defined, and as may alternatively herein also be referred to as "Option Periods," on the same terms and conditions applicable to the first Contract Period, except as may be expressly hereinafter provided by other terms of this Agreement. Company may exercise each of those Contract Period Options by sending the Artist a notice, in such form and manner as may be hereinafter provided, not later than the expiration date of the Contract Period or Option Period then in effect (the "Current Contract Period"). If Company exercises a Contract Period Option, the Option Period concerned shall commence upon the expiration of the prior Contract Period and shall continue until a date eight (8) months following USNRC Initial Release of the Album Delivered, in complete satisfaction of the Artist's Recording Commitment for that Option Period.**
>
> **Notwithstanding anything hereinabove to the contrary, in the event that Company shall not have formally exercised its option to**

262 Established artists generally want their contracts to have *fewer* options, rather than more. A contract for two albums "firm," with a single option for one or two additional albums — or no option at all — is preferable to a typical "six album" (five option) deal.

extend the Term for a further Contract Period as of the last day of the calendar month during which the date upon on which the then-current Contract Period would otherwise expire, the following shall apply:

(1) Artist shall send to Company, by Certified Mail, with Return Receipt, written notice (the "Option Expiration Warning") advising Company that the pending Option has not yet been formally exercised.

(2) Company shall have the right, but not the obligation, to exercise any Option provided for herein at any time up to and including a date thirty (30) business days (the "Option Extension Period") following Company's actual receipt of the Option Expiration Warning, as determined by Certified Mail Return Receipt.

(3) The then-current Contract Period shall continue until either the end of the Option Extension Period or Company's notice ("Termination Notice") to Artist that Company does not intend to exercise its option, whichever shall first occur, but in no event shall the Option Extension Period have the effect of extending any Contract Period beyond a term of seven (7) years.

(4) Notwithstanding anything in the foregoing to the contrary, nothing herein shall be deemed to limit Company's right to send a Termination Notice to Artist at any time, nor limit Company's right to exercise an Option at any time if Artist shall have failed to send a timely Option Expiration Warning in strict compliance with the procedure set forth hereinabove.

Option Provision — Recording Contract — Artist Favorable:

Company will have three (3) separate Options, each of which shall be designated as a "Contract Period Option" to extend the Term for additional Contract Periods, as hereinabove defined, and as may alternatively herein also be referred to as "Option Periods," on terms and conditions hereinafter provided in other provisions of this Agreement regarding Advances and Option Periods. Company may exercise each of those Contract Period Options by sending the Artist a notice, in such form and manner as may be hereinafter provided, not later than the expiration date of the Contract Period or Option Period then in effect (the "Current Contract Period"). If Company exercises a Contract Period Option, the Option Period concerned shall commence upon the expiration of the prior Contract Period and shall continue until a date four (4) months following the Initial Release in any market of the Album Delivered, in complete satisfaction of Artist's Recording Commitment for that Option Period., but in no event later than a date ten (10) months following Delivery of all Recordings constituting the Artist's Recording Commitment for that Option Period.

Notwithstanding anything hereinabove to the contrary, in the event that Company shall not have formally exercised its option to extend the Term for a further Contract Period as of the date upon which the then-current Contract Period would otherwise expire, the following shall apply:

(1) Artist shall send to Company written notice (the "Option Expiration Warning"), by regular mail, electronic mail, or facsimile transmission, reminding Company that the pending Option has not yet been formally exercised.

(2) Company shall have the right to exercise any Option provided for herein at any time up to and including a date five (5) business days (the "Option Extension Period") following the date of such Option Expiration Warning.

(3) The then-current Contract Period shall continue until either the end of the Option Extension Period or Company's notice ("Termination Notice") to Artist that Company does not intend to exercise its option, whichever shall first occur.

(4) Notwithstanding anything in the foregoing, nothing herein shall be deemed to limit Company's right to send a Termination Notice to Artist at any time, nor extend any Contract Period more than sixty (60) days beyond the date upon which such Period would expire by its own terms, regardless of whether or not Artist shall have sent an Option Expiration Warning as hereinabove provided.

◆ ◆ ◆

Penalty Provision

We have included this reference to a "Penalty Provision" because many contracts use the word "Penalty" to describe what is actually a liquidated damages provision. As has been noted in the discussion on liquidated damages, the law abhors attempts to impose punitive measures within contracts, and provisions which are, in fact, merely penalties intended solely to coerce performance by a threat of punitive consequences for non-performance — as distinguished from provisions intended to provide appropriate liquidated damages as reasonable compensation in the event of breach — are likely to be held unenforceable and severable.

Of course, mere use of the *word* "penalty" will not be dispositive of the issue, any more than would calling a punitive provision "liquidated damages." The court will look to the substance of the provision, not its name. Nonetheless, it is better practice to call these provisions Liquidated Damages, rather than Penalties, to avoid having an ill-chosen caption become an unnecessary additional issue upon which the court will need to rule.[263]

Regardless of the name used, some types of penalties are permissible, provided that they are not overly punitive and bear some reasonable relationship to the damage arising from a specific non-performance, such as a late payment penalty. As with broader liquidated liability provisions which address a fundamental, material breach, penalty clauses should include some reasonable basis justifying the penalty imposed.

263 If the contract fails to include a construction clause stating that captions are immaterial to the agreement, then use of the word "penalty" as the title for a section will have more weight in the court's deliberations construing that provision.

Penalty Provision — Late Delivery (Generic)

The parties having acknowledged that time is of the essence in respect hereto, and further agreeing hereby that unexcused delay in Delivery hereunder will necessarily and unavoidably result in inconvenience and some degree of financial loss to Company, the parties hereby agree that, for each full day following the scheduled Delivery Date herein provided, up to and including the date upon which Delivery shall be completed, Supplier shall be assessed a LATE DELIVERY PENALTY FEE of $500.00 per day, which Supplier hereby stipulates is reasonable, and which shall constitute a Credit in favor of Company in respect to any and all sums which Company might otherwise be obligated to pay to Supplier hereunder. In the event that the total of accrued penalties under this provision shall exceed the total indebtedness of Company to Supplier, then Supplier shall pay the sum of all such excess to Company, up to the full value of consideration received by Supplier hereunder, without waiver or limitation in respect to any other right, remedy, recourse, action or cause of action which Company has or may have, in law or in equity, with respect to any claim of deficient performance, non-performance, or breach in respect hereto.

◆ ◆ ◆

Personal Guaranty Provision

Looking back to an earlier discussion regarding the Statute of Frauds, you may recall that one of the traditional types of agreement which must be evidenced by a writing is a promise to answer for the debt of another. Such a promise — to be the surety of another's obligation — is referred to as a guaranty, and the person who gives such a promise is a guarantor.[264]

There is virtually no defense to an obligation arising by guaranty. About the only exception would be proving that the third party's allegedly defaulted obligation is, in fact, not owed.[265]

A guaranty may be *special* or *continuing*. Special guaranties are for a particular transaction, while continuing guaranties are for an unlimited number of past and future transactions. Guaranties may be limited or unlimited in respect to amount, as well.

Personal guaranty refers to a guaranty given by a person — usually but not necessarily a business owner, shareholder, or officer — making that person directly liable for an obligation in the event that the business should fail to perform. The liability shield afforded to corporations and other limited liability entities generally immunizes the principals of such entities from personal liability for the entity's debts. Many lenders and suppliers, aware of this so-called "corporate veil," will require a personal guaranty from a fiscally sound individual as a condition for extending credit to the entity.

Because the *word* "guaranty" is fraught with legal meaning, use of the *word alone* may carry with it all of the necessary elements to create an indefensible personal obligation to be responsible for the debt of another. Thus a contract may create a continuing personal guaranty (and indemnification) by whomever signs the contract on behalf of an entity by inclusion of a provision in which guaranty language is embedded.

Guarantors are not always individuals. A financially sound entity may guaranty the obligations of a subsidiary or affiliate entity. Such guaranties are sometimes referred to as *corporate* rather than personal. It should be noted that a guaranty is only valid with respect to *another's* obligations. Thus a general partner cannot be a guarantor of a partnership obligation, because he or she is *already* personally liable for that obligation, and such a guaranty would be a legal nullity.

264 The more familiar spelling — guarantee — has become confused in the public mind with another legal concept; warranty. Around 100 years ago, for no apparent reason (other than the likelihood that those responsible for advertisements and packaging were not lawyers), manufacturers and purveyors of services began to represent that their goods or services were "guaranteed." Strictly speaking, a "guarantee" is a person to whom someone else (the guarantor) has promised (*i.e.*, given a guaranty) to pay a third party's obligation, should that third party (the defaultor) fail to do so.

265 Upon paying the obligation, the guarantor becomes a creditor, and may seek reimbursement from the defaulting debtor.

While guaranties may be embedded within an agreement, or subscribed as endorsements to a contract, many can be complex, standalone contracts in their own right, setting forth terms, conditions and limitations with respect to what obligations are and are not being guarantied. The critical points to consider in drafting a guaranty are as follows:

- *Limitations:* A guaranty may be limited as to a maximum amount, beyond which the guarantor has no obligation, or limited as to a specific transaction (*special guaranty*) or a particular type or class of transactions (*qualified guaranty).* It may also include a time limitation, with automatic termination upon a certain date. Perhaps most critically, the guaranty may limited to an original, principal obligation, or extended to cover finance charges, costs, expenses (including attorney's fees) which may arise by reason of that obligation or attempts to collect the obligation from the primary debtor or from the guarantor.
- *Termination:* A guaranty may be irrevocable, or terminable at will. Generally, termination will require very specific and provable notice of termination, since the guarantor will remain liable for obligations incurred prior to termination notice.
- *Remedy procedures:* In the event of an apparent default, the guaranty may allow the creditor to make immediate demand upon the guarantor, or require exhaustion of all remedies as against the defaulted debtor before making any claim upon the guarantor.

In order to minimize the possibility of repudiation, and to satisfy a condition imposed by statute in a few jurisdictions, many personal guaranties will also require the addition of an "Acknowledgment," bearing the signature and seal of a Notary Public.

Guaranty — Subscribed Endorsement (Basic):

The undersigned ____________ ("Guarantor") hereby personally guaranties performance of all obligations required of {Entity} within or arising by reason of the foregoing Agreement:

Dated: _______   ________________________

Guarantor

Embedded Personal Guaranty (Generic):

Regardless of any subscribed capacity, the natural person(s) executing this Agreement on behalf of {Entity}, and each such individual, jointly and severally, hereby personally warrants, represents and guaranties that such natural person(s) is/are duly authorized and empowered to execute this Agreement on behalf of {Entity}, and to bind {Entity} thereby, and do(es) hereby likewise guaranty, indemnify, and hold Company harmless, from any and all loss, damage, harm, or liability which Company may incur or accrue through reliance upon any portion of this Agreement.

Continuing Personal Guaranty (Irrevocable):

The undersigned _________ residing at {Residence Address}, for and in consideration of Company's acceptance of and agreement to that certain {Title of Agreement} dated {Date of Agreement} ("Agreement") with {Entity}, of which Guarantor is {Title or other relationship to Entity}, does hereby personally guaranty to Company the payment at {City} in the state of ________ any obligation of {Entity} to Company, and Guarantor hereby agrees to be personally bound to pay Company, on demand, any sum which may become due to Company by {Entity} whenever {Entity} shall fail to pay the same. It is understood that this guaranty shall be a continuing and irrevocable guaranty and indemnity for such indebtedness of {Entity}. Guarantor hereby waives notice of default, nonpayment and notice thereof, and consents to any modification or renewal of the Agreement hereby guarantied.

Dated: ________ **__________________________**

Guarantor

SSN: ________________

Personal Guaranty (Comprehensive)
Beneficiary (Obligee) Favorable:

In order to induce *{Company Name}* (hereinafter "Company") to enter into that certain agreement entitled *{Title of Agreement}* with, and to grant a line of credit in the name of and to, *{Name of Obligated Entity}* (hereinafter "Obligor"), and for other good and valuable consideration, the receipt and sufficiency of all of which are hereby acknowledged, the undersigned *{Name of Guarantor}* (hereinafter"Guarantor"), unconditionally and irrevocably guarantees to Company the full and prompt payment and performance by Obligor of all obligations which Obligor presently has or may hereafter have to Company, including but not limited to, payment when and as due of all sums presently or hereafter owing by or from Obligor to Company, no matter how evidenced.

Guarantor further agrees to indemnify and hold harmless Company from and against any and all losses Company may sustain, and expenses it may incur or accrue, as a result of any default of Obligor with respect to the performance of Obligor and/or Guarantor's obligations to Company.

Guarantor agrees that it shall not be necessary, as condition precedent to the enforcement of this guaranty, that demand first be made of Obligor, that suit be first instituted against Obligor, or that any rights or remedies against Obligor be first exhausted.

It is understood and agreed that the liability of the Guarantor hereunder shall be primary, direct, and in all respects unconditional, immediately upon the occurrence of a condition of default in the obligations of Obligor to Company.

For purposes of this guaranty and indemnity, all sums owing to Company by Obligor shall be deemed to have become immediately due and payable if (a) Obligor fails to make any payment to Company required to be made at the time it is due to be made; (b) a petition under any chapter of Title 11 of the United States Code, as amended,[266] or for the appointment of a receiver of any part of the property of Obligor, be filed by or against Obligor and not be dismissed within thirty (30) days; (c) Obligor makes a general assignment for the benefit of its creditors, suspends business, or commits any act amounting to a business failure or admission of insolvency; or (d) an arrest, seizure or attachment be levied

266 The Bankruptcy Act. While the Bankruptcy Act and Federal Rules of Bankruptcy Procedure generally invalidate contract provisions which adversely impact *Debtor's* rights and property interests by reason of the filing of a bankruptcy petition (discussed earlier, see "Insolvency Provision"), there is no bar to such petition being a triggering event with respect to a third party, such as a guarantor.

or tax lien be filed against any of the property of Obligor, and the same, be it attachment, lien or judgment, not be discharged or have adequate and acceptable security posted therefor within ten (10) days.

This shall be a continuing guaranty and indemnity, and, irrespective of the lack of any notice to or consent of Guarantor, its obligations hereunder shall not be impaired in any manner whatsoever.

Guarantor hereby waives notice of Company's acceptance hereof, of default or nonpayment by Obligor, or presentment, protest and demand, and all other matters of which Guarantor otherwise might be entitled to notice.

The obligations of Guarantor hereunder shall be binding upon its respective heirs, executors, administrators, successors, assigns, and legal representatives.

Guarantor shall reimburse Company, on demand, for any and all expenses incurred by Company in the enforcement or attempted enforcement of any of Company's rights hereunder as against Obligor and/or Guarantor, including, but not limited to, legal expenses, investigative expenses, costs of experts and of expert witnesses, court costs, and reasonable attorneys' fees.

Failure or delay by Company to proceed against Guarantor in case of an occurrence of any condition of default of Obligor's obligations to Company shall not constitute a waiver of Guarantor's obligations or Company's rights hereunder. Guarantor expressly and irrevocably waives any claim and defense of "Laches" based upon any failure or delay by Company in respect to enforcement of Company's rights hereunder.

This guaranty and indemnity is assignable by Company without notice to Guarantor, shall be construed liberally in favor of Company, and shall inure to the benefit of Company's successors and assigns.

The undersigned Guarantor agrees that Guarantor is irrevocably bound by each and every covenant, obligation, and guaranty herein given, and that, in the event of any action by Company on said guaranty, Company, may proceed against Guarantor to collect and enforce each and every obligation guarantied hereby.

If any part, term, provision, condition, or other portion of this Guaranty shall be found to be invalid for any reason, the validity of the remainder hereof shall not be affected thereby, and the rights and obligations of the parties may be construed and enforced as though this Guaranty did not contain the portion found to be invalid.

All notices that shall or may be given shall be addressed to the parties as follows:

If to Company: *{Company's Address}*

If to Guarantor: *{Guarantor's Address}*

This Agreement shall be construed, governed and enforced in accordance with the laws of the State of _______.

IN WITNESS WHEREOF, the Guarantor has executed this Guaranty upon this ____ day of *{Month}*, *{Year}*, at *{City}*, *{State}*.

____

Guarantor

Acknowledgment

State of , }
} ss.
County of . }

In ______, on ________, 20__, before me, the undersigned ____________, a Notary Public in and for the above state and county, personally appeared *{Name of Guarantor}*, known to me or proven to me upon the basis of satisfactory evidence to be the person named in and who executed the foregoing instrument, and being first duly sworn, such person acknowledged having executed said instrument for the purposes therein contained as his or her free and voluntary act and deed.

WITNESS my hand and seal:

____

NOTARY PUBLIC

(SEAL) My Commission Expires: _________

Personal Guaranty (Revocable - Comprehensive) Guarantor Favorable:[267]

As an inducement to *{Company Name}* (hereinafter "Company") to enter into that certain agreement entitled *{Title of Agreement}* with, and to grant a line of credit in the name of and to, *{Name of Principal Entity}* (hereinafter"Obligor"), the undersigned *{Name of Guarantor}* (hereinafter "Guarantor"), guarantees to Company the performance by Obligor of

267 While no guaranty is beneficial to the guarantor, this sample provides (so far as reasonably possible) favorable terms aimed at protecting the guarantor from avoidable collateral costs, expenses, and inconvenience arising from the guaranty. It limits the guaranty to the principal amount of the obligation (without interest, collection costs, or attorney's fees), is terminable at will, and requires complete exhaustion of remedies reduced to a final judgment against the Obligor before it may be exercised.

obligations of Obligor to Company for payment when due of such principal sums as may hereafter become owing by or from Obligor to Company.

As a condition precedent to enforcement of this Guaranty, or commencement of any claim hereunder, all remedies which Company has or may have as against Obligor must be first exhausted, and reduced to a final judgment against Obligor.

Guarantor may terminate Guarantor's obligations hereunder by certified mail notice to Company, provided, however such termination shall not affect liability hereunder with respect to any obligations of Obligor to Company actually incurred prior to such notice.

This guaranty is assignable by Company upon notice to Guarantor, shall be binding upon and inure to the benefit of the parties' respective successors and assigns, and shall not be construed for or against either party by reason of one party being the drafter hereof.

If any part, term, provision, condition, or other portion of this Guaranty shall be found to be invalid for any reason, the entirety hereof shall be deemed invalid.

All notices that shall or may be given shall be addressed to the parties as follows:

If to Company: *{Address of Company}*

If to Guarantor: *{Address of Guarantor}*

This Agreement shall be construed, governed and enforced in accordance with the laws of the State of ______.

IN WITNESS WHEREOF, Guarantor has executed this Guaranty upon this ____ day of *{Month}*, *{Year}*, at *{City}*, *{State}*.

____
Guarantor

◆ ◆ ◆

Reasonable Person Clause

If you haven't just opened this book for the first time at random and hit upon this page, you may recall having seen the word "reasonable" and its variants several hundred times already. In almost every area of law situations will be analyzed upon the basis of "reasonableness." What would a hypothetical "reasonable person" understand or do in a similar situation? This "reasonable person" standard is applied to almost every contract dispute, in an effort to judge the propriety of fundamentally *subjective* conduct and relationships by comparison to a theoretically *objective* ideal.

A "reasonable person" standard is implied in almost every contract, but there will be some contracts where that standard, or a higher standard,[268] should be expressly established. This is particularly true in circumstances where one party will have broad discretion in respect to matters which affect the rights and interests of the other party, as will often be the case in management contracts. When used in such context, a reasonable person clause is akin to, and may be integrated with, a "best efforts," clause. In essence, the purpose of inserting this type of Reasonable Person clause is to require a party to use sound judgment in the exercise of that party's discretion, to require avoidance of unreasonable risk-taking, and to discourage unreasonable or capricious conduct.

The Reasonable Person standard will also likely appear in certain definitions and requirements within a contract, or within a Construction clause, providing a specific alternative to imposition of a different standard such as "industry custom and usage" or "good faith." If, for example, the word "satisfactory" appears in the contract, it may be appropriate to specify that "for the purposes hereof, 'satisfactory performance' shall be taken to mean only such level of performance as an ordinary, reasonable person would deem satisfactory under similar circumstances." This creates a different standard of performance than would exist if the subject matter of that contract is within the scope of an industry in which "satisfactory" has some other, commonly understood meaning, which may be a higher or lower standard than would be imposed under the Reasonable Person standard.

Not all states apply the theoretically-objective "Reasonable Person" standard to contracts, but instead utilize a subjective "good faith" test, particularly in regard to approval provisions appearing within a contract. Under a good-faith standard, when one party's performance of contract obligations is contingent upon the approval of another party, non-approval must be based upon an honest, good faith reason. Conversely, under the Reasonable Person standard,

---

268 In management agreements, particularly where the manager is given authority to make investments or discretionary expenditures using the principal's funds, a "Prudent Person" standard may be used, prohibiting expenditures or investments which a prudent (rather than merely reasonable) person would deem risky, unconventional, improvident, or unwise. A "Prudent Person" clause imposes a duty greater than is required of a "reasonable person," amd approaches the level of duty required of a fiduciary. If the contract includes a power of attorney, then fiduciary duty is implicit, but should nonetheless be expressed.

the party is required to approve, and may only disapprove, that which a hypothetical "reasonable person" would have approved or disapproved under the same or similar circumstances.

These two standards are fundamentally different. An individual who honestly holds an unreasonable belief might have a subjective, "good faith" reason for non-performance, even though no "reasonable person" would have acted similarly. That unreasonable belief would legally justify non-performance under the "good faith" standard, while in jurisdictions applying a "reasonable person" standard, it would not.

Another key difference between objective and subjective standards is essentially procedural. A judge may enter a dispositive ruling under an objective standard, as a matter of law. Conversely, a party's "good faith" or an industry's "customary practice," will often be a question of fact, and hence reserved for jury determination. Where circumstances or choice of law provisions dictate a forum in which a subjective standard will be the legal default condition (*e.g.*, Oklahoma), it is advisable to expressly include the "reasonable person" standard in the contract. This may be done as a standalone provision,[269] or it may appear as language within those clauses and provisions to which the standard is particularly applicable, such as in a delivery or approval clause.

Reasonable Person — Standalone Clause

> **In construing the instant agreement, and in determining performance of the parties' respective obligations hereunder, an objective, "reasonable person" standard shall be applied as the minimum standard in all instances unless a higher objective standard is specified.**

Reasonable Person — Integrated Standard (Example 1)

> **Delivery shall be deemed to be "satisfactory" hereunder if a reasonable person, similarly situated and under similar circumstances, would consider such delivery to be satisfactory.**

269 Best practice would recommend incorporating such provision into the contract's construction clause.

Reasonable Person — Integrated Standard (Example 2)

Artist shall not undertake any third-party engagement which would impair Artist's ability to timely perform any one or more of Artist's obligations hereunder, without first obtaining Company's consent, which consent shall not be unreasonably withheld. Any denial of such consent by Company shall be delivered to Artist, in writing, within five (5) days of Artist's request for such consent, and shall state with specificity the reason for such denial of consent. Failure to timely deliver such written denial of consent shall constitute Company's express consent to the third-party engagement. For the purposes hereof, "unreasonable" shall be taken to mean a stated reason which a reasonable person, similarly situated, would consider unreasonable.

Prudent Person Clause (Higher Standard) — Basic

In performing Manager's obligations hereunder, Manager shall at all times possess such knowledge and information as is normally possessed by a prudent person experienced in the ordinary course of similar business dealings, and shall undertake only such actions hereunder as such prudent person would consider reasonable, ordinary, and objectively justified.

◆ ◆ ◆

Relationship of Parties Clause

This provision is generally included in contracts as a stipulation between the parties to clarify the exact nature of their relationship. Frequently, the intention will be less to establish what that relationship *is*, than to assert what it is *not*. There are certain liabilities, obligations, and benefits which arise in a relationship between partners, or between an employer and employee, which are absent in an independent contractor relationship. Another set of liabilities may arise when a contract creates an agency relationship, or a joint venture, or a partnership. In consequence, contracting parties often find it advisable to expressly state the contract *does not* create and employer/employee, principal/agent, joint venture, or partnership relationship between them.

Employee, Partner, or Independent Contractor?

> *"Before you can determine how to treat payments you make for services, you must first know the business relationship that exists between you and the person performing the services."* (IRS website)

According to the IRS, an **independent contractor relationship** exists when the paying party has a right to control or direct *only the result of the work done*, and not the means or methods for accomplishing that result, while an **employment relationship** exists when the paying party *can* control *what* will be done and *how* it will be done. For the IRS, the default relationship is that of an employer/employee, and independent contractor status must be demonstrated to their satisfaction.

Simply *calling* someone an independent contractor will not suffice. If the relationship has the *indicia* of employment, then it *is* employment… no matter what the contract says. Similarly, where the parties' conduct is such as would lead a reasonable person to conclude that one party is the agent or partner of the other, then an agency or partnership exists, and a contract's disclaimer of such relationship is likely meaningless.

In the eyes of a court (or the IRS), there is a list of factors to be considered in determining whether an individual is an employee and *not* an "independent contractor," *regardless* of how the parties' contract may describe their relationship. In general terms, those factors fall into three categories: "Behavioral Control," "Financial Control," and "Functional Relationship."

Behavioral Control Factor

- One party giving the other party instructions as to when, where, and how obligations are to be performed, will indicate an employment relationship. Independent contractors should not be given specific directions with respect to the manner in which they perform their obligations, other than in broad terms or as end-result requirements.

- One party providing training to the other party tends to indicate an employment relationship. Independent contractors are expected to have all of the talents, equipment, and skills necessary to fulfil their contract obligations.
- A requirement that one party submit regular reports (other than periodic status reports or updates) to the other party, will tend to indicate an employment relationship.
- One party's ongoing supervision of the other will tend to indicate an employment relationship.
- Set hours during which one party is to perform that party's obligations will tend to indicate an employment relationship.

Financial Control Factor

- If a party has invested in equipment and supplies necessary to fulfillment of that party's obligations, it will tend to support a claim of independent contractor status. Independent contractors invest in themselves and their business interests. Maintaining a home office or recording studio would be a good example.
- Payment by one party of the other party's expenses such as, mileage, travel, lodging, telephone, *etc.*, as a separate item apart from regular compensation, will tend to indicate an employment relationship. Independent contractors cover their own overhead, and factor such expenses into the contract price which they negotiate. This does not, however, rule out contractual provisions for reimbursement of extraordinary expenses; merely overhead expenses and such costs and expenses as were foreseeable by a "reasonable person" as being within the scope of contract obligations at the time of its formation.
- Making identical or similar services generally available to others tends to indicate independent contractor status.
- Payment based on units of time (hour, week, or month) rather than on the basis of goods or services delivered, will tend to indicate an employment relationship.
- A party's risk of financial loss, coupled with a potential for profit, tends to indicate independent contractor status.
- A party's separate license to provide the type goods or services falling within the scope of the contract (*e.g.*, a business license) will tend to indicate independent contractor status.

Functional Relationship Factor

- A party's legal capacity as other than an individual (*i.e.*, a corporation or other legal entity) will strongly indicate an independent contractor relationship.
- A party's eligibility for, or receipt of, fringe benefits (*e.g.*, health insurance, pension plan, *etc.*) normally afforded to employees of the other party will tend to indicate an employment relationship.
- One party's hiring, firing, or supervising of others employed by the other party, will tend to indicate an employment relationship.
- An arrangement wherein all services provided by an individual party to the other must be provided by that individual party personally, and cannot be delegated, will tend to indicate an employment relationship. (This factor is only one of many, however, and does not, *ipso facto*, rule out exclusive personal services agreements.)
- Either party's ability to terminate the relationship at any time without incurring liability will tend to indicate an employment relationship.
- The existence of a written agreement expressly stating independent contractor status, while containing few requirements for conduct inconsistent with such status, will strongly support a finding of independent contractor relationship.

"Take this job and..." — The At Will Doctrine

Where the subject contract is an Employment Agreement, a different set of concerns will apply. Unless an employee has a specific employment agreement, or is a union member coming within the scope of a collective bargaining agreement, that employee is regarded as an employee-at-will, which means that the employee can quit, or be fired, at any time, for no reason at all, in most states. It's when there *is* a reason that things can get complicated.

Employees may come and go as they please, without legal constraint, unless such constraints arise from valid employment contracts. Employers, too, enjoy relative freedom of action under the At-Will Doctrine. They are free to hire, fire, transfer, promote, demote, berate, castigate, demean, harass, humiliate or abuse employees to their hearts' content ***provided*** the employer's conduct — or the conduct of those for whose conduct the employer is legally or vicariously responsible — does not cross the line into violations of applicable law or public policy. Unfortunately for temperamental employers, recent decades have redrawn that line so liberally that, in some states, it often requires a level of restraint and demeanor more in keeping with kindergarten than commerce. To put it another way, an employee-at-will may be treated as badly as the law will allow,[270] and fired for no reason, or for any good reason, but never for a *bad* reason.

270 *I.e.*, with kid gloves, in most jurisdictions.

Under the At-Will Doctrine, an unhappy employee's remedy is to find another job. If he or she is unable to do so, however, there may be a sudden realization that he or she didn't *really* quit. Instead, it was a "constructive termination" — the employee was *compelled* to quit by the conduct of an employer, supervisor, or co-worker who demoted, berated, castigated, demeaned, harassed, humiliated and/or abused him or her. The legal sufficiency of such a claim — *i.e.*, the former employee's ability to sue the employer and win — will vary widely from state to state.

Clearly it's important for employers to know just where these lines are drawn within the jurisdictions to which they are subject.[271] This is an issue to be discussed with an attorney experienced in labor law within the state in which the employment takes place. A Human Resources Policy Manual developed in conjunction with such an attorney — and *adherence to its policies* — will be the best defense to these kinds of lawsuits,[272] and will likely avoid most such suits altogether. Meanwhile, here are two broad categories of employment practices which will be generally prohibited and which create exceptions to the At Will doctrine:

- **Discrimination**: Violating any state or federal law with respect to treatment of employees in the workplace creates an exception to the At-Will Doctrine. "Discrimination" is a broad term — and getting broader. It may include any conduct with respect to an employee on the basis of age, disability, ethnicity, gender, genetics, medical condition or history, physical appearance, religion, or sexual orientation. Whether any particular class is protected within a specific jurisdiction — and the extent of such protection — is a question which must be addressed to an attorney familiar with the laws of that jurisdiction.
- **Public Policy Violations**: Some conduct is so repugnant to public conscience that it will create an exception to the At-Will doctrine in most states. In those states where a public policy exception exists, an employer may not terminate an employee for reasonably exercising a constitutional right, or for engaging in lawful, privileged conduct. For example, an employee cannot be fired for filing a Worker's Compensation claim, or for refusing to engage in illegal activities, or for fulfilling a civic obligation such as voting or reporting for jury duty. In 2002, a California jury awarded wrongful discharge damages of $1.2 million to an employee-at-will who was fired for refusing to sign an unenforceable covenant not to compete. There is a balancing issue however, where one employee's lawful conduct amounts to harassment or discrimination in respect to another employee. This is when having a skilled Human Resources staff (and a good labor lawyer) can be essential.

---

271 And this may include not only the state where the employee works, but possibly the business' state of domicile, or a federal jurisdiction, or other jurisdictions, depending on which particular "line" has been crossed.

272 Although a policy manual may also open the door to an "implied contract" exception to the At Will Doctrine in most states.

In addition to the foregoing law and public policy exceptions, there are also contract-based exceptions to the At-Will Doctrine.

- **Express Contract**: The existence of a formal employment agreement supplants "at will" status, and the employee (and employer) will instead be bound by the terms of that agreement. Such agreements normally provide for termination under stated circumstances, either "for cause," (*i.e.*, culpable conduct on the employee's part), or "not for cause," (*e.g.*, changed business circumstance; reorganization; relocation; inadequate — but not culpable — performance by employee.) Employment contracts generally state the responsibilities of the employer to the employee, and vice versa, as a matter of bargained for terms of the agreement.

- **Collective Bargaining**: When employees are members of a union, they will generally have all of the benefits of at-will employment, but the employer will be constrained by the terms of the applicable collective bargaining agreement in respect to termination. "For Cause" termination may require conforming to union-imposed procedures, while "not for cause" termination may be subject to a seniority system, hampering an employer's ability to lay off employees based upon their relative merit.

- **Implied Contract**: Most states also recognize an implied contract as an exception to at-will employment. Under this exception, an employer may not fire an employee when there is an implied contract between the employer and employee. The burden of proof will be on the discharged employee to demonstrate both (a) the existence, and (b) the terms of the alleged implied contract. This is where Human Resources Policy Manuals, employee handbooks, or other documents setting forth the employer's policies and practices may come into play. If company policy states that employees will only be fired "for cause," or provides for a grievance procedure or termination procedure which was not followed precisely, the employer may be found in breach of an implied employment contract.

- **Implied Covenant**: A few states have also applied the implied covenant of good faith and fair dealing to at-will employment. As discussed earlier, it is well settled that such a covenant does exist in every contract. Commencing with a 1980 California case, however, a few states have extended that implied-in-law covenant to embrace employment at will relationships, even where no implied contract had been alleged or proven. In practice, however, this exception is generally applied in situations approaching unconscionable conduct on the employer's part, such as terminating an employee just before a pension is due to vest, or when other benefits have accrued and are about to become due.

You may have noted that the foregoing discussion of at-will employment and exceptions contains references to "most states" or "some states" or "a few states." This was not unintentional nor was it because we don't know how many states, or which states, apply which exceptions. The reality is that, between the time this chapter is complete, and the time this book goes to press, and the time — right *now!* — that you read these words, those numbers will almost certainly have changed. The law within any jurisdiction is subject to constant amendment and reinterpretation, and we are dealing with at least fifty-one different bodies of U.S. law. This is one of the key reasons why consulting a lawyer conversant with the laws of your particular jurisdiction can be so critical.

Relationship of Parties (Generic Disclaimer):

> **Nothing in this Agreement shall be deemed or construed by the parties hereto, or by any third party, as creating a relationship of principal and agent, partnership, joint venture, or employment as between the parties hereto, it being understood and agreed that no provision contained herein, and no act of the parties hereto, shall be deemed to create any relationship between the parties hereto other than such relationship, and only such relationship, as is herein set forth.**

Relationship of Parties (Generic Disclaimer - Alternative):

> **The parties expressly agree and stipulate that nothing herein shall be construed as creating any joint venture or partnership as between the parties; the parties are not by reason hereof, and neither party shall be deemed to be, an agent, partner, principal, employee, or legal representative of the other party for any purpose; neither party shall have any right, power or authority to create any obligation or responsibility on behalf of the other, nor to bind the other party in respect to any matter.**

Relationship of Parties - Recording Contract:

> **It is understood and agreed that in entering into this agreement, and in rendering services pursuant thereto, Artist has, and shall have, the status of an independent contractor, and nothing contained herein shall contemplate or constitute Artist, or any individual member of Artist, as Company's employee, joint venturer, partner, representative, or agent.**

◆ ◆ ◆

Renewal Provision

Contracts often have a fixed term, generally stated either as a period of time from the commencement date of the contract, or by a specified termination date. For example,

> The term of this contract shall be one (1) year from the date first written above

or

> This contract shall terminate at 12:01 a.m., January 1, 2009.

Termination of a contract does not terminate *prior obligations* created by that contract, nor affect any ongoing *executory provisions* which survive expiration of the contract's term. Termination merely precludes wholly new obligations arising under that contract, and assumes that all non-executory provisions have been fully executed.

Many contracts contemplate that, once the term has expired, the parties may wish to continue their contractual relationship on the same terms, without the necessity of renegotiating an entirely new agreement. This is generally accomplished by a Renewal Provision, which will set forth the mechanism by which the contract will be renewed, either automatically or upon a specified form of notice.

Because renewal is so closely linked to a contract's term, the renewal provision may not always appear as a separate section, but rather as a part of the Term clause of the contract. Alternatively, because the concepts of renewal and option are closely related, renewals may appear under the caption "Option," although such "optional" renewal provisions usually allot the right to renew to only one party.

Since automatic renewal clauses allow an agreement to continue for an additional defined period if the existing agreement isn't cancelled or renegotiated within a specified time (measured from the expiration of the current contract) the term of renewal depends on the specific contract language. Such clauses generally provide that the contract shall be automatically renewed for a stated period unless either party, before some specified date (*e.g.*, 60 days before expiration), gives notice to the other of its desire to cancel renewal of the agreement.

Such clauses often appear in employment agreements, commercial services agreements, and leases. Because many automatic renewal provisions may have the effect of creating a new obligation without the obligated party being clearly aware of that fact, they are generally disfavored by public policy. A number of states have enacted laws which make such automatic renewals ineffective in respect to certain types of contracts, particularly residential leases and consumer service contracts, unless the other party gives specific written notice (usually no more than sixty days, nor less than thirty days prior to the automatic renewal date), advising the other party that an automatic renewal is scheduled to occur unless a cancellation notice is sent by a stated date.

With respect to residential leases in particular, a local attorney should be consulted because, while some states have laws which govern automatic renewal clauses, counties or municipalities within a state may also regulate such clauses, under rent control ordinances. Thus a renewal provision which might be valid under state law, but void or restricted under local law. For example, California law permits automatic renewal clauses but requires that they must be printed in eight-point or larger bold faced type to be enforceable. Certain cities within California, however, have enacted ordinances which impose additional restrictions on automatic renewal of residential leases.

Many collective bargaining agreements have a provision stating that if neither party gives timely notice of intent to renegotiate the agreement, the agreement will automatically renew itself for a period of a stated number of years.

In the music industry, automatic renewal provisions (as distinct from "options") are most often seen in personal management, talent agency, and publicist's agreements, providing that if neither party gives cancellation notice within a certain period prior to expiration of the term, the contract will be renewed for an additional, stated term.

Automatic Renewal *- (embedded in Term Clause):*

> **This agreement shall continue for _____ (__) year(s) (hereinafter the "Initial Term") from the date hereof, and shall thereafter be renewed for _____ (__) year periods (hereinafter "Renewal Period(s)") automatically unless either party shall give written notice of termination to the other not later than ______ (___) days prior to the expiration of the Initial Term or the then current Renewal Period, as applicable, subject to the terms and conditions hereof.**

Renewal Provision (Generic):

Upon expiration of the Term of this Agreement ("INITIAL TERM"), and upon the expiration of each "RENEWAL TERM" (as hereinafter defined) THIS AGREEMENT SHALL BE AUTOMATICALLY RENEWED FOR AN ADDITIONAL TERM OF ____ (__) YEAR(S) ("RENEWAL TERM") UNLESS EITHER PARTY SHALL HAVE GIVEN WRITTEN NOTICE TO THE OTHER, IN THE MANNER HEREIN PROVIDED, NOT LATER THAN ___ (__) DAYS, NOR MORE THAN ___ (__) DAYS, PRIOR TO THE EXPIRATION OF THE "INITIAL TERM" OR ANY THEN-CURRENT "RENEWAL TERM," OF THAT PARTY'S INTENTION TO CANCEL AND TO NOT RENEW THIS AGREEMENT.

Renewal Provision (Generic, with notice requirement):

Upon expiration of the Term of this Agreement ("Initial Term"), and upon the expiration of each "Renewal Term" (as hereinafter defined) thereafter this Agreement shall be automatically renewed for an additional term of ____ (__) year(s) ("renewal term") PROVIDED that {Party 1} shall have given written notice to {Party 2}, in the manner herein provided, not more than ___ (__) days, nor fewer than ___ (__) days, prior to the expiration of the "initial term" or any then-current "renewal term," advising {Party 2} of the impending automatic renewal, and further specifically advising that {Party 2} shall have the right to cancel or terminate any such Automatic Renewal at any time within ___ (__) days following receipt of such written notice.

◆ ◆ ◆

Re-Recording Restrictions

Re-recording restrictions are unique to recording agreements, and are faintly akin to non-competition clauses in their intended effect. Even though compulsory licensing permits anyone else to record a composition once it has been released as a phonorecord, the original recording artist (even if that artist owns the publishing rights) will be contractually prevented from making a new recording of that composition for a period of time after termination of the recording agreement.

Labels are understandably concerned about the possibility that, once a recording contract has terminated, the Artist would sign with another label to release an album of new — and arguably *improved* — recordings of hits which their original label continues to sell or license. Essentially, labels don't want to have their catalogue of master recordings in competition with new recordings of the same compositions by the same artists. To avoid this, the re-recording restriction prevents artists from re-recording such compositions for a period of time. This restriction is non-negotiable as to its inclusion in the contract, but negotiable as to its specific terms and as to the length of the restriction period.

The specified time for the restriction is usually based on two separate dates. One will invariably be the date upon which the recording contract terminates; the artist will be prohibited from re-recording for a negotiated number of years after the contract ends. The second date is more problematic, but will be linked to particular recordings rather than to the contract itself. The label will want the latest possible date for this component of the restriction while the artist will want the earliest possible date. In consequence, the date for the second component of the re-recording restriction may be the recording date, or the delivery date, or the release date of a particular recording.

For example, a re-recording restriction may be for one year from contract termination, or three years from "Delivery Date" (or recording date, or release date) whichever is *later*. Because of exclusivity, an artist cannot re-record a song *during* the contract, unless the contract's Territory is less than worldwide *and* there is a territorial limitation on the re-recording restriction.

The re-recording restriction extends that prohibition for a fixed term *after* the contract, and for a fixed term after each song was recorded/delivered/ released. It is to the Artist's benefit to limit these restrictions to: *(a)* recordings *released* by the Label under the contract, rather than recordings *delivered* by Artist under that contract, and *(b)* the Territory. This allows Artist to re-record compositions which the Label chose not to use, even though the Label continues to own unreleased master recordings of such compositions, and to record the same compositions for another label in other markets which are outside the Territory.

Also, even though this is referred to as a re-*recording* restriction, its prohibition should be aimed at the *release* of a new recording rather than at the recording process itself. That is, the

Artist should be able to re-record previously released songs, but with those new recordings prohibited from being *released* until the re-recording restriction expires.

It is sometimes possible to get the re-recording restriction waived at a later date, but labels are unpredictable in this regard, so the best practice is to negotiate acceptable terms for the restriction in the original contract. The best an artist will likely be able to obtain will be one year from termination or two years from recording date, whichever is later. Labels will want as much as three years from termination or five years from release date, whichever is later.

Labels will usually want the restriction to prevent a former artist from re-recording, anywhere in the world, any composition contained in a previously delivered master, until the later of two dates: *(a)* five years from the original release date, or *(b)* three years from termination of the recording contract.

About the best than can be negotiated for the Artist would be a restriction which prevents *releasing* (rather than *recording*), within the Territory of the original recording contract, a re-recording of a composition *released* under that recording contract, for a period of either *(a)* three years from the date that a master containing that composition was *originally recorded*, or *(b)* one year from contract termination, whichever is later.

Where the recording contract is other than worldwide, the re-recording restriction need to carve out an exception to allow the Artist to record at least some portion of identical material for other labels in other territories, during the Term. This may be coupled with a pre-agreed commitment requiring the original label to license recordings to the other label, usually on an override royalty basis.

Re-Recording Restriction (General):

> **During the Term of this agreement, Artist will not enter into any agreement which would interfere with the full and prompt performance of Artist's material obligations hereunder, and Artist will not perform or render any services for the purpose of making phonograph records or Master Recordings for any person other than Label, except as otherwise expressly permitted in this agreement. After the expiration of the Term of this Agreement, Artist will not, for any reason whatsoever, perform any composition which shall have been recorded hereunder for any Person other than Company for the purpose of making and releasing phonograph records or Master Recordings prior to the date five (5) years subsequent to the date of Delivery of the Master containing such composition or two (2) years subsequent to the expiration date of the Term. Except as otherwise expressly permitted in this Agreement, Artist will not at any time during the Term, or during the foregoing post-Term period of restriction, record,**

manufacture, distribute or sell, or authorize or knowingly permit Artist's performances to be recorded by any Person for any purpose, anywhere throughout the universe, without an express written agreement prohibiting the use of such recording on phonograph records in violation of the foregoing restrictions or the general terms of this Agreement.

Re-Recording Restriction (Territorial Limitation):

During the Term of this agreement, Artist will not enter into any agreement which would interfere with Artist's material obligations hereunder, and Artist will not perform or render any services for the purpose of making Master Recordings or distributing phonograph records within the Territory for any person other than Label, except as may be otherwise expressly permitted in this Agreement. After the expiration of the Term of this Agreement, Artist will not, for any reason whatsoever, perform any composition which shall have been recorded hereunder for any Person other than Company for the purpose of making and releasing phonograph records or Master Recordings within the Territory prior to the date five (5) years subsequent to the date of Delivery of the Master containing such composition or two (2) years subsequent to the expiration date of the Term. Except as otherwise expressly permitted in this Agreement, Artist will not at any time during the Term, or during the foregoing post-Term period of restriction, record, manufacture, distribute or sell, or authorize or knowingly permit Artist's performances to be recorded by any Person for any purpose without an express written agreement prohibiting the use of such recording on phonograph records within the Territory in violation of the foregoing restrictions or the general terms of this Agreement.

◆ ◆ ◆

Reservation of Rights Clause

Many, if not most, music-related contracts contain some grant of rights. While those rights, whether being conveyed or only licensed, will often be an important part of the subject matter and consideration of the agreement, of equal importance will be establishing which related rights are *not* being conveyed or licensed. This can be done expressly, by enumerating the rights which are specifically not being included in the grant, or as a general reservation of all rights which are not expressly included in the grant. Even when the first, express method is used, it is good practice to "backstop" the express reservations with a blanket reservation that "all rights not expressly granted hereinabove are generally and specifically reserved to [the granting party.]" General reservations of this nature have often proven to be the deciding factor in determining whether or not a grantee or licensee has exceeded the scope of the grant.

By way of example, when the American Broadcasting Company (ABC) obtained a license to re-broadcast three, 30-minute episodes of the BBC's "Monty Python" show, ABC subsequently edited those shows to eliminate "offensive" material and to fit American television time slots. The original production agreement between Monty Python's creators and the BBC had contained a reservation of rights, under which the writers retained a degree of artistic control over the programs. The writers filed suit for injunctive relief to stop the broadcast. Although U.S. law did not, at that time (1976), recognize "moral rights," the court held that ABC's removal of twenty-four minutes from the original ninety minutes of material created an unauthorized "derivative work," in violation of copyright law. Additionally, the court also found that the screen credit given to the Monty Python authors for the altered work was a separate violation under the Lanham Act's prohibition against false designations of origin or false descriptions or representations "in connection with any goods or services." (15 U.S.C. § 1127)[273]

The original Monty Python / BBC contract contained the following specific reservation of rights provision: "BBC shall not without the consent of the Writer or his agent (which consent shall not be unreasonably withheld) make any structural alterations as opposed to minor alterations to the script…"[274]

That contract also contained a *general* reservation of right, which reserved to the writers "any rights not granted to BBC."[275]

---

273 *Gilliam, et al., v. American Broadcasting Companies, Inc.*, (1976, 2nd Circ.) 538 F.2d 14

274 538 F.2d 17, fn. 2

275 "BBC was not entitled to make unilateral changes in the script and was not specifically empowered to alter the recordings once made; Monty Python, moreover, had reserved to itself any rights not granted to BBC. Since a grantor may not convey greater rights than it owns, BBC's permission to allow […] ABC to edit appears to have been a nullity." [*Gilliam v. ABC*, *supra*, 538 F.2d at 21, citing *Hampton v. Paramount Pictures Corp.*, (1960, 9th Cir.) 279 F.2d 100, cert. denied (1970) 364 U.S. 882; *Ilyin v. Avon Publications*, (1956, SD NY 1956) 144 F. Supp. 368, 372.]

Reservation of Rights (Specific):

> **The rights granted herein do not include any consent, permission, license or grant of any right in respect to *[list exclusions]*, each and all of which are expressly reserved**

Reservation of Rights (General):

> **Each, every, any and all rights not expressly granted herein are generally and specifically reserved to [Grantor], without exception.**

It is good practice to include *both* of the foregoing, where applicable, and to *always* include the latter reservation of all rights not expressly granted.

◆ ◆ ◆

Restrictions & Requirements Clause

Many contracts contain a section entitled "Restrictions" or "Restrictions & Requirements," while others may include restrictive covenants within a "Warranties and Representations" section. The purpose of such sections, wherever situated in the contract, will be to impose affirmative duties on a contracting party, requiring that they do — and refrain from doing — certain things which are generally collateral to the principle subject matter of the agreement. Recording contracts generally contain several such restrictions and requirements

Union Membership

All major labels are signatory to union contracts which require, among other things, that all of the recording artists signed to the label will be members of the unions, or will become members upon being signed to a union-signatory label. This also generally applies to distributed labels, which are signatories themselves, or which have ongoing distribution contracts which require union membership. While this provision may be absent from contracts with independent labels, it will be difficult to obtain major distribution without union affiliation.

Union Membership Requirement — Recording Contract — Company Favorable

Artist, and each individual comprising Artist hereunder, is or will become and will remain to the extent necessary to enable the performance of this agreement, a member in good standing of all labor unions or guilds, membership in which may be required by Company for the performance of Artist's services hereunder.

Union Membership Requirement — Recording Contract — Artist Favorable

Artist, and each individual comprising Artist hereunder, is or will become and will remain to the extent necessary to enable the performance of this agreement, a member of all labor unions or guilds, membership in which may be lawfully compulsory for the performance of Artist's services hereunder.

Re-Recording Restrictions

Labels are understandably concerned about the possibility that, once a recording contract has terminated, the Artist would sign with another label to issue compilations of new — and arguably *improved* — recordings of hits which had been recorded under the prior agreement, and which the original label continues to sell or license. Essentially, labels don't want to have their catalogue of master recordings in competition with new recordings of the same compositions by the same artists. To avoid this, the re-recording restriction prevents artists from re-recording such compositions for a period of time. This restriction is non-negotiable as to its inclusion in the contract, but negotiable as to its specific terms and as to the length of the restriction period. More critically, it should be limited to the Territory, so as to not unreasonably restrict Artist's ability to enter into contracts with other labels for countries outside the Territory.

The specified time for the restriction is usually based on two separate dates. One will invariably be the date upon which the recording contract terminates; the artist will be prohibited from re-recording for a negotiated number of years after the contract ends. The second date is more problematic, but will be linked to particular recordings rather than to the contract itself. The label will want the latest possible date for this component of the restriction while the artist will want the earliest possible date. In consequence, the date for the second component of the re-recording restriction may be the recording date, or the delivery date, or the release date of a particular recording.

For example, a re-recording restriction may be for one year from contract termination, or three years from "Delivery Date" (or recording date, or release date) whichever is *later*. Because of exclusivity, an artist cannot re-record a song *during* the contract. The re-recording restriction extends that prohibition for a fixed term *after* the contract, and for a fixed term after each song was recorded/delivered/released.

It is to the Artist's benefit to limit these restrictions to: *(a)* recordings *released* by the Label under the contract, rather than recordings *delivered* by Artist under that contract, and *(b)* the Territory. This allows Artist to re-record compositions which the Label chose not to use, even though the Label continues to own unreleased master recordings of such compositions, and to record the same compositions for another label in other markets which are outside the Territory.

Also, even though this is referred to as a re-*recording* restriction, its prohibition should be aimed at the *release* of a new recording rather than at the recording process itself. That is, the Artist should be able to re-record previously released songs, but with those new recordings prohibited from being *released* until the re-recording restriction expires.

It is sometimes possible to get the re-recording restriction waived at a later date, but labels are unpredictable in this regard, so the best practice is to negotiate acceptable terms for the restriction in the original contract. The best an artist will likely be able to obtain will be one year from termination or two years from recording date, whichever is later. Labels will want as much as three years from termination or five years from release date, whichever is later.

Re-Recording Restriction — Record Contract — Company Favorable

> **After the expiration of the Term of this agreement, Artist will not, for any reason whatsoever, perform any composition which shall have been recorded hereunder for any Person other than Label for the purpose of making and releasing phonograph records or Master Recordings prior to a date five (5) years subsequent to the date of Delivery to Label of the Master containing such composition or two (2) years subsequent to the expiration date of the Term, whichever shall be later.**

Re-Recording Restriction — Record Contract — Artist Favorable

> **After the expiration of the Term of this Agreement, Artist will not perform any composition which shall have been recorded hereunder and commercially released by Label hereunder for any Person other than Label for the purpose of releasing within the Territory phonograph records or Master Recordings prior to a date three (3) years subsequent to the date of Delivery to Label of the Master containing such composition or one (1) year subsequent to the expiration date of the Term hereof. Nothing herein shall preclude Artist from recording or re-recording any composition for commercial release outside the Territory, either during or subsequent to the Term of this Agreement.**

Performance Restrictions

In addition to re-recording of compositions which an artist has recorded under a recording contract, most record labels seek to exercise some level of control over their artists' public appearances and performances, as well as enforcing — and often expanding upon — the exclusivity provisions of their contracts in regard to recording services.

Performance Restrictions — Record Contract — Company Favorable

During the Term of this Agreement, Artist will not enter into any agreement with any Person which would interfere with the full and prompt performance of Artist's material obligations hereunder, and Artist will not perform or render any services for the purpose of making phonograph records or Master Recordings, nor render entertainment services of any kind or nature, for any Person, other than Company, except as otherwise expressly permitted in this agreement.

Except as otherwise expressly permitted in this agreement, Artist will not at any time record, manufacture, distribute or sell, or authorize or knowingly permit Artist's performances of any kind or nature to be recorded by any party and by any means, whether now known or unknown, for any purpose whatsoever, without the express written consent of Company.

Performance Restrictions — Record Contract — Artist Favorable

During the Term of this agreement, Artist will not, within the Territory, perform or render any services for the purpose of making phonograph records or Master Recordings for, nor enter into any agreement with, any Person (other than Company) for release within the Territory of phonograph records or Master Recordings, except as permitted under the terms of this agreement.

Except as otherwise expressly permitted in this agreement, Artist will not at any time record, manufacture, distribute or sell, or authorize, or knowingly permit Artist's performances to be recorded by any party for any commercial purpose within the Territory in violation of express restrictions contained herein.

Non-Musical Performances

Most record contracts carve out an automatic exception to their performance restrictions, allowing Artists to pursue separate careers in acting or other non-musical endeavors. As a practical matter, the exclusivity of the contract only applies to musical performances, anyway, so this is really not much of a concession on the part of the Label. Also, any public exposure by the Artist — as a model, actor, or talk-show host — can only help record sales. The only real issue has to do with appearances which *do* involve singing or instrumental performance, such as a theatrical stage performance in a musical production. If the Artist (or a member of Artist) has aspirations in that area, the solution is generally to limit the restriction to songs recorded under the contract, or to the *genre* of music which Artist records under the contract. Thus there would be no prohibition against a rock musician appearing in a Broadway production unless the musical portions are similar in style to Artist's recordings for the Label, as opposed to being "show tunes."

Non-Musical Performance Exceptions — Record Contract — Company Favorable

> **Artist may render non-musical performances in motion pictures or television shows provided that no such performance interferes with the full and prompt performance of Artist's material obligations under this agreement.**

Non-Musical Performance Exceptions — Record Contract — Artist Favorable

> **Artist may render performances in motion pictures, television shows, or legitimate stage productions, provided that no such performance interferes with the full and prompt performance of Artist's material obligations under this agreement. During the Term, no such performance shall include performance of any composition recorded by Artist hereunder, unless by the express consent of Label.**

Since the Artist will almost-invariably be signed on an "exclusive" basis, the contract prohibits the Artist from providing his or services as a recording artist to anyone other than the Label. There are two traditional, limited exceptions, however, which must nonetheless be included in the contract in order to be effective. One allows the Artist to participate as a "sideman" on another artist's recording, and the other allows the Artist to act as a producer for other artists' recordings.

<u>The Sideman & Producer Exceptions</u>

If the Artist has performed on another artist's recordings prior to entering into the recording contract, especially if those recordings have not been released, those performances should be disclosed in the exceptions portion of the "Scope of Services" or "Recording Services" portion of the contract. In order to participate in another artist's recording *after* being signed to the Label, the arrangements need to go through the Label's Legal Affairs or Business Affairs department. In effect, the Artist's services will become the subject of a "loan out" agreement, with the Label setting terms and restrictions under which the Artist can record for another label.

The Label's minimum demand will be the inclusion of an "appears courtesy of" credit on the other label's album. If the Artist's participation is minimal, such as merely playing an instrument or singing background vocals, the Label charges nothing for the Artist's services, other than requiring that the Artist receive at least union scale. If the Artist's participation is more substantial, however, the labels will negotiate additional terms, such as a royalty-sharing agreement, or other financial arrangement. Sometimes the arrangement will be a trade of artists, where each label will agree to allow one of its signed artists to appear on a recording for the other label. Getting these deal formalized in a written agreement is generally low priority for labels' lawyers, so brief "deal memos," usually in letter format, tend to be the norm. Generally, the most critical issue will be determining precisely how the "courtesy of" credit will appear. This involves not only the precise language to be used, but the type style, point size, and placement of the credit on the album.

An exception which allows a signed Artist to work as a producer for another artist and label is generally more complex — and harder to obtain — than a sideman exception, since many labels are reluctant to grant this type of exception. There are a number of factors to be weighed in determining whether or not this exception will be worth fighting for in negotiations.

First, does the Artist already have a track record or pending commitments as a record producer? If so, then obtaining a producer exception is likely essential to the Artist. For its part, the label will consider having an established producer under exclusive contract an important aspect of the overall deal. The Label will likely insist that the Artist agree to produce other artists who are signed to the Label, either exclusively or as a condition of being allowed to produce records for other labels. A common compromise will require the Artist to commit to producing one project for his or her own Label, for each one or two projects for any other label. The Label will also usually insist on a "courtesy of" credit, as well. Such arrangements ultimately benefit the Artist, both financially (by way of Producer advances and royalties), and in terms of a broader exposure throughout the industry.

Side-Performer and Producer Exceptions — Record Contract — Company Favorable

(1) Company may permit individuals included within the defined term "Artist" hereunder to perform as a background musician ("sideman") or backup vocalist ("side-vocalist") accompanying a featured artist for the purpose of making Phonograph Records for others, provided that all aspects of such recording shall be in accordance with all applicable Union rules and regulations, and further provided that:

(a) Artist shall have fulfilled all of Artist's obligations under this agreement, and the sideman or side-vocalist engagement does not in any way interfere with the availability of any member of Artist to perform any of Artist's obligations hereunder, or the prompt performance of any of Artist's ongoing or prospective obligations to Company, including, without limitation, any and all recording, promotional, publicity and touring commitments; and

(b) (1) No more than one individual member of Artist may perform as a sideman or side-vocalist on any recording (*i.e.*, "side") for another, nor shall members of Artist perform on more than five (5) sides on any one album for another, nor on more than one (1) side on any single or EP for another; and

(2) No member of Artist, while performing as a sideman or side-vocalist, shall render any solo or "step-out" performance, and

(3) The material recorded will not include any material, or any portion of any material, which Artist has recorded for Company, or which Artist is scheduled to record for Company; and

(4) The musical style and characteristics of the recording in which a member of Artist performs as a sideman or side-vocalist will be substantially different from the characteristic musical style of Recordings made by Artist for Company hereunder.

(c) Artist will not accept the sideman engagement unless the Person for whom the recordings are being made first agrees and warrants in a writing, directed to the Company, and for Company's express benefit, that:

(1) The member of Artist's name will appear with a courtesy credit to Company on the Album liners used for

such Records, in the same position as the credits accorded to other sidemen or side-vocalists, and in type identical thereto in size, prominence and all other respects; and

(2) Except as expressly provided in subsection __(1)(c)(1) above, neither Artist nor Artist's name (or any similar name), nor any picture, portrait or likeness of Artist, or of any member of Artist, will be used in connection with such Recordings, including, without limitation, on the front covers of Album containers, on sleeves or Companys used for Singles, or in videos, advertising, publicity or any other form of promotion or exploitation, without Company's express written consent, which Company may withhold in its unrestricted discretion.

(d) (1) Before any member of Artist accepts the sideman or side-vocalist engagement, Artist will notify Company of the name of the Person for whom the recordings are being made, and identify the record company which will have the right to distribute the Records.

(2) Individuals included within the defined term "Artist," hereunder, may accept employment as a producer for the purpose of making Phonograph Records for others, provided that all aspects of such recording shall be in accordance with all applicable Union rules and regulations, and further provided that:

(e) (1) Artist shall have fulfilled all of Artist's obligations under this agreement, and the employment as producer does not interfere with the continuing prompt performance of any of Artist's obligations to Company, including, without limitation, all recording, promotional, publicity and touring commitments; and

(2) Artist, or the member of Artist seeking to accept employment to produce a recording for another shall, and does hereby, agree to produce, for Company, at Company's sole option and upon Company's subsequent request, another recording of an artist to be selected by Company, for compensation commensurate with the average compensation which such individual has regularly received for his or her services as a record producer during the two (2) year period immediately preceding Company's request. Said individual will provide his or her "best efforts"

producing a recording for Company in fulfillment of this agreement.

(f) **(1)** No member of Artist will produce recordings of any material which Artist has recorded for Company; and

(2) If any member of Artist is a writer or co-writer of material produced by a member of Artist under this exception, then there shall be no restriction upon Artist recording that same material for Company, and no member of Artist, acting as a producer, shall agree to, or sign any contract containing, any such restriction; and

(g) No member of Artist may accept any producing engagement unless the Person for whom the recordings are being produced agrees in writing, for Company's benefit, that:

(1) The name of the member of Artist producing the recording may be used in advertising, Company and packaging credits comparable in size, prominence and placement to the credits generally accorded to record producers; and

(2) Except as expressly provided in subsection {_} (2)(c)(1) above, neither Artist nor Artist's name (or any similar name), nor any picture, portrait or likeness of Artist, nor of any member of Artist, will be used in connection with such Recordings, including, without limitation, on the front of any Record package or in any advertising, publicity or any other form of promotion or exploitation without Company's express written consent, which Company may withhold in its unrestricted discretion.

(h) Before any member of Artist may accept any producing engagement, Artist will notify Company of the name of the Person for whom the recordings are being produced and the record company which will have the right to distribute the Records; Notwithstanding the foregoing, Artist's inadvertent failure to so notify Company shall not be deemed a breach of this agreement. Upon notice from Company, Artist shall cure such failure on a prospective basis.

Side-Performer and Producer Exceptions — Record Contract — Artist Favorable

(1) Artist, or individuals included within the defined term "Artist" hereunder, may perform as background musician(s) ("sideman") or backup vocalist(s) ("side-vocalist") accompanying another artist or group for the purpose of making Phonograph Records for others, subject to the following.

(a) Artist shall have substantially completed all of Artist's then-current material obligations to Company under this agreement; and

(b) (1) No member of Artist, while performing as a sideman or side-vocalist, shall render any solo or "step-out" performance having a duration greater than twenty (20) seconds on any one track ("side"), and

(2) The material recorded will not include any composition which Artist has previously recorded for Company; and

(c) Artist will not accept the sideman engagement unless the Person for whom the recordings are being made agrees that the member of Artist's name will appear with a courtesy credit to Company on the Album liners used for such Records.

(d) Artist will notify Company of the name of the Person for whom the recordings are being made, and identify the record company which will have the right to distribute the Records.

(2) Artist, or individuals included within the defined term "Artist," hereunder, may accept employment as a producer for the purpose of making Phonograph Records for others, provided::

(a) That Artist shall have substantially completed all of Artist's then-current material obligations to Company under this Agreement; and

(b) No member of Artist will produce recordings of any composition which Artist has previously recorded for Company hereunder; and

(c) Artist will notify Company of the name of the Person for whom the recordings are being produced and the record company which will have the right to distribute the Records, and the

prospective schedule for such recording sessions. Company shall use its best efforts to avoid any scheduling conflicts.

Notwithstanding the foregoing, Artist's inadvertent failure to so notify Company shall not be deemed a material breach of this agreement.

Anti-Piracy Cooperation (The "Narc" Clause)

Most current record contracts include a requirement that the artist cooperate in regard to lawsuits for record piracy and illegal downloads. Since most piracy suits are handled by the RIAA, this cooperation generally requires no more than an occasional declaration or affidavit from the artist, although it is conceivable that the artist might have to appear as a witness if the matter goes to trial. Some labels go further by including language which imposes an affirmative duty upon artists to report any information which comes to their attention regarding record piracy or unauthorized downloading. It is difficult to imagine the circumstances under which such a provision could or would be enforced, but it has nonetheless become a not-uncommon addition to this provision in many current contracts.

Anti-Piracy Cooperation Requirement — Record Contract — Company Favorable

In the event that Artist, or any individual comprising Artist hereunder, shall become aware of any unauthorized recording, manufacture, distribution or sale by any third party contrary to any of the restrictions or requirements set forth herein, or constituting a misappropriation or infringement of any right of Company hereunder, Artist shall promptly notify Company thereof and shall cooperate fully with Company and those acting on Company's behalf in the event that Company, or a representative of Company, or a third party acting for the benefit of Company, commences any formal or informal action or proceeding against such third party.

Anti-Piracy Cooperation Requirement — Record Contract — Artist Favorable

> **In the event that Company shall become aware of any unauthorized recording, manufacture, distribution or sale by any third party which is contrary to the foregoing restrictions, Artist shall, at Company's sole expense, provide such cooperation as Company may reasonably request in support of any action or proceeding which Company may initiate against such third party.**

◆ ◆ ◆

Return Allowance Clause

While allowing retailers to return unsold merchandise for credit or refund is not unique to the music industry, most manufacturers with a return policy absorb its costs as an overhead expense, without passing that cost along to its suppliers. The music business generally offers a 100% return privilege at almost every level of normal retail channels, but requires the recording Artist to effectively subsidize that policy by withholding a fixed portion of the Artist's royalties.

Even though the Copyright Act calls for royalties to be paid for each unit *manufactured*, there is a certain fairness underlying an industry-wide custom of contractually agreeing that royalties will instead be paid on the basis of units actually sold. Even copyright law acknowledges this general industry custom and practice by incorporating a return allowance ("reserve") into the statutory requirements for compulsory licensing under 37 CFR § 201.19. The statutory provision allows for withholding of a portion of royalties for up to nine months, to allow for possible returns or exchanges. Recording contracts, on the other hand, usually incorporate a permanent fixed percentage which is to be retained for a year or longer.

In recording contracts, a return allowance is often incorporated by reference and integration of a Distributor's regular return policy. This is frequently reiterated in several different sections of the contract. For example, the definition of the word "sold" — which forms the fundamental basis for all royalty calculations — may include the following:

> "Sales", "Actually Sold" & "Records Sold" - are deemed to include One Hundred percent (100%) of all Records shipped hereunder for which Label is paid and **which are neither returned, nor exchanged, nor treated as returned to Distributor under Distributor's then current policy.**

Elsewhere in the contract, there is likely to be an integration clause which incorporates all of the terms and conditions of the Distribution Agreement, binding the Artist to such contract terms as exist between the Label and the Distributor. Distributors' "policy" will generally be to withhold 10% to 25% as a reserve for *possible* returns. That percentage will be "treated as returned" *even if not one single record is, in fact, ever returned.* Theoretically, the Artist should be entitled to receive any unused remainder of those reserved funds at the end of the stated term — usually two years — following the Royalty Accounting period during which the allowance was applied. In practical terms, however, the all or a substantial portion of the reserve allowance is more apt to evaporate in bookkeeping, somewhere between the distributor and the record company's royalty department. Since Artists seldom have a right to audit a

Distributor, directly, there will generally be no opportunity to verify the accuracy of royalties reported for accrued, unused return allowances.

A distribution agreement will typically include a definition of sales income which reflects a return allowance reserve provision, such as the following:

> The term "net billings" for purposes of determining Qualified Sales and Aggregate Sales in the United States, shall mean the gross wholesale receipts to Distributor from its customers on all records shipped less actual returns and a reasonable reserve for future returns

In almost every instance, as specific "Return Allowance" provision is unlikely to appear as a discrete contract provision unless the adversely affected party — usually the Artist — has sufficient negotiating power to insist upon a restrictive provision which establishes and enforces a "cap" on royalty deductions based on such an allowance. Absent such a cap, return allowances will generally be left as an open-ended, discretionary percentage set by the Distributor, and buried within contractual definitions of "sold" or in a section which establishes the basis for royalty calculations.

Return Allowance (Artist Favorable):

> **Notwithstanding any other provision hereof, the amount deducted from "sales" to allow for returns or potential returns in the calculation of royalties payable hereunder shall in no event be greater than fifteen percent (15%) of the number of saleable records shipped during any royalty period. Commencing one (1) year from the date of original release of each Record hereunder, and in respect to the Royalty Report for each such Record thereafter, Artist shall receive, in addition to royalties otherwise payable hereunder, payment of royalties for Records "treated as returned" (the "Return Allowance") for the period ending one year prior to the Reporting Date, but which Records were not, in fact, actually returned during that same earlier reporting period.**

Return Allowance (Company Favorable):

The percentage of Records shipped which are deemed returned or treated as returned under the Distributor's then-current policy shall under no circumstances be royalty-bearing, without regard to actual returns. In the event, however, that actual returns exceed the said percentage treated as returned under the Distributor's policy, then the percentage of actual returns shall instead be applied, and shall not bear royalties hereunder.

◆ ◆ ◆

Return Privilege Clause

While a return allowance clause provides for withholding of royalties based on the possibility of returned merchandise, a return privilege clause creates the policy and limitations under which merchandise may actually be returned to the distributor by retailers, either in exchange for other albums, or as credit toward future purchases. Thus a return *allowance* — or *reserve* — will generally appear in an contract with an artist or other party who is contractually entitled to receive royalties, to provide for a reduction in the number of "sold" albums upon which such royalties will be based, while a return *privilege* clause will appear in sales contracts with wholesalers and retailers who purchase product from the distributor, granting retailers a right to return all or some portion of that purchased merchandise.

The return privilege is likely to vary somewhat depending on the purchasing power and volume of the purchaser to whom it is extended. Record distributors generally allow their customers a 100% return privilege for recordings purchased wholesale in the form of CDs or other tangible configurations, although there has been a recent trend toward charging a "restocking fee" for returns in excess of a certain percentage of the original order. There are practical reasons for record distributors to maintain a liberal return policy, since it relieves retailers of concerns about being stuck with inventory they can't sell, and consequently encourages them to order significantly larger quantities than might otherwise be prudent for a product which has no track record. Because the music industry is far more trend-driven than most other businesses, record distributors need to be able to saturate the consumer marketplace with available product in coordination with the record company's promotional efforts, so that there is ample product available if and when consumer demand first occurs. Today's "must have" album is likely to be next week's vague memory, so if it's not "in stock" when demand hits, the opportunity for sale may be permanently lost.

In other industries, new products are often sold to retailers at deep discounts or with other inducements to encourage purchase of an unknown new product, and delivery to retailers is generally timed to coincide with a period of intense introductory advertising. A "wait-and-see" period follows. If there is sufficient repeat-customer and new-customer demand, retailers will order increased quantities of the product, and will continue to do so for so long as that demand continues. When the demand lessens, retailers will likely relegate the product to a "bargain bin," or sell off any remaining inventory to a discount outlet. That approach won't work when the product is sound recordings.

Record companies must have the product available in stores already, in substantial quantities, from the first date of release, in order to benefit from the narrow window of time coinciding with consumer demand created through promotion and airplay. After a few weeks or months, peak demand will fall off, and any inventory which remains unsold at that time becomes a burden for the retailer. This is why the return privilege is so critical. Record stores won't purchase huge quantities of a new album unless they know that they can return any unsold excess inventory with little or no penalty. The return privilege generally exists for as long as a particular title remains in the distributor's current music catalogue, and catalogue changes are generally made only after advance notice, allowing the retailer an opportunity to return excess inventory before a title is discontinued. Distributors' policies generally provide for unlimited returns of unopened items, but do not accept returns of opened merchandise on the same basis. Some distributors also impose a cap of 20% to 50% of the original order for unconditional returns of unopened merchandise, with a restocking fee of 5% to 20% of the wholesale price for returns in excess of that percentage. Some distributors absorb the shipping costs for returns, while others do not. A distributor's return policy is also likely to be far more liberal in regard to a major retailer than for a small, single store outlet. In general, the return privilege will be generously interpreted, since it encourages retailers to accept large shipments of albums by new artists with no sales history to justify such large purchases. Because a well-promoted single which generates public enthusiasm will likely result in immediate demand for copies of the album which contains that song, distributors offer the return privilege to be certain that retailers will have sufficient inventory on hand, if and when that demand occurs.

Return Privilege Clause — Distributor's Sales Contract

Purchaser shall have the right to return to Distributor any and all Merchandise purchased from Distributor hereunder at any time, provided that the particular returned merchandise consists exclusively of Titles currently available for sale within Distributor's Catalog as of the date upon which such returned merchandise is received by Distributor. Purchaser shall receive credit for such returned merchandise, applicable solely toward any pending or future purchases from Distributor, on the following basis:

(a) For unopened merchandise qualified as returnable hereunder, and returned in good order to Distributor, Purchaser shall be entitled to receive full credit for the purchase price actually paid by Purchaser for such merchandise. For the purposes hereof, "full credit" and "actually paid," shall incorporate proportional reductions to allow for any discounts or "free goods" provided to Purchaser in respect to the subject Title.

(b) Notwithstanding the foregoing, any unopened merchandise in excess of a quantity of any Title which is greater than thirty percent (30%) of the aggregate quantity of that Title purchased by Purchaser from Distributor during the six (six) months immediately preceding Purchaser's return of such merchandise shall be subject to a Re-Stocking fee, charged against return credits otherwise available hereunder, amounting to fifteen percent (15%) of the credit allowable for such excess returns.

(c) Merchandise which has been opened but which is otherwise undamaged may be returned on the same terms and conditions as hereinabove set forth, save that the credit allowable for such merchandise shall be seventy-five percent (75%) of the purchase price actually paid by Purchaser for such merchandise, and all such opened merchandise shall be further subject to the foregoing Re-Stocking fee.

◆ ◆ ◆

Reversion Provision

Reversion is the returning of property title to a prior owner. In the entertainment industry, where projects are often abandoned before completion, reversion clauses are a mechanism by which the creator of a work can retrieve his or her work when such an abandonment occurs.[276] Negotiating such a provision can be an intricate process, because the party who is required to restore ownership of a work to its prior owner or other interested party will likely have invested considerable time and money in the project, and will generally want to recover all or some portion of those expenditures as a condition of the reversion.

A primary example of such a situation would be when a record company decides not to release an album. The record company will have paid hundreds of thousands of dollars in advances and recording costs for the master recordings, which are contractually its property. The recording artist, on the other hand, has actually received money, and his or her investment is a matter of creative effort, coupled with an intense desire to have those recordings publicly released.

Reversion provisions are generally difficult for new artists to obtain, and only the most established artists have sufficient negotiating power to insist upon an outright, uncompensated reversion of master recordings if the record company fails to meet its release obligations. Somewhere between the two extremes of a free reversion and no reversion are more common provisions whereby the record company preserves a right to recoup all or some portion of its investment while allowing the master recordings to be released through a competing label.

Such mechanisms fall into two broad categories.

The most common, a royalty override, is not a reversion *per se*, but rather a commitment to license the master recordings to another label in consideration of receiving a royalty payment larger than the total royalty commitments which the original record company is obligated to pay for the recordings. If, for example, the original obligations were a fifteen percent all-in Artist's Royalty, plus mechanical royalties, then an override royalty license might require the new label to pay a total royalty of twenty to twenty-five percent, plus mechanical royalties to the original record company, which would the pay its obligations from the money received, and keep the difference. The key negotiating point in such arrangements will be the recoupment provisions. The royalty override should be set to terminate or be reduced once recoupment, or some other negotiated amount, has been reached. Also, if negotiated at the time of the original recording agreement, the Artist may be able to *exclude* retention of some portion of the Artist's Royalties from that recoupment scheme. As an alternative, to avoid recoupment concerns, the override royalty licence (and necessarily the commitment to grant

276 In the entertainment industry, reversion is often referred to as "turnaround," particularly when applied to materials which have been acquired on an optional basis. When the option is allowed to expire without having been exercised, the rights revert to the original owner, and the project is said to have "gone into turnaround."

such license which appears in the original recording contract) can make the Licensee (new label) responsible for direct payment of all royalties, so that the original label receives nothing but the override royalty, which it then applies toward recoupment.

There are a number of variations on royalty override arrangements, but the important point is that the broad outlines of a potential license should be set forth in the original recording contract as a provision related to the label's release commitment. At that point in time, everyone will be proceeding on the assumption that the recordings will be released by the original record company, making it much easier to obtain the most favorable terms for an unlikely event.

Record companies prefer royalty overrides to reversions, because such an arrangement does not forfeit the record company's ownership interest in the master recordings. Artists, on the other hand, prefer reversions, which restore ownership of the master recordings to them. Such reversion provisions are not always linked to non-release of an album. Established artists often negotiate for outright or partial ownership of master recordings, and such ownership interest lies at the heart of most "joint venture" or "distribution" recording agreements.

For newer artists, any reversion will be difficult to obtain, but will nonetheless be worth fighting for in negotiations. If nothing else, it may be the bargaining chip which can be traded for a favorable royalty override commitment, which will allow the artist to "shop" a completed album to other labels if his or her original label fails to release it. Few things are more frustrating for an artist than having an album "shelved" indefinitely... except possibly having it reluctantly released and un-promoted.

Recording contracts are not the only types of agreements where reversion rights should be included as a key point in the negotiations. Anyone whose consideration includes creative contributions — whether as a performer, as a songwriter, or other author of creative work — should strive for a provision which causes intellectual or other property to "revert" after a specified period of time, or upon the occurrence of a specified event or non-event. This is especially true for speculative or semi-speculative arrangements where little or no advance monies are received, such as so-called "demo" and "shopping" agreements.

In recording contracts, reversion provisions will focus on unreleased master recordings. This does not merely refer to unreleased *albums*, but to unreleased *tracks*. If, for example, a recording artist delivers sixteen finished recordings, but the resulting album contains only twelve of those recordings, the artist will want the right to recover the four unreleased recordings — or, at the very least, a right to re-record the compositions embodied in those recordings — when the contract terminates. Labels will generally resist a provision which conveys unreleased master recordings, arguing that they want to retain a right to commercially release such archived masters at some future date. Where the artist cannot obtain the master recordings themselves, the "re-recording restriction" provision of the contract should clearly allow for re-recording of songs based on *release* (rather than delivery or creation) during the original contract term.

In publishing agreements, songwriters should negotiate for a provision requiring that any song controlled by the publisher under that agreement will revert to the songwriter if it has not been commercially exploited by the publisher during the term of the agreement, or during another specified period. This is particularly important in"single-song" agreements where substantially all rights to the song will have been transferred. The availability of a reversion right will be largely dependent on the amount of any advance which the songwriter received from the publisher.

Record companies and publishers are understandably reluctant to surrender rights for which they have already paid large advances. In consequence, many reversion provisions take on aspects of a "buy-back" agreement, with either an immediate reimbursement of a portion of such advances, or a lien against future exploitation income from the reverted property, or a combination of both reimbursement and lien.

In a buy-back alternative, the Artist will be required to repay some percentage of the total Advance to the Label, and will thereafter own the Masters outright. Since recording artists are generally unlikely to have the cash on hand to do this, exercising this buy-back option may require bringing in a backer or other lender, who would be secured by a lien against the Masters. If it is a straight loan arrangement, then that lien would be released once the principal and interest had been paid. Often, however, a backer will want to recover principal (and possibly interest) from the first monies received (*i.e.*, from "Dollar One"), *and* retain an ongoing participatory interest in the Masters. These arrangements will be outside the scope of the release commitment section of the record contract, but should be considered by the artist in determining how to best structure the reversion/buy-back provisions of that section.

For the second, override royalty or licensing alternative, the label will retain the Masters, but allow the Artist to "shop" the masters, seeking another label or distributor willing to release the album under a license. If the Artist is successful, then the new label will be entitled to release the masters under license, in consideration of an "override royalty" payable to the old label from sales of the album. The exact terms of this royalty arrangement *will* need to be included in the reversion/buy-back provision of the release commitment section, so that there is an absolute obligation for the Label to license the masters on those pre-agreed terms, should they fail to meet the release commitment.

Reversion (Recording Contract) - Basic

In the event that this Agreement is terminated, all rights in and to any Master Recording not commercially released by Company within two (2) years following the termination of this Agreement, including any and all rights and licenses in and to composition embodied within such Masters, shall automatically revert to Artist. "Commercially released" shall mean traditional retail distribution in the United States and Canada by the Company through Normal Retail Channels.

Reversion (Publishing Agreement) - Basic

In the event that Publisher does not secure commercial exploitation of the Composition within two (2) years from the date of this Agreement, the Composition (and all rights, including copyright contained therein) shall automatically revert back to Songwriter. Commercial exploitation shall mean a use of the Composition that results in compensation to Songwriter (such as royalty payments) for the use of the Composition in sound recordings, film, television, or print, where such exploitation is the result of the direct efforts of Publisher.

Reversion (Recording Contract) - Comprehensive

Upon termination of this Agreement, all of Company's rights, title and interest in and to each and every Recording which was not timely released in each and every territory when and as specified in the Release Commitment, shall be irrevocably forfeit, and clear title in and to all such Recordings shall revert to the exclusive ownership, benefit and control of Artist, in fee. In accordance herewith, Company shall, upon Artist's request, promptly deliver all such Recordings, and all copies thereof, and all clearance and other documents related thereto, to Artist's designee, and Company shall further execute all such instruments as Artist may reasonably request to memorialize and facilitate such reversion and Company's forfeiture of rights with respect to all such unreleased Recordings.

Buy-Back & Royalty Override (Alternative to Reversion)

Upon termination of the Term of this Agreement, then Artist shall, for a period of one (1) year from the date upon which this Agreement terminates (the "Buy-Back Period"), have the option to purchase from the Company all unreleased Recordings hereunder, together with an assignment of all of Company's rights and interest therein and thereto, and Company's warranty of clear title thereto, for a sum equivalent to fifty percent (50%) of all unrecouped Advances received by Artist in regard to such unreleased Recordings. At any time during the Buy-Back Period, Artist may request, and Company shall promptly provide, an accounting setting forth the sum-certain purchase price which Artist must pay to the Company in consideration of conveyance of the said unreleased Recordings and relevant assignment of rights. If Artist disagrees with the sum specified by Company, then Artist may, at Artist's expense, retain the services of an independent, certified accountant, whom Company shall permit to examine the Company's account books and records. The purchase price calculated and certified by said independent accountant shall be dispositive in respect thereto. For the purposes hereof, "unreleased Recordings" shall be taken to mean recordings which Company failed to timely release in each, every and all territories in which Company was obliged to release such recordings under the terms of the Release Commitment hereinabove.

Without prejudice to the foregoing, Artist shall have an additional, concurrent option, for a period of one (1) year from the from the date upon which this Agreement terminates (the "Override Licensing Period") in which to solicit distribution of unreleased Recordings through an alternative Company or major distributor, upon the following terms and conditions:

(A) The alternative record company or distributor (hereinafter "Licensee") shall agree to pay Company all Artist's royalties and Mechanical Royalties which are due or which may become due by reason of Licensee's manufacture, distribution and sale of records embodying any of Artist's unreleased Recordings hereunder, plus an "override royalty" equal to ten percent (10%) of the aggregate of such Artist's Royalties and Mechanical Royalties; and

(B) Licensee shall, concurrently with execution of an exclusive Licensing Agreement between Licensee and Company in

respect hereto, deliver to Company an advance against the aforesaid royalty payment in the sum of $75,000.00; and

(C) Said Licensing Agreement shall require the Licensee to report sales and pay all royalties due to Company not more often than twice per calendar year; and

(D) The Initial Term of said Licensing Agreement shall be seven (7) years, and shall be perpetually renewable by extension periods of five (5) years each, at Licensee's option and upon Licensee's payment to Company of a renewal fee of $2,500 at the commencement of each five (5) year renewal period; and

(E) In consideration of the foregoing terms, Company shall lease the subject unreleased Recordings, and all rights therein, to Licensee, pursuant to a more formal Licensing Agreement embodying the foregoing essential terms.

All licensing and renewal fees, and override royalty payments received by Company from Licensee under the aforesaid Licensing Agreement shall be credited toward Recoupment hereunder, and shall be the sole source from which Company may obtain such Recoupment. Company may not make any deductions from royalties due to Artist from sales of records or licensing of Masters by Licensee hereunder for the purposes of Recoupment hereunder.

The term of the Buy-Back Period, as set forth above, shall be extended to run concurrently with the term of any Licensing Agreement hereunder, including all renewals thereof, and shall remain in force and effect until ninety (90) days following termination of any Licensing Agreement or lease of Master Recordings hereunder .

◆ ◆ ◆

Right to Audit Clause

When one party is dependent on another for accounting and payment of money, as with record royalties, or for other valuable assets (*e.g.*, inventory) there is an implicit right to compel an accounting of financial books and records through court action, either as an equitable remedy or (in some jurisdictions) as a statutory remedy. Given the costs and delay of litigation, the better practice is to establish a *contractual* right to audit, through inclusion of an express provision. As with most contract provisions, the language of a Right to Audit Clause may be slanted to favor one party or the other by limiting or expanding the right. In fact, the reason most companies include such a provision is to *limit* the right by overriding a broader, statutory scheme for comprehensive accounting. Care should therefore be exercised to be certain that the limitations imposed on the scope and timing of an audit do not preclude a meaningful audit conducted on reasonable terms which might have been available through the courts if there had been no audit provision in the contract.

This is not to say that a right to audit clause should not be included, but rather that it should be drafted in such a way as to not waive a party's right to audit all relevant books and records by limiting the scope of an audit to only a fraction of such records.

Right to Audit — Favorable to Company (Basic):

> **Company shall maintain books of account concerning the sale of phonograph records and other exploitations of the Master in accordance with the Company's usual and customary accounting practices. Artist's certified public accountant may, at Artist's sole expense, upon ninety (90) days written notice to Company, examine royalty statements sent to Artist by Company in connection with the sale of phonograph records hereunder, but solely with respect to those portions of such statements as may specifically pertain to royalties payable to Artist by Company, and no other artist. Company shall have no obligation to permit Artist to examine any such particular royalty statements more than once. Company's books relating to any particular royalty statement may be examined as aforesaid only during normal business hours in the place where such books and records are customarily located, and only once within any twelve (12) month period. Nothing herein shall be construed as allowing Artist any right to inspect any books or records of Company except as expressly provided hereinabove. The rights hereinabove granted to Artist shall constitute Artist's sole and exclusive rights to examine Company's books and records, and Artist waives any right to an accounting which is not hereinabove expressly enumerated.**

Right to Audit — Favorable to Company (Comprehensive):

Artist may, at Artist's own expense, audit only such books and records of Company as directly relate to this agreement and which report the exploitation of Masters for which royalties or other monies are payable hereunder. Artist may make such audit only for the purpose of verifying the accuracy of statements sent to Artist hereunder and only as provided herein. Artist may initiate such audit only by giving notice to Company at least thirty (30) lays prior to the date Artist intends to commence Artist's audit. Artist's audit will be conducted by a reputable accountant experienced in recording industry audits, in such a manner so as not to disrupt Artist's other functions or to interfere with the normal working of Company's royalty accounting department, and will be completed promptly. Artist may audit a particular statement only once and only within two (2) years after the date such statement is rendered as provided in subparagraph (4) above. Artist's audit may be conducted only during Company's usual business hours and at the place where Company keeps the books and records to be examined, or such other location as Company may designate. Artist will not be entitled to examine records that do not specifically report sales of Records or other exploitation of Masters on which royalties are payable to Artist hereunder for such accounting period as is the subject of the audit. Artist's auditor will review his tentative written findings with a member of Company's finance staff designated by Company before disclosing any preliminary results or rendering a report to Artist, and shall allow Company an opportunity to remedy any factual errors and clarify any issues that may have resulted from inadvertent error or misunderstanding, prior to completion of the audit.

In the event that an audit conducted in accordance with the foregoing results in a determination of underpayment or under-reporting of royalties due to Artist hereunder, Company shall have a period of sixty (60) days following Company's receipt of the final Auditor's Report during which to deliver to Artist, and Artist agrees to accept, without any admission of liability by Company, and solely to compromise any dispute and as liquidated damages, a sum equal to all allegedly-unpaid royalties reported by such audit, plus simple interest thereon at the rate of ten percent (10%) per year, calculated from the date of the relevant royalty statement in which any alleged under-reporting occurred, in full and complete settlement of any and all claims of any and every kind or nature, in law or in equity, which Artist then has or may have with respect to Company hereunder.

[Note: The last portion of the foregoing amounts to a combined cure and liquidated damages provision.]

Right to Audit — Favorable to Artist (Basic):

Company shall maintain books and records concerning the sale of records hereunder in accordance with Generally Accepted Accounting Principles.[277] An independent certified public accountant or attorney on Artist's behalf may, at Artist's own expense, during Company's normal business hours, at Company's place of business, and upon ten (10) days written notice to Company, examine and make extracts of the Company's books and records for the purpose of verifying the accuracy of accounting statements rendered by Company hereunder. Company's books and records relating to a particular royalty statement or other accounting may be examined at any time within five (5) years after the date rendered, except where audit discovers under-reporting or underpayment of royalties by Company during any two quarterly reporting periods within any twenty-four (24) month period, in which event all books and records relating to Artist may be examined for any period applicable to Artist.

Right to Audit — Favorable to Artist (Basic, continued)
Audit Penalty Provision:

In the event that audit discloses an under-reporting or underpayment to Artist of five percent (5%) or more during any twelve (12) month period, or by any sum greater than one-half percent (0.5%) during two (2) out of any four (4) successive twelve (12) month periods, then Company shall, in addition to immediate payment of all previously unpaid royalties, promptly reimburse to Artist, as a non-recoupable expense, all costs, expenses, and professional fees incurred by Artist in connection with the audit.

---

277 "Generally Accepted Accounting Principles" (or GAAP) is a term of art, with a commonly-understood legal meaning.

Right to Audit — Favorable to Artist (Comprehensive)

Artist may audit Company's books and records relating to this agreement regarding exploitation of Masters for which royalties or other monies are payable hereunder, for the purpose of verifying the accuracy of statements sent to Artist hereunder. Artist may initiate such audit by giving notice to Company at least fifteen (15) days prior to the date Artist intends to commence Artist's audit. Artist's audit will be conducted by a reputable accountant experienced in recording industry audits. Artist's audit may be conducted during Company's usual business hours and at the place where Company normally keeps the books and records to be examined. Artist will be permitted to examine any and all records which reflect the number of Records hereunder that are manufactured, the movement of Artist's inventory of such Records, and any credits or rebates that are given in respect of such Records, for each accounting period that is the subject of the audit.

In the event that an audit conducted in accordance with the foregoing subsection results in a determination of underpayment or under-reporting of royalties due to Artist hereunder, Company shall promptly deliver to Artist a sum equal to all previously-unpaid royalties reported by such audit, plus interest thereon at the rate of ten percent (10%) per year, compounded quarterly and calculated from the date of the relevant royalty statement in which such under-reporting of royalties occurred. Such payment shall not constitute liquidated damages, nor shall Artist's acceptance of such payment constitute a waiver or limitation of any further right, remedy or recourse which Artist may have, in law or in equity, all of which Artist hereby expressly reserves.

Notwithstanding the foregoing, if the amount of unpaid or under-reported royalties for any accounting period, as determined by audit hereunder, is a sum greater than or equal to ten percent (10%) of the royalties originally reported by the royalty statement for that accounting period, then Company shall, promptly upon Artist's request therefor, reimburse to Artist all costs and expenses for or related to the subject audit, which reimbursement shall be a non-recoupable expense of Company hereunder.

◆ ◆ ◆

Royalty Clause

The term "royalty" refers to a payment made to the owner of a right or privilege in compensation for a license to use some portion of that right or privilege.[278] For songwriters, royalties are essentially the sole source of their income, while for recording artists royalties are a primary source of income for so long as their recordings continue to sell.[279] While many artists never see any income beyond an original advance, it must be remembered that "advances" are actually prepaid royalties. Others in the industry, including producers, side-performers, publishers, agents, and managers also depend, to a greater or lesser extent, directly or indirectly, on royalties.

In consequence, Royalty clauses are critical to those whose income is largely based on receiving royalty payments. Generally, the clause will not only state the royalty rate, but also the underlying "base" to which that rate will apply, the frequency of payments, and other factors which will affect the actual monetary income — or "penny rate" — to which will a party will be entitled.

As discussed earlier, an ability to approximate the penny rate is a crucial negotiating skill, particularly in regard to recording contracts. Although the Royalty clause may appear reasonably straightforward, there are non-obvious adjustments to both the royalty rate and the royalty base which appear in *other* clauses and provisions of record contracts. Locating all of those various adjustment factors, and determining the resulting penny rate, is the only way of determining what the "actual" royalty will be.

Before looking at a typical Artist's Royalty clause from a recording contract, there are a number of terms and concepts which appear in such clauses which need to be discussed and understood.

The Artist's Royalty will be expressed as a percentage of either the retail (SRLP) or the wholesale (PPD) price of records, but that apparently-straightforward percentage can be — will be — grossly misleading to anyone not familiar with the music industry. The reason for confusion is simple: even though the *percent* appears to be immutably fixed, the base amount to which that percentage will be applied will shift radically. There are so many different tiers,

---

278 Etymologically, the word is derived from the ancient doctrine that all rights — and particularly all real property and mineral rights — vested solely in the king, and were used by others solely by the king's consent. A portion of the income derived from such use was therefore paid to the crown in consideration for a license or charter. This payment of a portion of derived income to the crown was the "royalty" fee. As societal changes permitted individuals to hold an outright ownership interest in such rights, giving them (rather than the crown) a right to grant others a license for use, the term "royalty" nonetheless continued to be applied to the portion of derived income paid for such licenses.

279 Supplemented by live performance income and ancillary sources, such as merchandising and endorsement income. Recording artists will likely experience a shift in these income sources after they cease actively recording and releasing albums. With the exception of those few superstar artists whose albums continue to sell well for decades, most artists who decide to continue performing will generate primary income from live performances, with royalties (if any) becoming supplemental income.

deductions, exceptions, exclusions, reductions, reserves and restrictions which appear in various other parts of the contract that it is impossible to determine with absolute certainty what the eventual penny rate will actually be. In consequence, a penny rate calculated at the time of negotiations will remain only a rough approximation.

The Basic Royalty Rate

The "Basic Royalty Rate" will usually be defined in the agreement's Royalty clause as a flat percentage which the artist is to be paid on sales, based on either the retail selling price, or on the wholesale price of each unit sold. Most European and other foreign countries calculate royalties based on the wholesale price, referred to variously as "Published Price to Dealer" or "Published Dealer Price" or sometimes as the "Net Dealer Price." Regardless of the nomenclature, the common acronym which is likely to appear in such contracts is "PPD." Most U.S. and Canadian record companies traditionally use the retail selling price, generally referred to as the Suggested Retail List Price ("SRLP"), or in some instances as the Suggested Manufacturer's List Price ("SMLP"), but many U.S. labels, and particularly independent labels, have more recently begun to base Artist's Royalties on the wholesale price, instead.

Artist's royalty rates calculated on a retail basis generally range from a first album percentage of 12% to 15% of SRLP. The rate escalates thereafter, generally increasing by 0.5% to 1% with each successive album, or in some cases after each two albums following the first album. (*I.e.*, the Artist's royalty rate would increase for the 2nd, 4th and 6th albums.) From the Artist's standpoint, there is little to be gained from trying to maximize the first-album royalty rate in contract negotiations. Instead, the Artist should try for a significant "bump" for the second album royalty rate (and Advance), and per-album increases thereafter. A higher first-album royalty rate only accelerates the recoupment process. If that first album is successful, then the label is likely to pick up the Artist's option. If the first album is unsuccessful, then the Artist will not be seeing any Artist's royalties from it anyway, regardless of the percentage. There are also various royalty rate increases based on sales performance, so that an SRLP-based Artist's royalty rate generally "tops-out" at around 20%.

Wholesale-based rates will naturally be for a larger percentage, starting at around 20% to 22% of PPD for new artists, up to around 30% for more established artists. For royalty calculations, the PPD is frequently an "uplift" price, which is calculated as being around 30% higher than the actual wholesale selling price. The Penny Rate, expressed as dollars or other currency, will remain approximately the same, regardless of whether the contract is based on retail or wholesale prices.

"All-In"

The term "all-in," abbreviates "all inclusive," and means that Artist's Royalty is the ***total royalty*** that the Label will pay for an album, excluding only the mechanical royalties. Generally the Producer will be entitled to a royalty and that royalty percentage will be deducted from the Artist's Royalty. Similarly, if the Artist owes another label an override royalty, that, too, will be deducted from the Artist's royalty unless the current contract expressly provides otherwise.[280] Not infrequently, certain performers who are not part of "Artist" under the contract will record under a separate contract which provides for royalty payments in addition to whatever fees they receive for their performances. Those royalties are also deducted from the Artist's Royalty. If "Artist" is a group, then the partners will eventually share among themselves whatever percentage of the Artist's royalty remains unallocated to others. Of course, there will still be managers, agents, lawyers and others who may be entitled to claim a percentage of the Artist's royalty income, as well.

Audiovisual Exception

There will invariably be a carve-out for audiovisual uses. The Royalty section is limited to royalties for use of the Artist's recordings in *phonorecords*. The artist's royalty or share of income from licensing of those recordings for other purposes, such as for videos and films, are covered in other sections of the contract related to licensing revenues.

Formats

Format refers to the number of recordings embodied on a Record, and should not be confused with *configuration*, which has an altogether different — but critical — meaning.[281] Singles and EP's will have a lower royalty rate than albums. For Singles, the SRLP-based royalty rate is typically 10% to 12%. EP's will be approximately the same, although EP's are seldom commercially released.

Territorial Rate Reductions

The Artist's Royalty Basic Rate applies only to sales within the United States.[282] All other territories will be paid at reduced rates specified in the contract. Moreover, the label receives less money from these foreign sales, and the artist is only paid based on the amount of money

---

280 This can get complex. If the masters are being licensed from another label on an override royalty basis, the Artist is likely to be entitled to a separate royalty or licensing share from that other label under a prior contract.

281 Formats are Singles, Long-Play Singles, EP's, Albums, *etc.* Configurations are Vinyl Discs, CD's, Cassette Tapes, *etc.*

282 It's important to clarify that "United States" means all 50 states, as well as U.S. territories and possessions, and U.S. military installations around the world. Failure to make this clear can result in having Alaska, Hawaii, and/or these other significant markets relegated to "ROW" ("rest of the world") status, which generally pays only 50% of the stated royalty rate. If the label will not agree to including these markets within the definition of United States, then they should be included as a separate "foreign market" with a stated reduction factor, so that they do not default into the ROW category.

which the label receives. In consequence, the Artist's Royalty on foreign sales will be a smaller percentage of a smaller base amount. It is sometimes possible to negotiate higher percentages for foreign territories where the Artist has a particularly strong fan base and sales, but 90% of the U.S. Basic Rate will be about the maximum that can be attained. For new artists these reductions will be pretty much non-negotiable. If sales of a first or second album are especially strong in a particular territory, then the reductions for that territory can most likely be renegotiated.

Sales Performance Escalations

These "automatic" increases in Artist Royalty Rate are generally standardized, and not worth worrying about, since they don't take effect until after the first half-million records have been sold in the United States, and are only applied to records sold after that sales plateau has been reached. The general rule is that one percent is added to the Basic Rate for each record sold *after* the first half million sales, and another one percent is added after the one-million sales plateau has been reached. If the Basic Rate is 15%, then that rate will be paid for the first 500,000 records sold (in the U.S.), and will escalate to 16% for the next 500,000 records sold, and then be raised to 17% for all U.S. sales after that point.

Budget and Mid-Tier Rates

For reasons having more to do with record companies' accounting departments than with contract issues, the reduction factors for Budget and Mid-Line record sales will not be readily subject to negotiation, or even subsequent renegotiation. The industry standard is a one-quarter (25%) royalty reduction for Mid-Priced records, and a one- third (33.33%) royalty reduction for Budget Records. About the only thing that an Artist can negotiate for in respect to these reductions is to seek an approval right before records can be sold as anything other than top-tier recordings, or — more likely — obtain time restrictions which prevent such sales for a designated period after release.

New Technologies

"New Technology" refers to commercial configurations other than the current primary configuration... at least in theory. The idea is that a label will pay a reduced royalty for records released in this new configuration, until it is determined that the configuration has established itself as a permanent one. There have be numerous configurations during the recording industry's 100-year-plus history. Some, such as vinyl, have withstood the test of time, while others such as 8-tracks and, more recently, cassettes, have enjoyed a brief preeminence, only to fall by the wayside as their deficiencies become apparent, or as they were supplanted by newer technologies.

This is another one of those areas where labels have discovered an increased revenue source that they are loathe to relinquish. Specifically, many labels still classify CD's as "new technology," or otherwise provide for a reduced royalty for CD sales, even though CD's are the overwhelmingly predominant configuration in today's market. While it makes sense to allow a royalty reduction for experimental configurations, there is no valid reason for discounting the royalties for CD's, and most labels will concede the point if confronted with it. Artists should attempt to insert "CD's" into the definition of LP or other benchmark definition which is used to establish full royalties, and should avoid any contract clauses which specifically or implicitly reduce the royalty rate for CD's.

As a general rule, the royalty rate for "new technology" will be reduced by 25% (*i.e.*, the label will only pay 75% of the Basic Rate), although there is frequently a provision which increases the royalty rate slightly if a new configuration achieves a significant share of total sales.

Calculating the "Penny Rate"

Labels have spent literally millions of dollars on elaborate — and often arcane — accounting software which does nothing but calculate artist's royalties, so the following is a gross oversimplification.

Adjusted Base = SRLP (or PPD) x [Reciprocal[283] of Container factor] x [Reciprocal of "Records sold" reserve factor] (*i.e.*, Free Goods, Breakage & Returns allowances, etc., generally from 15% to 30%)

Adjusted Rate = [Basic Rate - Producer's share - sideman royalty commitments] x [any rate reduction factors] (*e.g.*, a reduced CD rate, Mid-line release, etc.)

Penny Rate = [Adjusted Rate] x [Adjusted Base]

Assume a 15% "all-in" Artist's Royalty with a 3% Producer's Royalty, a 15% reserve for breakage, returns and free goods, a 25% container charge, and an SRLP of $16.95. The "penny rate" would be just under $1.30 ($1.296675). Of course, if the label has limited "top tier" sales to vinyl LPs, relegating the CD configuration to second- or even third-tier classification, then the penny rate would drop accordingly. If, for example, the contract provides that CD's only pay 90% of the Basic Royalty, then the penny rate would be just under $1.17 ($1.1670075) for the above example.

---

283 The "reciprocal" is derived by subtracting the stated factor from 1. If the reserve factor is 15%, then its reciprocal is 0.85. For a 30% reserve, the reciprocal is 0.7. The customary container factor of 25% has a reciprocal of 0.75)

One reason for determining the penny rate is because it is the only number which can be used to realistically estimate the potential for recoupment and the possibility of eventual actual income from Artist's royalties. Using the above $1.17 example, then, if the total Advances (including the Recording Fund) are $300,000.00, the recoupment point will more than 250,000 records "sold" — and over 300,000 of actual retail sales.[284] This "recoupment point" number can only go *up* however, since the label may elect to expend promotional money, half of which will likely be treated as additional recoupable advances.

284 Although not directly relevant at this point in the discussion, if the Artist is the songwriter/publisher in respect to the compositions on the album, and assuming there is a 75% controlled compositions clause with a 10 track cap, then the Artist's **mechanical** royalties would come to $0.6825 per album sold, at the current 9.1¢ statutory rate.

Royalty Clause — Record Contract - Typical

(1) Company will pay Artist an "all-in" royalty, computed at the applicable percentage indicated hereinbelow of the applicable Royalty Base Price in respect of Net Sales of Records (other than Audiovisual Records) consisting entirely of Master Recordings made under this agreement and sold through Normal Retail Channels:

(a) United States:

(i.) Standard Albums:

First Standard Album	**15%**
Second Standard Album	**15%**
Third Standard Album	**16%**
Fourth Standard Album	**16%**
Fifth Standard Album	**17%**
Sixth Standard Album	**17%**

(ii.) Other Formats:

Singles	**10%**
Long-Play Singles	**11%**
EPs	**12%**

(b) Foreign:

(i.) Canada: 90% of the otherwise applicable U.S. rate, without regard to any escalations.

(ii.) U.K.: 80% of the otherwise applicable U.S. rate, without regard to any escalations.

(iii.) Germany, France, BENELUX,[285] Japan and Australia: 75% of the otherwise applicable U.S. rate, without regard to any escalations.

(iv.) Italy, Greece, Portugal, Spain, Denmark, and Ireland: 66⅔% of the otherwise applicable U.S. rate, without regard to any escalations.

(v.) Rest of world (ROW): 50% of the otherwise applicable U.S. rate, without regard to any escalations.

(2) Notwithstanding anything to the contrary contained in subparagraph (1) above, with respect to top-line United States Normal Retail Channels ("USNRC") Net Sales of any Standard Album in excess of 500,000 units, Artist's basic royalty rate applicable to such excess units only shall be prospectively increased by one percent (1%), on an album-by-album basis. Notwithstanding

285 BENELUX is often used to designate the affiliated countries of Belgium, the Netherlands, and Luxembourg.

the foregoing, with respect to top-line USNRC Net Sales of any Standard Album in excess of 1,000,000 units, Artist's basic royalty rate applicable to such excess units only shall be increased prospectively by one percent (1%), on an album-by-album basis.

(3) The royalty rate on any Mid-priced Record will be seventy-five percent (75%) of the otherwise applicable royalty rate. The royalty rate on any Budget Record will be sixty-six and two-thirds percent (66.666%) of the otherwise applicable royalty rate.

(4) The royalty rate for any Record in a New Technology Configuration will be seventy-five percent (75%) of the otherwise applicable royalty rate hereunder. Notwithstanding the foregoing, the royalty rate for any Record in any Configuration constituting New Technology will be eighty percent (80%) commencing with the accounting period following the accounting period during which the number of Records sold pursuant to this Agreement in the United States in any such New Technology Configuration exceed twenty percent (20%) of all such sales in the United States.

Publishing royalties are far less complex. For compositions used in phonorecords, there is a statutory rate applicable to all licenses other than a first use (or "incept") license. In consequence, all mechanical license royalty clauses will generally make reference to the statutory rate, even if the rate being charged is other than that statutory rate. Thus a mechanical license which is discounted to only half the statutory rate will say precisely that. *I.e.*, "Royalty Rate: 50% Statutory."

Another aspect of using the statutory rate for mechanical licenses will be determining whether the royalty rate will change whenever the statutory rate changes. Some publishers will agree to a fixed-rate royalty (*i.e.*, based on the statutory rate in effect as of a certain specified date), while other publishers will insist that the royalty payable for any given accounting period will be based on the then-current statutory rate.

For publishing licenses other than mechanical licenses — *e.g.*, sync licenses, grand right, small right, print, electrical transcription, ringtones, *etc.* — there is no statutory rate, and the royalty will be whatever can be negotiated. In general, these will be stated as a penny rate (*i.e.*, as a dollar amount) within the license itself, although many will alternatively or additionally include a percentage of income derived from the use, or from potential future uses, of the licensed work. Thus sync licenses for motion pictures will state an initial fee, and additional fees to be paid upon the occurrence of certain prospective events, such as U.S. release of the film, foreign release, subsequent video/DVD sales, cable transmission (distinguishing basic cable from premium and pay-per-view), television broadcast, or common carrier (in-flight) exhibition of the film.

Royalty Clause — Single Song Agreement

In consideration of this agreement, Publisher agrees to pay to Writer(s) such royalties as are set forth hereinbelow:

(a) Ten cents (10¢) per copy with respect to regular piano copies separately sold and paid for in the United States and Canada.

(b) Fifteen percent (15%) of the net wholesale selling price of each copy of all other printed editions, if any, sold and paid for in the United States and Canada, excepting and excluding such printed editions as may be licensed for inclusion within folios or other composite works which are not published by Publisher.

(c) Fifty percent (50%) of all net sums actually received by Publisher from the licensing of electrical transcription, mechanical instrument, motion picture and television synchronization rights and all other rights in respect to any and all other forms of reproduction now known or hereafter to become known, including the use thereof in folios or other composite works licensed by Publisher, in the United States and Canada.

(d) No royalties shall be due for "promotional copies," "professional copies," or other complimentary copies disseminated for advertising or promotional purposes and which are not sold or resold.

(e) For use in folios or other composite works together with other compositions, the royalty rate hereinabove provided shall be prorated in the ratio of the subject musical composition(s) to all works (including the said musical composition(s)) in such publication, except that with respect to royalties for such usage provided in paragraph (c) hereinabove, such computation shall be based on the ratio between the subject musical composition(s) and the total number of compositions licensed by Publisher in the composite work.

(f) Fifty percent (50%) of all net sums actually received by Publisher from sales and uses in countries outside the United States and Canada. It is understood and agreed that in such outside countries publication may be made by an assignee, representative or licensee of Publisher.

(g) Writer(s) shall not be entitled to share in any sums distributed to Publisher by any performing rights organization (e.g., ASCAP, BMI, SESAC) which customarily makes a direct or indirect distribution to writers. Likewise, Publisher shall not be entitled to share in any sums distributed to Writer(s) by any such performing rights organization. If however, any small performance rights shall be administered directly

by Publisher or by its assignees, agents or licensees, Publisher shall pay to Writer(s) hereunder Fifty percent (50%) of all net sums received by Publisher on account of such licenses.

Royalty Clause — Mechanical License

In consideration of the within license, Licensee shall account to Publisher quarterly, within forty-five (45) days following the end of each calendar quarter, and shall pay royalties at ___% of the statutory rate which is current as of the end of the quarter to which such accounting relates, on the basis of all phonorecords made and/or distributed during such quarter.

If the royalty amount payable for any quarterly accounting period is less than One Hundred Dollars ($100.00), Licensee may carry the balance forward to the next statement. Quarterly statements shall be timely submitted regardless of whether any royalty payment is due in respect thereto. All accrued balances owing for royalty payments, regardless of amount, shall be paid to Publisher concurrently with the final royalty accounting statement for each calendar year. If payments are not received by the due date, Publisher may assess an interest charge against Licensee of 1.5% per month, and Licensee may be subject to further legal action including, but not limited to, revocation or suspension of this License.

A non-refundable Advance shall be due and payable to Publisher upon execution of this license, and prior to release of any phonorecord hereunder, which Advance shall in no event be less than the full amount of royalties due or which would become due for a total of 1,000 units distributed hereunder. For an initial release of 12,500 units or less, the Advance shall be 100% of the royalties attributable to the quantity of units comprising said initial release, or the aforesaid minimum Advance, whichever is greater. For an initial release in excess of 12,500 units, the Advance shall be the sum of $______.

◆ ◆ ◆

Scope of Agreement Clause

One of the essential elements of any contract is describable subject matter. The description of subject matter may also be regarded as a declaration of the principal objectives of the parties' agreement, and is often referred to as the *scope* of the contract.

Where the contract is for services, it is not unusual to include a separate section which is specifically entitled "Scope" in which to expressly set forth precisely what services are included — or excluded — from the commitments being undertaken.

Scope of Agreement — Legal Services Contract *(Example)*

> **Scope: Client has retained Attorney to undertake collection of royalties which Client believes are owing and unpaid to Client from [Record Company]. The services to be rendered hereunder shall include, and be limited to, communications with [Record Company] and its legal representatives; initiating and supervising an audit of [Record Company]'s books and records if informal negotiations with [Record Company] are unavailing; instituting such other means of investigation and verification as Attorney deems prudent to obtain evidence of underpayment; and commencing litigation or other adversarial proceeding against [Record Company] for collection of unpaid royalties if no mutually acceptable settlement is reached. "Litigation" shall be deemed to include all activities normally and customarily included within the scope of litigation or other adversarial process. Nothing herein shall obligate Attorney to initiate or undertake any appeal or other appellate process on Client's behalf.**

◆ ◆ ◆

Severability Provision

The severability doctrine is well established in contract law.[286] Courts will sever (*i.e.*, remove) an unlawful provision from an otherwise valid contract, while enforcing the lawful remainder of that contract, *if* the severed, unlawful clause is not essential to the parties' fundamental agreement.

While courts do not generally concern themselves with the *subject matter* of contracts, a court may void contractual provisions which are unlawful or contrary to public policy. When a contract contains an unlawful provision among several acceptable provisions, the court may choose one of three courses of action:

> ***Reformation:*** A court may rewrite the contract to make the terms comply with law and public policy. This is sometimes referred to as the "blue-pencil" remedy, and is disfavored because it so easily lends itself to abuse. In consequence, this approach is generally limited to restrictive covenants appearing in recorded deeds and similar public records, where avoidance of the entire document would be impossible or ill-advised.
>
> ***Avoidance:*** A court may hold the entire contract to be unenforceable and void. The court will likely elect this course whenever the general scope of the contract is unlawful, or where the lawful remainder following severance would negate the parties' clear contractual intentions, or deprive a party of a bargained-for consideration.
>
> ***Severance:*** A court may sever unlawful provisions and enforce the remaining terms of the contract. Because courts favor protecting parties' justified expectations, this third option, invoking the severability doctrine, will most often be the courts' preferred course of action.

In order for the court to sever an unlawful provision, it must determine that the unlawful provision is not essential to the overall agreement. To make that determination, the court will look first at the intent of the negotiating parties, as it appears within the four corners of the contract. The contract language alone is not necessarily dispositive, however, even where the contract specifically provides a severability clause or describes certain terms as being essential. Rather, the court may look to extrinsic evidence, such as the history of contract negotiations, to discern the intent of the parties. Such extrinsic evidence can overcome even the express language of a severability clause.

If the parties would have made the agreement without the unlawful provision, that provision is not essential to the contract, and the remaining contract can be enforced. If the court determines that the parties would <u>not</u> have entered into the agreement without the unlawful

286 The doctrine also applies to Public Law. Courts will sever an unconstitutional provision in a statute but enforce the remainder of the statute if the unconstitutional provision is not essential to the overall statute.

provision, then that provision *is* essential, in which case the entire contract fails and will be held to be unenforceable.

There is a "special case" to be considered in respect to the severability of *arbitration* provisions which appear in contracts. Even where an entire contract is deemed unenforceable, an arbitration provision will generally be deemed severable and enforceable unless there is a legal challenge which is directed specifically at the arbitration provision itself. Public policy and federal statutes favoring arbitration will require that such provision be enforced, regardless of the unenforceability of the remainder of the agreement. Where there has been a challenge to the legality of a contract which contains an arbitration provision, it is likely that a court will abstain and require that the arbitrator make the required determinations as to enforceability of the agreement. Where the legal challenge is to the arbitration provision itself, however, the court will make that determination and, if it finds the provision enforceable, transfer the remaining issues to the arbitrator for determination.

Since extrinsic evidence is permissible in making determinations under the severability doctrine, even the most carefully crafted severability provision may prove futile if the court determines that it cannot, in good conscience, hold the remaining provisions enforceable in light of an extrinsically demonstrated intention or common understanding of the parties.

Severability Clause — Basic

> **If any term, condition, or provision of this Agreement should be held by a court of competent jurisdiction to be void or unenforceable, in whole or in part, such provision or part thereof shall be treated as severable, leaving valid the remainder of the Agreement.**

Severability Clause — Basic (Alternate)

> **If any provision, clause, or paragraph of this Agreement or any document incorporated by reference shall be determined invalid by a court of competent jurisdiction, such determination shall not affect the other provisions, clauses, or paragraphs of this Agreement which are not affected by the determination. The provisions, clauses, or paragraphs of this Agreement and any documents incorporated herein by reference are declared severable.**

Severability Clause — Basic
(with "Breadth & Scope" provision)

In the event that any condition, covenant or other provision herein contained is held to be invalid or void by any court of competent jurisdiction, the same shall be deemed severable from the remainder of this Agreement and shall in no way affect any other condition, covenant or other provision herein contained. However, if such condition, covenant or other provision shall be deemed invalid due to its scope or breadth, such condition, covenant or other provision shall be deemed valid to the extent of the scope or breadth permitted by applicable law.

Severability Clause — Basic
(with "Reformation" provision)

The provisions of this Agreement are severable and, in the event that any one or more provisions are deemed illegal or unenforceable, the remaining provisions shall remain in full force and effect unless the deletion of such provision shall cause this Agreement to become materially adverse to either party, or deprive either party of a bargained for consideration hereunder, in which event the parties shall use reasonable efforts to arrive at an accommodation that best preserves for the parties the benefits and obligations of the offending provision, and hereby submit themselves to the jurisdiction of a court of competent jurisdiction to equitably reform the Agreement to accomplish such preservation should the parties be unable to do so without judicial intervention.

Severability Addendum to Essential Contract Provision
(to provide for its survivability)

Notwithstanding any other term or condition set forth in the within Agreement, this [clause <or> paragraph <or> section] {n} is severable from the rest of this agreement and shall remain in full force and effect notwithstanding any termination of this Agreement.

Severability Clause
with Stipulation as to Non-Severable Provisions,
and with Rescission/Restitution alternative to severance.

The provisions, clauses, or paragraphs of this Agreement and any documents incorporated herein by reference are declared severable except as to [clause(s) <or> paragraph(s) <or> section(s)] numbered {list of paragraph numbers} (hereinafter the "Essential Provisions") which the parties, as a bargained for consideration of this Agreement, have mutually determined and hereby stipulate to be essential and indispensable elements of material consideration in the within Agreement. In the event that any one or more of the aforesaid Essential Provisions is held by any court of competent jurisdiction to be invalid or void, in whole or in part, then the entire within Agreement shall be declared void, and the parties shall make restitution, each to the other, of all prior consideration hereunder, or of equivalent value, so as to return each party to *status quo ante* insofar as it may be possible so to do, and to equitably and proportionally divide between them any increases, revenues or value obtained by either of them by reason of the within Agreement prior to its avoidance. In the event that any condition, covenant or other provision herein contained other than the aforesaid Essential Provisions may be held to be invalid or void by any court of competent jurisdiction, then the same shall be deemed severable from the remainder of this Agreement and shall in no way affect any other condition, covenant or other provision herein contained.

◆ ◆ ◆

Side Letter (Inducement Letter)

There are a number of situations where it is necessary for there to be a "side agreement" which is separate from a primary contract, but nonetheless essential to one or more of the parties as an *inducement* to enter into the primary contract. This is especially true in regard to so-called "loan out" agreements.

In a loan-out, an Artist (or other party, such as a record producer) will not personally appear as a party to the primary agreement. Instead, there will be a corporation or other entity which appears as the contracting party. That entity's obligation under the primary agreement will be to furnish the other party with the services of the non-party. The acronyms "fso" ("furnishing the services of") or "pso" ("providing the services of") are often seen in such loan-out agreements. The identification of the contracting parties will therefore appear in a manner similar to the following:

> By and between QQQQ Records ("Company") and XYZ, Inc., fso
> Benjamin Tover ("Artist")

Even though the Artist (Ben Tover) is *identified* in the contract, he is not a *party* to that contract, because he has no personal obligations under the contract. Instead, he is part of the *subject matter* of the agreement.

Because the Artist has no personal obligation under the contract, there is nothing to prevent him from ignoring the contract obligations (since he has none), leaving the record company with no recourse against the Artist, but only against the loan-out company, which may be no more than a judgment-proof, empty shell. Record companies would consequently never enter into such agreements unless they had some way of assuring themselves that the Artist was obligated perform all of the contractual requirements. Hence a "side letter."

Even though the side letter is extra-contractual (*i.e.*, outside the contract), it creates a separate, binding promise by the Artist that he or she will perform all of the obligations of the loan-out agreement. These are often referred to as "inducement" letters because their purpose is to induce the record company to sign the loan out agreement. Even though the side letter is not integrated with the loan out agreement, and will often not even be mentioned in that agreement, it is nonetheless an indispensable element of the consideration which the record company receives under that loan out agreement.

Loan-outs are not the only situation where an extra-contractual letter agreement may be an essential element of a transaction. Record contracts frequently include a requirement that the Artist sign a side letter addressed to the Distributor, agreeing to be bound by the terms and conditions of the agreement between the record company and distributor. Such provisions generally take the following form:

> *Artist will sign any inducement letter or similar document required by Distributor as a guarantee that Artist will meet Artist's obligations under this Agreement, including obligations arising under any Distribution Agreement.*

Artist's should be careful to ascertain the terms and conditions of "any Distribution Agreement" before signing a contract which contains such a provision, or should insert language which imposes reasonable limits, such as the following:

> *Artist will sign an inducement letter or similar document required by Distributor as a guarantee that Artist will meet Artist's obligations under this Agreement, including obligations arising under any Distribution Agreement, provided that nothing therein or herein shall be deemed to impose upon Artist any obligation not expressly provided by the instant Agreement, nor diminish any benefit to which Artist would otherwise be entitled under this Agreement.*

Some labels attempt to circumvent Artist's ability to review and approve the terms of such a side letter, and the resulting integration of a Distribution Agreement, by appending power-of-attorney language to the above provisions, such as the following:

> [...] ***Label is hereby appointed Artist's attorney-in-fact and may sign such document in Artist's name.***

Artists need to avoid giving their record label any such authority.

Side Letter — re Loan-Out Recording Contract

> **In regard to that certain Record Contract dated _____ by and between [Record Company name] (hereinafter "Company") and [Loan Out Company name] (hereinafter "Loan Out"), for good and valuable consideration and as inducement to Company to enter into the aforesaid Record Contract, the undersigned {Artist's name}, hereby ratifies and affirms each and all of the warranties and representations made by Loan Out within the said Record Contract, and further agrees to personally perform each, every, any, and all obligations required of Loan Out or of "Artist" as set forth within the said Record Contract, and to be bound by all of the terms and conditions of said Record Contract applicable to Loan Out or "Artist" thereunder.**

An entirely different type of "side letter" refers to writings which are more properly referred to as letters of instruction or letters of direction. Such letters arise as the result of one contract, but become attachments to an entirely separate contract. For example, a "shopping agreement" may call for the "Company" to receive all or a portion of Artist's advances or royalties under a subsequently obtained recording contract. If that payment requirement is not specified in the recording contract itself, then a "side letter" directing the record company to make payments directly to the third party "Company" (rather than to Artist) may be sent to the record company, and be appended to the Artist's recording contract.

Most commonly, such letters of direction will be sent to the record company in regard to record producers or side-performers who are entitled to record royalties, instructing the record company to pay those third parties directly, and to deduct such payments from royalties otherwise payable to the Artist.[287] Most producers will insist upon such an arrangement, as they do not want to be dependent on having their payments passed through the Artist. Letters of direction provide for immediate and direct payment from the primary source, and thereby avoid both delay and possible disputes.

Letter of Direction — from Artist to Label re Producer[288]

I have engaged [{Name of Producer} <or> {Name of Producer's Loan Out Company} f/s/o {Name of Producer}] (hereinafter "Producer") to produce a recording of my performance on {number of compositions} (__) musical composition(s) entitled, "{Title(s) of Composition(s)}" (hereinafter "Recording") in connection with the album ("LP") which I am required to Deliver to you pursuant to that certain agreement between you and me dated _______ (hereinafter the "Agreement").

Notwithstanding that the Agreement requires me to pay for the services of the Producer, I hereby request and irrevocably authorize you to make payments on my behalf to Producer for services rendered in regard to the Recording, as follows:

(1) For recording sessions commenced hereunder pursuant to a recording budget [excluding any artist advances and the Producer Advance] (as defined below) approved by Artist and Company ("Approved Budget"). Producer was paid an advance for the Recording in the amount of _______ Dollars ($_______) (the "Producer Advance"), which is

287 Where a third-party agreement calls for royalty payments from "Dollar One," but the Artist only receives royalties post-recoupment, a side letter will be insufficient unless the record company agrees to the Dollar One payments, in which event such third-party, pre-recoupment disbursements will be *added* to the total of advances which must be recouped before the Artist begins receiving any royalty payments.

288 This letter will generally be an express requirement of the contract between Artist and Producer, and a copy will frequently be appended as an Exhibit to that contract.

deemed a non-returnable advance against and recoupable from all royalties payable to Producer hereunder. To the extent not so recouped, such advance may be recouped by you from any monies becoming payable to me, but all amounts so recouped from monies payable to me shall be credited to my royalty account if subsequently recouped from monies payable to the Producer. Fifty percent (50%) of the Producer Advance shall be paid upon commencement of recording of the Recording (or, if later, upon execution of this Agreement) and the remaining fifty percent (50%) of the Producer Advance shall be paid upon delivery and acceptance by Company of Delivery of a Master of said Recording, together with all necessary licenses and applicable approvals and consents required by Company (including but not limited to, any union or payroll forms) or, if later, upon execution of this Agreement. Producer shall be responsible and liable for any recording costs which are in excess of the Approved Budget [if such excess recording costs result directly from the failure of Producer to satisfactorily render services hereunder].

(2) A royalty (the "Producer's Royalty") on net sales of top-line, full-priced phonograph records sold through normal retail distribution channels in the U.S. derived from the Recording ("US Retail LP Sales"), computed, adjusted and paid in the same manner as the royalty payable to me under the Agreement, at the same times, and subject to the same conditions, but at a basic rate of ___ percent (__%) for the Recording instead of the rate fixed in the Agreement, with proportionate reductions and prorations on all sales for which reduced royalties are payable under the Agreement. If my royalty rate is computed on a basis other than the suggested retail list price, Producer's Royalty shall be adjusted accordingly so that the same "penny rate" is payable to Producer on such basis as though Producer had been paid on the suggested list retail price. [It is hereby acknowledged that {Name of Executive Producer} is entitled to a separate royalty ("Executive Producer's Basic LP Rate") for services rendered as executive producer of the LP and that Producer's Royalty shall not be reduced or prorated based on the services of Executive Producer by Executive Producer's Basic LP Rate.] Notwithstanding anything to the contrary contained herein, Producer's Royalties for the Recording may be reduced by royalties given in consideration for any services rendered by third party producers, mixers, or re-mixers.

(3) If a phonograph record embodying the Recording contains recordings produced by someone other than Producer, the Producer's Royalty rate shall be reduced by multiplying the otherwise applicable royalty rate by

a fraction, the numerator of which is the number of recordings embodied on the LP produced by Producer, and the denominator of which is the total number of recordings (inclusive of the Recording) contained on such phonograph record. The amount of the Producer's Royalty payable hereunder shall be deducted from all monies payable or becoming payable to me under the Agreement.

(4) The Producer's Royalty will not be payable until you have recouped all recording costs and advances attributable to the Recordings under the Agreement. Such recoupment will be computed at my net royalty rate as reduced to reflect the deduction of the Producing Royalty and the royalty payable to any other third party royalty participants paid in respect of the Recordings (including any Executive Producer of the LP and, if applicable, remixers). After such recoupment, the Producer's Royalty will be computed retroactively and paid on all such records from the first record sold; notwithstanding, the Producer's Royalty shall not be payable unless and until the advance(s) paid to Producer hereunder shall have been recouped by the royalties otherwise payable to Producer hereunder.

Your compliance with this authorization will constitute an accommodation to me alone, and nothing herein shall constitute the Producer a beneficiary of, or party to, the Agreement, this instrument, or any other agreement between you and me. All payments hereunder will constitute payments to me. You will have no liability by reason of any erroneous payment you may make pursuant to, or by reason of any failure to comply with, this authorization. I will indemnify and hold you harmless against any claims asserted against you and any damages, losses or expenses incurred by you by reason of your compliance herewith or reliance hereupon.

All monies becoming payable under this authorization will be remitted to the Producer at such address as the Producer may direct in writing, and shall be accompanied by statements with respect to such payments, contemporaneous copies of which statements shall also be sent to me or my designee.

◆ ◆ ◆

Supersedure & Novation Clause

Despite the parties best efforts, and sometimes because of them, it is not unusual for a contract to be modified or replaced before the end of its term. When new contract provisions *modify* existing contract clauses or provisions, the document which embodies those modifications is referred to as an *amendment* to the contract. When the changes consist of adding *new, additional* terms and conditions to the contract, then the document which contains those new terms is referred to as an *addendum* to the contract.

Frequently, the changes being introduced are too broad to be adequately (or comprehensibly) accomplished by amendments or addenda. In such cases, the better practice is to prepare an entirely new contract which will replace — or, in legal parlance, *supersede* — the existing agreement. An entirely new contract which completely supersedes a prior agreement is referred to as a *novation*. Thus a "short form" contract may be a novation of an earlier "deal memo," while a subsequent "long form" agreement would be a novation of that "short form" agreement.[289]

Where the subject matter of a contract does not fall within the Statute of Frauds or equivalent requirement that the agreement be evidenced by writing, it may be possible — but not advisable — to modify the terms of an existing agreement orally or by subsequent conduct. The better practice is to insert language which expressly provides that the agreement may *only* be modified by a subsequent writing, and that a party's waiver, ratification, or acquiescence on any particular occasion is not continuing and does not modify the contract's terms and conditions in respect to any subsequent occurrence.

Amendment — Preface

> **This writing (hereinafter "Amendment") constitutes an amendment to and modification of that certain agreement entitled {Title of Original Contract} dated ____ by and between {Party to Original Contract} and {Other Party to Original Contract} (hereinafter the "Agreement"). To the extent that any term, condition, clause or provision hereinafter set forth within this Amendment contradicts or is otherwise inconsistent with any term, condition, clause or provision of the Agreement, including any prior amendment thereto, then the instant Amendment shall supercede, take precedence over, and govern in respect to any such contradictory terms of the Agreement.**

289 For recording contracts, a Deal Memo may be 1 to 4 pages, a Short Form will likely be anywhere from 30 to 60 pages, and a Long Form may be 70 to 100 pages, or more.

Addendum — Preface

> **This writing (hereinafter "Addendum No. __") constitutes an addendum to that certain agreement entitled {Title of Original Contract} dated ____ by and between {Party to Original Contract} and {Other Party to Original Contract} (hereinafter the "Agreement"). To the extent that any term, condition, clause or provision of this Addendum No. __ contradicts or is otherwise inconsistent with any term, condition, clause or provision of the Agreement, as such terms and conditions may have been elsewhere amended, then the terms and conditions of the Agreement (as amended) shall take precedence over, and govern in respect to any contradictory terms appearing herein.**

Note the distinction between the two foregoing examples. An amendment *changes* the terms of the agreement, while an addendum merely *adds* new, non-contradictory terms to the contract. Thus an amendment will modify and supersede substantive provisions of the contract, while an addendum does not.

If it is more practical to scrap the existing contract and replace it with an entirely new agreement, then the new contract needs to include a Supersedure and Novation Clause.

Supersedure and Novation Clause — General

> **The instant agreement comprises the entire agreement between the parties hereto, and is a novation of, and wholly supersedes, any and all prior agreements by and between the parties hereto, including their respective successors, wherefore each and every one of such prior agreements, if any, is hereby repudiated by the parties, and by each of them, made entirely void, and without any legal force or effect.**

Supersedure and Novation Clause — Specific

> **The instant agreement is a novation of, and wholly supersedes, that certain agreement entitled {Title of Original Contract} dated ____ by and between {Party to Original Contract} and {Other Party to Original Contract} (hereinafter the "Prior Agreement"), wherefore, and upon execution hereof, said Prior Agreement is made entirely void, and without any legal force or effect**

◆ ◆ ◆

Sunset Provision

When a contract has been terminated, but there are outstanding benefits, either currently or prospectively, which in some manner attributable to efforts of the contracting parties, but payable to only one of them as a matter of right, it is advisable to include an executory provision which apportions such future income on a decreasing schedule. Such a provision — commonly referred to as a Sunset Provision — clarifies the entitlements of the terminated party, and thereby avoids potentially costly disputes. Agency and management agreements are the most obvious contracts in which such provisions are essential, but any contract in which a terminated party *might* have a legal or equitable claim to future income of the other party or parties, should likewise contain a Sunset Provision. Consider the following examples:

Hypothetical 1 — Artist's Management

> By contract, Manager is entitled to 15% of Artist's income from all sources in the entertainment industry. Artist is a recording artist, but is cast in a motion picture. The management contract terminates before the film begins production. When the Artist receives payment for the film, the Manager demands 15% of that money, plus 15% of all royalties which Artist has received, or will thereafter receive, for record sales of albums recorded before the contract terminated. Meanwhile, Artist has signed with a new manager who *also* demands 15% of that same income.

Without a Sunset Provision in the original contract, there is no good solution to this problem. Either the Artist ends up paying 30% in perpetuity, or spends a fortune litigating the dispute — which might still require that the 30% be paid, at least for some period of time.

Hypothetical 2 — Leaving Member

> Artist is a partnership consisting of five performers. One decides to leave and strike out on his own as a solo artist. The original group continues to perform and record with a session player taking the place of the departed member. The departed member claims that he is entitled to a share of the group's touring profits, because those profits are attributable to a tour which was booked, and to goodwill which was created, while he was still a member of the partnership.

Leaving member provisions are generally the most elaborate portion of any inter-band agreement and one of the most crucial parts of such leaving member sections will be Sunset Provisions which address and limit a leaving member's rights in respect to the group's future income.

In general, Sunset Provisions establish a schedule of decreasing percentages. The time periods of such a schedule are generally expressed as either six month or one year increments, and the percentages are negotiable, but they generally fall into the following ranges:

Period (each 6 or 12 months) following termination	Percentage of amount which would have been payable had contract not been terminated
1	50% to 100%
2	25% to 80%
3	10% to 75%
4	Up to 60%
5	Up to 50%
6	Up to 33-⅓%
7	Up to 25%
8	Up to 10%

For contracts such as Management Agreements, where there is a fixed percentage, it may be convenient for the Sunset Provision to convert that percentage directly. If the contract percentage is 15%, then the Sunset Provision might expressly state the reduced percentages over time. *I.e.,* 10% for first year following termination, 7½% for the second year, 5% for the third year, 2½% for the fourth year, and nothing thereafter. For agreements which are not based on a fixed percentage, then the Sunset Provision should state a percentage of the income to which the terminated party would have been entitled had the contractual relationship not been terminated.

Sunset Provision — Management Agreement (Fixed Percentage)

Upon termination of this Agreement, including expiration of the Term of this Agreement, Manager's commissions for the years succeeding termination of this Agreement shall be calculated and paid in all respects as provided in the Accounting Clause hereinabove, except that in lieu of any other consideration or percentage provided elsewhere in this Agreement the post-termination percentage to be paid to Manager hereunder shall be as follows:

(a) First year following termination 15%

(b) Second year following termination 12½%

(c) Third year following termination 10%

(d) Fourth year following termination 7½%

(e) Fifth year following termination 5%

The foregoing shall constitute the entire, maximum consideration to which Manager may be entitled following termination of this Agreement. Manager shall in no event receive any further commission or other consideration hereunder after the fifth (5th) year following termination of this Agreement.

Addendum to Sunset Provision — Management Agreement — Distinguishing "New" and "Old" Income Sources

Nothing herein shall be deemed to create any commission, right or interest of Manager in or to any portion of income or source of income other than such income as is derived solely from entertainment agreements which fall within the Scope of this Agreement and which agreements were entered into by or on behalf of Artist during the Term of this Agreement, or within six (6) months following a termination of this Agreement other than by expiration of the Term. For the purposes hereof, renewal of an entertainment agreement which falls within the foregoing limitation and definition shall be deemed to be a continuation of its predecessor agreement, and to likewise fall within the foregoing definition, except that any increase in consideration payable to Artist under such renewal shall be outside the scope of income hereunder, and any commission payable to Manager in respect to such renewal agreements shall be based solely upon the amount of consideration payable to Artist under a predecessor agreement entered into during the Term or during the above, six-month post-termination period.

Sunset Provision — General

Upon termination of this Agreement, and for a period of five (5) years thereafter, {Terminated Party} (hereinafter "Former Party") shall be entitled to receive a portion of such income as said Former Party would have received hereunder had the within Agreement not terminated (the "Entitlement Amount"), with such portion of said Entitlement Amount decreasing over the said five (5) year period, as follows:

(a) during the first six (6) months following termination, Former Party shall be entitled to receive one hundred percent (100%) of the Entitlement Amount;

(b) during the period from six (6) months to one (1) year following termination of the within Agreement, Former Party shall be entitled to receive seventy- five percent (75%) of the Entitlement Amount;

(c) during the period from one (1) year to three (3) years following termination of the within Agreement, Former Party shall be entitled to receive fifty percent (50%) of the Entitlement Amount; and

(d) during the period from three (3) years to five (5) years following termination of the within Agreement, Former Party shall be entitled to receive twenty-five percent (25%) of the Entitlement Amount.

Former Party shall under no circumstances be entitled to any payment hereunder after five (5) years from termination of the within Agreement, nor shall the sums upon which the Entitlement Amount is based include any revenue derived from agreements other than such agreements as were finalized, or for which an agreement in principle had been reached, prior to termination of the within Agreement.

◆ ◆ ◆

Term Clause

For most contracts, the "term" will be either obvious or subject to a simple determination. Typically, the contract will endure until a stated date, or for a stated period of time, or else will terminate upon the occurrence of a stated event or completion of the last of a series of events. Music industry contracts — and especially recording contracts — tend to have terms which are far more difficult to determine, and this is often a source of confusion for those new to the industry. Since many of these contracts are "exclusive" — it can sometimes be difficult to ascertain whether one is currently bound by a prior contract, or free to enter into a new contract.

Everyone talks about a "six album deal," but (with rare exceptions) the deal in question is only for one album, with a series of options for up to five more albums… or, more accurately, for one more… and one more… and so on, up to five more, with the choice being entirely up to the label as to whether or not to go forward with any of them. For so long as an option period has not expired, the contract remains in full force, and its "term" continues to run. This means that one must be able to determine when an option period expires, but that will likely be dependent on the "Delivery Date" of a prior obligation, which may itself be almost impossible to ascertain.

In the earliest days of the record business, performers were generally employees at will, unlikely to have any formal contract. Later, record contracts were for a set number of recordings ("sides"), and the contracts were often non-exclusive. Commencing around the 1950's, record companies began signing artists to exclusive contracts with fixed terms, typically one to three years. Any recordings an artist completed during that term would come within scope of the agreement, and there would generally be some minimum number of sides which the Artist was required to deliver during that term. There were seldom contracts which called for delivery of "albums," since the albums of that era were bulky, bound portfolios of cardboard sleeves into which a 78-rpm disc could be inserted. Such albums were sometimes released as a "special project" or "collectors' edition" containing eight to twelve previously-released singles by a particular artist.

Development of 33⅓-rpm LP's and stereo recordings shifted the industry's emphasis away from singles toward albums, which in their new, single-disk LP configuration were no longer unwieldy or overly expensive to manufacture, warehouse, and ship. It had also became possible to record multiple tracks in a relatively short time, which could later be edited and assembled by a record producer for delivery to the record company. This technology allowed signed artists more freedom to schedule tours, alternated with time spent in the recording studio. It also allowed record producers and engineers to continue work on an album, even if the performers were half a world away.

As a result of all of those changes in the industry, and especially in the nature of the recording process, the manner of determining the *term* of recording contracts changed as well.

In today's industry, the contract term will usually be a hybrid of both the number of masters to be delivered (the "Recording Commitment"), and a more-or-less unlimited period of time in which to do so, combined with option periods triggered by contract events such as Delivery and Release Dates. Other language in the contract may shift such dates to the first, last, or n^{th} day of the month during which an event occurred or may be scheduled to occur. As a result of all these shifting factors, determining the "term" of a record contract can be difficult, and often becomes less a matter of calculation and more a matter of opinion, opening the door to potential disputes based on differing calculations.

Most record contracts are for one album "firm," with a series of time-dependent options for additional subsequent albums. For established artists, the first *two* albums may be firm commitments, and options may likewise be for more than one album. Whether or not such options will be exercised, however, always lies solely within the discretion of the label — the *Artist* has no option. The truth is that most new artists will not get past their first album, and, if they are fortunate enough to get a chance at a second album, that second release is even more likely to be their last. The real problem for artists is that the label may have a year or more (depending on the contract language) in which to decide whether or not to exercise its option. For however long that period may be, the artist can do nothing but tour, rehearse, work on new material, promote the last album, and fret about whether or not his or her recording contract will be allowed to lapse. Until the option period expires, or the option is picked up, the Artist remains in a state of contractual limbo.

<u>*Personal Service Agreements*</u>

There is a "special case" in regard to the term of contracts for personal services which are to be performed in California. California Labor Code § 2855 provides that such contracts must have a maximum term of no more than seven (7) years, ***unless*** the contract is for "personal service in the production of phonorecords," [Cal. Labor Code § 2855.(b)] In its entirety, the statute reads as follows:

> (a) Except as otherwise provided in subdivision (b), a contract to render personal service, other than a contract of apprenticeship as provided in Chapter 4 (commencing with Section 3070), may not be enforced against the employee beyond seven years from the commencement of service under it. Any contract, otherwise valid, to perform or render service of a special, unique, unusual, extraordinary, or intellectual character, which gives it peculiar value and the loss of which cannot be reasonably or adequately compensated in damages in an action at law, may nevertheless be enforced against the person contracting to render the service, for a term not to exceed seven years from the commencement of service under it. If the employee voluntarily continues to serve under it beyond that time, the contract may be referred to as affording a presumptive measure of the compensation.

(b) Notwithstanding subdivision (a):

(1) Any employee who is a party to a contract to render personal service in the production of phonorecords in which sounds arc first fixed, as defined in Section 101 of Title 17 of the United States Code, may not invoke the provisions of subdivision (a) without first giving written notice to the employer in accordance with Section 1020 of the Code of Civil Procedure, specifying that the employee from and after a future date certain specified in the notice will no longer render service under the contract by reason of subdivision (a).

(2) Any party to a contract described in paragraph (1) shall have the right to recover damages for a breach of the contract occurring during its term in an action commenced during or after its term, but within the applicable period prescribed by law.

(3) If a party to a contract described in paragraph (1) is, or could contractually be, required to render personal service in the production of a specified quantity of the phonorecords and fails to render all of the required service prior to the date specified in the notice provided in paragraph (1), the party damaged by the failure shall have the right to recover damages for each phonorecord as to which that party has failed to render service in an action that, notwithstanding paragraph (2), shall be commenced within 45 days after the date specified in the notice. [Cal. Labor Code § 2855]

Every California contract which is for personal service — except for the personal services of a recording artist[290] — must be for no more than seven years. A number of other state legislatures are considering the enactment of similar limitations. The exception for recording artists — which was obtained through lobbying by the recording industry and RIAA — allows for an indefinite, occurrence based term in recording contracts. Under the exception, the term of a recording contract lasts until the Artist has "delivered" a fixed number of recordings. The artist may send a written notice stating that the contract will be terminated as of a particular date which is at least seven years from the commencement of the term, but failure to have "delivered" the required number of recordings prior to that date may constitute an actionable breach, although the record company will have only forty-five days from the specified termination date in which to commence litigation against the artist, if it chooses to do so.

---

290 As written, the subdivision applies to anyone rendering personal services "in the production of phonorecords," which would include recording engineers, producers, and others, in addition to recording artists. As a practical matter, the exception was aimed at, and is limited to, recording artists.

Term — Date Certain

This agreement shall become effective upon signing, and shall remain in full force and effect through {Month Day, Year}

Term — Stated Period

This contract shall remain in full force and effect for a term of {Number} ({n}) [Years <or> Months <or> Days] from and after the [last date subscribed hereto <or> date first written above <or> {Month Day, Year}].

Term — Occurrence Based

The term of this Agreement shall run, and the terms and conditions hereof shall continue in full force and effect, from the date first written above until such time as {Party 1} shall deliver to {Party 2}, in good order, and subject to {Party 2}'s full and unqualified acceptance thereof, {Description of Items to be delivered to complete contract obligations.}

Term — Recording Contract

The term of this agreement (hereinafter "Term") shall commence as of the date first written above and continue for a first Contract Period which shall terminate eight (8) months following initial release in the United States of the Album Delivered during such Contract Period, but in no event later than a date sixteen (16) months following Delivery of all Recordings comprising such Album. [In no event however shall the Initial Contract Period, nor any subsequent "Option Period," as hereinafter provided, have or create an aggregated term or span greater than seven (7) years from commencement of the Initial Term of this Agreement to its expiration.][291]

◆ ◆ ◆

---

291 The seven-year limitation is intended to avoid the exception under California Labor Code § 2855 subd. (b).

Termination Provision

Although contracts ideally continue in force throughout their stated Term, there will be circumstances under which it may become necessary, advisable or desirable to terminate the contract earlier. The conditions under which such an earlier termination may occur, and the procedures by which such termination will be effectuated, will be set forth in a Termination Provision.

Termination provisions are generally divided into two types: Discretionary or "at will" termination, and justifiable or "for cause" termination. Also, where there is an automatic renewal provision, either party must give timely notice to the other in order to terminate the agreement. Absent such notice, the contract will be automatically renewed. This has the effect of making the contract term perpetual, until such time as it has been expressly terminated by one of the parties.[292]

Many contracts allow one party, or sometimes either party, absolute discretion to terminate the contract at any time, for any reason, or for no reason at all, simply by giving notice to the other party of an intention to terminate the agreement. The contractual relationship between parties having such a discretionary right to terminate their agreement is said to be "at will."

Other contracts, however, only allow the contract to be terminated prior to expiration of its Term for serious (*i.e.*, "material") breaches of the agreement, such as failure to pay money owed. Such :for cause" termination provisions are often linked to notice and cure provisions which allow the breaching party an opportunity to avoid termination by prompt performance of their defaulted obligations. Additionally, such provisions may specify particular types of breach which will be considered material, and others which will not. Recitals of the materiality and non-materiality of particular contract obligations may prevent termination based upon a breach which only one party considers serious. Such recitals are not absolutely binding on a court, which may disregard them in determining which contract provisions should be considered "essential." This is especially true in making determinations under the severability doctrine. Such recitals are often abused in the music industry, where it is not unusual to find self serving contract provisions which declare that obviously essential and fundamental contract obligations are "not material."[293] Such recitals will have little if any effect on judicial analysis, as it will ultimately be for the court to say what is and what is not material.

Ideally, all parties should have some termination right, but the nature of the contract and the parties' respective obligations and bargaining power will dictate the extent to which such rights will be embodied in the agreement. In general, there will always be a requirement of

---

292 But note that there may be a limitation on the term of contracts for personal services. See, *e.g.*, earlier discussion regarding California Labor Code § 2855 in the "Term Clause" section.

293 *E.g.*, "Company's failure to account for or pay royalties to Artist hereunder shall not be deemed a material breach of this Agreement." (Quoted from a typical "Shopping Agreement.")

adequate notice of an intention to terminate. The notice may be an absolute election, or it may be conditionally required as part of a cure provision.

Caution should be exercised in giving termination notice. It is important to verify that the underlying contract provides for termination upon whatever grounds are stated in the notice. A bald statement that one party has decided to no longer perform contract obligations may give rise to a cause of action for anticipatory breach of contract, whereas a properly prepared termination notice which conforms to the contract's requirements will be regarded as a privileged act and not as grounds for a cause of action.[294]

Discretionary Termination — Bilateral

> **Subject only to such binding covenants as may be set forth herein, and further subject to any continuing executory obligations hereunder, it is understood and agreed that either party may terminate the within agreement at any time, without penalty, upon ten (10) days written notice.**

Discretionary Termination — Unilateral

> **Company shall have the right, exercisable at any time by notice to Artist, to terminate this Agreement without penalty and without further obligation to Artist.**

Automatic Renewal (with Notice of Termination required)

> **Upon expiration of the Initial Term, this Agreement shall be automatically renewed [on a month-by-month basis <or> for an additional Term of {Number} ({n}) {Years <or> Months <or> Weeks <or> Days}], and shall thereafter continue in full force and effect. Notwithstanding the foregoing, following expiration of the Initial Term, either party may terminate this Agreement by serving a thirty (30) day written notice of termination upon the other party, in the manner prescribed for notice herein.**

---

294 Of course, there's nothing to prevent the other party from filing suit, but "privilege" is an affirmative defense which should defeat any claim based solely on a properly drafted and contractually-compliant termination notice.

Termination for Cause - Commercial Contract (Comprehensive)

The non-defaulting party may terminate this Agreement if a Default, as defined below, by the other party has occurred and is continuing by giving written notice to the defaulting party. The term "Default" shall mean, without necessarily being limited to, any of the following: (a) failure by a party to comply with or perform any provision or condition of this Agreement that results in a material breach of this Agreement and, if such material breach can be cured, continuance of such failure for thirty (30) days after written notice to such party (if cure is not practicable, the thirty (30) day notice period is not required); (b) a party becomes insolvent, is unable to pay its debts as they mature, or is the subject of a petition in bankruptcy, whether voluntary or involuntary, or of any other proceeding under bankruptcy, insolvency or similar laws; or makes an assignment for the benefit of creditors; or is named in, or its property is subject to a suit for appointment of a receiver, or is dissolved or liquidated; or (c) any material warranty or representation made in this Agreement is breached, false or misleading in any material respect. In the event of such termination, the non-defaulting party shall be entitled to pursue any and all remedies provided in law and recover any damages it may have suffered by reason of such Default, provided, however, that {Party 2} expressly waives its right to seek equitable relief including, without limitation, seeking injunctive relief. Upon Default and/or termination hereunder, any Materials in {Party 1}'s possession at time of termination shall continue to be licensed under the terms of this Agreement until such Copies are returned to {Party 2} or purchased by {Party 1}.

Termination — Employment Contract (Comprehensive)

Employee agrees to work for the Company for a period of twenty-four (24) months commencing on the date of this Agreement. However, the Company may terminate the Employee's employment at any time, for any reason (or no reason), and With or Without Cause, by providing the Employee with seven (7) days' written notice. If Employee's employment continues following the end of the two (2)-year term of this Agreement (the "Term"), it will continue on an "at-will" basis, which means that either the Employee or the Company may terminate the Employee's employment at any time thereafter, for any reason (or no reason), and With or Without Cause, by providing the other party with seven (7) days' written notice.

If the Company terminates the Employee's employment Without Cause, or if the Employee resigns his employment for Good Reason, prior to the end of the Term, the Employee, or his legal representatives, as the case may be, shall receive: (i) all salary earned by the Employee through the last day of his employment; (ii) continuation of the Employee's base salary for a period of two (2) years after the date of the termination of the Employee's employment; and (iii) immediate vesting of all outstanding shares of the Employee's Company stock options, notwithstanding anything to the contrary in the agreement(s) granting such options. However, if: (i) the Employee resigns at any time Without Good Reason; (ii) the Company terminates the Employee's employment for Cause prior to the end of the Term; or (iii) the Company terminates the Employee's employment for any reason, with or Without Cause, or if the Employee resigns with or Without Good Reason, after the end of the Term, the Employee will only be entitled to all salary earned by him through the last day of his employment.

For purposes of this Agreement "Cause" shall mean a good faith determination by the Board of Directors of the Company, following a reasonable factual investigation, of the occurrence of any one or more of the following events or circumstances, provided however, such event or circumstance will not constitute Cause unless Employee has failed to cure such event or circumstance within 30 days after receipt by Employee of written notice thereof: (i) Employee willfully engages in wrongful conduct that results in material damage to the Company; (ii) any willful and material failure to perform Employee's duties hereunder; (iii) Employee is convicted of a felony, including a plea of no contest, (iv) employee engages in fraud or one or more acts of dishonesty which materially damages the Company; or (v) Employee materially breaches this Agreement or the Proprietary Information and Invention Agreement, which material breach results in actual damage to the Company. No act or failure to act on

Employee's part shall be deemed "willful" unless it is done, or omitted to be done, by Employee not in good faith and such that a reasonable person would believe that the act, or failure to act, was not in the best interests of the Company.

For the purposes of this Agreement, "Good Reason" for Employee's resignation will exist if Employee resigns within sixty days of any of the following: (i) any reduction in his base salary or bonus, if any; (ii) any material reduction in his benefits; (iii) a change in Employee's position with the Company or a successor company which materially reduces Employee's duties or level of responsibility; or (iv) any requirement that Employee's relocate his place of employment by more than thirty-five (35) miles from his then-current office, provided such reduction, change, or relocation is effected by the Company without Employee's prior written consent. A resignation by Employee under any other circumstances or for any other reasons will be a resignation "Without Good Reason."

This Agreement shall automatically terminate in the event of the Employee's death or Permanent Disability. "Permanent Disability" is defined as physical or mental incapacity rendering the Employee unable to perform substantially all of his duties for a period of at least four (4) consecutive months or an aggregate of at least six (6) months over any twelve (12) month period.

◆ ◆ ◆

Territory Clause

In music industry contracts which include exclusive rights, "Territory" is likely to be a critical issue, since it limits the geographical area in which the rights and privileges granted by the contract may be exercised and — by exclusion — defines those remaining areas where the granting party is free to contract separately — and "exclusively" — with a different party. Although this concept seems simple enough, there are a number of factors to be taken into consideration, particularly in regard to recording contracts and publishing agreements.

The simplest Territory is Worldwide, although current practice is to substitute the phrase "throughout the Universe" or the word "Universal." Referring to the "Universe" (rather than the "world") addresses very practical (if prospective) concerns about space-based distribution systems and non-terrestrial markets.

The most common (and desirable) Territory is the United States, but this, too, needs to be qualified. Royalties are generally subject to substantial reduction based on the country in which sales occur. Also, record companies and publishers often apply a "double standard" when it comes to determining what is meant by "United States." For the purposes of *their* exclusive rights, labels and publishers generally regard the "United States" as including all 50 states, plus all U.S. territories, possessions, protectorates, dominions, and military installations, wherever situated. When it comes to calculating royalties, however, they often define "United States" as referring only to the 50 states.[295] This leaves any undefined, excluded portions in the "Rest of the World" category, for which royalties are generally reduced by 50%. To avoid that, it's necessary to spell out precisely what is meant by "United States" in both Territorial and Royalty contexts.

The most common Territory for American recording artists is "U.S. and Canada." The next most common country to be included with the Territory for recording contracts is the United Kingdom. Other countries may also be expressly named as part of the Territory in a less-than-universal contract. Certain countries are prime markets for specific artists or musical genres. It is not unheard of for a contract to have a Territory of "U.S., Canada, the U.K., Germany, Sweden, and Japan."

It is to the record company's advantage to have the broadest possible Territory. A broad Territory is not disadvantageous to the Artist *provided* the contract includes a release commitment which includes all principal markets within the Territory. If it does not, then the Artist runs the risk of having no releases in countries where sales might be significant. Artists should seek to exclude from the Territory any significant potential market for which the Label is unwilling to guarantee a release. It is also good practice, in such situations, to pre-negotiate terms for a licensing agreement for master recordings for those excluded markets. Labels will

295 In fact, some labels narrow the definition (for royalty purposes) to the lower 48 states.

generally agree to this, although the Label may insist on a delay period so that foreign release is subsequent to U.S. release by some agreed-upon period.

In analyzing other portions of contracts which contain a Territory Clause, it is important to be certain that restrictive provisions are also linked to the Territory, rather than being universal. If, for example, a recording artist has an exclusive U.S. contract with one label, and an exclusive European contract with a different label, any re-recording restrictions could prevent the Artist from releasing the same compositions for both labels. Either the European label would have to license masters from the U.S. Label (or vice versa), or the Artist would have to record entirely different songs for each label.

Despite these pitfalls, the Territory Clause itself will generally be short and to the point.

Territory (Generic) — Worldwide (Universal)

As used herein, the word "Territory" shall mean any and all places and locations throughout the Universe.

Territory (Generic) — U.S. and Canada

As used herein, the word "Territory" shall mean the United States and Canada.

Territory (Generic) — Stated Countries

As used herein, the word "Territory" shall mean the United States, Canada, the United Kingdom, Germany, and Japan.

Universal Territory — Recording Contract (Company Favorable)

Artist hereby grants to Company the exclusive, irrevocable right (but not the obligation) during the Term (as herein defined), to distribute and sell Artist's Records, in any medium now known or hereafter developed, in any manner, including but not limited to normal record retail channels, digital distribution and e-commerce throughout the Universe (the "Territory").

Universal Territory — Recording Contract (Artist Favorable)

> **Company shall, during the Term (as hereinafter defined) distribute and sell Artist's Records through normal record retail channels, digital distribution and e-commerce throughout the world (the "Territory") as hereinafter provided. Notwithstanding the foregoing, Company shall have the non-exclusive right to sell Records through Company's website and/or any individual artist's website. Initial sales will be in the United States, followed by Canada, Europe, and the rest of appropriate world markets.**[296]

◆ ◆ ◆

296 The potential difficulties regarding "Territory" cannot be effectively addressed in the Territory Clause itself, but rather in the Restrictions and Release Commitment sections of the contract.

Time of the Essence Clause

As noted in the discussion on "severability," one of the most important aspects of judicial analysis of contracts is determining which provisions of the agreement are "essential," and which are not. Even though the parties' express recital of what are and what are not critical terms of their agreement will not be dispositive, such recitals are nonetheless helpful and may tip the analytical scale one way or the other in a questionable situation.

In many situations, the timeliness of contract performance is as crucial as the quality of that performance. It does no good for a shipping company to deliver the band's equipment to a venue in perfect condition… two days after the scheduled performance date.

The phrase which lawyers have traditionally used in contracts where timeliness of performance is an essential consideration has become ubiquitous and so familiar that it has entered common speech as a cliché. Here's the phrase:

Time is of the essence.

Because that phrase is so overused as to have lost much of its effectiveness, it is better practice to utilize a more comprehensive and specific statement.

Time of the Essence Clause (General):

> **The parties hereby acknowledge and agree that timeliness of performance is an expressly bargained for, material, and essential consideration of this Agreement, and that failure to timely perform or Deliver in accordance with the schedule(s) set forth herein, or in accordance with such schedule(s) as may hereafter be set forth in a separate writing, shall constitute a serious, material breach of this Agreement.**

Time of the Essence Clause (Specific):

The parties hereby acknowledge and agree that timeliness of performance is an expressly bargained for, material, and essential consideration of this Agreement, and that any [unexcused] failure of {Identification of Party} to timely {specific obligation(s) to be performed} on or before {Month Day, Year} shall constitute a serious, material breach of this Agreement. [For the purposes hereof, "excused" shall mean and be limited to such reason for non-performance as amounts to an event of force majeure.]

◆ ◆ ◆

Warranties and Representations

Generally referred to simply as the Warranties & Representations section in most contracts, this section is also the most common location for certain key restrictions and covenants which the contract imposes on the parties, as well as for the *indemnification provision* by which the party making representations and warranties agrees to bear all costs and expenses which may arise should any of those representations or warranties prove to be less than 100% accurate. Not all contracts combine these elements, however, and it is not unusual for "Restrictions" and/or "Indemnification" to appear as separate sections elsewhere in the agreement.

Each contracting party is supposed to have all of the necessary legal rights in regard to materials which are to be delivered by that party under the contract terms. In the music business, this most often refers to intellectual property and quasi-property rights including (but not necessarily limited to) lawful rights of ownership or control over compositions, recordings, artwork, photographs, logos, band name, and personality rights. When one party warrants these rights to another party, it is that other party which is likely to be directly liable should there be a third-party claim which challenges the warranting party's alleged rights.

It is because of that direct liability that the contract will contain express statements (representations) that the granting party has legal ownership or other rights to contract in regard to all material being provided, as well as legally-binding assurances (warranties) in respect to such rights. This allows the other party to "rely" on those representations and warranties and to demand indemnification should those representations prove untrue. (Misrepresentations of material fact may also lead to a civil action for fraud, seeking compensatory and punitive damages.)

While a party cannot avoid legal liability to third parties by the terms of a contract, the warranties section *can* minimize direct exposure in certain cases, particularly with respect to infringement claims, since reasonable reliance on warranties and representations generally demonstrates that infringement was unintentional rather than willful. (Willful infringement can trigger substantial punitive damages, on top of actual or statutory damages.) Further, under the indemnification provision (discussed below) all costs and expenses arising from any third party claim may be (theoretically) recovered from the warranting party, although (in practical terms) such recovery is generally limited to withholding royalties or other revenues which would be otherwise payable to the warranting party, until the indemnification amount is paid.

Artists are generally required to expressly warrant and represent that none of the elements incorporated into a recording or album will infringe in any way upon the rights of any third party. The term "Materials" is broadly inclusive, so the critical issue for the Artist is to be certain that this warranty is restricted to "materials" which have been furnished by the Artist. Without this limitation, the Artist might be held responsible for infringements over which he or she had no control, such as artwork, photographs, or text included as part of an album's packaging.

Labels will also generally require warranties that there are no unreleased master recordings by Artist which might surface later, in competition with the label's release of Artist's recordings. This generally only applies to new artists. For established artists who have previously recorded for other labels, there is a likelihood that those former labels may retain some previously unreleased masters. Under the terms of a prior recording agreement, a former label may or may not have a right to release previously-unreleased masters after the contract has terminated. In any event, that prior label likely *owns* those unreleased masters (unless there was a reversion provision in the prior agreement), and such masters have been known to find their way into public release. This required representation is one of those areas where an ill-advised Demo Deal or Shopping Agreement can cause problems. Under such deals, the other party (not the artist) likely owns the "demo" master recordings. Unless that original contract was carefully drafted with a reversion provision and/or a strict limitation prohibiting any commercial exploitation of such "demos" such recordings may suddenly find their way into public release. If the existence of those prior recordings has not been fully disclosed by the artist, they may result in a claim of material breach as to this part of the warranties and representations.

The best practice is to append a schedule of *all* prior master recordings to the record contract, indicating the ownership of each. Artists should claim ownership of any preexisting unreleased master recordings, if possible. This is one area where the "effective date" of the contract may be material, as the Artist will not want to surrender ownership of such prior masters on a theory that they fall within the term of the contract. If the label is interested in such earlier masters, it would be better practice to *license* or sell those masters to the Label through a separate agreement, rather than have them be considered to have been "recorded during the Term" by reason of a back-dated contract.

Apart from recording contracts, warranties and representations sections appear in almost all entertainment industry contracts, and most especially in those contracts which convey — or which purport to convey — some right or interest in intellectual property. The warranties may be broad or narrowly constrained, but the essence of each of them will be to create a material representation that the party conveying a particular right has all of the necessary legal rights to do so.

Limited Warranty — Sync License

The Licensor makes no warranty or representation, express or implied, except that the Licensor warrants that it has the right to grant such recording right and performing right licenses as are set forth herein, subject to the terms, conditions, limitations, restrictions and reservations herein contained, such licenses being granted without recourse for any other cause or in any other event whatsoever; the total liability of the Licensor under each such license being limited in any event to that part of the consideration paid hereunder by the Licensee to the Licensor for such license in respect to which such breach of warranty may relate.

Warranty of Authorship — Producer Agreement

Producer warrants that all music and other materials, including all compositions, tunes, lyrics, ideas, designs and inventions of Producer that are provided or selected by Producer in connection with the withing Project are, or will be, Producer's original, independent creations, or in the public domain throughout the world, and shall in no manner or degree infringe upon or violate any copyright, or impermissibly infringe upon or violate any privacy right, or any other right, of any person. Producer further warrants that Producer is free to grant all rights granted and make all agreements made by Producer herein. Producer agrees to hold Company and its affiliates, subsidiaries, successors, licensees and assigns harmless from and against all damages, losses, costs and expenses (including, without limitation, reasonable attorneys' fees and costs) which Company or any of its successors, licensees or assigns may suffer or incur by reason of any claim, demand, or action by a third party which is reduced to final judgment by a court of competent jurisdiction which contradicts any of the foregoing warranties, or which claim is settled with Producer's consent, which consent shall not be unreasonably withheld.

Songwriter's Warranty — Publishing Agreement

Writer represents, covenants and warrants that the Compositions are original works of Writer's independent creation, and that said Compositions do not and will not infringe upon or violate the rights of any person, firm, corporation, or other entity, and that Writer has the full and unencumbered right, power, and authority to grant to Publisher all of the publishing rights herein granted to Publisher.

Warranties and Representations — Record Contract — Company Favorable

Artist warrants and represents that

(1) Artist is not under any disability, restriction or prohibition, whether contractual or otherwise, with respect to (A) Artist's right to enter into this agreement, and (B) Artist's right to grant any and all of the rights granted to Company hereunder, and to perform each and every term and provision hereof and each and every obligation of Artist hereunder;

(2) Company shall not be required to make any payments of any kind or nature for, or in connection with, the acquisition, exercise or exploitation of rights by Company pursuant to this agreement, except those payments and expenditures which are specifically provided for within this Agreement. To the extent that Company shall, intentionally or inadvertently, make or cause to be made any payment or expenditure not thus specified herein, then Artist shall promptly reimburse the same to Company, upon demand.

(3) Artist, and each individual comprising Artist hereunder, is or will become and will remain to the extent necessary to enable the performance of this agreement, a member in good standing of all labor unions or guilds, membership in which may be required for the performance of Artist's services hereunder;

(4) Neither the "Materials" nor any use of the Materials by Company will violate or infringe upon the rights of any Person. "Materials" as used in this subparagraph means, but is not necessarily limited to, any musical, artistic and literary materials, ideas and other intellectual properties, furnished by or on behalf of Artist and/or contained in or used in connection with any Master Recordings made hereunder or in the packaging, sale, distribution, advertising, marketing, publicizing, or other exploitation thereof;

(5) There are now in existence no prior recorded performances by Artist unreleased within the United States or elsewhere in the world; and

(6) All of Artist's representations and warranties shall be true and correct upon execution hereof and upon delivery of each Master Recording hereunder, and shall remain in effect in perpetuity. Company's acceptance of Master Recordings or other materials hereunder shall not constitute a waiver of any of Artist's representations, warranties or agreements in respect thereto.

During the Term of this agreement, Artist will not enter into any agreement which would interfere with the full and prompt performance of Artist's material obligations hereunder, and Artist will not perform or render any services for the purpose of making phonograph records or Master Recordings, nor render entertainment services of any kind or nature, for any person other than Company, except as otherwise expressly permitted in this agreement

After the expiration of the Term of this agreement, for any reason whatsoever, Artist will not perform any composition which shall have been recorded hereunder for any Person other than Company for the purpose of making and releasing phonograph records or Master Recordings prior to a date five (5) years subsequent to the date of Delivery to Company of the Master containing such composition or two (2) years subsequent to the expiration date of the Term, whichever shall be later.

Except as otherwise expressly permitted in this agreement, Artist will not at any time record, manufacture, distribute or sell, or authorize or knowingly permit Artist's performances of any kind or nature to be recorded by any party and by any means, whether now known or unknown, for any purpose whatsoever, without the express written consent of Company.

Artist may render non-musical performances in motion pictures or television shows provided that no such performance interferes with the full and prompt performance of Artist's material obligations under this agreement.

Notwithstanding any of the terms and conditions of this Agreement, Artist, and each individual comprising Artist hereunder, shall comply with any other restriction, and shall grant any additional rights and do such other things, as may be required by the Distributor pursuant to the Distribution Agreement, so that Company may perform all of its obligations thereunder.

In the event that Artist, or any individual comprising Artist hereunder, shall become aware of any unauthorized recording, manufacture, distribution or sale by any third party contrary to the foregoing re-recording restrictions, Artist shall notify Company thereof and shall cooperate fully with Company in the event that Company, or a representative of Company, commences any action or proceeding against such third party.

Artist will at all times indemnify and hold harmless Company from and against any and all claims, losses, damages, liabilities, costs and expenses, including, without limitation, all legal expenses and attorneys' fees of any party or third party, arising out of or regarding any alleged breach or actual breach by Artist, or of any individual comprising Artist hereunder, or any person actually or ostensibly acting for or on behalf of Artist, of any warranty, representation or agreement made by Artist herein, which has resulted in a final judgment or has been settled with Artist's written consent (it being understood that Artist's consent is hereby given, in advance, to any settlement which does not exceed Twenty-Five Thousand ($25,000) Dollars). Notwithstanding the foregoing, if Artist withholds consent to any settlement which Company is willing to make, the foregoing indemnity shall apply and Company may settle such claim in its sole discretion unless Artist promptly assumes all costs of defending against such claim, demand or action including, without limitation, court costs, reasonable attorneys' fees, and direct expenses theretofore incurred by Company in connection with said claim, demand or action; provided that in the event Artist assumes said costs, Company shall nonetheless have the right to settle such claim, demand or action in its sole discretion without Artist's consent, provided that, in such event, the foregoing indemnification shall not apply with respect thereto. Artist will reimburse Company on demand for any payment made at any time after the date hereof in respect of any liability or claim in respect of which Company are entitled to be indemnified. Upon the making or filing of any such claim, action or demand, Company shall be entitled to withhold from any amounts payable under this agreement such amounts as are reasonably related to the potential liability in issue. Notwithstanding the foregoing, Company shall liquidate such withheld amounts if within twelve (12) months no lawsuit has been commenced and active settlement discussions are not then taking place. Notwithstanding the foregoing, Company shall release to Artist all such withheld payments upon Artist's posting of a bond in an amount equivalent to the sum being withheld by Company in respect of such third party claim with a good and sufficient surety approved by Company, provided that such surety agrees unconditionally, in writing, to pay all costs, fees, damages, etc. incurred by Company by reason of such

third party claim. Artist shall be promptly notified of any such third party claim, action or demand and shall have the right, at Artist's own expense, to participate in the defense thereof with counsel of Artist's own choosing; provided, however, that Company's decision in connection with the defense of any such claim, action or demand shall be final.

Artist, and each individual performer comprising Artist hereunder, shall execute and deliver to Company, upon Company's request therefore, a form of artist inducement and guarantee letter as may be required by a Distributor. If Artist shall fail or refuse to execute and deliver any such inducement letter promptly following Company's request therefore, Artist hereby appoints Company as Artist's true and lawful attorney-in-fact to execute such inducement letter in Artist's name and on Artist's behalf. Such power of attorney is irrevocable and is coupled with an interest.

Warranties and Representations — Record Contract — Artist Favorable

Artist warrants and represents that:

(a) Artist is not under any undisclosed disability, restriction or prohibition with respect to Artist's right to enter into this agreement, to make the grants of right contained herein, and to perform the obligations of Artist hereunder;

(b) Artist, and each individual comprising Artist hereunder, is or will become and will remain to the extent necessary to enable the performance of this agreement, a member of all labor unions or guilds, membership in which may be lawfully required for the performance of Artist's services hereunder;

(c) Neither the "Materials" nor any use of the Materials by Company will violate or infringe upon the rights of any Person. "Materials" as used in this subparagraph means and is limited to musical, artistic and literary materials, ideas and other intellectual properties furnished by Artist to Company, and thereafter contained in or used in connection with any Master Recordings made hereunder or in the packaging, sale, distribution, advertising, marketing, publicizing, or other exploitation thereof;

(d) To the best of Artist's knowledge, information, and belief, there are now in existence no prior recorded performances by Artist unreleased within the Territory, apart from "demo" recordings,

master recordings which are owned and controlled exclusively by Artist, and such other recordings as have been expressly disclosed by Artist to Company; and

(e) All of Artist's representations and warranties shall be true and correct upon execution hereof and upon delivery of each Master Recording hereunder, to the best of Artist's knowledge, information and belief at the time thereof.

During the Term of this Agreement, Artist will not enter into any agreement to perform or render any services for the purpose of making phonograph records or Master Recordings for any Person for release within the Territory, other than Company, except as permitted under the terms of this Agreement.

After the expiration of the Term of this agreement, Artist will not perform any composition which shall have been recorded hereunder for any Person other than Company for the purpose of releasing phonograph records or Master Recordings within the Territory prior to a date three (3) years subsequent to the date of Delivery to Company of the Master containing such composition or one (1) year subsequent to the expiration date of the Term hereof.

Except as otherwise expressly permitted in this agreement, Artist will not at any time record, manufacture, distribute or sell, or authorize or knowingly permit Artist's performances to be recorded by any party for any commercial purpose within the Territory in violation of express restrictions contained herein.

Artist may render performances in motion pictures, television shows, or legitimate stage productions, provided that no such performance interferes with the full and prompt performance of Artist's material obligations under this agreement. During the Term, no such performance shall include performance of any composition recorded by Artist hereunder, unless by the express consent of Company.

Artist, and each individual comprising Artist hereunder, shall comply with any other restriction, and shall grant any additional rights and do such other things, as may be required by the Distributor pursuant to the Distribution Agreement so that Company may perform all of its obligations thereunder, provided that such compliance, or the terms of such Distribution Agreement shall not have the effect of creating obligations not set forth herein, nor decreasing any benefit to Artist hereunder. Company shall consult with Artist regarding entering into a Distribution Agreement and shall procure a Distribution Agreement which

contains terms which are no less favorable to Artist than those contained herein.

In the event that Company, or a representative of Company, Artist, shall become aware of any unauthorized recording, manufacture, distribution or sale by any third party contrary to the foregoing re-recording restrictions, Artist shall cooperate with Company, at Company's sole expense, in the event that Company commences any action or proceeding against such third party.

Artist will indemnify and hold harmless Company from and against any claims, losses, damages, liabilities, costs and expenses, including, without limitation, legal expenses and reasonable third party attorneys' fees, arising out of any actual breach by Artist of any warranty, representation or agreement made by Artist herein, which has resulted in a final judgment or has been settled with Artist's written consent. Notwithstanding the foregoing, if Artist withholds consent to any settlement which Company is willing to make, the foregoing indemnity shall apply and Company may settle such claim in its sole discretion unless Artist promptly assumes all further costs of defending against such claim, demand or action including, without limitation, court costs, reasonable attorneys' fees, and direct expenses in connection with said claim, demand or action; provided that in the event Artist assumes said costs, Company shall nonetheless have the right to settle such claim, demand or action in its sole discretion without Artist's consent, provided that, in such event, the foregoing indemnification shall not apply with respect thereto. Artist shall be promptly notified of any such third party claim, action or demand and shall have the right, at Artist's own expense, to participate in the defense thereof with counsel of Artist's own choosing.

Subject to Artist's right to review and approve the terms and conditions of any Distribution Agreement which materially affects the rights and obligations of Artist hereunder, Artist, and each individual performer comprising Artist hereunder, shall execute and deliver to Company, upon Company's request therefore, a form of artist inducement and guarantee letter as may be required by a Distributor.

◆ ◆ ◆

Work For Hire Clause

As discussed at length in Chapter 3 ("A Primer on Copyright") Section 101 of the Copyright Act (17 USC § 101) defines a "work made for hire" as either "a work prepared by an employee within the scope of his or her employment" or "a work specially ordered or commissioned for use as a contribution to a collective work [etc.] **if the parties expressly agree in a written instrument signed by them** that the work shall be considered a work made for hire." Thus there are only two circumstances in which a *qualifying* creative work is a "work made for hire" under the current Copyright Act:

(1) When the creative work is part of an employee's regular duties;

-or-

(2) When there is a ***written*** agreement stating that a qualified type of work is being created or contributed to on a work-for-hire basis.

There are a number of qualifications included in the statutory definition, including a list of the *types* of creative work which may be considered to be works made for hire. This is particularly important for those in the music industry because the types of work which may qualify as a "work made for hire" *includes* songwriting, but *excludes sound recordings.*[297]

The Copyright Act provides that, "In the case of a work made for hire, the employer or other person for whom the work was prepared is considered the author for purposes of this title, and, unless the parties have expressly agreed otherwise in a written instrument signed by them, owns all of the rights comprised in the copyright."[298]

For works created under the current Copyright Act, there is a legal presumption that such works are ***not*** works made for hire. That presumption can only be rebutted by proving that the work falls within one of the two statutory categories listed above.

Even though it is generally the *employer* who is deemed to be the "author" of the work for copyright purposes, the "real" author may nonetheless negotiate for a contractual right to be acknowledged as an author or co-author of the work.[299] Depending on the contract terms, such acknowledgment may appear on or in the published work itself, or within the copyright registration, or both.

With regard to sound recordings, and despite the fact that they do not qualify to be regarded as works made for hire, the common practice is to nonetheless obtain work for hire

---

297 Confusingly, Copyright Form SR ("Sound Recordings") nonetheless asks *"Was this contribution to the work a 'work made for hire'?"*

298 17 USC § 201.(b). (Emphasis added.)

299 Work for hire agreements generally include a waiver of *droits moral*, one of which "moral rights" is the right of attribution (*"paternité"*)), which is the right to be acknowledged as the creator of a work.

agreements from those who contribute to such sound recordings. Since such an agreement is technically defective due to exclusion of sound recordings from 17 USC § 101, such agreements also generally include an *assignment, transfer* and/or *conveyance* of all rights, in *addition* to"work for hire" language. This is good practice for all work for hire agreements, not just those relating to sound recordings, because the Berne Convention does not recognize "work for hire," *per se,* but does recognize that copyright interests may be sold or assigned.

Work for Hire Clause — Recording Contract

> **Each, every, any, and all Recordings recorded by Artist during the Term of this Agreement, including all takes, outtakes, and any completed or incomplete recordings, as well as all Master Recordings, shall, from inception of the recording process, be Company's exclusive property, throughout the Universe, free from any claims by Artist or any person deriving or claiming to derive any rights or interest from or through Artist. Each such Recording shall at all times be deemed a "work-made-for-hire" for Company, of which Company shall be the sole Author for all copyright purposes. If any such Recording is determined not to be a "work-made-for-hire" each such Recording (together with all rights therein and to all other products of Artist's services in connection with its recording, other than mechanical rights with respect to any Composition embodied in such Recording) shall be deemed to have been hereby transferred, conveyed, and assigned exclusively to Company.**

Work for Hire Partial Exclusion Clause — Employment Agreement

> **Under the terms and conditions of this Agreement, the Scope of Employee's employment includes creative efforts which are likely to result in original works of authorship or invention subject to protection under copyright, trademark, or patent statutes, and which are "works made for hire" in and to which Employer shall have exclusive rights of authorship under applicable law. Notwithstanding the foregoing, it is expressly understood and agreed that, for the purposes hereof, any and all works of authorship or of invention created by Employee other than during normal working hours, and not directly commissioned or ordered by Employer in advance of such creation, will be and shall remain the sole and exclusive property of Employee, in which Employer shall have no right or interest.**

Work for Hire Partial Exclusion Side Letter — Employment at Will

Whereas {Employee Name} ("Employee") is an employee-at-will of {Employer's Name} ("Employer") and the Scope of Employee's employment includes creative efforts likely to result in original works of authorship or invention subject to protection under copyright, trademark, or patent statutes, and which are "works made for hire" in and to which Employer has exclusive rights of authorship under applicable law, it is nonetheless hereby expressly agreed by and between Employer and Employee, that any and all works of authorship or of invention created by Employee other than during normal working hours, and not directly commissioned or ordered by Employer in advance of such creation, will be and shall remain the sole and exclusive property of Employee, in which Employer shall have no right or interest.

Work for Hire Exclusion Clause — Employment Agreement

Notwithstanding that the Scope of Employee's employment hereunder may, from time to time, require creative efforts by Employee which may result in original works of authorship or invention subject to protection under copyright, trademark, or patent statutes, it is hereby expressly agreed that such works of authorship or invention will not be deemed "works made for hire" but rather the exclusive property of Employee, in which Employer shall have no right or interest, except as hereinafter provided.

As a bargained for consideration of this Agreement, Employer shall have an exclusive Right of First Refusal in respect to acquiring an interest in or right to use of such intellectual property from Employee, and Employee hereby agrees to license the same to Employer or, at Employee's option, to sell the same to Employer, on reasonable, commercially-competitive terms, which Employee shall not unreasonably refuse to accept. Employer's Right of First Refusal hereunder shall terminate thirty (30) days following written notice from Employee to Employer of the availability for licensing (or, at Employee's option, sale) of such intellectual property.

In the event that Employer's foregoing Right of First Refusal shall lapse, and Employee shall at any time thereafter obtain from a third party a bonafide offer to purchase, or to use by license, such intellectual property, then Employer shall have a limited Right of Second Refusal, by which Employer may agree to purchase or license for use the subject intellectual

property from Employer for a royalty (or purchase price) not less than five percent (5%) greater than that which is set forth in the bonafide third-party offer. Employer's Right of Second Refusal hereunder shall terminate ten (10) days after Employee has given Employer written notice of such third-party offer, and Employee shall under no circumstances accept any such third-party offer without disclosing Employer's foregoing Right of Second Refusal, and in no event prior to ten (10) days following written notice to Employer of such third-party offer.

Nothing herein shall be deemed to prevent or delay Employee from registering any copyright or mark, or from applying for patent protection, in respect to any intellectual property which is a subject hereof. Disclosures made by Employee to Employer hereunder in respect to intellectual property shall be treated as confidential by Employer, and shall not constitute public disclosure or publication in regard to any such intellectual property, or as to any portion thereof.

Work for Hire Agreement — General — Company ("Employer") Favorable

As between {Name of retained artist} ("Contractor") and {Name of employing entity} ("Employer"), the following sets forth the terms and conditions under which Contractor is employed to provide work more fully described as {description of services to be rendered by contractor, e.g., composing music, writing lyrics, providing editing services, graphic design services, etc.} (hereinafter, the "Work").

1. **Contractor agrees to deliver the Work to Employer no later than {date} in a manner and form satisfactory to Employer.**

2. **Upon Employer's acceptance of the Work, Employer agrees to pay Contractor the sum of {Amount} Dollars ($\{n\}) as full consideration for all rights in and to the Work. Contractor shall not be entitled to receive any further payment on account of the Work.**

3. **Contractor expressly acknowledges that the material contributed by Contractor hereunder, and Contractor's services hereunder, are specially ordered and commissioned by Employer for use in connection with {tentative title, description of work or of project into which Work will be integrated}. The Work contributed by Contractor hereunder shall be considered a "work made for hire" as such term is defined by the copyright laws of the United States (17 U.S.C. § 101). Employer**

shall be the sole and exclusive author, owner, and copyright proprietor of all rights and title in and to the results and proceeds of Contractor's services hereunder in whatever stage of completion. If, for any reason, the results and proceeds of Contractor's services hereunder are determined at any time not to be a "work made for hire," Contractor hereby irrevocably transfers and assigns to Employer all right, title and interest therein, including all copyrights, as well as all renewals and extensions thereof.

4. **Contractor agrees that Employer may make any changes or additions to the Work prepared by Contractor, which, in Employer's sole discretion, Employer may consider necessary, and may engage others to do any or all of the foregoing, with or without attribution to Contractor. Contractor further agrees to waive, and does hereby waive, any and all rights or interest which Contractor has or may have in and to any portion of the Work, including (but not limited to) any *droits moral* (i.e., moral rights), of any and every type or nature.**

5. **Contractor warrants and represents that, except with respect to material furnished to Contractor by Employer for inclusion in the Work, Contractor is the sole author of the Work and all of Contractor's contributions thereto are Contractor's original works of independent creation and not copied in whole or in part from any other work; Contractor further warrants and represents that the Work is not libelous or obscene, and does not knowingly violate rights of privacy or publicity, or any other rights, of any person, firm or entity.**

Work for Hire Agreement — General — Artist ("Employee") Favorable

As between {Name of retained artist} ("Contractor") and {Name of employing entity} ("Employer"), the following sets forth the terms and conditions under which Contractor is employed to provide work more fully described as {description of services to be rendered by contractor, e.g., composing music, writing lyrics, providing editing services, graphic design services, etc.} (hereinafter, the "Work").

1. **Contractor agrees to deliver the Work to Employer no later than {date} in a manner and form satisfactory to Employer.**
2. **Upon execution hereof, Employer shall pay Contractor the sum of {Amount} Dollars (${n}) as a non-refundable Advance in consideration of Contractor's agreement and allocation of time to undertake the Work hereunder.**
3. **Upon Contractor's delivery and Employer's acceptance of the Work, Employer agrees to pay Contractor the further sum of {Amount} Dollars (${n}) as final consideration for all rights in and to the Work. Contractor shall not be entitled to thereafter receive any further payment on account of the Work. In the event that Employer shall fail to make the required payment upon delivery, or shall for any reason refuse to accept Contractor's tender, then all rights in and to the Work, and all portions thereof, shall be deemed to irrevocably revert, be transferred to, and thereafter vest solely in and to Contractor, without prejudice or limitation in respect to any other right, recourse, remedy, action, or cause of action which Contractor has or may have, in law or in equity, either hereunder or in regard thereto.**
4. **Contractor expressly acknowledges that the material contributed by Contractor hereunder, and Contractor's services hereunder, are specially ordered and commissioned by Employer for use in connection with {tentative title, description of work or of project into which Work will be integrated}. Upon Employer's acceptance and payment of full consideration as hereinabove provided, the Work contributed by Contractor hereunder shall be considered a "work made for hire" as such term is defined by the copyright laws of the United States (17 U.S.C. § 101). Employer shall thereafter be the sole and exclusive author, owner, and copyright proprietor of all rights and title in and to the results and proceeds of Contractor's services as delivered hereunder. If, for any reason, the results and proceeds of Contractor's services delivered hereunder are thereafter determined not to be a "work made for hire," Contractor irrevocably transfers and assigns to**

Employer all right, title and interest therein, including all copyrights, as well as all renewals and extensions thereof.

5. **Contractor agrees that Employer may make any reasonable and necessary changes or additions to the Work prepared by Contractor, and may engage others implement such changes provided that Employer shall first afford Contractor a reasonable opportunity to implement such desired changes. Contractor further agrees to waive, and does hereby waive, any and all rights or interest which Contractor has or may have in and to any portion of the delivered Work, including (but not limited to) *droits moral* (i.e., moral rights), except with respect to the right of attribution. The Work, when and as published, shall include an accurate acknowledgment of Contractor's contribution to the published work in a manner no less prominent than is afforded to any other contributor, and in no event in less than 10-point type. Further, any copyright registration of the Work shall in all instances include Contractor's name as an author or co-author of the work, as a "work made for hire."**

6. **Contractor warrants and represents that, except with respect to material furnished to Contractor by Employer for inclusion in the Work, and any material within public domain, Contractor is the sole author of the Work as delivered hereunder, and all of Contractor's contributions thereto are Contractor's original works of independent creation.**

◆ ◆ ◆

SECTION III
REMEDIES

NA

CHAPTER 11

UNDERSTANDING REMEDIES

An ancient legal maxim states that, "For every wrong, there is a remedy." Note, however, that the maxim does *not* say that for every ***harm*** there is a remedy. Legal remedies are only available for losses or injuries which result from the improper conduct of another; or, in legal parlance, when another's misconduct is a *proximate cause* of the damage.

The broad, general categories of civil remedies include: injunctive relief, declaratory relief, contract damages, negligence damages, tort damages, statutory actions, special or consequential damages, and punitive or exemplary damages. Not all of these are available in every instance, and the facts underlying a particular claim will dictate which remedies may be available under the circumstances.

The jurisdiction and forum in which a claim will be pursued will also affect the availability of remedies. If, for example, a contract requires that the parties mediate any dispute prior to commencing litigation or arbitration, then there will be little need to reduce a claim to formal causes of action or prayers for relief unless and until the mediation fails.[300] Also, only *courts* have the power to issue injunctive relief. If a contract requires that disputes be mediated or arbitrated, yet injunctive relief is desired, then it may be necessary to file a strictly limited lawsuit seeking an injunction, while pursuing the remainder of the disputed issues through specified alternative methods of resolution.

A lawsuit may also be necessary to *compel* arbitration when one party refuses to participate in a contractually-agreed or statutorily-mandated arbitration process. In such an instance, the court is permitted to rule *only* on the issue of whether arbitration is required, and not upon any substantive issue of the underlying dispute.

The legal analysis and considerations which go into the process of forum selection and formalization of claims for relief are always best left to a qualified attorney, and beyond the scope of this book. Our purpose here is to provide an overview of how the system works, and an understanding of the usual methods of dispute resolution, as well as brief explanations of some of the more common causes of action and types of relief which often appear in contract litigation.

---

300 There is a "special case" consideration in regard to filing a lawsuit even though the contract requires mediation or arbitration. If the applicable statute of limitations is about to run out, and there is no agreement tolling the statute of limitations, then it is advisable to file the lawsuit, so as not to lose all rights to pursue the underlying claim. The suit can always be dismissed, later, if alternate dispute resolution is effective.

Mediation

Mediation is a process which seeks to resolve disputes between parties through an agreed settlement. Some contracts include a requirement that the parties attempt this method of dispute resolution before commencing arbitration or litigation. Where such a contractual requirement exists, failure to mediate may raise an affirmative defense against the claims of a party who failed or refused to mediate before initiating a lawsuit or arbitration proceeding. Also, in some contracts, mediation may be encouraged by including a condition precedent in the contract's attorney's fees provision, precluding any award of attorney's fees to a prevailing party which failed to mediate in good faith before commencing arbitration or litigation.

The principle benefit of mediation is that it is an inexpensive method for resolving disputes quickly. It may also prove useful in reducing the number of parties (and hence issues) in a multi-party dispute, in advance of the remaining parties proceeding to arbitration or litigation. The disadvantages are that it may be no more than a delaying tactic when there is no reasonable possibility of settlement between the parties, that there can be nothing gained beyond simple recovery (if that much), and that it requires early disclosure of some portion, at least, of the parties' respective legal theories, evidence, and trial strategies.

There are generally two formats in which mediation is conducted: the single-room format and the multi-room format. Not infrequently, a mediation may commence using one format, and shift to the alternative format at some point in the process. Each has its own advantages and disadvantages. Single-room mediation can often be concluded more quickly, but is more likely to erupt into recriminations or open hostility between the parties, and to fail to achieve a settlement. Multi-room mediation, with the mediator shuttling back and forth between the separated parties, can take considerably longer to conclude since arguments, offers, counteroffers, compromises and concessions are exchanged solely through the mediator, rather than directly between the parties or their counsel. Essentially, the mediator advocates on behalf of each party, separately, seeking to obtain concessions and compromises from each side sufficient to bring their contradictory claims into close enough proximity to allow a settlement.

Prior to the commencement of the mediation proceedings, the parties will generally provide the mediator with a mediation brief, outlining the factual and legal basis for that party's claims. Such briefs are often marked as "confidential," so that the other party does not see it, and the mediator cannot discuss its contents with the other party without express permission. This is generally done so that the mediator can understand the full strength of the briefing party's position, while not giving away trial strategies, legal theories, or undisclosed evidence to the other party in advance of trial, should the mediation fail.

Nothing which occurs in the course of a failed mediation can be used directly as evidence or for impeachment if the dispute proceeds to arbitration or litigation. Any admissions or concessions which were made during the mediation process are generally inadmissible in any later proceedings. This evidentiary rule is meant to encourage the parties to openly discuss all aspects of their dispute in an effort to achieve a compromise through mediation. This does not mean, however, that information obtained during the mediation cannot be used later to develop new admissible evidence through investigation or discovery, or to identify new witnesses or lines of questioning for use at a subsequent trial or arbitration.

It is essential that the individuals necessary to executing a final settlement agreement be present for the mediation process, either personally or through a representative with power of attorney granting the right to enter into a binding settlement agreement. Generally, no one leaves the mediation until it has become clear that no settlement is possible, or until there is a final, signed settlement agreement. It is not unusual for a mediation to continue through the night, seeking to reduce the disputed issues to a common agreement in the form of a final, executed settlement.

It's been said, with some justification, that a successful mediation is one from which the parties each emerge feeling equally screwed. No one "wins" in a mediation. Instead, it is a process of compromises through which each side agrees to give up some portion of that to which they believe they are fully entitled, in order to avoid further costs and expenses of pursuing their claims, and to eliminate the possibility of losing even more should they be unsuccessful in arbitration or litigation of their dispute.

Arbitration

In arbitration, a dispute is submitted to an impartial third person or persons, rather than to a court. Arbitrators are usually attorneys or retired judges who can be selected directly by the parties, or chosen in accordance with the terms of a contract in which the parties have previously agreed to a particular arbitration service or procedure, or they can be appointed by a court. If there is no contract and the parties decide to arbitrate rather than litigate their dispute, then one common procedure is for each party to choose an arbitrator, with those two arbitrators then selecting a third.

The arbitrators' decision is given after an informal, trial-like proceeding in which each side presents evidence and witnesses. When parties submit to arbitration, they can agree to be bound by and comply with the arbitrators' decision (binding arbitration) or they can reserve the right to reject the arbitrators' decision (non-binding arbitration) in which case they may thereafter elect to proceed to litigation if either party feels a better result might be obtained through a formal trial.

Dispute resolution through arbitration generally occurs in any of four situations:

(1) When a contract between parties provides for arbitration of disputes between them; or

(2) When the law requires that a particular type of dispute be submitted to arbitration prior to commencing litigation; or

(3) When the parties to an existing dispute agree to submit the matter to binding or non-binding arbitration; or

(4) When a court orders it, either in an attempt to seek resolution of a lawsuit without the expense of a formal trial, or when a party has petitioned the court for an order to compel the other party to participate in contract-based arbitration.

Arbitration proceedings are almost identical to what occurs in litigation, except that the procedural rules which govern most arbitration do not generally provide for a discovery process. Because arbitration is often based upon a contractual agreement however, this lack can be addressed by the parties, in advance, by providing (in their arbitration agreement or provision) that the applicable arbitration rules will be modified by inclusion of discovery, usually by stipulating that Federal or some specified state's statutory discovery procedures will be applicable.

The other key difference between arbitration and litigation is that arbitrators do not have authority to directly enforce their findings and awards. Following arbitration, those findings and award may be submitted to a court by the prevailing party, at which time the court will convert the monetary award into an enforceable judgment and *may* incorporate some or all of the arbitrators' findings as part of that judgment.

Awards obtained through arbitration are essentially limited to monetary damages, although an arbitrator's findings of fact and conclusions of law, if later adopted by the court, may have an equitable effect, such as to construe a contract or to compel performance of an obligation or duty. However, because of this lack of direct judicial authority, arbitration cannot be used to obtain injunctive relief. In consequence, a party contractually obliged to arbitrate disputes may nonetheless be entitled to file a court action for the limited purpose of obtaining an injunction, unless an underlying contract lawfully[301] waives or precludes injunctive relief.

Apart from those differences, arbitration is conducted in much the same manner as a trial. An initiating party pleads its claims, and the other party responds with denials of any disputed claims and, if it chooses, with counterclaims of its own, to which the other party responds. If discovery is allowed by the arbitration agreement, the parties use that process to develop additional evidence to support their position. The case is then presented before one or more arbitrators who hear the parties' legal arguments and evidence. If there is a single arbitrator, he or she will issue a decision in the form of written conclusions and an award in favor of the prevailing party. Where there are multiple arbitrators, they must deliberate to arrive at their decision by a majority. Where there is no unanimous decision, the minority may issue its own dissenting findings, but such dissents have no force nor legal effect, although they may

301 In some cases, a waiver or preclusion of injunctive relief within a contract has been held to be unconscionable or otherwise unenforceable. *However*, when such an issue arises in a contract which contains an arbitration clause, such determination may be held to be outside the court's jurisdiction to determine arbitrability, and instead lie within the exclusive jurisdiction of the arbitrator. In consequence, it may be necessary to obtain an ***arbitrator's*** ruling as to the propriety of a court-ordered injunction, first, before the court would issue such an injunction. Since injunctive relief is equitable, however, and frequently addresses emergency situations, many courts will issue a temporary order with injunctive effect to preserve the *status quo* until the arbitrator can hear and rule on the issue.

influence a reviewing court's thinking, or affect a party's acquiescence or rejection of a non-binding arbitration award.

Because judicial policy strongly favors dispute resolution without litigation and formal trial, the courts of most jurisdictions support the arbitration process in a number of ways. Not only will courts compel arbitration when there is a legal or contractual basis for doing so, but may also make the court's subpoena power available to compel attendance of witnesses and production of evidence to facilitate the arbitration process. Following arbitration, the arbitrator's findings of fact and conclusions of law may be adopted by the court, and the arbitrators' final award converted into an enforceable court judgment.

The principal advantage of arbitration is that it can generally be concluded in far less time than an average lawsuit. Up-front, out- of pocket costs, however, are likely to be greater in arbitration, since at least one of the parties will be required to pay all or a portion of the arbitration fees in advance.[302] Depending on the arbitration service used, the number of arbitrators involved, and the hourly rate charged by particular arbitrators, costs can range from several hundred to several thousand dollars per day for arbitration sessions. In addition to an initial fee paid at the outset when initiating the arbitration process, a sum equivalent to the estimated total fees for the arbitration must generally be deposited before the first session, with any unused balance refundable at the conclusion of the proceedings. Of course, each party will also have to pay its own attorney's costs and expenses. If there is no discovery in the arbitration, those legal expenses should be considerably less than for litigation of the same dispute. As with litigation, recovery of attorney's fees as part of an arbitration award will be dependent on the presence or absence of statutory authority or an attorney's fees provision within the underlying contract.

With non-binding arbitration, the parties will have some period of time — usually at least thirty days following the arbitrator's decision — to reject that outcome and proceed to civil litigation and a trial *de novo*, which retries the issues as though an arbitration or earlier trial had never taken place.

Civil Litigation

Litigation — that is, the presentation by adversaries of argument, evidence and testimony before a judge or jury empowered by the government to impose penalties and grant relief — has been the traditional method of nonviolent[303] dispute resolution since the dawn of civilization. The forms in which such litigation is commenced, prosecuted, tried, and

---

302 Most commonly, each party pays its proportional share of the arbitration fees, which may be recoverable by the prevailing party as part of the arbitrator's award. In some instances, however, the underlying contract may specify than one party — usually the party with greater financial resources — will advance all arbitration costs, regardless of which party initiates the arbitration process.

303 Traditional *violent* forms of dispute resolution (*e.g.*, battery, murder, war, trial by combat, *etc.*) are far older, presumably predating civilization itself, but outside the scope of our discussion.

concluded have changed considerably over millennia, even though our current adversarial system retains some slight vestiges of its trial-by-combat origins. Distinct differences in procedure, applicable laws, and nomenclature are also apparent when comparing various countries' litigation methods. Such differences even exist between separate jurisdictions in a single country, particularly in respect to procedural rules but also as to some substantive laws.

Civil litigation begins with an aggrieved party's filing of a complaint, petition, or claim which sets forth allegations of fact and the specific relief to which the complaining party believes he or she is entitled, based on those alleged facts. In most instances, the complaining party will be referred to as "Plaintiff," but in other situations or jurisdictions he or she may be called the Petitioner, Claimant, or Complainant.[304] Upon filing of the complaint (called a "petition" or "claim" in some jurisdictions), the court will issue a summons, directed to the named defendants, informing them that a suit has been filed and commanding them to respond in writing within a stated period of time. That time period begins to run when the summons and complaint have been served on each named defendant.[305] If a served defendant fails to file a written response within the allotted time, a default may be entered against that defendant. Once a defendant has answered the complaint, the case is said to be "at issue," and the parties will enter the "discovery" phase of litigation, in which they seek to gather evidence for trial. If undisputed facts show that, as a matter of law, judgment should enter for one party or the other, the case may be disposed of by the court on a motion for summary judgment or equivalent motion. Otherwise the case will proceed to trial. The judge will be the final determiner of all equitable claims and of all issues of law. If there is a jury, then the jury will determine all of the *facts* of the case.[306] If there is no jury, then the judge will be the trier of fact, as well as the trier of law.

The body of American law is drawn in largest part from the Common Law of England, and British legal precedents and traditions continue to influence federal jurisprudence, as well as the legal systems of almost all[307] of the United States. The American system can be especially confusing to outsiders — particularly since it is not a single system at all, but rather an

---

304 To avoid confusion, the initiating party will hereafter be referred to as "plaintiff" and the party being sued will be referred to as "defendant," with the reminder that such nomenclature is by no means universally used.

305 Personal service may be waived however, either by an express agreement ("waiver of service") or by a voluntary appearance, either in person or by counsel, in which the defendant argues the merits of the case without reserving the right to challenge jurisdiction.

306 In *criminal* cases, jurors also have the power — although arguably not the *right* — to rule upon issues of law as well as issues of fact by refusing to enforce laws which are unjust. This disfavored practice of acquitting defendants who are technically guilty is referred to as "jury nullification." While it is now an almost-universally condemned practice, and modern juries are seldom informed that they have this power, jury nullification was successfully used in the past to denounce unpopular laws. *E.g.*, Northern juries consistently refused to convict anyone charged with violating the Fugitive Slave Act.

307 The notable exception is Louisiana, which preserves its heritage as a French possession under the Napoleonic Code which embodied legal traditions at variance with English Common Law's reliance upon trial by jury, judicial precedent, and the doctrine of *stare decisis*. The Supremacy Clause of the U.S. Constitution required Louisiana to integrate a number of common law elements into its state constitution and laws, but much of the French legal system's legacy remains within its statutes and procedures.

agglomeration of more than fifty similar-but-different systems of individual legal codes, operating under the aegis of a unifying Federal system which may, under certain circumstances, preempt and override state laws. Some understanding of this diverse system is necessary to a discussion of remedies because not every remedy is available in every jurisdiction, and selecting the proper forum can be crucial to successful litigation.

Conduct which will justify an award of damages or other judicial relief is referred to as "actionable conduct." However, as we have seen, conduct which is actionable under the laws of one state may be a complete non-issue across the invisible boundary which divides that state from its neighbor.[308] Forum selection is therefore an important part of the legal analysis which precedes civil litigation.

There are a number of possible grounds for establishing jurisdiction for civil litigation. Here are a few of the most common:

- The county or judicial district in which one or more of the named defendants maintains a principal residence or place of business;
- The county or judicial district where the contract underlying a dispute was entered into;
- The county or judicial district where obligations of the disputed contract were (or were to have been) performed;
- The county or judicial district where obligations under the terms of the disputed contract were incurred;
- The county or judicial district where disputed real property is situated;
- The county or judicial district where an actionable incident occurred;
- A county or judicial district and court specified within a contract which underlies the dispute (provided there is some logical nexus and legal ground for the forum selection).

Some types of actions may only be brought in federal court, while others may only be brought in state court. This does not mean, however, that two separate cases must be filed. Instead, where there is a basis for federal jurisdiction, all of the state law causes of action can be included in the federal complaint, and a federal court will try the all of the claims, applying federal *procedure* to the entire case, but interpreting the applicable state's substantive laws as to the state law claims. When a federal court tries state law causes of action, it is exercising what is referred to as "pendent" jurisdiction. A case may be filed in federal court under the following circumstances:

308 Publicity rights cases provide a prime example of the inconsistencies in substantive law between various states. (See Chapter 2 , "Name & Likeness")

- When at least one cause of action is based on a claim under *federal* law, such as an action for copyright infringement under Title 17 of the U.S. Code, or where the matter at issue affects interstate commerce;
- When the United States government, or an agency of the U.S. Government, is named as a party to the action;
- When *none* of the plaintiffs are residents of the same state as *any* of the named defendants.[309]

Regardless of the forum selected, and allowing for differences in procedure and nomenclature between jurisdictions, civil litigation will generally proceed in the following manner:

A) ***Pleading Phase***

(1) Plaintiff prepares and files complaint.

(2) Court clerk issues summons.

(3) Plaintiff has summons and complaint served on defendants.

(4) Either,

(a) Defendant fails to file a timely response, in which case a default may be entered against the non-responding defendant and plaintiff may obtain an enforceable judgment against that defendant; or

(b) Defendant files an Answer or other responsive pleading. (Defendants may respond in a number of ways, discussed below. The simple, ultimate response, however, will be a defendant's "Answer" to the complaint, at which point the case is said to be "at issue" before the court.)

B) ***Discovery Phase***[310]

(1) The parties gather evidence by a number of methods which include:

(a) Written interrogatories to a party;

(b) Requests for admissions by a party;

---

309 This is referred to as "complete diversity of citizenship" (or simply "diversity") jurisdiction, as provided by Article III section 2 of the U.S. Constitution. The district court will apply federal procedural rules, but will adjudicate the matter in accordance with the substantive laws of whichever state would have otherwise had jurisdiction over the case. Under diversity jurisdiction, the case will usually be filed in the federal district in which one or more of the named defendants maintains a principal residence or place of business, unless there are legal grounds for selecting another federal district.

310 In federal cases, the discovery process is streamlined by Rule 26 of the Federal Rules of Civil Procedure, which requires (among other things) that the parties meet informally and exchange discoverable evidence early in the litigation process. Only after having done so may the parties initiate the more formal, traditional forms of discovery.

(c) Demands for a party to produce documents or other tangible things for inspection and copying, or to permit examination of places or of persons;

(d) Deposition testimony of parties and of non-parties, including requirements for production of documents or other tangible things at deposition. (Note that non-parties must be personally served with court-authorized subpoenas commanding them to appear and/or to produce documents.);

(e) Exchange of expert witness information and depositions of expert witnesses.

(2) ***Law & Motion Phase***

(a) Discovery motions. (Formal presentation to the court of discovery issues which the parties — or their counsel – cannot resolve informally between themselves. *E.g.*, a motion to compel responses to interrogatories.);

(b) Motions seeking imposition of sanctions against the other party or their counsel for improper conduct. Sanctions can include a monetary award, preclusion of evidence, preclusion of an issue, striking of an answer, dismissal of the case, or such other sanction as the court deems appropriate to the circumstances.

(c) Motions for summary judgment or summary adjudication, which (if granted) can have the effect of ending the case entirely, or of eliminating certain causes of action pled by the complaint.

(d) Other dispositive motions, varying by jurisdiction, such as a motion for judgment on the pleadings.

(e) Other motions, varying by jurisdiction, and usually procedural in nature.

C) ***Pretrial Phase***

(1) Conferences with court, seeking to minimize the number of issues which will be presented at trial;

(2) Voluntary or mandatory settlement conferences, attempting to resolve case without trial;

(3) Exchange of witness lists, or preparation of a joint witness list;

(4) Exchange of exhibit lists, or preparation of a joint exhibit list;

(5) Submission of proposed written jury instructions (if there is to be a jury.)

D) ***Trial Phase.***

(1) Any last-minute motions (motions *in limine*) will be heard, usually for the purpose of limiting issues or precluding certain evidence or testimony at trial.

(2) If a jury trial, then jury selection will precede any presentation of evidence or testimony.

(3) Counsel for each side may make an opening statement.

(4) Plaintiff's counsel will then call witnesses to be examined and cross-examined. If there is any physical evidence, it must be introduced through the testimony of witnesses who can establish a foundation for that evidence.

(5) Once plaintiff's counsel has finished presenting plaintiff's case, defendant's counsel may make an opening statement, if none was given earlier and the right to do so was reserved.

(6) Defendant may call witnesses to be examined and cross-examined, and may introduce additional evidence through those witnesses.

(7) After the defense rests, plaintiff's counsel may call additional witnesses to rebut the testimony or evidence introduced by the defense.

(8) Closing statements are made by plaintiff's counsel, then by defendant's counsel, and then (usually) plaintiff's counsel is permitted a final statement.

(9) If there is a jury, the court will read the jury instructions which they are to follow in deliberating on the facts of the case and reaching their verdict. If there is no jury, then the judge will determine the facts and issue a verdict.

(10) The judge will enter a final judgment which will, in most cases,[311] embody the verdict.

E) ***Post-judgment phase.***

(1) The defeated party may file a notice of appeal in a higher court within a prescribed period of time following entry of judgment;[312]

(2) The prevailing party may commence efforts to enforce the judgment, potentially including seizure of funds or other property to satisfy any monetary award.

---

311 In civil cases, a judge may decide to override a jury verdict which the court finds to be contrary to law or unsupported by the evidence. Such "Judgment Notwithstanding Verdict" ("JNOV" or Judgment *non obstante veredicto*) is unusual, and will almost invariably be appealed to a higher court. In criminal cases, the judge may also overrule a jury verdict of *conviction* by entering a acquittal JNOV, but a jury verdict of acquittal is sacrosanct and may not be overturned except upon a showing that it was fraudulently obtained, in which exceptional circumstance the acquittal may be vacated and an entirely new trial may be held, if no jeopardy attached in the original proceeding.

312 If the judgment is *monetary*, a notice of appeal will not stop collection of that judgment. The party appealing may, however, obtain a *bond* (undertaking) which will stop attempts at judgment collection during the pendency of the appeal.

Of course, this is a very simplified and cursory overview of litigation proceedings, and it can sometimes take years between the filing of the complaint and entry of judgment following trial. A subsequent appeal — which will have its own procedural framework — can extend that time for additional years. The time and expense of litigation is one of the reasons why nearly 80% of all civil lawsuits end in settlement rather than trial.[313] Another reason is that, in the course of discovery, it is not unusual to discover that your case is not quite as strong as originally believed. Add to those concerns the fact that the outcome of a trial is *never* certain, and settlement begins to look more attractive, particularly as legal costs and expenses continue to mount.

> "Rare, indeed, is the litigant who doesn't lose some skirmishes on the way to winning the war. Lawsuits usually involve many reasonable disputed issues and a lawyer who takes on only those battles he is certain of winning is probably not serving his client vigorously enough..." Cabrales v. Los Angeles (1991, 9th Cir.) 935 F.2d 1050, 1053

In the next chapter, we will discuss some of the more common types of relief available through civil litigation. Before doing so, however, here is a closer look at the pleading phase during which a plaintiff's complaint introduces those specific causes of action or claims for relief into the proceedings.

Historically, there were very strict rules regarding pleading, as the common law recognized only few specific forms of action, and a plaintiff had to fit the facts of his or her case into one of those limited forms, or risk having the action terminated without any trial on the merits. A complaint could be challenged, amended, and challenged yet again, almost indefinitely, until it had been reduced to a single issue of law or fact which could proceed to trial.

Additionally, under the common law as it existed prior to the 1870's, English courts of law and courts of equity were two completely separate systems. To seek relief in equity, a plaintiff had to demonstrate that there was no remedy *at law* which could provide adequate relief. Vestiges of that separation remain in our present system, and equitable remedies may not be available when legal remedies are deemed sufficient.[314]

---

313 Although all trial lawyers know this, it remains impossible to determine which one case out of five will go all the way to trial. In consequence, *every* case must be dealt with and prepared for as though it were going all the way. Clients, anticipating settlement, are often resentful of the amounts which their lawyers may charge them for discovery and trial preparation. No matter how likely settlement may be, lawyers have a duty of zealous representation which requires that they adequately prepare for all foreseeable contingencies. Clients would be far more resentful if their case went to trial and their lawyer had failed to obtain admissible evidence through discovery, or was otherwise unprepared to present a complete and effective case.

314 Trial by jury was available only in courts of law, while in courts of equity the judge was the sole trier of fact as well as of law. The same remains true today, despite merger of the two types of court; all issues of equity will be decided by the judge, even when a jury is empaneled as the trier of fact for other issues within the same case.

Common law pleading was eventually supplanted by code pleading, which merged law and equity, and eliminated the strict limitation on causes of action which had existed under the common law. In code pleading, the important emphasis was on alleging the facts of the case.

Pleadings, whether by plaintiff or by defendant, serve four traditional functions:

(1) To give notice of each particular claim or defense; and

(2) To allege the underlying facts which each party believes to exist; and

(3) To identify and restrict the issues to be adjudicated; and

(4) On the basis of the foregoing, to allow for the prompt disposition of frivolous claims and insubstantial defenses.

In code pleading states, a pleader is required to plead the "ultimate facts" of the case. For example, the California Code of Civil Procedure requires that a complaint provide "a statement of the facts constituting the cause of action in ordinary and concise language."[315] This is also referred to as "fact" pleading.

Conversely, the Federal Rules of Civil Procedure require only "a short and plain statement of the claim showing that the pleader is entitled to relief."[316] This is referred to as "notice" pleading, and fulfils only the first of the four traditional roles of pleading, eliminating elaborate fact pleading. Nonetheless, federal pleadings cannot be wholly devoid of the factual elements of the underlying claim. In Bell Atlantic Corp. v. Twombly (2007) 127 S. Ct. 1955, the United States Supreme Court addressed the issue of sufficiency of pleadings, holding that a federal complaint "requires more than labels and conclusions [...] Factual allegations must be enough to raise a right to relief above the speculative level..." [127 S. Ct. at 1965] Justice Souter, writing for the majority, summarized the opinion as follows: "[W]e do not require heightened fact pleading of specifics, but only enough facts to state a claim to relief that is plausible on its face." [Id., at 1974]

At a bare minimum, a complaint should contain the following elements:

(1) A statement of jurisdiction, alleging the grounds upon which the case is filed in a particular court;

(2) An identification of the parties to the litigation, both plaintiff and defendant, stating their respective capacities and domicile. In most jurisdictions, it is permissible to include pseudonymous defendants ("DOES") to preserve plaintiff's right to amend by inclusion of previously-unknown persons.[317]

---

315 California Code of Civil Procedure § 425.10.(a)

316 F.R.Civ.P. Rule 8.(a)(2)

317 Such fictitiously-named defendants are not allowed in cases filed in federal court on the basis of "diversity" jurisdiction, since it is impossible to establish than an unidentified defendant does not, in fact, reside in the same states as a plaintiff.

(3) A statement of each claim or cause of action asserted by the plaintiff, and sufficient allegations of fact to demonstrate that the claims are at least plausible; and

(4) A prayer stating the relief which plaintiff seeks to obtain through the action.

The foregoing will satisfy the requirements of "notice pleading," but in "code pleading" jurisdictions the complaint must also include a concise recital of facts which plaintiff alleges to be true and which include an allegation of each and every essential element of each cause of action pled. Failure to allege an essential element may cause the complaint to be dismissed — albeit usually with leave to amend — for "failure to allege facts sufficient to state a cause of action." That is, assuming each and every allegation of the complaint to be true, some essential factual element to a particular cause of action is nonetheless absent.

For example, the essential elements for a cause of action for breach of contract are (1) the existence of a written/oral/implied contract between plaintiff and defendant; (2) plaintiff's performance of all of plaintiff's obligations except those which plaintiff was excused or prevented from performing; (3) defendant's breach of that contract on or around a particular date, by some stated action or failure to act; and (4) that plaintiff has suffered loss, damage or harm as a proximate result of defendant's breach. A complaint which fails to include all four of those necessary factual allegations, and to thereby to put each of those alleged facts into issue, would be facially defective in a code pleading jurisdiction.

Obviously, in order to plead a viable claim for relief in such jurisdictions, the pleader must first know the **essential elements** of the causes of action upon which his or her claim or claims may be based. Plaintiff cannot, as a practical matter, allege the existence or nonexistence of each and every factor which might affect the outcome of the litigation, so the general rule is that each party bears the responsibility for pleading those matters upon which that party must produce proof at trial: plaintiff must plead all of the essential elements for each cause of action alleged in the complaint, and defendant must plead each appropriate affirmative defense. Thus Plaintiff's omission of an "essential element" of a cause of action in the complaint may render that cause of action ineffective and subject to demurrer, motion to strike. or an affirmative defense. Likewise, defendant's failure to plead a particular affirmative defense in his or her answer to the complaint may constitute a waiver of that defense.

Of course, a defendant's initial response to the complaint need not necessarily be an answer, but may be any one or more of several alternative responsive pleadings including (without limitation) the following.

- Motion for change of venue, challenging the jurisdiction of the forum selected by plaintiff, and seeking to have the case transferred to another court for trial.[318]

318 A motion for change of venue may also be brought after filing of an answer, on different grounds, most usually having to do with the selected forum being inconvenient for necessary witnesses.

- Notice of removal to federal court, on the grounds that there is a federal question, complete diversity of citizenship, or other grounds for federal jurisdiction.[319]
- A motion to strike all or portions of the pleading as being contrary to law, superfluous, or on other legal grounds.
- A general or special demurrer, which challenges the legal sufficiency of the pleading by asking the court to find that, even assuming all allegations of the pleading to be true, the pleading fails to allege all of the essential elements necessary to state a valid claim for which relief can be obtained.[320]

Certain defenses, such as lack of jurisdiction over the defendant, improper venue, insufficiency of process, and insufficiency of service of process may be deemed to have been waived if not brought by motion in lieu of an answer, or contemporaneously with an answer.

Because the law favors trial on the merits of a case, the outcome of most hearings on responsive pleading motions and demurrers will be to either deny the motion, requiring the defendant to answer the complaint as originally pled, or to grant[321] the motion "with leave to amend," allowing the plaintiff to correct perceived defects in the pleading, after which the defendant must file a timely answer or other responsive pleading to the amended complaint. It is not unusual for this process to be repeated several times, and for a case to eventually go to trial on the basis of a complaint which was repeatedly amended before the defendant was ever required to file an answer.

The purpose of an answer it to place into issue those allegations of plaintiff's complaint which defendant contends are untrue, and to plead affirmative defenses which provide legal and factual grounds which excuse defendant from some or all liability to plaintiff. Answers generally take one of two forms: a "general denial" or "specific denials."

A "general denial" usually consists of a single sentence which simply states that "defendant generally denies each and every allegation of plaintiff's complaint." A general denial is commonly used when defendant contests the basic substance of the complaint, even though many or the allegations may be true. But general denials are not permissible in every instance. For example, federal courts limit the use of general denials to cases in which defendant actually

---

319 Such notice (theoretically) stays all proceedings in a state court where the complaint was originally filed. Any challenge to the removal must be heard in the federal court to which the case was removed, or the federal judge to whom it is assigned may, on the court's own motion or that of a party, order the case remanded to state court, either for lack of federal jurisdiction or under an abstention doctrine.

320 Under the Federal Rules of Civil Procedure ("F.R.Civ.P."), demurrers have been abolished and replaced by a motion to dismiss for failure to state a claim [F.R.Civ.P. Rule 12.(b)(6)] which operates as a general demurrer. However, because F.R.Civ.P. Rule 8 requires only "a short and plain statement of the claim showing that the pleader is entitled to relief," complaints are only likely to be dismissed under Rule 12(b)(6) if plaintiff's case fails completely, as a matter of law, such as by reason of a statute of limitations or where the statute of frauds precludes enforcement of a contract.

321 Technically, a demurrer is a form of objection, and is therefore "overruled" or "sustained," rather than "denied" or "granted."

intends to controvert *each and every one of plaintiff's allegations.*[322] Since it will be an exceedingly rare complaint in which *none* of the facts alleged is true, general denials are disfavored in federal court. There are also other restrictions on general denials in certain states. For example, in California, if a complaint is verified,[323] the answer must be verified as well, and cannot be a general denial.[324]

Conversely, "specific denials" involve an allegation-by-allegation analysis of the complaint, denying only those allegations which defendant actually intends to contest, usually by reference to the paragraph numbers in which such allegations appear. This can become somewhat challenging, however, where a numbered paragraph in the complaint actually contains multiple allegations, since failure to deny an allegation is deemed to be an *admission* as to the truth of that allegation. If the responding party has no knowledge as to the truth of an allegation, it is permissible (and best practice) to deny that allegation on the stated grounds of "lack of information or belief."

Even if plaintiff's allegations are true, defendant may still be able to present additional facts which establish a defense. Such affirmative defenses must be specifically pled in defendant's answer so that plaintiff is on notice of defendant's allegations and has an opportunity to prepare to refute them. An affirmative defense is a statement which introduces matters which do not deny plaintiff's claims, but instead offer a factual or legal excuse which avoids defendant's liability or bars plaintiff from some or all relief. With few exceptions, an affirmative defense cannot be introduced at trial if it has not been pled by the defendant's answer, although the court may, in its discretion, grant leave to amend the answer to add affirmative defenses, either prior to trial or at the time of trial.[325]

Rule 8.(c) of the Federal Rules of Civil Procedure lists nineteen affirmative defenses which must be specifically pled to avoid waiver, but that list is far from complete. In fact, Rule 8.(c) concludes with "... and any other matter constituting an avoidance or affirmative defense."[326] There are literally hundreds of other affirmative defenses which a defendant may offer in answering a complaint. These include equitable defenses, which appeal to basic notions of equity and fairness. Equitable defenses may include illegality, such as a contract for purchase of illegal goods, or fraud. Another example is defendant's claim that the plaintiff has "unclean hands," meaning that the plaintiff acted in a malicious or wrongful manner in regard to the

322 See F.R.Civ.P. Rule 8.(b)

323 "Verified" refers to an attached statement — a "verification" — signed by the party under penalty of perjury, attesting that he or she is familiar with the facts of the case, and that the contents of the attached pleading are true.

324 See California Code of Civil Procedure § 431.30.(d)

325 Certain fundamental jurisdictional defects, such as a plaintiff's lack of standing to sue, cannot be waived and may be introduced at any time.

326 The affirmative defenses listed by F.R.Civ.P. Rule 8.(c) are: "...accord and satisfaction; arbitration and award; assumption of risk; contributory negligence; discharge in bankruptcy; duress; estoppel; failure of consideration; fraud; illegality; injury by fellow servant; laches; license; payment; release; res judicata; statute of frauds; statute of limitations; waiver; and any other matter constituting an avoidance or affirmative defense."

transactions that form the basis of plaintiff's claim. It should be borne in mind that defendant (or defendant's counsel) is bound by the "doctrine of truthful pleading," and may be required to certify to the court that there is a legal and factual basis for each defense pled.[327] Moreover, adversaries are certain to inquire through discovery as to the evidentiary basis upon which a party relies in respect to each allegation or defense pled.

In addition to answering the complaint, a defendant may also seek affirmative *relief* by a cross-complaint or counterclaim. This will in most respects be the same as a complaint, with only the designations of the parties changed. That is, instead of "plaintiff" it will refer to the "cross-complainant" or "counter-claimant" and, instead of "defendants" it will refer to "cross-defendants" or "counter-defendants." If it adds new persons (not previously parties to the action) as cross-defendants, a summons will need to be obtained from the court. Those newly-added parties will need to be served, usually by personal service, but parties who have already appeared in the lawsuit are deemed served by mailing a copy to their addresses of record in the action. As with a complaint, the cross-defendants must file an answer or other responsive pleading to the cross-complaint. Once answered, the allegations and claims of the cross-complaint are also "at issue" before the court, and will be determined at trial, unless disposed of by settlement or summary adjudication prior to trial.

Taking a case to trial can be an expensive proposition for several reasons, and the foregoing barely hints at the complexities involved. Nonetheless, litigation is often the only viable means for obtaining relief. Before commencing a lawsuit, it's essential to analyze the facts of the case objectively and, on the basis of those facts — and the ability to support those facts by admissible evidence — determine what specific causes of action apply and are likely to succeed at trial.

As we've said repeatedly, "Anyone can sue *anyone*, at *any* time, for *any* reason, or *for no reason at all*." There are penalties for frivolous lawsuits, and such suits seldom survive the pleading phase, but all it takes is a brief, written complaint and a filing fee to commence litigation. However, just because one *can* do something doesn't mean one *should*. Pre-pleading analysis of a potential case requires several steps, including, but not limited to:

(1) Determining the supportable facts. For this purpose "facts" are limited to concrete events: something that someone said or did (or was required to do but did not), something that happened (or will happen) as a result, and some specific, non-speculative damage that resulted or will result.

(2) Developing a cogent legal theory of the case. This requires determining causal links by analyzing how what someone else said or did (or failed to do) actually

327 F.R.Civ.P. Rule 11 states, in part: "By presenting [...] a pleading [...] or other paper, an attorney or unrepresented party is certifying that [...] the claims, defenses, and other legal contentions therein are warranted by [...] law; [that] the allegations and other factual contentions have evidentiary support [...]; and the denials of factual contentions are warranted on the evidence or, if specifically so identified, are reasonably based on a lack of information or belief." Some states also have equivalent rules. (*E.g.*, California CCP § 128.7) Sanctions for violation of Rule 11 can be severe.

caused damage, and ascertaining what legal duties (if any) the parties owed each other.

(3) Comparing the facts and legal analysis to the essential elements required for potential causes of action.

(4) Selecting those causes of action which are most likely to succeed on the basis of the supportable facts.

(5) Determining the appropriate jurisdiction and forum.[328]

While the law permits individuals[329] to act as their own lawyers in civil matters, it is not a particularly good idea to try to "do it yourself" for several reasons, not the least of which is that you are likely too close to the issues and emotions of the case to be objective. An attorney provides both the legal expertise and the professional detachment necessary to analyze, plead, and present your case effectively.

Damages

With the exception of equitable causes of action which may seek relief through some form of judicial order, most litigation seeks relief through an award of money. Such an award is referred to as "damages," which fall into several different, overlapping categories.

- **General damages** are the natural, necessary, and unavoidable result of the conduct or occurrence underlying the action.

- **Actual damages** or **compensatory damages** are those which are sufficient to fully recompense plaintiff for the actual loss, injury or harm suffered, but not more than that.

- **Consequential damages** are a form of special damages, awardable for loss or injury which does not flow directly from defendant's actions, but rather from consequences or subsequent result of such actions. That is, "but for" the damages proximately resulting from defendant's conduct, the consequential loss would not have occurred. Consequential damages must be specially pled and proven.

---

328 There is an additional, overriding factor which will seldom, if ever, be discussed in an academic environment. Is there a "deep pocket" on the other side of the case? As a practical matter, it makes little sense to pursue an action against someone who cannot afford to pay an eventual judgment against them.

329 But not corporations or other legal entities, which must be represented by a licensed attorney except in narrow exceptions such as "small claims" actions.

- **Direct damages** are those which occur immediately and unavoidably as a result of the conduct or occurrence underlying the action.

- **Exemplary damages** or **punitive damages** are intended to punish wrongdoing and to discourage the defendant and others from engaging in similar conduct in the future. Such damages are only available in certain types of action, and generally require a finding that defendant's conduct was "wanton, willful, oppressive, malicious, or shocking to the conscience." Punitive and exemplary damages are not available in contract causes of action, but are available for contract-related torts, such as fraud.[330]

- **Incidental damages** are commercially reasonable costs and expenses which arise as a consequence of a breach of contract in certain commercial transactions.

- **Irreparable damages** are those for which no amount of money would be sufficient to offset the harm suffered, so that a monetary award would be an inadequate remedy. The term "irreparable damage" does not refer to a monetary award, but is instead generally seen in equitable actions for injunctive relief, where the inadequacy of monetary damages is an element in determining whether an injunction is appropriate. Irreparable damage may also appear as a predicate to punitive damages.

- **Nominal damages** are a small sum awarded where it is difficult or impossible to correlate a compensatory sum to loss or injury, or insufficient proof of the extent of loss or injury, yet where there has nonetheless been some real invasion of rights, or some loss or injury. Nominal damages are a technicality most often used to allow for a further award of punitive or special damages, or an award of attorney's fees.

- **Special damages** are those which are an actual, but not inescapable, result of the conduct or occurrence complained of. That is, they as a natural and proximate consequence of such conduct or occurrence in a particular case by reason of special circumstances or conditions not usual to such types of cases generally. To be entitled to special damages, they and the conditions which might permit them must be pled and proven.

- **Statutory damages** are those which are set by legislative enactment for certain specified causes of action. Generally, in actions where statutory damages are established (*e.g.*, for infringement of copyright), plaintiff may elect to accept those damages in lieu of proving "actual" damages.

---

330 The terms "punitive damages" and "exemplary damages" are synonymous in *effect*, but differ in the rationale which underlies them. Punitive damages are retributory, and intended to punish the defendant for past conduct. Exemplary damages are intended as a deterrent to similar wrongful conduct in the future, by making a cautionary example of the defendant.

Distinguishing "Law" and "Equity"

If you have no interest in the historical and academic aspects of our legal system, you may want to skip ahead to the next chapter on specific remedies and causes of action.

On the other hand, understanding how two completely separate, and fundamentally incompatible systems of judicial administration came about and were ultimately — but imperfectly — merged, may clarify an essential distinction which still confounds most people who try to fathom our present system of justice.

In those U.S. states which began as English colonies, the dual system of equity courts separate from courts of law was embodied in the earliest statutes, and, even today that system continues to operate in a few states.[331] Other states, (*e.g.*, Spanish colonies, such as California) never had separate courts of law and equity,[332] although the laws of all states (except Louisiana, a former French colony) still derive certain elements from the English common law system. Total merger of law and equity into a single form of civil action remains an ongoing ideal, which is not likely to achieve completion any time in the foreseeable future.

Because the merger is still incomplete, some principles have successfully migrated from law to equity (or vice versa), while others have not. Thus differences between law and equity remain, and the nature of those differences can best be grasped by understanding their history, and how two distinct, simultaneous systems of justice came into being.

Traditionally, the judicial officer in a law court was (and is) a "Judge," while the bench officer in equity courts was commonly known as a "Chancellor." In fact, many equity courts are referred to as Chancery courts, even today.[333] Here's how that came about.

Under the ancient religious doctrine of "divine right," *all* governmental power — executive, legislative, and judicial — was vested solely and entirely in the king. Medieval English courts therefore had and exercised only such authority as had been delegated to them by the Crown. However, under Saxon rule, England had no central judicial system or single body of law. Apart from crimes against the Crown, such as high treason, laws were primarily matters of local custom, administered by independent, local courts. It was only after the Norman Conquest in

331 Many northern states eliminated separate equity courts following the American Revolution, although most Southern and mid-Atlantic states did not. Federal courts continued to maintain wholly separate courts of law and courts of equity until 1938, when the Federal Rules of Civil Procedure were first implemented.

332 Most states have separate *divisions* where strictly equitable matters are tried within a merged court system. However, the *types* of cases which are deemed to be strictly equity matters differs from state to state. Thus, a case which might be heard as a matter of law in one jurisdiction might sound in equity in a different jurisdiction. For example, some states (*e.g.*, Delaware) treat corporate law cases as matters of equity, since a corporation is a legal fiction flowing from the law of trusts, which is equitable. Other types of cases which are traditionally regarded as exclusively equitable (rather than legal) include probate matters (*e.g.*, wills and trusts), and family law (*e.g.*, divorces and adoptions)

333 Delaware's Court of Chancery, which hears cases involving Delaware corporations, is a notable example.

1066 that a system of royal courts began to emerge. Over a period lasting more than a century, local courts slowly lost jurisdiction as the King's Council began a practice of sending judges around the country to hold *assizes* (sittings) to hear cases locally. This enabled the King's judges to collect the best of local laws and customs — such as trial by jury — and to merge them into a uniform system which they could then apply in every locale. This harmonized collection of local laws formed the core of what came to be known as the "Common Law of England."

Because of the clergy's literacy, most royal administration (including the administration of justice) was delegated to various bishops, abbots, and other clerics. The royal office of "Lord Chancellor" — roughly equivalent to the modern title, "Prime Minister" — is believed to have first been created during the reign of the penultimate Saxon king, Edward the Confessor (1042-1066). By the reign of Henry II (1154-1189), a system of law courts had been established throughout England. These courts of law were presided over by judges appointed by the crown, generally from the higher ranks of the clergy, since the practice of law as a separate profession was unknown. Instead, priests, monks, or laymen served as counsel to the parties, or the parties appeared and presented their own cases, personally.

The right to resort to the king's courts was obtained by purchasing a "writ" from the king. The writ authorized and directed the king's courts to hear the case and to grant appropriate relief. These royal writs formed a template which both created and constrained the court's authority to grant relief, based upon the circumstances of the case for which the writ had been obtained. Procedurally, trials might be by physical combat, or by presentation of argument and evidence.

When an applicant's case contained unprecedented circumstances the Chancery (which was essentially nothing more than the king's secretarial department) could create new forms of writ to address those new issues of law. This provided flexibility in the system by designing remedies appropriate to the circumstances of the specific case for which the writ had been obtained. There was at that time no distinction between "law" and "equity" — there was only the "king's justice," which was absolute. The distinction between "law" and "equity" — which continues to perplex law students and laymen to this day — developed over the next few hundred years. Looking at the particular dispute being considered, the Chancery would draft a writ setting forth the procedural rules for a trial of that issue, and the relief which might be awarded to the victor.

Although Hollywood has repeatedly cast King John (r. 1199-1216) in the role of an incompetent, untrustworthy villain, there is little historical evidence to support that characterization. It is undoubtedly true that it was King John who, under political and financial pressure from his nobles, signed the Magna Carta in 1215, limiting the crown's theretofore absolute power over the entire populace, and forming the initial foundation upon which all constitutional governments have since been based.

By 1258, a series of reforms had been embodied in the Provisions of Oxford which, among other restrictions, specifically prohibited the creation of new forms of writ by the Chancellor.

This prohibition against new writs limited the relief granted in English courts of law to money damages based on previously-existing forms of writ. The Chancery was forbidden from formulating new remedies to be applied by the courts of law, which had become rigidly formalized.[334] This lack of flexibility left the English legal system with three major inadequacies:

(1) There was no ability to compel performance of contractual obligations before damage had been caused. The only available remedy was an award of money damages after the fact for actual loss suffered from the breach of contract.

(2) There was no method for prevention of a threatened injury to property. Instead, the injured party was limited to an award of money damages for the injury, after it had actually occurred.

(3) All contracts were construed exactly as originally written; no correction could be made to the language of a contract or other instrument, no matter how compelling the evidence that the written instrument did not truly reflect the parties' actual intent, or that a party's agreement had been coerced or fraudulently obtained.

In 1207, members of the clergy had been prohibited by canon law (*i.e.*, church law) from continuing to act as counsel in the king's courts. In consequence, a series of royal commissions were appointed and, in 1292, upon the recommendation of those commissions, the crown decreed that students "apt and eager" should be assembled and trained in the law. Those students were accordingly located in what became known as the Inns of Court and Chancery, where they studied law and theology,[335] among other subjects which today would be considered "liberal arts," such as dancing, singing, and playing instrumental music. Their training in one of the several Inns continued for approximately seven years, after which they might be "called to the bar," and awarded the degree of barrister, permitting them to practice law before the court.

Because legal remedies were by then limited to only such forms of writ as had existed prior to 1258, legal education placed a great deal of emphasis on developing an ability to imaginatively conform the facts of any particular case to meet the constraints of one of the few available forms of traditional writ. Even the most creative of legal fictions could not, however, force the facts of some cases into the mold necessary to permit a case to proceed under the limited forms of writ then available. Some form of extraordinary relief was therefore necessary to obtain justice in those cases. Since all jurisprudence still fell within the "king's justice," at

---

334 *E.g.*, all pleadings and oral argument before the courts of law at that time were required to be presented in Latin, rather than in English.

335 The vast body of written laws and judicial precedents upon which we now rely did not yet exist, and the "legal authority" often cited in court opinions were quotations from the Bible. *E.g.*, "By the Law of God, he that builds a House ought to dwell in it; and he that plants a Vineyard ought to gather the Grapes thereof; and it was a Curse upon the Wicked, that they should build Houses and not dwell in them, and plant Vineyards and not gather the Grapes thereof. Deut. 28. v.30." *Earl of Oxford's Case in Chancery* (1615)

least until the mid-17th century, petitions for such extraordinary relief were addressed to the Crown, through the Chancellor.

The fact that the medieval Chancellors had all been members of the clergy trained in Canon Law and moral precepts of the Roman Catholic Church is significant in the development of equity.[336] In fact, the Lord Chancellor was often referred to as "Keeper of the King's Conscience" and, by the 14th century, the Chancellor's courts came to be called "Courts of Conscience." Thus Chancellors administered a more adaptable jurisprudence than did law courts operating under traditional "common law" writs. However, this flexibility had a significant limitation: courts of law could quash (*i.e.,* invalidate) the extraordinary writs and orders issued by a Court of Chancery. Among other things, this hierarchy ultimately resulted in the maxim that "equity follows the law," although, for around 250 years, the reverse was true in English courts.[337] The maxim now prevails however: where the law has spoken on an issue, equity cannot interfere. Notwithstanding, it remains possible to collaterally attack a judgment of law on equitable grounds when the underlying judgment was obtained through a fraud on the court. Such suits are not common, but this extraordinary remedy, which pits equity against law in an effort to do justice, remains available under certain circumstances.

Another maxim, that "equity acts *in personam*" arose because Chancery jurisdiction was theoretically limited to persons (*in personam* jurisdiction) with no direct jurisdiction over property or things (*in rem* jurisdiction.) However, as a practical matter, Chancery courts had substantial *indirect* power over property through the ability to make orders which *affected* property, and to punish disobedience of those orders as contempt. Equitable liens and servitudes are now commonly enforced against property, but the maxim nonetheless still limits certain types of equitable actions.

The primary limitation on courts of equity was the doctrine that equity should not intervene whenever legal remedies were sufficient. But the standard legal remedy was (and still is) an award of money damages, which is clearly insufficient to address every possible dispute, particularly those disputes which seek injunctive or declaratory relief to *prevent* a damage from occurring, or where the subject matter is non-fungible, so that monetary damages are categorically inadequate. Nonetheless, the availability of *any* legal remedy often acted as a bar to seeking equitable relief, especially when the courts of law and courts of equity were wholly separate entities, so that two completely different suits would need to be filed and prosecuted in separate courts in order to obtain both forms of relief. While the doctrine is no longer

---

336 The first exception was Sir Thomas More, a layman who was appointed Chancellor in 1530 by King Henry VIII, after the death of Cardinal Wolsey. Although More had studied law in one of the Inns of Court and Chancery (Lincoln's Inn), and had become a barrister in 1501, he spent several subsequent years living in a monastery, and was the author of a number of religious works. His strongly held religious beliefs eventually put him at odds with Henry VIII in 1534, and his refusal to swear to the Act of Succession and Oath of Supremacy (repudiating any authority of the Pope over the king) led to his execution for treason in 1535. More was subsequently canonized as a Catholic saint.

337 See, *Earl of Oxford's Case* (1616) 1 Rep Ch 1, holding that in cases of conflict between law and equity, equity was to prevail. That dictum remained operative in England until the 1870's, when English courts of law and equity were merged.

absolute, it remains in force even today, and equity will not act where legal remedies are sufficient.

Although distinctions between legal and equitable causes of action have been minimized by unification of the courts, one critical difference remains: **there is no right to trial by jury in an equitable action.** However, the line between the two types of action has become so blurred that determination that a particular remedy is "legal" may trigger a right to a jury trial, while a contrary determination that the same remedy is instead "equitable" may foreclose that right. Legal analysis of these distinctions can be both subtle and complex. For example, where a complaint seeks restitution of some unjust enrichment, courts have come down on both sides of the question. "Restitution" is a measure of damage and therefor a legal remedy; on the other hand, "unjust enrichment" (and the consequent need for restitution) falls squarely within the realm of equity (*e.g.*, establishment and enforcement of involuntary trusts.) A particular court's view of the action as being "equitable" or "legal" will determine whether or not there is a right to trial by jury.

Both the federal and state constitutions guarantee the right to a trial by jury in a civil action at law when certain minimum conditions have been met,[338] but neither state nor federal constitutional guaranties, nor history, allow any right to jury trial in a suit seeking equitable relief. Instead, suits in equity have historically been tried solely by a court in what are generally referred to as "bench trials" or "trials at bench."

With merged courts, analysis of a right to jury trial may be difficult in cases where plaintiff seeks both legal and equitable relief based on the same set of operative facts, or where a cross-complaint seeks both legal and equitable remedies.

Determination of whether a jury trial is available and, if so, whether it will precede or follow a bench trial, or run concurrently with it, can be a vital aspect of litigation strategy. In cases where both legal and equitable remedies are founded on the same operative facts (*e.g.*, a contract between the parties) the identity of the trier of fact can be crucial. Judges are often believed to be more receptive to technical legal arguments, while juries are more apt to ignore legal technicalities if a party is otherwise sympathetic. However, once a fact has been "found" by a competent trier of fact, any subsequent trier of fact is legally bound to accept the found fact as true.

For example, if one party refuses to perform an alleged contract based on a belief that no contract was formed between the parties, and seeks declaratory relief (an equitable remedy) to that effect, and the defendant cross-complains for damages for breach of that same contract, then the identity of the trier of the "fact" of the contract is critical. If the court rules on the

338 The primary condition is generally that the amount in controversy must be over a minimum sum. The Bill of Rights (Amendment VII) states: "In Suits at common law, where the value in controversy shall exceed twenty dollars, the right of trial by jury shall be preserved, and no fact tried by a jury, shall be otherwise re-examined in any Court of the United States, than according to the rules of the common law." Failure to timely demand a jury trial may constitute a waiver of the right, however.

equitable declaratory relief action first and determines that no valid contract existed between the parties, then an essential element of the legal action for contract damages is missing and the cause of action for breach is made moot. Conversely, if a jury decides the breach of contract claim first and awards damages to the cross-complainant, there is an implicit finding of fact that a binding contract existed (since there would otherwise have been nothing to breach), barring the judge from making a contrary finding on the declaratory relief action, unless the court is prepared to overrule the jury's verdict on legal grounds.[339]

To add to the confusion, many states have codified equitable causes of action, thereby — in some instances — converting them to legal remedies. The rule of thumb is that statutory enactments have greater authority than does case law, and that courts have discretion to do equity, as they see fit, provided that no statute or legal precedent has preempted the issue. Of course constitutions, as interpreted by the courts, take precedence over statutory enactments, and federal laws take precedence over (and in some instances entirely preempt) state laws.

◆ ◆ ◆

All in all, the law is an immense, intricate, antique tapestry which has been frequently mended and altered over the centuries. Despite its broken threads and imperfections, it remains vibrant and beautiful — when viewed from a distance.

---

339 Except in criminal cases where a jury returns a verdict of acquittal, a court may overrule a jury's verdict. Such rulings are referred to as "Judgment Notwithstanding Verdict," or, more commonly by the acronym "JNOV" which incorporates the Latin phrase *non obstante veredicto.* In criminal cases, acquittals are immutable, unless obtained fraudulently, such as by jury tampering, intimidation, or bribery, in which event they, too, may be set aside.

A byproduct of the inviolability of jury acquittal in criminal cases is the phenomenon known as "jury nullification," which occurs when a jury chooses to ignore the dictates of a law which it believes is either unjust or being wrongly applied by returning a verdict of "Not Guilty" regardless of defendant's "legal" guilt.

Juries unquestionably have the *power* to nullify, but whether they also have a *right* to nullify is debatable. Prior to the mid- to late-19th century, judges often informed jurors of their nullification right. This led to a number of cases where juries refused to convict defendants of violating laws which the populace generally disapproved. In the 19th century, defendants were frequently acquitted when charged under laws such as the Alien & Sedition Act and the Fugitive Slave Act. In the 20th Century, defendants were seldom convicted for violating the Volstead Act, which prohibited importation, manufacture, possession and sale of alcoholic beverages. Not surprisingly, most laws which juries nullified were later amended or repealed by legislatures, or overturned by the courts.

Currently, in most jurisdictions, judges instruct jurors that it is their duty to follow the law exactly as it is given to them by the judge, regardless of whether they agree with that law or not. Only a few states allow jurors to be instructed that they have the power to judge the law as well as the facts of a case. Most courts forbid attorneys from informing jurors of their nullification power, and many judges will replace a juror (prior to verdict) if they learn that he or she has suggested nullification. The practice nonetheless continues, as when those who assist in the suicide of terminally ill patients are acquitted of criminal charges, nullifying penal laws which expressly forbid a defendant's admitted conduct.

CHAPTER 12

A FEW SPECIFIC REMEDIES

Legal actions fall into several broad categories, including: contract actions, statutory actions, tort actions, negligence actions, and actions for equitable relief. There are few clear demarcations between them however, since a single lawsuit may contain multiple — and what may appear to be contradictory — causes of action. While it is not permissible to plead inconsistent *facts*, it is permissible — and often necessary — to plead inconsistent *legal theories* of recovery.

Contract actions are those which (not surprisingly) arise from a contract. The most common of these are for breach of contract, but there are also other causes of action which are said to "sound in contract" such as specific performance, rescission, and actions for declaratory and injunctive relief, as well as many others.

Statutory actions are those which are specifically authorized by a particular statute, enumerating the elements of the cause of action and establishing a formula or fixed sum for calculating awardable damages. Such statutes often provide for an award of attorney's fees, as well.[340]

Tort actions seek damages for certain types of wrongful conduct, including fraud, conversion, defamation, and misappropriation. In general, torts are the civil equivalent of crimes; *i.e.*, the same conduct which might justify a criminal prosecution may also be prosecuted privately, in civil court, as a tort. Note, however, that the names given to such actions are not always the same in a civil suit as they would be in a criminal charge. For example, the crime of "larceny" (*i.e.*, theft), is the tort of "conversion," and the crime of "manslaughter" is the tort of "wrongful death."

Negligence actions are for damages arising by reason of an unintentional breach of a recognized legal duty. Malpractice actions and accident cases sound in negligence.

Equitable actions cover a broad range of relief in which the court, acting without a jury, seeks to fairly resolve disputed issues. Injunctive relief and declaratory relief (among others) are equitable actions.

There are other categories as well, such as criminal actions and governmental actions, which are outside the scope of this book. Even within the categories mentioned above, there are potential causes of action and remedies which are far too numerous to be listed and discussed in any single volume, and "new" causes of action can be created through innovative

340 As a reminder, under the so-called "American Rule," attorney's fees may only be awarded to a prevailing party if specifically provided for by a contract or by a statute.

pleading and through sociological changes which introduce newly-distinguished rights and obligations.

Statutes of Limitations

All civil actions must be commenced by filing a complaint with an appropriate court within a certain, set period of time following the occurrence upon which the complaint is based. The precise amount of time varies depending on both the specific nature of particular cause of action being pled and on the jurisdiction in which the actionable conduct occurred or is to be prosecuted.

The laws which set forth these time limits in respect to particular causes of action are referred to as *statutes of limitations*, and can vary substantially from state to state. Failure to file suit within the time period specified by the applicable statute of limitations will create an absolute defense to any cause of action which is time barred by statute. This is a critical factor in determining when or if to file a civil complaint.

For example, in California, a complaint for breach of a *written* contract must be filed within four years from the *date of alleged breach*, while an action for breach of an *oral* or *implied* contract must be filed within two years from the date of alleged breach.

Statutes of limitations may appear straightforward, but they are frequently expanded or shortened by other statutes in respect to particular types of cases, on a state by state basis.[341] For example, the specific nature or subject matter of a contract may alter the statute of limitations. *E.g.*, if the action is against a California building contractor for breach by latent defect it must be commenced within ten years (instead of four), but if it is for breach arising from termination of a California personal service contract for recording phonorecords, it must be brought within forty-five days of the noticed termination date.

In New York, Tennessee, and several other states, a breach of either a written or oral contract must be brought within six years. For breach of contract, the current statutes of limitations for the various states range from a minimum of two years[342] to a maximum of twenty years for written contracts "with attestment" or "under seal."[343] Determining the

341 *E.g.*, Vermont has a three year statute for personal injuries, unless the injury was caused by skiing (either the plaintiff or the defendant or both were skiing at the time of the injury), in which case the statute is shortened to one year. Snowboarding, ice skating, and other winter sports are not included in the shortened statute.

342 For breach of oral or implied contracts in California, Colorado, Delaware, and Kansas

343 A few states make a distinction between a written contract and a "contract under seal," which is considered to be an even more formal and binding agreement. Even though valuable consideration is necessary to make an enforceable contract, ancient decisions held that a seal itself amounted to good consideration, and created an irrebuttable presumption of obligation. Historically, seals were melted wax impressed with a signet or device, while modern seal are generally an impression stamped or embossed on paper by a corporation or notary to authenticate a document or signature. Some states allow longer statutes of limitations on actions arising from a contract "under seal": Alabama, Alaska, and North Carolina, 10 years; South Carolina, 15 years; New Hampshire and Rhode Island, 20 years.

applicable choice of law will establish which jurisdiction's statute of limitations will apply in respect to each cause of action which is being considered. Each state has its own vagaries in this respect, and causes of action which would be viable in one state may be time-barred in another. It is therefore essential to consult with an attorney who is well-versed in the laws of the particular jurisdiction in which the case is to be filed.

As a very approximate set of guidelines — and subject to the whims of various state legislatures — the statutes of limitations for some of the more common causes of action currently fall within the following ranges:

Type of Action	Range of Statutes of Limitations
Personal injury (Negligence)	1 to 3 years
Personal injury (Intentional tort)	1 to 6 years
Breach of oral or implied contract	2 to 6 years
Breach of written contract	3 to 6 years,
Breach of written contract "under seal"	up to 20 years
Professional negligence (legal malpractice)	1 to 3 years from date of discovery, or a maximum of 2 to 5 years from the date of the wrongful act, or date upon which damage occurs by reason of wrongful act.
Fraud (negligent or through mistake)	3 to 6 years (from *discovery* of fraud or mistake, *not* occurrence)
Fraud (per se; by concealment; by intentional misrepresentation; by promise without intent)	3 to 6 years from discovery
Any claim against a government entity	6 months to 1 year (generally)
Enforcement of civil judgment:	5 to 25 years

Again, the foregoing are only *approximate ranges*, and the specific statute of limitations applicable in a particular state with respect to a particular case and cause of action may fall anywhere within the given range, and should be determined promptly upon discovery of potentially actionable conduct. Such determinations should be made by an attorney who regularly practices in the relevant state or jurisdiction. If no complaint has been filed before the applicable statute date for a particular cause of action, the underlying claim becomes effectively worthless.

◆ ◆ ◆

Before discussing specific causes of action, we need to reiterate an important truth and caveat about *all* civil litigation and other adversary proceedings: There are no guaranties, and it will be a rare case which doesn't hand each party occasional unpleasant surprises. At the end of the day, it's all up to the judge, and whether the ultimate judgment is "right" or "wrong" in a party's opinion… it's still the *judgment.*

◆ ◆ ◆

There's an old story about a reporter interviewing three major league baseball umpires; a rookie umpire, a journeyman umpire, and a venerable umpire nearing retirement. He asked each of them the same question: "How do you tell a ball from a strike?"

The rookie replied, "I call 'em the way I see 'em."

The journeyman said, "*I* call 'em the way they *are.*"

The venerable umpire just smiled. "Ain't *nothin'* 'til I say."

And so, too, with litigation. *Nothing* is certain, until the judge says otherwise.

◆ ◆ ◆

Following, are brief explanations and discussions of a few of the more common civil causes of action which may arise in music-industry litigation.

Breach of Contract

This cause of action arises when one party to a contract has failed or refused to perform one or more of the obligations required under that contract.

To recover damages for breach of contract, plaintiff must allege and prove all of the following essential elements:

1. That plaintiff and defendant entered into a contract;[344]
2. That plaintiff performed all, or substantially all, of the significant things that the contract required plaintiff to do, except for such things as plaintiff was prevented or excused from doing;
3. That all conditions required in order to allow defendant's performance had occurred (*i.e.*, that defendant was not prevented or excused from performing);
4. That on or about some (approximate or exact) date, defendant failed to do something that the contract required defendant to do; and
5. That plaintiff was harmed by that failure.

Generally, plaintiff's damages will be limited to the value which plaintiff would have received had defendant not breached the contract. The court may allow prejudgment interest on the award, accruing from the date on which the court finds that the obligation became due. If the contract provides for an interest rate, that rate will apply to prejudgment interest, otherwise such interest will be at the current "legal rate" allowed by state or federal law. Attorney's fees will only be awarded to the prevailing party if the contract included an attorney's fees provision *and* a party alleged that provision and prayed for an award of attorney's fees in pleading their complaint or answer.

◆ ◆ ◆

344 At the time of pleading, it is *essential* to state whether the contract was written, oral, or implied by conduct. Failure to do so opens the complaint to attack by demurrer (or motion for dismissal) on the grounds of uncertainty.

Anticipatory Breach

A party may commit an actionable breach of contract even before performance is required by clearly and positively indicating, through words or conduct, that he or she will not or cannot fulfill the requirements of the contract. Thus the essential elements of anticipatory breach of contract are almost identical to those for breach of contract:

1. That plaintiff and defendant entered into a [written -or- oral -or- implied] contract;
2. That plaintiff did all, or substantially all of the significant things that the contract required plaintiff to do, except for such things as plaintiff was prevented or excused from doing;
3. That all conditions required in order to allow defendant's performance had occurred (*i.e.*, that defendant was not prevented or excused from performing);
4. That on or about some particular (approximate of exact) date, defendant clearly and positively indicated, by words or conduct, that defendant would not or could not meet the contract requirements;
5. That plaintiff would have been able to fulfill, and would have fulfilled, all the terms of the contract if defendant had not clearly and positively indicated that defendant would not or could not meet the contract requirements; and
6. That plaintiff has been or will be harmed by defendant's failure to perform.

Contract damages for anticipatory breach will generally be limited to the net sum which plaintiff would have obtained had defendant performed the contract. That is, plaintiff is entitled to the value of the consideration which would have been due to plaintiff, less the value of consideration which plaintiff was excused or prevented from delivering or performing by reason of the anticipated breach.

◆ ◆ ◆

"Common Counts"

The so-called "common counts" are a bundle of causes of action to collect contract and quasi-contract damages, echoing the ancient common law writ of *assumpsit.*[345] Common counts may include a claim for money due to plaintiff based on any one or more of the following grounds:

(a) For money owed on an open book account;

(b) Where there is a written account stated between plaintiff and defendant in which it was agreed that defendant was indebted to plaintiff;

(c) For money received by defendant which was intended for the use and benefit of the plaintiff;

(d) For work, labor, services, and/or materials supplied at the request of defendant and for which defendant promised to pay plaintiff;

(e) For money lent by plaintiff to defendant at defendant's request;

(f) For money paid out by plaintiff to third parties for defendant's benefit and at defendant's request; and

(g) Any other circumstance in which defendant should be morally and legally obliged to pay money to plaintiff because defendant requested that money be given or expended, or that labor be performed, and defendant received the benefit thereof. (See, "Quantum Meruit," *infra.*)

Damages for common counts will be limited to the money actually owed, or the reasonable value of services and material provided. Attorney's fees will generally only be awarded if a contract so provides, although statutory attorney's fees may be available in some jurisdictions under certain circumstances. The court may also allow prejudgment interest on the award, calculated from the date when the obligation was first incurred.

◆ ◆ ◆

345 Assumpsit — from the Latin *assumere* ("he has undertaken") — was a common law writ seeking damages by reason of non-performance of a simple contract, express or implied, and oral written, but subject to a Statute of Frauds affirmative defense. Assumpsit became obsolete in federal courts after the 1938 enactment of the F.R.Civ.P., although many states continue to recognize assumpsit as a common law or statutory cause of action. (Assumpsit had become obsolete in the U.K. in the 1870's.)

You Don't want money; You want what they agreed to Do!

Specific Performance

This equitable cause of action may arise when one party to a contract refuses to perform, and is perhaps most often seen in transactions where a seller receives a "better offer" after having already accepted a lesser offer. In such circumstances, the court may command the defaulting party to perform the original contract.

The essential elements of specific performance are:

1. That a valid contract was formed between plaintiff and defendant;
2. That Plaintiff is ready, willing and able to perform Plaintiff's obligations under the contract;
3. That Defendant has refused to perform Defendant's obligations under the contract;
4. That performance of defendant's obligations under the contract is still possible.

Specific performance is, in effect, a form of mandatory injunction, seeking relief by a judicial order commanding defendant to perform the contract. Monetary damages occasioned by a delay in performance may also be awarded, as may attorneys' fees if the underlying contract provides for such award.

This is one cause of action in which a paradox regarding attorneys' fees may easily arise. If plaintiff alleges that a contract provides for attorneys' fees, but the court finds that no enforceable contract was ever formed, the prevailing defendant may nonetheless be entitled to an award of attorney's fees under the (nonexistent) contract provision pled by plaintiff.

This outcome results from application of the equitable Doctrine of Reciprocity, which has been characterized as a legal formulation of the Golden Rule, "Do as you would be done by," and "What's sauce for the goose…" By placing a claim to attorneys' fees in issue, and seeking the potential benefit thereof, a plaintiff is deemed to have submitted to a contrary result in favor of the other party. In effect, a pleading's allegation of an attorneys' fees clause is itself treated as an attorneys' fees clause, binding upon the pleader.

◆ ◆ ◆

Rescission & Restitution

Under certain limited circumstances, it is possible to cancel (rescind) a contract and recover consideration already delivered under that agreement, returning the parties to the relative positions that they had with respect to each other prior to the contract (*status quo ante.*)[346] Rescission is an equitable cause of action directed to that end, where one party wishes to rescind the agreement but the other party refuses. The grounds for rescission are generally limited to:

(1) fraud in the inducement;[347]

(2) mistake; or

(3) failure of consideration.

These categories are somewhat misleading, and there are subtle legal nuances which should be explored prior to attempting rescission through litigation. Because rescission sounds in equity, the court may decline to rescind a contract if one party has affirmed it by his or her actions, or where there has been partial or substantial performance in implementing the contract, or if a third party has acquired some rights by reason of the contract.

◆ ◆ ◆

346 It is, of course, always permissible for the contracting parties to *voluntarily* rescind the agreement between them by their mutual consent, *provided* that there is no third-party beneficiary who would be damaged thereby.

347 Notwithstanding that rescission is an equitable cause of action, a jury may be empaneled in some cases for the limited purpose of trying the factual issue of an alleged fraud or other "fact" questions pled as the basis for rescission. Even if the jury finds that there was fraud or other factual basis for rescission, it remains solely an issue within the discretion of the judge, sitting in equity, to determine if rescission is proper.

Declaratory Relief

Declaratory relief is the most basic and all-encompassing form of equitable remedy, having but a single essential element:

(1) An actual, non-trivial controversy currently exists as between plaintiff and defendant.

The "actual controversy" can be virtually anything, provided that it is real and that some non-trivial[348] value can be attributed to the outcome or subject matter of the dispute. Typically, declaratory relief may be sought to resolve ambiguous contract provisions, to determine if a contract even exists, to ascertain the legal ownership of property, or to obtain a judicial finding to determine specific obligations or excuse performance of an obligation. In essence, each side presents its own factual and legal arguments, along with evidence supporting its contentions, and the court makes a determination as to the truth of the matter and the legal rights and obligations of the parties with respect to each other.

Most equitable remedies fall within the broad scope of declaratory relief, even though they may be pled as separate, distinct causes of action. Among these are:

- Actions to quiet title, in which plaintiff seeks to have the court determine the true ownership of property and, by decree, invalidate (*i.e.*, "quiet") defendants' competing claims of interest.

- Actions for an accounting, in which plaintiff seeks to have the court determine that defendant is required to account to plaintiff for money or other things, and for a court order compelling that accounting.

- For cancellation of instrument, in which plaintiff seeks to have the court find that a written instrument should be held invalid and order that it be cancelled, usually by an order directed to the County Recorder or other person charged with maintaining official records.

- For reformation of instrument, in which plaintiff contends that the language of a writing does not reflect the true terms agreed to, or that it contains terms which are contrary to law or public policy and should be severed, and seeks to have the court order the terms of the writing suitably modified to conform to the facts and law. As with cancellation, this is generally accomplished by court order directed to the County Recorder or other person charged with maintaining official records.

---

348 One of the long standing maxims of jurisprudence states, "*de minimus non curat lex,*" which is generally translated as "The law does not deal with trifles."

The list of specialized forms of declaratory relief goes well beyond the foregoing examples, but the gist of all of them is that the court makes a determination of facts and implements (or invents) a remedy designed to effectuate that determination. Whenever there is a non-trivial dispute between parties that is outside the scope of established legal remedics, it can usually be addressed through declaratory relief.

◆ ◆ ◆

Injunctive Relief

Injunctive Relief is probably the most familiar form of common equitable remedy. Injunctions fall into two broad categories: prohibitory injunctions and mandatory injunctions.

Prohibitory injunctions are court orders which either forbid someone from commencing some contemplated action, or which command that they cease some current, ongoing action, or that they abate some present condition or circumstance.

A mandatory injunction, on the other hand, commands that the party to whom it is directed must perform some specified act, duty, or obligation.[349]

Injunctive relief may be obtained by petition to the court, or — where injunction is only a portion of the relief being sought — it may be pled as a cause of action within a complaint which contains additional causes of action, as well. Where the injunction being sought is to enjoin some act only until all of the relevant issues of a case have been adjudicated, it is referred to as a "preliminary injunction." If the injunction is intended to continue indefinitely, it is referred to as a "permanent injunction."

Another familiar form of injunctive relief is found in temporary orders intended to prevent certain actions until the court can conduct a full hearing as to whether or not a more formal injunction should issue. These "temporary restraining orders" are generally only granted as an interim measure when there is a true emergency justifying them, such as when there is a threat of imminent harm to persons, property, or rights. The duration of such orders is usually limited to a short period of time, but with an included order that the enjoined party has only until that time to demonstrate to the court why the temporary order should not be made permanent when the temporary order expires.

As a general rule, the party obtaining a restraining order or preliminary injunction may be required to post a bond before the injunction will issue. This is intended to protect the interests of the enjoined party should they eventually prevail on the issue. However, as we have previously noted, it may be possible — depending on the circumstances and the jurisdiction — to waive or limit the bond requirement, in advance, within the terms of an underlying contract.

The essential elements which will normally justify an injunction are:

---

349 A special form of mandatory injunction called a "writ of mandate," (*mandamus*) may be directed to governmental agencies or to lower courts, commanding that they perform some required act. Such writs may be peremptory (absolutely commanding compliance) or in the form of an alternative writ under which the official or agency to whom the writ is directed must either perform the commanded act or else appear before the issuing court and show cause why they should not be compelled to do so. In practice, the official or agency is seldom required to respond directly, as most such writs are issued in the course of adversary proceedings, and the adverse party will respond as a "real party in interest" on behalf of the official or agency to whom or which an alternative writ has been directed.

1. The likelihood of *imminent* harm;
2. An award of money damages — *i.e.*, legal remedies — would be insufficient (*i.e.* harm is "irreparable" as well as "imminent"); and
3. A likelihood that plaintiff will prevail as to the ultimate claims of the action.

◆ ◆ ◆

Negligence

Each and every person owes a duty to every other person to act in a reasonable and prudent manner so as to avoid causing harm. This is known as the duty of due care (or "ordinary care" or "reasonable care"), and negligence arises when a breach of that duty results in injury to another person or to property.

"Due care" simply means the degree of prudence which an "ordinary person" would use in order to avoid injury to themselves or others under similar circumstances. The hypothetical "ordinary person" whose conduct sets this standard is not an especially cautious individual, nor an exceptionally skillful one. One may be held to have been negligent if a person of ordinary prudence, in the same situation, and possessed of the same knowledge, would have foreseen or anticipated that someone might be injured by or as a consequence of his or her action or inaction.[350] The phrase "reasonably foreseeable," is often seen in negligence pleadings.

Every person who is exercising ordinary care has a right to assume that every other person will also perform his or her duty and obey the law. In the absence of reasonable cause for thinking otherwise, it is not negligence to fail to anticipate an accident which can occur only as a result of another person's violation of law or through breach of the duty of care.

The amount of caution required of a person in the exercise of ordinary care also depends on any special qualifications which that person may have. Professionals such as lawyers, physicians, accountants, architects, and engineers, among others, are held to a higher standard with respect to matters falling within their areas of expertise. So-called "malpractice" actions are therefore more properly termed actions for "professional negligence."

Someone who has been injured or who has suffered some property loss or damage as a result of another's negligent conduct may bring an action for negligence. Most accident-related cases sound in negligence. The essential elements of a negligence cause of action are:

1. That defendant owed a specified duty to the plaintiff; and
2. That defendant breached that duty by some specific action or inaction (*i.e.*, that defendant was negligent); and
3. That defendant's negligence was a proximate cause of injury, loss, damage or harm to the plaintiff.

350 It should be noted that minors are not held to the same standard of conduct as are adults. Minors are only required to exercise the degree of care which ordinarily is exercised by those of equivalent maturity, intelligence and capacity under similar circumstances.

Note that there is no allegation that the defendant ***intended*** to cause such injury. Intent is not an element of negligence. There are a number of specific causes of action which sound in negligence, such as negligent misrepresentation (fraud) and negligent breach of fiduciary duty, where intent is not an element of the actionable conduct. In each such instance, there will be some specific duty which has been violated, resulting in damage to the plaintiff.

◆ ◆ ◆

Trespass

The ancient tort of trespass refers to unauthorized entry onto, or use of, another's property.[351] Any interference with an owner's or tenant's right to the exclusive use and enjoyment of their property, such as by using another's facilities, or by unauthorized dumping on another's property will sound in trespass. (*E.g.*, golf balls landing in someone's swimming pool have been held to constitute a trespass.) While trespass traditionally relates to entry onto real property, the doctrine has been expanded in recent years to include the tort of "trespass to chattels," which concerns the unauthorized use of another's *personal* property, such as computers and other equipment. The essential elements of trespass are:

1. That plaintiff had the right to quiet use and enjoyment of the subject property;
2. That defendant had no such right;
3. That defendant entered onto or used the subject property without permission, license or other valid authority; and
4. That plaintiff suffered loss, damage, or harm as a result of defendant's trespass.

In addition to monetary damages, the court may also grant an injunction prohibiting any further, continuing, repeated, or permanent trespass.

◆ ◆ ◆

351 If the trespass is with an illegal intent, such as to commit an unlawful act, trespass itself is also chargeable as a separate criminal offense.

Nuisance

Nuisance is the use of one's own property in a manner which interferes with the rights of others. It is akin to trespass in that the damages arise through interference with others' quiet use and enjoyment of their own property, or with the use and enjoyment of public property,[352] but without the element of physical incursion which constitutes a trespass. For example, playing loud music on one's own property may create an actionable nuisance with respect neighboring property owners, or even casual passers-by. Similarly, erecting walls or planting trees which block a neighbor's view, or which create a potential hazard to a neighbor's property, may constitute an actionable nuisance in certain cases.

As with trespass, nuisance may be grounds for the issuance of an injunction to abate the nuisance by prohibiting any further, continuing, or repeated conduct, or by imposing limits on certain conduct, such as times of day when the conduct is permissible.

The essential elements of nuisance are:

1. That defendant has engaged in certain specified conduct, or has caused or allowed a specified condition to exist or persist;
2. That the specified conduct or condition interferes with plaintiff's quiet use and enjoyment of plaintiff's property; and
3. That plaintiff has been damaged by reason of defendant's conduct.

From the standpoint of the music industry, nuisance actions generally arise from noise complaints, most frequently brought by neighbors of "garage bands" which rehearse late into the night in less-than-perfectly-insulated facilities, or by those living near performance venues whose patrons, on entering or leaving the venue, may also be something less than perfect.

◆ ◆ ◆

352 Public nuisance may also be prosecuted as a criminal offense.

Fraud

In its broad, general sense, fraud includes anything which is intended to deceive, including all statements, acts, concealments and omissions involving a breach of a legal or equitable duty, trust or confidence, which results in injury to someone who has justifiably relied on the candor, truthfulness or fidelity of the other person. There is no absolute or fixed rule for determining what facts will constitute fraud. Whether or not particular conduct is found to have been fraudulent depends on the facts of each case.

Fraud generally falls into three categories: *(1)* misrepresentation of material facts; *(2)* concealment or suppression of material facts; and *(3)* promise without intent to perform. Actionable fraud can also be either actual fraud or constructive fraud.

Actual fraud occurs when a party to a contract, or another person acting in concert with a contracting party, acts with the intent to deceive another party to the contract, or to induce him or her to enter into the contract, by doing any of the following:

- Suggesting that some statement of fact is true, while believing that it is not true;
- Positively asserting that some statement of fact is true, without having sufficient information to justify such assertion, even if the person making the assertion believes it to be true;
- Suppressing or concealing a true fact, while having knowledge of that fact;
- Making a promise about a material matter without any intention of performing it; or,
- Committing any other act which has deceptive effect.

Constructive fraud occurs when there is a breach of duty which, without actually having a fraudulent intent, nonetheless gains an advantage for the person at fault, or for anyone deriving benefit through such person, by misleading another to his or her detriment, or to the detriment of another reliant upon him or her. Also, certain acts or omissions which the law expressly declares to be fraudulent in certain circumstances fall within the category of constructive fraud, without any intentional or actual fraud having occurred.

The most fundamental element of fraud is "detrimental reliance." That is, that the plaintiff justifiably relied upon defendant and was damaged as a proximate result. Actual fraud is always a question of fact, and the facts which are alleged to have constituted fraudulent conduct must be pled with specificity.

Proof of actual fraud is difficult, since the defendant's *intent to defraud at the time the fraud was committed* is an essential element of the tort. Also, the measure of proof is by "clear and convincing evidence" of the essential elements, which are as follow:

- ***Fraud by Intentional or Negligent Misrepresentation:***

 1. On or around some particular date, defendant made certain representations of material fact (which representations must be specifically pled in the complaint);
 2. Those representations were false;
 3. The true facts (which must also be pled with specificity) were … ;
 4. When defendant made the false representations, defendant …
    (a) *(Intentional)* … knew they were false; or
    (b) *(Negligent)* … had no reasonable ground for believing them to be true;
 5. Defendant made the representations…
    (a) *(Intentional)* … with the intent to defraud, and
    (b) *(Negligent & Intentional)* … to induce plaintiff to act (or refrain from acting) in a particular manner (which must be pled with specificity);
 6. At the time plaintiff acted (or refrained from acting) in the stated manner, plaintiff did not know that defendant's representations were false, but believed them to be true.
 7. Had plaintiff known the true facts at the time, plaintiff would not have acted (or refrained from acting) in the specified manner, but would instead have acted in another manner (which must also be pled with reasonable specificity, *e.g.*, "plaintiff would not have entered into any contract with defendant.");
 8. As a direct and proximate result of defendant's fraudulent conduct, plaintiff suffered loss, damage, and/or harm in a certain sum or according to proof;
 9. *(For special or consequential damages)* As a further result and unavoidable consequence of defendant's fraud, plaintiff suffered additional loss, damage, and/or harm (the particulars of which must be specifically pled);
 10. *(For punitive damages)* Defendant's fraudulent conduct was wanton, willful, malicious, oppressive, and/or shocking to the conscience.

- ***Fraud by Concealment:***

 1. On or around some particular date, defendant concealed or suppressed certain material fact (which facts must be specifically pled in the complaint);
 2. Defendant concealed of suppressed those material facts…

(a) ... by telling plaintiff other true facts which were intended to mislead and did mislead plaintiff and prevent plaintiff from discovering the concealed or suppressed facts; or

(b) ... which defendant had a legal duty to disclose to plaintiff. (The basis of defendant's legal duty of disclosure must be specifically pled.)

3. Defendant concealed or suppressed those facts with the intent to defraud, and to induce plaintiff to act (or refrain from acting) in a particular manner (which must be pled with specificity);

4. At the time plaintiff acted (or refrained from acting) in the stated manner, plaintiff was unaware of the concealed or suppressed facts;

5. Had plaintiff known of the concealed or suppressed facts at the time, plaintiff would not have acted (or refrained from acting) in the specified manner, but would instead have acted in another manner (which must also be pled with reasonable specificity);

6. As a direct and proximate result of defendant's fraudulent conduct, plaintiff suffered loss, damage, and/or harm in a certain sum or according to proof;

7. *(For special or consequential damages)* As a further result and unavoidable consequence of defendant's fraud, plaintiff suffered additional loss, damage, and/or harm (the particulars of which must be specifically pled);

8. *(For punitive damages)* Defendant's fraudulent conduct was wanton, willful, malicious, oppressive, and/or shocking to the conscience.

- ***Fraud by Promise Without Intent to Perform***

1. On or around some particular date, defendant made a promise about a material matter (the particulars of which promise must be specifically pled in the complaint);

2. At the time that defendant made that promise, defendant had no intention of performing that promise;

3. Defendant made that promise with the intent to defraud, to induce plaintiff to rely upon the promise and to act (or refrain from acting) in a particular manner (which must be pled with specificity);

4. At the time plaintiff acted (or refrained from acting) plaintiff was unaware that defendant had no intention of performing the promise, but believed that defendant would perform that promise. Plaintiff acted in justifiable reliance upon defendant's promise;

5. Had plaintiff known at the time that defendant did not intend to perform the promise, plaintiff would not have acted (or refrained from acting) in the specified manner, but would instead have acted in another manner (which must also be pled with reasonable specificity);
6. As a direct and proximate result of defendant's fraudulent conduct, plaintiff suffered loss, damage, and/or harm in a certain sum or according to proof;
7. *(For special or consequential damages)* As a further result and unavoidable consequence of defendant's fraud, plaintiff suffered additional loss, damage, and/or harm (the particulars of which must be specifically pled);
8. *(For punitive damages)* Defendant's fraudulent conduct was wanton, willful, malicious, oppressive, and/or shocking to the conscience.

◆ ◆ ◆

Since prevailing on a cause of action for fraud generally requires proving the relevant essential elements by clear and convincing evidence (rather than the lower standard of "preponderance of evidence"), the cause of action should only be pled if such evidence is available to plaintiff, or can be reasonably anticipated to be discoverable before trial. In some jurisdictions, fraud complaints must be verified. That is, the plaintiff must attest under penalty of perjury that the alleged facts are true to the best of plaintiff's knowledge, information, and belief.

◆ ◆ ◆

Conversion

The civil tort of conversion is equivalent to the penal offense of larceny or theft. Any non-permissive taking or retention of another's property will sound in conversion. Here are the essential elements:

1. That Plaintiff is the owner of certain described property;
2. That on or about a certain date, defendant took possession of the described property...
   (a) ... with plaintiff's permission; or
   (b) ... without plaintiff's permission;
3. That on or about a certain date, plaintiff demanded that defendant return the described property to plaintiff;
4. That, despite demand, defendant has failed and refused, and continues to fail and refuse, to restore possession of the property to plaintiff (defendant exercises dominion and control over the property, without plaintiff's consent);
5. That, prior to the filing of the lawsuit, plaintiff incurred and accrued certain cost and expenses in reasonable and justified, good-faith efforts to recover the described property from defendant;[353]
6. That plaintiff is entitled to have the property restored to plaintiff, or to have restitution in a sum equal to the fair market value of the described property;[354]
7. That plaintiff is entitled to recover compensatory damages for loss of use of the described property for the period of time that defendant withheld it from plaintiff.
8. *(For punitive damages)* That defendant's act of conversion was wanton, willful, malicious, oppressive, and/or shocking to the conscience.

◆ ◆ ◆

353 This is the foundation for special damages, which may include attorney's fees incurred prior to the pleading and filing of the complaint. That is, the attorney's fees and other monies spent in attempting to recover the property *without* a lawsuit may be recoverable as special or consequential damages.

354 If the property is unique or irreplaceable (non-fungible), this must be specially pled.

Breach of Fiduciary Duty

Fiduciary duty is the highest standard of care imposed under both equity and law. A fiduciary is expected to be unswervingly loyal to the person (the "principal" or "beneficiary") to whom the duty is owed, and a fiduciary must never put his or her personal interests before that duty.

Thus a fiduciary is obliged to always act in the best interests of another person. For instance, a trustee has a fiduciary duty to the trust's beneficiaries, a lawyer has a fiduciary duty to his or her client, an attorney-in-fact (under a power of attorney) has a fiduciary duty to his or her principal, and a corporate director has a fiduciary duty to the corporation's shareholders. Partners (including band members, where the group is a partnership) owe a fiduciary duty to each other.

A fiduciary obligation exists whenever one person (the principal or beneficiary) places special trust and confidence in another person, and relies upon that person (the fiduciary) to exercise his or her discretion or expertise in acting for the principal, provided that the fiduciary knowingly accepts that trust and confidence and thereafter undertakes to act on behalf of the principal by exercising his or her (the fiduciary's) own discretion and expertise.

A business relationship alone does not necessarily establish a fiduciary relationship. If one person employs another and directs, supervises or approves the employee's actions, there is no fiduciary obligation formed. Rather, it is only when one party reposes, and the other accepts, a special trust and confidence involving the exercise of expertise or discretion that a fiduciary relationship may come into being.

Whenever a person undertakes to act for another in a fiduciary capacity, the law forbids the fiduciary from acting in any manner adverse or contrary to the interests of the principal, or from acting for the fiduciary's own benefit in relation to the subject matter, except with the principal's express, informed consent. The principal is entitled to the fiduciary's best efforts on the principal's behalf and the fiduciary must exercise all of the skill, care and diligence at his or her disposal when acting on behalf of the principal. Moreover, a person acting in a fiduciary capacity is required to make truthful and complete disclosures to those placing trust in the fiduciary, and is forbidden from obtaining any unreasonable advantage at the principal's expense. Case law has generally held that those who collect and are responsible for distributing royalties are *not* acting in a fiduciary capacity. Unless and until a statute is enacted imposing a fiduciary duty on royalty administrators, malfeasance with respect to royalty accounting and payments will not support this cause of action *unless* there is a contract provision in which the parties expressly agree and acknowledge the existence of a fiduciary relationship and duty in respect to royalty accounting and payments.

Breach of fiduciary duty is especially reprehensible and repugnant to the law, and will generally justify the imposition of punitive damages in addition to compensatory damages and, where appropriate, the imposition of an involuntary, equitable trust.

The essential elements to be pled and proven in a cause of action for breach of fiduciary duty are:

1. That on or about a certain date a fiduciary relationship was formed between plaintiff (as principal) and defendant (as fiduciary);
2. That on or about a certain date defendant breached the fiduciary duty owed to plaintiff by certain specific acts of commission or of omission;
3. That plaintiff suffered specified damages by reason of defendant's breach of the fiduciary duty;
4. That plaintiff incurred and accrued particular costs and expenses, prior to suit, in reasonable, justified and good faith efforts to recover assets and mitigate damages, and should be awarded consequential or special damages on account thereof;
5. *(Where defendant holds property obtained through abuse of the fiduciary relationship)* That certain specified property obtained by defendant is, in fact, held by defendant only as an involuntary trustee, for the benefit of plaintiff, and the property should be turned over to plaintiff's exclusive ownership, possession and control;
6. Defendant's breach of fiduciary duty was wanton, willful, malicious, oppressive, and/or shocking to the conscience, justifying punitive or exemplary damages in such sum as accords with proof and as allowable by law.

◆ ◆ ◆

Infringement of Copyright

In the chapters on copyright and copyright registration we discussed the advantages of registering works with the Copyright Office. Actions for infringement are where the principal advantage of registration is most notable.

The current Copyright Act preempts state action for copyright infringement, with only very narrow exceptions having to do with contract, fraud, and other state law causes of action which may arise from copyright-related issues. What this means is that any action for infringement of copyrighted work must be filed in a federal district court, rather than in state court, and a state court action which does not fall into one of the narrow exceptions to preemption is subject to dismissal if not removed to federal court.

The owner of an unregistered copyright will be limited to seeking injunctive relief to prevent further infringement, and actual, provable damages, but will not be entitled to seek statutory damages or additional relief. For the owners of registered copyrights, however, in addition to injunction, the United States Code provides:

Either…

(a) "The copyright owner is entitled to recover the actual damages suffered by him or her as a result of the infringement, and any profits of the infringer that are attributable to the infringement and are not taken into account in computing the actual damages. In establishing the infringer's profits, the copyright owner is required to present proof only of the infringer's gross revenue, and the infringer is required to prove his or her deductible expenses and the elements of profit attributable to factors other than the copyrighted work." [17 USC § 504.(b)];

… or …

(b) "… the copyright owner may elect, at any time before final judgment is rendered, to recover, instead of actual damages and profits, an award of statutory damages for all infringements involved in the action, with respect to any one work, for which any one infringer is liable individually, or for which any two or more infringers are liable jointly and severally, in a sum of not less than $750 or more than $30,000 as the court considers just. For the purposes of this subsection, all the parts of a compilation or derivative work constitute one work." [17 USC § 504.(c)(1)];

… and …

(c) "In a case where […] infringement was committed willfully, the court in its discretion may increase the award of statutory damages to a sum of not more than $150,000. [However] [if] such infringer was not aware and had no reason to believe that his or her acts constituted an infringement of copyright, the court in its discretion may reduce the award of statutory damages to a sum of not less than $200." [17 USC § 504.(c)(2)]

In order to obtain these damages, the copyright must be fully registered with the Copyright Office. The essential elements to be pled and proven in an action for copyright infringement are:

1. That plaintiff is the owner or exclusive licensee of the registered copyright;
2. That defendant's use is identical or substantially similar to the plaintiff's copyright work;
3. That defendant had the opportunity to have prior knowledge of the existence plaintiff's work;
4. That defendant has used the copyrighted material without plaintiff's consent in a manner not permitted under copyright law (*i.e.*, that defendant has infringed upon one or more of the five exclusive rights granted by the Copyright Act, and the use does not qualify for exemption from liability);[355]
5. *(For punitive damages)* That defendant's infringement was willful; and
6. That plaintiff has been damaged by the infringement.

Note that an action for preliminary and permanent injunction is also an available remedy to stop infringement and prevent future infringement by the same parties. This injunctive remedy may be available even when the copyright is not registered.

◆ ◆ ◆

355 When dealing with works of original composition, there is a two-step proof. First, the allegedly infringing work must be **similar** to the copyrighted work and, second, the defendant must have had **opportunity** to have been familiar with the copyrighted work. Independent creation of similar works is not an infringement. "Independent creation" is therefore an affirmative defense to an action for infringement of copyright.

Misappropriation of Personality

As we've noted in discussions of personality and publicity rights ("name and likeness") in earlier chapters, this cause of action does not even *exist* in some jurisdictions, while in others (*e.g.*, New York) it is limited to a statutory action, and in still others it is available only as a common law remedy. In some states it may be pled cumulatively as two separate causes of action; one under common law, and the other under a statutory scheme (*e.g.*, California Civil Code § 3344).

In general, the statutory provisions require intent as an element of the cause of action, whereas the common law protection generally does not. Also, the particular, specific elements of personality which are protected by statutes vary from state to state, whereas the common law looks to anything which is part of, or derived from, an individual's persona. Further, statutory protection generally applies only to commercial misappropriations, with exceptions for certain commercial uses such as news reporting, matters of public interest, sports coverage, and similar uses, whereas the common law applies a broader standard as to the type of use which is actionable. Finally, some states' laws only protect the personality rights of living persons, while in other states personality rights are descendible.

A full discussion of the essential elements of various states' statutory schemes is outside the scope of this book, and should in any event be a matter for discussion with counsel in the jurisdiction where any contemplated suit is likely to be filed, since forum selection will be critical to determining whether or not the cause of action can even be pled.

Bearing in mind that not all jurisdictions recognize even a common law cause of action for misappropriation of personality, the essential elements of that common law claim are:

1. Defendant used some element or aspect of plaintiff's identity;
2. Defendant's appropriation of plaintiff's identity was to defendant's advantage, commercially or otherwise;
3. Plaintiff never consented to the use; and
4. Plaintiff suffered some loss, damage or harm as a result of the use.

In general, misappropriation of personality rights will be actionable whenever the unauthorized use is commercial in nature, and particularly when the plaintiff is a public figure who regularly receives payment for public appearances, performances, and commercial endorsements. Since such uses usually involve interstate commerce, it will likely be possible to bring the action in a jurisdiction such as California where the cause of action is well-settled and misappropriations of personality are subject to both common law and statutory remedies.

◆ ◆ ◆

Infringement of Trademark

An action for infringement of trademark can take any one or more of several forms, in either state or federal courts. In essence, each of these will be an action for "unfair competition" in some manner, and the phrase "confusingly similar" will be the touchstone for each of them.

Although the most fundamental element of a trademark (or service mark) is that it be used in commerce, and registration is optional, there are definite benefits to registration which are most apparent when seeking relief through the courts. The Lanham Act (15 USC §§ 1051, *et seq.*) protects both federally-registered marks and unregistered common-law marks. As with copyright, however, the relief available is significantly greater for registered marks.

For an unregistered mark, the relief available will generally be limited to *(a)* actual damages suffered; and *(b)* injunctive relief. For registered marks, the available relief is *(a)* injunctive relief [15 USC § 1116]; *(b)* the *greater* of actual damages suffered -or- total income received by the infringing party as a result of the infringement [15 USC § 1117(a)]; *(c)* if the infringement is intentional, a further sum of three times the greater of damage suffered or profits realized [15 USC § 1117(b)]; and *(d)* an award of attorney's fees [15 USC § 1117(b)]. The court also has discretion to increase or decrease these awards, based on the circumstances of the case.

In some cases, however, it is impossible to prove either actual damages or the amount of profit realized from the infringement. The Lanham Act therefore provides for *statutory* damages in that circumstance of not less than $500.00, nor more than $1,000,000.00 per registered mark, at the discretion of the judge [15 USC § 1117(c)], further subject to punitive damages and an award of attorney's fees if the infringement was intentional.

The essential elements of the claim would include:

1. That Plaintiff is the owner or exclusive licensee of the mark;
2. *(For registered marks)* That the mark is registered;
3. That on or about a certain date, defendant used ...
    - (a) ... the mark ... or
    - (b) ... a mark confusingly similar to plaintiff's mark
4. That defendant's use was without plaintiff's permission;
5. That consumers were confused or deceived by defendant's use of the mark, or were likely to be confused or deceived by defendant's use of the mark,
6. That defendant sought to profit, or did profit, from use of the mark;
7. That plaintiff was damaged as a result of defendant's use of the mark. (Note that "irreparable injury" is presumed in trademark infringement. Damages

arise by reason of dilution of value of the mark and of the goodwill associated with that mark, as well as any provable losses.)

8. *(For intentional infringement)* That defendant's use of the mark was intended to confuse and deceive consumers, and was a willful infringement of plaintiff's mark for such purpose.

Remember, the Lanham Act embraces two distinct mandates: (1) protection of the mark, as a property right; and (2) protection of the public from being deceived through unauthorized use of the mark, or use of confusingly similar marks, by someone other than the publicly-recognized owner of the mark.

Each state also has its own set of statutes protecting marks and addressing unfair competition. Since each state's laws are different in regard to this area, an attorney who practices within a particular state is best qualified to determine whether a state, rather than federal, remedy is appropriate to the circumstances presented by a particular case. Additionally, since the Lanham Act is not preemptive, it may be pled as a *state court* cause of action, in addition to whatever state law unfair competition or trademark remedies are available. A Lanham Act claim may be pled in federal court *only* if (1) the mark is federally registered, *or* (2) the unauthorized use complained of is a use which "affects interstate commerce," *or* (3) no plaintiff is a resident of the same state as any defendant (under which diversity jurisdiction, state law will be applied).

◆ ◆ ◆

Interference with Contractual Relationship

Despite its name, this is a tort action rather than one sounding in contract. The essence of the claim is that plaintiff was in a contractual relationship, and that defendant interfered with that relationship to plaintiff's detriment. Such interference can take several forms, ranging from defamatory statements about plaintiff, to converting property which prevents plaintiff from performing a contractual obligation. The tort can be committed intentionally or negligently but, as with any negligence-based claim, negligent interference requires the existence of some duty, the breach of which duty was an element of the interference. The elements of the claim are:

1. Plaintiff was in a contractual relationship with a third party;
2. *(Intentional)* Defendant had actual or constructive knowledge of that contractual relationship;
3. *(Negligent)* Defendant had a duty under which Defendant was obliged to do, or refrain from doing, some specific thing (pled with specificity.)
4. Defendant did (or failed to do) something (or refrained from doing something defendant was duty bound to do or to refrain from doing) (pled with specificity.)
5. Defendant's actions (as specifically alleged), interfered with plaintiff's contractual relationship (specifically pled manner in which conduct amounted to interference.)
6. As a proximate result of defendant's interference with plaintiff's contractual relationship, plaintiff was damaged by (plead specific form of damage.)
7. *(Intentional)* Defendant's actions, (as specifically alleged) were done with the intention to interfere with plaintiff's contractual relationship.
8. *(For punitive damages, where intentional)* Defendant's acts of interference were willful, wanton, malicious, oppressive, and shocking to the conscience.

◆ ◆ ◆

For an Accounting

This equitable cause of action is almost-invariably seen only as an adjunct to other causes of action, and in many instances is regarded as a *remedy* or prayer for relief, rather than as a cause of action in its own right. In consequence, it often appears only in the prayer (rather than the body) of a complaint, and therefore is not invoked until entry of judgment which orders an accounting as part of that judgment.

Nonetheless, it may be pled as a separate cause of action, having the following elements:

1. Defendant has received money or other property which is rightfully the property of plaintiff (the underlying basis for this allegation must be pled with specificity);
2. Plaintiff has no remedy at law by which to quantify the extent or amount of plaintiff's property or funds received or retained by defendant.
3. Plaintiff is entitled to equitable relief by a judicial order compelling defendant to account to plaintiff for all sums and other things of value received by defendant which are rightfully the property of plaintiff, and to deliver to plaintiff the property and sums determined by that accounting.

Tactically, pleading it as a separate cause of action may be useful in jurisdictions which permit partial summary judgment or summary adjudication upon single causes of action. If uncontested facts will justify an accounting, then obtaining a partial-judgment order compelling that accounting early in the litigation can be worthwhile.

As a practical matter, the accounting is usually performed under a court order by an auditor or forensic accountant retained by the plaintiff (or sometimes by the court), but with the costs of such accounting usually paid by the defendant. In the music industry, actions for an accounting (or a judgment which includes an order for an accounting) are common, although sometimes limited by contract provisions which restrict the allowable scope of an audit. Venues whose payments to promoters or performers may be questionable; record labels required to report and pay royalties; agents or managers who collect their clients' income from various sources; these, and others, are legally required to account for the money or other property which they have received on another's behalf.

The "right to audit" clause which appears in most entertainment contract therefore does not *create* a right to audit. That right exists as a matter of law and equity. Instead, the contract clause is intended to *limit* the right, bypassing the judicial process, while restricting the scope and frequency of audits. On the other hand, it may take months or years to obtain a court order for an accounting, whereas the contract-based audit usually only requires a stated period (usually thirty days') advance notice. If the results of a contract-based audit are unsatisfactory, the equitable remedy may still remain available, depending on the specific language of the subject contract and the particular circumstances of the case.

◆ ◆ ◆

Claim & Delivery (Replevin)

If you didn't skip the earlier section on "Distinguishing Law and Equity," then it may be of interest to know that this remedy is one of those ancient, common-law writs discussed in that section. Although now more frequently referred to as "claim and delivery," a writ of replevin is an order by which a court compels a defendant to surrender specific property at the outset of an action. Replevin can therefore be a powerful tactical tool in a case where the defendant is wrongfully holding plaintiff's property, since it not only protects that property from disappearing in the course of the proceedings, but also deprives defendant of the *use* of that property while the case is awaiting trial.

In order to invoke the remedy, the plaintiff must produce sufficient evidence to show that the property in question is more likely plaintiff's lawful property than defendant's, and post a bond or undertaking with the court to protect the defendant's possible interests should judgment on the issue ultimately favor defendant's claims. This is often done on an ex parte basis, without the defendant's participation and often without advance notice to the defendant. Once the bond has been posted, the usual procedure is for the sheriff serve the defendant with the writ, and to seize and hold the property pending a full hearing and a court determination as to whether the property should be delivered to the plaintiff, returned to the defendant, or retained by the sheriff pending final adjudication of the case.

One music-industry situation in which replevin can be useful is during band break-ups, where there is a dispute as to former band-members' respective rights of ownership or possession in regard to band equipment or other assets. Having the sheriff seize such property before it can find its way to a swap meet or online auction may be the only practical method for preserving assets pending final adjudication. Controversy over possession of master recordings is another circumstance in which replevin may provide an appropriate remedy to prevent the subject matter of a dispute from changing hands while that dispute is still in the process of being resolved.

◆ ◆ ◆

Quantum Meruit

In an earlier discussion regarding the divergent history of common law and equity, we examined the imperfect merger of those two forms of justice, and how certain remedies contain elements of each. Quantum Meruit — which translates from Latin as "as much as deserved" — is a perfect example. Although akin to the ancient common-law writ of *assumpsit*, quantum meruit is an action in *quasi*-contract, with overtones of an equitable remedy, as well.

Equity abhors unjust enrichment, which would often be the result where a contract is deemed void or voidable as a matter of law, or where no contract was properly established. Under such circumstance, one party might receive a benefit, without being contractually or legally obligated to tender consideration for that benefit. To address this potential inequity, a cause of action for *Quantum Meruit* says, in effect "Forget the contract, or lack of contract. Take a look at the consideration which plaintiff gave to the defendant, calculate the fair value of that consideration, and order the defendant to pay plaintiff that amount."

There are some circumstances, however, where statutes preclude even a *quantum meruit* award, and — as we've mentioned earlier — established doctrine requires that where the law has spoken, equity must remain silent.

In general, such circumstances arise in contracts where a licence was required, but not obtained. In that situation, the law will generally forbid recovery of any consideration for those unlicensed services, regardless of their value, as a matter of public policy. Thus an unlicensed doctor, lawyer, accountant, booking agent, or construction contractor, may be barred from *any* award, as a matter of public policy.

However, in a recent case before the California Supreme Court,[356] the doctrine of severability was applied in a case involving unlicensed talent booking by an artist's manager. The court held that plaintiff was entitled to recover for those contract services which did *not* require a license, and that recovery was barred only in respect to such services rendered under the management contract which amounted to unlicensed talent booking. This overruled forty years of precedent in California court opinions and Labor Commission rulings which had uniformly held that whenever an unlicensed manager had procured or attempted to procure even one employment opportunity for an artist in violation of the Talent Agencies Act, the entire contract was void, and the manager barred from recovering *any* commissions for services under that contract. The California Supreme Court's recent application of the severability doctrine in *Blasi* has opened the door for managers who have violated the Act to nonetheless enforce their contracts to recover commissions for bookings procured by or in cooperation with a licensed agent (rather than by the manager acting alone), as well as for any non-booking-related consideration provided under the contract.

---

356 Marathon v. Blasi (2008) 42 Cal.4th 974

Arguably, under this rationale, a plaintiff barred by the absence of a license with respect to only a portion of contract damages would nonetheless be entitled to seek severance and recovery for such goods and services as did not require a license. Whether or not the judicial policy and rationale announced in *Blasi* would be applied in respect to other occupations — particularly in light of strong public policies against unlicensed practitioners — and whether it would permit quantum meruit recovery in such cases, remains to be seen.[357]

In any event, quantum meruit should probably be pled as an equitable alternative in any action for collection of an outstanding obligation — either separately or within "common counts" — especially when a challenge to the validity of an underlying contract is anticipated.

◆ ◆ ◆

357 *E.g.*, California attorneys are required to have written contracts with their clients (other than for "emergency" representation), and to provide the client with a fully signed copy of such agreement promptly upon its signing. Failure to comply with these requirements renders the contract voidable (at the client's sole option) and reduces the attorney's claim for fees to *quantum meruit* only, by statute. (See, *e,g,*, California Business & Professions Code § 6148)

There are far more commonly-recognized causes of action available than those few we have outlined here. Indeed, there are multi-volume legal publications which contain nothing but civil causes of action, explaining each of them and their essential elements in far greater detail than can be included in this brief overview.

We began this section with the maxim that "For every wrong, there is a remedy." Under the doctrine arising from that maxim, it is often possible to *invent* a new cause of civil action where none previously existed, subject only to law and public policy considerations. If a skilled attorney can plead facts sufficient to justify relief, courts will generally find a way to grant that relief, if at all possible.

To return, to the main thrust of this book, contract-based causes of action can only succeed if, in fact, there has been some violation of law, or of the terms of the underlying contract. Thus the first step must always be to negotiate and form a contract which contains everything to which the parties have agreed and nothing to which they haven't agreed. After that, it's simply a matter of meeting one's contractual obligations as expressed by the agreed terms and conditions. A well-considered and carefully-crafted agreement is therefore the first and best defense against having to become involved contract litigation. To conclude with a final reiteration of an earlier caveat: The cost of untangling a poorly-drafted contract will always exceed the cost of having it properly prepared in the first place.

Afterword, Tables, & Index

Afterword

Three and a half years ago, we thought that putting this book together would be a relatively simple matter of assembling, updating, and collating a decade's worth of lecture notes and handouts that we'd prepared for various music law and music business seminars and courses we had previously designed and conducted.

We were wrong.

For those of you — colleagues, students, and former students — who have been listening to us repeatedly promise that we'd have a final, published edition ready for you by "next semester," we hope that the foregoing pages will prove to have been worth the wait. Also, with our apologies, we're *still* not finished with everything that we'd promised to deliver.

As we noted in our Introduction, we came to an unexpected and unavoidable conclusion in the process of putting this book together... it turns out that all of the information we had compiled — and which we considered indispensable to the comprehensive overview of the music industry which we had envisioned (and promised) — couldn't be encompassed by a single volume. We had to either abandon our original intention, dispensing with substantial amounts of accumulated content, or resign ourselves to the idea of a multiple-volume approach. After a fair amount of soul searching, we decided that this was a case where "half a loaf" was not sufficient, and that omitting potentially-crucial material was an unacceptable alternative.

Although the remaining volumes of this series are not yet ready for publication, several lengthy chapters which were included in our originally-intended, single-volume manuscript had been completed before being extracted from what has now become this "Volume One." Those extracted chapters analyze, *inter alia*, interband agreements, recording contracts, songwriter agreements, and publishing contracts and licenses, and now form the core of Volumes Two and Three. We consequently expect to have Volume Two ready for release by early 2009, and to have the final volumes published before the end of 2010.

Those of you in the legal profession will recognize that the potential for changes in law is an ongoing concern. We have, in some instances, referred to superseded laws and opinions for their historical relevance, while noting that these authorities have been supplanted by subsequent opinions and enactments. We have also sought to incorporate the most current opinions and laws into this book, particularly where they have had a superseding effect. While future editions will undoubtedly reflect any interim changes that may occur, we strongly recommend verifying the currency of authorities before citing them in pleadings. (Or, you can cite us directly, and let us take the heat if there's been a post-publication change in law.)

While this book is intended to be authoritative and citable, its primary benefit for lawyers is in familiarizing them with the unconventional (and occasionally bizarre) realities of the music industry and its transactional customs and practices. Later volumes in this series contain detailed, paragraph-by-paragraph analyses of specific music industry contracts, along with sample forms of agreement, practice guides, and side-by-side comparisons of "company favorable" and "artist favorable" sample clauses and provisions for each form of contract.

For non-lawyers, the fundamental information contained in this first volume in the series should be read, re-read, and mastered before even attempting to negotiate or form an important contract without an attorney's guidance. In fact, once this information has been thoroughly mastered, non-lawyers are even more likely to recognize the need for having an attorney with them throughout the contract negotiation and formation process. Fortunately, such mastery will also allow them to communicate informedly and succinctly with their attorney, thereby saving substantial time and effort (*i.e.*, money) and a great deal of frustration on both sides of the attorney-client relationship. Likewise, the information on remedies and dispute resolution will enable non-lawyers to more fully appreciate the intricacies of adversary proceedings, and allow them to work more smoothly with their counsel if and when they find themselves — voluntarily or otherwise — a party to such proceedings. (Unfortunately, it's become virtually impossible to achieve any level of success in this business without being sued, or having to sue someone else, for *something*.)

All in all, this book has been an excitingly tedious pursuit. In retrospect, it represents more than 3,000 hours of otherwise-billable research and drafting time. (We just did the math, and that comes to well over $1-million that we *weren't* able to invoice to clients. We're going to have to sell a lot of books to justify the effort. On the other hand, that sum also represents a fair estimate of value for the professionally researched materials and original work compressed into this volume.)

Again, to all of you who have been clamoring for us to keep our word and get this book into print, we apologize for the delay, and here it is. And, at the risk of having to issue a further apology some time in the near future, we *promise* that the remainder of the series will be published soon... or as soon as humanly possible, anyway. Meanwhile, we hope that our efforts will prove both informative and useful.

Robert J. Nathan &
Burgundy Morgan
August 28, 2008

TABLE OF CITED CASES

Index of Forms, Clauses & Provisions

INDEX